The Humanities in the Western Tradition

Readings in Literature and Thought

VOLUME II

Marvin Perry
Baruch College, City University of New York

J. Wayne Baker
The University of Akron

Pamela Pfeiffer Hollinger
The University of Akron

Houghton Mifflin Company   Boston   New York

Senior Sponsoring Editor: Nancy Blaine
Development Editor: Julie Dunn
Senior Project Editor: Bob Greiner
Editorial Assistant: Wendy Thayer
Production/Design Assistant: Bethany Schlegel
Manufacturing Manager: Florence Cadran
Senior Marketing Manager: Sandra McGuire

Printed in the USA

ISBN: 0-395-84815-6

123456789-b-07 06 05 04 03

Contents

Preface

The Humanities in the Western Tradition: Readings in Literature and Thought surveys thought and literature from antiquity to the present with an assortment of sources. Instructors in Humanities courses have long recognized the pedagogical value of primary sources in exploring the profound questions of human experience and understanding the historical stages of the Western tradition. These selections have been carefully chosen and edited to fit the needs of a survey of the Humanities and to supplement standard textbooks in literature and histories of the West.

We have based our choice of readings for the two volumes on several criteria. As an aid for understanding the dominant ideals of the Western tradition this reader emphasizes primarily the foremost thinkers and authors who shaped the Western tradition. In their choice of readings, the editors hope to convey to students that the Western heritage is a living, vital tradition and that studying these primary sources in literature and thought will enrich their lives. Even though the reader focuses on great thinkers, the great ideas, and great works of literature, it also includes a sampling of works that capture the social, political, and economic outlook of an age so that students derive a sense of movement and development in Western history. While some readings are included in their entirety, such as Sophocles' *Oedipus the King* and Chaucer's "The Nun's Priest's Tale," the other readings are of sufficient length to convey their essential meaning and main ideas.

An important feature of the reader is the use of the constellation, the grouping of several related documents illuminating a single theme; such constellations reinforce the student's understanding of important themes and invites comparison, analysis, and interpretation. For example, in Volume I, Chapter 3, Section 3, the constellation "Humanism" contains three interrelated readings: "The Pursuit of Excellence" by Pindar, "Lauding Human Talents" by Sophocles, and "The Funeral Oration of Pericles" by Thucydides. In Volume II, Chapter 15, Section 8, the constellation "American Realism" contains three readings: *The Adventures of Huckleberry Finn* by Mark Twain, *Leaves of Grass* by Walt Whitman, and "Selected Poems" by Emily Dickinson.

An overriding concern for the editors in preparing this compilation was to make the documents accessible—to enable students to comprehend and to interpret both literary works and historical documents on their own. To facilitate this aim, we have provided several pedagogical features. Introductions of three types explain the historical setting, the authors' intents, and the meaning and significance of the readings. First, introductions to each chapter provide comprehensive overviews to each period considered. Second, introductions to each numbered section or grouping treat the historical background for the reading(s) that follow(s). Third, each reading has a brief headnote that provides specific details about that reading.

Within some readings, interlinear notes, clearly set off from the text of the document, serve as transitions and suggest the main themes of the passage that follow. Used primarily in longer extracts, these interlinear notes help to guide students through the readings. Moreover, to assist students' comprehension, brief, bracketed editorial definitions or notes that explain unfamiliar or foreign terms or phrases are inserted into the running text. When terms or concepts in the documents require fuller explanations, these appear at the bottom of the pages as editors' footnotes. Where helpful, we have retained the notes of authors, translators, or editors from whose works the documents were acquired.

For ancient sources, we have generally selected recent translations that are both faithful to the text and readable. For some seventeenth- and eighteenth-century English documents, the archaic spelling has been retained, when this does not preclude comprehension, to demonstrate to students how the English language has evolved over time.

It is our hope that this reader enhances the appreciation of Western literature and thought and enriches the study of the Humanities. The selection and compilation of sources is not an easy task and the authors wish to thank the following instructors for their helpful suggestions and advice:

Robert Eisner, *San Diego State University*

David Fenimore, *University of Nevada, Reno*

Sandi S. Landis, *St. Johns River Community College, Orange Park Campus*

Charlie McAllister, *Catawba College*

Merry Ovnick, *California State University, Northridge*

Richard A. Voeltz, *Cameron University*

M. P.

J. W. B.

P. P. H.

PART III

CHAPTER

10

The Renaissance

From the fifteenth through the seventeenth centuries, medieval attitudes and institutions broke down, and distinctly modern cultural, economic, and political forms emerged. For many historians, the Renaissance, which originated in the city-states of Italy, marks the starting point of the modern era. The Renaissance was characterized by a rebirth of interest in the humanist culture and outlook of ancient Greece and Rome. Although Renaissance individuals did not repudiate Christianity, they valued worldly activities and interests to a much greater degree than did the people of the Middle Ages, whose outlook was dominated by Christian otherworldliness. Renaissance individuals were fascinated by *this* world and by life's possibilities; they aspired to live a rich and creative life on earth and to fulfill themselves through artistic and literary activity.

Individualism was a hallmark of the Renaissance. The urban elite sought to demonstrate their unique talents, to assert their own individuality, and to gain recognition for their accomplishments. The most-admired person during the Renaissance was the multitalented individual, the "universal man," who distinguished himself as a writer, artist, linguist, athlete. Disdaining Christian humility, Renaissance individuals took pride in their talents and worldly accomplishments—"I can work miracles," said the great Leonardo da Vinci.

During the High Middle Ages there had been a revival of Greek and Roman learning. Yet there were two important differences between the period called the Twelfth-Century Awakening and the Renaissance. First, many more ancient works were restored to circulation during the Renaissance than during the cultural revival of the Middle Ages. Second, medieval scholastics had tried to fit the ideas of the ancients into a Christian framework; they used Greek philosophy to explain Christian teachings. Renaissance scholars, on the other hand, valued ancient works for their own sake, believing that Greek and Roman authors could teach much about the art of living.

A distinguishing feature of the Renaissance period was the humanist movement, an educational and cultural program based on the study of ancient Greek and Latin literature. By studying the humanities—history, literature, rhetoric, moral and political philosophy—humanists aimed to revive the worldly spirit of the ancient Greeks and Romans, which they believed had been lost in the Middle Ages.

Humanists were thus fascinated by the writings of the ancients. From the works of Thucydides, Plato, Cicero, Seneca, and other ancient authors, humanists sought guidelines for living life well in this world and looked for stylistic models for their own literary efforts. To the humanists, the ancients had written brilliantly, in an incomparable literary style, on friendship, citizenship, love, bravery, statesmanship, beauty, excellence, and every other topic devoted to the enrichment of human life.

Like the humanist movement, Renaissance art also marked a break with medieval culture. The art of the Middle Ages had served a religious function; its purpose was to lift the mind to God. It depicted a spiritual universe in which the supernatural was the supreme reality. The Gothic cathedral, with its flying buttresses, soared toward heaven, rising in ascending tiers; it reflected the medieval conception of a hierarchical universe with God at its apex. Painting also expressed gradations of spiritual values. Traditionally, the left side of a painting portrayed the damned, the right side the saved; dark colors expressed evil, light colors good. Spatial proportion was relative to spirituality—the less spiritually valuable a thing was, the less form it had (or the more deformed it was). Medieval art perfectly expressed the Christian view of the universe and the individual. The Renaissance shattered the dominance of religion over art, shifting attention from heaven to the natural world and to the human being. Renaissance artists often dealt with religious themes, but they placed their subjects in a naturalistic setting. Renaissance art also developed a new concept of visual space that was defined from the standpoint of the individual observer. It was a quantitative space in which the artist, employing reason and mathematics, portrayed the essential form of the object as it appeared in three dimensions to the human eye; that is, it depicted the object in perspective.

The Renaissance began in the middle of the fourteenth century in the northern Italian city-states, which had grown prosperous from the revival of trade in the Middle Ages. Italian merchants and bankers had the wealth to acquire libraries and fine works of art and to support art, literature, and scholarship. Surrounded by reminders of ancient Rome—amphitheaters, monuments, and sculpture—the well-to-do took an interest in classical culture and thought. In the late fifteenth and the sixteenth centuries, Renaissance ideas spread to Germany, France, Spain, and England through books available in great numbers due to the invention of the printing press.

1 The Humanists' Fascination with Antiquity

Humanists believed that a refined person must know the literature of Greece and Rome. They strove to imitate the style of the ancients, to speak and write as eloquently as the Greeks and Romans. Toward these ends, they sought to read, print, and restore to circulation every scrap of ancient literature that could still be found.

Petrarch
THE FATHER OF HUMANISM[1]

During his lifetime, Francesco Petrarca, or Petrarch (1304–1374), had an astounding reputation as a poet and scholar. Often called the "father of humanism," he inspired other humanists through his love for classical learning; his criticism of medieval Latin as barbaric in contrast to the style of Cicero, Seneca, and other Romans; and his literary works based on classical models. Petrarch saw his own age as a restoration of classical brilliance after an interval of medieval darkness.

A distinctly modern element in Petrarch's thought is the subjective and individualistic character of his writing. In talking about himself and probing his

---

[1]Throughout the text, titles original to the source appear in italics. Titles added by the editors are not italicized.

own feelings, Petrarch demonstrates a self-consciousness characteristic of the modern outlook.

Like many other humanists, Petrarch remained devoted to Christianity: "When it comes to thinking or speaking of religion, that is, of the highest truth, of true happiness and eternal salvation," he declared, "I certainly am not a Ciceronian or a Platonist but a Christian." Petrarch was a forerunner of the Christian humanism best represented by Erasmus. Christian humanists combined an intense devotion to Christianity with a great love for classical literature, which they much preferred to the dull and turgid treatises written by scholastic philosophers and theologians. In the following passage, Petrarch criticizes his contemporaries for their ignorance of ancient writers and shows his commitment to classical learning.

. . . O inglorious age! that scorns antiquity, its mother, to whom it owes every noble art—that dares to declare itself not only equal but superior to the glorious past. I say nothing of the vulgar, the dregs of mankind, whose sayings and opinions may raise a laugh but hardly merit serious censure. . . .

. . . But what can be said in defense of men of education who ought not to be ignorant of antiquity and yet are plunged in this same darkness and delusion?

You see that I cannot speak of these matters without the greatest irritation and indignation. There has arisen of late a set of dialecticians [experts in logical argument], who are not only ignorant but demented. Like a black army of ants from some old rotten oak, they swarm forth from their hiding places and devastate the fields of sound learning. They con-

demn Plato and Aristotle, and laugh at Socrates and Pythagoras.[2] And, good God! under what silly and incompetent leaders these opinions are put forth. . . . What shall we say of men who scorn Marcus Tullius Cicero,[3] the bright sun of eloquence? Of those who scoff at Varro and Seneca,[4] and are scandalized at what they choose to call the crude, unfinished style of Livy and Sallust [Roman historians]?[5] . . .

Such are the times, my friend, upon which we have fallen; such is the period in which we live and are growing old. Such are the critics of today, as I so often have occasion to lament and complain—men who are innocent of knowledge and virtue, and yet harbour the most exalted opinion of themselves. Not content with losing the words of the ancients, they must attack their genius and their ashes. They rejoice in their ignorance, as if what they did not know were not worth knowing. They give full rein to their license and conceit, and freely introduce among us new authors and outlandish teachings.

---

[2]The work of Aristotle (384–322 B.C.), a leading Greek philosopher, had an enormous influence among medieval and Renaissance scholars. A student of the philosopher Socrates, Plato (c. 427–347 B.C.) was one of the greatest philosophers of ancient Greece. His work grew to be extremely influential in the West during the Renaissance period, as new texts of his writings were discovered and translated into Latin and more Westerners could read the originals in Greek. Pythagoras (c. 582– c. 507 B.C.) was a Greek philosopher whose work influenced both Socrates and Plato. (Throughout the text, the editors' notes carry numbers, whereas notes from the original sources are indicated by asterisks, daggers, et cetera. An exception is made for editorial notes pertaining to Scriptures, which have symbols rather than numbers.)

[3]Cicero (106–43 B.C.) was a Roman statesman and rhetorician. His Latin style was especially admired and emulated during the Renaissance.
[4]Varro (116–27 B.C.) was a Roman scholar and historian. Seneca (4 B.C.–A.D. 65) was a Roman statesman, dramatist, and Stoic philosopher whose literary style was greatly admired during the Renaissance.
[5]Throughout the text, words in brackets have been added as glosses by the editors. Brackets around glosses from the original sources have been changed to parentheses to distinguish them.

Leonardo Bruni
STUDY OF GREEK LITERATURE AND A HUMANIST EDUCATIONAL PROGRAM

Leonardo Bruni (1374–1444) was a Florentine humanist who extolled both intellectual study and active involvement in public affairs, an outlook called civic humanism. In the first reading from his *History of His Own Times in Italy,* Bruni expresses the humanist's love for ancient Greek literature and language.

In a treatise, *De Studiis et Literis* (On Learning and Literature), addressed to the noble lady Baptista di Montefeltro (1383–1450), daughter of the Count of Urbino, Bruni outlines the basic course of studies that the humanists recommended as the best preparation for a life of wisdom and virtue. In addition to the study of Christian literature, Bruni encourages a wide familiarity with the best minds and stylists of ancient Greek and Latin cultures.

LOVE FOR GREEK LITERATURE

Then first came a knowledge of Greek, which had not been in use among us for seven hundred years. Chrysoloras the Byzantine,[1] a man of noble birth and well versed in Greek letters, brought Greek learning to us. When his country was invaded by the Turks, he came by sea, first to Venice. The report of him soon spread, and he was cordially invited and besought and promised a public stipend, to come to Florence and open his store of riches to the youth. I was then studying Civil Law,[2] but . . . I burned with love of academic studies, and had spent no little pains on dialectic and rhetoric. At the coming of Chrysoloras I was torn in mind, deeming it shameful to desert the law, and yet a crime to lose such a chance of studying Greek literature; and often with youthful impulse I would say to myself: "Thou, when it is permitted thee to gaze on Homer, Plato and Demosthenes,[3] and the other [Greek] poets, philosophers, orators, of whom such glorious things are spread abroad, and speak with them and be instructed in their admirable teaching, wilt thou desert and rob thyself? Wilt thou neglect this opportunity so divinely offered? For seven hundred years, no one in Italy has possessed Greek letters; and yet we confess that all knowledge is derived from them. How great advantage to your knowledge, enhancement of your fame, increase of your pleasure, will come from an understanding of this tongue? There are doctors of civil law everywhere; and the chance of learning will not fail thee. But if this one and only doctor of Greek letters disappears, no one can be found to teach thee." Overcome at length by these reasons, I gave myself to Chrysoloras, with such zeal to learn, that what through the wakeful day I gathered, I followed after in the night, even when asleep.

ON LEARNING AND LITERATURE

. . . The foundations of all true learning must be laid in the sound and thorough knowledge of Latin: which implies study marked by a broad spirit, accurate scholarship, and careful attention to details. Unless this solid basis be secured it is useless to attempt to rear an enduring edifice. Without it the great monuments of literature are unintelligible, and the art of composition impossible. To attain this essential knowledge we must never relax our careful attention to the grammar of the language, but perpetually confirm and extend our acquaintance with it until it is thoroughly our own. . . . To this end we must be supremely careful in our choice of authors, lest an inartistic and debased style infect our own writing and degrade our taste; which danger is best avoided by bringing a keen, critical sense to bear upon select works, observing the sense of each passage, the structure of the sentence, the force of every word down to the least important particle. In this way our reading reacts directly upon our style. . . .

But we must not forget that true distinction is to be gained by a wide and varied range of such studies as conduce to the profitable enjoyment of life, in which, however, we must observe due proportion in the attention and time we devote to them.

First amongst such studies I place History: a subject which must not on any account be neglected by one who aspires to true cultivation. For it is our duty to understand the origins of our own history and its development; and the achievements of Peoples and of Kings.

For the careful study of the past enlarges our foresight in contemporary affairs and affords to citizens and to monarchs lessons of incitement or warning in the ordering of public policy. From History, also, we draw our store of examples of moral precepts.

In the monuments of ancient literature which have come down to us History holds a position of great distinction. We specially prize such [Roman] authors as Livy, Sallust and Curtius;[4] and, perhaps even above these, Julius Caesar; the style of whose Commentaries, so elegant and so limpid, entitles them to our warm admiration. . . .

The great Orators of antiquity must by all means be included. Nowhere do we find the virtues more warmly extolled, the vices so fiercely decried. From them we may learn, also, how to express consolation, encouragement, dissuasion or advice. If the principles which orators set forth are portrayed for us by philosophers, it is from the former that we learn how to employ the emotions—such as indignation, or

---

[1]Chrysoloras (c. 1355–1415), a Byzantine writer and teacher, introduced the study of Greek literature to the Italians, helping to open a new age of Western humanistic learning.

[2]Civil Law refers to the Roman law as codified by Emperor Justinian in the early sixth century A.D. and studied in medieval law schools.

[3]Demosthenes (384–322 B.C.) was an Athenian statesman and orator whose oratorical style was much admired by Renaissance humanists.

[4]Q. Curtius Rufus, a Roman historian and rhetorician of the mid–first century A.D., composed a biography of Alexander the Great.

pity—in driving home their application in individual cases. Further, from oratory we derive our store of those elegant or striking turns of expression which are used with so much effect in literary compositions. Lastly, in oratory we find that wealth of vocabulary, that clear easy-flowing style, that verve and force, which are invaluable to us both in writing and in conversation.

I come now to Poetry and the Poets. . . . For we cannot point to any great mind of the past for whom the Poets had not a powerful attraction. Aristotle, in constantly quoting Homer, Hesiod, Pindar, Euripides and other [Greek] poets, proves that he knew their works hardly less intimately than those of the philosophers. Plato, also, frequently appeals to them, and in this way covers them with his approval. If we turn to Cicero, we find him not content with quoting Ennius, Accius,[5] and others of the Latins, but rendering poems from the Greek and employing them habitually. . . . Hence my view that familiarity with the great poets of antiquity is essential to any claim to true education. For in their writings we find deep speculations upon Nature, and upon the Causes and Origins of things, which must carry weight with us both from their antiquity and from their authorship. Besides

---

[5]Ennius (239–169 B.C.) wrote the first great Latin epic poem, which was based on the legends of Rome's founding and its early history. Accius (c. 170–c. 90 B.C.), also a Roman, authored a history of Greek and Latin literature.

these, many important truths upon matters of daily life are suggested or illustrated. All this is expressed with such grace and dignity as demands our admiration. . . . To sum up what I have endeavoured to set forth. That high standard of education to which I referred at the outset is only to be reached by one who has seen many things and read much. Poet, Orator, Historian, and the rest, all must be studied, each must contribute a share. Our learning thus becomes full, ready, varied and elegant, available for action or for discourse in all subjects. But to enable us to make effectual use of what we know we must add to our knowledge the power of expression. These two sides of learning, indeed, should not be separated: they afford mutual aid and distinction. Proficiency in literary form, not accompanied by broad acquaintance with facts and truths, is a barren attainment; whilst information, however vast, which lacks all grace of expression, would seem to be put under a bushel or partly thrown away. Indeed, one may fairly ask what advantage it is to possess profound and varied learning if one cannot convey it in language worthy of the subject. Where, however, this double capacity exists— breadth of learning and grace of style—we allow the highest title to distinction and to abiding fame. If we review the great names of ancient [Greek and Roman] literature, Plato, Democritus, Aristotle, Theophrastus, Varro, Cicero, Seneca, Augustine, Jerome, Lactantius, we shall find it hard to say whether we admire more their attainments or their literary power.

Petrus Paulus Vergerius
THE IMPORTANCE OF LIBERAL STUDIES

In *On the Manners of a Gentleman and Liberal Studies,* written in 1392, Petrus Paulus Vergerius (1370–1444), a prominent Paduan scholar, upheld the importance of classical study and made astute observations regarding the educational process. He urged teachers to provide "examples of living men known and respected for their worth" for students to imitate. At an early age, students should learn moral discipline: they should be taught to disdain "arrogance or intolerable self-conceit," "untruthfulness," "idleness of mind," and overindulgence in food, drink, and sleep. They should also be imbued with respect for elders and the ceremonies of the church.

In the following passage from his education treatise, Vergerius discusses the nature and value of a liberal education.

We call those studies *liberal* which are worthy of a free man; those studies by which we attain and practise virtue and wisdom; that education which calls forth, trains and develops those highest gifts of body and of mind which ennoble men, and which are rightly judged to rank next in dignity to virtue only. For to a vulgar temper gain and pleasure are the one aim of existence, to a lofty nature, moral worth and fame. It is, then, of the highest importance that even from infancy this aim, this effort, should constantly be kept alive in growing minds. For I may affirm with fullest conviction that we shall not have attained wisdom in our later years unless in our earliest we have sincerely entered on its search. Nor may we for a moment admit, with the unthinking crowd, that those who give early promise fail in subsequent fulfilment. This may, partly from physical causes, happen in exceptional cases. But there is no doubt that nature has endowed some children with so keen, so ready an intelligence, that without serious effort they attain to a notable power of reasoning and conversing upon grave and lofty subjects, and by aid of right guidance and sound learning reach in manhood the highest distinction. On the other hand, children of modest powers demand even more attention, that their natural defects may be supplied by art. But all alike must in those early years, . . . whilst the mind is supple, be inured to the toil and effort of learning. Not that education, in the broad sense, is exclusively the concern of youth. Did not Cato[1] think it honourable to learn Greek in later life? Did not Socrates, greatest of philosophers, compel his aged fingers to the lute?

Our youth of to-day, it is to be feared, is backward to learn; studies are accounted irksome. Boys hardly weaned begin to claim their own way, at a time when every art should be employed to bring them under control and attract them to grave studies. The Master [teacher] must judge how far he can rely upon emulation, rewards, encouragement; how far he must have recourse to sterner measures. Too much leniency is objectionable; so also is too great severity, for we must avoid all that terrifies a boy. . . . Not seldom it happens that a finely tempered nature is thwarted by circumstances, such as poverty at home, which compels a promising youth to forsake learning for trade: though, on the other hand, poverty is less dangerous to lofty instincts than great wealth. Or again, parents encourage their sons to follow a career traditional in their family, which may divert them from liberal studies: and the customary pursuits of the city in which we dwell exercise a decided influence on our choice. So that we may say that a perfectly unbiassed decision in these matters is seldom possible, except to certain select natures, who by favour of the gods, as the poets have it, are unconsciously brought to choose the right path in life. . . . For us it is the best that can befall, that either the circumstances of our life, or the guidance and exhortations of those in charge of us, should mould our natures whilst they are still plastic. . . .

[My father], Jacopo da Carrara, who, though a patron of learning, was not himself versed in Letters, died regretting that opportunity of acquiring a knowledge of higher studies had not been given him in youth; which shews us that, although we may in old age long for it, only in early years can we be sure of attaining that learning which we desire. So that it is no light motive to youthful diligence that we thereby provide

ourselves with precious advantages against on-coming age, a spring of interest for a leisured life, a recreation for a busy one. Consider the necessity of the literary art to one immersed in reading and speculation: and its importance to one absorbed in affairs. To be able to speak and write with elegance is no slight advantage in negotiation, whether in public or private concerns. Especially in administration of the State, when intervals of rest and privacy are accorded to a prince, how must he value those means of occupying them wisely which the knowledge of literature affords to him! Think of Domitian:[2] the son of Vespasian though he was, and brother of Titus, he was driven to occupy his leisure by *killing flies!* . . .

Indeed the power which good books have of diverting our thoughts from unworthy or distressing themes is another support to my argument for the study of letters. Add to this their helpfulness on those occasions when we find ourselves alone, without companions and without preoccupations—what can we do better than gather our books around us? In them we see unfolded before us vast stores of knowledge, for our delight, it may be, or for our inspiration. In them are contained the records of the great achievements of men; the wonders of Nature; the works of Providence in the past, the key to her secrets of the future. And, most important of all, this Knowledge is not liable to decay. With a picture, an inscription, a coin, books share a kind of immortality. In all these memory is, as it were, made permanent; although, in its freedom from accidental risks, Literature surpasses every other form of record.

Literature indeed exhibits not facts alone, but thoughts, and their expression. Provided such thoughts be worthy, and worthily expressed, we feel assured that they will not die: although I do not think that thoughts without style will be likely to attract much notice or secure a sure survival. What greater charm can life offer than this power of making the past, the present, and even the future, our own by means of literature? How bright a household is the family of books! we may cry, with Cicero. In their company is no noise, no greed, no self-will: at a word they speak to you, at a word they are still: to all our requests their response is ever ready and to the point. Books indeed are a higher—a wider, more tenacious—memory, a store-house which is the common property of us all.

I attach great weight to the duty of handing down this priceless treasure to our sons. . . .

We come now to the consideration of the various subjects which may rightly be included under the name of "Liberal Studies." Amongst these I accord the first place to History, on grounds both of its attractiveness and of its utility, qualities which appeal equally to the scholar and to the statesman. Next in importance ranks Moral Philosophy, which indeed is, in a peculiar sense, a "Liberal Art," in that its purpose is to teach men the secret of true freedom. History, then, gives us the concrete examples of the precepts incul-

---

[1]Greek writers such as Plutarch stressed Cato the Elder's anti-Hellenic sentiments (see vol. I page 84), but in *On Old Age* Cicero asserted that Cato learned Greek in his later years as a source of intellectual stimulation.

[2]The Roman emperor Domitian (A.D. 51–96), the son of the emperor Vespasian, succeeded his elder brother Titus as emperor in 81.

cated by philosophy. The one shews what men should do, the other what men have said and done in the past, and what practical lessons we may draw therefrom for the present day. I would indicate as the third main branch of study, Eloquence, which indeed holds a place of distinction amongst the refined Arts. By philosophy we learn the essential truth of things, which by eloquence we so exhibit in orderly adornment as to bring conviction to differing minds. And history provides the light of experience—a cumulative wisdom fit to supplement the force of reason and the persuasion of eloquence. For we allow that soundness of judgment, wisdom of speech, integrity of conduct are the marks of a truly liberal temper. . . .

The Art of Letters . . . is a study adapted to all times and to all circumstances, to the investigation of fresh knowledge or to the re-casting and application of old. Hence the importance of grammar and of the rules of composition must be recognised at the outset, as the foundation on which the whole study of Literature must rest: and closely associated with these rudiments, the art of Disputation or Logical argument. The function of this is to enable us to discern fallacy from truth in discussion. Logic, indeed, as setting forth the true method of learning, is the guide to the acquisition of knowledge in whatever subject. Rhetoric comes next, and is strictly speaking the formal study by which we attain the art of eloquence; which, as we have just stated, takes the third place amongst the studies specially important in public life. . . .

After Eloquence we place Poetry and the Poetic Art, which though not without their value in daily life and as an aid to oratory, have nevertheless their main concern for the leisure side of existence.

As to Music, the Greeks refused the title of 'Educated' to anyone who could not sing or play. Socrates set an example to the Athenian youth, by himself learning to play in his old age; urging the pursuit of music not as a sensuous indulgence, but as an aid to the inner harmony of the soul. In so far as it is taught as a healthy recreation for the moral and spiritual nature, music is a truly liberal art, and, both as regards its theory and its practice, should find a place in education.

Arithmetic, which treats of the properties of numbers, Geometry, which treats of the properties of dimensions, lines, surfaces, and solid bodies, are weighty studies because they possess a peculiar element of certainty. The science of the Stars, their motions, magnitudes and distances, lifts us into the clear calm of the upper air. There we may contemplate the fixed stars, or the conjunctions of the planets, and predict the eclipses of the sun and the moon. The knowledge of Nature—animate and inanimate—the laws and the properties of things in heaven and in earth, their causes, mutations and effects, especially the explanation of their wonders (as they are popularly supposed) by the unravelling of their causes—this is a most delightful, and at the same time most profitable, study for youth. With these may be joined investigations concerning the weight of bodies, and those relative to the subject which mathematicians call "Perspective."

I may here glance for a moment at the three great professional Disciplines: Medicine, Law, Theology. Medicine, which is applied science, has undoubtedly much that makes it attractive to a student. But it cannot be described as a Liberal study. Law, which is based upon moral philosophy, is undoubtedly held in high respect. Regarding Law as a subject of study, such respect is entirely deserved: but Law as practised becomes a mere trade. Theology, on the other hand, treats of themes removed from our senses, and attainable only by pure intelligence.

2 Human Dignity

In his short lifetime, Giovanni Pico della Mirandola (1463–1494) mastered Greek, Latin, Hebrew, and Arabic and aspired to synthesize the Hebrew, Greek, and Christian traditions. His most renowned work, *Oration on the Dignity of Man,* has been called the humanist manifesto.

Pico della Mirandola
Oration on the Dignity of Man

In the opening section of the *Oration,* Pico declares that unlike other creatures, human beings have not been assigned a fixed place in the universe. Our destiny is not determined by anything outside us. Rather, God has bestowed upon us a unique distinction: the liberty to determine the form and value our lives shall acquire. The notion that people have the power to shape their own lives is a key element in the emergence of the modern outlook.

I have read in the records of the Arabians, reverend Fathers, that Abdala the Saracen,[1] when questioned as to what on this stage of the world, as it were, could be seen most worthy of wonder, replied: "There is nothing to be seen more wonderful than man." In agreement with this opinion is the saying of Hermes Trismegistus: "A great miracle, Asclepius, is man."[2] But when I weighed the reason for these maxims, the many grounds for the excellence of human nature reported by many men failed to satisfy me—that man is the intermediary between creatures, the intimate of the gods, the king of the lower beings, by the acuteness of his senses, by the discernment of his reason, and by the light of his intelligence the interpreter of nature, the interval between fixed eternity and fleeting time, and (as the Persians say) the bond, nay, rather, the marriage song of the world, on David's [biblical king] testimony but little lower than the angels. Admittedly great though these reasons be, they are not the principal grounds, that is, those which may rightfully claim for themselves the privilege of the highest admiration. For why should we not admire more the angels themselves and the blessed choirs of heaven? At last it seems to me I have come to understand why man is the most fortunate of creatures and consequently worthy of all admiration and what precisely is that rank which is his lot in the universal chain of Being—a rank to be envied not only by brutes but even by the stars and by minds beyond this world. It is a matter past faith and a wondrous one. Why should it not be? For it is on this very account that man is rightly called and judged a great miracle and a wonderful creature indeed. . . .

. . . God the Father, the supreme Architect, had already built this cosmic home we behold, the most sacred temple of His godhead, by the laws of His mysterious wisdom. The region above the heavens He had adorned with Intelligences, the heavenly spheres He had quickened with eternal souls, and the excrementary and filthy parts of the lower world He had filled with a multitude of animals of every kind. But, when the work was finished, the Craftsman kept wishing that there were someone to ponder the plan of so great a work, to love its beauty, and to wonder at its vastness. Therefore, when everything was done (as Moses and Timaeus[3] bear witness), He finally took thought concerning the creation of man. But there was not among His archetypes that from which He could fashion a new offspring, nor was there in His treasurehouses anything which He might bestow on His new son as an inheritance, nor was there in the seats of all the world a place where the latter might sit to contemplate the universe. All was now complete; all things had been assigned to the highest, the middle, and the lowest orders. But in its final creation it was not the part of the Father's power to fail as though exhausted. It was not the part of His wisdom to waver in a needful matter through poverty of counsel. It was not the part of His kindly love that he who was to praise God's divine generosity in regard to others should be compelled to condemn it in regard to himself.

At last the best of artisans [God] ordained that that creature to whom He had been able to give nothing proper to himself should have joint possession of whatever had been peculiar to each of the different kinds of being. He therefore took man as a creature of indeterminate nature and, assigning him a place in the middle of the world, addressed him thus: "Neither a fixed abode nor a form that is thine alone nor any function peculiar to thyself have we given thee, Adam, to the end that according to thy longing and according to thy judgment thou mayest have and possess what abode, what form, and what functions thou thyself shalt desire. The nature of all other beings is limited and constrained within the bounds of laws prescribed by Us. Thou, constrained by no limits, in accordance with thine own free will, in whose hand We have placed thee, shalt ordain for thyself the limits of thy nature. We have set thee at the world's center that thou mayest from thence more easily observe whatever is in the world. We have made thee neither of heaven nor of earth, neither mortal nor immortal, so that with freedom of choice and with honor, as though the maker and molder of thyself, thou mayest fashion thyself in whatever shape thou shalt prefer. Thou shalt have the power to degenerate into the lower forms of life, which are brutish. Thou shalt have the power, out of thy soul's judgment, to be reborn into the higher forms, which are divine."

O supreme generosity of God the Father, O highest and most marvelous felicity of man! To him it is granted to have whatever he chooses, to be whatever he wills. Beasts as soon as they are born (so says Lucilius[4]) bring with them from their mother's womb all they will ever possess. Spiritual beings [angels], either from the beginning or soon thereafter, become what they are to be for ever and ever. On man when he came into life the Father conferred the seeds of all kinds

---

[1]Abdala the Saracen possibly refers to the eighth-century A.D. writer Abd-Allah Ibn al-Muqaffa.

[2]Ancient writings dealing with magic, alchemy, astrology, and occult philosophy were erroneously attributed to an assumed Egyptian priest, Hermes Trismegistus. Asclepius was a Greek god of healing.

[3]Timaeus, a Greek Pythagorean philosopher, was a central character in Plato's famous dialogue *Timaeus*.

[4]Lucilius, a first-century A.D. Roman poet and Stoic philosopher, was a close friend of Seneca, the philosopher-dramatist.

and the germs of every way of life. Whatever seeds each man cultivates will grow to maturity and bear in him their own fruit. If they be vegetative, he will be like a plant. If sensitive, he will become brutish. If rational, he will grow into a heavenly being. If intellectual, he will be an angel and the son of God. And if, happy in the lot of no created thing, he withdraws into the center of his own unity, his spirit, made one with God, in the solitary darkness of God, who is set above all things, shall surpass them all.

3 Break with Medieval Political Theory

Turning away from the religious orientation of the Middle Ages, Renaissance thinkers discussed the human condition in secular terms and opened up possibilities for thinking about moral and political problems in new ways. Thus, Niccolò Machiavelli (1469–1527), a Florentine statesman and political theorist, broke with medieval political theory. Medieval political thinkers held that the ruler derived power from God and had a religious obligation to rule in accordance with God's precepts. Machiavelli, though, ascribed no divine origin to kingship, nor did he attribute events to the mysterious will of God; and he explicitly rejected the principle that kings should adhere to Christian moral teachings. For Machiavelli, the state was a purely human creation. Successful kings or princes, he asserted, should be concerned only with preserving and strengthening the state's power and must ignore questions of good and evil, morality and immorality. Machiavelli did not assert that religion was supernatural in origin and rejected the prevailing belief that Christian morality should guide political life. For him, religion's value derived from other factors: a ruler could utilize religion to unite his subjects and to foster obedience to law.

Niccolò Machiavelli
The Prince

In contrast to medieval thinkers, Machiavelli did not seek to construct an ideal Christian community but to discover how politics was *really* conducted. He studied politics in the cold light of reason, as the following passage from *The Prince* illustrates.

It now remains to be seen what are the methods and rules for a prince as regards his subjects and friends. And as I know that many have written of this, I fear that my writing about it may be deemed presumptuous, differing as I do, especially in this matter, from the opinions of others. But my intention being to write something of use to those who understand, it appears to me more proper to go to the real truth of the matter than to its imagination; and many have imagined republics and principalities which have never been seen or known to exist in reality; for how we live is so far removed from how we ought to live, that he who abandons what is done for what ought to be done, will rather learn to bring about his own ruin than his preservation.

Machiavelli removed ethics from political thinking. A successful ruler, he contended, is indifferent to moral and religious considerations. But will not the prince be punished on the Day of Judgment for violating Christian teachings? In startling contrast to medieval theorists, Machiavelli simply ignored the question. The action of a prince, he said, should be governed solely by necessity.

A man who wishes to make a profession of goodness in everything must necessarily come to grief among so many who are not good. Therefore it is necessary for a prince, who wishes to maintain himself, to learn how not to be good, and to use this knowledge and not use it, according to the necessity of the case.

Leaving on one side, then, those things which concern only an imaginary prince, and speaking of those that are real, I state that all men, and especially princes, who are placed at a greater height, are reputed for certain qualities which bring them either praise or blame. Thus one is considered liberal, another . . . miserly; . . . one a free giver, another rapacious; one cruel, another merciful; one a breaker of his word, another trustworthy; one effeminate and pusillanimous, another fierce and high-spirited; one humane, another haughty; one lascivious, another chaste; one frank, another astute; one hard, another easy; one serious, another frivolous; one religious, another an unbeliever, and so on. I know that every one will admit that it would be highly praiseworthy in a prince to possess all the above-named qualities that are reputed good, but as they cannot all be possessed or observed, human conditions not permitting of it, it is necessary that he should be prudent enough to avoid the scandal of those vices which would lose him the state, and guard himself if possible against those which will not lose it [for] him, but if not able to, he can indulge them with less scruple. And yet he must not mind incurring the scandal of those vices, without which it would be difficult to save the state, for if one considers well, it will be found that some things which seem virtues would, if followed, lead to one's ruin, and some others which appear vices result in one's greater security and wellbeing. . . .

. . . I say that every prince must desire to be considered merciful and not cruel. He must, however, take care not to misuse this mercifulness. Cesare Borgia was considered cruel, but his cruelty had brought order to the Romagna,[1] united it, and reduced it to peace and fealty. If this is considered well, it will be seen that he was really much more merciful than the Florentine people, who, to avoid the name of cruelty, allowed Pistoia[2] to be destroyed. A prince, therefore, must not mind incurring the charge of cruelty for the purpose of keeping his subjects united and faithful; for, with a very few examples, he will be more merciful than those who, from excess of tenderness, allow disorders to arise, from whence spring bloodshed and rapine; for these as a rule injure the whole community, while the executions carried out by the prince injure only individuals. . . .

Machiavelli's rigorous investigation of politics led him to view human nature from the standpoint of its

limitations and imperfections. The astute prince, he said, recognizes that human beings are by nature selfish, cowardly, and dishonest, and regulates his political strategy accordingly.

From this arises the question whether it is better to be loved more than feared, or feared more than loved. The reply is, that one ought to be both feared and loved, but as it is difficult for the two to go together, it is much safer to be feared than loved, if one of the two has to be wanting. For it may be said of men in general that they are ungrateful, voluble, dissemblers, anxious to avoid danger, and covetous of gain; as long as you benefit them, they are entirely yours; they offer you their blood, their goods, their life, and their children, as I have before said, when the necessity is remote; but when it approaches, they revolt. And the prince who has relied solely on their words, without making other preparations, is ruined; for the friendship which is gained by purchase and not through grandeur and nobility of spirit is bought but not secured, and at a pinch is not to be expended in your service. And men have less scruple in offending one who makes himself loved than one who makes himself feared; for love is held by a chain of obligation which, men being selfish, is broken whenever it serves their purpose; but fear is maintained by a dread of punishment which never fails.

Still, a prince should make himself feared in such a way that if he does not gain love, he at any rate avoids hatred; for fear and the absence of hatred may well go together, and will be always attained by one who abstains from interfering with the property of his citizens and subjects or with their women. And when he is obliged to take the life of any one, let him do so when there is a proper justification and manifest reason for it; but above all he must abstain from taking the property of others, for men forget more easily the death of their father than the loss of their patrimony. Then also pretexts for seizing property are never wanting, and one who begins to live by rapine will always find some reason for taking the goods of others, whereas causes for taking life are rarer and more fleeting.

But when the prince is with his army and has a large number of soldiers under his control, then it is extremely necessary that he should not mind being thought cruel; for without this reputation he could not keep an army united or disposed to any duty. Among the noteworthy actions of Hannibal[3] is numbered this, that although he had an enormous army, composed of men of all nations and fighting in foreign countries, there never arose any dissension either among them or against the prince, either in good fortune or in bad. This could not be due to anything but his inhuman cruelty, which together with his infinite other virtues, made him always venerated and terrible in the sight of his soldiers, and

---

[1] Cesare Borgia (c. 1476–1507) was the bastard son of Rodrigo Borgia, then a Spanish cardinal, and later Pope Alexander VI (1492–1503). With his father's aid he attempted to carve out for himself an independent duchy in north-central Italy, with Romagna as its heart. Through cruelty, violence, and treachery, he succeeded at first in his ambition, but ultimately his principality collapsed. Romagna was eventually incorporated into the Papal State under Pope Julius II (1503–1513).

[2] Pistoia, a small Italian city in Tuscany, came under the control of Florence in the fourteenth century.

[3] Hannibal (247–182 B.C.) was a brilliant Carthaginian general whose military victories almost destroyed Roman power. He was finally defeated at the battle of Zama in 202 B.C. by the Roman general Scipio Africanus.

without it his other virtues would not have sufficed to produce that effect. Thoughtless writers admire on the one hand his actions, and on the other blame the principal cause of them. . . .

> Again in marked contrast to the teachings of Christian (and ancient) moralists, Machiavelli said that the successful prince will use any means to achieve and sustain political power. If the end is desirable, all means are justified.

How laudable it is for a prince to keep good faith and live with integrity, and not with astuteness, every one knows. Still the experience of our times shows those princes to have done great things who have had little regard for good faith, and have been able by astuteness to confuse men's brains, and who have ultimately overcome those who have made loyalty their foundation.

You must know, then, that there are two methods of fighting, the one by law, the other by force: the first method is that of men, the second of beasts; but as the first method is often insufficient, one must have recourse to the second. It is therefore necessary for a prince to know well how to use both the beast and the man. . . .

A prince being thus obliged to know well how to act as a beast must imitate the fox and the lion, for the lion cannot protect himself from traps, and the fox cannot defend himself from wolves. One must therefore be a fox to recognise traps, and a lion to frighten wolves. Those that wish to be only lions do not understand this. Therefore, a prudent ruler ought not to keep faith when by so doing it would be against his interest, and when the reasons which made him bind himself no longer exist. If men were all good, this precept would not be a good one; but as they are bad, and would not observe their faith with you, so you are not bound to keep faith with them. Nor have legitimate grounds ever failed a prince who wished to show [plausible] excuse for the non-fulfilment of his promise. Of this one could furnish an infinite number of modern examples, and show how many times peace has been broken, and how many promises rendered worthless, by the faithlessness of princes, and those that have been best able to imitate the fox have succeeded best. But it is necessary to be able to disguise this character well, and to be a great feigner and dissembler; and men are so simple and so ready to obey present necessities, that one who deceives will always find those who allow themselves to be deceived. . . .

. . . Thus it is well to seem merciful, faithful, humane, sincere, religious, and also to be so; but you must have the mind so disposed that when it is needful to be otherwise you may be able to change to the opposite qualities. And it must be understood that a prince, and especially a new prince, cannot observe all those things which are considered good in men, being often obliged, in order to maintain the state, to act against faith, against charity, against humanity, and against religion. And, therefore, he must have a mind disposed to adapt itself according to the wind, and as the variations of fortune dictate, and, as I said before, not deviate from what is good, if possible, but be able to do evil if constrained.

A prince must take great care that nothing goes out of his mouth which is not full of the above-named five qualities, and, to see and hear him, he should seem to be all mercy, faith, integrity, humanity, and religion. And nothing is more necessary than to seem to have this last quality, for men in general judge more by the eyes than by the hands, for every one can see, but very few have to feel. Everybody sees what you appear to be, few feel what you are, and those few will not dare to oppose themselves to the many, who have the majesty of the state to defend them; and in the actions of men, and especially of princes, from which there is no appeal, the end justifies the means. Let a prince therefore aim at conquering and maintaining the state, and the means will always be judged honourable and praised by every one, for the vulgar is always taken by appearances and the issue of the event; and the world consists only of the vulgar, and the few who are not vulgar are isolated when the many have a rallying point in the prince. A certain prince of the present time, whom it is well not to name, never does anything but preach peace and good faith, but he is really a great enemy to both, and either of them, had he observed them, would have lost him state or repuation on many occasions.

4 The Ideal Gentleman

By the early sixteenth century, the era of the republics had come to an end in Italy, and the princely courts were the new social and political ideal. At the same time that Machiavelli was defining the new *political* ideal in his *Prince,* Baldassare Castiglione (1478–1529) was describing the new *social* ideal—the Renaissance courtier who served princes—in his *Book of the Courtier* (1528). Born into an illustrious Lombard family near Mantua, Castiglione received a humanist education in Latin and Greek, and had a distinguished career serving in the courts of Italian dukes and Charles V in Spain. Castiglione's handbook became one of the most influential books of the day, providing instruction to aristocrats and nonaristocrats alike about how to be the perfect courtier or court lady. By the end of the sixteenth century, it had been translated into every major European language, making Castiglione the arbiter of aristocratic manners throughout Europe.

Like Greco-Roman moralists, Castiglione sought to overcome brutish elements in human nature and to shape a higher type of individual through reason. To structure the self artistically, to live life with verve and style, and to achieve a personal dignity were the humanist values that Castiglione's work spread beyond Italy.

Baldassare Castiglione
The Book of the Courtier

Castiglione chose the court of Urbino as the setting for his *Book of the Courtier,* which he wrote in the form of a conversation among the courtiers and ladies of the court. The participants—such as Guidobaldo, Duke of Urbino; the Duchess, Elisabetta Gonzaga; Count Ludovico da Canossa; and Cardinal Pietro Bembo— were all real people who in Castiglione's day had actual conversations at the court. In the first two books of *The Courtier,* Castiglione describes the ideal courtier as an example of the Renaissance "universal man," a well-rounded person with breadth of interest and versatility of accomplishment. In the following excerpt, Count Ludovico describes the courtier as a person of noble birth, a man who is skilled in weaponry, an expert horseman, and adept at all sorts of games.

"Thus, I would have our Courtier born of a noble and genteel family; because it is far less becoming for one of low birth to fail to do virtuous things than for one of noble birth, who, should he stray from the path of his forebears, stains the family name, and not only fails to achieve anything but loses what has been achieved already. For noble birth is like a bright lamp that makes manifest and visible deeds both good and bad, kindling and spurring on to virtue as much for fear of dishonor as for hope of praise. And since this luster of nobility does not shine forth in the deeds of the lowly born, they lack that spur, as well as that fear of dishonor, nor do they think themselves obliged to go beyond what was done by their forebears; whereas to the wellborn it seems a reproach not to attain at least to the mark set them by their ancestors. Hence, it almost always happens that, in the profession of arms as well as in other worthy pursuits, those who are most distinguished are men of noble birth, because nature has implanted in everything that hidden seed which gives a certain force and quality of its own essence to all that springs from it, making it like itself: as we can see not only in breeds of horses and other animals, but in trees as well, the shoots of which nearly always resemble the trunk; and if they sometimes degenerate, the fault lies with the husbandman. And so it happens with men, who, if they are tended in the right way, are almost always like those from whom they spring, and often are better; but if they lack someone to tend them properly, they grow wild and never attain their full growth. . . .

"[B]esides his noble birth, I would wish the Courtier favored in this other respect, and endowed by nature not only with talent and with beauty of countenance and person, but with that certain grace which we call an 'air,' which shall make him at first sight pleasing and lovable to all who see him; and let this be an adornment informing and attending all his actions, giving the promise outwardly that such a one is worthy of the company and the favor of every great lord. . . .

"But to come to some particulars: I hold that the principal and true profession of the Courtier must be that of arms; which I wish him to exercise with vigor; and let him be known among the others as bold, energetic, and faithful to whomever he serves. And the repute of these good qualities will be earned by exercising them in every time and place, inasmuch as one may not ever fail therein without great blame. And, just as among women the name of purity, once stained, is never restored, so the reputation of a gentleman whose profession is arms, if ever in the least way he sullies himself through cowardice or other disgrace, always remains defiled before the world and covered with ignominy. Therefore, the more our Courtier excels in this art, the more will he merit praise. . . .

"Then, coming to bodily frame, I say it is enough that it be neither extremely small nor big, because either of these conditions causes a certain contemptuous wonder, and men of either sort are gazed at in much the same way that we gaze at monstrous things. And yet, if one must sin in one or the other of these two extremes, it is less bad to be on the small side than to be excessively big; because men who are so huge of body are often not only obtuse of spirit, but are also unfit for every agile exercise, which is something I very much desire in the Courtier. And hence I would have him well built and shapely of limb, and would have him show strength and lightness and suppleness, and know all the bodily exercises that befit a warrior. And in this I judge it his first duty to know how to handle every kind of weapon, both on foot and on horse, and know the advantages of each kind; and be especially acquainted with those arms that are ordinarily used among gentlemen, because, apart from using them in war (where perhaps so many fine points are not necessary), there often arise differences between one gentleman and another, resulting in duels, and quite often those weapons are used which happen to be at hand. Hence, knowledge of them is a very safe thing. Nor am I one of those who say that skill is forgotten in the hour of need; for he who loses his skill at such times shows that out of fear he has already lost his heart and head. . . .

"Weapons are also often used in various exercises in time of peace, and gentlemen are seen in public spectacles before the people and before ladies and great lords. Therefore I wish our Courtier to be a perfect horseman in every kind of saddle; and, in addition to having a knowledge of horses and what pertains to riding, let him put every effort and diligence into outstripping others in everything a little, so that he may be always recognized as better than the rest. . . .

"I have this Courtier of ours excel all others in what is the special profession of each. And as it is the peculiar excellence of the Italians to ride well with the rein, to manage wild horses especially with great skill, to tilt and joust, let him be among the best of the Italians in this. In tourneys, in holding a pass, in attacking a fortified position, let him be among the best of the French. In stick-throwing, bull-fighting, in casting spears and darts, let him be outstanding among the Spaniards. But, above all, let him temper his every action with a certain good judgment and grace, if he would deserve that universal favor which is so greatly prized.

"There are also other exercises which, although not immediately dependent upon arms, still have much in common therewith and demand much manly vigor; and chief among these is the hunt, it seems to me, because it has a certain resemblance to war. It is a true pastime for great lords, it befits a Courtier, and one understands why it was so much practiced among the ancients. He should also know how to swim, jump, run, throw stones; for, besides their usefulness in war, it is frequently necessary to show one's prowess in such things, whereby a good name is to be won, especially with the crowd (with whom one must reckon after all). Another noble exercise and most suitable for a man at court is the game of tennis which shows off the disposition of body, the quickness and litheness of every member, and all the qualities that are brought out by almost every other exercise. Nor do I deem vaulting on horseback to be less worthy, which, though it is tiring and difficult, serves more than anything else to make a man agile and dexterous; and besides its use-

fulness, if such agility is accompanied by grace, in my opinion it makes a finer show than any other." . . .

Not only should the courtier be physically gifted, but he should be well educated. In the following passages, Count Ludovico declares that he should be learned in the humanities, the new educational curriculum of the Renaissance humanists. Moreover, in the spirit of the "universal man," he should be a musician, and he should display a knowledge of drawing and painting.

"I would have him more than passably learned in letters, at least in those studies which we call the humanities. Let him be conversant not only with the Latin language, but with Greek as well, because of the abundance and variety of things that are so divinely written therein. Let him be versed in the poets, as well as in the orators and historians, and let him be practiced also in writing verse and prose, especially in our own vernacular; for, besides the personal satisfaction he will take in this, in this way he will never want for pleasant entertainment with the ladies, who are usually fond of such things. And if, because of other occupations or lack of study, he does not attain to such a perfection that his writings should merit great praise, let him take care to keep them under cover so that others will not laugh at him, and let him show them only to a friend who can be trusted; because at least they will be of profit to him in that, through such exercise, he will be capable of judging the writing of others. For it very rarely happens that a man who is unpracticed in writing, however learned he may be, can ever wholly understand the toils and industry of writers, or taste the sweetness and excellence of styles, and those intrinsic niceties that are often found in the ancients. . . .

"Gentlemen, you must know that I am not satisfied with our Courtier unless he be also a musician, and unless, besides understanding and being able to read music, he can play various instruments. For, if we rightly consider, no rest from toil and no medicine for ailing spirits can be found more decorous or praiseworthy in time of leisure than this; and especially in courts where, besides the release from vexations which music gives to all, many things are done to please the ladies, whose tender and delicate spirits are readily penetrated with harmony and filled with sweetness. Hence, it is no wonder that in both ancient and modern times they have always been particularly fond of musicians, finding music a most welcome food for the spirit." . . .

Then the Count said: "Before we enter upon that subject, I would discuss another matter which I consider to be of great importance and which I think must therefore, in no way be neglected by our Courtier: and this is a knowledge of how to draw and an acquaintance with the art of painting itself."

Castiglione also portrays the ideal court lady. She should have many of the same attributes as the courtier, and, in addition, she should be able to manage her house and her children, as well as being able to provide gracious entertainment for the men at court. In the following passage, the speaker is the Magnifico Giuliano de' Medici.

". . . I hold that many virtues of the mind are as necessary to a woman as to a man; also, gentle birth; to avoid affectation, to be naturally graceful in all her actions, to be mannerly, clever, prudent, not arrogant, not envious, not slanderous, not vain, not contentious, not inept, to know how to gain and hold the favor of her mistress and of all others, to perform well and gracefully the exercises that are suitable for women. And I do think that beauty is more necessary to her than to the Courtier, for truly that woman lacks much who lacks beauty. Also she must be more circumspect, and more careful not to give occasion for evil being said of her, and conduct herself so that she may not only escape being sullied by guilt but even by the suspicion of it, for a woman has not so many ways of defending herself against false calumnies as a man has. But since Count Ludovico has set forth in great detail the chief profession of the Courtier, and has insisted that this be arms, I think it is also fitting to state what I judge that of the Court Lady to be, and when I have done this I shall think to have discharged the greater part of my assignment.

"Leaving aside, then, those virtues of the mind which she is to have in common with the Courtier (such as prudence, magnanimity, continence, and many others), as well as those qualities that befit all (such as kindness, discretion, ability to manage her husband's property and house and children, if she is married, and all qualities that are requisite in a good mother), I say that, in my opinion, in a Lady who lives at court a certain pleasing affability is becoming above all else, whereby she will be able to entertain graciously every kind of man with agreeable and comely conversation suited to the time and place and to the station of the person with whom she speaks, joining to serene and modest manners, and that to comeliness that ought to inform all her actions, a quick vivacity of spirit whereby she will show herself a stranger to all boorishness; but with such a kind manner as to cause her to be thought no less chaste, prudent, and gentle than she is agreeable, witty, and discreet: thus, she must observe a certain mean (difficult to achieve and, as it were, composed of contraries) and must strictly observe certain limits and not exceed them. . . .

"And since words that have no subject matter of importance are vain and puerile, the Court Lady must have not only the good judgment to recognize the kind of person with whom she is speaking, but must have knowledge of many things, in order to entertain that person graciously; and let her know how in her talk to choose those things that are suited to the kind of person with whom she is speaking, and be careful lest, unintentionally, she might sometimes utter words that could offend him. Let her take care not to disgust him by indiscreet praise of herself or by being too prolix [verbose]. Let her not proceed to mingle serious matters with playful or humorous discourse, or mix jests and jokes with serious talk. Let her not show ineptitude in pretending to know what she does not know, but let her seek modestly to do herself credit in what she does know—in all things avoiding affectation, as has been said. In this way she will be adorned with good manners; she will perform with surpassing grace the bodily exercises that are proper to women; her discourse will be fluent and most prudent virtuous, and pleasant; thus, she will be not only loved but revered by everyone, and perhaps worthy of being considered the equal of this great Courtier, both in qualities of mind and of body."

5 The Spread of the Renaissance

The Renaissance spread from Italy to Germany, France, England, and Spain. Exemplifying the Renaissance spirit in France was François Rabelais (c. 1495–c. 1553), a Benedictine monk (until he resigned from the order), a physician, and a humanist scholar. *Gargantua and Pantagruel,* Rabelais' satirical epic, attacked clerical education and monastic orders and expressed an appreciation for secular learning and a confidence in human nature. Like other Renaissance humanists, Rabelais criticized medieval philosophy for its overriding concern with obscure, confused, and irrelevant questions and censured a narrow-minded clergy which deprived people of life's joys. Expressing his aversion to medieval asceticism, he attacked monasticism as life-denying and extolled worldly pleasure as a legitimate need and aim of human nature.

François Rabelais
CELEBRATION OF THE WORLDLY LIFE

The following reading from *Gargantua and Pantagruel* contains a description of life at an imagined monastery, the abbey of Thélème, whose rules differed markedly from those of traditional medieval monasteries. Here Rabelais expressed the Renaissance celebration of the worldly life.

THE RULES ACCORDING TO WHICH THE THÉLÈMITES LIVED

All their life was regulated not by laws, statutes, or rules, but according to their free will and pleasure. They rose from bed when they pleased, and drank, ate, worked, and slept when the fancy seized them. Nobody woke them; nobody compelled them either to eat or to drink, or to do anything else whatever. So it was that Gargantua has established it. In their rules there was only one clause:

DO WHAT YOU WILL

because people who are free, well-born, well-bred, and easy in honest company have a natural spur and instinct which drives them to virtuous deeds and deflects them from vice; and this they called honour. When these same men are depressed and enslaved by vile constraint and subjection, they use this noble quality which once impelled them freely towards virtue, to throw off and break this yoke of slavery. For we always strive after things forbidden and covet what is denied us.

Making use of this liberty, they most laudably rivalled one another in all of them doing what they saw pleased one. If some man or woman said, "Let us drink," they all drank; if he or she said, "Let us play," they all played; if it was "Let us go and amuse ourselves in the fields," everyone went there. If it were for hawking or hunting, the ladies, mounted on fine mares, with their grand palfreys following, each carried on their daintily gloved wrists a sparrow-hawk, a lanneret, or a merlin, the men carrying the other birds.[1]

So nobly were they instructed that there was not a man or woman among them who could not read, write, sing, play musical instruments, speak five or six languages, and compose in them both verse and prose. Never were seen such worthy knights, so valiant, so nimble both on foot and horse; knights more vigorous, more agile, handier with all weapons than they were. Never were seen ladies so good-looking, so dainty, less tiresome, more skilled with the fingers and the needle, and in every free and honest womanly pursuit than they were. . . .

Gargantua writes to his son Pantagruel, studying in Paris; in the letter, he describes a truly liberal education, one befitting a Renaissance humanist.

Now every method of teaching has been restored, and the study of languages has been revived: of Greek, without which it is disgraceful for a man to call himself a scholar, and of Hebrew, [other ancient Semitic languages], and Latin. The elegant and accurate art of printing, which is now in use, was invented in my time, by divine inspiration; as, by contrast, artillery was inspired by diabolical suggestion. The whole world is full of learned men, of very erudite tutors, and of most extensive libraries, and it is my opinion that neither in the time of Plato, of Cicero, nor of Papinian[2] were there such facilities for study as one finds today. No one, in future, will risk appearing in public or in any company, who is not well polished in Minerva's [Roman goddess of wisdom] workshop. I find robbers, hangmen, freebooters, and grooms nowadays more learned than the doctors and preachers were in my time.

Why, the very women and girls aspire to the glory and reach out for the celestial manna[3] of sound learning. So much so that at my present age I have been compelled to learn Greek, which I had not despised like Cato,[4] but which I had not the leisure to learn in my youth. Indeed I find great delight in reading the *Morals* of Plutarch, Plato's magnificent *Dialogues*, the *Monuments* of Pausanias, and the *Antiquities* of

---

[1]*Palfreys* and *lanneret,* archaic terms, refer respectively to a saddle horse usually ridden by women and to a small male falcon native to the Mediterranean area. A merlin is a small black and white European falcon, now also called a pigeon hawk.

[2]Papinian was a Roman jurist of the late second to early third century A.D. whose legal opinions were considered authoritative in late Roman law.

[3]*Manna* refers to a food miraculously provided by God for the Hebrews during their exodus out of Egypt during Moses' time (Exodus 16:14–36).

[4]Cato the Elder (234–149 B.C.), a Roman statesman, was noted for his conservative morals and hostility to Greek influences in Roman society.

Athenaeus,[5] while I wait for the hour when it will please God, my Creator, to call me and bid me leave this earth.

Therefore, my son, I beg you to devote your youth to the firm pursuit of your studies and to the attainment of virtue. You are in Paris. There you will find many praiseworthy examples to follow. You have Epistemon for your tutor, and he can give you living instruction by word of mouth. It is my earnest wish that you shall become a perfect master of languages. First of Greek, as Quintilian [Roman educational theorist] advises; secondly, of Latin; and then of Hebrew, on account of the Holy Scriptures; also of Chaldean and Arabic, for the same reason; and I would have you model your Greek style on Plato's and your Latin on that of Cicero. Keep your memory well stocked with every tale from history, and here you will find help in the Cosmographes[6] of the historians. Of the liberal arts, geometry, arithmetic, and music, I gave you some smattering when you were still small, at the age of five or six. Go on and learn the rest, also the rules of astronomy. But leave divinatory astrology and Lully's[7] art alone, I beg of you, for they are frauds and vanities. Of Civil Law I would have you learn the best texts by heart, and relate them to the art of philosophy. And as for the knowledge of Nature's works, I should like you to give careful attention to that too; so that there may be no sea, river, or spring of which you do not know the fish. All the birds of the air, all the trees, shrubs, and bushes of the forest, all the herbs of the field, all the metals deep in the bowels of the earth, the precious stones of the whole East and the South—let none of them be unknown to you.

Then scrupulously peruse the books of the Greek, Arabian, and Latin doctors once more, not omitting the Talmudists and Cabalists,[8] and by frequent dissections gain a perfect knowledge of that other world which is man. At some hours of the day also, begin to examine the Holy Scriptures. First the New Testament and the Epistles of the Apostles in Greek; and then the Old Testament, in Hebrew. In short, let me find you a veritable abyss of knowledge. For, later, when you have grown into a man, you will have to leave this quiet and repose of study, to learn chivalry and warfare, to defend my house, and to help our friends in every emergency against the attacks of evildoers.

---

[5]Pausanias was a travel writer famous for his guides to the ancient monuments of Greece, and Athenaeus was a compiler of literary and philosophical writings. Both were Greeks of the second century A.D.
[6]Cosmographes are books on geography, geology, and astronomy.
[7]Lully alludes to Ramon Lull (c. 1236–1315), a Franciscan friar, a mystic, and a philosopher, who was falsely reputed to have authored various books on magic and alchemy.

[8]Talmudists are students of the collection of writings on Jewish civil and religious laws, and Cabalists refers to students of a medieval Jewish occult tradition based on a mystical interpretation of the Hebrew Scriptures.

6 Thomas More: Prince of English Humanists

The most distinguished of the early English humanists was Thomas More (1478–1535). A lawyer by profession, More was a member of Parliament, counselor to King Henry VIII, speaker of the House of Commons, and lord chancellor of England. However, as a devout Catholic, he disapproved of Henry's divorce from Catherine of Aragon, and in 1532, he resigned as lord chancellor. More's dilemma became acute after Parliament made Henry the Supreme Head of the Church of England. More's refusal to accept Henry as the supreme head of the church led to his execution in 1535.

By 1520, More had wide repute as a humanist, not only in England but also on the Continent. His works include poems, a biography of Pico (see page 7), a history of King Richard III, correspondence extolling humanist educational values, and various religious writings. But he is most famous for his masterpiece, *Utopia,* published in 1516. Influenced by *The Republic* of Plato, *Utopia*—which means "no place"—was the first modern description of a perfect society. More's *Utopia* gave rise to a new literary genre in the West. Particularly in the late eighteenth and early nineteenth centuries, theorists drew up plans for an ideal society that would remedy current misery.

Thomas More
Utopia

In Book One, More meets Raphael, the narrator of Book Two, who tells him that he sailed to the New World where he discovered the perfect society on the island of Utopia. In Book Two, excerpted herein, Raphael describes Utopia as a communal society where there is neither poverty nor social or economic injustices. Since the Utopians share all things, there is no need for a money economy, and there is no private property. No one is idle, everyone works, but Raphael assures the reader that the work is not onerous.

[N]o one has to exhaust himself with endless toil from early morning to late at night as if he were a beast of burden. Such wretchedness, really worse than slavery, is the common lot of workmen in all countries, except Utopia. Of the day's twenty-four hours, the Utopians devote only six to work. They work three hours before noon, when they go to lunch. After lunch they rest for a couple of hours, then go to work for another three hours. Then they have supper, and at eight o'clock (counting the first hour after noon as one), they go to bed and sleep eight hours.

The other hours of the day, when they are not working, eating, or sleeping, are left to each man's individual discretion, provided he does not waste them in roistering or sloth, but uses them busily in some occupation that pleases him. Generally these periods are devoted to intellectual activity. For they have an established custom of giving public lectures before daybreak; attendance at these lectures is required only of those who have been specially chosen to devote themselves to learning, but a great many other people, both men and women, choose voluntarily to attend. Depending on their interests, some go to one lecture, some to another. But if anyone would rather devote his spare time to his trade, as many do who don't care for the intellectual life, this is not discouraged; in fact, such persons are commended as especially useful to the commonwealth.

After supper, they devote an hour to recreation, in their gardens when the weather is fine, or during winter weather in the common halls where they have their meals. There they either play music or amuse themselves with conversation. They know nothing about gambling with dice, or other such foolish and ruinous games. They do play two games not unlike our own chess. One is a battle of numbers, in which one number captures another. The other is a game in which the vices fight a battle against the virtues. The game is set up to show how the vices oppose one another, yet readily combine against the virtues; then, what vices oppose what virtues, how they try to assault them openly or undermine them insidiously; how the virtues can break the strength of the vices or turn their purposes to good; and finally, by what means one side or the other gains the victory.

But in all this, you may get a wrong impression, if we don't go back and consider one point more carefully. Because they allot only six hours to work, you might think the necessities of life would be in scant supply. This is far from the case. Their working hours are ample to provide not only enough but more than enough of the necessities and even the conveniences of life. You will easily appreciate this if you consider how large a part of the population in other countries exists without doing any work at all. In first place, hardly any of the women, who are a full half of the population, work: or, if they do, then as a rule their husbands lie snoring in bed. Then there is a great lazy gang of priests and so-called religious men. Add to them all the rich, especially the landlords, who are commonly called gentlemen and nobility. Include with them their retainers, that mob of swaggering bullies. Finally, reckon in with these the sturdy and lusty beggars, who go about feigning some disease as an excuse for their idleness. You will certainly find that the things which satisfy our needs are produced by far fewer hands than you had supposed.

In telling about their social and economic relations, Raphael explains that since there is plenty of everything, no one is greedy or selfish.

But to return to their manner of living. The oldest of every household, as I said, is the ruler. Wives are subject to their husbands, children to their parents, and generally the younger to their elders. Every city is divided into four equal districts, and in the middle of each district is a market for all kinds of commodities. Whatever each household produces is brought here, and stored in warehouses, each kind of goods in its own place. Here the head of each household looks for what he or his family needs, and carries off what he wants without any sort of payment or compensation. Why should anything be refused him? There is plenty of everything, and no reason to fear that anyone will claim more than he needs. Why would anyone be suspected of asking for more than is needed, when everyone knows there will never be any shortage? Fear of want, makes every living creature greedy and avaricious—and, in addition, man develops these qualities out of pride, pride which glories in putting down others by a superfluous display of possessions. But this kind of vice has no place whatever in the Utopian way of life.

In the following passage, More demonstrates his humanistic appreciation of ancient wisdom. Even though the Utopians had never come into contact with European philosophy, using their natural reason they learned the same principles. But when Raphael introduced them to Greek literature and philosophy, they were very appreciative.

The people in general are easygoing, cheerful, clever, and fond of leisure. When they must, they can stand heavy labor, but otherwise they are not much given to it. In intellectual pursuits, they are tireless. When they heard from us about the literature and learning of the Greeks (for we thought there was nothing in Latin except the historians and poets that they would enjoy), it was wonderful to behold how eagerly they sought to be instructed in Greek. We therefore began to study a little of it with them, at first more to avoid seeming lazy than out of any expectation that they would profit by it. But after a short trial, their diligence convinced us that our efforts would not be wasted. They picked up the forms of the letters so quickly, pronounced the language so aptly, memorized it so quickly, and began to recite so accurately that it seemed like a miracle. Most of our pupils were established scholars, of course, picked for their unusual ability and mature minds; and they studied with us, not just of their own free will, but at the command of the senate. Thus in less than three years they had perfect control of the language, and could read the best Greek authors fluently, unless the text was corrupt. I suspect they picked up Greek more easily because it was somewhat related to their own tongue. Though their language resembles the Persian in most respects, I suspect them of deriving from Greece because their language retains quite a few vestiges of Greek in the names of cities and in official titles.

Although the Utopians had never come into contact with Christianity, most of them had come to believe in a single, all-powerful god. Therefore, when Raphael introduced them to Christianity, many of them recognized it as the true religion.

There are different forms of religion throughout the island, and in each particular city as well. Some worship as a god the sun, others the moon, and still others one of the planets. There are some who worship a man of past ages who was conspicuous either for virtue or glory: they consider him not only a god but the supreme god. Most of the Utopians, however, and among these all the wisest, believe nothing of the sort: they believe in a single power, unknown, eternal, infinite, inexplicable, far beyond the grasp of the human mind, and diffused throughout the universe, not physically, but in influence. Him they call father, and to him alone they attribute the origin, increase, progress, change, and end of all visible things; they do not offer divine honors to any other.

Though the other sects of the Utopians differ from this main group in various particular doctrines, they all agree in this single head, that there is one supreme power, the maker and ruler of the universe, whom they all call in their native language Mithra. Different people define him differently, and each supposes the object of his worship is the special vessel of that great force which all people agree in worshipping. But gradually they are coming to forsake this mixture of superstitions, and to unite in that one religion which seems more reasonable than any of the others. And there is no doubt that the other religions would have disappeared long ago, except for various unlucky accidents that befell certain Utopians who were thinking about changing their religion. All the others immediately construed these events as a sign of heavenly anger, not chance, as if the deity who was being abandoned were avenging an insult against himself.

But after they had heard from us the name of Christ, and learned of his teachings, his life, his miracles, and the no less marvelous devotion of the many martyrs who shed their blood to draw nations far and near into the Christian fellowship, you would not believe how they were impressed. Either through the mysterious inspiration of God, or because Christianity is very like the religion already prevailing among them, they were well disposed toward it from the start. But I think they were also much influenced by the fact that Christ had encouraged his disciples to practice community of goods, and that among the truest groups of Christians, the practice still prevails. Whatever the reason, no small number of them chose to join our communion, and received the holy water of baptism.

Scholars disagree about More's intentions in writing *Utopia*. Is it a plan to impose a monastic sort of life on the entire society? Is it a precursor of modern socialism? Or is it a prospectus for a just and equitable society? The clearest statement of what may have been More's purpose is found in this passage at the very end of *Utopia*.

Now I have described to you as accurately as I could the structure of that commonwealth which I consider not only the best but the only one that can rightfully claim that name. In other places men talk very liberally of the common wealth, but what they mean is simply their own wealth; in Utopia, where there is no private business, every man zealously pursues the public business. And in both places, men are right to act as they do. For among us, even though the state may flourish, each man knows that unless he makes separate provision for himself, he may perfectly well die of hunger. Bitter necessity, then, forces men to look out for themselves rather than for others, that is, for the people. But in Utopia, where everything belongs to everybody, no man need fear that, so long as the public warehouses are filled, he will ever lack for anything he needs. Distribution is simply not one of their problems; in Utopia no men are poor, no men are beggars. Though no man owns anything, everyone is rich.

For what can be greater riches than for a man to live joyfully and peacefully, free from all anxieties, and without worries about making a living? . . .

Now here I'd like to see anyone try to compare this justice of the Utopians with the so-called justice that prevails among other peoples—among whom let me perish if I can discover the slightest scrap of justice or fairness. What kind of justice is it when a nobleman or a goldsmith or a money-lender, or someone else who makes his living by doing either nothing at all or something completely useless to the public, gets to live a life of luxury and grandeur? In the meantime, a laborer, a carter, a carpenter, or a farmer works so hard and so constantly that even a beast of burden would perish under the load; and this work of theirs is so necessary that no commonwealth could survive a year without it. Yet they earn so meager a living and lead such miserable lives that a beast of burden would really be better off. Beasts do not have to work every minute, and their food is not much worse: in fact they like it better. And, besides, they do not have to worry about their future. But workingmen not only have to sweat and suffer without present reward, but agonize over the prospect of a penniless old age. Their daily wage is inadequate even for their present needs, so there is no possible chance of their saving toward the future.

Now isn't this an unjust and ungrateful commonwealth? It lavishes rich rewards on so-called gentry, bankers and goldsmiths and the rest of that crew, who don't work at all, are mere parasites, or purveyors of empty pleasures. And yet it makes no provision whatever for the welfare of farmers and colliers, laborers, carters, and carpenters, without whom the commonwealth would simply cease to exist. After the state has taken the labor of their best years, when they are worn out by age and sickness and utter destitution, then the thankless state, forgetting all their pains and services, throws them out to die a miserable death. What is worse, the rich constantly try to grind out of the poor part of their meager wages, not only by private swindling, but by public tax-laws. It is basically unjust that people who deserve most from the commonwealth should receive least. But now they have distorted and debased the right even further by giving their extortion the color of law; and thus they have palmed injustice off as "legal." When I run over in my mind the various commonwealths flourishing today, so help me God, I can see nothing in them but a conspiracy of the rich, who are fattening up their own interests under the name and title of the commonwealth. They invent ways and means to hang onto whatever they have acquired by sharp practice, and then they scheme to oppress the poor by buying up their toil and labor as

cheaply as possible. These devices become law as soon as the rich, speaking through the commonwealth—which, of course, includes the poor as well—say they must be observed.

And yet, when these insatiably greedy and evil men have divided among themselves goods which would have sufficed for the entire people, how far they remain from the happiness of the Utopians, who have abolished not only money but with it greed! What a mass of trouble was uprooted by that one step! What a multitude of crimes was pulled up by the roots! Everyone knows that if money were abolished, fraud, theft, robbery, quarrels, brawls, seditions, murders, treasons, poisonings, and a whole set of crimes which are avenged but not prevented by the hangman would at once die out. If money disappeared, so would fear, anxiety, worry, toil, and sleepless nights. Even poverty, which seems to need money more than anything else for its relief, would vanish if money were entirely done away with. . . .

Even the rich, I'm sure, understand this. They must know that it's better to have enough of what we really need than an abundance of superfluities, much better to escape from our many present troubles than to be burdened with great masses of wealth. And in fact I have no doubt that every man's perception of where his true interest lies, along with the authority of Christ our Saviour (whose wisdom could not fail to recognize the best, and whose goodness would not fail to counsel it), would long ago have brought the whole world to adopt Utopian laws, if it were not for one single monster, the prime plague and begetter of all others—I mean Pride.

Pride measures her advantages not by what she has but by what other people lack. Pride would not condescend even to be made a goddess, if there were no wretches for her to sneer at and domineer over. Her good fortune is dazzling only by contrast with the miseries of others, her riches are valuable only as they torment and tantalize the poverty of others. Pride is a serpent from hell which twines itself around the hearts of men; and it acts like the suckfish in holding them back from choosing a better way of life.

Pride is too deeply fixed in the hearts of men to be easily plucked out. So I am glad that the Utopians at least have been lucky enough to achieve this commonwealth, which I wish all mankind would imitate. The institutions they have adopted have made their community most happy, and as far as anyone can tell, capable of lasting forever. . . .

More, however, has the final word.

When Raphael had finished his story, it seemed to me that not a few of the customs and laws he had described as existing among the Utopians were quite absurd. Their methods of waging war, their religious ceremonies, and their social customs were some of these, but my chief objection was to the basis of their whole system, that is, their communal living and their moneyless economy. This one thing alone takes away all the nobility, magnificence, splendor, and majesty which (in the popular view) are considered the true ornaments of any nation. But I saw Raphael was tired with talking, and I was not sure he could take contradiction, in these matters. . . .

So with praise for the Utopian way of life and his account of it, I took him by the hand and led him in to supper. But first I said that we would find some other time for thinking of these matters more deeply, and for talking them over in more detail. And I still hope such an opportunity will present itself some day.

Meanwhile, though he is a man of unquestioned learning, and highly experienced in the ways of the world, I cannot agree with everything he said. Yet I confess there are many things in the Commonwealth of Utopia that I wish our own country would imitate—though I don't really expect it will.

7 Skepticism and Fideism

Michel de Montaigne (1533–1592), the greatest French literary figure of the sixteenth century, lived during a time of great upheaval. An eminent humanist, he had a great interest in the thinkers of ancient Greece and Rome and in the relevance of their ideas for his own day. But he also was acutely affected by the Reformation: Religious warfare raged in France between Calvinists and Catholics for most of his adult life. Even his own family was divided, as his father remained a staunch Catholic, while his mother and siblings became Calvinists. Montaigne himself continued to be a Catholic, although an extremely tolerant one. Montaigne was a skeptic, who doubted that reason could arrive at absolute certainty. Partially as a result of his doubts, a crisis in thought developed among French philosophers which, in the following century, René Descartes (see page 75) tried to resolve. At the age of thirty-eight, Montaigne retired to his country estate where, between 1571 and 1580, he wrote his *Essays.* The first two books appeared in 1580, and the third in 1588, just four years before his death. In his *Essays,* which are considered by many to be the finest example of the genre ever written, Montaigne reflects on the human condition and explores humanity's strengths and weaknesses. In his *Apology for Raymond Sebond,* by far the longest of the essays, he argues that religious truth lay only in faith, not in reason.

Michel de Montaigne
An Apology for Raymond Sebond

Raymond Sebond was a fifteenth-century theologian who, in *Natural Theology,* argued that humans—using their reason, and observing nature and its inherently divine order—could discover all the essential truths about God and Christianity. At his father's request, Montaigne translated Sebond's treatise into French, and then he wrote the *Apology* (Defense). In the first few pages, Montaigne considers the two common objections to Sebond's work. In reply to the first objection, that Christianity ought to be based purely on faith, not on reason, Montaigne agrees that faith is the foundation of Christianity, but he also acknowledges that Sebond's rational argument might be useful in defending the faith. This, however, was the full extent of Montaigne's "defense" of Sebond. For, in reply to the second objection—that Sebond's arguments are so weak that they can easily be overcome—Montaigne asserts that all human reasoning is unsound. He believed that human reason cannot ascertain the truth; no one can find absolute certainty through reason. Indeed, Montaigne wonders, why do humans consider themselves to be the greatest creatures in the universe? Are humans even superior to the animals?

Presumption is our natural and original malady. The most vulnerable and frail of all creatures is man, and at the same time the most arrogant. He feels and sees himself lodged here, amid the mire and dung of the world, nailed and riveted to the worst, the deadest and the most stagnant part of the universe, on the lowest story of the house and the farthest from the vault of heaven, . . . and in his imagination he goes planting himself above the circle of the moon, and bringing the sky down beneath his feet. It is by the vanity of this same imagination that he equals himself to God, attributes to himself divine characteristics, picks himself out and separates himself from the horde of other creatures, carves out their shares to his fellows and companions the animals, and distributes among them such portions of faculties and powers as he sees fit. How does he know, by the force of his intelligence, the secret internal stirrings of animals? By what comparison between them and us does he infer the stupidity that he attributes to them?

When I play with my cat, who knows if I am not a pastime to her more than she is to me? . . .

Montaigne then develops his answer to the question, "What do I know?" Among the ancient philosophers, some claimed to have found the truth and others said that the truth cannot be discovered. In his discussion, Montaigne declares that he is a follower of the ancient skeptics, Pyrrho (c. 360–275 B.C.) and Sextus Empiricus (A.D. 160–210), who said that they still were searching for the truth.

Pyrrho and other Skeptics . . . say that they are still in search of the truth. These men judge that those who think they have found it are infinitely mistaken; and that there is also an overbold vanity in that second class that assures us that human powers are not capable of attaining it. . . .

Ignorance that knows itself, that judges itself and condemns itself, is not complete ignorance: to be that, it must be ignorant of itself. So that the profession of the Pyrrhonians is to waver, doubt, and inquire, to be sure of nothing, to answer for nothing.

Now this attitude of their judgment, straight and inflexible, taking all things in without adherence or consent, leads them to their Ataraxy, which is a peaceful and sedate condition of life, exempt from the agitations we receive through the impression of the opinion and knowledge we think we have of things.

Is it not an advantage to be freed from the necessity that curbs others? Is it not better to remain in suspense than to entangle yourself in the many errors that the human fancy has produced? Is it not better to suspend your conviction than to get mixed up in these seditious and quarrelsome divisions?

What am I to choose? What you like, provided you choose! There is a stupid answer, to which nevertheless all

dogmatism seems to come, by which we are not allowed not to know what we do not know. . . .

The Pyrrhonians have kept themselves a wonderful advantage in combat, having rid themselves of the need to cover up. It does not matter to them that they are struck, provided they strike; and they do their work with everything. If they win, your proposition is lame; if you win, theirs is. If they lose, they confirm ignorance; if you lose, you confirm it. If they prove that nothing is known, well and good; if they do not know how to prove it, just as good. *So that, since equal reasons are found on both sides of the same subject, it may be the easier to suspend judgment on each side* [Cicero].

And they set store by the fact that they can find much more easily why a thing is false than that it is true; and what is not than what is; and what they do not believe than what they believe.

Their expressions are: "I establish nothing; it is no more thus than thus, or than neither way; I do not understand it; the appearances are equal on all sides; it is equally legitimate to speak for and against. Nothing seems true, which may not seem false." Their sacramental word is ἐπέχω, that is to say, "I hold back, I do not budge." Those are their refrains, and others of similar substance. Their effect is a pure, complete, and very perfect postponement and suspension of judgment. They rise their reason to inquire and debate, but not to conclude and choose. Whoever will imagine a perpetual confession of ignorance, a judgment without leaning or inclination, on any occasion whatever, he has a conception of Pyrrhonism.

I express this point or view as well as I can, because many find it difficult to conceive; and its authors themselves represent it rather obscurely and diversely. . . .

Our speech has its weaknesses and its defects, like all the rest. Most of the occasions for the troubles of the world are grammatical. Our lawsuits spring only from debate over the interpretation of the laws, and most of our wars from the inability to express clearly the conventions and treaties of agreement of princes.

Let us take the sentence that logic itself offers us as the clearest. If you say "It is fine weather," and if you are speaking the truth, then it is fine weather. Isn't that a sure way of speaking? Still it will deceive us. To show this let us continue the example. If you say "I lie," and if you are speaking the truth, then you lie. The art, the reason, the force, of the conclusion of this one are the same as in the others; yet there we are stuck in the mud.

I can see why the Pyrrhonian philosophers cannot express their general conception in any manner of speaking; for they would need a new language. Ours is wholly formed of affirmative propositions, which to them are utterly repugnant; so that when they say "I doubt," immediately you have them by the throat to make them admit that at least they know and are sure of this fact, that they doubt. Thus they have been constrained to take refuge in this comparison from medicine, without which their attitude would be inexplicable: when they declare "I do not know" or "I doubt," they say that this proposition carries itself away with the rest, no more nor less than rhubarb, which expels evil humors and carries itself off with them.

This idea is more firmly grasped in the form of interrogation: "What do I know?"—the words I bear as a motto, inscribed over a pair of scales.

In the concluding paragraphs of his essay, Montaigne reveals himself as a *fideist*—one who simply believes in God without objective, rational proof of his existence. Unable to establish truth through reason, he makes a leap of faith. By denying that there is any objective basis for truth, Montaigne created a skeptical crisis that continued to plague philosophers in the next century in their quest for certainty.

But then what really is? That which is eternal: that is to say, what never had birth, nor will ever have an end; to which time never brings any change. For time is a mobile thing, which appears as in a shadow, together with matter, which is ever running and flowing, without ever remaining stable or permanent. To which belong the words *before* and *after,* and *has been* or *will be,* which at the very first sight show very evidently that time is not a thing that *is;* for it would be a great stupidity and a perfectly apparent falsehood to say that that *is* which is not yet in being, or which already has ceased to be. And as for these words, *present, immediate, now,* on which it seems that we chiefly found and support our understanding of time, reason discovering this immediately destroys it; for she at once splits and divides it into future and past, as though wanting to see it necessarily divided in two.

The same thing happens to nature that is measured, as to time that measures it. For there is nothing in it either that abides or is stable; but all things in it are either born, or being born, or dying. For which reason it would be a sin to say of God, who is the only one that *is,* that he *was* or *will be.* For those terms represent declinings, transitions, or vicissitudes of what cannot endure or remain in being. Wherefore we must conclude that God alone *is*—not at all according to any measure of time, but according to an eternity immutable and immobile, not measured by time or subject to any decline; before whom there is nothing, nor will there be after, nor is there anything more new or more recent; but one who really *is*—who by one single *now* fills the *ever;* and there is nothing that really is but he alone—nor can we say "He has been," or "He will be"—without beginning and without end.

To this most religious conclusion of a pagan I want to add only this remark of a witness of the same condition, for an ending to this long and boring discourse, which would give me material without end: "O what a vile and abject thing is man," he says, "if he does not raise himself above humanity!"[1]

That is a good statement and a useful desire, but equally absurd. For to make the handful bigger than the hand, the armful bigger than the arm, and to hope to straddle more than the reach of our legs, is impossible and unnatural. Nor can man raise himself above himself and humanity; for he can see only with his own eyes, and seize only with his own grasp.

He will rise, if God by exception lends him a hand; he will rise by abandoning and renouncing his own means, and letting himself be raised and uplifted by purely celestial means.

It is for our Christian faith, not for his Stoical virtue, to aspire to that divine and miraculous metamorphosis.

---

[1]Seneca.

8 Human Nature and the Human Condition

William Shakespeare (1564–1616) is widely regarded as the West's foremost playwright. He expressed the Renaissance spirit by dealing with classical themes and figures, using settings from Renaissance Italy and ancient Greece, and probing the full range of people's motives, actions, and feelings. Shakespeare wrote poems, historical plays, and comedies, but his tragedies were his crowning achievement. In all of his tragic masterpieces, Shakespeare plumbs the depths of human nature and the human condition with the beauty of his poetic language, the carefulness of his characterizations, and the spontaneity of his creative imagination. The most popular of all of his plays is *The Tragedy of Hamlet, Prince of Denmark,* which was first performed in 1600 at the Globe theater in London.

William Shakespeare
*The Tragedy of Hamlet, Prince of Denmark**

The main characters of *Hamlet* are Hamlet himself; Queen Gertrude, Hamlet's mother; Claudius, Hamlet's uncle; Horatio, Hamlet's loyal friend; Ophelia, an innocent young woman whom Hamlet loves; Ophelia's father, Polonius; and her brother, Laertes. The intrigue of *Hamlet* centers on the death of the king of Denmark—Hamlet's father—who was the victim of a conspiracy between the adulterous Queen Gertrude and Claudius, now the new king. Vowing to avenge his father's death, Hamlet feigns madness to discover the truth. *Hamlet* is known for its soliloquies—lengthy monologues that expose Hamlet's inner torment and allow us to think about our own struggle to exist in a world which often seems to conspire against us. One of the most famous soliloquies is excerpted below, where Hamlet reflects on the place of human beings in the Great Chain of Being, questions the optimistic outlook of the Renaissance humanists, and reveals the melancholy he has felt since learning of his father's death.

I have of late—but wherefore I know not—lost all my mirth, forgone all custom of exercises[1]; and indeed it goes so heavily with my disposition, that this goodly frame, the earth, seems to me a sterile promontory; this most excellent canopy, the air, look you, this brave[2] o'erhanging firmament, this majestical roof fretted[3] with golden fire, why, it appeareth nothing to me but a foul and pestilent congregation of vapors. What [a] piece of work[4] is a man, how noble in reason, how infinite in faculties, in form and moving, how express[5] and admirable in action, how like an angel in apprehension, how like a god! the beauty of the world; the paragon of animals; and yet to me what is this quintessence[6] of dust? Man delights not me—nor women neither. . . .

(Act 2, Scene 2, lines 295–309)

The timelessness of Shakespeare's masterpiece is largely due to his ability to portray the struggle waged within Hamlet's soul—his dream of revenge and the forces that deprive him of it, including his own indecisiveness. In the scene below, which contains Shakespeare's most famous soliloquy, Hamlet's madness seems apparent as he considers suicide, tells Ophelia that he does not love her, and orders her to enter a monastery.

HAM.
To be, or not to be, that is the question:
Whether 'tis nobler in the mind to suffer

The slings and arrows of outrageous fortune,
Or to take arms against a sea of troubles,
And by opposing, end them. To die, to sleep—
No more, and by a sleep to say we end
The heart-ache and the thousand natural shocks
That flesh is heir to; 'tis a consummation[7]
Devoutly to be wish'd. To die, to sleep—
To sleep, perchance to dream—ay, there's the rub,[8]
For in that sleep of death what dreams may come,
When we have shuffled off[9] this mortal coil,[10]
Must give us pause; there's the respect[11]
That makes calamity of so long life[12]:
For who would bear the whips and scorns of time,[13]
Th' oppressor's wrong, the proud man's contumely,†
The pangs of despis'd love, the law's delay,
The insolence of office, and the spurns
That patient merit of th' unworthy takes,
When he himself might his quietus make[14]
With a bare bodkin[15]; who would fardels[16] bear,
To grunt and sweat under a weary life,
But that the dread of something after death,
The undiscover'd country, from whose bourn[17]
No traveller returns, puzzles[18] the will,
And makes us rather bear those ills we have,
Than fly to others that we know not of?

---

*For this reading only, numbered footnotes are from the original source and editor's notes are indicated by asterisks, daggers, et cetera.

1. **custom of exercises:** my usual athletic activities.
2. **brave:** splendid. 3. **fretted:** ornamented as with fretwork.
4. **piece of work:** masterpiece. 5. **express:** exact.
6. **quintessence:** finest and purest extract.

7. **consummation:** completion, end.
8. **rub:** obstacle (a term from the game of bowls).
9. **shuffled off:** freed ourselves from. 10. **this mortal coil:** the turmoil of this mortal life. 11. **respect:** consideration.
12. **of . . . life:** so long-lived. 13. **time:** the world. †**contumely:** scorn.
14. **his quietus make:** write paid to his account.
15. **bare bodkin:** mere dagger. 16. **fardels:** burdens.
17. **bourn:** boundary, i.e. region. 18. **puzzles:** paralyzes.

Thus conscience[19] does make cowards [of us all],
And thus the native hue[20] of resolution
Is sicklied o'er with the pale cast[21] of thought,[22]
And enterprises of great pitch[23] and moment
With this regard their currents turn awry,
And lose the name of action.—Soft you now,
The fair Ophelia. Nymph, in thy orisons[24]
Be all my sins rememb'red.

OPH.
Good my lord,
How does your honor for this many a day?

HAM.
I humbly thank you, well, [well, well].

OPH.
My lord, I have remembrances of yours
That I have longed long to redeliver.
I pray you now receive them.

HAM.
No, not I,
I never gave you aught.

OPH.
My honor'd lord, you know right well you did,
And with them words of so sweet breath compos'd
As made these things more rich. Their perfume lost,
Take these again, for to the noble mind
Rich gifts wax poor when givers prove unkind.
There, my lord.

HAM.
Ha, ha! are you honest?[25]

OPH.
My lord?

HAM.
Are you fair?

OPH.
What means your lordship?

HAM.
That if you be honest and fair, [your honesty] should admit
no discourse to your beauty.

OPH.
Could beauty, my lord, have better commerce than with honesty?

HAM.
Ay, truly, for the power of beauty will sooner transform honesty from what it is to a bawd than the force of honesty can translate beauty into his likeness. This was sometime[26] a paradox,[27] but now the time gives it proof. I did love you once.

OPH.
Indeed, my lord, you made me believe so.

HAM.
You should not have believ'd me, for virtue cannot so [inoculate] our old stock but we shall relish of it.[28] I lov'd you not.

OPH.
I was the more deceiv'd.

HAM.
Get thee [to] a nunn'ry, why wouldst thou be a breeder of sinners? I am myself indifferent honest,[29] but yet I could accuse me of such things that it were better my mother had not borne me: I am very proud, revengeful, ambitious, with more offenses at my beck than I have thoughts to put them in, imagination to give them shape, or time to act them in. What should such fellows as I do crawling between earth and heaven? We are arrant knaves, believe none of us. Go thy ways to a nunn'ry. Where's your father?

OPH.
At home, my lord.

HAM.
Let the doors be shut upon him, that he may play the fool no where but in 's own house. Farewell.

OPH.
O, help him, you sweet heavens!

HAM.
If thou dost marry, I'll give thee this plague for thy dowry: be thou chaste as ice, as pure as snow, thou shalt not escape calumny. Get thee to a nunn'ry, farewell. Or if you wilt needs marry, marry a fool, for wise men know well enough what monsters[30] you[31] make of them. To a nunn'ry, go, and quickly too. Farewell.

OPH.
Heavenly powers, restore him!

HAM.
I have heard of your paintings, well enough. God hath given you one face, and you make yourselves another. You jig and amble, and you [lisp,] you nick-name God's creatures[32] and make your wantonness [your] ignorance.[33] Go to, I'll no more

---

19. **conscience:** reflection (but with some of the modern sense, too)
20. **native hue:** natural (ruddy) complexion.
21. **pale cast:** pallor.   22. **thought:** i.e. melancholy thought, brooding.
23. **pitch:** loftiness (a term from falconry, signifying the highest point of a hawk's flight).   24. **orisons:** prayers.
25. **honest:** chaste.

26. **sometime:** formerly.   27. **paradox:** tenet contrary to accepted belief.
28. **virtue . . . it:** virtue, engrafted on our old stock (of viciousness), cannot so change the nature of the plant that no trace of the original will remain.
29. **indifferent honest:** tolerably virtuous.
30. **monsters.** Alluding to the notion that the husbands of unfaithful wives grew horns.   31. **you:** you women.
32. **You . . . creatures:** i.e. you walk and talk affectedly.
33. **make . . . ignorance:** excuse your affectation as ignorance.

on't, it hath made me mad. I say we will have no moe[34] marriages. Those that are married already (all but one) shall live,
the rest shall keep as they are. To a nunn'ry, go.

Exit.

OPH.
O, what a noble mind is here o'erthrown!
The courtier's, soldier's, scholar's, eye, tongue, sword,
Th' expectation[35] and rose[36] of the fair[37] state,
The glass[38] of fashion and the mould of form,[39]
Th' observ'd of all observers,[40] quite, quite down!
And I, of ladies most deject and wretched,
That suck'd the honey of his [music] vows,
Now see [that] noble and most sovereign reason
Like sweet bells jangled out of time, and harsh;
That unmatch'd form and statue of blown[41] youth
Blasted[42] with ecstasy.[43] O, woe is me
T' have seen what I have seen, see what I see!

(Act 3, Scene 1, lines 55–161)
[*Ophelia withdraws.*]

When Ophelia learns that Hamlet has accidentally
killed her father (when he stabbed a person hiding
behind a curtain thinking it was his Uncle Claudius),
she goes mad with grief and dies by drowning. In
the following scene, a grieving Laertes leaps into his
sister's grave. Hamlet then attacks Laertes, declaring
that he had always loved Ophelia.

LAER.
Lay her i' th' earth,
And from her fair and unpolluted flesh
May violets spring! I tell thee, churlish priest,
A minist'ring angel shall my sister be
When thou liest howling.

HAM.
What, the fair Ophelia!

QUEEN.
[*Scattering flowers.*] Sweets[44] to the sweet, farewell!
I hop'd thou shouldst have been my Hamlet's wife.
I thought thy bride-bed to have deck'd, sweet maid,
And not have strew'd thy grave.

LAER.
O, treble woe
Fall ten times [treble] on that cursed head
Whose wicked deed thy most ingenious[45] sense

Depriv'd thee of! Hold off the earth a while,
Till I have caught her once more in mine arms.
[*Leaps in the grave.*]
Now pile your dust upon the quick and dead,
Till of this flat a mountain you have made
T' o'ertop old Pelion,[46] or the skyish head
Of blue Olympus.

HAM.
[*Coming forward.*] What is he whose grief
Bears such an emphasis, whose phrase[47] of sorrow
Conjures[48] the wand'ring stars[49] and makes them stand
Like wonder-wounded hearers? This is I,
Hamlet the Dane![50] [*Hamlet leaps in after Laertes.*]

LAER.
The devil take thy soul! [*Grappling with him.*]

HAM.
Thou pray'st not well.
I prithee take thy fingers from my throat.
For though I am not splenitive[51] [and] rash,
Yet have I in me something dangerous,
Which let thy wisdom fear. Hold off thy hand!

KING.
Pluck them asunder.

QUEEN.
Hamlet, Hamlet!

ALL.
Gentlemen!

HOR.
Good my lord, be quiet.
[*The Attendants part them, and they come out of the grave.*]

HAM.
Why, I will fight with him upon this theme
Until my eyelids will no longer wag.

QUEEN.
O my son, what theme?

HAM.
I lov'd Ophelia. Forty thousand brothers
Could not with all their quantity of love
Make up my sum. What wilt thou do for her?

KING.
O, he is mad, Laertes.

QUEEN.
For love of God, forbear him.

---

34. **moe:** more.
35. **expectation:** hope.   36. **rose:** ornament.   37. **fair.** Probably proleptic: "(the kingdom) made fair by his presence."
38. **glass:** mirror.   39. **mould of form:** pattern of (courtly) behavior.
40. **observ'd . . . observers.** Shakespeare uses *observe* to mean not only "behold, mark attentively" but also "pay honor to."
41. **blown:** in full bloom.   42. **Blasted:** withered.   43. **ecstasy:** madness.   44. **Sweets:** flowers.   45. **ingenious:** intelligent.

46. **Pelion, Olympus:** mountains in northeastern Greece.
47. **emphasis, phrase.** Rhetorical terms, here used in disparaging reference to Laertes' inflated language.
48. **Conjures:** puts a spell upon.   49. **wand'ring stars:** planets.
50. **the Dane.** This title normally signifies the King.
51. **splenitive:** impetuous.

HAM.
'Swounds, show me what thou't[52] do.
Woo't[53] weep, woo't fight, woo't fast, woo't tear thy self?
Woo't drink up eisel,[54] eat a crocadile?[55]
I'll do't. Dust [thou] come here to whine?
To outface me with leaping in her grave?
Be buried quick with her, and so will I.
And if thou prate of mountains,[56] let them throw
Millions of acres on us, till our ground,
Singeing his pate against the burning zone,[57]
Make Ossa[58] like a wart! Nay, and thou'lt mouth,
I'll rant as well as thou.

QUEEN.
This is mere[59] madness,
And [thus] a while the fit will work on him;
Anon, as patient[60] as the female dove,
When that her golden couplets[61] are disclosed,[62]
His silence will sit drooping.

HAM.
Hear you, sir,
What is the reason that you use me thus?
I lov'd you ever. But it is no matter.
Let Hercules himself do what he may,
The cat will mew, and dog will have his day.[63]
Exit Hamlet.
(Act 5, Scene 1, lines 238–292)

Knowing that Hamlet plans to kill him, Claudius concocts a plan to use Laertes to kill Hamlet. He tells Osric, a young courtier, to arrange a fencing match. Claudius poisons Laertes' blade so that Hamlet will die if Laertes wounds him. Then the king prepares a poisoned drink which he will give to Hamlet if it appears that Hamlet is winning the match. In the following selection, from the final scene of the play, the match has just begun, Hamlet has made a hit, and Claudius has just offered him a drink of wine.

HAM.
I'll play this bout first, set it by a while.
Come. [*They play again.*] Another hit; what say you?

LAER.
[A touch, a touch,] I do confess't.

KING.
Our son shall win.

QUEEN.
He's fat,[64] and scant of breath.
Here, Hamlet, take my napkin, rub thy brows.
The Queen carouses[65] to thy fortune, Hamlet.

HAM.
Good madam!

KING.
Gertrude, do not drink.

QUEEN.
I will, my lord, I pray you pardon me.

KING.
[*Aside.*] It is the pois'ned cup, it is too late.

HAM.
I dare not drink yet, madam; by and by.

QUEEN.
Come, let me wipe thy face.

LAER.
My lord, I'll hit him now.

KING.
I do not think't.

LAER.
[*Aside.*] And yet it is almost against my conscience.

HAM.
Come, for the third, Laertes, you do but dally.
I pray you pass with your best violence;
I am sure you make a wanton of me.[66]

LAER.
Say you so? Come on. [*They play.*]

OSR.
Nothing, neither way.
LAER.
Have at you now!
[*Laertes wounds Hamlet; then, in scuffling, they change rapiers.*]

KING.
Part them, they are incens'd

HAM.
Nay, come again.
[*Hamlet wounds Laertes. The Queen falls.*]

52. **thou't:** thou wilt.
53. **Woo't:** wilt thou.
54. **eisel:** vinegar. 55. **crocadile:** crocodile.
56. **if . . . mountains.** Referring to lines 251–54.
57. **burning zone:** sphere of the sun.
58. **Ossa:** another mountain in Greece, near Pelion and Olympus. **mouth:** talk bombast (synonymous with *rant* in the next line).
59. **mere:** utter. 60. **patient:** calm.
61. **golden couplets:** pair of baby birds, covered with yellow down.
62. **disclosed:** hatched.
63. **Let . . . day:** i.e. nobody can prevent another from making the scenes he feels he has a right to.

64. **fat:** sweaty. 65. **carouses:** drinks a toast.
66. **make . . . me:** i.e. are holding back in order to let me win, as one does with a spoiled child (*wanton*).

OSR.
Look to the Queen there ho!

HOR.
They bleed on both sides. How is it, my lord?

OSR.
How is't, Laertes?

LAER.
Why, as a woodcock to mine own springe,[67] Osric:
I am justly kill'd with mine own treachery.

HAM.
How does the Queen?

KING.
She sounds[68] to see them bleed.

QUEEN.
No, no, the drink, the drink—O my dear Hamlet—
The drink, the drink! I am pois'ned. [*Dies.*]

HAM.
O villainy! Ho, let the door be lock'd!
Treachery! Seek it out.

LAER.
It is here, Hamlet. [Hamlet,] thou art slain.
No med'cine in the world can do thee good;
In thee there is not half an hour's life.
The treacherous instrument is in [thy] hand,
Unbated[69] and envenom'd. The foul practice[70]
Hath turn'd itself on me. Lo here I lie,
Never to rise again, Thy mother's pois'ned.
I can no more—the King, the King's to blame.

HAM.
The point envenom'd too!
Then, venom, to thy work. [*Hurts*[71] *the King.*]

ALL.
Treason! treason!

KING.
O, yet defend me, friends, I am but hurt.

HAM.
Here, thou incestious, [murd'rous], damned Dane,
Drink [off] this potion! Is [thy union] here?
Follow my mother! [*King dies.*]

LAER.
He is justly served,
It is a poison temper'd[72] by himself.
Exchange forgiveness with me, noble Hamlet.

Mine and my father's death come not upon thee
Nor thine on me! [*Dies.*]

HAM.
Heaven make thee free of it! I follow thee.
I am dead, Horatio. Wretched queen, adieu!
You that look pale, and tremble at this chance,
That are but mutes or audience[73] to this act,
Had I but time—as this fell[74] sergeant,[75] Death,
Is strict in his arrest—O, I could tell you—
But let it be. Horatio, I am dead,
Thou livest. Report me and my cause aright
To the unsatisfied.

HOR.
Never believe it;
I am more an antique Roman[76] than a Dane.
Here's yet some liquor left.

HAM.
As th' art a man,
Give me the cup. Let go! By heaven, I'll ha't!
O God, Horatio, what a wounded name,
Things standing thus unknown, shall I leave behind me!
If thou didst ever hold me in thy heart,
Absent thee from felicity a while,
And in this harsh world draw thy breath in pain
To tell my story. [*A march afar off and a shot within*]. What
    warlike noise is this? [*Osric goes to the door and returns.*]

OSR.
Young Fortinbras, with conquest come from Poland,
To th' embassadors of England gives
This warlike volley.

HAM.
O, I die, Horatio,
The potent poison quite o'er-crows[77] my spirit.[78]
I cannot live to hear the news from England,
But I do prophesy th' election lights
On Fortinbras, he has my dying voice.[79]
So tell him, with th' occurrents[80] more and less
Which have solicited[81]—the rest is silence. [*Dies.*]

HOR.
Now cracks a noble heart. Good night, sweet prince,
And flights of angels sing thee to thy rest!   [*March within.*]
(Act 5, Scene 2, lines 284–361)

---

67. **springe:** snare.   68. **sounds:** swoons.
69. **Unbated:** not blunted.   70. **foul practice:** vile plot.
71. s.d. **Hurts:** wounds.   72. **temper'd:** mixed.

73. **mutes or audience:** silent spectators.
74. **fell:** cruel.   75. **sergeant:** sheriff's officer.
76. **antique Roman:** i.e. one who will commit suicide on such an occasion.
77. **o'er-crows:** triumphs over (a term derived from cockfighting).
78. **spirit:** vital energy.   79. **voice:** vote.
80. **occurrents:** occurrences.   81. **solicited:** instigated.

9 The Golden Age of Spanish Literature

Despite the chilling effect of the persecution of individuals suspected of being Protestants by the Spanish Inquisition, the sixteenth and seventeenth centuries are known as Spain's "Golden Age" of literature. Spain's most illustrious author during the Golden Age was Miguel de Cervantes (1547–1616). Following a decade of military adventures and tragedies, including losing the use of his left hand and having to serve as a galley slave, Cervantes married a nineteen-year-old girl and began to write plays at the age of thirty-seven. For the next fifteen years, he was only minimally successful, but then, between 1603 and 1605, he wrote his masterpiece, *Don Quixote of La Mancha,* which is considered to be the first modern novel.

Miguel de Cervantes
Don Quixote of La Mancha

Cervantes' *Don Quixote of La Mancha* is a parody of the popular romances of the day that glorified medieval chivalry. The style of *Don Quixote* draws on the *picaresque* narrative form which developed in Spain during the sixteenth century. A picaresque narrative involves a *picaro*—a knave or rogue—who gallivants from one escapade to another, and it also has a narrator who, on the surface, appears to be relating his own autobiography. In the first chapter, the reader is introduced to Don Quixote who devotes all his time to reading books about knighthood and chivalry. The following excerpt relates how he begins to imagine himself to be a gallant knight.

In resolution, he plunged himself so deeply in his reading of these books, as he spent many times in the lecture of them whole days and nights; and in the end, through his little sleep and much reading, he dried up his brains in such sort as he lost wholly his judgment. His fantasy was filled with those things that he read, of enchantments, quarrels, battles, challenges, wounds, wooings, loves, tempests, and other impossible follies. And these toys did so firmly possess his imagination with an infallible opinion that all that *machina* of dreamed inventions which he read was true, as he accounted no history in the world to be so certain and sincere as they were. He was wont to say, that the Cid Ruy Diaz was a very good knight, but not to be compared to the Knight of the Burning Sword, which, with one thwart blow, cut asunder two fierce and mighty giants. He agreed better with Bernardo del Carpio, because he slew the enchanted Roland in Roncesvalles. He likewise liked of the shift Hercules used when he smothered Anteon, the son of the earth, between his arms. He praised the giant Morgant marvellously, because, though he was of that monstrous progeny, who are commonly all of them proud and rude, yet he was affable and courteous. But he agreed best of all with Reinauld of Mount

Alban; and most of all then, when he saw him sally out of his castle to rob as many as ever he could meet; and when, moreover, he robbed the idol of Mahomet, made all of gold, as his history recounts, and would be content to give his old woman, yea, and his niece also, for a good opportunity on the traitor Galalon, that he might lamb-skin and trample him into powder.

Finally, his wit being wholly extinguished, he fell into one of the strangest conceits that ever madman stumbled on in this world; to wit, it seemed unto him very requisite and behooveful, as well for the augmentation of his honour as also for the benefit of the commonwealth, that he himself should become a knight-errant, and go throughout the world, with his horse and armour, to seek adventures, and practise in person all that he had read was used by knights of yore; revenging of all kinds of injuries, and offering himself to occasions and dangers, which, being once happily achieved, might gain him eternal renown. The poor soul did already figure himself crowned, through the valour of his arm, at least Emperor of Trapisonda; and led thus by these soothing thoughts, and borne away with the exceeding delight he found in them, he hastened all that he might, to effect his urging desires.

Subsequently, Don Quixote polishes his armor, renames his worn-out barn horse Rozinante, and selects Dulcinea as his lady-love—a peasant woman who does not know that he loves her and who never makes an actual appearance in the novel. Then he ventures forth seeking knightly glory. Along the way, he chooses a simple peasant, Sancho Panza, to be his squire, promising to make him governor of an island. Part of the pleasure that is derived from reading *Don Quixote* comes from Cervantes' treatment of the relationship between Don Quixote and Sancho. Rather than creating stock characters patterned after a chivalric code that formally defined the interaction between a high-born knight and his underling squire, Cervantes deals with their relationship as friends, especially as the strengths of one complement the other's weaknesses. The following excerpt relates one of Don Quixote's most famous adventures—his battle with giants, which were, in reality, windmills.

As they discoursed, they discovered some thirty or forty windmills, that are in that field; and as soon as Don Quixote espied them, he said to his squire, "Fortune doth address our affairs better than we ourselves could desire; for behold there, friend Sancho Panza, how there appears thirty or forty monstrous giants, with whom I mean to fight, and deprive them all of their lives, with whose spoils we will begin to be rich; for this is a good war, and a great service unto God, to take away so bad a seed from the face of the earth." "What giants?" quoth Sancho Panza. "Those that thou seest there," quoth his lord, "with the long arms; and some there are of that race whose arms are almost two leagues long." "I pray you understand," quoth Sancho Panza, "that those which appear there are no giants, but windmills; and that which seems in them to be arms, are their sails, that, swung about by the wind, do also make the mill go." "It seems well," quoth Don Quixote, "that thou art not yet acquainted with matter of adventures. They are giants; and, if thou beest afraid, go aside and pray, whilst I enter into cruel and unequal battle with them." And, saying so, he spurred his horse Rozinante, without taking heed to his squire Sancho's cries, advertising him how they were doubtless windmills that he did assault, and no giants; but he went so fully persuaded that they were giants as he neither heard his squire's outcries, nor did discern what they were, although he drew very near to them, but rather said, as loud as he could, "Fly not, ye cowards and vile creatures! for it is only one knight that assaults you."

With this the wind increased, and the mill sails began to turn about; which Don Quixote espying, said, "Although thou movest more arms than the giant Briareus thou shalt stoop to me." And, after saying this, and commending himself most devoutly to his Lady Dulcinea, desiring her to succor him in that trance, covering himself well with his buckler, and setting his lance on his rest, he spurred on Rozinante, and encountered with the first mill that was before him, and, striking his lance into the sail, the wind swung it about with such fury, that it broke his lance into shivers, carrying him and his horse after it, and finally tumbled him a good way off from it on the field in evil plight. Sancho Panza repaired presently to succor him as fast as his ass could drive; and when he arrived, he found him not able to stir, he had gotten such a crush with Rozinante. "Good God!" quoth Sancho, "did I not foretell unto you that you should look well what you did, for they were none other than windmills? nor could any think otherwise, unless he had also windmills in his brains."

Ever since, "tilting at windmills" has referred to nonsensical, often delusional, encounters with imaginary rivals. Another disastrous incident, when Don Quixote mistakes two flocks of sheep for two armies about to go into battle, is excerpted below.

In these discourses Don Quixote and his squire rode; when Don Quixote, perceiving a great and thick dust to arise in the way wherein he travelled, turning to Sancho, said, "This is, Sancho, the day wherein shall be manifest the good which fortune hath reserved for me. This is the day wherein the force of mine arm must be shown as much as in any other whatsoever; and in it I will do such feats as shall for ever remain recorded in the books of fame. Dost thou see, Sancho, the dust which ariseth there? Know that it is caused by a mighty army, and sundry and innumerable nations, which come marching there." "If that be so," quoth Sancho, "then must there be two armies; for on this other side is raised as great a dust." Don Quixote turned back to behold it, and seeing it was so indeed, he was marvellous glad, thinking that they were doubtlessly two armies, which came to fight one with another in the midst of that spacious plain; for he had his fantasy ever replenished with these battles, enchantments, successes, ravings, loves, and challenges which are rehearsed in books of knighthood, and all that ever he spoke, thought, or did, was addressed and applied to the like things. And the dust which he had seen was raised by two great flocks of sheep, that came through the same field by two different ways, and could not be discerned, by reason of the dust, until they were very near. Don Quixote did affirm that they were two armies with so very good earnest as Sancho believed it, and demanded of him, "Sir, what then shall we two do?" "What shall we do," quoth Don Quixote, "but assist the needful and weaker side? For thou shalt know, Sancho, that he who comes towards us is the great emperor Alifamfaron, lord of the great island of Trapobana; the other, who marcheth at our back, is his enemy, the king of the Garamantes, Pentapolin of the naked arm, so called because he still entereth in battle with his right arm naked." "I pray you, good sir," quoth Sancho, "to tell me why these two princes hate one another so much?" "They are enemies," replied Don Quixote, "because that this Alifamfaron is a furious pagan, and is enamoured of Pentapolin's daughter, who is a very beautiful and gracious princess, and, moreover, a Christian; and her father refuseth to give her to the pagan king, until first he abandon Mahomet's false sect, and become one of his religion." "By my beard," quoth Sancho, "Pentapolin hath reason, and I will help him all that I may." "By doing so," quoth Don Quixote, "thou performest thy duty; for it is not requisite that one be a knight to the end he may enter into such battles." "I do apprehend that myself," quoth Sancho, "very well; but where shall we leave this ass in the meantime, that we may be sure to find him again after the conflict?—for I think it is not the custom to enter into battle mounted on such a beast." "It is true," quoth Don Quixote; "that which thou mayst do is to leave him to his adventures, and care not whether he be lost or found; for we shall have so many horses, after coming out of this battle victors, that very Rozinante himself is in danger to be changed for another. But be attentive; for I mean to describe unto thee the principal knights of both the armies; and to the end thou mayst the better see and note all things, let us retire ourselves there to that little hillock, from whence both armies may easily be descried." . . .

Good God! how many provinces repeated he at that time! and how many nations did he name, giving to every one of them, with marvellous celerity and briefness, their proper attributes, being swallowed up and engulfed in those things which he had read in his lying books! Sancho Panza stood suspended at his speech, and spoke not a word, but only would now and then turn his head, to see whether he could mark those knights and giants which his lord had named; and, by reason he could not discover any, he said, "Sir, I give to the devil any man, giant, or knight, of all those you said, that appeareth; at least, I cannot discern them. Perhaps all is but enchantment, like that of the ghosts of yesternight." "How sayst thou so?" quoth Don Quixote. "Dost not thou hear the horses neigh, the trumpets sound, and the noise of the drums?" "I hear nothing else," said Sancho, "but the great bleating of many sheep." And so it was, indeed; for by this time the two flocks did approach them very near. "The fear that thou conceivest, Sancho," quoth Don Quixote, "maketh thee that thou canst neither hear nor see aright; for one of the effects of fear is to trouble the senses, and make things appear otherwise than they are; and, seeing thou fearest so much, retire thyself out of the way; for I alone am sufficient to give the victory to that part which I shall assist." And, having ended his speech, he set spurs to Rozinante, and, setting his lance in the rest, he flung down from the hillock like a thunderbolt. Sancho cried

to him as loud as he could, saying, "Return, good sir Don Quixote! for I vow unto God, that all those which you go to charge are but sheep and muttons; return, I say. Alas that ever I was born! what madness is this? Look; for there is neither giant nor knight, nor cats, nor arms, nor shields parted nor whole, nor pure azures nor devilish. What is it you do? wretch that I am!" For all this Don Quixote did not return, but rather rode, saying with a loud voice, "On, on, knights! all you that serve and march under the banners of the valorous emperor Pentapolin of the naked arm; follow me, all of you, and you shall see how easily I will revenge him on his enemy, Alifarmfaron of Trapobana." And, saying so, he entered into the midst of the flock of sheep, and began to lance them with such courage and fury as if he did in good earnest encounter his mortal enemies.

The shepherds that came with the flock, cried to him to leave off; but, seeing their words took no effect, they unloosed their slings, and began to salute his pate with stones as great as one's fist. But Don Quixote made no account of their stones, and did fling up and down among the sheep, saying, "Where art thou, proud Alifamfaron? where art thou? come to me; for I am but one knight alone, who desire to prove my force with thee man to man, and deprive thee of thy life, in pain of the wrong thou dost to the valiant Pentapolin, the Garamante." At that instant a stone gave him such a blow on one of his sides, as did bury two of his ribs in his body. He beholding himself so ill dight [treated], did presently believe that he was either slain or sorely wounded; and, remembering himself of his liquor, he took out his oil-pot, and set it to his mouth to drink; but ere he could take as much as he thought requisite to cure his hurts, there cometh another almond, which struck him so full upon the hand and oil-pot, as it broke it into pieces, and carried away with it besides three or four of his cheek teeth, and did moreover bruise very sorely two of his fingers. Such was the first and the second blow, as the poor knight was constrained to fall down off his horse. And the shepherds arriving, did verily believe they had slain him; and therefore, gathering their flock together with all speed, and carrying away their dead muttons, which were more than seven, they went away without verifying the matter any further.

At the end of the novel, after many other such adventures, Don Quixote and Sancho return home. The legacy of Cervantes' novel is most evident in the widespread use of the term "quixotic" to refer to a person who is foolishly impractical, particularly in pursuit of some kind of lofty, romantic ideals or goals.

11

The Reformation

The reformation of the church in the sixteenth century was rooted in demands for spiritual renewal and institutional change. These pressures began as early as the late fourteenth century and came from many sources.

The papacy and orthodox Catholic theology were challenged by English theologian John Wycliffe (c. 1320–1384) and Czech theologian John Huss (c. 1369–1415). Both attacked the bishops' involvement in temporal politics and urged a return to the simple practices of the early apostolic church, and both, claiming that the Bible alone—not the church hierarchy—was the highest authority for Christians, emphasized study of the Holy Scriptures by the laity and sermons in the common language of the people. Wycliffe, though not Huss, also undermined the clergy's authority by denying the priests' power to change the bread and wine into Christ's body and blood during the Mass. Despite severe persecution by church and state, followers of Wycliffe's and Huss's beliefs continued to exist and participated in the sixteenth-century Protestant movement.

Institutional reform from within was attempted through the Conciliar movement, which endeavored to restrict the pope's power through regular meetings of general councils of bishops. The Council of Constance (1414–1418) declared that a general council, not the papacy, was the supreme authority within the church and called for regular assemblies of bishops to consider the church's problems and initiate necessary reforms.

By the mid–fifteenth century, the Conciliar movement had collapsed, and the papacy, unreformed, freely exercised its supremacy. Fearful of losing its autonomy and power, the papacy resisted calling a new council from 1437 until 1512, when the Fifth Lateran Council met in Rome under close papal supervision. The council issued decrees aimed at improving education of the clergy, eliminating many abuses in church administration, and summoning a church council every five years. But the council's decrees were not implemented after the last session ended in 1517, the same year Martin Luther first challenged the papacy, thus starting the Protestant reform movement.

The principal source of the reform spirit was a widespread popular yearning for a more genuine spirituality. It took many forms: the rise of new pious practices, greater interest in mystical experiences and in the study of the Bible, the development of communal ways for lay people to live and work following the apostles' example, and a heightened search for ways within secular society to imitate more perfectly the life of Christ—called the New Devotion movement.

Several secular factors contributed to this heightening of spiritual feeling. The many wars, famines, and plagues of the late fourteenth and the fifteenth centuries had traumatized Europe. The increasing educational level of the urban middle class and skilled laborers and the invention of the printing press allowed the rapid and relatively inexpensive spread of new ideas. Finally, there was the influence of the humanist movement, particularly in northern Europe and Spain. Many humanists dedicated themselves to promoting higher levels of religious education. They stimulated public interest in biblical study by publishing new editions of the Holy Scriptures and the writings of the church fathers, along with new devotional literature. Nearly all the religious reformers of the sixteenth century were deeply influenced by the ideals and methods of the Christian humanist movement.

In Germany, a spirit of discontent with social and economic conditions coincided with the demand for reform of the church and religious life. For several decades before Luther's revolt against the papacy, the economic conditions of the knights, the peasants, and the lower-class urban workers had deteriorated. The knights' grievances included loss of their political power to the centralizing governments of the German princes and increasing restrictions on their customary feudal privileges. Peasants protested that lords had steadily withdrawn certain of their customary rights and had added burdens, increasing the lords' income and control over their estates. The knights and peasants were squeezed into an ever-worsening social and economic niche. In the cities, the lower-class artisans and laborers were similarly oppressed. Those in the urban upper classes, who controlled town governments, enhanced their own economic privileges at the expense of lower-class citizens. The church, which was a major landowner and active in commercial enterprises in the towns, played an important role in these conflicts. All these grievances formed the explosive background to Martin Luther's challenge to the authority of the church and the imperial government.

The success of the reformers, both Protestant and Catholic, depended on support from the ruling political forces in the various kingdoms, principalities, and city-states of Europe. Usually, the rulers' religious preference determined whether the church remained Catholic or became Lutheran, Calvinist, or some combination of all three, as in England. The rulers of large parts of Germany, especially the imperial city-states, and of the Scandinavian kingdoms adopted the Lutheran reform. The Austrian and Spanish Hapsburg emperors and the French kings remained Catholic, although Calvinism had many adherents in France. In eastern Europe, Protestantism was successful at first, but, under the influence of the Catholic reform movement, Catholicism later recovered its dominance. In Switzerland, allegiance was divided among Catholics and the followers of John Calvin, reformer of the church in Geneva, and of Huldrych Zwingli, reformer of the church in Zurich. Calvinism took root in Scotland, and its influence also grew in England where it inspired the Puritan movement.

These divisions in the Christian church marked a turning point in European history and culture, ending forever the coherent world-view of medieval Christendom. The Reformation split the peoples of Europe into two broad political, intellectual, and spiritual camps: Protestant and Catholic. With the moral, political, and ideological power of the church significantly diminished, post-Reformation society was open to increasing secularization on all fronts. By ending the religious unity of the Middle Ages and weakening the Catholic Church, the Reformation contributed significantly to the rise of modernity.

1 Erasmus: A Catholic Critic of the Church

The greatest scholar and most popular humanist author of the early sixteenth century was Desiderius Erasmus (1466–1536). Educated under the influence of the New Devotion and well trained in the new humanistic studies, Erasmus dedicated his life to purifying the Latin and Greek texts of the Bible and those of the early fathers of the church. He used his wit and humanistic learning in his writings to advocate a simple yet more intense Christian life modeled on Christ. Erasmus castigated those who pandered to the superstitions of people by encouraging magical beliefs about relics, the cults of the saints, indulgences (see next reading), and other abuses of pious practices. He was also hostile to the excessive influence of scholastic philosophers on the church's theology, believing that in their quibbling over obscure philosophical-theological issues, they mocked the Christian faith as revealed in the New Testament. An Augustinian monk who preferred to live outside the monastery, Erasmus severely criticized the lax practices of monks and clergy. He argued, too, that salvation was not based on ascetic and ceremonial acts, but on deeds of love.

Erasmus had a large following of younger admirers trained in the humanities. When Martin Luther (1483–1546) appeared on the scene, many people regarded him as one of these younger humanists: Both men criticized current theology, condemned abuses in the church, and proclaimed the need for reform. Soon, however, Erasmus realized that Luther was going far beyond what Erasmus felt was wise or necessary. Instead he urged reform within the church's framework. In 1524, he felt it necessary to separate himself publicly from Luther. Consequently, he wrote a reasoned defense of the role of free will in the process of salvation, taking a Catholic position on this difficult theological problem. Luther, furious with Erasmus, responded with a treatise on the bondage of the will, and Erasmus found himself abused by zealots from both camps. To the end, he remained a devout, loyal, but critical Catholic reformer. His piety and literary scholarship exemplified the ideas of Christian humanism.

Erasmus

In Praise of Folly

One of Erasmus' most famous works was *In Praise of Folly,* written in 1509, before Luther's challenge to the church. In the following passages, speaking through the voice of Folly, Erasmus castigates monks, theologians, and other Christians for failing to discern the true purpose of the Christian life: the imitation of Christ.

As for the theologians, perhaps it would be better to pass them over in silence, *"not stirring up the hornets' nest"* and *"not laying a finger on the stinkweed,"* since this race of men is incredibly arrogant and touchy. For they might rise up en masse and march in ranks against me with six hundred conclusions and force me to recant. And if I should refuse, they would immediately shout "heretic." For this is the thunderbolt they always keep ready at a moment's notice to terrify anyone to whom they are not very favorably inclined. . . .

. . . They are so blessed by their Selflove as to be fully persuaded that they themselves dwell in the third heaven, looking down from high above on all other mortals as if they were earth-creeping vermin almost worthy of their pity. They are so closely hedged in by rows of magistral definitions, conclusions, corollaries, explicit and implicit propositions, they have so many *"holes they can run to,"* that Vulcan [Roman god of fire] himself couldn't net them tightly enough to keep them from escaping by means of distinctions, with which they cut all knots as cleanly as the fine-honed edge of "the headsman's axe"—so many new terms have they thought up and such monstrous jargon have they coined. . . .

In all of these there is so much erudition, so much difficulty, that I think the apostles themselves would need to be inspired by a different spirit if they were forced to match wits on such points with this new breed of theologians. Paul could

provide a living example of faith, but when he said "Faith is the substance of things to be hoped for and the evidence of things not seen," his definition was not sufficiently magisterial. So too, he lived a life of perfect charity, but he neither distinguished it nor defined it with sufficient dialectical precision in the first epistle to the Corinthians, chapter 13. . . .

. . . But Christ, interrupting their boasts (which would otherwise never come to an end), will say, "Where did this new race of Jews [quibbling theologians] come from? The only law I recognize as truly mine is the only one I hear nothing about. Long ago, not speaking obliquely in parables but quite openly, I promised my Father's inheritance not to hoods [worn by monks], or trifling prayers, or fasts, but rather deeds of faith and charity. Nor do I acknowledge those who too readily acknowledge their own deeds: those who want to appear even holier than I am can go dwell in the heavens of the Abraxasians[1] if they like, or they can order that a new heaven be built for them by the men whose petty traditions they have placed before my precepts." When they hear this and see sailors and teamsters chosen in preference to them, how do you suppose their faces will look as they stare at each other? . . .

_____
[1] A heretical sect that believed there were 365 "heavens."

Almost as happy as the theologians are those men who are commonly called "religious" and "monks"—though both names are quite incorrect, since a good part of them are very far removed from religion and no one is encountered more frequently everywhere you go. I cannot imagine how anything could be more wretched than these men. . . . For even though everyone despises this breed of men so thoroughly that even a chance meeting with one of them is considered unlucky, still they maintain a splendid opinion of themselves. First of all, they consider it the very height of piety to have so little to do with literature as not even to be able to read. Moreover, when they roar out their psalms in church like braying asses (counting their prayers indeed, but understanding them not at all), then (of all things!) they imagine that the listening saints are soothed and caressed with manifold delight. Among them are some who make a great thing out of their squalor and beggary, who stand at the door bawling out their demands for bread—(indeed there is no inn or coach or ship where they do not make a disturbance), depriving other beggars of no small share of their income. And in this manner these most agreeable fellows, with their filth, ignorance, coarseness, impudence, recreate for us, as they say, an image of the apostles. . . .

Closely related to such men are those who have adopted the very foolish (but nevertheless quite agreeable) belief that if they look at a painting or statue of that huge . . . Christopher, they will not die on that day; or, if they address a statue of Barbara with the prescribed words, they will return from battle unharmed, or, if they accost Erasmus on certain days, with certain wax tapers, and in certain little formulas of prayer, they will soon become rich.[2] Moreover, in George they have discovered a new Hercules. . . .[3] They all but worship George's horse, most religiously decked out in breastplates and bosses [ornaments], and from time to time oblige him with some little gift. To swear by his bronze helmet is thought to be an oath fit for a king.

Now what shall I [Folly] say about those who find great comfort in soothing self-delusions about fictitious pardons for their sins, measuring out the times in purgatory down to the droplets of a waterclock, parceling out centuries, years, months, days, hours, as if they were using mathematical ta-

bles. Or what about those who rely on certain little magical tokens and prayers thought up by some pious impostor for his own amusement or profit? They promise themselves anything and everything: wealth, honor, pleasure, an abundance of everything, perpetual health, a long life, flourishing old age, and finally a seat next to Christ among the saints, though this last they don't want for quite a while yet—that is, when the pleasures of this life, to which they cling with all their might, have finally slipped through their fingers, then it will be soon enough to enter into the joys of the saints. Imagine here, if you please, some businessman or soldier or judge who thinks that if he throws into the collection basket one coin from all his plunder, the whole cesspool of his sinful life will be immediately wiped out. He thinks all his acts of perjury, lust, drunkenness, quarreling, murder, deception, dishonesty, betrayal are paid off like a mortgage, and paid off in such a way that he can start off once more on a whole new round of sinful pleasures.

Now who could be more foolish—rather, who could be happier—than those who assure themselves they will have the very ultimate felicity because they have recited daily those seven little verses from the holy psalms? A certain devil—certainly a merry one, but too loose-lipped to be very clever—is believed to have mentioned them to St. Bernard,[4] but the poor devil was cheated by a clever trick. Such absurdities are so foolish that even I am almost ashamed of them, but still they are approved not only by the common people but even by learned teachers of religion. . . .

But why have I embarked on this vast sea of superstitions?

Not if I had a hundred tongues, a hundred mouths,
A voice of iron, could I survey all kinds
Of fools, or run through all the forms of folly.[5]

So rife, so teeming with such delusions is the entire life of all Christians everywhere. And yet priests are not unwilling to allow and even foster such delusions because they are not unaware of how many emoluments accumulate from this source. In the midst of all this, if some odious wiseman should stand up and sing out the true state of affairs: "You will not die badly if you live well. You redeem your sins if to the coin you add a hatred of evil deeds, then tears, vigils, prayers, fasts, and if you change your whole way of life. This saint will help you if you imitate his life"—if that wiseman were to growl out such assertions and more like them, look how much happiness he would immediately take away from the minds of mortals, look at the confusion he would throw them into!

---

[2]Christopher refers to Saint Christopher, a popular legendary giant and the patron saint of travelers. Barbara was a widely venerated but legendary early Christian martyr and saint. Erasmus, an Italian bishop and also a saint, was martyred in about A.D. 303.

[3]George, the patron saint of England and of the Crusaders, was believed to have been martyred in about A.D. 300. Saint George's battle with a dragon was a popular legend. Hercules, a Greek hero, performed twelve difficult tasks that won him immortality as a gift of the gods. He was himself worshiped as a god by later Greeks and Romans.

[4]Saint Bernard (1091–1153) was a leading theologian, Cistercian monk, and preacher.
[5]Virgil's *Aeneid* 6.625–627.

Erasmus
"Paraclesis"

One of Erasmus' greatest contributions to the revival of the writings of *Christian* antiquity was his Greek New Testament, published in 1516, the year before Luther challenged the church. Hoping to clarify the meaning of the Greek text, Erasmus also included, in a parallel column, his own Latin translation. In the "Paraclesis" (the Greek word for "exhortation")—the preface to his New Testament—Erasmus admonishes the reader to follow "the philosophy of Christ"—the teachings of Jesus contained in the New Testament.

The most radical concept in the "Paraclesis" is one with which the Protestant reformers agreed—the New Testament should be translated into the vernacular languages, making it available to all Christians. The New Testament was not the exclusive property of theologians and the clergy to read and study; all Christians should be able to read it and come to an understanding of the wisdom of Christ and the apostles. Instead of quibbling over theological details and paying so much attention to relics and images, all Christians should embrace the philosophy of Christ which will bring them a transforming happiness. Erasmus' stress on drawing religious inspiration directly from the New Testament undermined clerical authority and would become a major feature of Protestant theology. Following are excerpts from the "Paraclesis."

I exhort all men to the most holy and wholesome study of Christian philosophy and summon them as if with the blast of a trumpet, that an eloquence far different than Cicero's be given me: an eloquence certainly much more efficacious, if less ornate than his. . . .

Why do not all of us ponder within ourselves that this must be a new and wonderful kind of philosophy since, in order to transmit it to mortals, He who was God became man, He who was immortal became mortal, He who was in the heart of the Father descended to earth? It must be a great matter, and in no sense a commonplace one, whatever it is, because that wondrous Author came to teach after so many families of distinguished philosophers, after so many remarkable prophets. Why, then, out of pious curiosity do we not investigate, examine, explore each tenet? . . .

Indeed, I disagree very much with those who are unwilling that Holy Scripture, translated into the vulgar tongue, be read by the uneducated, as if Christ taught such intricate doctrines that they could scarcely be understood by very few theologians, or as if the strength of the Christian religion consisted in men's ignorance of it. The mysteries of kings, perhaps, are better concealed, but Christ wishes his mysteries published as openly as possible. I would that even the lowliest women read the Gospels and the Pauline Epistles. And I would that they were translated into all languages so that they could be read and understood not only by Scots and Irish but also by Turks and Saracens. . . .

He is not a Platonist who has not read the works of Plato; and is he a theologian, let alone a Christian, who has not read the literature of Christ? Who loves me, Christ says, keeps my word, a distinguishing mark which He himself prescribed. . . . Only a very few can be learned, but all can be Christian, all can be devout, and—I shall boldly add—all can be theologians. . . . The first step, however, is to know what He taught; the next is to carry it into effect. Therefore, I believe, anyone should not think himself to be Christian if he disputes about instances, relations, quiddities, and formalities with an obscure and irksome confusion of words, but rather if he holds and exhibits what Christ taught and showed forth. Not that I condemn the industry of those who not without merit employ their native intellectual powers in such subtle discourse, for I do not wish anyone to be offended, but that I think, and rightly so, unless I am mistaken, that that pure and genuine philosophy of Christ is not to be drawn from any source more abundantly than from the evangelical books and from the Apostolic Letters, about which, if anyone should devoutly philosophize, praying more than arguing and seeking to be transformed rather than armed for battle, he would without a doubt find that there is nothing pertaining to the happiness of man and the living of his life which is not taught, examined, and unraveled in these works. . . .

Let us all, therefore, with our whole heart covet this literature, let us embrace it, let us continually occupy ourselves with it, let us fondly kiss it, at length let us die in its embrace, let us be transformed in it, since indeed studies are transmuted into morals. As for him who cannot pursue this course (but who cannot do it, if only he wishes?), let him at least reverence this literature enveloping, as it were, His divine heart. If anyone shows us the footprints of Christ, in what manner, as Christians, do we prostrate ourselves, how we adore them! But why do we not venerate instead the living and breathing likeness of Him in these books? If anyone displays the tunic of Christ, to what corner of the earth shall we not hasten so that we may kiss it? Yet were you to bring forth His entire wardrobe, it would not manifest Christ more clearly and truly than the Gospel writings. We embellish a wooden or store statue with gems and gold for the love of Christ. Why not, rather, mark with gold and gems and with ornaments of greater value than these, if such there be, these writings which bring Christ to us so much more effectively than any paltry image? The latter represents only the form of the body—if indeed it represents anything of Him—but these writings bring you the living image of His holy mind and the speaking, healing, dying, rising Christ himself, and thus they render Him so fully present that you would see less if you gazed upon Him with your very eyes.

2 The Lutheran Reformation

By the middle of the fifteenth century, many Christians were angered by the luxurious lifestyle of the upper clergy and the behavior of Renaissance popes who enhanced their political power at the expense of other rulers and who seemed more concerned with land and wealth than with Christ's message. Concerned Christians yearned to revive the intense spirituality displayed by the first followers of Christ. This quest for a deeper commitment to the essential Christian mission took several forms: a growing interest in mysticism as a way of communicating directly with the divine; the study of the Bible to arrive at a greater understanding of Christ's life and teachings; the development of communal ways for lay people to live and to work following the apostles' example; a heightened search for ways within secular society to imitate more perfectly the life of Christ; and a revival of pious practices, such as veneration of the saints, acquisition of relics, and popular support for the cult of Mary. In addition, the reformist spirit was buttressed by the humanists' dedication to religious education and their interest in biblical study; nearly all the religious reformers of the sixteenth century were influenced by the methods and ideals of the Christian humanist movement.

In addition to the quest of the pious for religious renewal—for a return to the spiritual sincerity and vitality expressed by Jesus' early followers—other signs of discontent proliferated in German lands. Townspeople resented money from German lands flowing to Rome in the form of church taxes and payment for church offices. To many Germans, the church was a foreign power that dominated and exploited Germans. In the countryside, peasants groaned under the increasing weight of taxes imposed on them by both lay and ecclesiastical lords. Lower-class townspeople were often oppressed by the urban upper classes that dominated political and economic life. This combination of spiritual uneasiness and social and economic abuses led many Germans to find hope in a movement for religious reform.

All these grievances formed the explosive background to the challenge of Martin Luther (1483–1546) to the authority of the church and the imperial government.

Martin Luther

Address to the Christian Nobility, The Babylonian Captivity of the Church, and *The Freedom of the Christian*
CHALLENGING THE CHURCH

Due to his father's wishes, Luther entered law school, but he soon dropped out because of a deep-seated spiritual despondency. Like many of his contemporaries, Luther sought to save his soul from the temptations of the flesh, the devil, and the world. He often tormented himself with the question: Why would a righteous God choose a sinner like me to be saved? In 1505, Luther entered the Augustinian monastery at Erfurt, but although he was a fastidiously conscientious monk, he did not find the spiritual solace he was seeking. Nonetheless, he persevered as a monk, was ordained into the priesthood in 1507, went on to study theology, and became a professor and preacher in Wittenberg.

In 1507, Pope Julius II proclaimed an indulgence[1] to finance the construction of the new Saint Peter's basilica in Rome. The indulgence promised Christians, living or dead, the remission of ecclesiastical penalties for sin and thus the possibility of avoiding purgatory. By April 1517, John Tetzel, a Dominican monk, was preaching the indulgence near Wittenberg, but he preached that the indulgence was itself a means to salvation, which could easily be purchased. Tetzel, playing on the emotions of those who had lost loved ones, reputedly said, "As soon as the coin in the box rings, the soul from purgatory to heaven springs." To sincere Christians it seemed as if the church was espousing an abhorrent idea— that people could buy their way into heaven. That same year, Luther denounced the abuses connected with the preaching of the indulgence in his *Ninety-Five Theses Concerning the Efficacy of Indulgences,* written in Latin, which he posted on the north door of the Castle Church on All Saints' Eve (October 31). This quarrel led quickly to other and more profound theological issues.

In August 1520, Luther attacked the whole system of papal governance in the following selection taken from his *Address to the Christian Nobility of the German Nation Concerning the Reform of the Christian Estate,* the first of his so-called "Reformation tracts," written in German. He argues that the Romanists (traditional Catholics loyal to the papacy) have built "three walls" that effectively block any reform of the church. Consequently, Luther appeals to the nobility and the leaders of the imperial cities in Germany to intervene by summoning a "free council" to reform the church.

---

[1]According to the Roman Catholic teaching concerning the sacrament of penance, the priest absolved the truly contrite sinner from the guilt of sin but gave the sinner a temporal penalty, or penance, to fulfill. If the penance was either insufficient or not completed before one's death, the remainder would be fulfilled in purgatory—the place where sinners made recompense for their sins before being allowed into heaven. In theory, an indulgence allowed a sinner to draw upon the treasury of merit accrued by Christ, the Virgin Mary, and the saints to remit the temporal punishment for sins.

ADDRESS TO THE CHRISTIAN NOBILITY

The Romanists, have very cleverly built three walls around themselves. Hitherto they have protected themselves by these walls in such a way that no one has been able to reform them. As a result, the whole of Christendom has fallen abominably.

In the first place, when pressed by the temporal power they have made decrees and declared that the temporal power had no jurisdiction over them, but that, on the contrary, the spiritual power is above the temporal. In the second place, when the attempt is made to reprove them with the Scriptures, they raise the objection that only the pope may interpret the Scriptures. In the third place, if threatened with a council, their story is that no one may summon a council but the pope.

In this way they have cunningly stolen our three rods from us, that they may go unpunished. They have ensconced themselves within the sage stronghold of these three walls so that they can practice all the knavery and wickedness which we see today. Even when they have been compelled to hold a council they have weakened its power in advance by putting the prince under oath to let them remain as they were. In addition, have given the pope full authority over all decisions of a council, so that it is all the same whether there are many councils or no councils. They only deceive us with puppet shows and sham fights. They fear terribly for their skin in a really free council! They have so intimidated kings and princes with this technique that they believe it would be an offense against God not to be obedient to the Romanists in all their knavish and ghoulish deceits. . . .

The second wall is still more loosely built and less substantial. The Romanists want to be the only masters of Holy Scripture, although they never learn a thing from the Bible all their life long. They assume the sole authority for themselves, and quite unashamed, they play about with words before our very eyes, trying to persuade us that the pope cannot err in matters of faith, regarding less of whether he is righteous or wicked. Yet they cannot point to a single letter. This is why so many heretical and un-Christian, even unnatural, ordinances stand in the canon law. But there is no need to talk about these ordinances at present. Since these Romanists think the Holy Spirit never leaves them, no matter how ignorant and wicked they are, they become bold and decree only what they want. . . .

But so as not to fight them with mere words, we will quote the Scriptures. St. Paul says in Corinthians 14 [:30], "If something better is revealed to anyone, though he is already sitting and listening to another in God's word, then the one who is speaking shall hold his peace and give place." What would be the point of this commandment if we were compelled to believe only the man who does the talking or the man who is at the top? Even Christ said in John 6 [:45] that all Christians shall be taught by God. If it were to happen that the pope and his cohorts were wicked and not true Christians, were not taught by God and were without under-

standing, why should the pope not follow the obscure man? Has the pope not erred many times? Who would help Christendom when the pope erred if we did not have somebody who had the Scriptures on his side?

Therefore, their claim that only the pope may interpret Scripture is an outrageous fancied fable. They cannot produce a single letter [of Scripture] to maintain that the interpretation of Scripture or the confirmation of its interpretation belongs to the pope alone. They themselves have usurped this power. . . .

The third wall falls of itself when the first two are down. When the pope acts contrary to the Scriptures, it is our duty to stand by the Scriptures, to reprove him and to constrain him, according to the word of Christ, Matthew 18 [:15–17], "If your brother sins against you, go and tell it to him, between you and him alone; if he does not listen to you, then take one or two others with you; if he does not listen to them, tell it to the church; if he does not listen to the church, consider him a heathen." Here every member is commanded to care for every other. How much more should we do this when the member that does evil is responsible for the government of the church, and by his evil-doing is the cause of much harm and offense to the rest! But if I am to accuse him before the church, I must naturally call the church together.

The Romanists have no basis in Scripture for their claim that the pope alone has the right to call or confirm a council. This is just their own ruling, and it is only valid as long it is not harmful to Christendom or contrary to the laws of God. Now when the pope deserves punishment, this ruling no longer obtains, for not to punish him by authority of a council is harmful to Christendom.

Luther believed that the only authority for the Christian is holy Scripture, God's word to men and women, and he viewed Christianity as a personal relationship between the individual and God. Whereas the Roman Catholic Church taught that the clergy were intermediaries between human beings and God, that a person reached God by going through the clergy, as for example, when confessing to a priest, Luther asserted that the clergy were no different from and possessed no more power than the laity. In effect, all believers are priests. This means that the Christian's path to God is direct; no clerical intermediary is required. Luther also dismissed the authority of canon law, ecclesiastical courts, and the exclusive power of the clergy to interpret the Scriptures. Luther likened the situation of Christians during his own age to that of the Jews who were forcibly taken into captivity by the Babylonians in 586 B.C. in the second of his "Reformation tracts," *The Babylonian Captivity of the Church.* In the following passage, he speaks on behalf of Christian liberty, and not only refers to the "tyranny of the pope" but equates him with the Antichrist—a secular king who is to rule the world in the years immediately prior to Christ's Second Coming before the Last Judgment and the end of the world.

THE BABYLONIAN CAPTIVITY OF THE CHURCH

I lift my voice simply on behalf of liberty and I confidently cry: No law, whether of man or of angels, may rightfully be imposed upon Christians without their consent, for we are free of all laws. And if any laws are imposed upon us, we must bear them in such a way as to preserve that sense of freedom which knows and affirms with certainty that an injustice is being done to it, even though it glories in bearing this injustice—so taking care neither to justify the tyrant nor to murmur against his tyranny. . . .

Nevertheless, since but few know . . . the blessedness of Christian liberty, and cannot know them because of the tyranny of the pope, I for one will disengage myself, and keep my conscience free by bringing this charge against the pope and all his papists: Unless they will abolish their laws and ordinances, and restore to Christ's churches their liberty and have it taught among them, they are guilty of all the souls that perish under this miserable captivity, the papacy is truly the kingdom of Babylon and of the very Antichrist. For who is "the man of sin" and "the son of perdition" [II Thess. 2:3] but he who with his doctrines and his laws increases the sins and perdition of souls in the church, while sitting in the church as if he were God? [II Thess. 2:4]. All this the papal tyranny has fulfilled, and more than fulfilled, these many centuries. It has extinguished faith, obscured the sacraments and oppressed the gospel; but its own laws, which are not only impious and sacrilegious, but even barbarous and foolish, it has decreed and multiplied without end.

Luther's idea that the individual reaches God and attains salvation without clerical intermediaries diminished the importance of the institutional church and its clergy. Luther also dismissed the authority of canon law, ecclesiastical courts, and retained only two of the seven sacraments—baptism and the Eucharist. While lecturing at the university on the Apostle Paul's Epistle to the Romans, Luther formulated his distinctive teaching of *justification by faith alone, through God's grace alone.* "Justification," a theological term, is derived from two Latin words—*iustus* (righteous) and *facere* (to make)—and means "to make a person righteous." For Luther, however, justification was a *passive righteousness,* attained by God granting an individual faith, and not through any human efforts. His new evangelical theology of *justification by faith alone through God's grace alone* brought him further conflict with the Roman Catholic Church that maintained that *both* faith, a sincere human belief in God, and good works— church attendance, acts of charity, fasting, and pilgrimages—were necessary to achieve salvation. For Luther, however, good works did not bring a person closer to salvation, for faith alone was the avenue to

heaven. A person of faith, he said, does good works—for example, demonstrating active love toward one's neighbor—in thanksgiving to God, but such actions are not rewarded with eternal life. In the following selection from his final "Reformation tract"—*The Freedom of the Christian*—Luther reflects on faith, works, and what it means to be righteous in the eyes of God.

THE FREEDOM OF THE CHRISTIAN

You may ask, "What then is the Word of God, and how shall it be used, since there are so many words of God?" I answer: The Apostle explains this in Romans 1. The Word is the gospel of God concerning his Son, who was made flesh, suffered, rose from the dead, and was glorified through the Spirit who sanctifies. To preach Christ means to feed the soul, make it righteous, set it free, and save it, provided it believes the preaching. Faith alone is the saving and efficacious use of the Word of God, according to Rom. 10 (:9): "If you confess with your lips that Jesus is Lord and believe in your heart that God raised him from the dead, you will be saved." Furthermore, "Christ is the end of the law, that every one who has faith may be justified" (Rom. 10:4). Again, in Rom. 1 (:17), "He who through faith is righteous shall live." The Word of God cannot be received and cherished by any works whatever but only by faith. Therefore it is clear that, as the soul needs only the Word of God for its life and righteousness, so it is justified by faith alone and not any works; for if it could be justified by anything else, it would not need the Word, and consequently it would not need faith.

This faith cannot exist in connection with works—that is to say, if you at the same time claim to be justified by works, whatever their character—for that would be the same as "limping with two different opinions" (I Kings 18:21), as worshipping Baal and kissing one's own hand (Job 31:27–28), which, as Job says, is a very great iniquity. Therefore the moment you begin to have faith you learn that all things in you are altogether blameworthy, sinful, and damnable, as the Apostle says in Rom. 3 (:23), "Since all have sinned and fall short of the glory of God," and, "None is righteous, no, not one; . . . all have turned aside, together they have gone wrong" (Rom. 3:10–12). When you have learned this you will know that you need Christ, who suffered and rose again for you so that, if you believe in him, you may through this faith become a new man in so far as your sins are forgiven and you are justified by the merits of another, namely, of Christ alone.

Since, therefore, this faith can rule only in the inner man, as Rom. 10 (:10) says, "For man believes with his heart and so is justified," and since faith alone justifies, it is clear that the inner man cannot be justified, freed, or saved by any outer work or action at all, and that these works, whatever their character, have nothing to do with this inner man. On the other hand, only ungodliness and unbelief of heart, and no outer work, make him guilty and a damnable servant of sin. Wherefore it ought to be the first concern of every Christian to lay aside all confidence in works and increasingly to strengthen faith alone and through faith to grow in the knowledge, not of works, but of Christ Jesus, who suffered and rose for him, as Peter teaches in the last chapter of his first Epistle (1 Pet. 5:10). No other work makes a Christian. . . .

Our faith in Christ does not free us from works but from false opinions concerning works, that is, from the foolish presumption that justification is acquired by works. Faith redeems, corrects, and preserves our consciences so that we know that righteousness does not consist in works, although works neither can nor ought to be wanting; just as we cannot be without food and drink and all the works of this mortal body, yet our righteousness is not in them, but in faith; and

yet those works of the body are not to be despised or neglected on that account. In this world we are bound by the needs of our bodily life, but we are not righteous because of them. "My kingship is not of this world" (John 18:36), says Christ. He does not, however, say, "My kingship is not here, that is, in this world." And Paul says, "Though we live in the world we are not carrying on a worldly war" (II Cor. 10:3), and in Gal. 2 (:20), "The life I now live in the flesh I live by faith in the Son of God." Thus what we do, live, and are in works and ceremonies, we do because of the necessities of this life and of the effort to rule our body. Nevertheless we are righteous, not in these, but in the faith of the Son of God.

3 The Origins of Reformed Protestantism

Reformed Protestantism, as distinct from Lutheranism, began in 1523, when Huldrych Zwingli (1484–1531) became the reformer of Zurich. When Zwingli accepted a position as preacher at the main church in Zurich in 1518, he was an admirer and follower of Erasmus. Five years later, he broke with Erasmus and came to a Protestant understanding of Christianity through his own study of the New Testament and the church fathers. The Reformation in Zurich was completed by 1525, when the council, the governing body of the city, ordered the churches cleared of all images and abolished the Catholic Mass. The simple Reformed communion service, which was celebrated only four times a year, replaced the Mass. In that same year, the council created the new Marriage Court, which replaced the Bishop's court in Constance, where all legal problems concerning marriage had previously been judged. The Zurich Marriage Court, the first Protestant morals court, had six judges: Four were laymen and two were clergymen, chosen by the Council. The sole appeal was to the Council. As the Zwinglian Reformation spread to other parts of Switzerland, similar courts were established in other Swiss cities. When John Calvin (1509–1564) arrived in Basel in 1534, he discovered such a court there.

After embracing Protestantism, Calvin found it necessary to flee from his native France. In Basel, he composed a summary of his new Protestant theology, *The Institutes of the Christian Religion,* which went through several editions during Calvin's lifetime. Written in the elegant Latin style favored by humanists, the work was translated into French and soon became one of the most important theological texts for Protestants in France, the Netherlands, Scotland, and England. Calvin himself settled in Geneva where his influence dominated the civil and religious life of the townspeople. From Geneva, Calvin carried on an active mission, spreading the Reformed faith throughout his native France and elsewhere.

In 1536, the newly Protestant-controlled government of Geneva asked Calvin to draw up a public confession of the Reformed faith, a catechism, and rules for worship. But the government's demand that all citizens be forced to subscribe to the new confession resulted in a change of government in the elections in 1538. Calvin withdrew to Basel and then to Strassburg. By 1541, the political situation had changed again; Calvin was recalled, and his recommendations for a new government for the church were put into law. He remained the spiritual leader of Geneva until his death. Calvinism was especially influential in England and Scotland, giving rise to the Puritan movement in seventeenth-century England and the Presbyterian Church in Scotland and Ireland. Both of these religious traditions exercised great influence on the settlers of the English colonies in North America.

John Calvin
The Institutes of the Christian Religion
PREDESTINATION

One doctrine that assumed greater and greater importance in the revised editions of Calvin's *Institutes* was predestination: the belief that each person's salvation or damnation was already decided before birth. Luther and Zwingli also taught that God had chosen those who would have faith. But they did not agree with Calvin concerning those who were to be damned, holding that those who refused to believe did so of their own volition. Calvin taught that salvation was only offered to the elect—the chosen few who were predestined to be saved by God's sovereign will—and that the reprobate (the damned) could not believe. Some argued that Calvin's doctrine implied that God was a tyrant; others said that it intimated that God was the author of sin. To many Christians, this doctrine diminished the justice and mercy of God and made meaningless the idea of freedom of choice in the matter of salvation. Calvin's answer to these criticisms was that we cannot know the mind of God—we are not able to understand why God chooses some humans and condemns others. We must trust in God's wisdom and justice.

In actual fact, the covenant of life is not preached equally among all men, and among those to whom it is preached, it does not gain the same acceptance either constantly or in equal degree. In this diversity the wonderful depth of God's judgment is made known. For there is no doubt that this variety also serves the decision of God's eternal election. If it is plain that it comes to pass by God's bidding that salvation is freely offered to some while others are barred from access to it, at once great and difficult questions spring up, explicable only when reverent minds regard as settled what they may suitably hold concerning election and predestination. A baffling question this seems to many. For they think nothing more inconsistent than that out of the common multitude of men some should be predestined to salvation, others to destruction. But how mistakenly they entangle themselves will become clear in the following discussion. . . .

No one who wishes to be thought religious dares simply deny predestination, by which God adopts some to hope of life, and sentences others to eternal death. But our opponents, especially those who make foreknowledge its cause, envelop it in numerous petty objections. We, indeed, place both doctrines in God, but we say that subjecting one to the other is absurd.

When we attribute foreknowledge to God, we mean that all things always were, and perpetually remain, under his eyes, so that to his knowledge there is nothing future or past, but all things are present. And they are present in such a way that he not only conceives them through ideas, as we have before us those things which our minds remember, but he truly looks upon them and discerns them as things placed before him. And this foreknowledge is extended throughout the universe to every creature. We call predestination God's eternal decree, by which he determined with himself what he willed to become of each man. For all are not created in equal condition; rather, eternal life is foreordained for some, eternal damnation for others. Therefore, as any man has been created to one or the other of these ends, we speak of him as predestined to life or to death. . . .

As Scripture, then, clearly shows, we say that God once established by his eternal and unchangeable plan those whom he long before determined once for all to receive into salvation, and those whom, on the other hand, he would devote to destruction. We assert that, with respect to the elect, this plan was founded upon his freely given mercy, without regard to human worth; but by his just and irreprehensible but incomprehensible judgment he has barred the door of life to those whom he has given over to damnation. Now among the elect we regard the call as a testimony or election. Then we hold justification another sign of its manifestation, until they come into the glory in which the fulfillment of that election lies. But as the Lord seals his elect by call and justification, so, by shutting off the reprobate from knowledge of his name or from the sanctification of his Spirit, he, as it were, reveals by these marks what sort of judgment awaits them. Here I shall pass over many fictions that stupid men have invented to overthrow predestination. They need no refutation, for as soon as they are brought forth they abundantly prove their own falsity. I shall pause only over those which either are being argued by the learned or may raise difficulty for the simple, or which impiety speciously sets forth in order to assail God's righteousness.

John Calvin
Ecclesiastical Ordinances
REGULATORY BEHAVIOR

Calvin's *Ecclesiastical Ordinances,* the foundation for the organization of the church, were accepted by the citizens and the government of Geneva on November 20, 1541, two months after his return to Geneva. There were four offices in the church: ministers, teachers, elders, and deacons. The ministers preached and administered the sacraments of baptism and the Eucharist. The teachers, who were also clergy, taught children and ministerial candidates. The elders were laymen whose task it was to closely supervise the morals of the citizens. The deacons cared for the poor and the sick. An especially important innovation was the consistory, a church court that was inspired by the morals courts in Basel and Zurich. The consistory was composed of the ministers and elders who met weekly to hear accusations against individuals and to discipline those whose conduct was contrary to the church's moral teachings. Like the Zurich Marriage Court, the Consistory was a morals court with both clergy and laymen as judges. However, unlike the Zurich Marriage Court, the Genevan Consistory was a church court only. Its sole punishment was to bar individuals from partaking of the Eucharist; persistent offenders were turned over to the city authorities for further punishment. The *Ecclesiastical Ordinances* illuminate the character of the Calvinist system of public regulation of morals through community pressure and state power.

The Duties of Elders, or Presbyters

The office of the elders is to watch over the conduct of every individual, to admonish lovingly those whom they see doing wrong or leading an irregular life. When there is need, they should lay the matter before the body deputed to inflict paternal discipline (i.e. the consistory), of which they are members. . . .

The Consistory, or Session The elders, who have been described, shall assemble once a week with the ministers, namely Thursday morning, to see if there be any disorders in the Church and discuss together such remedies as shall be necessary. . . . If any one shall in contempt refuse to appear before them, it shall be their duty to inform the [town] council, so that it may supply a remedy. . . .

EXTRACTS FROM CALVIN'S REGULATIONS FOR THE VILLAGES ABOUT GENEVA

The whole household shall attend the sermons on Sunday, except when some one shall be left at home to tend the children or cattle.

If there is preaching on week days, all who can must come,—unless there be some good excuse,—so that at least one from each household shall be present. Those who have men-servants or maid-servants shall bring them when it is pos-sible, so that they shall not live like beasts without instruction. . . . Should any one come after the sermon has begun, let him be warned. If he does not amend, let him pay a fine of three sous [coins]. Let the churches be closed except during service, so that no one may enter them at other hours from superstitious motives. If any one be discovered engaged in some superstition within or near the church, let him be admonished. If he will not give up his superstition, let him be punished.

Persecution of Catholics Those who are found to have rosaries or idols to adore, let them be sent before the consistory, and in addition to the reproof they receive there, let them be sent before the council. Let the same be done with those who go on a pilgrimage. Those who observe feasts or papistical fasts shall only be admonished. Those who go to mass shall, besides being admonished, be sent before the council, and it shall consider the propriety of punishing the offenders by imprisonment or special fines, as it judges best.

He who blasphemes, swearing by the body or blood of our Lord, or in like manner, shall kiss the earth for the first offense, pay five sous for the second and ten for the third. He who contradicts the word of God shall be sent before the consistory for reproof, or before the council for punishment, as the case may require. If any one sings indecent, licentious songs, or dances . . . he shall be kept in prison three days and then sent to the council.[*]

[*]There are similar provisions for drunkenness, gambling, quarreling, taking more than five percent interest, etc.

Commentary on the Book of the Prophet Daniel
RESISTANCE TO TYRANNY

Like Luther and Zwingli, Calvin admonished Christians to obey all civil authorities. Although he tended to be skeptical about any good coming from kings, Calvin believed that all authority comes from God and that bad kings or tyrants were to be accepted as an expression of God's just punishment for the sins of the people.

Nonetheless, by 1561, Calvin was forced by circumstances (the severe persecution of Calvinists in France and elsewhere) to moderate his position. In his *Commentary on the Book of the Prophet Daniel,* Calvin justified disobeying rulers who deny the rights of God (as understood by the Protestant reformers). Calvin comments on the story of the Hebrew prophet Daniel, who clearly refused to obey the Persian king's order that he not worship the god of Israel. Calvin denies that Daniel had committed any offense against the king and explains this apparent contradiction by affirming the traditional Christian view that obedience to divine law takes precedence over obligations to obey the law of earthly rulers. Calvin's teaching here laid the basis for civil disobedience and even revolutionary action by Calvinists in France, the Netherlands, England, and Scotland. Furthermore, the Puritans in America challenged political authorities who they thought contravened God's law. Thus they developed two habits crucial to the development of political liberty—dissent and resistance. During the American Revolution, these Puritan tendencies led Americans to resist authority that they considered unjust. The following passage starts with a biblical quote in which Daniel addresses the Persian king.

. . . And even before thee, O king, I have committed nothing wrong. It is clear that the Prophet had violated the king's edict. Why, then, does he not ingenuously confess this? Nay, why does he contend that he has not transgressed against the king? Because he conducted himself with fidelity in all his duties, he could free himself from every [false charge] by which he knew himself oppressed, as if he had despised the king's sovereignty. But Daniel was not so bound to the king of the Persians when [the king] claimed for himself as a god what ought not to be offered to him. We know how earthly empires are constituted by God, only on the condition that [God] deprives himself of nothing, but shines forth alone, and all magistrates must be set in regular order, and every authority in existence must be subject to his glory. Since, therefore, Daniel could not obey the king's edict without denying God, as we have previously seen, he did not transgress against the king by constantly persevering in that exercise of piety to which he had been accustomed, and by calling on his God three times a-day. To make this the more evident, we must remember that passage of [the Apostle] Peter, "Fear God, honour the king" (1 Pet. 2:17). The two commands are connected together, and cannot be separated from one another. The fear of God ought to precede, that kings may obtain their authority. For if any one begins his reverence of an earthly prince by rejecting that of God, he will act preposterously, since this is a complete perversion of the order of nature. Then let God be feared in the first place, and earthly princes will obtain their authority, if only God shines forth, as I have already said. Daniel, therefore, here defends himself with justice, since *he had not committed any crime against the king;* for he was compelled to obey the command of God, and he neglected what the king had ordered in opposition to it. For earthly princes lay aside all their power when they rise up against God, and are unworthy of being reckoned in the number of mankind. We ought rather utterly to defy than to obey them whenever they are so restive and wish to spoil God of his rights, and, as it were, to seize upon his throne and draw him down from heaven.

4 The Catholic Response to Protestantism

The criticisms of Catholic beliefs and practices by Luther, Calvin, and other Protestant reformers generated a host of theological defenses of traditional Catholicism. However, there was a general admission that grave abuses in Catholic clerical morals and discipline had been allowed to go uncorrected. Almost everyone agreed that a new general council of the church was necessary to clarify and affirm Catholic doctrine and institute reforms in clerical discipline and practices. Despite many promises to summon such a council, the popes delayed. Political conditions never seemed right, and the papacy, remembering the challenge to its power attempted by councils in the fifteenth century, feared that prematurely summoning a council could be a disaster for papal authority.

The council was finally convened in 1545 at the Alpine city of Trent, on the borders between the German lands and Italy. The papacy was firmly in control and no Protestant theologians participated in the conciliar sessions. The council was suspended several times, the longest hiatus lasting for ten years (1552–1562), and concluded its work in 1563.

The council fathers confessed their responsibility for the evils that had grown up in the church and committed themselves to institutional reforms that would raise the standards of morality and learning among future bishops and clergy. The most significant pastoral reforms included creating an official catechism outlining the orthodox beliefs of the Roman church, establishing seminaries to direct the education of future clergy, and reforming the bishop's office by increasing his responsibilities for the pastoral life of his diocese. On doctrinal matters, the council gave an authoritative Catholic response to Protestant teachings on a host of issues.

For example, the council condemned the Protestant view that faith alone was necessary for salvation and insisted on the integration of both faith and good works in the process of salvation. This position allowed the council to defend such traditional Catholic practices as monasticism, indulgences, masses for the dead, alms giving, pilgrimages, veneration of saints, and other pious works.

Saint Ignatius Loyola
The Spiritual Exercises

Even before the Council of Trent had been called to respond to the challenge of Protestant teachings, the Basque nobleman Saint Ignatius Loyola (1491–1556) founded a new religious order, the Society of Jesus, popularly called the Jesuits. A former soldier, Ignatius underwent a spiritual conversion in 1521–1522 and, after seeking guidance about his vocation, decided to become a priest. Later, while studying at the University of Paris, Ignatius and several companions decided to found their order and received papal recognition in 1540.

The new Jesuit order was characterized by three unusual features. First, the members took a special oath of obedience to the pope, which bound them to support the papacy and its programs with special devotion. Second, they rejected the traditional monastic ideal of a life of contemplation and instead espoused a life of active service in the world. Third, they were especially committed to the Christian education of youth and to missionary work among pagans and heretics.

The Jesuits soon became the vanguard of the Roman Catholic Church's effort to resist what it believed to be Protestant errors and to hasten the restoration of Catholicism in those lands where it no longer was the dominant religion. Ignatius himself thought it vital for his followers, and for the Catholic laity as well, to "think with the mind of the Church." To help Catholics achieve a higher spiritual life, Ignatius composed a book during 1521–1535 called *The Spiritual Exercises.* It became a guide for Jesuit confessors or counselors in leading penitents to a greater spiritual maturity. It was a summary of practical ways to order one's life through the imitation of Christ.

In the last section of *The Spiritual Exercises,* written during the early 1530s, Ignatius gives final instructions to his followers: a set of rules for "thinking with the Church." These guidelines reflect the response of reformed Catholicism to the great theological issues raised by Luther, Calvin, and other Protestants.

RULES FOR THINKING WITH THE CHURCH

In order to have the proper attitude of mind in the Church Militant [all active, living Christians] we should observe the following rules:

1. Putting aside all private judgment, we should keep our minds prepared and ready to obey promptly and in all things the true spouse of Christ our Lord, our Holy Mother, the hierarchical Church.

2. To praise sacramental confession and the reception of the Most Holy Sacrament [the Eucharist] once a year, and much better once a month, and better still every week, with the requisite and proper dispositions.

3. To praise the frequent hearing of Mass, singing of hymns and psalms, and the recitation of long prayers, both in and out of church; also the hours arranged for fixed times for the whole Divine Office, for prayers of all kinds and for the canonical hours.

4. To praise highly religious life, virginity, and continence; and also matrimony, but not as highly, as any of the foregoing.

5. To praise the vows of religion, obedience, poverty, chastity, and other works of perfection and supererogation.[1] It must be remembered that a vow is made in matters that lead to evangelical perfection. It is therefore improper to make a vow in matters that depart from this perfection; as, for example, to enter business, to get married, and so forth.

6. To praise the relics of the saints by venerating them and by praying to these saints. Also to praise the stations, pilgrimages, indulgences, jubilees,[2] Crusade indulgences, and the lighting of candles in the churches.

7. To praise the precepts concerning fasts and abstinences, such as those of Lent, Ember Days,[3] Vigils, Fridays, and Saturdays; likewise to praise acts of penance, both interior and exterior.

8. To praise the adornments and buildings of churches as well as sacred images, and to venerate them according to what they represent.

9. Finally, to praise all the precepts of the church, holding ourselves ready at all times to find reasons for their defense, and never offending against them.

10. We should be more inclined to approve and praise the directions and recommendations of our superiors as well as their personal behavior. Although sometimes these may not be or may not have been praiseworthy, to speak against them when preaching in public or in conversation with people would give rise to murmuring and scandal rather than to edification. As a result, the people would be angry with their superiors, whether temporal or spiritual. Still, while it does harm to our superiors in their absence to speak ill of them in the presence of the people, it might be useful to speak of their bad conduct to those who can apply a remedy.

11. To praise both positive and scholastic theology, for as it is more characteristic of the [early church] doctors, such as St. Augustine, St. Jerome, St. Gregory, and others, to encourage the affections to greater love and service of God our Lord in all things, so it also is more characteristic of the [medieval] scholastic doctors, such as St. Thomas, St. Bonaventure, and the Master of the

---

[1]The performance of good works beyond what God requires.

[2]*Stations* refers to a set of prayers recited while meditating on certain moments in the passion and death of Christ. Jubilees were certain years set aside by the papacy during which special indulgences were offered to pilgrims attending certain shrines, particularly that of Saint Peter in Rome.

[3]Three Ember Days were set aside by the church each season for special prayers and fasting.

Sentences,[4] etc., to define and explain for our times the things necessary for eternal salvation, and to refute and expose all errors and fallacies. Also, the scholastic doctors, being of more recent date, not only have a clearer understanding of the Holy Scripture and of the teachings of the [early church] doctors, but also, being enlightened and inspired by the Divine Power, they are helped by the Councils, Canons, and Constitutions of our Holy Mother Church. . . .

13. If we wish to be sure that we are right in all things, we should always be ready to accept this principle: I will believe that the white that I see is black, if the hierarchical Church so defines it. For, I believe that between the Bridegroom, Christ our Lord, and the Bride, His Church, there is but one spirit, which governs and directs us for the salvation of our souls, for the same Spirit and Lord, who gave us the Ten Commandments, guides and governs our Holy Mother Church.

14. Although it be true that no one can be saved unless it be predestined and unless he have faith and grace, still we must be very careful of our manner of discussing and

---

[4]*Master of the Sentences* is a reference to Peter Lombard (c. 1100–c. 1160), an Italian theologian whose book *Sentences* was the most widely used theology textbook in the medieval universities.

speaking of these matters. [See Calvin's *Institutes,* page 41.]

15. We should not make predestination an habitual subject of conversation. If it is sometimes mentioned we must speak in such a way that no person will fall into error, as happens on occasion when one will say, "It has already been determined whether I will be saved or lost, and in spite of all the good or evil that I do, this will not be changed." As a result, they become apathetic and neglect the works that are conducive to their salvation and to the spiritual growth of their souls.

16. In like manner, we must be careful lest by speaking too much and with too great emphasis on faith, without any distinction or explanation, we give occasion to the people to become indolent and lazy in the performance of good works, whether it be before or after their faith is founded in charity.

17. Also in our discourse we ought not to emphasize the doctrine that would destroy free will. We may therefore speak of faith and grace to the extent that God enables us to do so, for the greater praise of His Divine Majesty. But, in these dangerous times of ours, it must not be done in such a way that good works or free will suffer any detriment or be considered worthless.

Age of the Baroque

The Age of the Baroque encompasses the period roughly from the last decades of the sixteenth century to the opening decades of the eighteenth century. To art historians, the *Baroque Age* was primarily defined during the seventeenth century when popes, kings, and aristocrats, eager to demonstrate their wealth and power, appropriated an artistic style characterized by majesty, opulence, sensuality, tension, and drama. The preeminent expression of the Baroque style in France is Louis XIV's extravagant palace complex at Versailles. Because Louis recognized the relevance of the arts in furthering his concept of royal glory, his Versailles fuses architecture, sculpture, painting, and gardens to create an awe-aspiring whole.

The Age of Baroque coincided with the Age of Absolutism, as monarchs sought to strengthen royal power by asserting authority over both aristocracy and clergy. During much of the Middle Ages, royal absolutism was effectively resisted by lords, townspeople, and the church. However, by the late 1500s monarchs, maintaining that their right to rule stemmed from God, had increasingly asserted power over their kingdom.

The symbol of absolutism was Louis XIV (1643–1715). During his seventy-two-year reign, France gained greater unity and central authority than it had ever known. To prevent the great nobles from challenging royal authority, Louis XIV chose many of his ministers and provincial administrators from the middle class. The great nobles, "princes of the blood," enjoyed considerable social prestige but exercised no real power in the government. The king encouraged these "people of quality" to live at court where they contended with each other for his favor.

As the symbol of France and the greatest ruler of Europe, Louis insisted that the social life at Versailles provide an appropriate setting for his exalted person. During his long reign, France set the style for the whole of Europe. The splendor of Versailles was the talk of Europe, and other monarchs sought to imitate the fashions and manners of the Sun King's court.

In England, James I (1603–1625) made it clear from the beginning of his reign that, as God's lieutenant on earth, he was the supreme ruler and legislator, a belief that his son, Charles I (1625–1649), shared. However, things turned out differently in England. The English Parliament rebelled against the king; the Civil War began in 1642 and ended with the execution of Charles in 1649. Oliver Cromwell ruled the Puritan Commonwealth until his death in 1658. In 1660, the monarchy was restored, but the Glorious Revolution of 1688–1689 secured the rights of Parliament and the rule of law and permanently limited the monarch's power.

Writers during the Baroque Age drew heavily from both the Greco-Roman and Christian traditions. English authors John Milton and John Bunyan expressed a Puritan concern with sin and salvation, and French Catholic playwrights Corneille and Molière were influenced by the content and form of classical Greek drama.

1 Justification of Absolute Monarchy by Divine Right

Effectively blocking royal absolutism in the Middle Ages were the dispersion of power between kings and feudal lords, the vigorous sense of personal freedom and urban autonomy of the townspeople, and the limitations on royal power imposed by the church. However, by the late sixteenth century, monarchs were asserting their authority over competing groups with ever-greater effectiveness. In this new balance of political forces, European kings implemented their claim to absolute power as monarchs chosen by and responsible to God alone. This theory, called the divine right of kings, became the dominant political ideology of seventeenth- and eighteenth-century Europe.

Bishop Jacques-Benigne Bossuet
Politics Drawn from the Very Words of Holy Scripture

Louis XIV was the symbol of absolutism, a term applied to those early modern states where monarchs exercised power free of constitutional restraints. Theorists of absolutism like Bishop Jacques-Benigne Bossuet (1672–1704) argued that monarchs received their authority directly from God. Following are excerpts from Bossuet's *Politics Drawn from the Very Words of Holy Scripture.*

THIRD BOOK, IN WHICH ONE BEGINS TO EXPLAIN THE NATURE AND THE PROPERTIES OF ROYAL AUTHORITY

Article II, Royal Authority is Sacred

1st Proposition, God establishes kings as his ministers, and reigns through them over the peoples
We have already seen that all power comes from God.

"The prince, St. Paul adds, is God's minister to thee for good. But if thou do that which is evil, fear: for he beareth not the sword in vain. For he is God's minister: an avenger to execute wrath upon him that doth evil."

Thus princes act as ministers of God, and his lieutenants on earth. It is through them that he exercises his Empire. . . .

It is in this way that we have seen that the royal throne is not the throne of a man, but the throne of God himself. "God hath chosen Solomon my son, to sit upon the throne of the kingdom of the Lord over Israel." And again: "Solomon sat on the throne of the Lord."

And in order that no one believe that it was peculiar to the Israelites to have kings established by God, here is what Ecclesiasticus says: "Over every nation he set a ruler." . . .

Thus he governs all peoples, and gives them, all of them, their kings; though he governs Israel in a more particular and announced fashion.

2nd Proposition, The person of kings is sacred It appears from all this that the person of kings is sacred, and that to attempt anything against them is a sacrilege. . . . [T]hey are sacred through their charge, as being the representatives of divine majesty, deputized by his providence for the execution of his plans. It is thus that God calls Cyrus his anointed. . . .

One must protect kings as sacred things; and whoever neglects to guard them is worthy of death. . . .

3rd Proposition, One must obey the prince by reason of religion and conscience . . . Even if rulers do not acquit themselves of this duty [punishment of evildoers and praise of the good], one must respect in them their charge and their ministry. "Servants, be subject to your masters with all fear, not only to the good and gentle, but also to the angry and unjust."

There is thus something religious in the respect one gives to the prince. The service of God and respect for kings are inseparable things, and St. Peter places these two duties together: "Fear God, Honor the King."

God, moreover, has put something divine into kings. "I have said: You are Gods, and all of you the sons of the most High." It is God himself whom David makes speak in this way. . . .

4th Proposition, Kings should respect their own power, and use it only for the public good   Their power coming from on high, as has been said, they must not believe that they are the owners of it, to use it as they please; rather must they use it with fear and restraint, as something which comes to them from God, and for which God will ask an accounting of them.

FOURTH BOOK, ON THE CHARACTERISTICS OF ROYALTY (CONTINUATION)

First Article, Royal Authority is Absolute

1st Proposition, The prince need account to no one for what he ordains   . . . Without this absolute authority, he can neither do good nor suppress evil: his power must be such that no one can hope to escape him; and, in fine, the sole defense of individuals against the public power, must be their innocence. . . .

2nd Proposition, When the prince has decided, there can be no other decision   The judgments of sovereigns are attributed to God himself. . . .

[N]o one has the right to judge or to review after him.

One must, then, obey princes as if they were justice itself, without which there is neither order nor justice in affairs.

They are gods, and share in some way in divine independence. "I have said: You are gods, and all of you the sons of the most High."

Only God can judge their judgments and their persons. . . .

It follows from this that he who does not want to obey the prince, is . . . condemned irremissibly to death as an enemy of public peace and of human society. . . .

The prince can correct himself when he knows that he has done badly; but against his authority there can be no remedy except his authority.

3rd Proposition, There is no co-active force against the prince   One calls co-active [coercive] force a power to constrain and to execute what is legitimately ordained. To the prince alone belongs legitimate command; to him alone belongs co-active force as well.

It is for that reason also that St. Paul gives the sword to him alone. "If thou do that which is evil, fear; for he beareth not the sword in vain."

In the state only the prince should be armed: otherwise everything is in confusion, and the state falls back into anarchy.

He who creates a sovereign prince puts everything together into his hands, both the sovereign authority to judge and all the power of the state.

James I
True Law of Free Monarchies
AND A SPEECH TO PARLIAMENT

One of the most articulate defenders of the divine right of monarchy was James VI, who was king of Scotland (1567–1625), and as James I (1603–1625) also was king of England. A scholar as well as a king, in 1598 James anonymously published a widely read book called the *True Law of Free Monarchies*. He claimed that the king alone was the true legislator. James's notions of the royal prerogative and of the role of Parliament are detailed in the following passages from the *True Law* and a speech to Parliament.

True Law of Free Monarchies

Prerogative and Parliament

According to these fundamental laws already alleged, we daily see that in the parliament (which is nothing else but the head court of the king and his vassals) the laws are but craved by his subjects, and only made by him at their [proposal] and with their advice: for albeit the king make daily statutes and ordinances, [imposing] such pains thereto as he thinks [fit], without any advice of parliament or estates, yet it lies in the power of no parliament to make any kind of law or statute, without his sceptre [that is, authority] be to it, for giving it the force of a law. . . . And as ye see it manifest that the king is over-lord of the whole land, so is he master over every person that inhabiteth the same, having power over the life and death of every one of them: for although a just prince will not take the life of any of his subjects without a clear law, yet the same laws whereby he taketh them are made by himself or his predecessors; and so the power flows always from himself. . . . Where he sees the law doubtsome or rigorous, he may interpret or mitigate the same, lest otherwise *summum jus* be *summa injuria* [the greatest right be the greatest wrong]: and therefore general laws made publicly in parliament may upon . . . [the king's] authority be mitigated and suspended upon causes only known to him.

As likewise, although I have said a good king will frame all his actions to be according to the law, yet is he not bound thereto but of his good will, and for good example-giving to his subjects. . . . So as I have already said, a good king, though he be above the law, will subject and frame his actions thereto, for example's sake to his subjects, and of his own free will, but not as subject or bound thereto. . . .

In a speech before the English Parliament in March 1610, James elaborated on his exalted theory of the monarch's absolute power.

A Speech to Parliament

. . . The state of monarchy is the supremest thing upon earth: for kings are not only God's lieutenants upon earth and sit upon God's throne, but even by God himself they are called gods. There be three principal [comparisons] that illustrate the state of monarchy: one taken out of the word of God, and the two other out of the grounds of policy and philosophy. In the Scriptures kings are called gods, and so their power after a certain relation compared to the Divine power. Kings are also compared to fathers of families: for a king is truly *parens patriae* [parent of the country], the politic father of his people. And lastly, kings are compared to the head of this microcosm of the body of man. . . .

I conclude then this point touching the power of kings with this axiom of divinity, That as to dispute what God may do is blasphemy, . . . so is it sedition in subjects to dispute what a king may do in the height of his power. But just kings will ever be willing to declare what they will do, if they will not incur the curse of God. I will not be content that my power be disputed upon; but I shall ever be willing to make the reason appear of all my doings, and rule my actions according to my laws. . . .

Now the second general ground whereof I am to speak concerns the matter of grievances. . . . First then, I am not to find fault that you inform yourselves of the particular just grievances of the people; nay I must tell you, ye can neither be just nor faithful to me or to your countries that trust and employ you, if you do it not. . . . But I would wish you to be careful to avoid [these] things in the matter of grievances.

First, that you do not meddle with the main points of government: that is my craft . . . to meddle with that, were to lessen me. I am now an old king . . . ;

I must not be taught my office.

Secondly, I would not have you meddle with such ancient rights of mine as I have received from my predecessors, possessing them *more majorum* [as ancestral customs]: such things I would be sorry should be accounted for grievances. All novelties are dangerous as well in a politic as in a natural body: and therefore I would be loath to be quarrelled in my ancient rights and possessions: for that were to judge me unworthy of that which my predecessors had and left me.

2 A Secular Defense of Absolutism

Thomas Hobbes (1588–1679), a British philosopher and political theorist, witnessed the agonies of the English civil war, including the execution of Charles I in 1649. These developments fortified Hobbes' conviction that absolutism was the most desirable and logical form of government. Only the unlimited power of a sovereign, said Hobbes, could contain human passions that disrupt the social order and threaten civilized life; only absolute rule could provide an environment secure enough for people to pursue their individual interests.

Leviathan (1651), Hobbes' principal work of political thought, broke with medieval political theory. Medieval thinkers assigned each group of people—clergy, lords, serfs, guildsmen—a place in a fixed social order; an individual's social duties were set by ancient traditions believed to have been ordained by God. During early modern times, the great expansion of commerce and capitalism spurred the new individualism already pronounced in Renaissance culture; group ties were shattered by competition and accelerating social mobility. Hobbes gave expression to a society where people confronted each other as competing individuals.

Thomas Hobbes
Leviathan

Hobbes was influenced by the new scientific thought that saw mathematical knowledge as the avenue to truth. Using geometry as a model, Hobbes began with what he believed were self-evident axioms regarding human nature, from which he deduced other truths. He aimed at constructing political philosophy on a scientific foundation and rejected the authority of tradition and religion as inconsistent with a science of politics. Thus, although Hobbes supported absolutism, he dismissed the idea advanced by other theorists of absolutism that the monarch's power derived from God. He also rejected the idea that the state should not be obeyed when it violated God's law. *Leviathan* is a rational and secular political statement. In this modern approach, rather than in Hobbes' justification of absolutism, lies the work's significance.

Hobbes had a pessimistic view of human nature. Believing that people are innately selfish and grasping, he maintained that competition and dissension, rather than cooperation, characterize human relations. Even when reason teaches that cooperation is more advantageous than competition, Hobbes observed that people are reluctant to alter their ways, because passion, not reason, governs their behavior. In the following passages from *Leviathan,* Hobbes described the causes of human conflicts.

Nature hath made men so equall, in the faculties of body, and mind; as that though there bee found one man sometimes manifestly stronger in body, or of quicker mind than another; yet when all is reckoned together, the difference between man, and man, is not so considerable, as that one man can thereupon claim to himselfe any benefit, to which another may not pretend, as well as he. For as to the strength of body, the weakest has strength enough to kill the strongest, either by secret machination, or by confederacy with others, that are in the same danger with himselfe. . . .

And as to the faculties of the mind . . . men are . . . [more] equall than unequall. . . .

From this equality of ability, ariseth equality of hope in the attaining of our Ends. And therefore if any two men desire the same thing, which nevertheless they cannot both enjoy, they become enemies; and in the way to their End, . . . endeavour to destroy, or subdue one another. . . . If one plant,

sow, build, or possesse a convenient Seat, others may probably be expected to come prepared with forces united, to dispossesse, and deprive him, not only of the fruit of his labour, but also of his life, or liberty. . . .

So that in the nature of man, we find three principall causes of quarrell. First, Competition; Secondly, Diffidence; Thirdly, Glory.

The first, maketh men invade for Gain; the second, for Safety; and the third, for Reputation. The first use Violence, to make themselves Masters of other men's persons, wives, children, and cattell; the second, to defend them; the third, for trifles, as a word, a smile, a different opinion, and any other signe of undervalue, either direct in their Persons, or by reflexion in their Kindred, their Friends, their Nation, their Profession, or their Name.

Hereby it is manifest, that during the time men live without a common Power to keep them all in awe, they are in that condition which is called Warre; and such a warre, as is of every man, against every man. . . .

Hobbes then described a state of nature—the hypothetical condition of humanity prior to the formation of the state—as a war of all against all. For Hobbes, the state of nature is a logical abstraction, a device employed to make his point. Only a strong ruling entity—the state—will end the perpetual strife and provide security. For Hobbes, the state is merely a useful arrangement that permits individuals to exchange goods and services in a secure environment. The ruling authority in the state, the sovereign, must have supreme power, or society will collapse and the anarchy of the state of nature will return.

Whatsoever therefore is consequent to a time of Warre, where every man is Enemy to every man; the same is consequent to the time, wherein men live without other security, than what their own strength, and their own invention shall furnish them withall. In such condition, there is no place for Industry; because the fruit thereof is uncertain: and consequently no Culture of the Earth; no Navigation, nor use of the commodities that may be imported by Sea; no commodious Building; no Instruments of moving, and removing such things as require much force; no Knowledge of the face of the Earth; no account of Time; no Arts; no Letters; no Society; and which is worst of all, continuall feare, and danger of violent death; And the life of man, solitary, poore, nasty, brutish, and short. . . .

The Passions that encline men to Peace, are Feare of Death; Desire of such things as are necessary to commodious living; and a Hope by their Industry to obtain them. And Reason suggesteth convenient Articles of Peace, upon which men may be drawn to agreement. . . .

And because the condition of Man, (as hath been declared in the precedent Chapter) is a condition of Warre of every one against every one; in which case every one is governed by his own Reason; and there is nothing he can make use of, that may not be a help unto him, in preserving his life against his enemyes; It followeth, that in such a condition, every man has a Right to every thing; even to one another's body. And therefore, as long as this naturall Right of every man to every thing endureth, there can be no security to any man, (how strong or wise soever he be,) of living out the time, which Nature ordinarily alloweth men to live. . . .

. . . If there be no Power erected, or not great enough for our security; every man will and may lawfully rely on his own strength and art, for caution against all other men. . . .

The only way to erect . . . a Common Power, as may be able to defend them from the invasion of [foreigners] and the injuries of one another, and thereby to secure them in such sort, as that by their owne industrie, and by the fruites of the

Earth, they may nourish themselves and live contentedly; is, to conferre all their power and strength upon one Man, or upon one Assembly of men, that may reduce all their Wills, by plurality of voices, unto one Will . . . and therein to submit their Wills, every one to his Will, and their Judgements, to his Judgment. This is more than Consent, or Concord; it is a reall Unitie of them all, in one and the same Person, made by Covenant of every man with every man, in such manner, as if every man should say to every man, *I Authorise and give up my Right of Governing my selfe, to this Man, or to this Assembly of men, on this condition, that thou give up thy Right to him, and Authorise all his Actions in like manner.* This done, the Multitude so united in one Person, is called a COMMON-WEALTH. . . . For by this Authorite, given him by every particular man in the Common-wealth, he hath the use of so much Power and Strength . . . conferred on him, that by terror thereof, he is inabled to forme the wills of them all, to Peace at home, and mutuall [aid] against their enemies abroad. And in him consisteth the Essence of the Common-wealth; which (to define it,) is *One Person, of whose Acts a great Multitude, by mutuall Covenants one with another, have made themselves every one the Author, to the end he may use the strength and means of them all, as he shall think expedient, for their Peace and Common Defence.*

And he that carryeth this Person, is called SOVERAIGNE, and said to have *Soveraigne Power;* and every one besides, his SUBJECT. . . .

. . . They that have already Instituted a Commonwealth, being thereby bound by Covenant . . . cannot lawfully make a new Covenant, amongst themselves, to be obedient to any other, in any thing whatsoever, without his permission. And therefore, they that are subjects to a Monarch, cannot without his leave cast off Monarchy, and return to the confusion of a disunited Multitude; nor transferre their Person from him that beareth it, to another Man, or other Assembly of men: for they . . . are bound, every man to every man, to [acknowledge] . . . that he that already is their Soveraigne, shall do, and judge fit to be done; so that [those who do not obey] break their Covenant made to that man, which is injustice: and they have also every man given the Soveraignty to him that beareth their Person; and therefore if they depose him, they take from him that which is his own, and so again it is injustice. . . . And whereas some men have pretended for their disobedience to their Soveraign, a new Covenant, made, not with men, but with God; this also is unjust: for there is no Covenant with God, but by mediation of some body that representeth God's Person; which none doth but God's Lieutenant, who hath the Soveraignty under God. But this pretence of Covenant with God, is so evident a [lie], even in the pretenders own consciences, that it is not onely an act of an unjust, but also of a vile, and unmanly disposition. . . .

. . . Consequently none of [the sovereign's] Subjects, by any pretence of forfeiture, can be freed from his Subjection.

3 Seventeenth-Century English Literature

The seventeenth century was dominated by religious and political conflicts that shattered the orderly hierarchy of authority which had characterized the Elizabethan state. Although the governmental system that emerged with the Glorious Revolution was more tolerant of differences between political, social, and religious opponents, it remained strict enough to uphold the essentials of social order, private property, and Christian orthodoxy. The literature of the age reflected these trends, pondering political, constitutional, and religious issues. Prose, epic poems, and plays embraced the idea of the Christian "calling" to do God's will on earth. Tempered by the ideals of the Protestant Reformation, this manifests itself in a certain belief that individuals must *decide for themselves* what it is that God intends for them to do.

The writers of the seventeenth century also sought to build on the foundation laid by their predecessors by emphasizing diversity, individuality, decorum, and *copia* (fullness). Through diversity and individuality, they meant to fashion a unique *English* literary style—making use of their own language in philosophy, science, religion, and the arts. Decorum referred to doing that which is proper, fitting, or seemly, and the literature reflects a unity of purpose in theme, subject matter, symbolism, and narrator of a work. *Copia* was intended to provide a rich cache of images, based not only on tradition, but also on classical allusions drawn from antiquity. Writers were expected to be knowledgeable about all of the arts in order to create a universal, ideal character capable of influencing those who read their works.

John Milton
Paradise Lost

The course of contemporary English history found its fullest expression in the works of the writer, John Milton (1608–1674). He demonstrated his facility for Hebrew, Greek, and Latin while in school and immersed himself in Latin verse and in classical tragedies and comedies at Christ College, Cambridge, where he received both his bachelor's and master's degrees. In his early poems, Milton showed himself to be a master of poetic image, grace, and style, but because of his scholarly gifts, his family and friends assumed he would become a minister. Instead, he retired to his family's homes at Hammersmith and Horton to cultivate the sort of humanist education he had not received at Cambridge. While at Horton, Milton wrote the poem "At a Solemn Music" which hints at the grandiose theme of good versus evil that was to culminate in his monumental poem, *Paradise Lost,* the heroic epic for which he would forever be remembered.

In 1642, when his wife left him, Milton wrote a series of pamphlets, arguing that divorce should be granted not only for adultery, but also in cases of incompatibility or a loveless marriage. He also published two of his most famous pamphlets—*On Education,* a discourse on the value of a humanistic education, and *Aeropagitica,* a plea for freedom of the press and an indictment of royal censorship. In his first political treatise, *The Tenure of Kings and Magistrates,* following the public execution of Charles I (an event that Milton reportedly attended), he asserted the right of the people to execute a tyrannical king. However, Milton's excitement at the fall of the Stuarts was tempered by the loss of his eyesight (probably from glaucoma) which left him totally blind by the age of forty-three. During the Restoration Period, Milton wrote his last political tract, *The Readie and Easie Way to Establish a Free Commonwealth,* an indictment of the English people who chose to become slaves of the monarchy. Subsequently, Royalists in Parliament issued a warrant for Milton's arrest, imprisoned him briefly, and forced him to pay an exorbitant fine.

Although the prodigious output of prose during Milton's life is four times greater than his entire poetic production, it is for his poetry that he is remembered. During his later life, Milton began to dictate *Paradise Lost,* and while he worked, he closely identified himself with the ancient poet Homer, who also was reputedly blind when he composed the *Iliad* and the *Odyssey.* Milton composed the epic in blank verse, which rarely appeared outside of drama. Blank verse is unrhymed iambic pentameter which is the most natural form of English verse. An iambic foot is an unstressed syllable followed by a stressed one, and pentameter means that there are five iambic feet per line. For example, one of the most famous lines in the poem is read as follows: "and jús/ti-fý/ the wáys of God to men." The subject of *Paradise Lost* is humanity's fall from God's grace, and with a note of irony attached, Milton chose Satan as an atypical protagonist, a type of antihero, to assert Eternal Providence and justify the ways of God to men. Milton's overwhelming sense of human guilt and sinfulness is drawn directly from the Protestant reformers who viewed human nature as corrupt, but the abundance of classical allusions demonstrates his affinity for the Renaissance. Consequently, the epic not only demonstrates how Milton overcame despair and found meaning in suffering, but it also reflects the power of his Protestant faith and his humanist belief in the capacity of the human soul to prevail against adversity.

The setting of the epic poem is Paradise, and the period of time is just before The Fall, until Adam and Eve are expelled from Paradise. The plot is, however, secondary to the ruminations and reflections of Milton's characters, including Gabriel, Adam, Eve, and, most importantly, Satan. Milton's powerful characterization of Satan actually induces sympathy from readers for the wrongs he incurs following his battle against tyranny in heaven. The rhythm and tone of the epic poem causes it to be counted as one of the great masterpieces of the English language. Moreover, Milton's theme of the fall of the human race inspired the classical composer Franz Josef Haydn's (1732–1809) oratorio *The Creation* and the Romantic poem "Enydmion" by John Keats (1795–1821), as well as many other authors and composers who are indebted to Milton for their style and theme. A number of scholars and critics have also come to recognize that many people who speak about the reality of Satan—his deportment, exploits, and expressions—have drawn their understanding, not as much from the Bible, as from a cultural perception that is traceable to Milton's *Paradise Lost.*

In the following selection from Book IX, Milton states "The Argument" for this particular section of the epic poem, dealing with The Fall of the human race occasioned by Adam and Eve in the Garden of Eden, eating of the fruit of the Tree of Knowledge, following Eve's temptation by the Serpent (the incarnation of evil).

THE ARGUMENT.—Satan, having compassed the Earth, with meditated guile returns as a mist by night into Paradise; enters into the Serpent sleeping. Adam and Eve in the morning go forth to their labours, which Eve proposes to divide in several places, each labouring apart: Adam consents not, alleging the danger lest that Enemy of whom they were forewarned should attempt her found alone. Eve, loth to be thought not circumspect or firm enough, urges her going apart, the rather desirous to make trial of her strength; Adam at last yields. The Serpent finds her alone: his subtle approach, first gazing, then speaking, with much flattery extolling Eve above all other creatures. Eve, wondering to hear the Serpent speak, asks how he attained to human speech and such understanding not till now; the Serpent answers that by tasting of a certain Tree in the Garden he attained both to speech and reason, till then void of both. Eve requires him to bring her to that tree, and finds it to be the Tree of Knowledge forbidden: the Serpent, now grown bolder, with many wiles and arguments induces her at length to eat. She, pleased with the taste, deliberates a while whether to impart thereof to Adam or not; at last brings him of the fruit; relates what persuaded her to eat thereof. Adam, at first amazed, but perceiving her lost, resolves, through vehemence of love, to perish with her, and, extenuating the trespass, eats also of the fruit. The effects thereof in them both; they seek to cover their nakedness; then fall to variance and accusation of one another.

In the passage that follows, Satan reveals his bitterness about being expelled from heaven (for leading a rebellion of angels) and his desire to reap vengeance on God by destroying his creation of six nights and days, particularly Adam, "this Man of Clay," whom God formed from the dust of the earth.

"O Earth, how like to Heaven, if not preferred
More justly, seat worthier of Gods, as built
With second thoughts, reforming what was old!
For what God, after better, worse would build?
Terrestrial Heaven, danced round by other Heavens,
That shine, yet bear their bright officious[1] lamps,
Light above light, for thee alone, as seems,
In thee concentring all their precious beams
Of sacred influence! As God in Heaven
Is centre, yet extends to all, so thou
Centring receiv'st from all those orbs; in thee,
Not in themselves, all their known virtue appears,
Productive in herb, plant, and nobler birth
Of creatures animate with gradual life
Of growth, sense, reason, all summed up in Man.
With what delight could I have walked thee round,
If I could joy in aught—sweet interchange
Of hill and valley, rivers, woods, and plains,
Now land, now sea, and shores with forest crowned,
Rocks, dens, and caves! But I in none of these
Find place or refuge; and the more I see
Pleasures about me, so much more I feel
Torment within me, as from the hateful siege
Of contraries; all good to me becomes

Bane, and in Heaven much worse would be my state.
But neither here seek I, nor in Heaven,
To dwell, unless by maistring[2] Heaven's Supreme;
Nor hope to be myself less miserable
By what I seek, but others to make such
As I, though thereby worse to me redound.
For only in destroying I find ease
To my relentless thoughts; and him destroyed,
Or won to what may work his utter loss,
For whom all this was made, all this will soon
Follow, as to him linked in weal or woe:
In woe then, that destruction wide may range!
To me shall be the glory sole among
The Infernal Powers, in one day to have marred
What he, Almighty styled, six nights and days
Continued making, and who knows how long
Before had been contriving? though perhaps
Not longer than since I in one night freed
From servitude inglorious well nigh half
The Angelic Name, and thinner left the throng
Of his adorers. He, to be avenged,
And to repair his numbers thus impaired—
Whether such virtue, spent of old, now failed
More Angels to create (if they at least
Are his created), or to spite us more—
Determined to advance into our room
A creature formed of earth, and him endow,
Exalted from so base original,
With heavenly spoils, our spoils. What he decreed
He effected; Man he made, and for him built
Magnificent this World, and Earth his seat,
Him Lord pronounced, and, O indignity!
Subjected to his service Angel-wings
And flaming ministers, to watch and tend
Their earthly charge. Of these the vigilance
I dread, and to elude, thus wrapt in mist
Of midnight vapour, glide obscure, and pry
In every bush and brake, where hap may find
The Serpent sleeping, in whose mazy folds
To hide me, and the dark intent I bring.
O foul descent! that I, who erst contended
With Gods to sit the highest, am now constrained
Into a beast, and, mixed with bestial slime,
This essence to incarnate and imbrute,[3]
That to the highth of Deity aspired!
But what will not ambition and revenge
Descend to? Who aspires must down as low
As high he soared, obnoxious, first or last,
To basest things. Revenge, at first though sweet,
Bitter ere long back on itself recoils.

---

[1]*Officious* means ready to serve, or obliging.

[2]*Maistring* means mastering.
[3]*Imbrute* means to reduce to brutality.

Let it; I reck[4] not, so it light well aimed,
Since higher I fall short, on him who next
Provokes my envy, this new favourite
Of Heaven, this Man of Clay, son of despite,
Whom, us the more to spite, his Maker raised
From dust: spite then with spite is best repaid."

When Adam and Eve part from one another to perform their daily tasks, the Serpent finds the opportunity to tempt Eve while she is alone. Fascinated by
his ability to speak, Eve asks the serpent how he
came to possess such a quality. The Serpent tells her
how he ate the "fair Apples, of fairest colours mixed,
ruddy and gold." When he tells her that the tree is
not far away, Eve asks the Serpent to lead her to the
tree—only to discover it is the tree the fruit of which
God has forbidden Adam and Eve to eat, lest they
die. Undaunted, the Serpent lures Eve to eat of the
forbidden fruit by telling her that she will not die, but
rather, she will be like God and possess knowledge
of both good and evil.

Which when she saw, thus to her guide she spake:—
    "Serpent, we might have spared our coming hither,
Fruitless to me, though fruit be here to excess,
The credit of whose virtue rest with thee—
Wondrous, indeed, if cause of such effects!
But of this tree we may not taste nor touch;
God so commanded, and left that command
Sole daughter of his voice: the rest, we live
Law to ourselves; our Reason is our Law."
    To whom the Tempter guilefully replied:—
"Indeed! Hath God then said that of the fruit
Of all these garden-trees ye shall not eat,
Yet lords declared of all in Earth or Air?"
    To whom thus Eve, yet sinless:—"Of the fruit
Of each tree in the garden we may eat;
But of the fruit of this fair Tree, amidst
The Garden, God hath said, 'Ye shall not eat
Thereof, nor shall ye touch it, lest ye die.'"
    She scarce had said, though brief, when now more bold
The Tempter, but, with shew of zeal and love
To Man, and indignation at his wrong,
New part puts on, and, as to passion moved,
Fluctuates disturbed, yet comely, and in act
Raised, as of some great matter to begin.
As when of old some orator renowned
In Athens or free Rome, where eloquence
Flourished, since mute, to some great cause addressed,
Stood in himself collected, while each part,
Motion, each act, won audience ere the tongue
Sometimes in highth began, as no delay

Of preface brooking through his zeal of right:
So standing, moving, or to highth upgrown,
The Tempter, all impassioned, thus began:—
"O sacred, wise, and wisdom-giving Plant,
Mother of science! now I feel thy power
Within me clear, not only to discern
Things in their causes, but to trace the ways
Of highest agents, deemed however wise.
Queen of this Universe! do not believe
Those rigid threats of death. Ye shall not die
How should ye? By the Fruit? it gives you life
To knowledge. By the Threatener? look on me,
Me who have touched and tasted, yet both live,
And life more perfet have attained than Fate
Meant me, by venturing higher than my lot.
Shall that be shut to Man which to the Beast
Is open? or will God incense his ire
For such a petty trespass, and not praise
Rather your dauntless virtue, whom the pain
Of death denounced, whatever thing Death be,
Deterred not from achieving what might lead
To happier life, knowledge of Good and Evil?
Of good, how just! of evil—if what is evil
Be real, why not known, since easier shunned?
God, therefore, cannot hurt ye and be just;
Not just, not God; not feared then, nor obeyed:
Your fear itself of death removes the fear.
Why, then, was this forbid? Why but to awe,
Why but to keep ye low and ignorant,
His worshipers? He knows that in the day
Ye eat thereof your eyes, that seem so clear,
Yet are but dim, shall perfectly be then
Opened and cleared, and ye shall be as Gods,
Knowing both good and evil, as they know,
That ye should be as Gods, since I as Man,
Internal Man, is but proportion meet—
I, of brute, human; ye, of human, Gods.
So ye shall die perhaps, by putting off
Human, to put on Gods—death to be wished,
Though threatened, which no worse than this can bring!
And what are Gods, that Man may not become
As they, participating godlike food?
The Gods are first, and that advantage use
On our belief, that all from them proceeds.
I question it; for this fair Earth I see,
Warmed by the Sun, producing every kind;
Them nothing. If they all things, who enclosed
Knowledge of Good and Evil in this Tree,
That whoso eats thereof forthwith attains
Wisdom without their leave? and wherein lies
The offence, that Man should thus attain to know?
What can your knowledge hurt him, or this Tree
Impart against his will, if all be his?
Or is it envy? and can envy dwell
In Heavenly breasts? These, these and many more

---

[4]*Reck* means to have concern or care.

Causes import your need of this fair Fruit,
Goddess humane, reach, then, and freely taste!" . . .

*Milton recounts the effect Eve's disobedience to God
had upon Adam when she tells him of her deed.*

Thus Eve with countenance blithe her story told;
But in her cheek distemper flushing glowed.
On the other side, Adam, soon as he heard
The fatal trespass done by Eve, amazed,
Astonied stood and blank, while horror chill
Ran through his veins, and all his joints relaxed.
From his slack hand the garland wreathed for Eve
Down dropt, and all the faded roses shed.
Speechless he stood and pale, till thus at length
First to himself he inward silence broke:—
    "O fairest of Creation, last and best
Of all God's works, creature in whom excelled
Whatever can to sight or thought be formed,
Holy, divine, good, amiable, or sweet!
How art thou lost! how on a sudden lost,
Defaced, deflowered, and now to death devote!
Rather, how hast thou yielded to transgress
The strict forbiddance, how to violate
The sacred Fruit forbidden? Some cursed fraud
Of enemy hath beguiled thee, yet unknown,
And me with thee hath ruined; for with thee
Certain my resolution is to die.
How can I live without thee? . . .

*Despite his reservations, Adam, spurred on by Eve,
decides to eat of the forbidden fruit, and the couple
then submits to their carnal desires for each other.*

He scrupled not to eat,
Against his better knowledge, not deceived,
But fondly overcome with female charm.
Earth trembled from her entrails, as again
In pangs, and Nature gave a second groan;
Sky loured, and, muttering thunder, some sad drops
Wept at completing of the mortal Sin
Original; while Adam took no thought,
Facing his fill, nor Eve to iterate
Her former trespass feared, the more to soothe
Him with her loved society; that now,
As with new wine intoxicated both,
They swim in mirth, and fancy that they feel
Divinity within them breeding wings
Wherewith to scorn the Earth. But that false Fruit
Far other operation first displayed,
Carnal desire inflaming. He on Eve
Began to cast lascivious eyes; she him
As wantonly repaid. . . .

*Milton recounts their shame when they recognize
what they have done, and Book IX closes with
Adam blaming Eve, and she him, for their loss of
innocence.*

Soon as the force of that fallacious Fruit,
That with exhilarating vapour bland
About their spirits had played, and inmost powers
Made err, was now exhaled, and grosser sleep,
Bred of unkindly fumes, with conscious dreams
Incumbered, now had left them, up they rose
As from unrest, and, each the other viewing,
Soon found their eyes how opened, and their minds
How darkened. Innocence, that as a veil
Had shadowed them from knowing ill, was gone;
Just confidence, and native righteousness,
And honour, from about them, naked left
To guilty Shame: he covered, but his robe
Uncovered more. So rose the Danite strong,
Herculean Samson, from the harlot-lap
Of Philistean Dalilah,[5] and waked
Shorn of his strength; they destitute and bare
Of all their virtue. Silent, and in face
Confounded, long they sat, as strucken mute;
Till Adam, though not less than Eve abashed,
At length gave utterance to these words constrained:—
    "O Eve, in evil hour thou didst give ear
To that false Worm, of whomsoever taught
To counterfeit Man's voice—true in our fall,
False in our promised rising; since our eyes
Opened we find indeed, and find we know
Both good and evil, good lost and evil got:
Bad Fruit of Knowledge, if this be to know,
Which leaves us naked thus, of honour void,
Of innocence, of faith, of purity,
Our wonted ornaments now soiled and stained,
And in our faces evident the signs
Of foul concupiscence; whence evil store,
Even shame, the last of evils; of the first
Be sure then. How shall I behold the face
Henceforth of God or Angel, erst with joy
And rapture so oft beheld? Those Heavenly Shapes
Will dazzle now this earthly with their blaze
Insufferably bright. Oh, might I here
In solitude live savage, in some glade
Obscured, where highest woods, impenetrable
To star or sunlight, spread their umbrage broad,
And brown as evening. Cover me, ye pines!

---

[5]The reference here is to the Old Testament story (Judges 16) of the Danite strong man, Samson, whose strength reputedly was in his hair, and the Philistine temptress, Deliah, who seduced him and cut his hair.

Ye cedars, with innumerable boughs
Hide me, where I may never see them more!
But let us now, as in bad plight, devise
What best may, for the present, serve to hide
The parts of each other that seem most
To shame obnoxious, and unseemliest seen—
Some tree, whose broad smooth leaves, together sewed,
And girded on our loins, may cover round
Those middle parts, that this new comer, Shame,
There sit not, and reproach us as unclean." . . .
      To whom, soon moved with touch of blame, thus
         Eve:—
"What words have passed thy lips, Adam severe?
Imput'st thou that to my default, or will
Of wandering, as thou call'st it, which who knows
But might as ill have happened thou being by,
Or to thyself perhaps? Hadst thou been there,
Or here the attempt, thou couldst not have discerned
Fraud in the Serpent, speaking as he spake;
No ground of enmity between us known
Why he should mean me ill or seek to harm.
Was I to have never parted from thy side?
As good have grown there still, a lifeless rib.
Being as I am, why didst not thou, the Head,
Command me absolutely not to go,
Going into such danger, as thou saidst?
Too facile then, thou didst not much gainsay,
Nay, didst permit, approve, and fair dismiss.
Hadst thou been firm and fixed in thy dissent,

Neither had I transgressed, nor thou with me."
      To whom, then first incensed, Adam replied:—
"Is this the love, is this the recompense
Of mine to thee, ingrateful Eve, expressed
Immutable when thou wert lost, not I—
Who might have lived, and joyed immortal bliss,
Yet willingly chose rather death with thee?
And am I now upbraided as the cause
Of thy transgressing? not enough severe,
It seems, in thy restraint! What could I more?
I warned thee, I admonished thee, foretold
The danger, and the lurking Enemy
That lay in wait; beyond this had been force,
And force upon free will hath here no place.
But confidence then bore thee on, secure
Either to meet no danger, or to find
Matter of glorious trial; and perhaps
I also erred in overmuch admiring
What seemed in thee so perfet that I thought
No evil durst attempt thee. But I rue
That error now, which is become my crime,
And thou the accuser. Thus it shall befall
Him who, to worth in women overtrusting,
Lets her will rule: restraint she will not brook;
And, left to herself, if evil thence ensue,
She first his weak indulgence will accuse."
      Thus they in mutual accusation spent
The fruitless hours, but neither self-condemning;
And of their vain contest appeared no end.

John Bunyan
The Pilgrim's Progress

John Bunyan (1628–1688) combined everyday speech with the eloquent prose of the King James Version of the Bible into a vivid narrative style. Like Luther and Milton, he understood human nature to be corrupt, and throughout his life, he sought assurance of his salvation from sin. Bunyan had little formal education and participated in the English civil war. Although he saw little actual fighting, he suffered lifelong guilt over the death of the young man who came to replace him. After his discharge from the army, Bunyan married a fervently pious woman and entered into a period of spiritual crises which lasted about five years. During this time he often felt that he was assailed by devils, physically abused, and threatened with damnation. He recounted these painful encounters in his spiritual autobiography, *Grace Abounding to the Chief of Sinners*. Bunyan eventually recovered from his dark night of despair and became an electrifying preacher. However, when he refused to conform to the liturgy of the Church of England, Bunyan was sent to prison, where he remained for the greater part of twelve years. During his imprisonment, Bunyan preached to his fellow prisoners, studied, and supported his family by making and selling shoelaces. Most important, he began *The Pilgrim's Progress*—a book that was destined to become the most successful allegory ever written in English. Part I of *The Pilgrim's Progress* is told in the guise of a dream as it details the spiritual journey of Christian (the leading character) to the Celestial City. On his journey, Christian must overcome despair, fear, corruption, the burden of sin, "Vanity Fair," and the "Valley of the Shadow of Death" before finding Faithful, who leads him into the knowledge of God's grace.

The following passage contains one of the most compelling images in the allegory—the loss of Christian's "burden," which he carries on his shoulders, symbolizing the burden of sin. When it falls from his shoulders into a sepulchre (symbolizing the empty tomb of Christ's resurrection), Christian leaps for joy.

Now, I saw in my dream that the highway up which Christian was to go was fenced on either side with a wall that was called Salvation.[*] Up this way, therefore, did burdened Christian run, but not without great difficulty, because of the load on his back.

He ran thus till he came to a place somewhat ascending; and upon that place stood a cross, and a little below, in the bottom, a sepulchre. So I saw in my dream, that just as Christian came up with the cross, his burden loosed from off his shoulders, and fell from off his back, and began to tumble, and so continued to do till it came to the mouth of the sepulchre, where it fell in, and I saw it no more.

When God releases us of our guilt and burden, we are as those that leap for joy.

Then was Christian glad and lightsome, and said with a merry heart, "He hath given me rest by His sorrow, and life by His Death." Then he stood still awhile to look and wonder; for it was very surprising to him that the sight of the cross should thus ease him of his burden. He looked, therefore, and looked again, even till the springs that were in his head sent the water down his cheeks.[†] Now, as he stood looking and weeping, behold, three Shining Ones came to him, and saluted him with "Peace be to thee." So the first said to him, "Thy sins be forgiven thee";[‡] the second stripped him of his rags, and clothed him with a change of raiment,[§] the third also set a mark on his forehead[‖] and gave him a roll with a seal upon it, which he bade him look on as he ran, and that he should give it in at the celestial gate: so they went their way. Then Christian gave three leaps for joy, and went on, singing:

"Thus far did I come laden with my sin;
Nor could aught ease the grief that I was in.
Till I came hither: what a place is this!
Must here be the beginning of my bliss?
Must here the burden fall from off my back?

Must here the strings that bound it to me crack?
Blest cross! blest sepulchre! blest rather be
The Man that was there put to shame for me!"

Christian then finds Hopeful, and they nearly succumb to a Flood of Temptation, before meeting the Giant Despair and his wife, Diffidence, who beat them and imprison them in Doubting Castle. Hopeful and Christian escape when Christian finds the key called Promise, which unlocks any door, including the door of the dungeon. Together, Hopeful and Christian encounter further temptation, conquer Conceit, and overcome Ignorance and Guilt before arriving at the gate of the Celestial City. They cannot enter the Celestial City, however, until they cross the River of Death—symbolizing an individual's fear of death—a river that can only be crossed by believing in Jesus Christ.

Death is not welcome to nature, though by it we pass out of this world into glory.

The pilgrims then began to inquire if there was no other way to the gate; to which they answered, "Yes; but there hath not any save two, to wit, Enoch and Elijah,[1] been permitted to tread that path since the foundation of the world, nor shall until the last trumpet shall sound." The pilgrims then, especially Christian, began to despond in his mind, and looked this way and that; but no way could be found by them by which they might escape the river. Then they asked the men if the waters were all of a depth. They said, "No"; yet they could not help them in that case; "for," said they, "you shall find it deeper or shallower as you believe in the King of the place."

They then addressed themselves to the water; and, entering, Christian began to sink, and crying out to his good friend Hopeful, he said, "I sink in deep waters; the billows go over my head; all His waves go over me. Selah."[2]

---

[*]Isa. 26:1
[†]Zech. 12:10.
[‡]Mark 2:5.
[§]Zech. 3:4.
[‖]Eph. 1:13.

---

[1]Enoch and Elijah are Old Testament prophets.
[2]*Selah* is a word that occurs often in Psalms which probably is a musical term.

Then said the other, "Be of good cheer, my brother; I feel the bottom, and it is good." Then said Christian, "Ah! my friend, the sorrows of death have compassed me about; I shall not see the land that flows with milk and honey." And, with that, a great darkness and horror fell upon Christian, so that he could not see before him. Also here he in a great measure lost his senses, so that he could neither remember nor orderly talk of any of those sweet refreshments that he had met with in the way of his pilgrimage. But all the words that he spake still tended to discover that he had horror of mind, and heart-fears that he should die in that river, and never obtain entrance in at the gate. Here also, as they that stood by perceived, he was much in the troublesome thoughts of the sins that he had committed, both since and before he began to be a pilgrim. It was also observed that he was troubled with apparitions of hobgoblins and evil spirits; forever and anon he would intimate so much by words.

Christian delivered from his fears in death.

Hopeful, therefore, here had much ado to keep his brother's head above water; yea, sometimes he would be quite gone down, and then, ere a while, he would rise up again half dead. Hopeful would also endeavor to comfort him, saying, "Brother, I see the gate, and men standing by to receive us"; but Christian would answer, "It is you, it is you they wait for: you have been hopeful ever since I knew you." "And so have you," said he to Christian. "Ah, brother," said he, "surely, if I were right, He would now arise to help me; but for my sins He hath brought me into this snare, and hath left me." Then said Hopeful, "My brother, you have quite forgot the text where it is said of the wicked, "There are no bands in their death, but their strength is firm; they are not troubled as other men, neither are they plagued like other men."[3] These troubles and distresses that you go through in these waters are no sign that God hath forsaken you; but are sent to try you, whether you will call to mind that which hitherto you have received of His goodness, and live upon Him in your distresses."

---

[3]Biblical reference Psalms 73:4, 5.

Then I saw in my dream that Christian was in a muse[4] awhile. To whom also Hopeful added these words, "Be of good cheer, Jesus Christ maketh thee whole." And, with that, Christian brake out with a loud voice, "Oh, I see Him again; and He tells me, 'When thou passest through the waters, I will be with thee; and through the rivers, they shall not over-flow thee.'"[5] Then they both took courage; and the enemy was, after that, as still as a stone, until they were gone over. Christian, therefore, presently found ground to stand upon; and so it followed that the rest of the river was but shallow. Thus they got over. . . .

In a poem at the end of Part I, Bunyan admonishes the reader to interpret the metaphors of his dream correctly.

Now, reader, I have told my dream to thee,
See if thou canst interpret it to me,
Or to thyself or neighbor; but take heed
Of misinterpreting; for that, instead
Of doing good, will but thyself abuse:
By misinterpreting, evil ensues.
    Put by the curtains, look within my veil,
Turn up my metaphors and do not fail,
There, if thou seekest them, such things to find
As will be helpful to an honest mind.

In 1684, Bunyan published Part II of *The Pilgrim's Progress*—detailing the journey of Christiana, Christian's wife, and their children. Written in a lighter tone than Part I, Christiana and her children meet Mr. Sagacity and the characters of Mercy and Prudence. After they pass through the Valley of Humiliation, they encounter "a sweet grace," Humility. Later, they are greeted by shepherds—Knowledge, Experience, Watchful, and Sincere—and join with Great-Heart to kill Giant Despair and to demolish Doubting Castle. Finally the pilgrims cross the River of Death and are welcomed joyfully into the Celestial City.

---

[4]To muse is to reflect or to meditate in silence.
[5]Biblical reference Isaiah 43:2.

4 French Theater

The seventeenth century witnessed the creation of the classical tradition in French theater. Based on rules from ancient Greece (by way of Renaissance Italy), the classical tradition stipulated that a tragedy should have five acts; that it should be written in poetry, not in prose; that it should have a serious and lofty theme; and that there should be no violence on stage. Additionally, the concept of "the three unities" demanded that there be a single plot that takes place in one location during a twenty-four-hour period. It was within this general framework that Corneille, the master of classical French tragedy, wrote his dramas. The master of classical comedy, the second genre in seventeenth-century French theater, was Molière.

Pierre Corneille
Le Cid

Although he also wrote comedies, Pierre Corneille (1606–1684) is best known as the father of French tragedy. His first tragic masterpiece, *Le Cid* (lord, chief), was based on the Spanish legend about the eleventh-century warrior who fought against the Moors. Corneille's version emphasizes the virtues of passionate devotion to family, honor, and loyalty—this was his lofty theme. The plot revolves around the love between the major characters—Rodrigo (later the Cid), the son of Don Diego, and Ximena, the daughter of the count. Nothing can quench their love—not the Infanta, the king's daughter, who loves Rodrigo, nor Don Sancho who loves Ximena. But when Don Diego and the count have a quarrel, their love is threatened. During the quarrel, the elderly and feeble Don Diego is slapped by the count. Don Diego, who feels that his honor must be defended, tells Rodrigo that he must avenge the insult by killing the count in a duel. In the following passage, Rodrigo despairs because he must choose between his love for Ximena and his duty to his family.

RODRIGO:
A sudden, lethal thrust has pierced my heart.
The cause is just—I should avenge my father—
That is my duty—duty's laws are harsh—
Inhuman—I their hapless, helpless victim.
I cannot act.
I cannot move. My will has ebbed away.
I was about to see my hopes fulfilled.
But now—oh, God!—what anguish I must suffer!
My father has been wronged, and who has wronged him?
Ximena's. What a bitter battle rages
In here, where passion is at war with honour!
One bids me act, the other gives me pause.
Must I avenge my father, lose Ximena?
I'm forced to choose, and yet find I cannot.
The choice is this: betray my love or live
With shame.
In either case my grief is limitless.
I am in Hell now. What am I to do?
Kill my beloved's father, or permit
The gravest of affronts to go unpunished?
Father! Mistress! Honour! Love! Where can I turn?
My duty binds me fast, and rightly so;
Its bonds are cruel, though: it demands of me
That I give up the woman I adore
And lead a wretched life. Yet if I don't—
But spare the Count, I'll be unfit to live—
Disgraced.
My sword, on you all hope of vengeance rests;

By you all hope of love will be destroyed!
Death—death alone—can free me from this torment.
I owe as much allegiance to my bride
As to my father—if I do kill hers
Her righteous anger will descend on me;
But if I let him live—remain dishonoured—
She'll scorn me.
I must give up what happiness I know
Or prove unworthy of her. Either way
My case is desperate and to seek to soothe it
Can only make my suffering ten times worse.
Come then, Rodrigo!
Death takes us all at last—if so, I'll find it
By my own hand, rather than wrong Ximena.
But then to die without revenge! To seek
An end that spells the end of my good name!
To heed a love my tortured soul can see
Is doomed!
Leave Spain to spit on me when I am gone
As a traitor to the honour of my house!
No! That shall never be! It's time to act!
I must uphold my name, I have no choice.
I am ashamed now at my indecision.
No matter what, Ximena will be lost.
My father's honour has received a stain.
Her father's death must make it clean again.

Rodrigo is victorious in the duel, and Ximena is obligated by the code of honor to demand justice from the king. She insists that Rodrigo must be punished for killing her father, the king's greatest warrior. Later, Ximena confesses to her governess, Elvira, that even though she now hates Rodrigo, she also still loves him. Rodrigo, who has heard them talking, confronts Ximena in the following scene.

RODRIGO:
(*Emerging from hiding.*) No need to hunt me down.
I'm here. Kill me.

XIMENA:
What's this? Rodrigo? No! It cannot be!

RODRIGO:
Do what you want. I'll not resist. Enjoy
The sweetness of revenge. Act now! Destroy
Your enemy!

XIMENA:
You've killed me, Rodrigo.

RODRIGO:
Ximena . . . !

XIMENA:
Leave me! Let me die! Go! Go!

RODRIGO:
No! Let me speak. I ask but one brief word.
Then you may give your answer—with this sword.

XIMENA:
Stained with my father's life-blood, where it gored His
side . . .

RODRIGO:
Ximena . . . !

XIMENA:
Hide it from my sight!

RODRIGO:
No. Look at it. I want it to invite
Your hatred and your fury—then it will
Hasten the death I seek.

XIMENA:
It's dripping still
With blood—my blood.

RODRIGO:
Bathe it in mine. Make good
Your wrongs. Let blood efface the taint of blood.

XIMENA:
Cruel sword! Two people will have perished by it:
My father by the blade—I by the sight.

RODRIGO:
Ximena, listen—let me seize the chance
To end my wretched life at your fair hands.

Yet while I seek it, I may not repent
A noble act and earn my own contempt.
To deal a man of honour such a blow
Disgraces all his family, and so
His son must hunt the man who struck him; then
Avenge their tarnished name. I would again
If ever the necessity arose.
My love fought long and hard for you, God knows,
Against both him and me. Though the offence
Was grave, I found so many arguments
Against revenge. You see your power? I faced
The choice: to break with you or live disgraced.
I held a high place in your heart—and why?
I was a man of honour. But were I
To lose that honour—heed love's siren voice—
I would become unworthy of your choice:
I wronged you, but how else could I erase
The taint of shame and merit you. That pays
My debt to honour, to my father. Now
I've come to give you satisfaction—how?
By offering you my life. I had to do
What I did then—I have to do this too,
Your father's death has led you to seek mine.
I am the willing victim—it is time:
Be brave. Now do it.

XIMENA:
No. I tell you this:
Although we may be mortal enemies,
I cannot find it in my heart to blame
A son who fights to save his father's name.
Whatever voice I give to my distress,
It is my pain, not anger I express.
I know you're noble, brave and spirited—
I know what honour asks of you. You did
What any good man always has to do:
Your duty—I have learned my own from you.
Your valour and your fateful victory
Have taught me it. You shrank from infamy—
Avenged your father—I must do the same:
Avenge *my* father and uphold my name.
But how I love you! What a price I pay!
Oh, had he only died some other way
The joy of seeing you would then have brought
Such comfort to my desperate mind. Distraught,
I should have found such solace had my tears
Been wiped away by one I held so dear.
But now I've lost him I must lose you too:
My honour rules me and I must subdue
My love. For duty, whose inhuman laws
Mean death to me, has forced me to seek yours.
I love you, but you must expect to pay
In blood—no place for pardon here today.
I'll act as you have—with nobility.
You wronged me, but you also proved to me

That you were wholly worthy of my love:
You did your duty—I'll do mine—I'll prove
That I deserve you—by destroying you.

RODRIGO:
Then do what honour now compels you to.
Don't wait: if you must have my life, it's yours—
Sacrifice it in a noble cause.
I'll welcome both the sentence and the blow.
The sluggish course of justice is too slow
For such a crime as mine. Then why delay
Your vengeance and my punishment? This way—
Killed by the one I worship—I die
Content.

XIMENA:
I cried for justice. Now must I
Inflict the penalty myself? I may
Demand your life—to give that life away
Is not your part. No, there are others who
Must make the gift: I seek your death, it's true,
But I could never think of killing you.

RODRIGO:
You must be brave enough to act; you must
Yourself exact revenge and not entrust
That task to others. Do as I have done:
Who could avenge a father but his son?
Who could avenge your father? Only you.

XIMENA:
These words of yours are cruel—they're wasted, too.
You hound me. Why? If you, and you alone,
Avenged your father, I'll avenge my own
Without your help—do as you did: I dare.
I'll not give in to love, or your despair—
My father, and my honour, must not owe
A debt to either.

RODRIGO:
                Heartless honour! So,
Do what I will your answer is the same:
Refusal. Then, in your dead father's name,
And in your love's, avenge him—pity me;
Punish your wretched lover, who would be
Less miserable by far were he to die
Now, at your hands, than live on, hated by
One he adores.

XIMENA:
                I cannot hate you. No!

RODRIGO:
You have no choice.

XIMENA:
                I cannot, Rodrigo!

RODRIGO:
You fear no censure—no wild rumours, then?
How envious, lying tongues will gossip when
The world hears what I've done—and that your love
Endures in spite of it! Kill me! Remove
This threat to your good name. Thwart slander now.
No more delay.

XIMENA:
                But my good name will show
A greater lustre if I let you go.
I'll make the poisonous tongue of envy pour
Its praises on my glory and deplore
My suffering, since I feel such tenderness
Towards you, yet desire your death. Distress
Consumes me. Leave! I cannot bear to see
A man I've lost, who means my life to me.

RODRIGO:
Then I shall go.

XIMENA:
                Despite the love that I—
For all my burning rage—am tortured by,
I'll do all within my power to satisfy
My father's honour. Yet despite the hard
Demands of justice, deep within my heart
I pray I lack the power to punish you.

RODRIGO:
Our love is boundless!

XIMENA:
                Sorrow's boundless too.

RODRIGO:
Fathers who cause their children such distress!
So many tears!

XIMENA:
                A strange reversal!

RODRIGO:
                                Yes.

XIMENA:
We were so close to peace—to happiness.

RODRIGO:
Too late for all regrets. Lament in vain.

XIMENA:
No more. Just go. And never come again.

RODRIGO:
A living death is what my life will be
Till you succeed in taking it from me.

XIMENA:
When I accomplish that, then I shall die
Upon the instant. This I swear. Goodbye.

ELVIRA:
Madam . . .

XIMENA:
      No. Leave me. To lament my plight
I seek the endless silence of the night.

Rodrigo is then triumphant in a battle with the Moors—he saves the kingdom and thus becomes the Cid. Afterward, to settle the dispute between Ximena and Rodrigo, the king decides that Rodrigo will face one challenger, Don Sancho. Whoever wins, will marry Ximena. After disarming Don Sancho and thus winning the match, Rodrigo refuses to kill him. In the final scene of the play, Ximena and Rodrigo are reconciled and the king appoints Rodrigo commander of the royal armies.

Enter RODRIGO, the INFANTA.

INFANTA:
Ximena, dry your tears now, and receive
This conquering hero from me. Cease to grieve.

RODRIGO:
Sire, in your presence, if you don't object
Both as a mark of love and of respect,
I'll kneel before her. (*To XIMENA.*) What I've come here for
Is not the spoils of victory, but once more
To offer you my life. Despite my love
I don't intend to take advantage of
The terms of combat or the King's decree:
Your father hasn't had enough from me?
Why, then, how are you to be satisfied?
How many thousand rivals must I fight?
Must I seize cities? Put whole hordes to flight?
Travel the world accomplishing great deeds?
Surpass the fabled heroes with my feats?
Knowing that I have given you offence
I dare—I can—do all to make amends.
But if your honour and your pride are still
Wholly implacable—if nothing will
Appease them but to see the offender dead,
Don't make me fight with champions. My head
Is at your feet—take your revenge on me
With your hands—they alone can rightfully
Vanquish the invincible: make good
Vengeance no other person living could.
Let death be punishment enough for you—

Don't banish me from your remembrance too.
My end ensures your glory—in return
Preserve my memory, and while you mourn
Say to yourself: "He loved me—otherwise
He would be living now."

XIMENA:
      Rodrigo, rise.
Your love—your courage—wipe away my hate.
But, Sire, must your commands still be obeyed.
And is the marriage that you plan for me
Acceptable to you? How can it be?
Will you reward Rodrigo's services
With me? Essential to you though he is?
Although he's won me with this victory
Must I let future ages say of me:
"Her father's blood was on her hands."?

DON FERNANDO:
      But time
Can cleanse what might at first be thought a crime
Of blame. He won you and you must be his.
But while his valour has accomplished this,
It would be an affront to you, were I
To let him take the spoils of victory
So soon. The terms of combat, while they state
That you must marry him, impose no date.
Wait for a year—grief's scars will then have healed.
During that time, Rodrigo, take the field:
Now let my armies, under your command,
Pursue the routed Moors, lay waste their land.
But while you do great deeds, be true to her—
Return still worthy of her—worthier:
Let glorious exploits bring you such acclaim
That marriage to you will enhance her name.

RODRIGO:
To win Ximena, Sire, and to serve you
What can you ask of me that I'll not do?
A year without the sight of her will be
Hard to endure, but you have given me
Hope, and at least the chance of happiness.

DON FERNANDO:
Have faith in me and in your own prowess:
Your mistress' heart you certainly possess—
 Her honour, which still prompts her to rebel,
Time, your great valour, and your King shall quell.

The End.

Molière
Tartuffe

Jean-Baptiste Poquelin (1622–1673), better known by his stage name Molière, brought comedy to its highest level since antiquity. Molière received his degree in law in 1642, but the very next year, he joined an acting troupe, where he developed his skills as an actor, director, and playwright. In 1658, the brother of Louis XIV became Molière's patron, and he and his company were given their own theater in Paris. Throughout his career, Molière felt the ire of the religious authorities, who viewed his plays as scandalous attacks on religion. This was particularly true of *Tartuffe, or The Imposter*—a comedy that attacks religious hypocrisy. The church was able to prevent its performance for five years, until 1669. The main character of the play is Orgon, a wealthy, middle-aged man of the bourgeoisie, who is captivated by Tartuffe, whom he sees as a holy and devout man who teaches authentic Christian beliefs. Orgon invites Tartuffe to be an esteemed guest in his home. Others in Orgon's household—his son, Damis; his brother-law, Cleante; and his wife, Elmire—try to warn him that Tartuffe is a hypocrite, but Orgon continues in his conviction that he is a devout man. In the following excerpt, Orgon extolls Tartuffe's piety to Cleante.

CLEANTE, ORGON

CLEANTE:
Well, brother, she was laughing at you to your face.
Now, don't be cross, but I believe she's got a case.
In fact, to be quite frank, I think the girl is right.
I never thought I'd ever witness such a sight:
Did he use magic to persuade you to forget
Important things, and love a person you've just met?
You've spent a fortune rescuing him from despair,
And now, it seems, you want . . .

ORGON:
                  Brother-in-law, stop there!
You don't know anything about him. Stop your chat.

CLEANTE:
All right, so I don't know him, I'll allow you that.
But if I'm to find out what kind of man he is . . .

ORGON:
Oh, if you knew him well, you'd be in ecstasies!
You'd never stop adoring him once you began.
    He is a man . . . who . . . er . . . in short, a man . . .
    a man.
If you sat at his feet, he'd bring you peace, for sure;
The world would seem to you a great heap of manure.
I've learnt from him, the truth is clearer in my eyes.
He's taught me to reject the things I used to prize.
The people that I thought I loved, I now deny,
And I could watch my mother, children, wife all die,
And, shall I tell you what? I just couldn't care less.

CLEANTE:
What warmth, my brother, what compassion you express!

ORGON:
I wish you'd seen how it turned out when first we met!
Like me, you'd have been drawn to him from the outset.
He came to church, and every day I saw that he
Fell on his knees and bowed his head in front of me.
The congregation as a whole became aware
Of how much ardour he would pour into his prayer.
He heaved great heavy sighs, and waved his arms around,
And often he'd bend very low and kiss the ground.
When I went out, he'd always hurry on before
To offer me some holy water by the door.
He has a servant, who's under his influence,
He's told me of his station, and his indigence.
I gave him money; with becoming modesty,
He always tried to give some of it back to me.
'No, it's too much', said he, 'Oh, it's too much by half.
I don't deserve your sympathy on my behalf.'
When I refused to take it back, he would ensure,
In front of me, that it was given to the poor.
At last I was inspired by Heaven to take him in.
Since that day, we've all prospered through his discipline.
He watches everything, my honour is his life,
And he's become inseparable from my wife:
He tells me if young fellows give her the glad eye,
The man's a lot more jealous and concerned than I.
But you wouldn't believe the ardour of his zeal:
The sin that any trivial action can reveal
Disturbs him. A mere nothing shocks him to the core.
The other day, he said that he had to deplore

The fact that, when at prayer, he chanced to catch a flea,
And having caught it, killed it, much too angrily.

CLEANTE:
Good Lord! What's this I hear? Have you gone raving mad?
Or was that speech a joke, and have I just been had?
You must be teasing me. So, what does all that mean?

ORGON:
Ugh! Brother, that's the language of the libertine.
You must work hard to keep your spirit free of crimes—
Or else, as I've explained to you a dozen times,
You may end up in dreadful trouble, very soon.

CLEANTE:
It's typical of people like you to impugn
The attitudes of others. Just because I've seen
What you can't see, you choose to call me libertine.
You say I've no respect for any sacred thing
Because I find your empty cant embarrassing.
You won't get me worked up, I take it in good part:
I know what I believe, and God sees in my heart.
A man who rules the rest by putting on such airs
Can be a hypocrite for all his fervent prayers.
When battle's joined, and men of honour come to fight,
The quiet men are brave, the boasters may take fright;
So truly pious men, whom people must admire,
Will not make such a song and dance about hell-fire.
Oh, Heavens! Can't you see there's a distinction
Between hypocrisy and true devotion?
You want the two of them to share a single space;
You can't see one's a mask, the other a true face.
You mix up artifice with real sincerity,
And try to take appearance for reality,
Respecting empty phantoms more than flesh and blood,
And bogus coinage more than currency that's good!
My fellow human beings are the strangest crew:
They can't be moderate and calm in what they do.
So, rational behaviour's not what they expect;
They set it on one side, and show it no respect.
They're all out to exaggerate and maximize,
They manage to destroy the noblest enterprise—
In passing, brother-in-law, I say this in your ear.

ORGON:
I daresay you're a doctor we should all revere:
You know the lot; in short, you're the embodiment
Of holy wisdom, and of true enlightenment.
Yes, you're an oracle, a Cato of our time.
Compared with us poor foolish dolts, Sir, you're sublime.

CLEANTE:
No, brother, no! I'm not a doctor to revere,
And all man's earthly wisdom isn't lodged up here.
No, all my learning can be summed up in a word:
I can tell truth from falsehood, see through what's absurd.
Of all my heroes, I find certain men stand out,

And I admire them: men who seem truly devout.
There's nothing nobler, nothing worthier, I feel,
Than holy fervour, genuine religious zeal.
But then, by contrast, nothing is more odious
Than all the trappings of belief that's dubious,
Those charlatans whose fervent piety's for show,
Who sacrilegiously pretend to mop and mow,
And make a mockery, with cool impertinence,
Of everything that we should hold in reverence,
Who show off their beliefs like some grotesque parade,
Who buy and sell devotion like a kind of trade,
Who strive for all the dignities that they can earn
And wink, nod, make affected gestures in return.
Those men are wildly eager to receive their pay:
They rush to make their fortunes, following God's way.
They drip with holy unction, yet they can be bought,
Extol the joys of solitude, but love the court.
They reconcile their pious notions with their vice,
They're spiteful, hasty, insincere, and cold as ice.
If they want to destroy a man, they boldly claim
That it's God's will that he's brought low, and put to shame.
They're dangerous because their anger doesn't show:
They make use of religious faith to bring us low.
They're much admired for their beliefs, and so they try
To smite us with the sword of faith and let us die.
There are a lot too many of this two-faced crew,
But it's not difficult to tell if faith is true. . . .

Orgon comes increasingly under Tartuffe's spell, so much so that he is about to break his promise to his daughter Mariane that she will marry Valere, the young man she truly loves. Instead, Orgon decides that she will marry Tartuffe. At this point, Elmire, Orgon's wife, arranges a meeting with Tartuffe to convince him not to marry Mariane. However, when they are alone in the following scene, Tartuffe reveals his attraction to Elmire, and he tries to seduce her.

TARTUFFE, ELMIRE

TARTUFFE:
May gracious Heaven grant you true spiritual wealth,
And bring your body and your soul abundant health!
May all your days be blest! These are the true desires
Of quite the humblest mortal Heaven's grace inspires.

ELMIRE:
Thanks for that pious wish. You really are too kind.
We'll be more comfortable sitting down, you'll find.

TARTUFFE:
Now, have you quite recovered from your illness, pray?

ELMIRE:
My fever came down quickly, I feel well today.

TARTUFFE:
I've little merit, and my prayers are much too base
To bring about this evidence of Heaven's grace—
But every prayer I made to him who reigns supreme
Had your full convalescence as its only theme.

ELMIRE:
You didn't need to take such trouble, show such zeal.

TARTUFFE:
Well, your good health is dear to me. I truly feel
I'd give mine to help you in your infirmity.

ELMIRE:
Oh, what a fine display of Christian charity!
I owe you something for your kindness, now, that's true.

TARTUFFE:
But you deserve much more than I can do for you.

ELMIRE:
I've got a secret, and I'd like to sound you out.
I must say that I'm glad that nobody's about.

TARTUFFE:
I too am very glad, I too feel no regret.
Madame, I'm so delighted with our tête-à-tête.
To be alone with you has been my ardent plea,
Which till now Heaven never has accorded me.

ELMIRE:
I'd like a quiet word with you. Can I appeal
To you to be quite frank, and tell me how you feel?

TARTUFFE:
The one grace I implore, for you must know the whole,
Is humbly to expose to you my naked soul,
To swear to you that all that public fuss I made
When, drawn by your attractions, your admirers paid
Their visits, was not due to hatred of you, nay
'Twas more a holy zeal which carried me away,
Disinterested urge . . .

ELMIRE:
I take it like that too.
You want to save my soul, that governs what you do.

TARTUFFE:
(*squeezing her fingers.*) Oh, yes, indeed, Madame. The ardour
that I feel . . .

ELMIRE:
Ouch! Don't squeeze me so hard!

TARTUFFE:
It's through excess of zeal.
I never could harm you deliberately, and
In fact, I'd much prefer . . .   (*He puts his hand on her knee.*)

ELMIRE:
Monsieur, what's this? Your hand . . .

TARTUFFE:
I'm just touching your gown: the fabric is so rich.

ELMIRE:
Well, please let go of me, I'm rather ticklish.
(*She pushes back her chair, and* TARTUFFE *pushes his forward.*)

TARTUFFE:
Oh, goodness, what fine lace! It's really marvellous!
This new embroidery is quite miraculous.
They never used to do this kind of thing so well.

ELMIRE:
That's so, but I think we should stick to business. Tell
Me, is it true my husband plans to break his word,
And give his daughter's hand to you? That's what I've
heard.

TARTUFFE:
He's mentioned it; but, to reveal my true desires,
That's not the happiness to which my soul aspires.
A much more marvellous attraction conquers me,
Felicity for which I long most ardently.

ELMIRE:
You don't give in to earthly passions like the rest.

TARTUFFE:
A heart that's made of stone does not beat in my breast.

ELMIRE:
You care for Heaven alone, love God for all you're worth.
Your interest is fixed by nothing on this earth.

TARTUFFE:
The passion for eternal beauty which I feel
Does not mean that my earthly passions are less real.
Our senses can be charmed—to us it may be given
To look on perfect beauty as a gift from Heaven.
In Heaven, a woman's beauty strikes an answering chord—
But you are the most wonderful work of the Lord.
He's taken such great pains over your countenance,
That all hearts must be won by such magnificence.
You perfect creature, every time I look at you
I see Divine Creation shining forth anew.
When I see you my heart with passion overflows—
You are a portrait for which God himself did pose.
I fought this secret love, I thought I was undone—
I feared that I was tempted by the Evil One.
I even thought it best to shun your lovely eyes,
For fear they might prevent me winning Heaven's prize.
But then, exquisite creature, I saw it would prove
That there was nothing sinful in my ardent love,
And I could reconcile it with my modesty,
And so I gave way to my feelings totally.
I do admit that it is somewhat staggering
To dare to make my heart a holy offering.

My dearest wish is that you will be well disposed,
That my infirmities will never be exposed.
In you are all my hopes, my wealth, my quietude:
On you rests my despair or my beatitude.
It all depends on you, and I can't rest until
I'm happy if you wish, or wretched if you will.

ELMIRE:

Well! That's a declaration not to be despised!
You know, to tell the truth, I am a bit surprised:
It seems to me that you should fight your instincts more,
And think what you are doing carefully, before
You say such things. You're so devout, I think you can . . .

TARTUFFE:

Although I am devout, I am no less a man.
When we are faced with heavenly beauty such as yours,
Our hearts are smitten straightaway, we cannot pause.
I know that what I say sounds strange coming from me,
But then, Madame, I am no angel, as you see;
Perhaps my declaration does put me to shame,
But then, your own bewitching beauty is to blame.
The moment that I saw your lovely looks, I knew
That I had lost my heart—its queen had to be you.
Your heavenly gaze, that glows like light ineffable,
Made all resistance from my heart impossible.
I fasted, prayed, and wept, but nothing I could do
Could overcome the charms that I could see in you.
My looks, my sighs, told you my feelings were sincere;
But now I can speak out, I'll make them still more clear.
If you look kindly on me, as I humbly crave,
And pity my distress, since I'm your abject slave,
If your kind eyes can gaze on me without a frown,
And, pitying my dismal plight, deign to look down,
O marvel most delectable, you'll always be
An object of unique devotion to me.
Your honour runs no risk if you give me your heart:
You needn't fear the least exposure on my part.
Those courtiers, ladies' men whom women can't resist,
Talk all the time—no juicy gossip can be missed.
They boast of how their love affairs are getting on.
If you give in to them, it's commented upon.
You can't rely on them, their tongues are volatile;
The altar where they sacrifice they soon defile.
But men like us burn with a fire that's more discreet.
Your secret's safe with us. We never will repeat
What's happened, for our reputation matters so,
That those we love are kept quite safe from every foe.
You'll find, if you accept the heart I offer here,
A love that's scandal-free, and pleasure without fear.

ELMIRE:

I've listened to your rhetoric, and what I hear
Has put your case. Yes, your position's very clear.
Doesn't it worry you that I might feel I ought
To tell my husband all about your paying court
To me? If I tell him about this interview,

Might it affect the way that he feels about you?

TARTUFFE:

I know that you're so full of Christian charity,
That you'll see fit to pardon my temerity.
Yes, you'll excuse the human weakness that I show,
Which brought about this outburst. Though you're hurt, I
know,
Consider your good looks, and try to bear in mind
That I'm a man of flesh and blood, and far from blind.

ELMIRE:

Another woman might perhaps decide to treat
You differently, but I intend to be discreet.
Yes, I'll make sure my husband doesn't get to learn
Of this, but let me ask a favour in return:
First, promise me your firm support in our affair,
I mean the marriage of Mariane and Valere.
Don't use the unjust power you've won as a pretence
To help you to get rich at other folks' expense.
And . . .

All the while, Orgon's son, Damis, has been listening from an adjoining room. Damis denounces Tartuffe to his father but Orgon refuses to believe him. Orgon disowns Damis, and, in order to mollify the wounded guest, gives Tartuffe all of his property. Elmire wonders if Orgon will believe Tartuffe's duplicity if he sees it with his own eyes and hears it with his own ears. She convinces Orgon to hide under a table while she meets again with Tartuffe. After Elmire pretends that she will submit to Tartuffe's advances, she asks him to check outside the door to make sure that no one is nearby. In the following scene, Tartuffe's duplicity becomes obvious to Orgon.

TARTUFFE, ELMIRE, ORGON

TARTUFFE:

So now the time has come. My rapture is profound,
Madame. I've been outside, and had a good look round.
There's nobody about, and, oh! I'm all on fire . . .

ORGON:

[interrupting]. Hold on, before surrendering to your desire.
Your promises of love have come out much too pat.
Ah, ah! An honest man, to hoodwink me like that!
It's scarcely fighting sin, the way you planned your life,
As husband to my girl, and lover to my wife!
For ages I could not believe that this was real,
I kept on hoping that you would amend your spiel.
But no—I've heard you out, and I've had quite enough.
I need no other proof, it's time to call your bluff.

ELMIRE:

[*to* TARTUFFE]. You know, I'd really rather not have done all this. Too bad there had to be so much unpleasantness.

TARTUFFE:

What? Can you really think? . . .

ORGON:

Oh, stop fooling about. I've had enough of this. It's high time you got out.

TARTUFFE:

No, listen to my plan . . .

ORGON:

There's nothing to discuss. Get out of here, and do it quick. Don't make a fuss

TARTUFFE:

No, you get out. Go on. You're not the master here.

This house belongs to me, as everyone will hear.
I've had enough. It's time to make you understand.
Don't try your dirty tricks on me—it's underhand.
You thought you could insult me, didn't realize
That I can punish you, and cut you down to size.
Now God will be avenged, and you will soon repent
The folly that led you to say it's time I went.

Soon afterward an official arrives at the house to evict Orgon and his family; then Valere informs Orgon that Tartuffe and an officer from the king are on their way to arrest him. As it turns out, however, the king has recognized Tartuffe as a criminal, so the officer arrests Tartuffe instead, and in the end, all is well for Orgon.

13

Intellectual Transformations: The Scientific Revolution and the Age of Enlightenment

The Scientific Revolution of the sixteenth and seventeenth centuries replaced the medieval view of the universe with a new cosmology and produced a new way of investigating nature. It overthrew the medieval conception of nature as a hierarchical order ascending toward a realm of perfection. Rejecting reliance on authority, the thinkers of the Scientific Revolution affirmed the individual's ability to know the natural world through the method of mathematical reasoning, the direct observation of nature, and carefully controlled experiments.

The medieval view of the universe had blended the theories of Aristotle and Ptolemy, two ancient Greek thinkers, with Christian teachings. In that view, a stationary earth stood in the center of the universe just above hell. Revolving around the earth were seven planets: the moon, Mercury, Venus, the sun, Mars, Jupiter, and Saturn. Because people believed that earth did not move, it was not considered a planet. Each planet was attached to a transparent sphere that turned around the earth. Encompassing the universe was a sphere of fixed stars; beyond the stars lay three heavenly spheres, the outermost of which was the abode of God. An earth-centered universe accorded with the Christian idea that God had created the universe for men and women and that salvation was the aim of life.

Also agreeable to the medieval Christian view was Aristotle's division of the universe into a lower, earthly realm and a higher realm beyond the moon. Two sets of laws operated in the universe, one on earth and the other in the celestial realm. Earthly objects were composed of four elements: earth, water, fire, and air; celestial objects were composed of the divine ether—a substance too pure, too clear, too fine, too spiritual to be found on earth. Celestial objects naturally moved in perfectly circular orbits around the earth; earthly objects, composed mainly of the heavy elements of earth and water, naturally fell downward, whereas objects made of the lighter elements of air and fire naturally flew upward toward the sky.

The destruction of the medieval world picture began with the publication in 1543 of *On the Revolutions of the Heavenly Spheres,* by Nicolaus Copernicus, a Polish mathematician, astronomer, and clergyman. In Copernicus' system, the sun was in the center of the universe, and the earth was another planet that moved around the sun. Most thinkers of the time, committed to the Aristotelian-Ptolemaic system and to the biblical statements that seemed to support it, rejected Copernicus' conclusions.

The work of Galileo Galilei, an Italian mathematician, astronomer, and physicist, was decisive in the shattering of the medieval cosmos and the shaping of the modern scientific outlook. Galileo advanced the modern view that knowledge of nature derives from direct observation and from mathematics. For Galileo, the universe was a "grand book which . . . is written in the language of mathematics, and its characters are triangles, circles, and other geometric figures without which it is humanly impossible to understand a single word of it." Galileo also pioneered experimental physics, advanced the modern idea that nature is uniform throughout the universe, and attacked reliance on scholastic authority rather than on experimentation in resolving scientific controversies.

Johannes Kepler, a contemporary of Galileo, discovered three laws of planetary motion that greatly advanced astronomical knowledge. Kepler showed that the path of a planet was an ellipse, not a circle as Ptolemy (and Copernicus) had believed, and that planets do not move at uniform speed but accelerate as they near the sun. He devised formulas to calculate accurately both a planet's speed at each point in its orbit around the sun and a planet's location at a particular time. Kepler's laws provided further evidence that Copernicus had been right, for they made sense only in a sun-centered universe, but Kepler could not explain why planets stayed in their orbits rather than flying off into space or crashing into the sun. The resolution of that question was left to Sir Isaac Newton.

Newton's great achievement was integrating the findings of Copernicus, Galileo, and Kepler into a single theoretical system. In *Principia Mathematica* (1687), he formulated the mechanical laws of motion and attraction that govern celestial and terrestrial objects.

The creation of a new model of the universe was one great achievement of the Scientific Revolution; another accomplishment was the formulation of the scientific method. The scientific method encompasses two approaches to knowledge, which usually complement each other: the empirical (inductive) and the rational (deductive). Although all sciences use both approaches, the inductive method is generally more applicable in such descriptive sciences as biology, anatomy, and geology, which rely on the accumulation of data. In the inductive approach, general principles are derived from analyzing external experiences—observations and the results of experiments. In the deductive approach, used in mathematics and theoretical physics, truths are derived in successive steps from indubitable axioms. Whereas the inductive method builds its concepts from an analysis of sense experience, the deductive approach constructs its ideas from self-evident principles that are conceived by the mind itself without external experience. The deductive and inductive approaches to knowledge, and their interplay, have been a constantly recurring feature in Western intellectual history since the rationalism of Plato and the empiricism of Aristotle. The success of the scientific method in modern times arose from the skillful synchronization of induction and deduction by such giants as Leonardo da Vinci, Copernicus, Kepler, Galileo, and Newton.

The Scientific Revolution was instrumental in shaping the modern outlook. It destroyed the medieval conception of the universe and established the scientific method as the means for investigating nature and acquiring knowledge, even in areas having little to do with the study of the physical world. By demonstrating the powers of the human mind, the Scientific Revolution gave thinkers great confidence in reason and led eventually to a rejection of traditional beliefs in magic, astrology, and witches. In the eighteenth century, the Age of Enlightenment, this growing skepticism led thinkers to question miracles and other Christian beliefs that seemed contrary to reason.

The Enlightenment of the eighteenth century culminated the movement toward modernity that started in the Renaissance era. The thinkers of the Enlightenment, called *philosophes,* attacked medieval otherworldliness, dethroned theology from its once-proud position as queen of the sciences, and based their understanding of nature and society on reason alone, unaided by revelation or priestly authority.

From the broad spectrum of Western history, several traditions flowed into the Enlightenment: the rational spirit born in classical Greece, the Stoic emphasis on natural law that applies to all human beings, and the Christian belief that all individuals are equal in God's eyes. A more immediate influence on the Enlightenment was Renaissance humanism, which focused on the individual and worldly human accomplishments and which criticized medieval theology-philosophy for its preoccupation with questions that seemed unrelated to the human condition. In many ways, the Enlightenment grew directly out of the Scientific Revolution. The philosophes praised both Newton's discovery of the mechanical laws that govern the universe and the scientific method that made this discovery possible. They wanted to transfer the scientific method—the reliance on experience and the critical use of the intellect—to the realm of society. They maintained that independent of clerical authority, human beings through reason could grasp the natural laws that govern the social world, just as Newton had uncovered the laws of nature that operate in the physical world. The philosophes said that those institutions and traditions that could not meet the test of reason, because they were based on authority, ignorance, or superstition, had to be reformed or dispensed with.

For medieval philosophers, reason had been subordinate to revelation; the Christian outlook determined the medieval concept of nature, morality, government, law, and life's purpose. During the Renaissance and Scientific Revolution, reason increasingly asserted its autonomy. For example, Machiavelli rejected the principle that politics should be based on Christian teachings; he recognized no higher world as the source of a higher truth. Galileo held that on questions regarding nature, one should trust to observation, experimentation, and mathematical reasoning and should not rely on Scripture. Descartes rejected reliance on past authority and maintained that through thought alone one could attain knowledge that has absolute certainty. Agreeing with Descartes that the mind is self-sufficient, the philosophes rejected the guidance of revelation and its priestly interpreters. They believed that through the use of reason, individuals could comprehend and reform society.

The Enlightenment philosophes articulated basic principles of the modern outlook: confidence in the self-sufficiency of the human mind, belief that individuals possess natural rights that governments should not violate, and the desire to reform society in accordance with rational principles. Their views influenced the reformers of the French Revolution and the Founding Fathers of the United States.

1 Critique of Authority

The brilliant Italian scientist Galileo Galilei (1564–1642), who had embraced Copernicanism, appealed to the Roman Catholic authorities to halt their actions against the theories of Copernicus, but was unsuccessful. His support of Copernicus aroused the ire of both clergy and scholastic philosophers. In 1616, the church placed Copernicus' book on the Index of Forbidden Books, and Galileo was ordered to cease his defense of the Copernican theory. In 1632, Galileo published *Dialogue Concerning the Two Chief World Systems* in which he upheld the Copernican view. Widely distributed and acclaimed, the book antagonized Galileo's enemies, who succeeded in halting further printing. Summoned to Rome, the aging and infirm scientist was put on trial by the Inquisition and ordered to renounce the Copernican theory. Galileo bowed to the Inquisition, which condemned the *Dialogue* and sentenced him to life imprisonment—largely house arrest at his own villa near Florence, where he was treated humanely.

Galileo Galilei

Letter to the Grand Duchess Christina and *Dialogue Concerning the Two Chief World Systems—Ptolemaic and Copernican*

The first reading illustrates Galileo's active involvement in a struggle for freedom of inquiry many years before the *Dialogue* was published. In 1615, in a letter addressed to Grand Duchess Christina of Tuscany, Galileo argued that passages from the Bible had no authority in scientific disputes.

The second reading (from the *Dialogue*) reveals Galileo's views on Aristotle. Medieval scholastics regarded Aristotle as the supreme authority on questions concerning nature, an attitude that was perpetuated by early modern scholastics. Galileo insisted that such reliance on authority was a hindrance to scientific investigation, that it is through observation, experiment, and reason that one arrives at physical truth.

LETTER

Biblical Authority

Some years ago, as Your Serene Highness well knows, I discovered in the heavens many things that had not been seen before our own age. The novelty of these things, as well as some consequences which followed from them in contradiction to the physical notions commonly held among academic philosophers, stirred up against me no small number of professors—as if I had placed these things in the sky with my own hands in order to upset nature and overturn the sciences. They seemed to forget that the increase of known truths stimulates the investigation, establishment, and growth of the arts; not their diminution or destruction.

Showing a greater fondness for their own opinions than for truth, they sought to deny and disprove the new things which, if they had cared to look for themselves, their own senses would have demonstrated to them. To this end they hurled various charges and published numerous writings filled with vain arguments, and they made the grave mistake of sprinkling these with passages taken from places in the Bible which they had failed to understand properly, and which were ill suited to their purposes. . . .

. . . Men who were well grounded in astronomical and physical science were persuaded as soon as they received my first message. There were others who denied them or remained in doubt only because of their novel and unexpected character, and because they had not yet had the opportunity to see for themselves. These men have by degrees come to be

satisfied. But some, besides allegiance to their original error, possess I know not what fanciful interest in remaining hostile not so much toward the things in question as toward their discoverer. No longer being able to deny them, these men now take refuge in obstinate silence, but being more than ever exasperated by that which has pacified and quieted other men, they divert their thoughts to other fancies and seek new ways to damage me. . . .

. . . Possibly because they are disturbed by the known truth of other propositions of mine which differ from those commonly held, and therefore mistrusting their defense so long as they confine themselves to the field of philosophy, these men have resolved to fabricate a shield for their fallacies out of the mantle of pretended religion and the authority of the Bible. These they apply, with little judgment, to the refutation of arguments that they do not understand and have not even listened to.

First they have endeavored to spread the opinion that such propositions in general are contrary to the Bible and are consequently damnable and heretical. . . . Hence they have had no trouble in finding men who would preach the damnability and heresy of the new doctrine from their very pulpits with unwonted confidence, thus doing impious and inconsiderate injury not only to that doctrine and its followers but to all mathematics and mathematicians in general. . . .

. . . They go about invoking the Bible, which they would have minister to their deceitful purposes. Contrary to the sense of the Bible and the intention of the holy [Church] Fathers, if I am not mistaken, they would extend such authorities until even in purely physical matters—where faith is not involved—they would have us altogether abandon reason and the evidence of our senses in favor of some biblical passage, though under the surface meaning of its words this passage may contain a different sense.

I hope to show that I proceed with much greater piety than they do, when I argue not against condemning [Copernicus'] book, but against condemning it in the way they suggest—that is, without understanding it, weighing it, or so much as reading it. For Copernicus never discusses matters of religion or faith, nor does he use arguments that depend in any way upon the authority of sacred writings which he might have interpreted erroneously. He stands always upon physical conclusions pertaining to the celestial motions, and deals with them by astronomical and geometrical demonstrations, founded primarily upon sense experiences and very exact observations. He did not ignore the Bible, but he knew very well that if his doctrine were proved, then it could not contradict the Scriptures when they were rightly understood. . . .

The reason produced for condemning the opinion that the earth moves and the sun stands still is that in many places in the Bible one may read that the sun moves and the earth stands still. Since the Bible cannot err, it follows as a necessary consequence that anyone takes an erroneous and heretical position who maintains that the sun is inherently motionless and the earth movable.

With regard to this argument, I think in the first place that it is very pious to say and prudent to affirm that the holy Bible can never speak untruth—whenever its true meaning is understood. But I believe nobody will deny that it is often very abstruse, and may say things which are quite different from what its bare words signify. Hence in expounding the Bible if one were always to confine oneself to the unadorned grammatical meaning, one might fall into error. . . .

. . . Now the Bible, merely to condescend to popular capacity, has not hesitated to obscure some very important pronouncements, attributing to God himself some qualities extremely remote from (and even contrary to) His essence. Who, then, would positively declare that this principle has been set aside, and the Bible has confined itself rigorously to the bare and restricted sense of its words, when speaking but casually of the earth, of water, of the sun, or of any other created thing? Especially in view of the fact that these things in no way concern the primary purpose of the sacred writings, which is the service of God and the salvation of souls—matters infinitely beyond the comprehension of the common people.

This being granted, I think that in discussions of physical problems we ought to begin not from the authority of scriptural passages, but from sense-experiences and necessary demonstrations. . . . Nothing physical which sense-experience sets before our eyes, or which necessary demonstrations prove to us, ought to be called in question (much less condemned) upon the testimony of biblical passages which may have some different meaning beneath their words. . . .

. . . I do not feel obliged to believe that that same God who has endowed us with senses, reason, and intellect has intended to forgo their use and by some other means to give us knowledge which we can attain by them. He would not re-quire us to deny sense and reason in physical matters which are set before our eyes and minds by direct experience or necessary demonstrations. . . .

It is obvious that such [anti-Copernican] authors, not having penetrated the true senses of Scripture, would impose upon others an obligation to subscribe to conclusions that are repugnant to manifest reason and sense, if they had any authority to do so. God forbid that this sort of abuse should gain countenance and authority, for then in a short time it would be necessary to proscribe all the contemplative sciences. People who are unable to understand perfectly both the Bible and the sciences far outnumber those who do understand. The former, glancing superficially through the Bible, would arrogate to themselves the authority to decree upon every question of physics on the strength of some word which they have misunderstood, and which was employed by the sacred authors for some different purpose. And the smaller number of understanding men could not dam up the furious torrent of such people, who would gain the majority of followers simply because it is much more pleasant to gain a reputation for wisdom without effort or study than to consume oneself tirelessly in the most laborious disciplines.

DIALOGUE

Galileo attacked the unquestioning acceptance of Aristotle's teachings in his *Dialogue Concerning the Two Chief World Systems—Ptolemaic and Copernican.* In the *Dialogue,* Simplicio is an Aristotelian and Salviati is a spokesman for Galileo; Sagredo, a third participant, introduces the problem of relying on the authority of Aristotle.

Aristotelian Authority

SAGREDO   One day I was at the home of a very famous doctor in Venice, where many persons came on account of their studies, and others occasionally came out of curiosity to see some anatomical dissection performed by a man who was truly no less learned than he was a careful and expert anatomist. It happened on this day that he was investigating the source and origin of the nerves, about which there exists a notorious controversy between the Galenist and Peripatetic doctors.[1] The anatomist showed that the great trunk of nerves, leaving the brain and passing through the nape, extended on down the spine and then branched out through the whole body, and that only a single strand as fine as a thread arrived at the heart. Turning to a gentleman whom we knew to be a Peripatetic philosopher, and on

---

[1]Galenist doctors followed the medical theories of Galen (A.D. 129–c. 199), a Greek anatomist and physician whose writings had great authority among medieval and early modern physicians. Peripatetic doctors followed Aristotle's teachings.

whose account he had been exhibiting and demonstrating everything with unusual care, he asked this man whether he was at last satisfied and convinced that the nerves originated in the brain and not in the heart. The philosopher, after considering for awhile, answered: "You have made me see this matter so plainly and palpably that if Aristotle's text were not contrary to it, stating clearly that the nerves originate in the heart, I should be forced to admit it to be true." . . .

SIMPLICIO   But if Aristotle is to be abandoned, whom shall we have for a guide in philosophy? Suppose you name some author.

SALVIATI   We need guides in forests and in unknown lands, but on plains and in open places only the blind need guides. It is better for such people to stay at home, but anyone with eyes in his head and his wits about him could serve as a guide for them. In saying this, I do not mean that a person should not listen to Aristotle; indeed, I applaud the reading and careful study of his works, and I reproach only those who give themselves up as slaves to him in such a way as to subscribe blindly to everything he says and take it as an inviolable decree without looking for any other reasons. This abuse carries with it another profound disorder, that other people do not try harder to comprehend the strength of his demonstrations. And what is more revolting in a public dispute, when someone is dealing with demonstrable conclusions, than to hear him interrupted by a text (often written to some quite different purpose) thrown into his teeth by an opponent? If, indeed, you wish to continue in this method of studying, then put aside the name of philosophers and call yourselves historians, or memory experts; for it is not proper that those who never philosophize should usurp the honorable title of philosopher.

2   The Autonomy of the Mind

René Descartes (1596–1650), a French mathematician and philosopher, united the new currents of thought initiated during the Renaissance and the Scientific Revolution. Descartes said that the universe was a mechanical system whose inner laws could be discovered through mathematical thinking and formulated in mathematical terms. With Descartes' assertions on the power of thought, human beings became fully aware of their capacity to comprehend the world through their mental powers. For this reason he is regarded as the founder of modern philosophy.

The deductive approach stressed by Descartes presumes that inherent in the mind are mathematical principles, logical relationships, the principle of cause and effect, concepts of size and motion, and so on—ideas that exist independently of human experience with the external world. Descartes, for example, would say that the properties of a right-angle triangle ($a^2 + b^2 = c^2$) are implicit in human consciousness prior to any experience one might have with a triangle. These innate ideas, said Descartes, permit the mind to give order and coherence to the physical world. Descartes held that the mind arrives at truth when it "intuits" or comprehends the logical necessity of its own ideas and expresses these ideas with clarity, certainty, and precision.

René Descartes
Discourse on Method

In the *Discourse on Method* (1637), Descartes proclaimed the mind's autonomy and importance and its ability and right to comprehend truth. In this work he offered a method whereby one could achieve certainty and thereby produce a comprehensive understanding of nature and human culture. In the following passage from the *Discourse on Method,* he explained the purpose of his inquiry. How he did so is almost as revolutionary as the ideas he wished to express. He spoke in the first person, autobiographically, as an individual employing his own reason, and he addressed himself to other individuals, inviting them to use their reason. He brought to his narrative an unprecedented confidence in the power of his own judgment and a deep disenchantment with the learning of his times.

PART ONE

From my childhood I lived in a world of books, and since I was taught that by their help I could gain a clear and assured knowledge of everything useful in life, I was eager to learn from them. But as soon as I had finished the course of studies which usually admits one to the ranks of the learned, I changed my opinion completely. For I found myself saddled with so many doubts and errors that I seemed to have gained nothing in trying to educate myself unless it was to discover more and more fully how ignorant I was.

Nevertheless I had been in one of the most celebrated schools in Europe, where I thought there should be wise men if wise men existed anywhere on earth. I had learned there everything that others learned, and, not satisfied with merely the knowledge that was taught, I had perused as many books as I could find which contained more unusual and recondite [obscure] knowledge. . . . And finally, it did not seem to me that our times were less flourishing and fertile than were any of the earlier periods. All this led me to conclude that I could judge others by myself, and to decide that there was no such wisdom in the world as I had previously hoped to find. . . .

I revered our theology, and hoped as much as anyone else to get to heaven, but having learned on great authority that the road was just as open to the most ignorant as to the most learned, and that the truths of revelation which lead thereto are beyond our understanding, I would not have dared to submit them to the weakness of my reasonings. I thought that to succeed in their examination it would be necessary to have some extraordinary assistance from heaven, and to be more than a man.

I will say nothing of philosophy except that it has been studied for many centuries by the most outstanding minds without having produced anything which is not in dispute and consequently doubtful. I did not have enough presumption to hope to succeed better than the others; and when I noticed how many different opinions learned men may hold on the same subject, despite the fact that no more than one of them can ever be right, I resolved to consider almost as false any opinion which was merely plausible. . . .

This is why I gave up my studies entirely as soon as I reached the age when I was no longer under the control of my teachers. I resolved to seek no other knowledge than that which I might find within myself, or perhaps in the great book of nature. I spent a few years of my adolescence traveling, seeing courts and armies, living with people of diverse types and stations of life, acquiring varied experience, testing myself in the episodes which fortune sent me, and, above all, thinking about the things around me so that I could derive some profit from them. For it seemed to me that I might find much more of the truth in the cogitations [reflections] which each man made on things which were important to him, and where he would be the loser if he judged badly, than in the cogitations of a man of letters in his study, concerned with speculations which produce no effect, and which have no consequences to him. . . .

. . . After spending several years in thus studying the book of nature and acquiring experience, I eventually reached the decision to study my own self, and to employ all my abilities to try to choose the right path. This produced much better results in my case, I think, than would have been produced if I had never left my books and my country. . . .

PART TWO

. . . As far as the opinions which I had been receiving since my birth were concerned, I could not do better than to reject them completely for once in my lifetime, and to resume them afterwards, or perhaps accept better ones in their place, when I had determined how they fitted into a rational scheme. And I firmly believed that by this means I would succeed in conducting my life much better than if I built only upon the old foundations and gave credence to the principles which I had acquired in my childhood without ever having examined them to see whether they were true or not. . . .

. . . Never has my intention been more than to try to re-form my own ideas, and rebuild them on foundations that would be wholly mine. . . . The decision to abandon all one's preconceived notions is not an example for all to follow. . . .

As for myself, I should no doubt have . . . [never attempted it] if I had had but a single teacher or if I had not known the differences which have always existed among the most learned. I had discovered in college that one cannot imagine anything so strange and unbelievable but that it has been upheld by some philosopher; and in my travels I had found that those who held opinions contrary to ours were neither barbarians nor savages, but that many of them were at least as reasonable as ourselves. I had considered how the same man, with the same capacity for reason, becomes different as a result of being brought up among Frenchmen or Germans than he would be if he had been brought up among Chinese or cannibals; and how, in our fashions, the thing which pleased us ten years ago and perhaps will please us again ten years in the future, now seems extravagant and ridiculous; and I felt that in all these ways we are much more greatly influenced by custom and example than by any certain knowledge. Faced with this divergence of opinion, I could not accept the testimony of the majority, for I thought it worthless as a proof of anything somewhat difficult to discover, since it is much more likely that a single man will have discovered it than a whole people. Nor, on the other hand, could I select anyone whose opinions seemed to me to be preferable to those of others, and I was thus constrained to embark on the investigation for myself.

Nevertheless, like a man who walks alone in the darkness, I resolved to go so slowly and circumspectly that if I did not get ahead very rapidly I was at least safe from falling. Also, I did not want to reject all the opinions which had slipped irrationally into my consciousness since birth, until I had first spent enough time planning how to accomplish the task which I was then undertaking, and seeking the true method of obtaining knowledge of everything which my mind was capable of understanding. . . .

> Descartes' method consists of four principles that place the capacity to arrive at truth entirely within the province of the human mind. First one finds a self-evident principle, such as a geometric axiom. From this general principle, other truths are deduced through logical reasoning. This is accomplished by breaking a problem down into its elementary components and then, step by step, moving toward more complex knowledge.

. . . I thought that some other method [beside that of logic, algebra, and geometry] must be found to combine the advantages of these three and to escape their faults. Finally, just as the multitude of laws frequently furnishes an excuse for vice, and a state is much better governed with a few laws which are strictly adhered to, so I thought that instead of the great number of precepts of which logic is composed, I would have enough with the four following ones, provided that I made a firm and unalterable resolution not to violate them even in a single instance.

The first rule was never to accept anything as true unless I recognized it to be evidently such: that is, carefully to avoid precipitation and prejudgment, and to include nothing in my conclusions unless it presented itself so clearly and distinctly to my mind that there was no occasion to doubt it.

The second was to divide each of the difficulties which I encountered into as many parts as possible, and as might be required for an easier solution.

The third was to think in an orderly fashion, beginning with the things which were simplest and easiest to understand, and gradually and by degrees reaching toward more complex knowledge, even treating as though ordered materials which were not necessarily so.

The last was always to make enumerations so complete, and reviews so general, that I would be certain that nothing was omitted. . . .

What pleased me most about this method was that it enabled me to reason in all things, if not perfectly, at least as well as was in my power. In addition, I felt that in practicing it my mind was gradually becoming accustomed to conceive its objects more clearly and distinctly. . . .

> Descartes was searching for an incontrovertible truth that could serve as the first principle of philosophy. His arrival at the famous dictum "I think, therefore I am" marks the beginning of modern philosophy.

PART FOUR

. . . As I desired to devote myself wholly to the search for truth, I thought that I should . . . reject as absolutely false anything of which I could have the least doubt, in order to see whether anything would be left after this procedure which could be called wholly certain. Thus, as our senses deceive us at times, I was ready to suppose that nothing was at all the way our senses represented them to be. As there are men who make mistakes in reasoning even on the simplest topics in geometry, I judged that I was as liable to error as any other, and rejected as false all the reasoning which I had previously accepted as valid demonstration. Finally, as the same precepts which we have when awake may come to us when asleep without their being true, I decided to suppose that nothing that had ever entered my mind was more real than the illusions of my dreams. But I soon noticed that while I thus wished to think everything false, it was necessarily true that I who thought so was something. Since this truth, *I think, therefore I am,* was so firm and assured that all the most extravagant suppositions of the sceptics[1] were unable to shake it, I judged that I could safely accept it as the first principle of the philosophy I was seeking.

---

[1]The skeptics belonged to the ancient Greek philosophic school that held true knowledge to be beyond human grasp and treated all knowledge as uncertain.

Discourse on Method: Descartes by Lafleur, © 1956. Reprinted by permission of Pearson Education, Inc., Upper Saddle River, NJ, pages 3–7, 9–12, 20–21.

3   The Outlook of the Philosophes

The philosophes attacked the abuses of the society of their day, including religious persecution, torture, slavery, and the suppression of freedom. In particular, they assailed organized religion for propagating beliefs that seemed contrary to reason and for fostering fanaticism and intolerance. By asserting that through reason society could be reformed, the philosophes were instrumental in shaping the liberal-democratic tradition.

Voltaire
A PLEA FOR TOLERANCE AND REASON

François Marie Arouet (1694–1778), known to the world as Voltaire, was the recognized leader of the French Enlightenment. Few of the philosophes had a better mind, and none had a sharper wit. A relentless critic of the Old Regime (the social structure in prerevolutionary France), Voltaire attacked superstition, religious fanaticism and persecution, censorship, and other abuses of eighteenth-century French society. Spending more than two years in Great Britain, Voltaire acquired a great admiration for English liberty, toleration, commerce, and science. In *Letters Concerning the English Nation* (1733), he drew unfavorable comparisons between a progressive Britain and a reactionary France.

Voltaire's angriest words were directed against established Christianity, to which he attributed many of the ills of modern society. Voltaire regarded Christianity as "the Christ-worshiping superstition" that someday would be destroyed "by the weapons of reason." He rejected revelation and the church hierarchy and was repulsed by Christian intolerance, but he accepted Christian morality and believed in God as the prime mover who set the universe in motion.

The following passages compiled from Voltaire's works—grouped according to topic—provide insight into the outlook of the philosophes. The excerpts come from sources that include his *Treatise on Tolerance* (1763), *The Philosophical Dictionary* (1764), and *Commentary on the Book of Crime and Punishments* (1766).

TOLERANCE

It does not require any great art or studied elocution to prove that Christians ought to tolerate one another. I will go even further and say that we ought to look upon all men as our brothers. What! call a Turk, a Jew, and a Siamese, my brother? Yes, of course; for are we not all children of the same father, and the creatures of the same God?

What is tolerance? . . . We are all full of weakness and errors; let us mutually pardon our follies. This is the last law of nature. . . .

It is clear that every private individual who persecutes a man, his brother, because he is not of the same opinion, is a monster. . . .

Of all religions, the Christian ought doubtless to inspire the most tolerance, although hitherto the Christians have been the most intolerant of all men.

. . . Tolerance has never brought civil war; intolerance has covered the earth with carnage. . . .

What! Is each citizen to be permitted to believe and to think that which his reason rightly or wrongly dictates? He should indeed, provided that he does not disturb the public order; for it is not contingent on man to believe or not to believe; but it is contingent on him to respect the usages of his country; and if you say that it is a crime not to believe in the dominant religion, you accuse then yourself the first Christians, your ancestors, and you justify those whom you accuse of having martyred them.

You reply that there is a great difference, that all religions are the work of men, and that the Apostolic Roman Catholic Church is alone the work of God. But in good faith, ought our religion because it is divine reign through hate, violence, exiles, usurpation of property, prisons, tortures, murders, and thanksgivings to God for these murders? The more the Christian religion is divine, the less it pertains to man to require it; if God made it, God will sustain it without you. You know that intolerance produces only hypocrites or rebels; what distressing alternatives! In short, do you want to sustain through executioners the religion of a God whom executioners have put to death and who taught only gentleness and patience?

―――――――

I shall never cease, my dear sir, to preach tolerance from the housetops, despite the complaints of your priests and the outcries of ours, until persecution is no more. The progress of reason is slow, the roots of prejudice lie deep. Doubtless, I shall never see the fruits of my efforts, but they are seeds which may one day germinate.

DOGMA

. . . Is Jesus the Word? If He be the Word, did He emanate from God in time or before time? If He emanated from God, is He co-eternal and consubstantial with Him, or is He of a similar substance? Is He distinct from Him, or is He not? Is He made or begotten? Can He beget in His turn? Has He paternity? or productive virtue without paternity? Is the Holy Ghost made? or begotten? or produced? or proceeding from the Father? or proceeding from the Son? or proceeding from both? Can He beget? can He produce? is His hypostasis consubstantial with the hypostasis of the Father and the Son? and how is it that, having the same nature—the same essence as the Father and the Son, He cannot do the same things done by these persons who are Himself?

Assuredly, I understand nothing of this; no one has ever understood any of it, and that is why we have slaughtered one another.

The Christians tricked, cavilled, hated, and excommunicated one another, for some of these dogmas inaccessible to human intellect.

FANATICISM

Fanaticism is to superstition what delirium is to fever, what rage is to anger. He who has ecstasies and visions, who takes dreams for realities, and his own imaginations for prophecies is an enthusiast; he who reinforces his madness by murder is a fanatic. . . .

The most detestable example of fanaticism is that exhibited on the night of St. Bartholomew,[1] when the people of Paris rushed from house to house to stab, slaughter, throw out of the window, and tear in pieces their fellow citizens who did not go to mass.

There are some cold-blooded fanatics; such as those judges who sentence men to death for no other crime than that of thinking differently from themselves. . . .

Once fanaticism has infected a brain, the disease is almost incurable. I have seen convulsionaries who, while speaking of the miracles of Saint Paris [a fourth-century Italian bishop], gradually grew heated in spite of themselves. Their eyes became inflamed, their limbs shook, fury disfigured their face, and they would have killed anyone who contradicted them.

There is no other remedy for this epidemic malady than that philosophical spirit which, extending itself from one to another, at length softens the manners of men and prevents the access of the disease. For when the disorder has made any progress, we should, without loss of time, flee from it, and wait till the air has become purified.

PERSECUTION

What is a persecutor? He whose wounded pride and furious fanaticism arouse princes and magistrates against innocent men, whose only crime is that of being of a different opinion. "Impudent man! you have worshipped God; you have preached and practiced virtue; you have served man; you have protected the orphan, have helped the poor; you have changed deserts, in which slaves dragged on a miserable existence, into fertile lands peopled by happy families; but I have discovered that you despise me, and have never read my controversial work. You know that I am a rogue; that I have forged G[od]'s signature, that I have stolen. You might tell these things; I must anticipate you. I will, therefore, go to the confessor [spiritual counselor] of the prime minister, or the magistrate; I will show them, with outstretched neck and twisted mouth, that you hold an erroneous opinion in relation to the cells in which the Septuagint was studied; that you have even spoken disrespectfully ten years ago of Tobit's dog,[2] which you asserted to have been a spaniel, while I proved that it was a greyhound. I will denounce you as the enemy of God and man!" Such is the language of the persecutor; and if precisely these words do not issue from his lips, they are engraven on his heart with the pointed steel of fanaticism steeped in the bitterness of envy. . . .

O God of mercy! If any man can resemble that evil being who is described as ceaselessly employed in the destruction of your works, is it not the persecutor?

SUPERSTITION

In 1749 a woman was burned in the Bishopric of Würzburg [a city in central Germany], convicted of being a witch. This

―――――――

[1]St. Bartholomew refers to the day of August 24, 1572, when the populace of Paris, instigated by King Charles IX at his mother's urging, began a week-long slaughter of Protestants.

[2]The Septuagint, the version of the Hebrew Scriptures used by Saint Paul and other early Christians, was a Greek translation done by Hellenized Jews in Alexandria sometime in the late third or the second century B.C. *Tobit's dog* appears in the Book of Tobit, a Hebrew book contained in the Catholic version of the Bible.

is an extraordinary phenomenon in the age in which we live. Is it possible that people who boast of their reformation and of trampling superstition under foot, who indeed supposed that they had reached the perfection of reason, could nevertheless believe in witchcraft, and this more than a hundred years after the so-called reformation of their reason?

In 1652 a peasant woman named Michelle Chaudron, living in the little territory of Geneva [a major city in Switzerland], met the devil going out of the city. The devil gave her a kiss, received her homage, and imprinted on her upper lip and right breast the mark that he customarily bestows on all whom he recognizes as his favorites. This seal of the devil is a little mark which makes the skin insensitive, as all the demonographical jurists of those times affirm.

The devil ordered Michelle Chaudron to bewitch two girls. She obeyed her master punctually. The girls' parents accused her of witchcraft before the law. The girls were questioned and confronted with the accused. They declared that they felt a continual pricking in certain parts of their bodies and that they were possessed. Doctors were called, or at least, those who passed for doctors at that time. They examined the girls. They looked for the devil's seal on Michelle's body—what the statement of the case called *satanic marks*. Into them they drove a long needle, already a painful torture. Blood flowed out, and Michelle made it known, by her cries, that satanic marks certainly do not make one insensitive. The

judges, seeing no definite proof that Michelle Chaudron was a witch, proceeded to torture her, a method that infallibly produces the necessary proofs: this wretched woman, yielding to the violence of torture, at last confessed every thing they desired.

The doctors again looked for the satanic mark. They found a little black spot on one of her thighs. They drove in the needle. The torment of the torture had been so horrible that the poor creature hardly felt the needle; thus the crime was established. But as customs were becoming somewhat mild at that time, she was burned only after being hanged and strangled.

In those days every tribunal of Christian Europe resounded with similar arrests. The [twigs] were lit everywhere for witches, as for heretics. People reproached the Turks most for having neither witches nor demons among them. This absence of demons was considered an infallible proof of the falseness of a religion.

A zealous friend of public welfare, of humanity, of true religion, has stated in one of his writings on behalf of innocence, that Christian tribunals have condemned to death over a hundred thousand accused witches. If to these judicial murders are added the infinitely superior number of massacred heretics, that part of the world will seem to be nothing but a vast scaffold covered with torturers and victims, surrounded by judges, guards and spectators.

Denis Diderot
Encyclopedia
COMPENDIUM OF KNOWLEDGE

A 38-volume *Encyclopedia,* whose 150 or more contributors included leading Enlightenment thinkers, was undertaken in Paris during the 1740s as a monumental effort to bring together all human knowledge and to propagate Enlightenment ideas. The *Encyclopedia*'s numerous articles on science and technology and its limited coverage of theological questions attest to the new interests of eighteenth-century intellectuals. Serving as principal editor, Denis Diderot (1713–1784) steered the project through difficult periods, including the suspension of publication by French authorities. After the first two volumes were published, the authorities denounced the work for containing "maxims that would tend to destroy royal authority, foment a spirit of independence and revolt, . . . and lay the foundations for the corruption of morals and religion." In 1759, Pope Clement XIII condemned the *Encyclopedia* for having "scandalous doctrines [and] inducing scorn for religion." It required careful diplomacy and clever ruses to finish the project and still incorporate ideas considered dangerous by religious and governmental authorities. With the project's completion in

1772, Diderot and Enlightenment opinion triumphed over clerical censors and powerful elements at the French court.

The *Encyclopedia* was a monument to the Enlightenment, as Diderot himself recognized. "This work will surely produce in time a revolution in the minds of man, and I hope that tyrants, oppressors, fanatics, and the intolerant will not gain thereby. We shall have served humanity." Some articles from the *Encyclopedia* follow.

Encyclopedia . . . In truth, the aim of an *encyclopedia* is to collect all the knowledge scattered over the face of the earth, to present its general outlines and structure to the men with whom we live, and to transmit this to those who will come after us, so that the work of past centuries may be useful to the following centuries, that our children, by becoming more educated, may at the same time become more virtuous and happier, and that we may not die without having deserved well of the human race. . . .

. . . We have seen that our *Encyclopedia* could only have been the endeavor of a philosophical century. . . .

I have said that it could only belong to a philosophical age to attempt an *encyclopedia;* and I have said this because such a work constantly demands more intellectual daring than is commonly found in [less courageous periods]. All things must be examined, debated, investigated without exception and without regard for anyone's feelings. . . . We must ride roughshod over all these ancient puerilities, overturn the barriers that reason never erected, give back to the arts and sciences the liberty that is so precious to them. . . . We have for quite some time needed a reasoning age when men would no longer seek the rules in classical authors but in nature. . . .

Fanaticism . . . is blind and passionate zeal born of superstitious opinions, causing people to commit ridiculous, unjust, and cruel actions, not only without any shame or remorse, but even with a kind of joy and comfort. *Fanaticism,* therefore, is only superstition put into practice. . . .

Fanaticism has done much more harm to the world than impiety. What do impious people claim? To free themselves of a yoke, while *fanatics* want to extend their chains over all the earth. Infernal zealomania! . . .

Government . . . The good of the people must be the great purpose of the *government.* The governors are appointed to fulfill it; and the civil constitution that invests them with this power is bound therein by the laws of nature and by the law of reason, which has determined that purpose in any form of *government* as the cause of its welfare. The greatest good of the people is its liberty. Liberty is to the body of the state what health is to each individual; without health man cannot enjoy pleasure; without liberty the state of welfare is excluded from nations. A patriotic governor will therefore see that the right to defend and to maintain liberty is the most sacred of his duties. . . .

If it happens that those who hold the reins of *government* find some resistance when they use their power for the destruction and not the conservation of things that rightfully belong to the people, they must blame themselves, because the public good and the advantage of society are the purposes of establishing a *government.* Hence it necessarily follows that power cannot be arbitrary and that it must be exercised according to the established laws so that the people may know its duty and be secure within the shelter of laws, and so that governors at the same time should be held within just limits and not be tempted to employ the power they have in hand to do harmful things to the body politic. . . .

History . . . On the usefullness of history. The advantage consists of the comparison that a statesman or a citizen can make of foreign laws, morals, and customs with those of his country. This is what stimulates modern nations to surpass one another in the arts, in commerce, and in agriculture. The great mistakes of the past are useful in all areas. We cannot describe too often the crimes and misfortunes caused by absurd quarrels. It is certain that by refreshing our memory of these quarrels, we prevent a repetition of them. . . .

Humanity . . . is a benevolent feeling for all men, which hardly inflames anyone without a great and sensitive soul. This sublime and noble enthusiasm is troubled by the pains of other people and by the necessity to alleviate them. With these sentiments an individual would wish to cover the entire universe in order to abolish slavery, superstition, vice, and misfortune. . . .

Intolerance . . . Any method that would tend to stir up men, to arm nations, and to soak the earth with blood is impious.

It is impious to want to impose laws upon man's conscience: this is a universal rule of conduct. People must be enlightened and not constrained. . . .

What did Christ recommend to his disciples when he sent them among the Gentiles? Was it to kill or to die? Was it to persecute or to suffer? . . .

Which is the true voice of humanity, the persecutor who strikes or the persecuted who moans?

Peace . . . War is the fruit of man's depravity; it is a convulsive and violent sickness of the body politic. . . .

If reason governed men and had the influence over the heads of nations that it deserves, we would never see them inconsiderately surrender themselves to the fury of war; they would not show that ferocity that characterizes wild beasts. . . .

Political Authority   No man has received from nature the right to command others. Liberty is a gift from heaven, and each individual of the same species has the right to enjoy it as soon as he enjoys the use of reason. . . .

The prince owes to his very subjects the *authority* that he has over them; and this *authority* is limited by the laws of nature and the state. The laws of nature and the state are the conditions under which they have submitted or are supposed to have submitted to its government. . . .

Moreover the government, although hereditary in a family and placed in the hands of one person, is not private property, but public property that consequently can never be taken from the people, to whom it belongs exclusively, fundamentally, and as a freehold. Consequently it is always the people who make the lease or the agreement: they always intervene in the contract that adjudges its exercise. It is not the state that belongs to the prince, it is the prince who belongs to the state: but it does rest with the prince to govern in the state, because the state has chosen him for that purpose: he has bound himself to the people and the administration of affairs, and they in their turn are bound to obey him according to the laws. . . .

The Press   [*press* includes newspapers, magazines, books, and so forth] . . . People ask if freedom of the *press* is advantageous or prejudicial to a state. The answer is not difficult. It is of the greatest importance to conserve this practice in all states founded on liberty. I would even say that the disadvantages of this liberty are so inconsiderable compared to its advantages that this ought to be the common right of the universe, and it is certainly advisable to authorize its practice in all governments. . . .

The Slave Trade   [This trade] is the buying of unfortunate Negroes by Europeans on the coast of Africa to use as slaves in their colonies. This buying of Negroes, to reduce them to slavery, is one business that violates religion, morality, natural laws, and all the rights of human nature.

Negroes, says a modern Englishman full of enlightenment and humanity, have not become slaves by the right of war; neither do they deliver themselves voluntarily into bondage, and consequently their children are not born slaves. Nobody is unaware that they are bought from their own princes, who claim to have the right to dispose of their liberty, and that traders have them transported in the same way as their other goods, either in their colonies or in America, where they are displayed for sale.

If commerce of this kind can be justified by a moral principle, there is no crime, however atrocious it may be, that cannot be made legitimate. Kings, princes, and magistrates are not the proprietors of their subjects: they do not, therefore, have the right to dispose of their liberty and to sell them as slaves.

On the other hand, no man has the right to buy them or to make himself their master. Men and their liberty are not objects of commerce; they can be neither sold nor bought nor paid for at any price. We must conclude from this that a man whose slave has run away should only blame himself, since he had acquired for money illicit goods whose acquisition is prohibited by all the laws of humanity and equity.

There is not, therefore, a single one of these unfortunate people regarded only as slaves who does not have the right to be declared free, since he has never lost his freedom, which he could not lose and which his prince, his father, and any person whatsoever in the world had not the power to dispose of. Consequently the sale that has been completed is invalid in itself. This Negro does not divest himself and can never divest himself of his natural right; he carries it everywhere with him, and he can demand everywhere that he be allowed to enjoy it. It is, therefore, patent inhumanity on the part of judges in free countries where he is transported, not to emancipate him immediately by declaring him free, since he is their fellow man, having a soul like them.

4   Protection of Natural Rights

"Every age has its dominant idea," wrote Diderot; "that of our age seems to be Liberty." Eighteenth-century political thought is characterized by a thoroughgoing secularism; an indictment of despotism, the divine right of kings, and the special privileges of the aristocracy and the clergy; a respect for English constitutionalism because it enshrined the rule of law; and an affirmation of John Locke's theory that government had an obligation to protect the natural rights of its citizens. Central to the political outlook of the philosophes was the conviction that political solutions could be found for the ills that afflicted society.

In general, the philosophes favored constitutional government that protected citizens from the abuse of power. With the notable exception of Rousseau, the philosophes' concern for liberty did not lead them to embrace democracy, for they placed little trust in the masses. Several philosophes, notably Voltaire, placed their confidence in reforming despots, such as Frederick II of Prussia, who were sympathetic to enlightened ideas. However, the philosophes were less concerned with the form of government—monarchy or republic—than they were with preventing the authorities from abusing their power.

John Locke
Second Treatise on Government

John Locke (1632–1704), a British statesman, philosopher, and political theorist, was a principal source of the Enlightenment. Eighteenth-century thinkers were particularly influenced by Locke's advocacy of religious toleration, his reliance on experience as the source of knowledge, and his concern for liberty. In his first *Letter Concerning Toleration,* Locke declared that Christians who persecute others in the name of religion vitiate Christ's teachings. Locke's political philosophy as formulated in the *Two Treatises on Government* (1690) was a rational and secular attempt to understand and improve the human condition. The Lockean spirit pervades the American Declaration of Independence, Constitution, and Bill of Rights and is the basis of the liberal tradition that aims to protect individual liberty from despotic state authority.

Viewing human beings as brutish and selfish, Thomas Hobbes (see page 51) the British philosopher and political theorist, had prescribed a state with unlimited power; only in this way, he said, could people be protected from each other and civilized life preserved. Locke, regarding people as essentially good and humane, developed a conception of the state differing fundamentally from Hobbes'. Locke held that human beings are born with natural rights of life, liberty, and property; they establish the state to protect these rights. Consequently, neither executive nor legislature, neither king nor assembly has the authority to deprive individuals of their natural rights. Whereas Hobbes justified absolute monarchy, Locke explicitly endorsed constitutional government in which the power to govern derives from the consent of the governed and the state's authority is limited by agreement.

Locke said that originally, in establishing a government, human beings had never agreed to surrender their natural rights to any state authority. The state's founders intended the new polity to preserve these natural rights and to implement the people's will. Therefore, as the following passage from Locke's *Second Treatise on Government* illustrates, the power exercised by magistrates cannot be absolute or arbitrary.

. . . *Political power* is that power, which every man having in the state of nature, has given up into the hands of the society, and therein to the governors, whom the society hath set over itself, with this express or tacit trust, that it shall be employed for their good, and the preservation of their property: now this *power,* which every man has *in the state of nature,* and which he parts with to the society in all such cases where the society can secure him, is to use such means, for the preserving of his own property, as he thinks good, and nature allows him; and to punish the breach of the law of nature in others, so as (according to the best of his reason) may most conduce to the preservation of himself, and the rest of mankind. So that the *end and measure of this power,* when in every man's hands in the state of nature, being the preservation of all of his society, that is, all mankind in general, it can have no other *end or measure,* when in the hands of the magistrate, but to preserve the members of that society in their lives, liberties, and possessions; and so cannot be an absolute, arbitrary power over their lives and fortunes, which are as much as possible to be preserved; but a *power to make laws,* and annex such *penalties* to them, as may tend to the preservation of the whole, by cutting off those parts, and those only, which are so corrupt, that they threaten the sound and healthy, without which no severity is lawful. And this *power has its original only from compact,* and agreement, and the mutual consent of those who make up the community. . . .

These are the *bounds,* which the trust, that is put in them by the society, and the law of God and nature, have *set to the legislative* power of every common-wealth, in all forms of government.

First, They are to govern by *promulgated established laws,* not to be varied in particular cases, but to have one rule for rich and poor, for the favourite at court, and the country man at plough.

Secondly, These *laws* also ought to be designed *for no other end ultimately, but the good of the people.*

Thirdly, They must *not raise taxes* on the *property of the people, without the consent of the people,* given by themselves, or their deputies. And this properly concerns only such governments, where the *legislative* is always in being, or at least where the people have not reserved any part of the legislative to deputies, to be from time to time chosen by themselves.

Fourthly, The *legislative* neither must *nor can transfer the power of making laws* to any body else, or place it any where, but where the people have. . . .

If government fails to fulfill the end for which it was established—the preservation of the individual's right to life, liberty, and property—the people have a right to dissolve that government.

. . . The *legislative acts against the trust* reposed in them, when they endeavour to invade the property of the subject, and to make themselves, or any part of the community, masters, or arbitrary disposers of the lives, liberties, or fortunes of the people.

The reason why men enter into society, is the preservation of their property; and the end why they chuse and authorize a legislative, is, that there may be laws made, and rules set, as guards and fences to the properties of all the members of the society, to limit the power, and moderate the dominion of every part and member of the society: for since it can never be supposed to be the will of the society, that the legislative should have a power to destroy that which every one designs to secure, by entering into society, and for which

the people submitted themselves to legislators of their own making; whenever the *legislators endeavour to take away, and destroy the property of the people,* or to reduce them to slavery under arbitrary power, they put themselves into a state of war with the people, who are thereupon absolved from any farther obedience, and are left to the common refuge, which God hath provided for all men, against force and violence. Whensoever therefore the *legislative* shall transgress this fundamental rule of society; and either by ambition, fear, folly or corruption, *endeavour to grasp* themselves, *or put into the hands of any other, an absolute power* over the lives, liberties, and estates of the people; by this breach of trust they *forfeit the power* the people had put into their hands for quite contrary ends, and it devolves to the people, who have a right to resume their original liberty, and, by the establishment of a new legislative, (such as they shall think fit) provide for their own safety and security, which is the end for which they are in society. What I have said here, concerning the legislative in general, holds true also concerning the supreme executor, who having a double trust put in him, both to have a part in the legislative, and the supreme execution of the law, acts against both, when he goes about to set up his own arbitrary will as the law of the society. He *acts* also *contrary to his trust,* when he either employs the force, treasure, and offices of the society, to corrupt the *representatives,* and gain them to his purposes; or openly pre-engages the *electors,* and prescribes to their choice, such, whom he has, by sollicitations, threats, promises, or otherwise, won to his designs; and employs them to bring in such, who have promised beforehand what to vote, and what to enact. . . .

Locke responds to the charge that his theory will produce "frequent rebellion." Indeed, says Locke, the true rebels are the magistrates who, acting contrary to the trust granted them, violate the people's rights.

. . . Such *revolutions happen* not upon every little mismanagement in public affairs. *Great mistakes* in the ruling part, many wrong and inconvenient laws, and all the *slips* of human frailty, will be *borne by the people* without mutiny or murmur. But if a long train of abuses, prevarications and artifices, all tending the same way, make the design visible to the people, and they cannot but feel what they lie under, and see whither they are going; it is not to be wondered at, that they should then rouze themselves, and endeavour to put the rule into such hands which may secure to them the ends for which government was at first erected. . . .

. . . I answer, that *this doctrine* of a power in the people of providing for their safety a-new, by a new legislative, when their legislators have acted contrary to their trust, by invading their property, is *the best defence against rebellion,* and the probablest means to hinder it: for *rebellion* being an opposition, not to persons, but authority, which is founded only in the constitutions and laws of the government; those, whoever they be, who by force break through, and by force justify their violation of them, are truly and properly *rebels:* for when men, by entering into society and civil government, have excluded force, and introduced laws for the preservation of property, peace, and unity amongst themselves, those who set up force again in opposition to the laws, do [rebel], that is, bring back again the state of war, and are properly rebels: which they who are in power, (by the pretence they have to authority, the temptation of force they have in their hands, and the flattery of those about them) being likeliest to do; the properest way to prevent the evil, is to shew them the danger and injustice of it, who are under the greatest temptation to run into it.

The end of government is the good of mankind; and which is *best for mankind,* that the people should always be exposed to the boundless will of tyranny, or that the rulers should be sometimes liable to be opposed, when they grow exorbitant in the use of their power, and employ it for the destruction, and not the preservation of the properties of their people?

Thomas Jefferson
Declaration of Independence

Written by Thomas Jefferson (1743–1826) to justify the American colonists' break with Britain, the Declaration of Independence enumerated principles that were quite familiar to English statesmen and intellectuals. The preamble to the Declaration, excerpted below, articulated clearly Locke's philosophy of natural rights. Locke had viewed life, liberty, and property as the individual's essential natural rights; Jefferson substituted the "pursuit of happiness" for property.

A DECLARATION BY THE REPRESENTATIVES OF THE UNITED STATES OF AMERICA, IN GENERAL CONGRESS ASSEMBLED.

When in the Course of human Events, it becomes necessary for one People to dissolve the Political Bands which have connected them with another, and to assume among the Powers of the Earth, the separate and equal Station to which the Laws of Nature and of Nature's God entitle them, a decent Respect to the Opinions of Mankind requires that they should declare the causes which impel them to the Separation.

We hold these Truths to be self-evident, that all Men are created equal, that they are endowed by their Creator with certain unalienable Rights, that among these are Life, Liberty, and the Pursuit of Happiness—That to secure these Rights, Governments are instituted among Men, deriving their just Powers from the Consent of the Governed, That whenever any Form of Government becomes destructive of these Ends, it is the Right of the People to alter or to abolish it, and to institute new Government, laying its Foundation on such Principles, and organizing its Powers in such Form, as to them shall seem most likely to effect their Safety and Happiness. Prudence, indeed, will dictate that Governments long established should not be changed for light and transient Causes; and accordingly all Experience hath shewn, that Mankind are more disposed to suffer, while Evils are sufferable, than to right themselves by abolishing the Forms to which they are accustomed. But when a long Train of Abuses and Usurpations, pursuing invariably the same Object, evinces a Design to reduce them under absolute Despotism, it is their right, it is their duty, to throw off such Government, and to provide new Guards for their future Security. Such has been the patient Sufferance of these Colonies; and such is now the Necessity which constrains them to alter their former Systems of Government. The History of the present King of Great-Britain is a History of repeated Injuries and Usurpations, all having in direct Object the Establishment of an absolute Tyranny over these States. . . .

5   Literature As Satire: Critiques of European Society

The French philosophes, particularly Voltaire, Diderot, and Montesquieu, often used the medium of literature to decry the ills of their society and advance Enlightenment values. In the process they wrote satires that are still read and admired for their literary merits and insights into human nature and society. The eighteenth century also saw the publication of Jonathan Swift's *Gulliver's Travels,* one of the greatest satirical works written in English.

Voltaire
Candide

Several eighteenth-century thinkers, including German philosopher Gottfried Wilhelm Leibnitz (1646–1716) and English poet Alexander Pope, subscribed to the view that God had created the best of all possible worlds, that whatever evil or misfortune existed served a purpose—it contributed to the general harmony of the universe. This is the meaning of Pope's famous lines in his *Essay on Man*: "One truth is clear, WHATEVER IS IS RIGHT." This view, known as philosophical optimism implied that individuals must accept their destiny and make no attempt to change it. In *Candide* (1759), his most important work of fiction, Voltaire bitterly attacked and ridiculed philosophical optimism. In effect Voltaire asked: "In a world where we constantly experience cruelty, injustice, superstition, intolerance, and a host of other evils, how can it be said that this is the best of all possible worlds?" But Voltaire does not resign himself to despair, for he is an ardent reformer who believes that through reason human beings can improve society.

An immediate inspiration for Voltaire's response to philosophical optimism was the catastrophic earthquake that struck Lisbon, Portugal, on November 1, 1755, claiming sixty thousand victims. How does such a catastrophe fit into the general harmony of things in this best of all possible worlds? Like the biblical Book of Job, *Candide* explored the question: Why do the innocent suffer? And because Voltaire delved into this mystery with wit, irony, satire, and wisdom, the work continues to be hailed as a literary masterpiece.

The illegitimate Candide (son of the sister of the baron in whose castle he lives in Westphalia) is tutored by the philosopher Pangloss, a teacher of "metaphysico-theologo-cosmolonigology," that is, a person who speaks nonsense. The naive Pangloss clings steadfastly to the belief that all that happens, even the worst misfortunes, are for the best.

Candide falls in love with Cunegund, the beautiful daughter of the baron of the castle; but the baron forcibly removes Candide from the castle when he discovers their love. Candide subsequently suffers a series of disastrous misfortunes, but he continues to adhere to the belief firmly instilled in him by Pangloss, that everything happens for the best and that this is the best of all possible worlds. Later, he meets an old beggar, who turns out to be his former teacher, Pangloss, who tells Candide that the Bulgarians have destroyed the castle and killed Cunegund and her family. Candide and Pangloss then travel together to Lisbon, where they survive the terrible earthquake, only to have

Pangloss hanged (but he escapes death) by the Inquisition. Soon thereafter, Candide is reunited with Cunegund, who, although having been raped and sold into prostitution, had not been killed. Following further adventures and misfortunes, the lovers are again separated when Cunegund is captured by pirates.

After experiencing more episodes of human wickedness and natural disasters, Candide abandons the philosophy of optimism, declaring "that we must cultivate our gardens." By this Voltaire meant that we can never achieve utopia, but neither should we descend to the level of brutes. Through purposeful and honest work, and the deliberate pursuit of virtue, we can improve, however modestly, the quality of human existence.

The following excerpt from *Candide* starts with Candide's first misfortune after being driven out of the castle at Westphalia. In addition to ridiculing philosophical optimism, Voltaire expresses his revulsion for militarism.

CHAPTER II
WHAT BEFELL CANDIDE AMONG THE BULGARIANS

Candide, thus driven out of this terrestrial paradise, wandered a long time, without knowing where he went; sometimes he raised his eyes, all bedewed with tears, toward Heaven, and sometimes he cast a melancholy look toward the magnificent castle where dwelt the fairest of young baronesses. He laid himself down to sleep in a furrow, heartbroken and supperless. The snow fell in great flakes, and, in the morning when he awoke, he was almost frozen to death; however, he made shift to crawl to the next town, which was called Waldberghoff-trarbk-dikdorff, without a penny in his pocket, and half dead with hunger and fatigue. He took up his stand at the door of an inn. He had not been long there before two men dressed in blue fixed their eyes steadfastly upon him.

"Faith, comrade," said one of them to the other, "yonder is a well-made young fellow, and of the right size."

Thereupon they went up to Candide, and with the greatest civility and politeness invited him to dine with them.

"Gentlemen," replied Candide, with a most engaging modesty, "you do me much honor, but, upon my word, I have no money."

"Money, sir!" said one of the men in blue to him. "Young persons of your appearance and merit never pay anything. Why, are not you five feet five inches high?"

"Yes, gentlemen, that is really my size," replied he with a low bow.

"Come then, sir, sit down along with us. We will not only pay your reckoning, but will never suffer such a clever young fellow as you to want money. Mankind were born to assist one another."

"You are perfectly right, gentlemen," said Candide; "that is precisely the doctrine of Master Pangloss; and I am convinced that everything is for the best."

His generous companions next entreated him to accept a few crowns, which he readily complied with, at the same time offering them his note for the payment, which they refused, and sat down to table.

"Have you not a great affection for—"

"Oh, yes!" he replied. "I have a great affection for the lovely Miss Cunegund."

"Maybe so," replied one of the men, "but that is not the question! We are asking you whether you have not a great affection for the King of the Bulgarians?"*

"For the King of the Bulgarians?" said Candide. "Not at all. Why, I never saw him in my life."

"Is it possible! Oh, he is a most charming king! Come, we must drink his health."

"With all my heart, gentlemen," Candide said, and he tossed off his glass.

"Bravo!" cried the blues. "You are now the support, the defender, the hero of the Bulgarians; your fortune is made; you are on the high road to glory."

So saying, they put him in irons and carried him away to the regiment. There he was made to wheel about to the right, to the left, to draw his ramrod, to return his ramrod, to present, to fire, to march, and they gave him thirty blows with a cane. The next day he performed his exercise a little better, and they gave him but twenty. The day following he came off with ten and was looked upon as a young fellow of surprising genius by all his comrades.

Candide was struck with amazement and could not for the soul of him conceive how he came to be a hero. One fine spring morning, he took it into his head to take a walk, and he marched straight forward, conceiving it to be a privilege of the human species, as well as of the brute creation, to make use of their legs how and when they pleased. He had not gone above two leagues when he was overtaken by four other heroes, six feet high, who bound him neck and heels, and carried him to a dungeon. A court-martial sat upon him, and he was asked which he liked best, either to run the gauntlet six and thirty times through the whole regiment, or to have his brains blown out with a dozen musket balls. In vain did he remonstrate to them that the human will is free, and that he chose neither. They obliged him to make a choice, and he determined, in virtue of that divine gift called free will, to run the gauntlet six and thirty times. He had gone through his

_____
*I.e., Prussians.

discipline twice, and the regiment being composed of two thousand men, they composed for him exactly four thousand strokes, which laid bare all his muscles and nerves, from the nape of his neck to his rump. As they were preparing to make him set out the third time, our young hero, unable to support it any longer, begged as a favor they would be so obliging as to shoot him through the head. The favor being granted, a bandage was tied over his eyes, and he was made to kneel down. At that very instant, his Bulgarian Majesty, happening to pass by, inquired into the delinquent's crime, and being a prince of great penetration, he found, from what he heard of Candide, that he was a young meta-physician, entirely ignorant of the world. And, therefore, out of his great clemency, he condescended to pardon him, for which his name will be celebrated in every journal, and in every age. A skillful surgeon made a cure of Candide in three weeks by means of emollient unguents prescribed by Dioscorides. His sores were now skinned over, and he was able to march when the King of the Bulgarians gave battle to the King of the Abares.*

Chapter III
How Candide Escaped from the Bulgarians, and What Befell Him Afterwards

Never was anything so gallant, so well accoutered, so brilliant, and so finely disposed as the two armies. The trumpets, fifes, oboes, drums, and cannon, made such harmony as never was heard in hell itself. The entertainment began by a discharge of cannon, which, in the twinkling of an eye, laid flat about six thousand men on each side. The musket bullets swept away, out of the best of all possible worlds, nine or ten thousand scoundrels that infested its surface. The bayonet was next the sufficient reason for the deaths of several thousands. The whole might amount to thirty thousand souls. Candide trembled like a philosopher and concealed himself as well as he could during this heroic butchery.

At length, while the two kings were causing *Te Deum* to be sung in each of their camps, Candide took a resolution to go and reason somewhere else upon causes and effects. After passing over heaps of dead or dying men, the first place he came to was a neighboring village, in the Abarian territories, which had been burned to the ground by the Bulgarians in accordance with international law. Here lay a number of old men covered with wounds, who beheld their wives dying with their throats cut, and hugging their children to their breasts all stained with blood. There several young virgins, whose bellies had been ripped open after they had satisfied the natural necessities of the Bulgarian heroes, breathed their last; while others, half burned in the flames, begged to be

dispatched out of the world. The ground about them was covered with the brains, arms, and legs of dead men.

Candide made all the haste he could to another village, which belonged to the Bulgarians, and there he found that the heroic Abares had treated it in the same fashion.† From thence continuing to walk over palpitating limbs or through ruined buildings, at length he arrived beyond the theater of war, with a little provision in his pouch, and Miss Cunegund's image in his heart. When he arrived in Holland his provisions failed him; but having heard that the inhabitants of that country were all rich and Christians, he made himself sure of being treated by them in the same manner as at the Baron's castle before he had been driven from thence through the power of Miss Cunegund's bright eyes.

He asked charity of several grave-looking people, who one and all answered him that if he continued to follow this trade, they would have him sent to the house of correction, where he should be taught to earn his bread.

He next addressed himself to a person who had just been haranguing a numerous assembly for a whole hour on the subject of charity. The orator, squinting at him under his broad-brimmed hat, asked him sternly what brought him thither and whether he was for the good cause.

"Sir," said Candide, in a submissive manner, "I conceive there can be no effect without a cause; everything is necessarily concatenated and arranged for the best. It was necessary that I should be banished from the presence of Miss Cunegund, that I should afterward run the gauntlet, and it is necessary I should beg my bread till I am able to earn it: all this could not have been otherwise."

"Hark you, friend," said the orator, "do you hold the Pope to be Antichrist?"

"Truly, I never heard anything about it," said Candide, "but whether he is or not, I am in want of something to eat."

"You deserve not to eat or to drink," replied the orator, "wretch, monster that you are! Hence! Avoid my sight and never come near me again while you live."

The orator's wife happened to put her head out of the window at that instant, when, seeing a man who doubted whether the Pope was Antichrist, she discharged upon his head a chamber pot full of——. Good heavens, to what excess does religious zeal transport the female kind!

A man who had never been christened, an honest Anabaptist‡ named James, was witness to the cruel and ignominious treatment showed to one of his brethren, to a two-footed featherless being, who had a soul.§ Moved with pity, he carried him to his own house, cleaned him up, gave him meat and drink, and made him a present of two florins,

---

*I.e., French. The Seven Years' War had begun in 1756.

†Voltaire was not noted for his patriotism. His detachment enables him to flay both sides.

‡Voltaire looked with favor on the sixteenth-century sect (which was persecuted by both Catholics and Protestants).

§The Anabaptist adds the soul to the famous definition of man of a Greek philosopher, to whom Antisthenes, the Cynic, thereupon presented a plucked chicken.

at the same time proposing to instruct him in his own trade of weaving Persian silks which are fabricated in Holland. Candide threw himself at his feet, crying:

"Now I am convinced that Master Pangloss told me truth, when he said that everything was for the best in this world, for I am infinitely more affected by your extraordinary generosity than by the inhumanity of that gentleman in the black cloak and his wife."

The next day, as Candide was walking out, he met a beggar all covered with scabs, his eyes were sunk in his head, the end of his nose was eaten off, his mouth drawn on one side, his teeth as black as coal, snuffling and coughing most violently, and every time he attempted to spit, out dropped a tooth.

Chapter IV
How Candide Found His Old Master in Philosophy, Dr. Pangloss, Again and What Happened to Them

Candide, divided between compassion and horror, but giving way to the former, bestowed on this shocking figure the two florins which the honest Anabaptist James had just before given to him. The specter looked at him very earnestly, shed tears, and threw his arms about his neck Candide started back aghast.

"Alas!" said the one wretch to the other, "don't you know your dear Pangloss?"

"What do I hear? Is it you, my dear master! You I behold in this piteous plight? What dreadful misfortune has befallen you? What has made you leave the most magnificent and delightful of all castles? What is become of Miss Cunegund, the mirror of young ladies and nature's masterpiece?"

"Oh, Lord!" cried Pangloss, "I am so weak I cannot stand."

Thereupon Candide instantly led him to the Anabaptist's stable, and procured him something to eat. As soon as Pangloss had a little refreshed himself, Candide began to repeat his inquiries concerning Miss Cunegund.

"She is dead," replied the other.

Candide immediately fainted away. His friend recovered him by the help of a little bad vinegar which he found by chance in the stable. Candide opened his eyes.

"Dead! Miss Cunegund dead!" he said. "Ah, where is the best of worlds now? But of what illness did she die? Was it for grief upon seeing her father kick me out of his magnificent castle?"

"No," replied Pangloss, "her belly was ripped open by the Bulgarian soldiers after they had ravished her as much as it was possible for a damsel to be ravished. They knocked the Baron her father on the head for attempting to defend her; my lady her mother was cut in pieces; my poor pupil was served just in the same manner as his sister; and as for the cas-

tle, they have not left one stone upon another; they have destroyed all the ducks, and the sheep, the barns, and the trees. But we have had our revenge, for the Abares have done the very same thing in a neighboring barony, which belonged to a Bulgarian lord."

At hearing this, Candide fainted away a second time, but having come to himself again, he said all that it became him to say. He inquired into the cause and effect, as well as into the sufficient reason, that had reduced Pangloss to so miserable a condition.

"Alas!" replied the other. "It was love: love, the comfort of the human species; love, the preserver of the universe, the soul of all sensible beings. Love! Tender love!"

"Alas," replied Candide, "I have had some knowledge of love myself, this sovereign of hearts, this soul of souls. Yet it never cost me more than a kiss and twenty kicks on the backside. But how could this beautiful cause produce in you so hideous an effect?"

Pangloss made answer in these terms: "Oh, my dear Candide, you must remember Pacquette, that pretty wench, who waited on our noble Baroness. In her arms I tasted the pleasures of paradise, which produced these hell-torments with which you see me devoured. She was infected with the disease and perhaps is since dead of it. She received this present of a learned Franciscan monk, who derived it from the fountainhead; he was indebted for it to an old countess, who had it of a captain of horse, who had it of a marchioness, who had it of a page; the page had it of a Jesuit, who, during his novitiate, had it in a direct line from one of the fellow-adventurers of Christopher Columbus. For my part I shall give it to nobody, I am a dying man."

"Oh, Pangloss," cried Candide, "what a strange genealogy is this! Is not the devil the root of it?"

"Not at all," replied the great man. "It was a thing unavoidable, a necessary ingredient in the best of worlds,[*] for if Columbus had not, in an island of America, caught this disease, which contaminates the source of generation, and frequently impedes propagation itself, and is evidently opposite to the great end of nature, we should have had neither chocolate nor cochineal.[†] It is also to be observed that, even to the present time in this continent of ours, this malady, like our religious controversies, is peculiar to ourselves. The Turks, the Indians, the Persians, the Chinese, the Siamese, and the Japanese are entirely unacquainted with it; but there is a sufficient reason for them to know it in a few centuries. In the meantime, it is making prodigious progress among us, especially in those armies composed of well-disciplined hirelings, who determine the fate of nations; for we may safely affirm that, when an army of thirty thousand men fights another equal in number, there are about twenty thousand of them poxed on each side."

---

*Voltaire mocks Pope's "all partial evil, universal good."
†A dye made from insects indigenous to Central America.

"Very surprising, indeed," said Candide. "But you must get cured."

"How can I?" said Pangloss. "My dear friend, I have not a penny in the world; and you know one cannot be bled or have a clyster [enema] without a fee."

This last speech had its effect on Candide. He flew to the charitable Anabaptist James, he flung himself at his feet, and gave him so touching a picture of the miserable situation of his friend that the good man, without any further hesitation, agreed to take Dr. Pangloss into his house and to pay for his cure. The cure was effected with only the loss of one eye and an ear. As he wrote a good hand and understood accounts tolerably well, the Anabaptist made him his bookkeeper. At the expiration of two months, being obliged to go to Lisbon about some mercantile affairs, he took the two philosophers with him in the same ship. Pangloss, during the voyage, explained to him how everything was so constituted that it could not be better. James did not quite agree with him on this point.

"Mankind," said he, "must, in some things, have deviated from their original innocence; for they were not born wolves, and yet they worry one another like those beasts of prey. God never gave them twenty-four pounders nor bayonets, and yet they have made cannon and bayonets to destroy one another. To this account I might add not only bankruptcies but the law, which seizes on the effects of bankrupts only to cheat the creditors."

"All this was indispensably necessary," replied the one-eyed doctor, "for private misfortunes are public benefits; so that the more private misfortunes there are, the greater is the general good."

While he was arguing in this manner, the sky was overcast, the winds blew from the four quarters of the compass, and the ship was assailed by a most terrible tempest, within sight of the port of Lisbon.

Chapter VI
How the Portuguese Made a Superb Auto-Da-Fé* to Prevent Any Future Earthquakes, and How Candide Underwent Public Flagellation

After the earthquake which had destroyed three-quarters of the city of Lisbon, the sages of that country could think of no

means more effectual to preserve the kingdom from utter ruin, than to entertain the people with an *auto-da-fé,* it having been decided by the University of Coimbra that burning a few people alive by a slow fire and with great ceremony is an infallible secret to prevent earthquakes.

In consequence thereof they had seized on a Biscayan for marrying his godmother,[†] and on two Portuguese for taking out the bacon of a larded pullet they were eating.[‡] After dinner, they came and secured Dr. Pangloss and his pupil Candide, the one for speaking his mind and the other for seeming to approve what he had said. They were conducted to separate apartments, extremely cool, where they were never incommoded with the sun. Eight days afterward they were each dressed in a *sanbenito,*[§] and their heads were adorned with paper miters. The miter and *sanbenito* worn by Candide were painted with flames reversed and with devils that had neither tails nor claws; but Dr. Plangloss' devils had both tails and claws, and his flames were upright. In these habits they marched in procession, and heard a very pathetic sermon, which was followed by a chant, beautifully intoned. Candide was flogged in regular cadence while the chant was being sung. The Biscayan and the two men who would not eat bacon were burned, and Pangloss was hanged, although this is not a common custom at these solemnities. The same day there was another earthquake, which made most dreadful havoc.[‖]

Candide, amazed, terrified, confounded, astonished, and trembling from head to foot, said to himself, "If this is the best of all possible worlds, what are the others? If I had only been whipped, I could have put up with it, as I did among the Bulgarians. But, O my dear Pangloss! You greatest of philosophers! That ever I should live to see you hanged, without knowing for what! O my dear Anabaptist, you best of men, that it should be your fate to be drowned in the very harbor! O Miss Cunegund, you mirror of young ladies! That it should be your fate to have your belly ripped open."

He was making the best of his way from the place where he had been preached to, whipped, absolved, and received benediction, when he was accosted by an old woman, who said to him, "Take courage, my son, and follow me."

---
*A ceremonial public execution held by the Inquisition. The one referred to here took place on June 20, 1756.

[†]This was held to contravene the established spiritual relationship.
[‡]This was considered by the Inquisition to be an infallible sign of belonging to the Jewish faith.
[§]A black sackcloth garment, painted with figures of devils, etc., identifying the several crimes.
[‖]A second tremor had actually occurred on December 21, 1755. Voltaire takes poetic license with the dates.

Denis Diderot
Supplement to the Voyage of Bouganville

Enlightenment thinkers often used examples from the non-European world in order to attack European values that seemed contrary to nature and reason. Denis Diderot reviewed Louis Antoine de Bouganville's *Voyage Around the World* (1771) and later wrote *Supplement to the Voyage of Bouganville.* In this work, Diderot explored some ideas, particularly the sex habits of Tahitians, treated by the French explorer. Diderot also denounced European imperialism and the exploitation of non-Europeans, and questioned traditional Christian sexual standards. In *Supplement,* Diderot constructed a dialogue between a Tahitian (Orou), who possesses the wisdom of a French philosophe, and a chaplain, whose defense of Christian sexual mores reveals Diderot's critique of the Christian view of human nature. Diderot thus used a representative of an alien culture to attack those European customs and beliefs that the philosophes detested. In the opening passage, before Orou's dialogue, a Tahitian elder rebukes Bouganville and his companions for bringing the evils of European civilization to his island.

"We [Tahitians] are free—but see where you [Europeans] have driven into our earth the symbol of our future servitude. You are neither a god nor a devil—by what right, then, do you enslave people? Orou! You who understand the speech of these men, tell every one of us, as you have told me, what they have written on that strip of metal—'This land belongs to us.' This land belongs to you! And why? Because you set foot in it? If some day a Tahitian should land on your shores, and if he should engrave on one of your stones or on the bark of one of your trees: 'This land belongs to the people of Tahiti,' what would you think? You are stronger than we are! And what does that signify? When one of our lads carried off some of the miserable trinkets with which your ship is loaded, what an uproar you made, and what revenge you took! And at that very moment you were plotting, in the depths of your hearts, to steal a whole country! You are not slaves; you would suffer death rather than be enslaved, yet you want to make slaves of us! Do you believe, then, that the Tahitian does not know how to die in defense of his liberty? This Tahitian, whom you want to treat as a chattel, as a dumb animal—this Tahitian is your brother. You are both children of Nature—what right do you have over him that he does not have over you?

"You came; did we attack you? Did we plunder your vessel? Did we seize you and expose you to the arrows of our enemies? Did we force you to work in the fields alongside our beasts of burden? We respected our own image in you. Leave us our own customs, which are wiser and more decent than yours. We have no wish to barter what you call our ignorance for your useless knowledge. We possess already all that is good or necessary for our existence. Do we merit your scorn because we have not been able to create superfluous wants for ourselves? When we are hungry, we have something to eat; when we are cold, we have clothing to put on. You have been

in our huts—what is lacking there, in your opinion? You are welcome to drive yourselves as hard as you please in pursuit of what you call the comforts of life, but allow sensible people to stop when they see they have nothing to gain but imaginary benefits from the continuation of their painful labors. If you persuade us to go beyond the bounds of strict necessity, when shall we come to the end of our labor? When shall we have time for enjoyment? We have reduced our daily and yearly labors to the least possible amount, because to us nothing seemed more desirable than leisure. Go and bestir yourselves in your own country; there you may torment yourselves as much as you like; but leave us in peace, and do not fill our heads with a hankering after your false needs and imaginary virtues. Look at these men—see how healthy, straight and strong they are. See these women—how straight, healthy, fresh and lovely they are. Take this bow in your hands—it is my own—and call one, two, three, four of your comrades to help you try to bend it. I can bend it myself. I work the soil, I climb mountains, I make my way through the dense forest, and I can run four leagues [about 12 miles] on the plain in less than an hour. Your young comrades have been hard put to it to keep up with me, and yet I have passed my ninetieth year. . . .

"Woe to this island! Woe to all the Tahitians now living, and to all those yet to be born, woe from the day of your arrival! We used to know but one disease—the one to which all men, all animals and all plants are subject—old age. But you have brought us a new one [venereal disease]: you have infected our blood. We shall perhaps be compelled to exterminate with our own hands some of our young girls, some of our women, some of our children, those who have lain with your women, those who have lain with your men. Our fields will be spattered with the foul blood that has passed from your veins into ours. Or else our children, condemned to die, will nourish and perpetuate the evil disease that you have given their fathers and mothers, transmitting it forever to their descendants." . . .

Before the arrival of Christian Europeans, love-making was natural and enjoyable. Europeans introduced an alien element, guilt.

But a while ago, the young Tahitian girl blissfully abandoned herself to the embraces of a Tahitian youth and awaited impatiently the day when her mother, authorized to do so by her having reached the age of puberty, would remove her veil and uncover her breasts. She was proud of her ability to excite men's desires, to attract the amorous looks of strangers, of her own relatives, of her own brothers. In our presence, without shame, in the center of a throng of innocent Tahitians who danced and played the flute, she accepted the caresses of the young man whom her young heart and the secret promptings of her senses had marked out for her. The notion of crime and the fear of disease have come among us only with your coming. Now our enjoyments, formerly so sweet, are attended with guilt and terror. That man in black [a priest], who stands near to you and listens to me, has spoken to our young men, and I know not what he has said to our young girls, but our youths are hesitant and our girls blush. Creep away into the dark forest, if you wish, with the perverse companion of your pleasures, but allow the good, simple Tahitians to reproduce themselves without shame under the open sky and in broad daylight.

In the following conversation between Orou and the chaplain, Christian sexual mores and the concept of God are questioned. Orou addresses the chaplain.

[OROU] "You are young and healthy and you have just had a good supper. He who sleeps alone, sleeps badly; at night a man needs a woman at his side. Here is my wife and here are my daughters. Choose whichever one pleases you most, but if you would like to do me a favor, you will give your preference to my youngest girl, who has not yet had any children."

The mother said: "Poor girl! I don't hold it against her. It's no fault of hers."

The chaplain replied that his religion, his holy orders, his moral standards and his sense of decency all prevented him from accepting Orou's invitation.

Orou answered: "I don't know what this thing is that you call 'religion,' but I can only have a low opinion of it because it forbids you to partake of an innocent pleasure to which Nature, the sovereign mistress of us all, invites everybody. It seems to prevent you from bringing one of your fellow creatures into the world, from doing a favor asked of you by a father, a mother and their children, from repaying the kindness of a host, and from enriching a nation by giving it an additional citizen. I don't know what it is that you call 'holy or-

ders,' but your chief duty is to be a man and to show gratitude. . . . I hope that you will not persist in disappointing us. Look at the distress you have caused to appear on the faces of these four women—they are afraid you have noticed some defect in them that arouses your distaste. But even if that were so, would it not be possible for you to do a good deed and have the pleasure of honoring one of my daughters in the sight of her sisters and friends? Come, be generous!"

THE CHAPLAIN You don't understand—it's not that. They are all four of them equally beautiful. But there is my religion! My holy orders! . . .

. . . [God] spoke to our ancestors and gave them laws; he prescribed to them the way in which he wishes to be honored; he ordained that certain actions are good and others he forbade them to do as being evil.

OROU I see. And one of these evils actions which he has forbidden is that of a man who goes to bed with a woman or girl. But in that case, why did he make two sexes?

THE CHAPLAIN In order that they might come together—but only when certain conditions are satisfied and only after certain initial ceremonies have been performed. By virtue of these ceremonies one man belongs to one woman and only to her; one woman belongs to one man and only to him.

OROU For their whole lives?

THE CHAPLAIN For their whole lives.

OROU So that if it should happen that a woman should go to bed with some man who was not her husband, or some man should go to bed with a woman that was not his wife . . . but that could never happen because the workman [God] would know what was going on, and since he doesn't like that sort of thing, he wouldn't let it occur.

THE CHAPLAIN No. He lets them do as they will, and they sin against the law of God (for that is the name by which we call the great workman) and against the law of the country; they commit a crime.

OROU I should be sorry to give offense by anything I might say, but if you don't mind, I'll tell you what I think.

THE CHAPLAIN Go ahead.

OROU I find these strange precepts contrary to nature, and contrary to reason. . . . Furthermore, your laws seem to me to be contrary to the general order of things. For in truth is there anything so senseless as a precept that forbids us to heed the changing impulses that are inherent in our being, or commands that require a degree of constancy which is not possible, that violate the liberty of both male and female by chaining them perpetually to one another? Is there anything more unreasonable than this perfect fidelity that would restrict us, for the enjoyment of pleasures so capricious, to a single partner—than an oath of immutability taken by two individuals made of flesh and blood under a sky that is not the same for a moment, in a cavern that threatens to collapse upon them, at the foot of a cliff that is crumbling into dust, under a tree that is withering, on a bench of stone that is being worn away? Take my word for it, you have reduced human beings to a worse condition than that of the animals. I don't know what your great workman is, but I am very happy that he never spoke to our forefathers, and I hope that he never speaks to our children, for if he does, he may tell them the same foolishness, and they may be foolish enough to believe it. . . .

OROU Are monks faithful to their vows of sterility?

THE CHAPLAIN No.

OROU I was sure of it. Do you also have female monks?

THE CHAPLAIN Yes.

OROU As well behaved as the male monks?

THE CHAPLAIN They are kept more strictly in seclusion, they dry up from unhappiness and die of boredom.

OROU So nature is avenged for the injury done to her! Ugh! What a country! If everything is managed the way you say, you are more barbarous than we are.

Montesquieu
The Persian Letters

Like the other philosophes, Charles Louis de Secondat, baron de la Brède et de Montesquieu (1689–1755), was an ardent reformer who used learning, logic, and wit to denounce the abuses of his day. His principal work, *The Spirit of the Laws* (1748), was a contribution to political liberty. To safeguard liberty from despotism, which he regarded as a pernicious form of government that institutionalizes cruelty and violence, Montesquieu advocated the principle of separation of powers, that is, the legislative, executive, and judiciary should not be in the hands of one person or body. Montesuieu's humanitarianism and tolerant spirit is also seen in an earlier work, *The Persian Letters* (1721), published anonymously in Holland. In the guise of letters written by imaginary Persian travelers in Europe, Montesquieu makes a statement. He denounces French absolutism, praises English parliamentary government, and attacks religious persecution, as in this comment on the Spanish Inquisition excepted below.

LETTER XXIX

Rica to Ibben, at Smyrna

. . . I have heard that in Spain and Portugal there are dervishes who do not understand a joke, and who have a man burned as if he were straw. Whoever falls into the hands of these men is fortunate only if he has always prayed to God with little bits of wood in hand, has worn two bits of cloth attached to two ribbons, and has sometimes been in a province called Galicia!* Otherwise, the poor devil is really in trouble. Even though he swears like a pagan that he is orthodox, they may not agree, and burn him for a heretic. It is useless for him to submit distinctions, for he will be in ashes before they even consider giving him a hearing.

Other judges presume the innocence of the accused; these always presume him guilty. In doubt they hold to the rule of inclining to severity, evidently because they consider mankind as evil. On the other hand, however, they hold such a high opinion of men that they judge them incapable of lying, for they accept testimony from deadly enemies, notorious women, and people living by some infamous profession. In passing sentence, the judges pay those condemned a little compliment, telling them that they are sorry to see them so poorly dressed in their brimstone shirts,† that the judges themselves are gentle men who abhor bloodletting, and are in despair at having to condemn them. Then, to console themselves, they confiscate to their own profit all the possessions of these poor wretches.

*The references are to a rosary, a scapular, and the pilgrimage shrine of St. James of Campostello in the Spanish province of Galicia.

†Those condemned by the Inquisition appeared for sentencing dressed in shirts colored to suggest the flames of their presumed post-mortem destination.

Happy the land inhabited by the children of the prophets! There these sad spectacles are unknown.* The holy religion brought by the angels trusts truth alone for its defense, and does not need these violent means for its preservation.

Paris, the 4th of the moon of Chalval, 1712

Montesquieu ridicules French sexual morality and French women.

Letter LII

Rica to Usbek, at ————

I was much amused at a social gathering the other day. There were women of all ages present: one of eighty, another of sixty, and one of forty, who had a niece of about twenty or twenty-one. Instinct led me to choose the youngest, and she whispered to me, "What do you think of my aunt, who at her age tries to play the beauty and wants to have lovers?" "She is wrong," I said. "Such plans become only you." A moment later, I found myself talking to the aunt. "What do you think," she asked me, "of that woman over there, who is at least sixty, but who spent more than an hour today in prettying herself?" "It is a waste of time," I told her. "One must have your charms to justify caring for them." I then went over to the unfortunate woman of sixty, pitying her deeply until she whispered, "Have you ever seen anything so absurd? Look at that woman of eighty, wearing flame-colored ribbons! She wants to look young and has succeeded only in being childish." "Ah! Good Lord!" I said to myself. "Do we feel only the ridiculousness of others? And yet perhaps it is a good thing." I thought further, "that we can find some consolation in the follies of others." However, I was in a mood to be amused, and I told myself that, having mounted sufficiently high, we might now try the descent. I began with the oldest. "Madame, you so closely resemble that woman to whom I was just talking that you seem to be sisters, I suppose of about the same age." "Quite right, sir," the said. "When one of us dies the other should have real cause for alarm, for I doubt that we are two days apart in age." Leaving this decrepit creature I went over to the one of sixty. "Madame, you must settle a bet I have made. I have wagered that you and that lady over there," indicating the woman of forty, "were the same age." "Upon my word," she said, "I don't believe there is a difference of six months." So far, so good; let us continue. I descended further, this time to the woman of forty. "Madame, would you please tell me if you are joking when you call that girl, over at the other table, your niece? You are surely as young as she; there is even something faded about her face that is quite missing in yours, and the lively colors of your complexion. . . ." "Listen," she said, "I am really her aunt, but her mother was at least twenty-five years older than I. We were not even of the same

marriage, and I have heard my departed sister say that her daughter and I were born the same year." "Just as I had said, madame; my astonishment was justified."

My dear Usbek, women who feel that the loss of their charms is prematurely aging them long to be young again. And how can they help deceiving others when they make such an effort to deceive themselves and to rid their minds of this most painful of all thoughts?

Paris, the 3rd of the moon of Chalval, 1713

Letter LV

Rica to Ibben, at Smyrna

Among the French there are certain unhappy men whom no one consoles—jealous husbands. There are men hated by everyone—jealous husbands. And there are men universally scorned—also jealous husbands.

Consequently there is no country with fewer jealous husband than France. Their tranquillity, however, is not based upon confidence in their wives but on the poor opinion they have of them. . . .

. . . Here husbands accept their lot with good grace and regard infidelities as fated by the stars. Any husband desiring to possess his wife to the exclusion of everyone else would be considered disruptive of the public happiness, a madman wanting to enjoy the sunlight and to forbid it to all others. . . .

A man who generally tolerates the infidelities of his wife is not disapproved but praised for his prudence; only in particular cases is he felt to be dishonored.

It is not that there are no virtuous women; there are, and one may say that they are distinguished. My guide always pointed them out to me, but they were all so ugly that one would have to be a saint not to hate virtue.

After what I have said of the manners of this country, you will readily see that the French do not admire constancy much. They believe it is as ridiculous to swear abiding love to one woman as it is to maintain that they will forever be in good health, or invariably happy.

Paris, the 7th of the moon of Zilcade, 1714

Letter XCIX

Rica to Rhedi, at Venice

I find the caprices of fashion among the French astonishing. They have forgotten how they were dressed last summer and have even less idea of how they will be dressed this winter; but the truly unbelievable thing is the cost to a husband of maintaining his wife in fashion.

What would be the use of my describing to you their dress and ornaments? A new fashion would come along and

---

*The Persians are the most tolerant of all the [Muslims].

destroy all my work and that of their workmen; before you received my letter, everything would be changed.

A woman leaving Paris for six months in the country returns as old-fashioned as if she had disappeared for thirty years. The son does not recognize the portrait of his mother, so alien to him are the clothes in which she is painted; he supposes the picture is of some American, or that the painter has indulged one of his fantasies.

Sometimes coiffures go up gradually, to be lowered all at once by a style revolution. At one time their immense height put the woman's face in her middle. At another, her feet are there, with her pedestal heels holding them high in the air. Who would believe it? Architects have often been obliged to raise, lower, and enlarge their doors according to the exigen-cies of dress style, which the rules of their art must be bent to serve. Sometimes you see an immense number of beauty patches on a face; the next day they are all gone. Formerly women had figures and teeth; today they are of no importance. In this changeable nation, whatever the jokers may say, daughters are made differently from their mothers.

As with style in dress, so it is with customs and fashions of living: the French change their manners with the age of the king. The monarch could even make this nation serious if he tried to do so. The prince impresses his characteristics on the court, the court upon the city, and the city upon the provinces. The soul of the sovereign is a mold which forms all the others.

PARIS, THE 8TH OF THE MOON OF SAPHAR, 1717

Jonathan Swift
Gulliver's Travels

As one of the greatest satirists of the English language, Jonathan Swift (1667–1745) is best known for *Travels into Several Remote Nations of the World,* better known as *Gulliver's Travels,* which was first published in 1726. Parodying a travelogue, the four books of Swift's masterpiece tell of the voyages of Lemuel Gulliver. His first voyage takes Gulliver to Lilliput, where the Lilliputians are only six inches tall and Gulliver is the giant; the situation is reversed, however, during Gulliver's second voyage, to Brobdingnag, a land of giants. The third voyage takes Gulliver to the floating island of Laputa, and Book IV, the most famous, describes Gulliver's voyage to the land of the Houyhnhnms (rational, virtuous horses), who tolerate and use the race of Yahoos (vicious and disgusting human beings) for menial services.

Gulliver's four voyages provided Swift with the opportunity to scrutinize the social, political, and economic institutions of his day, which seem hauntingly familiar even in today's world. In the land of the Lilliputians, Gulliver discovers that these miniature creatures by whom he is initially amused are, in reality, callous, cutthroat, back stabbing, and vengeful. Similarly, Gulliver assumes that the gigantic Brobdingnags must be contrary brutes, only to find that they live in an ideal society that is governed by a humane "philosopher-king," who places moral virtue ahead of maintaining political power. In his attack on the land of Laputa, Swift uses much of Book III to satirize the administration of Sir Robert Walpole, a Whig minister. Swift's finest satire is reserved for the Yahoos, atrocious exaggerations of the human race possessing virtually no rational sense. Today, the term *yahoo* is used as an epithet to describe any brutish, uncouth, or vicious person.

Just prior to the publication of *Gulliver's Travels,* Swift wrote a letter to Alexander Pope in which he proclaimed that in general he hated "that animal called man," although he loved individual humans. He declared that he would prove false the idea that the human being is an *"animal rationale* [rational animal]" and would, instead, show that a human being is really "only *rationis capax* [capable of reason]. Upon this great foundation of Misanthropy . . . the whole building of my Travells is erected." Therefore, on the one hand, Swift was simply restating the age-old Christian idea of original sin—humans are yahoos. But on the other hand, he was also expressing a mitigated optimism about humans—that they are capable of being rational—an idea that blossomed during the Enlightenment.

In the following passage from *Gulliver's Travels*, Gulliver discusses with a wise Houyhnhnm how "yahoos" behave in his native England. Here Swift is at his best in exposing and lampooning the foibles of his fellow Englishmen.

He asked me what were the usual causes or motives that made one country go to war with another. I answered they were innumerable, but I should only mention a few of the chief. Sometimes the ambition of princes, who never think they have land or people enough to govern; sometimes the corruption of ministers, who engage their master in a war in order to stifle or divert the clamour of the subjects against their evil administration. Difference in opinions hath cost many millions of lives: for instance, whether flesh be bread, or bread be flesh; whether the juice of a certain berry be blood or wine; whether whistling be a vice or a virtue; whether it be better to kiss a post, or throw it into the fire; what is the best colour for a coat, whether black, white, red, or gray; and whether it should be long or short, narrow or wide, dirty or clean; with many more. Neither are any wars so furious and bloody, or of so long continuance, as those occasioned by difference in opinion, especially if it be in things indifferent.

Sometimes the quarrel between two princes is to decide which of them shall dispossess a third of his dominions, where neither of them pretend to any right. Sometimes one prince quarrelleth with another, for fear the other should quarrel with him. Sometimes a war is entered upon, because the enemy is too strong, and sometimes because he is too weak. Sometimes our neighbours want the things which we have, or have the things which we want; and we both fight, till they take ours or give us theirs. It is a very justifiable cause of a war to invade a country after the people have been wasted by famine, destroyed by pestilence, or embroiled by factions among themselves. It is justifiable to enter into war against our nearest ally, when one of his towns lies convenient for us, or a territory of land, that would render our dominions round and complete. If a prince sends forces into a nation where the people are poor and ignorant, he may lawfully put half of them to death, and make slaves of the rest, in order to civilize and reduce them from their barbarous way of living. It is a very kingly, honourable, and frequent practice, when one prince desires the assistance of another to secure him against an invasion, that the assistant, when he hath driven out the invader, should seize on the dominions himself, and kill, imprison or banish the prince he came to relieve. Alliance by blood or marriage is a frequent cause of war between princes; and the nearer the kindred is, the greater is their disposition to quarrel: poor nations are hungry, and rich nations are proud; and pride and hunger will ever be at variance. For these reasons, the trade of a soldier is held the most honourable of all others; because a soldier is a Yahoo hired to kill in cold blood as many of his own species, who have never offended him, as possibly he can.

There is likewise a kind of beggarly princes in Europe, not able to make war by themselves, who hire out their troops to richer nations, for so much a day to each man; of which they keep three fourths to themselves, and it is the best part of their maintenance; such are those in Germany and other northern parts of Europe. . . .

. . . And being no stranger to the art of war, I gave him a description of cannons, culverins, muskets, carabines, pistols, bullets, powder, swords, bayonets, battles, sieges, retreats, attacks, undermines, countermines, bombardments, sea fights; ships sunk with a thousand men, twenty thousand killed on each side; dying groans, limbs flying in the air, smoke, noise, confusion, trampling to death under horses' feet; flight, pursuit, victory; fields strewed with carcases left for food to dogs, and wolves, and birds of prey; plundering, stripping, ravishing, burning, and destroying. And to set forth the valour of my own dear countrymen, I assured him that I had seen them blow up a hundred enemies at once in a siege, and as many in a ship, and beheld the dead bodies come down in pieces from the clouds, to the great diversion of the spectators.

I was going on to more particulars, when my master commanded me silence. He said whoever understood the nature of Yahoos might easily believe it possible for so vile an animal to be capable of every action I had named, if their strength and cunning equalled their malice. But as my discourse had increased his abhorrence of the whole species, so he found it gave him a disturbance in his mind, to which he was wholly a stranger before. He thought his ears being used to such abominable words, might by degrees admit them with less detestation. That although he hated the Yahoos of this country, yet he no more blamed them for their odious qualities, than he did a *gnnayh* (a bird of prey) for its cruelty, or a sharp stone for cutting his hoof. But when a creature pretending to reason could be capable of such enormities, he dreaded lest the corruption of that faculty might be worse than brutality itself. He seemed therefore confident, that instead of reason, we were only possessed of some quality fitted to increase our natural vices; as the reflection from a troubled stream returns the image of an ill-shapen body, not only larger, but more distorted.

He added, that he had heard too much upon the subject of war, both in this and some former discourses. There was another point which a little perplexed him at present. I had informed him, that some of our crew left their country on account of being ruined by *Law;* that I had already explained the meaning of the word; but he was at a loss how it should come to pass, that the law which was intended for every man's preservation, should be any man's ruin. Therefore he desired to be farther satisfied what I meant by law, and the dispensers thereof, according to the present practice in my own country; because he thought nature and reason were sufficient guides for a reasonable animal, as we pretended to be, in showing us what we ought to do, and what to avoid.

I assured his Honour that law was a science wherein I had not much conversed, further than by employing advocates, in vain, upon some injustices that had been done me: however, I would give him all the satisfaction I was able.

I said there was a society of men among us, bred up from their youth in the art of proving by words multiplied for the purpose, that white is black, and black is white, according as they are paid. To this society all the rest of the people are slaves. For example, if my neighbour hath a mind to my cow, he hires a lawyer to prove that he ought to have my cow from me. I must then hire another to defend my right, it being against all rules of law that any man should be allowed to speak for himself. Now in this case I who am the right owner lie under two great disadvantages. First, my lawyer, being practised almost from his cradle in defending falsehood, is quite out of his element when he would be an advocate for justice, which as an office unnatural, he always attempts with ill-will. The second disadvantage is that my lawyer must proceed with great caution, or else he will be reprimanded by the judges, and abhorred by his brethren, as one that would lessen the practice of the law. And therefore I have but two methods to preserve my cow. The first is to gain over my adversary's lawyer with a double fee, who will then betray his client by insinuating that he hath justice on his side. The second way is for my lawyer to make my cause appear as unjust as he can, by allowing the cow to belong to my adversary: and this, if it be skillfully done, will certainly bespeak the favour of the bench.

Now, your Honour is to know that these judges are persons appointed to decide all controversies of property, as well as for the trial of criminals, and picked out from the most dexterous lawyers, who are grown old or lazy, and having been biassed all their lives against truth and equity, are under such a fatal necessity of favouring fraud, perjury, and oppression, that I have known several of them refuse a large bribe from the side where justice lay, rather than injure the faculty, by doing any thing unbecoming their nature or their office.

It is a maxim among these lawyers, that whatever hath been done before may legally be done again: and therefore they take special care to record all the decisions formerly made against common justice and the general reason of mankind. These, under the name of *precedents,* they produce as authorities, to justify the most iniquitous opinions; and the judges never fail of directing accordingly.

In pleading they studiously avoid entering into the merits of the cause, but are loud, violent, and tedious in dwelling upon all circumstances which are not to the purpose. For instance, in the case already mentioned, they never desire to know what claim or title my adversary hath to my cow; but whether the said cow were red or black, her horns long or short, whether the field I graze her in be round or square, whether she was milked at home or abroad, what diseases she is subject to, and the like; after which they consult precedents, adjourn the cause from time to time, and in ten, twenty, or thirty years, come to an issue.

It is likewise to be observed, that this society hath a peculiar cant [dialect] and jargon of their own, that no other mortal can understand, and wherein all their laws are written, which they take special care to multiply; whereby they have wholly confounded the very essence of truth and falsehood, of right and wrong; so that it will take thirty years to decide whether the field left me by my ancestors for six generations belongs to me, or to a stranger three hundred miles off.

In the trial of persons accused for crimes against the state the method is much more short and commendable: the judge first sends to sound the disposition of those in power, after which he can easily hang or save the criminal, strictly preserving all due forms of law.

Here my master interposing, said it was a pity that creatures endowed with such prodigious abilities of mind as these lawyers, by the description I gave of them, must certainly be, were not rather encouraged to be instructors of others in wisdom and knowledge. In answer to which I assured his Honour that in all points out of their own trade, they were the most ignorant and stupid generation among us, the most despicable in common conversation, avowed enemies to all knowledge and learning, and equally disposed to pervert the general reason of mankind in every other subject of discourse, as in that of their own profession.

My master was yet wholly at a loss to understand what motives could incite this race of lawyers to perplex, disquiet, and weary themselves, and engage in a confederacy of injustice, merely for the sake of injuring their fellow-animals; neither could he comprehend what I meant in saying they did it for hire. Whereupon I was at much pains to describe to him the use of money, the materials it was made of, and the value of the metals, that when a Yahoo had got a great store of this precious substance, he was able to purchase whatever he had a mind to; the finest clothing, the noblest houses, great tracts of land, the most costly meats and drinks, and have his choice of the most beautiful females. Therefore since money alone was able to perform all these feats, our Yahoos thought they could never have enough of it to spend or save, as they found themselves inclined from their natual bent either to profusion or avarice. That the rich man enjoyed the fruit of the poor man's labour, and the latter were a thousand to one in proportion to the former. That the bulk of our people were forced to live miserably, by labouring every day for small wages to make a few live plentifully.

6 The French Revolution and Human Rights

In August 1789, the opening stage of the French Revolution, the newly created National Assembly adopted the Declaration of the Rights of Man and of Citizens, which expressed the liberal and universal ideals of the Enlightenment. The Declaration proclaimed that sovereignty derives from the people, that is, that the people are the source of political power; that men are born free and equal in rights; and that it is the purpose of government to protect the natural rights of the individual. Because these ideals contrasted markedly with the outlook of an absolute monarchy, a privileged aristocracy, and an intolerant clergy, some historians view the Declaration of Rights as the death knell of the Old Regime. Its affirmation of liberty, reason, and natural rights inspired liberal reformers in other lands.

The abolition of the special privileges of the aristocracy and the ideals proclaimed by the Declaration of the Rights of Man and of Citizens aroused the hopes of reformers in several areas: in what was considered radicalism, even by the framers of the Declaration of the Rights of Man, some women began to press for equal rights; humanitarians called for the abolition of the slave trade; and Jews, who for centuries had suffered disabilities and degradation, petitioned for full citizenship.

Declaration of the Rights of Man and of Citizens

Together with John Locke's *Second Treatise on Government,* the American Declaration of Independence, and the Constitution of the United States, the Declaration of the Rights of Man and of Citizens, which follows, is a pivotal document in the development of modern liberalism.

The Representatives of the people of FRANCE, formed into a NATIONAL ASSEMBLY, considering that ignorance, neglect, or contempt of human rights, are the sole causes of public misfortunes and corruptions of Government, have resolved to set forth in a solemn declaration, these natural, imprescriptible, and unalienable rights: that this declaration, being constantly present to the minds of the members of the body social, they may be ever kept attentive to their rights and their duties: that the acts of the legislative and executive powers of Government, being capable of being every moment compared with the end of political institutions, may be more respected: and also, that the future claims of the citizens, being directed by simple and incontestible principles, may always tend to the maintenance of the Constitution, and the general happiness.

For these reasons the NATIONAL ASSEMBLY doth recognize and declare, in the presence of the Supreme Being, and with the hope of his blessing and favor, the following *sacred* rights of men and of citizens:

I. *Men are born, and always continue, free, and equal in respect of their rights. Civil distinctions, therefore, can be founded only on public utility.*

II. *The end of all political associations, is, the preservation of the natural and imprescriptible rights of man; and these rights are liberty, property, security, and resistance of oppression.*

III. *The nation is essentially the source of all sovereignty; nor can any* INDIVIDUAL *or* ANY BODY OF MEN, *be entitled to any authority which is not expressly derived from it.*

IV. Political Liberty consists in the power of doing whatever does not injure another. The exercise of the natural rights of every man, has no other limits than those which are necessary to secure to every *other* man the free exercise of the same rights; and these limits are determinable only by the law.

V. The law ought to prohibit only actions hurtful to society. What is not prohibited by the law, should not be hindered; nor should any one be compelled to that which the law does not require.

VI. The law is an expression of the will of the community. All citizens have a right to concur, either personally, or by their representatives, in its formation. It should be the same to all, whether it protects or punishes; and *all being equal in its sight, are equally eligible to all honors, places, and employments, according to their different abilities, without any other distinction than that created by their virtues and talents.*

VII. No man should be accused, arrested, or held in confinement, except in cases determined by the law, and according to the forms which it has prescribed. All who promote, solicit, execute, or cause to be executed, arbitrary orders, ought to be punished; and every citizen called upon or apprehended by virtue of the law, ought immediately to obey, and renders himself culpable by resistance.

VIII. The law ought to impose no other penalties but such as are absolutely and evidently necessary; and no one ought to be punished, but in virtue of a law promulgated before the offence, and legally applied.

IX. Every man being presumed innocent till he has been convicted, whenever his detention becomes indispensible, all rigor [harshness] to him, more than is necessary to secure his person, ought to be provided against by the law.

X. No man ought to be molested on account of his opinions, not even on account of his *religious* opinions, provided his avowal of them does not disturb the public order established by the law.

XI. The unrestrained communication of thoughts and opinions being one of the most precious rights of man, every citizen may speak, write, and publish freely, provided he is responsible for the abuse of this liberty in cases determined by the law.

XII. A public force being necessary to give security to the rights of men and of citizens, that force is instituted for the benefit of the community, and not for the particular benefit of the persons with whom it is entrusted.

XIII. A common contribution being necessary for the support of the public force, and for defraying the other expenses of government, it ought to be divided equally among the members of the community, according to their abilities.

XIV. Every citizen has a right, either by himself or his representative, to a free voice in determining the necessity of public contributions, the appropriation of them, and their amount, mode of assessment and duration.

XV. Every community has a right to demand of all its agents, an account of their conduct.

XVI. Every community in which a separation of powers and a security of rights is not provided for, wants a constitution.

XVII. The rights to property being inviolable and sacred, no one ought to be deprived of it, except in cases of evident public necessity, legally ascertained, and on condition of a previous just indemnity.

Mary Wollstonecraft
A Vindication of the Rights of Woman

When in 1789 the French revolutionaries issued their Declaration of the Rights of Man, it was only a matter of time before a woman published a Declaration of the Rights of Woman. That feat was accomplished in the same year in France by Olympic de Gouges. In England, Mary Wollstonecraft (1759–1797), strongly influenced by her, published her own statement, *A Vindication of the Rights of Woman* in 1792. Her protest against the prevailing submissiveness of women was reinforced by the philosophy of the Enlightenment and the ideals of the French Revolution, which she observed firsthand from 1792 to 1794. A career woman, she made her living as a prolific writer closely associated with the radicals of her time, one of whom, William Godwin, she married shortly before her death. Wollstonecraft became famous for her vigorous protests against the subjection of women. Children, husbands, and society generally, she pleaded in *A Vindication of the Rights of Woman,* were best served by well-educated, self-reliant, and strong women capable of holding their own in the world.

. . . I have turned over various books written on the subject of education, and patiently observed the conduct of parents and the management of schools; but what has been the result?—a profound conviction that the neglected education of my fellow creatures is the grand source of the misery I deplore, and that women, in particular, are rendered weak and wretched. . . . The conduct and manners of women, in fact, evidently prove that their minds are not in a healthy state. . . . One cause of this . . . I attribute to a false system of education, gathered from the books written on this subject by men who, considering females rather as women than human creatures, have been more anxious to make them alluring mistresses than affectionate wives and rational mothers. . . .

. . . A degree of physical superiority of men cannot . . . be denied, and it is a noble prerogative! But not content with this natural preeminence, men endeavour to sink us still lower, merely to render us alluring objects for a moment. . . .

My own sex, I hope, will excuse me, if I treat them like rational creatures, instead of flattering their *fascinating* graces, and viewing them as if they were in a state of perpetual childhood, unable to stand alone. I earnestly wish to point out in what true dignity and human happiness consists. I wish to persuade women to endeavour to acquire strength, both of mind and body. . . .

Dismissing, then, those pretty feminine phrases, which the men condescendingly use to soften our slavish dependence, and despising that weak elegancy of mind, exquisite sensibility, and sweet docility of manners, supposed to be the sexual characteristics of the weaker vessel, I wish to show that elegance is inferior to virtue, that the first object of laudable ambition is to obtain a character as a human being, regardless of the distinction of sex. . . .

The education of women has of late been more attended to than formerly; yet they are still reckoned a frivolous sex, and ridiculed or pitied by the writers who endeavour by satire or instruction to improve them. It is acknowledged that they spend many of the first years of their lives in acquiring a smattering of accomplishments; meanwhile strength of body and mind are sacrificed to libertine notions of beauty, to the desire of establishing themselves—the only way women can rise in the world—by marriage. And this desire making mere animals of them, when they marry they act as such children may be expected to act,—they dress, they paint, and nickname God's creatures. Surely these weak beings are only fit for a seraglio [harem]! Can they be expected to govern a family with judgment, or take care of the poor babes whom they bring into the world? . . .

Contending for the rights of woman, my main argument is built on this simple principle, that if she be not prepared by education to become the companion of man, she will stop the progress of knowledge and virtue; for truth must be common to all, or it will be inefficacious with respect to its influence on general practice. And how can woman be expected to co-operate unless she knows why she ought to be virtuous? unless freedom strengthens her reason till she comprehends her duty, and see in what manner it is connected with her real good. If children are to be educated to understand the true principle of patriotism, their mother must be a patriot; and the love of mankind, from which an orderly train of virtues spring, can only be produced by considering the moral and civil interest of mankind; but the education and situation of woman at present shuts her out from such investigations. . . .

Consider—I address you as a legislator—whether, when men contend for their freedom, and to be allowed to judge for themselves respecting their own happiness, it be not inconsistent and unjust to subjugate women, even though you firmly believe that you are acting in the manner best calculated to promote their happiness? Who made man the exclusive judge, if woman partake with him of the gift of reason?

In this style argue tyrants of every denomination, from the weak king to the weak father of a family; they are all eager to crush reason, yet always assert that they usurp its throne only to be useful. Do you not act a similar part when you *force* all women, by denying them civil and political rights, to remain immured [imprisoned] in their families groping in the dark? for surely, sir, you will not assert that a duty can be binding which is not founded on reason? If, indeed, this be their destination, arguments may be drawn from reason; and thus augustly supported, the more understanding women acquire, the more they will be attached to their duty—comprehending it—for unless they comprehend it, unless their morals be fixed on the same immutable principle as those of man, no authority can make them discharge it in a virtuous manner. They may be convenient slaves, but slavery will have its constant effect, degrading the master and the abject dependent.

But if women are to be excluded, without having a voice, from a participation of the natural rights of mankind, prove first, to ward off the charge of injustice and inconsistency, that they [lack] reason, else this flaw in your NEW CONSTITUTION will ever show that man must, in some shape, act like a tyrant, and tyranny, in whatever part of society it rears its brazen front, will ever undermine morality. . . .

In what does man's pre-eminence over the brute creation consist? The answer is as clear as that a half is less than the whole, in Reason. . . . Yet . . . deeply rooted processes have clouded reason. . . . Men, in general, seem to employ their reason to justify prejudices, which they have imbibed, they can scarcely trace how, rather than to root them out.

The power of generalising ideas, of drawing comprehensive conclusions from individual observations . . . has not only been denied to women; but writers have insisted that it is inconsistent, with a few exceptions, with their sexual character. Let men prove this, and I shall grant that woman only exists for man. I must, however, previously remark, that the power of generalising ideas, to any great extent, is not very common amongst men or women. But this exercise is the true cultivation of the understanding; and everything conspires to render the cultivation of the understanding more difficult in the female than the male world. . . .

I shall not go back to the remote annals of antiquity to trace the history of woman; it is sufficient to allow that she has always been either a slave or a despot, and to remark that each of these situations equally retards the progress of reason. The grand source of female folly and vice has ever appeared to me to arise from narrowness of mind; and the very constitution of civil governments has put almost insuperable obstacles in the way to prevent the cultivation of the female understanding; yet virtue can be built on no other foundation. . . .

When do we hear of women who, starting out of obscurity, boldly claim respect on account of their great abilities or daring virtues? Where are they to be found? . . .

With respect to women, when they receive a careful education, they are either made fine ladies, brimful of sensibility, and teeming with capricious fancies, or mere notable women. The latter are often friendly, honest creatures, and have a shrewd kind of good sense, joined with worldly prudence, that often render them more useful members of society than the fine sentimental lady, though they possess neither greatness of mind nor taste. The intellectual world is shut against them. Take them out of their family or neighbourhood, and they stand still; the mind finding no employment, for literature affords a fund of amusement which they have never sought to relish, but frequently to despise. The sentiments and taste of more cultivated minds appear ridiculous, even in those whom chance and family connections have led them to love; but in mere acquaintance they think it all affectation.

A man of sense can only love such a woman on account of her sex, and respect her because she is a trusty servant. He lets her, to preserve his own peace, scold the servants, and go to church in clothes made of the very best materials. . . . [W]omen, whose minds are not enlarged by cultivation, or . . . by reflection, are very unfit to manage a family, for, by an undue stretch of power, they are always tyrannising to support a superiority that only tests on the arbitrary distinction of fortune.

Women have seldom sufficient serious employment to silence their feelings; a round of little cares, or vain pursuits frittering away all strength of mind and organs, they become naturally only objects of sense. In short, the whole tenor of female education (the education of society) tends to render the best disposed romantic and inconstant; and the remainder vain and [contemptible]. In the present state of society this evil can scarcely be remedied, I am afraid, in the slightest degree; should a more laudable ambition ever gain ground they may be brought nearer to nature and reason, and become more virtuous and useful as they grow more respectable. . . .

Women . . . all want to be ladies. Which is simply to have nothing to do, but listlessly to go they scarcely care where, for they cannot tell what.

But what have women to do in society? I may be asked, but to loiter with easy grace. . . . Women might certainly study the art of healing, and be physicians as well as nurses. . . . They might also study politics . . . for the reading of history will scarcely be more useful than the study of romances. . . . Business of various kinds, they might likewise pursue, if they were educated in a more orderly manner, which might save many from common and legal prostitution. . . . The few employments open to a woman, so far from being liberal, are menial. . . .

Some of these women might be restrained from marrying by a proper spirit of delicacy, and others may not have had it in their power to escape in this pitiful way from servitude; is not that Government then very defective, and very unmindful of the happiness of one-half of its members, that does not provide for honest, independent women, by encouraging them to fill respectable stations? . . .

It is a melancholy truth; yet such is the blessed effect of civilisation! the most respectable women are the most oppressed; and, unless they have understandings far superior to the common run of understandings, taking in both sexes, they must, from being created like contemptible beings, become contemptible. How many women thus waste life away the prey of discontent, who might have practised as physicians, regulated a farm, managed a shop, and stood erect, supported by their own industry, instead of hanging their heads. . . .

Would men but generously snap our chains, and be content with rational fellowship instead of slavish obedience, they would find us more observant daughters, more affectionate sisters, more faithful wives, more reasonable mothers—in a word, better citizens. We should then love them with true affection, because we should learn to respect ourselves; and the peace of mind of a worthy man would not be interrupted by the idle vanity of his wife, nor the babes sent to nestle in a strange bosom, having never found a home in their mother's. . . .

. . . The sexual distinction which men have so warmly insisted upon, is arbitrary. . . . Asserting the rights which women in common with men ought to contend for, I have not attempted to [make light of] their faults; but to prove them to be the natural consequence of their education and station in society. If so, it is reasonable to suppose that they will change their character, and correct their vices and follies, when they are allowed to be free in a physical, moral, and civil sense.

Let woman share the rights, and she will emulate the virtues of man; for she must grow more perfect when emancipated. . . .

Society of the Friends of Blacks

ADDRESS TO THE NATIONAL ASSEMBLY IN FAVOR OF THE ABOLITION OF THE SLAVE TRADE

Planters in the French West Indies and shipbuilding and sugar refining interests opposed any attempts to eliminate slavery or the slave trade since they profited handsomely from these institutions. On February 5, 1790, the Society of the Friends of Blacks, using the language of the Declaration of the Rights of Man, called for the abolition of the slave trade. Recognizing the power of proslavery forces, the society made it clear that it was not proposing the abolition of slavery itself. In 1791, the slaves of Saint Domingue revolted, and in 1794, the Jacobins in the National Convention abolished slavery in the French colonies. The island's white planters resisted the decree, and in 1801 Napoleon sent twenty thousand troops to Saint Domingue in an unsuccessful attempt to restore slavery. In 1804, the black revolutionaries established the independent state of Haiti.

Following are excerpts from the Society of the Friends of Blacks' address to the National Assembly.

The humanity, justice, and magnanimity that have guided you in the reform of the most profoundly rooted abuses gives hope to the Society of the Friends of Blacks that you will receive with benevolence its demand in favor of that numerous portion of humankind, so cruelly oppressed for two centuries.

This Society, slandered in such cowardly and unjust fashion, only derives its mission from the humanity that induced it to defend the blacks even under the past despotism. Oh! Can there be a more respectable title in the eyes of this august Assembly which has so often avenged the rights of man in its decrees?

You have declared them, these rights; you have engraved on an immortal monument that all men are born and remain free and equal in rights; you have restored to the French people these rights that despotism had for so long despoiled, . . . you have broken the chains of feudalism that still degraded a good number of our fellow citizens; you have announced the destruction of all the stigmatizing distinctions that religious or political prejudices introduced into the great family of humankind. . . .

We are not asking you to restore to French blacks those political rights which alone, nevertheless, attest to and maintain the dignity of man; we are not even asking for their liberty. No; slander, bought no doubt with the greed of the shipowners, ascribes that scheme to us and spreads it everywhere; they want to stir up everyone against us, provoke the planters and their numerous creditors, who take alarm even at gradual emancipation. They want to alarm all the French,

to whom they depict the prosperity of the colonies as inseparable from the slave trade and the perpetuity of slavery.

No, never has such an idea entered into our minds; we have said it, printed it since the beginning of our Society, and we repeat it in order to reduce to nothing this grounds of argument, blindly adopted by all the coastal cities, the grounds on which rest almost all their addresses [to the National Assembly]. The immediate emancipation of the blacks would not only be a fatal operation for the colonies; it would even be a deadly gift for the blacks, in the state of abjection and incompetence to which cupidity has reduced them. It would be to abandon to themselves and without assistance children in the cradle or mutilated and impotent beings.

It is therefore not yet time to demand that liberty; we ask only that one cease butchering thousands of blacks regularly every year in order to take hundreds of captives; we ask that one henceforth cease the prostitution, the profaning of the French name, used to authorize these thefts, these atrocious murders; we demand in a word the abolition of the slave trade. . . .

In regard to the colonists, we will demonstrate to you that if they need to recruit blacks in Africa to sustain the population of the colonies at the same level, it is because they wear out the blacks with work, whippings, and starvation; that, if they treated them with kindness and as good fathers of families, these blacks would multiply and that this population, always growing, would increase cultivation and prosperity. . . .

Have no doubt, the time when this commerce will be abolished, even in England, is not far off. It is condemned there in public opinion, even in the opinion of the ministers. . . .

If some motive might on the contrary push them [the blacks] to insurrection, might it not be the indifference of the National Assembly about their lot? Might it not be the insistence on weighing them down with chains, when one consecrates everywhere this eternal axiom: *that all men are born free and equal in rights.* So then therefore there would only be fetters and gallows for the blacks while good fortune glimmers only for the whites? Have no doubt, our happy revolution must re-electrify the blacks whom vengeance and resentment have electrified for so long, and it is not with

punishments that the effect of this upheaval will be repressed. From one insurrection badly pacified will twenty others be born, of which one alone can ruin the colonists forever.

It is worthy of the first free Assembly of France to consecrate the principle of philanthropy which makes of humankind only one single family, to declare that it is horrified by this annual carnage which takes place on the coasts of Africa, that it has the intention of abolishing it one day, of mitigating the slavery that is the result, of looking for and preparing, from this moment, the means.

Petition of the Jews of Paris, Alsace, and Lorraine to the National Assembly, January 28, 1790

After several heated debates, the National Assembly granted full citizenship to the Jews on September 27, 1791. Influenced by the French example, almost all European states in the nineteenth century would also emancipate the Jews dwelling within their borders. In the following *Petition of the Jews of Paris, Alsace, and Lorraine to the National Assembly, January 28, 1790,* the Jews pointed to historic wrongs and invoked the ideals of the Revolution as they called for equal rights.

A great question is pending before the supreme tribunal of France. *Will the Jews be citizens or not?*

Already, this question has been debated in the National Assembly; and the orators, whose intentions were equally patriotic, did not agree at all on the result of their discussion. Some wanted Jews admitted to civil status. Others found this admission dangerous. A third opinion consisted of preparing the complete improvement of the lot of the Jews by gradual reforms.

In the midst of all these debates, the national assembly believed that it ought to adjourn the question. . . .

It was also said that the adjournment was based on the necessity of knowing with assurance what were the true desires of the Jews; given, it was added, the disadvantages of according to this class of men rights more extensive than those they want.

But it is impossible that such a motive could have determined the decree of the national assembly.

First, the wish of the Jews is perfectly well-known, and cannot be equivocal. They have presented it clearly in their addresses of 26 and 31 August, 1789. The Jews of Paris repeated it in a *new address* of 24 December. They ask that all

the degrading distinctions that they have suffered to this day be abolished and that they be declared CITIZENS. . . .

Their desires, moreover, as we have just said, are well known; and we will repeat them here. They ask to be CITIZENS. . . .

In truth, [the Jews] are of a religion that is condemned by the one that predominates in France. But the time has passed when one could say that it was only the dominant religion that could grant access to advantages, to prerogatives, to the lucrative and honorable posts in society. For a long time they confronted the Protestants with this maxim, worthy of the Inquisition, and the Protestants had no civil standing in France. Today, they have just been reestablished in the possession of this status; they are assimilated to the Catholics in everything; the intolerant maxim that we have just recalled can no longer be used against them. Why would they continue to use it as an argument against the Jews?

In general, civil rights are entirely independent from religious principles. And all men of whatever religion, whatever sect they belong to, whatever creed they practice, provided that their creed, their sect, their religion does not offend the principles of a pure and severe morality, all these men, we say, equally able to serve the fatherland, defend its interests, contribute to its splendor, should all equally have the title and the rights of citizen. . . .

[The Jews] are reproached at the same time for the vices that make them unworthy of civil status and the principles which render them at once unworthy and incompetent. A rapid glance at the bizarre as well as cruel destiny of these unfortunate individuals will perhaps remove the disfavor with which some seek to cover them. . . .

Always persecuted since the destruction of Jerusalem, pursued at times by fanaticism and at others by superstition, by turn chased from the kingdoms that gave them an asylum and then called back to these same kingdoms, excluded from all the professions and arts and crafts, deprived even of the right to be heard as witnesses against a Christian, relegated to separate districts like another species of man with whom one fears having communication, pushed out of certain cities which have the privilege of not receiving them, obligated in others to pay for the air that they breathe as in Augsburg where they pay a *florin* an hour or in Bremen a *ducat* a day, subject in several places to shameful tolls. Here is the list of a part of the harassment still practiced today against the Jews.

And [critics of the Jews] would dare to complain of the state of degradation into which some of them can be plunged! They would dare to complain of their ignorance and their vices! Oh! Do not accuse the Jews, for that would only precipitate onto the Christians themselves all the weight of these accusations. . . .

Let us now enter into more details. The Jews have been accused of the crime of usury. But first of all, all of them are not usurers; and it would be as unjust to punish them all for the offense of some as to punish all the Christians for the usury committed by some of them and the speculation of many. . . .

Reflect, then, on the condition of the Jews. Excluded from all the professions, ineligible for all the positions, deprived even of the capacity to acquire property, not daring and not being able to sell openly the merchandise of their commerce, to what extremity are you reducing them? You do not want them to die, and yet you refuse them the means to live: you refuse them the means, and you crush them with taxes. You leave them therefore really no other resource than usury. . . .

Everything that one would not have dared to undertake, moreover, or what one would only have dared to undertake with an infinity of precautions a long time ago, can now be done and one must dare to undertake it in this moment of universal regeneration, when all ideas and all sentiments take a new direction; and we must hasten to do so. Could one still fear the influence of a prejudice against which reason has appealed for such a long time, when all the former abuses are destroyed and all the former prejudices overturned? Will not the numerous changes effected in the political machine uproot from the people's minds most of the ideas that dominated them? Everything is changing; the lot of the Jews must change at the same time; and the people will not be more surprised by this particular change than by all those which they see around them everyday. This is therefore the moment, the true moment to make justice triumph: attach the improvement of the lot of the Jews to the revolution; amalgamate, so to speak, this partial revolution to the general revolution. Your efforts will be crowned with success, and the people will not protest, and time will consolidate your work and render it unshakable.

CHAPTER

14

Age of Romanticism

In 1815 the European scene had changed. Napoleon was exiled to the island of St. Helena, and a Bourbon king, in the person of Louis XVIII, again reigned in France. The Great Powers of Europe, meeting at Vienna, had drawn up a peace settlement that awarded territory to the states that had fought Napoleon and restored to power some rulers dethroned by the French emperor. The Congress of Vienna also organized the Concert of Europe to guard against a resurgence of the revolutionary spirit that had kept Europe in turmoil for some twenty-five years. The conservative leaders of Europe wanted no more Robespierres who resorted to terror and no more Napoleons who sought to dominate the continent.

However, reactionary rulers' efforts to turn the clock back to the Old Regime could not contain the forces unleashed by the French Revolution. Between 1820 and 1848, a series of revolts rocked Europe. The principal causes were liberalism, which demanded constitutional government and the protection of the freedom and rights of the individual citizen, and nationalism, which called for the reawakening and unification of the nation and its liberation from foreign domination.

In the 1820s, the Concert of Europe crushed a quasi-liberal revolution in Spain and liberal uprisings in Italy, and Tsar Nicholas I subdued liberal officers who challenged tsarist autocracy. The Greeks, however, successfully fought for independence from the Ottoman Turks.

Between 1830 and 1832, another wave of revolutions swept over Europe. Italian liberals and nationalists failed to free Italy from foreign rule or to wrest reforms from autocratic princes, and the tsar's troops crushed a Polish bid for independence from Russian rule. But in France, rebels overthrew the reactionary Bourbon Charles X in 1830 and replaced him with a more moderate ruler, Louis Philippe; a little later Belgium gained its independence from Holland.

The year 1848 was decisive in the struggle for liberty and nationhood. In France, democrats overthrew Louis Philippe and established a republic that gave all men the right to vote. However, in Italy and Germany, revolutions attempting to unify each land failed, as did a bid in Hungary for independence from the Hapsburg Empire. After enjoying initial successes, the revolutionaries were crushed by superior might, and their liberal and nationalist objectives remained largely unfulfilled. By 1870, however, many nationalist aspirations had been realized. The Hapsburg Empire granted Hungary autonomy in 1867, and by 1870–1871, the period of the Franco-Prussian War, Germany and Italy became unified states. That authoritarian and militaristic Prussia unified Germany, rather than liberals like those who had fought in the revolutions of 1848, affected the future of Europe.

In the early nineteenth century, a new cultural orientation, Romanticism, emphasized the liberation of human emotions and the free expression of personality in artistic creations. The Romantics' attack on the rationalism of the Enlightenment and their veneration of the past influenced conservative thought, and their concern for a people's history and traditions contributed to the development of nationalism. By encouraging innovation in art, music, and literature, the Romantics greatly enriched European cultural life.

1 Conservatism

In the period after 1815, conservatism was the principal ideology of those who repudiated the Enlightenment and the French Revolution. Conservatives valued tradition over reason, aristocratic and clerical authority over equality, and the community over the individual. Edmund Burke (1729–1797), a leading Anglo-Irish statesman and political thinker, was instrumental in shaping the conservative outlook. His *Reflections on the Revolution in France* (1790) attacked the violence and fundamental principles of the Revolution. Another leading conservative was Joseph de Maistre (1753–1821), who fled his native Sardinia in 1792 (and again in 1793) after it was invaded by the armies of the new French Republic. De Maistre denounced the Enlightenment for spawning the French Revolution, defended the church as a civilizing agent that made individuals aware of their social obligations, and affirmed tradition as a model more valuable than instant reforms embodied in "paper constitutions."

The symbol of conservatism in the first half of the nineteenth century was Prince Klemens von Metternich (1773–1859) of Austria. A bitter opponent of Jacobinism and Napoleon, he became the pivotal figure at the Congress of Vienna (1814–1815), where European powers met to redraw the map of Europe after their victory over France. Metternich said that the Jacobins had subverted the pillars of civilization and that Napoleon, by harnessing the forces of the Revolution, had destroyed the traditional European state system. No peace was possible with Napoleon, who championed revolutionary doctrines and dethroned kings, and whose rule rested not on legitimacy but on conquest and charisma. No balance of power could endure an adventurer who obliterated states and sought European domination.

Edmund Burke
Reflections on the Revolution in France

Burke regarded the revolutionaries as wild-eyed fanatics who had uprooted all established authority, tradition, and institutions, thereby plunging France into anarchy. Not sharing the faith of the philosophes in human goodness, Burke held that without the restraints of established authority, people revert to savagery. For Burke, monarchy, aristocracy, and Christianity represented civilizing forces that tamed the beast in human nature. By undermining venerable institutions, he said, the French revolutionaries had opened the door to anarchy and terror. Burke's *Reflections,* excerpts of which follow, was instrumental in the shaping of conservative thought.

. . . You [revolutionaries] chose to act as if you had never been moulded into civil society, and had every thing to begin anew. You began ill, because you began by despising every thing that belonged to you. . . . If the last generations of your country appeared without much lustre in your eyes, you might have passed them by, and derived your claims from a more early race of ancestors. Under a pious predilection for those ancestors, your imaginations would have realized in them a standard of virtue and wisdom, beyond the vulgar practice of the hour: and you would have risen with the example to whose imitation you aspired. Respecting your fore-fathers, you would have been taught to respect yourselves. You would not have chosen to consider the French as a people of yesterday, as a nation of low-born servile wretches, until the emancipating year of 1789. . . . By following wise examples you would have given new examples of wisdom to the world. You would have rendered the cause of liberty venerable in the eyes of every worthy mind in every nation. . . . You would have had a free constitution; a potent monarchy; a disciplined army; a reformed and venerated clergy; a mitigated but spirited nobility, to lead your virtue. . . .

Compute your gains: see what is got by those extravagant and presumptuous speculations which have taught your leaders to despise all their predecessors, and all their contemporaries, and even to despise themselves, until the moment in which they became truly despicable. By following those false lights, France has bought undisguised calamities at a higher price than any nation has purchased the most unequivocal blessings! . . . France, when she let loose the reins of regal authority, doubled the licence, of a ferocious dissoluteness in manners, and of an insolent irreligion in opinions and practices; and has extended through all ranks of life, . . . all the unhappy corruptions that usually were the disease of wealth and power. This is one of the new principles of equality in France. . . .

. . . The science of government being therefore so practical in itself, and intended for such practical purposes, a matter which requires experience, and even more experience than any person can gain in his whole life, however sagacious and observing he may be, it is with infinite caution that any man ought to venture upon pulling down an edifice which has answered in any tolerable degree for ages the common purposes of society, or on building it up again, without having models and patterns of approved utility before his eyes. . . .

. . . The nature of man is intricate; the objects of society are of the greatest possible complexity; and therefore no simple disposition or direction of power can be suitable either to man's nature, or to the quality of his affairs.

When ancient opinions of life are taken away, the loss cannot possibly be estimated. From that moment we have no compass to govern us; nor can we know distinctly to what port we steer. . . .

. . . Nothing is more certain than that our manners, our civilization, and all the good things which are connected with manners and with civilization have, in this European world of ours, depended for ages upon two principles and were, indeed, the result of both combined: I mean the spirit of a gentleman and the spirit of religion. . . .

Burke next compares the English people with the French revolutionaries.

. . . Thanks to our sullen resistance to innovation, thanks to the cold sluggishness of our national character, we still bear the stamp of our forefathers. . . . We are not the converts of Rousseau; we are not the disciples of Voltaire; Helvetius has made no progress amongst us.[1] Atheists are not our preachers; madmen are not our lawgivers. We know that *we* have made no discoveries, and we think that no discoveries are to be made, in morality, nor many in the great principles of government. . . . We fear God; we look up with awe to kings, with affection to parliaments, with duty to magistrates, with reverence to priests, and with respect to nobility. . . .

. . . We are afraid to put men to live and trade each on his own private stock of reason, because we suspect that this stock in each man is small, and that the individuals would do better to avail themselves of the general bank and capital of nations and of ages.

---

[1]Rousseau, Voltaire, and Helvétius were French philosophes of the eighteenth century noted, respectively, for advocating democracy, attacking the abuses of the Old Regime, and applying scientific thinking to moral principles.

Klemens von Metternich
THE ODIOUS IDEAS OF THE PHILOSOPHES

Two decades of revolutionary warfare had shaped Metternich's political thinking. After the fall of Napoleon, Metternich worked to restore the European balance and to suppress revolutionary movements. In the following memorandum to Tsar Alexander I, dated December 15, 1820, Metternich denounces the French philosophes for their "false systems" and "fatal errors" that weakened the social fabric and gave rise to the French Revolution. In their presumption, the philosophes forsook the experience and wisdom of the past, trusting only their own thoughts and inclinations.

The progress of the human mind has been extremely rapid in the course of the last three centuries. This progress having been accelerated more rapidly than the growth of wisdom (the only counterpoise to passions and to error); a revolution prepared by the false systems . . . has at last broken out. . . .

. . . There were . . . some men [the philosophes], unhappily endowed with great talents, who felt their own strength, and . . . who had the art to prepare and conduct men's minds to the triumph of their detestable enterprise—an enterprise all the more odious as it was pursued without regard to results, simply abandoning themselves to the one feeling of hatred of God and of His immutable moral laws.

France had the misfortune to produce the greatest number of these men. It is in her midst that religion and all that she holds sacred, that morality and authority, and all connected with them, have been attacked with a steady and systematic animosity, and it is there that the weapon of ridicule has been used with the most ease and success.

Drag through the mud the name of God and the powers instituted by His divine decrees, and the revolution will be prepared! Speak of a social contract,[2] and the revolution is accomplished! The revolution was already completed in the palaces of Kings, in the drawing-rooms and boudoirs of certain cities, while among the great mass of the people it was still only in a state of preparation. . . .

. . . The French Revolution broke out, and has gone through a complete revolutionary cycle in a very short period, which could only have appeared long to its victims and to its contemporaries. . . .

. . . The revolutionary seed had penetrated into every country. . . . It was greatly developed under the *régime* of the military despotism of Bonaparte. His conquests displaced a number of laws, institutions, and customs; broke through bonds sacred among all nations, strong enough to resist time itself; which is more than can be said of certain benefits conferred by these innovators.

---

[2]The social contract theory consisted essentially of the following principles: (1) people voluntarily enter into an agreement to establish a political community; (2) government rests on the consent of the governed; and (3) people possess natural freedom and equality, which they do not surrender to the state. These principles were used to challenge the divine right of kings and absolute monarchy.

2 Liberalism

Conservatism was the ideology of the old order that was hostile to the Enlightenment and the French Revolution; in contrast, liberalism aspired to carry out the promise of the philosophes and the Revolution. Liberals called for a constitution that protected individual liberty and denounced censorship, arbitrary arrest, and other forms of repression. They believed that through reason and education, social evils could be remedied. Liberals rejected an essential feature of the Old Regime—the special privileges of the aristocracy and the clergy—and held that the individual should be judged on the basis of achievement, not birth. At the core of the liberal outlook lay the conviction that the individual would develop into a good and productive human being and citizen if not coerced by governments and churches.

John Stuart Mill
On Liberty

Freedom of thought and expression were principal concerns of nineteenth-century liberals. The classic defense of intellectual freedom is *On Liberty* (1859), written by John Stuart Mill (1806–1873), a prominent British philosopher. Mill argued that no individual or government has a monopoly on truth, for all human beings are fallible. Therefore, the government and the majority have no legitimate authority to suppress views, however unpopular; they have no right to interfere with a person's liberty so long as that person's actions do no injury to others. Nothing is more absolute, contended Mill, than the inviolable right of all adults to think and live as they please so long as they respect the rights of others. For Mill, toleration of opposing and unpopular viewpoints is a necessary trait in order for a person to become rational, moral, and civilized.

The object of this essay is to assert one very simple principle, as entitled to govern absolutely the dealings of society with the individual. . . . That principle is that the sole end for which mankind are warranted, individually or collectively, in interfering with the liberty of action of any of their number is self-protection. That the only purpose for which power can be rightfully exercised over any member of a civilized community, against his will, is to prevent harm to others. His own good, either physical or moral, is not a sufficient warrant. He cannot rightfully be compelled to do or forbear because it will be better for him to do so, because it will make him happier, because, in the opinions of others, to do so would be wise or even right. These are good reasons for remonstrating with him, or reasoning with him, or persuading him, or entreating him, but not for compelling him or visiting him with any evil in case he do otherwise. To justify that, the conduct from which it is desired to deter him must be calculated to produce evil to someone else. The only part of the conduct of anyone for which he is amenable to society is that which concerns others. In the part which merely concerns himself, his independence is, of right, absolute. Over himself, over his own body and mind, the individual is sovereign. . . .

. . . This, then, is the appropriate region of human liberty. It comprises, first, the inward domain of consciousness, demanding liberty of conscience in the most comprehensive sense, liberty of thought and feeling, absolute freedom of opinion and sentiment on all subjects, practical or speculative, scientific, moral, or theological. The liberty of expressing and publishing opinions may seem to fall under a different principle, since it belongs to that part of the conduct of an individual which concerns other people, but, being almost of as much importance as the liberty of thought itself and testing in great part on the same reasons, is practically inseparable from it. Secondly, the principle requires liberty of tastes and pursuits, of framing the plan of our life to suit our own character, of doing as we like, subject to such consequences as may follow, without impediment from our fellow creatures, so long as what we do does not harm them, even though they should think our conduct foolish, perverse, or wrong. Thirdly, from this liberty of each individual follows the liberty, within the same limits, of combination among individuals; freedom to unite for any purpose not involving harm to others: the persons combining being supposed to be of full age and not forced or deceived.

No society in which these liberties are not, on the whole, respected is free, whatever may be its form of government; and none is completely free in which they do not exist absolute and unqualified. The only freedom which deserves the name is that of pursuing our own good in our own way, so long as we do not attempt to deprive others of theirs or impede their efforts to obtain it. Each is the proper guardian of his own health, whether bodily *or* mental and spiritual. Mankind are greater gainers by suffering each other to live as seems good to themselves than by compelling each to live as seems good to the rest. . . .

. . . Let us suppose, therefore, that the government is entirely at one with the people, and never thinks of exerting any power of coercion unless in agreement with what it conceives to be their voice. But I deny the right of the people to exercise such coercion, either by themselves or by their government. The power itself is illegitimate. The best government has no more title to it than the worst. It is as noxious, or more noxious, when exerted in accordance with public opinion than when in opposition to it. If all mankind minus one were of one opinion, mankind would be no more justified in silencing that one person than he, if he had the power, would be justified in silencing mankind. Were an opinion a personal possession of no value except to the owner, if to be obstructed in the enjoyment of it were simply a private injury, it would make some difference whether the injury was inflicted only on a few persons or on many. But the peculiar evil of silencing the expression of an opinion is that it is robbing the human race, posterity as well as the existing generation—those who dissent from the opinion, still more than those who hold it. If the opinion is right, they are deprived of the opportunity of exchanging error for truth; if wrong, they lose, what is almost as great a benefit, the clearer perception and livelier impression of truth produced by its collision with error.

3   English Romantic Poetry

Romantics attacked the outlook of the Enlightenment, protesting that the philosophes' excessive intellectualizing and their mechanistic view of the physical world and human nature distorted and fettered the human spirit and thwarted cultural creativity. The rationalism of the philosophes, said the romantics, had reduced human beings to soulless thinking machines, and vibrant nature to lifeless wheels, cogs, and pulleys. In contrast to the philosophes' scientific and analytic approach, the romantics asserted the intrinsic value of emotions and imagination and extolled the spontaneity, richness, and uniqueness of the human spirit. To the philosophes, the emotions obstructed clear thinking.

For romantics, feelings and imagination were the human essence, the source of cultural creativity, and the avenue to true understanding. Their beliefs led the romantics to rebel against strict standards of aesthetics that governed artistic creations. They held that artists, musicians, and writers must trust their own sensibilities and inventiveness and must not be bound by textbook rules; the romantics focused on the creative capacities inherent in the emotions and urged individuality and freedom of expression in the arts. In the Age of Romanticism, the artist and poet succeeded the scientist as the arbiters of Western civilization.

Deeply influenced by the French Revolutions, English literary figures recognized that the same revolutionary zeal, which had swept aside a traditional political and social order, was capable of inspiring fresh literary ventures. In direct contrast to the neoclassical tradition of John Dryden, Alexander Pope, and Samuel Johnson, who viewed poetry as an art form created according to formal rules of rhyme and meter and filled it with classical allusions and scholarly artifices, a new breed of English poets asserted that artists must not be bound by the textbook rules and ancient models but should trust their own sensibilities and inventiveness. For the great English poet William Wordsworth, and his like-minded contemporaries, a poem was not a technically proficient literary form, but, rather, a creative expression of the imagination. Moreover, they believed that Nature could stimulate creativity and teach human beings a higher form of knowledge. They were particularly taken by the ideas of the ancient Greek philosopher, Plato, who postulated a somewhat mystical World of Being wherein all pure forms—such as Goodness, Truth, Beauty, and Justice—resided. Romantic poets were captivated by the link between the wonders of Nature (which they often personified) and Plato's mystical World of Being, and they asserted that Nature was as close to a perfect expression of the pure Forms that human beings could ever find in their earthly life.

William Wordsworth
"The Tables Turned"

The works of William Wordsworth (1770–1850) exemplify many tendencies of the Romantic Movement. In the interval during which he tried to come to grips with his disenchantment with the French Revolution, Wordsworth's creativity reached its height.

Both the theory and practice of writing poetry were revolutionized when Wordsworth and Samuel Taylor Coleridge (1772–1834) published their *Lyrical Ballads, with a Few Other Poems,* in 1798. In his Preface to the second edition of *Lyrical Ballads* (1800), Wordsworth delineated the difference between poetry that is "formally conceived" and poetry that is the result of "the spontaneous overflow of powerful feelings." Commenting on the purpose and style of the poems contained in the *Lyrical Ballads,* he stated, "I have said that each of these poems has a purpose: . . . namely to illustrate the manner in which our feelings and ideas are associated in a state of excitement." The Preface to *Lyrical Ballads* became known as the manifesto of Romanticism, demonstrating a shift in perspective, comparable to the shift begun by Descartes in philosophy, but for Wordsworth imagination and feeling, not mathematics and logic, yielded highest truth.

The philosophes had regarded nature as a giant machine, all of whose parts worked in perfect precision and whose laws could be uncovered through the scientific method. The Romantics rejected this mechanical model. To them, Nature was a living organism fitted with beautiful forms whose inner meaning was grasped through the human imagination; they sought from Nature a higher truth than mechanical law. In "The Tables Turned," Wordsworth exalts Nature as humanity's teacher.

Up! up! my Friend, and quit your books;
Or surely you'll grow double:
Up! up! my Friend, and clear your looks;
Why all this toil and trouble?

The sun, above the mountain's head,
A freshening lustre mellow
Through all the long green fields has spread,
His first sweet evening yellow.

Books! 'tis a dull and endless strife:
Come, hear the woodland linnet [Old World finch],
How sweet his music! on my life,
There's more of wisdom in it.

And hark! how blithe the throstle [thrush] sings!
He, too, is no mean preacher:
Come forth into the light of things,
Let Nature be your Teacher.

She has a world of ready wealth,
Our minds and hearts to bless—
Spontaneous wisdom breathed by health,
Truth breathed by cheerfulness.

One impulse from a vernal wood
May teach you more of man,
Of moral evil and of good,
Than all the sages can.

Sweet is the lore which Nature brings;
Our meddling intellect
Mis-shapes the beauteous forms of things:—
We murder to dissect.

Enough of Science and of Art;
Close up those barren leaves [book pages];
Come forth, and bring with you a heart
That watches and receives.

William Wordsworth
Ode: Intimations of Immortality from Recollections of Early Childhood

Much of Wordsworth's poetry is autobiographical. For example, from 1791 until 1792, Wordsworth traveled throughout France, savoring the sights and sounds of freedom. But when French radicals seized control of the government and began their Reign of Terror, Wordsworth felt betrayed and became despondent. On the verge of a total mental collapse, Wordsworth's sister, Dorothy, and Coleridge suggested that he return to the Wye River Valley (where England meets Wales) to recapture his poetic muse by communing with Nature. In 1802, Wordsworth began to compose his "Ode: Intimations of Immortality from Recollections of Early Childhood," and he wrote about the subject matter of the poem and the circumstances under which he wrote the poem:

Nothing was more difficult for me in childhood than to admit the notion of death as a state applicable to my own being. . . . I used to brood over the stories of Enoch and Elijah[1] and almost to persuade myself that whatever might become of others I'd be translated in something of the same way to heaven. . . . [T]he poem rests entirely upon two recollections of childhood, one that of a splendour in the objects of sense which is passed away, and the other an indisposition to bend to the law of death as applying to our own particular case. A Reader who has not a vivid recollection of these feelings having existed in his mind cannot understand the poem.

The original title of the poem was simply "Ode" followed by an inscription from Virgil's *Ecologue IV:* "Let us sing of somewhat higher things." Today, however, the poem has a longer title and opens with three lines taken from the concluding lines of Wordsworth's poem, "My Heart Leaps Up":

The Child is father of the Man;
And I could wish my days to be
Bound each to each by natural piety.

In the quoted lines of Wordsworth's poem, he reflects on his belief (adapted from Plato) that the human soul exists independently of the body and that it pre-existed before becoming incarnate in the body. Moreover, Wordsworth purported that when the soul is put in a body it gradually loses its vision of that which is immortal. Thus, he asserts "the Child is Father of the Man," and wishes that he could be in possession of the absolute truths he once possessed when he existed only as pure soul.

Like Plato, Wordsworth also believed that a human being's soul is immortal; therefore, death is nothing more than the soul's separation from the body. These reflections are at the heart of Wordsworth "Ode" which opens with him thinking about the time when everything on earth seemed completely new—Plato's concept of pure Forms. He then ponders the beauty of the cycle of Nature—how the rainbow and rose fade, the moon ceases to shine during the day, birds and lambs mature, and how Nature continually regenerates her beauties. Wordsworth then pens some of his most memorable lines pertaining to the human experience:

Not in entire forgetfulness,
And not in utter nakedness,
But trailing clouds of glory do we come
From God, who is our home . . .

The lines excerpted below illustrate how human beings gradually lose their vision of immortality by becoming imprisoned in a material body ("her Inmate Man"), which causes them to forget the eternal truths of the "imperial palace" of God's heaven—similar to Plato's World of Being.

There was a time when meadow, grove, and stream,
The earth, and every common sight,
   To me did seem
    Apparell'd in celestial light,
The glory and the freshness of a dream.

It is not now as it has been of yore;—
   Turn wheresoe'er I may,
    By night or day.
The things which I have seen I now can see no more.

---

[1]According to the Old Testament, Enoch, a descendant of Adam, and the prophet, Elijah, did not die a typical human death, but, rather, they were transported to heaven in some kind of miraculous way. "Enoch walked with God, and he was not; for God took him" (Genesis 5:24) and "Elijah went up by a whirlwind into heaven" (II Kings 2:11). Similarly, in the New Testament, the Apostle Paul refers to Enoch's being "taken": "and he [Enoch] was not found, because God had taken him" (Hebrews 11:5).

The Rainbow comes and goes,
And lovely is the Rose,
The Moon doth with delight
Look round her when the heavens are bare:
Waters on a starry night
Are beautiful and fair:
The sunshine is a glorious birth;
But yet I know, where'er I go,
That there hath pass'd away a glory from the earth.
Now, while the Birds thus sing a joyous song,
And while the young Lambs bound
As to the tabor's sound,

To me alone there came a thought of grief:
A timely utterance gave that thought relief,
And I again am strong.
The Cataracts blow their trumpets from the steep,
No more shall grief of mine the season wrong;
I hear the Echoes through the mountains throng,
The Winds come to me from the fields of sleep,
And all the earth is gay,
Land and sea
Give themselves up to jollity,
And with the heart of May
Doth every Beast keep holiday,
Thou Child of Joy,
Shout round me, let me hear thy shouts. thou happy Shepherd Boy!

Ye blessed Creatures, I have heard the call
Ye to each other make; I see
The heavens laugh with you in your jubilee;
My heart is at your festival,
My head hath it's coronal,
The fullness of your bliss, I feel—I feel it all.
Oh evil day! if I were sullen
While the Earth herself is adorning,
This sweet May-morning,
And the Children are pulling,
On every side,
In a thousand vallies far and wide,
Fresh flowers; while the sun shines warm,
And the Babe leaps up on his mother's arm:—
I heal, I hear, with joy I hear!
—But there's a Tree, of many one,
A single Field which I have look'd upon,
Both of them speak of something that is gone:
The Pansy at my feet
Doth the same tale repeat:
Whither is fled the visionary gleam?
Where is it now, the glory and the dream?
Our birth is but a sleep and a forgetting:
The Soul that rises with us, our life's Star,
Hath had elsewhere it's setting,
And cometh from afar:
Not in entire forgetfulness,

And not in utter nakedness,
But trailing clouds of glory do we come
From God, who is our home:
Heaven lies about us in our infancy!
Shades of the prison-house begin to close
Upon the growing Boy,
But He beholds the light, and whence it flows,
He sees it in his joy;
The Youth, who daily farther from the East
Must travel, still is Nature's Priest,
And by the vision splendid
Is on his way attended;
At length the Man perceives it die away,
And fade into the light of common day.
Earth fills her lap with pleasures of her own;
Yearnings she hath in her own natural kind,
And, even with something of a Mother's mind,
And no unworthy aim,
The homely nurse doth all she can
To make her foster-child, her Inmate Man,
Forget the glories he hath known,
And that imperial palace whence he came.

The concluding lines from Wordsworth's "Ode" demonstrate further his affinity for Plato's philosophy and his understanding of the concept of *recollection*— whereby a soul remembers (at least in part) what it once knew so completely—particularly by pondering the beauty of the natural world. Wordsworth, however, cautions that we can never totally recapture the immortal truths we once knew, for "nothing can bring back the hour / Of splendour in the grass, or glory in the flower."

A place of thought where we in waiting lie;
Thou little Child, yet glorious in the might
Of untam'd pleasures, on thy Being's height,
Why with such earnest pains dost thou provoke
The Years to bring the inevitable yoke,
Thus blindly with thy blessedness at strife?
Full soon thy Soul shall have her earthly freight,
And custom lie upon thee with a weight,
Heavy as frost, and deep almost as life!

O joy! that in our embers
Is something that doth live,
That nature yet remembers
What was so fugitive!
The thought of our past years in me doth breed
Perpetual benedictions: not indeed
For that which is most worthy to be blest;
Delight and liberty, the simple creed
Of Childhood, whether fluttering or at rest,
With new-born hope for ever in his breast:—

Not for these I raise
    The song of thanks and praise;
    But for those obstinate questionings
    Of sense and outward things,
    Fallings from us, vanishings;
    Blank misgivings of a Creature
Moving about in worlds not realiz'd,
High instincts, before which our mortal Nature
Did tremble like a guilty Thing surpriz'd:
    But for those first affections,
    Those shadowy recollections,
        Which, be they what they may,
Are yet the fountain light of all our day,
Are yet a master light of all our seeing;
        Uphold us, cherish us, and make
Our noisy years seem moments in the being
Of the eternal Silence: truths that wake,
        To perish never;
Which neither listlessness, nor mad endeavour,
        Nor Man nor Boy,
Nor all that is at enmity with joy,
Can utterly abolish or destroy!
        Hence, in a season of calm weather,
        Though inland far we be,
Our Souls have sight of that immortal sea
        Which brought us hither,
        Can in a moment travel thither,
And see the Children sport upon the shore,
And hear the mighty waters rolling evermore.

Then, sing ye Birds, sing, sing a joyous song!
        And let the young Lambs bound
        As to the tabor's sound!
    We in thought will join your throng,

Ye that pipe and ye that play,
Ye that through your hearts to day
Feel the gladness of the May!

What though the radiance which was once so bright
Be now for ever taken from my sight,
        Though nothing can bring back the hour
Of splendour in the grass, of glory in the flower;
        We will grieve not, rather find
        Strength in what remains behind.
        In the primal sympathy
        Which having been must ever be,
        In the soothing thoughts that spring
        Out of human suffering,
        In the faith that looks through death,
In years that bring the philosophic mind.

And oh ye Fountains, Meadows, Hills, and Groves,
Think not of any severing of our loves!
Yet in my heart of hearts I feel your might;
I only have relinquish'd one delight
To live beneath your more habitual sway.
I love the Brooks which down their channels fret,
Even more than when I tripp'd lightly as they;
The innocent brightness of a new-born Day
        Is lovely yet;
The Clouds that gather round the setting sun
Do take a sober colouring from an eye
That hath kept watch o'er man's mortality;
Another race hath been, and other palms are won.
Thanks to the human heart by which we live,
Thanks to its tenderness, its joys, and fears,
To me the meanest flower that blows can give
Thoughts that do often lie too deep for tears.

William Blake
"Milton"

William Blake (1757–1827) was a British engraver, poet, and religious mystic. He also affirmed the creative potential of the imagination and expressed distaste for the rationalist-scientific outlook of the Enlightenment, as is clear from these lines in his poem "Milton."

. . . the Reasoning Power in Man:
This is a false Body; an Incrustation [scab] over my Immortal
Spirit; a Selfhood, which must be put off & annihilated alway[s]
To cleanse the Face of my Spirit by Self-examination,
To bathe in the Waters of Life, to wash off the Not Human,
I come in Self-annihilation & the grandeur of Inspiration,

To cast off Rational Demonstration by Faith in the Saviour,
To cast off the rotten rags of Memory by Inspiration,
To cast off Bacon, Locke & Newton from Albion's covering[1] . . .

---

[1]Bacon, Locke, and Newton were British thinkers who valued reason and science, and Albion is an ancient name for England.

John Keats
"La Belle Dame Sans Merci"

In this so-called "Great Year" of 1818, John Keats (1795–1821) composed two of his most remarkable poems: "La Belle Dame Sans Merci" and "Ode on a Grecian Urn," portions of which follow. In the spring of 1821, Keats' good friend, Percy Bysshe Shelley, learned of his death at the age of twenty-five from tuberculosis. Keats was buried at the Protestant Cemetery in Rome, and, at his request, no name nor date appeared on his headstone, only the inscription "Here lies one whose name was writ in water"—meaning that he did not expect to be remembered. As fate would have it, water also was the cause of Shelley's death, for on July 8, 1822, during a violent storm, he drowned while piloting his small boat, the *Don Juan.* When his body finally washed up on the shore, Shelley was identified by a volume of poetry he had in his pocket, for the page was turned to Keats' poem "The Eve of St. Agnes."

The title of "La Belle Dame Sans Merci" comes from a medieval poem, "The Lovely Lady Without Pity," written by Alain Chartier (c. 1385–c. 1433), which details the sad tale of a mortal man being devastated by his love for a supernatural woman. Keats' version of the story details the love a knight has for a faery (or fairy), and he uses the form of dialogue associated with folk ballads—the first three verses are directed to the knight, the victim of love, by an unnamed observer of the scene, and the remainder of the poem consists of the knight's response. The tragedy of a lost love was a recurrent theme among Romantic writers, as was their fascination with the mystical, or supernatural, which heightened one's emotions.

I

Ah, what can ail thee, wretched wight,
    Alone and palely loitering;
The sedge[1] is wither'd from the lake,
    And no birds sing.

II

Ah, what can ail thee, wretched wight,
    So haggard and so woe-begone?
The squirrel's granary is full,
    And the harvest's done.

III

I see a lilly on thy brow,
    With anguish moist and fever dew;
And on thy cheek a fading rose
    Fast withereth too.

IV

I met a lady in the meads[2]
    Full beautiful, a faery's child;
Her hair was long, her foot was light,
    And her eyes were wild.

V

I set her on my pacing steed,
    And nothing else saw all day long;
For sideways would she lean, and sing
    A faery's song.

VI

I made a garland for her head,
    And bracelets too, and fragrant zone;[3]
She look'd at me as she did love,
    And made sweet moan.

[1]*Sedge* is a grasslike plant without a stem that grows in a clump, usually in a marshlike area.

[2]*Meads* are meadows.
[3]*Zone* means girdle.

VII

She found me roots of relish sweet,
    And honey wild, and manna dew;
And sure in language strange she said,
    I love thee true.

VIII

She took me to her elfin grot,[4]
    And there she gaz'd and sighed deep,
And there I shut her wild sad eyes—
    So kiss'd to sleep.

IX

And there we slumber'd on the moss,
    And there I dream'd, ah woe betide,
The, latest[5] dream I ever dream'd
    On the cold hill side.

---

[4]An *elfin grot* refers to an elf's small dwelling place.
[5]*Latest* means last.

X

I saw pale kings, and princes too,
    Pale warriors, death-pale were they all;
Who cry'd—"La belle Dame sans merci
    Hath thee in thrall!"

XI

I saw their starv'd lips in the gloam[6]
    With horrid warning gaped wide,
And I awoke, and found me here
    On the cold hill side.

XII

And this is why I sojourn here
    Alone and palely loitering,
Though the sedge is wither'd from the lake,
    And no birds sing.

---

[6]*Gloam* refers to the time of day called dusk, which signals the arrival of night.

John Keats
"Ode on a Grecian Urn"

The Grecian urn of Keats' ode existed only in his imagination, but what a fascinating image it is: young lovers are seen in "mad pursuit," and although they never kiss, neither does their love ever fade; trees never lose their leaves; and musicians never tire of playing their melodies. In essence, the images on the urn reveal to Keats a sense of immortality, for the images, which would have been nothing but "fleeting moments" in the natural world, have been captured on the urn for all eternity to share. Each verse captures Keats' fascination with a different scene, and each question begs the reader to appreciate what Keats is seeing in his mind's eye. The poem is brought to a close with the dictum, "Beauty is truth, truth beauty," for Keat this eternal verity is "all ye need to know." These concluding lines are counted among some of the most famous, and oft-quoted lines, in the history of the English language.

I

Thou still unravish'd bride of quietness,
    Thou foster-child of silence and slow time,
Sylvan[1] historian, who canst thus express
    A flowery tale more sweetly than our rhyme:
What leaf-fring'd legend haunts about thy shape
    Of deities or mortals, or of both,
        In Tempe or the dales of Arcady?[2]
    What men or gods are these? What maidens loth?
What mad pursuit? What struggle to escape?
    What pipes and timbrels? What wild ecstasy?

II

Heard melodies are sweet, but those unheard
    Are sweeter; therefore, ye soft pipes, play on;
Not to the sensual ear,[3] but, more endear'd,
    Pipe to the spirit ditties of no tone:
Fair youth, beneath the trees, thou canst not leave
    Thy song, nor ever can those trees be bare;
        Bold Lover, never, never canst thou kiss,
Though winning near the goal—yet, do not grieve;
    She cannot fade, though thou hast not thy bliss,
        For ever wilt thou love, and she be fair!

III

Ah, happy, happy boughs! that cannot shed
    Your leaves, nor ever bid the Spring adieu:
And, happy melodist, unwearied,

For ever piping songs for ever new;
More happy love! more happy, happy love!
    For ever warm and still to be enjoy'd,
        For ever panting, and for ever young;
All breathing human passion far above,
    That leaves a heart high-sorrowful and cloy'd,
        A burning forehead, and a parching tongue.

IV

Who are these coming to the sacrifice?
    To what green altar, O mysterious priest,
Lead'st thou that heifer lowing at the skies,
    And all her silken flanks with garlands drest?
What little town by river or sea shore,
    Or mountain-built with peaceful citadel,
        Is emptied of this folk, this pious morn?
And, little town, thy streets for evermore
    Will silent be; and not a soul to tell
        Why thou art desolate, can e'er return.

V

O Attic[4] shape! Fair attitude! with brede
    Of marble men and maidens overwrought,[5]
With forest branches and the trodden weed;
    Thou, silent form, dost tease us out of thought
As doth eternity: Cold Pastoral!
    When old age shall this generation waste,
        Thou shalt remain, in midst of other woe
Than ours, a friend to man, to whom thou sayst,
    "Beauty is truth, truth beauty,"[6]—that is all
        Ye know on earth, and all ye need to know.

---

[1]*Sylvan* references that which is rustic, representing a forest or woodland.
[2]*Tempe* is a lush valley in Greece that often is used to mean sylvan beauty, and *Arcady* refers to the place in ancient Greece that was associated with pastoral perfection.
[3]*Sensual ear* refers to the physical sense of hearing, rather than the "spiritual ear" which is the essence of much of the music Keats imagines when contemplating the urn.

[4]*Attic* refers to the region in Greece where its capital, Athens, is located.
[5]*Overwrought* in this verse refers to the ornamentation of the urn, including its interwoven patterns called "brede."
[6]"Beauty is truth, truth beauty" are lines found in a volume of Keats poetry from 1820, *Annals of the Fine Arts.*

Percy Bysshe Shelley
"Sonnet"

Like his close friend Byron, Percy Bysshe Shelley (1792–1822) was born into an aristocratic family, suffered ridicule during his early schooling, led a tempestuous life, and died young—at the age of twenty-nine. The two great influences on

Shelley's thought were the ancient Greek philosopher, Plato, and William God-win, a radical social philosopher. Even while he was married to his first wife, Harriet Westbrook, Shelley fell in love with Godwin's daughter, Mary, whose mother was Mary Wollstonecraft, author of *A Vindication of the Rights of Woman* (see page 99). In 1813, Shelley abandoned Harriet and eloped to France with Mary Godwin. But during the autumn, Harriet drowned herself in London, and Shelley subsequently lost custody of their two children. Shelley finally married Mary, and they moved to Italy, but in 1819, tragedy struck when their two children died within nine months of each other. In such a desperate situation, Shelley penned *Prometheus Unbound: A Lyrical Drama in Four Acts.*

The following poem, "Sonnet," reflects the Romantics' fascination with truth and love. In it, a disheartened man searches for something to love that will brighten the "gloomy scene." In spite of his quest, however, Shelley reveals that such a truth remains as inscrutable to him as it does to "the Preacher"—a reference to the fatalistic author of the biblical book of Ecclesiastes.

Lift not the painted veil which those who live
Call Life: though unreal shapes be pictured there,
And it but mimic all we would believe
With colours idly spread,—behind, lurk Fear
And Hope, twin Destinies; who ever weave
Their shadows, o'er the chasm, sightless and drear.
I knew one who had lifted it—he sought,

For his lost heart was tender, things to love,
But found them not, alas! nor was there aught
The world contains, the which he could approve.
Through the unheeding many he did move,
A splendour among shadows, a bright blot
Upon this gloomy scene, a Spirit that strove
For truth, and like the Preacher found it not.

Percy Bysshe Shelley
"Ode to the West Wind"

In 1819, while in Italy, Shelley composed what many readers regard to be his finest poem—"Ode to the West Wind."* The Romantic poets, including Shelley, not only associated the changing of the wind with the cycle of the seasons, but they also regarded wind as a metaphor for one's soul or spirit—in this case, "the breath of Autumn's being"—that appears to destroy things in the fall so that it can regenerate new life in the springtime of the year. For this poem, Shelley invented a unique type of stanza, consisting of four tercets (three-line verses) which conclude with a couplet (two-line verse) that rhymes with the middle line of the tercet that immediately precedes it.

---

*This poem was conceived and chiefly written in a wood that skirts the Arno, near Florence, and on a day when that tempestuous wind, whose temperature is at once mild and animating, was collecting the vapours which pour down the autumnal rains. They began, as I foresaw, at sunset with a violent tempest of hail and rain, attended by that magnificent thunder and lightning peculiar to the Cisalpine regions.

The phenomenon alluded to at the conclusion of the third stanza is well known to naturalists. The vegetation at the bottom of the sea, of rivers, and of lakes, sympathizes with that of the land in the change of seasons, and is consequently influenced by the winds which announce it.

I

O wild West Wind, thou breath of Autumn's being,
Thou, from whose unseen presence the leaves dead
Are driven, like ghosts from an enchanter fleeing,

Yellow, and black, and pale, and hectic red,
Pestilence-stricken multitudes: O thou,
Who chariotest to their dark wintry bed

The wingèd seeds, where they lie cold and low,
Each like a corpse within its grave, until
Thine azure sister of the Spring[1] shall blow

Her clarion[2] o'er the dreaming earth, and fill
(Driving sweet buds like flocks to feed in air)
With living hues and odours plain and hill:

Wild Spirit, which art moving everywhere;
Destroyer and preserver; hear, oh, hear!

II

Thou on whose stream, mid the steep sky's commotion,
Loose clouds like earth's decaying leaves are shed,
Shook from the tangled boughs of Heaven and Ocean,[3]

Angels of rain and lightning: there are spread
On the blue surface of thine aëry surge,
Like the bright hair uplifted from the head

Of some fierce Maenad,[4] even from the dim verge
Of the horizon to the zenith's height,
The locks of the approaching storm. Thou dirge

Of the dying year, to which this closing night
Will be the dome of a vast sepulchre,
Vaulted with all thy congregated might

Of vapours, from whose solid atmosphere
Black rain, and fire, and hail will burst: oh, hear!

III

Thou who didst waken from his summer dreams
The blue Mediterranean, where he lay,
Lulled by the coil of his crystàlline streams,[5]

Beside a pumice isle in Baiae's bay,[6]
And saw in sleep old palaces and towers
Quivering within the wave's intenser day,

All overgrown with azure moss and flowers
So sweet, the sense faints picturing them! Thou
For whose path the Atlantic's level powers

Cleave themselves into chasms, while far below
The sea-blooms and the oozy woods which wear
The sapless foliage of the ocean, know

Thy voice, and suddenly grow gray with fear,
And tremble and despoil themselves: oh, hear!

IV

If I were a dead leaf thou mightest bear;
If I were a swift cloud to fly with thee;
A wave to pant beneath thy power, and share

The impulse of thy strength, only less free
Than thou, O uncontrollable! If even
I were as in my boyhood, and could be

The comrade of thy wanderings over Heaven,
As then, when to outstrip thy skiey speed
Scarce seemed a vision; I would ne'er have striven

As thus with thee in prayer in my sore need.
Oh, lift me as a wave, a leaf, a cloud!
I fall upon the thorns of life! I bleed!

A heavy weight of hours has chained and bowed
One too like thee: tameless, and swift, and proud.

---

[1]*Sister of the Spring* refers to the regenerative power of the spring wind, as opposed to the autumn wind that Shelley is considering in the poem.
[2]*Clarion* refers to a high-pitched trumpet sound.
[3]*Heaven and Ocean* is Shelley's way of linking the natural rise of water vapor from the oceans into the sky to create the puffy clouds in the heavens.
[4]A *maenad* was a mythical woman whose frenzied dance was in honor of Dionysus, the Greek god of wine, intoxication, and fertility. One myth speaks of his death in the autumn only to be raised again to life in the spring.

---

[5]*Crystalline streams* connotes the visibly colored streams that flow into the Mediterranean Sea.
[6]*Baiae's bay* is a reference to an area west of Naples which was formed from volcanic stone call pumice and served as the site for estates of ancient Roman emperors.

V

Make me thy lyre,[7] even as the forest is:
What if my leaves are falling like its own!
The tumult of thy mighty harmonies

Will take from both a deep, autumnal tone,
Sweet though in sadness. Be thou, Spirit fierce,
My spirit! Be thou me, impetuous one!

Drive my dead thoughts over the universe
Like withered leaves to quicken a new birth!
And, by the incantation of this verse,

Scatter, as from an unextinguished hearth
Ashes and sparks, my words among mankind!
Be through my lips to unawakened earth

The trumpet of a prophecy! O, Wind,
If Winter comes, can Spring be far behind?

[7]This reference to *lyre* corresponds to the Aeolian lyre, known as a wind harp, which creates musical harmony when the wind blows through it.

George Gordon—Lord Byron
Childe Harold's Pilgrimage

Throughout the nineteenth century, Europeans viewed George Gordon (1788–1824), better known as Lord Byron, as the one person who embodied the fundamental attributes of Romanticism, and they sought to emulate him. Byron led an adventurous life, disdained convention, and epitomized the creative genius in rebellion against society. From the beginning of his life, Byron knew ridicule, and, later in life, he learned to mock those members of "polite society" who had given him such great grief. He critically satirized the social conventions that allowed them to think that they were better than he was. Byron was a descendant of two aristocratic families, and during the first ten years of his life, he lived in Aberdeen, Scotland, where his mother raised him as a strict Calvinist. Byron, however, soon rebelled against his dogmatic upbringing. Disabled by congenital lameness, he spent much of his early life trying to overcome it by swimming, boxing, fencing, and becoming an expert horseman. At Trinity College in Cambridge, he became self-indulgent and sexually promiscuous.

In 1809, after attaining his master of arts degree, Byron and a close friend journeyed to Turkey, Albania, Greece, Malta, Spain, and Portugal. These travels served as the basis for his first masterpiece, *Childe Harold's Pilgrimage,* excerpts of which appear below. With the publication of the first two books, in 1812, Byron became an overnight sensation. He added Book III to the poem, in 1816, after visiting Waterloo (where Napoleon, who fascinated Byron, suffered his great defeat) and journeying up the Rhine River into Switzerland. During his stay at Lake Geneva, Byron became good friends with another English Romantic poet—Percy Bysshe Shelley. Byron then crossed the Alps into Italy, where he visited Venice and Rome and all points in between. These wanderings became the basis for the fourth, and final, book of *Childe Harold's Pilgrimage.*

Although "Canto the First" begins with a description of how "Childe Harold" came to leave England to travel to Portugal, it is best remembered for the following verses that express Byron's outrage with Napoleon's invasion of Spain in 1808.

XXXVIII

Hark! heard you not those hoofs of dreadful note?
Sounds not the clang of conflict on the heath?
Saw ye not whom the reeking sabre smote;
Nor saved your brethren ere they sank beneath
Tyrants and tyrants' slaves? . . .

LIII

And must they fall? the young, the proud, the brave,
To swell one bloated Chief's unwholesome reign?
No step between submission and a grave?
The rise of rapine and the fall of Spain?
And doth the Power that man adores ordain
Their doom, nor heed the suppliant's appeal?
Is all that desperate Valour acts in vain?
And Counsel sage, and patriotic Zeal,
The Veteran's skill, Youth's fire, and Manhood's heart of
    steel?

"Canto the Third" contains a particularly moving description of the emotions Childe Harold (Byron included) feels when he arrives at Waterloo, the place of Napoleon Bonaparte's demise.

XVIII

And Harold stands upon this place of skulls,
The grave of France, the deadly Waterloo!
How in an hour the power which gave annuls
Its gifts, transferring fame as fleeting too!
In "pride of place" here last the eagle flew,
Then tore with bloody talon the rent plain,
Pierced by the shaft of banded nations through;
Ambition's life and labours all were vain;
He wears the shatter'd links of the world's broken chain.

XIX

Fit retribution! Gaul may champ the bit
And foam in fetters;—but is Earth more free?
Did nations combat to make *One* submit;
Or league to teach all kings true sovereignty?
What! shall reviving Thraldom again be
The pach'd-up idol of enlighten'd days?
Shall we, who struck the Lion down, shall we
Pay the Wolf homage? proffering lowly gaze
And servile knees to thrones? No; *prove* before ye praise!

XX

If not, o'er one fallen despot boast no more!
In vain fair cheeks were furrow'd with hot tears
For Europe's flowers long rooted up before
The trampler of her vineyards; in vain years
Of death, depopulation, bondage, fears,
Have all been borne, and broken by the accord
Of roused-up millions.

In the final canto, Childe Harold contemplates the ruins of Venice and Rome, but his melancholic ruminations only superficially mask his appreciation for the cause of "Freedom," especially the American Revolution, and he wonders aloud if the whole of Europe is now destined to submit to the authoritarian powers reinstated by the Congress of Vienna in 1815.

XCIII

What from this barren being do we reap?
Our senses narrow, and our reason frail,
Life short, and truth a gem which loves the deep,
And all things weigh'd in custom's falsest scale;
Opinion an omnipotence,—whose veil
Mantles the earth with darkness, until right
And wrong are accidents, and men grow pale
Lest their own judgments should become too bright,
And their free thoughts be crimes, and earth have too much
    light.

XCIV

And thus they plod in sluggish misery,
Rotting from sire to son, and age to age,
Proud of their trampled nature, and so die,
Bequeathing their hereditary rage
To the new race of inborn slaves, who wage
War for their chains, and rather than be free,
Bleed gladiator-like, and still engage
Within the same arena where they see
Their fellows fall before, like leaves of the same tree.

XCV

I speak not of men's creeds—they rest between
Man and his Maker—but of things allow'd,
Averr'd, and known,—and daily, hourly seen—
The yoke that is upon us doubly bow'd,
And the intent of tyranny avow'd,
The edict of Earth's rulers, who are grown

The apes of him who humbled once the proud,
And shook them from their slumbers on the throne;
Too glorious, were this all his mighty arm had done.

XCVI

Can tyrants but by tyrants conquer'd be,
And Freedom find no champion and no child
Such as Columbia[1] saw arise when she
Sprung forth a Pallas[2] arm'd and undefiled?
Or must such minds be nourish'd in the wild,
Deep in the unpruned forest, 'midst the roar
Of cataracts, where nursing Nature smiled
On infant Washington?[3] Has Earth no more
Such seeds within her breast, or Europe no such shore?

XCVII

But France got drunk with blood to vomit crime,
And fatal have her Saturnalia[4] been

[1]*Columbia* is a reference to the United States.
[2]*Pallas* refers to Pallas Athene—patron goddess of ancient Athens.
[3]*Washington* is a reference to George Washington—the first president of the United States.
[4]*Saturnalia* was an ancient Roman festival characterized by revelry and feasting.

To Freedom's cause, in every age and clime;
Because the deadly days which we have seen,
And vile Ambition, that built up between
Man and his hopes an adamantine[5] wall,
And the base pageant last upon the scene,
Are grown the pretext for the eternal thrall
Which nips life's tree, and dooms man's worst—his second
    fall.

XCVIII

Yet, Freedom! yet thy banner, torn, but flying,
Streams like the thunder-storm *against* the wind;
Thy trumpet voice, though broken now and dying,
The loudest still the tempest leaves behind;
Thy tree hath lost its blossoms, and the rind,
Chopp'd by the axe, looks rough and little worth,
But the sap lasts, and still the seed we find
Sown deep, even in the bosom of the North;
So shall a better spring less bitter fruit bring forth.

[5]*Adamantine* means unyielding or impenetrable.

4 German Romanticism

German Romanticism began in the early 1770s with the literary movement known as *Sturm und Drang* (Storm and Stress) which decried both social convention and the inordinate emphasis placed on rational thought by the Enlightenment thinkers, the philosophes. *Sturm und Drang* authors celebrated the subjective and wrote literature that stressed imagination, spontaneity, feeling, and passion. The movement also advanced the idea of the creative youthful genius who rebels against accepted standards of society.

Johann Wolfgang von Goethe
Faust: A Tragedy

Sturm und Drang was closely associated with the writings of Germany's greatest poet, the young Johann Wolfgang von Goethe (1749–1832). Goethe's best known work, *Faust: A Tragedy,* was published in two parts, in 1808 and 1832. By Goethe's day, the legend of Faust and the Faustian theme of selling one's soul to the devil was already centuries old. One of its most important themes, the one that had a great appeal to the Romantic temperament, is that of the seeker, a person who strives to transcend all limits and to break through all the restraints that prevent one from experiencing everything life has to offer.

The Prologue to Goethe's *Faust* occurs in heaven where God and Mephistopheles, as a manifestation of the Devil, enter into a wager. God allows Mephistopheles to try to lure Faust away from the course of good. But if he fails, Mephistopheles must acknowledge that humanity is not as corrupt as he believed. The opening scene is in the study of the learned Dr. Heinrich Faust. He is master of all knowledge but is spiritually anguished. He yearns for the innocence and life-affirming wisdom of youth, the inspiration of nature, and the joy and excitement of life's experiences. Science, philosophy, and theology no longer stimulate the troubled professor. In the opening scene, Faust acknowledges that his life is devoid of understanding and inner joy. Longing for some sort of inner meaning, Faust laments the emptiness of his life. The following excerpts are from a prose translation of Goethe's verse play.

FAUST (*sitting at his desk, restless.*)

Look at me. I've worked right through philosophy, right through medicine and jurisprudence, as they call it, and that wretched theology too. Toiled and slaved at it and know no more than when I began. I have my master's degree and my doctor's and it must be ten years now that I've led my students by the nose this way and that, upstairs and downstairs, and all the time I see plainly that we don't and can't know anything. It eats me up. Of course I'm ahead of these silly scholars, these doctors and clerics and what not. I have no doubts or scruples to bother me, and I snap my fingers at hell and the devil. But I pay the price. I've lost all joy in life. I don't delude myself. I shall never know anything worth knowing, never have a word to say that might be useful to my fellow men. I own nothing, no money, no property, I have no standing in the world. It's a dog's life and worse. And this is why I've gone over to magic, to see if I can get secrets out of the spirit world and not have to go on sweating and saying things I don't know, discover, it may be, what it is that holds the world together, behold with my own eyes its innermost workings, and stop all this fooling with words.

Oh if this were the last time the full moon found me here in my agony. How often have I sat at this desk among my books watching for you in the deep of night till at last, my melancholy friend, you came. Oh to be out on the hilltops in your lovely light, floating among spirits at some cavern's mouth or merging into your meadows in the dimness. Oh to be clear, once and for all, of this pedantry, this stench, and to wash myself in your dew and be well again.

But where am I? Still a prisoner in this stifling hole, these walls, where even the sunlight that filters in is dimmed and discoloured by the painted panes, surrounded from floor to ceiling by dusty, worm-eaten bookshelves with this sooty paper stuck over them, these instruments everywhere, these beakers, these retorts, and then, on top of that, my family goods and chattels. Call that a world?

Is it any wonder that your heart should quail and tremble and that this ache, this inertia, should thwart your every impulse? When God created man he put him in the midst of nature's growth and here you have nothing round you but bones and skeletons and mould and grime.

Up then. Out into the open country. And what better guide could I have than this strange book that Nostradamus[1] wrote. With its help I shall follow the movement of the stars. Nature may teach me how spirits talk to spirits. It is futile to brood drily here over the magic signs. You spirits, hovering about me, hear me and answer.

(*He opens the book and sees the sign of macrocosm.[2]*)

What a vision is this, flooding all senses with delight, racing through my nerves and veins with the fire and the freshness of youth. Was it a god who set down these signs that hush my inner fever, fill my poor heart with happiness, and with mysterious power make visible the forces of nature about me. Am I myself a god? Such light is given to me. In these pure lines I see the working of nature laid bare. Now I know what the philosopher meant: "The spirit-world is not closed. It is your mind that is shut, your heart that is inert. Up, my pupil, be confident, bathe your breast in the dawn."

(*He contemplates the sign.*)

Oh what a unity it is, one thing moving through another, the heavenly powers ascending and descending, passing the golden vessels up and down, flying from heaven to earth on fragrant wings, making harmonious music in the universe. What a spectacle. But ah, only a spectacle. Infinite nature, how shall I lay hold of you? How shall I feed at these breasts, these nurturing springs, for which I yearn, on which all life depends? When these are offered, must I thirst in vain?

Mephistopheles later appears in Faust's study. They make a pact, sealed in blood, in which Mephistopheles promises to fulfill Faust's every desire in this life. In return, however, Faust must, upon his death, become Mephistopheles' servant in hell. This scene has given rise to the widely used term, "Faustian bargain."

---

[1]Nostradamus (1505–1566) was a French astrologer and prophet.
[2]Sign of the macrocosm was a Renaissance diagram of the universe using concentric circles.

FAUST   A knock. Come in. Who's pestering me now?

MEPHISTOPHELES   It's me.

FAUST   Come in.

MEPHISTOPHELES   You have to say it three times.

FAUST   Oh well then, come in.

MEPHISTOPHELES   That's the way. I trust we shall hit it off together. You see, I want to cheer you up and so I've put on the costume of a nobleman, red with gold braid, a cape of stiff silk, a cock's feather in my hat, and a long rapier. And I want you to wear the same, so that you may feel completely on the loose, free and ready to find out what life is like.

FAUST   No matter what I wear, I shall feel the misery of our petty, earthly existence just the same. I'm too old to take it lightly, too young to back down altogether. What has the world to offer me? Renunciation. You can't do this, you can't do that. This is the eternal refrain that rings and jangles in our ears hour by hour all our life long. When I wake in the morning, I wake with horror. I could shed bitter tears to think of the day beginning that will not grant me one thing I wish for, no not one, the day that with senseless carping will nip all pleasure in the bud and thwart every generous impulse with its ugliness and its mockery. When I lie down on my bed at night I am full of fears. There will be no repose, wild dreams will come to terrify me. The divinity that resides in me, master of my powers, can shake me to the depths, but that is all. It effects nothing outwardly. And so life to me is a burden, and death what I desire.

MEPHISTOPHELES   And yet death when it comes is never wholly welcome, never.

FAUST   Oh happy man whom death reaches at the moment of victory to twine the bloody laurels about his brow, or it finds him after the mad whirl of the dance lying in a girl's embrace. Oh would that I had collapsed and died in ecstasy under the earth-spirit's impact.

MEPHISTOPHELES   Someone I know didn't drain his draught that particular night.

FAUST   Spying round is your game, it seems.

MEPHISTOPHELES   I don't know everything, but I know a lot.

FAUST   I was fooled. Sweet, familiar music, thoughts of happy days, awoke what was left of the child in me and lifted me out of my horrible confusion. But not again. Now I put my curse on everything, the decoys, the enticements, that confront us on every side, all the trumpery and flattery that detains us in this vale of misery. I curse the high and mighty notion the mind has of itself; I curse the dazzle of the outer world that assails our senses; I curse the dreams we dream, the hypocrisy of them; I curse the illu-

sion that our names can last and make us famous. I curse property in every form, be it wife and child or man and plough. I curse Mammon, whether he incites us to action with promise of rewards or smoothes the pillow for us in our lazy moments. I curse the winecup and its comforts. I curse love and its heights. I curse hope. I curse faith. And, most of all, patience I curse.

SPIRIT CHORUS   *(invisible.)*
Alas, alas for the lovely world destroyed. A demi-god has shattered it with a mighty blow. See, it is falling, crumbling. We carry the remnants over into limbo and lament the beauty lost. Man in your strength build it again. Build it better. Build it in your heart. Begin a new life with clear mind and let new songs be sung.

MEPHISTOPHELES   These are my lesser minions. Note how shrewdly they urge you to be active and cheerful. They want to draw you out of your stagnant solitude into the wide world.

Stop playing with this misery that gnaws at your life like a vulture. Any company, the meanest, will make you feel that you're a man among men. Not that I propose to thrust you among riff-raff. I'm not one of the great, but if you care to join forces with me for life, I shall be happy to oblige you on the spot. I'll be your companion and, if I suit, I'll be your servant, your slave.

FAUST   And what have I to do in return?

MEPHISTOPHELES   There's plenty of time for that.

FAUST   Not a bit of it. The devil's an egoist and not disposed to help others free gratis. State your terms. You're not the safest of servants.

MEPHISTOPHELES   I pledge myself to your service here and will always be at your beck and call. If we meet over there, you can do the same for me.

FAUST   Over there is no concern of mine. If you can shatter this world to pieces, let the other come. My joys and sorrows belong to this earth and this sunlight. When I part with them, the rest can follow, whatever it is. There may be top and bottom in that other place; people there may go on loving and hating. I simply don't care.

MEPHISTOPHELES   I see no difficulty in that. Come, agree. My tricks will delight you. I'll show you things no one has ever seen before.

FAUST   You poor devil, what can you have to show me? Did the likes of you ever comprehend the mind of man and all its great endeavour. But come on. Perhaps you have food that never fills you; red gold that trickles through your fingers like quicksilver; a game at which you can't win; a girl who while lying in the arms of one lover with the wink of an eye picks up someone else; honours that lift you to the seventh heaven and then go out like shooting stars. Come along with your fruit that rots in the hand when you try to pick it, and your trees that grow new leaves and shed them every day.

MEPHISTOPHELES There's nothing there that I don't feel equal to. Entertainments like those are just in my line. But, my friend, the day will come when we shall want to relax and savour a good thing quietly.

FAUST If ever I lie down in idleness and contentment, let that be the end of me, let that be final. If you can delude me into feeling pleased with myself, if your good things ever get the better of me, then may that day be my last day. This is my wager.

MEPHISTOPHELES Agreed.

FAUST And shake again. If ever the passing moment is such that I wish it not to pass and I say to it "You are beautiful, stay a while," then let that be the finish. The clock can stop. You can put me in chains and ring the death-bell. I shall welcome it and you will be quit of your service.

MEPHISTOPHELES Consider what you're saying. We shan't forget.

FAUST Quite right. I haven't committed myself wildly. If I come to a stop, if I stagnate, I'm a slave. Whether yours or another's, what does it matter?

MEPHISTOPHELES There's the doctoral dinner this very day. I shall be there as your servant. But, to meet all emergencies, could I have a word in writing?

FAUST So you want it in writing, do you, you pedant [nitpicker]? Don't you know the worth of a man, the worth of a man's word? Isn't it enough that my given word is to rule my life for the rest of my days? I know that, when you see the world raging along like so many torrents, you may well ask why a mere promise should bind me. But this is the way we are. We cherish the illusion and cling to it, it keeps us clear, and clean-spirited, and responsible. But a parchment all filled out and stamped is a spectre that everyone dreads. The written word dies, leather and sealing-wax take over. What do you want, you devil? Bronze, marble, parchment, paper? Shall I write with a style or a chisel or a pen? Take your choice.

MEPHISTOPHELES Why do you get so heated and exaggerate so when you start speechifying? Any scrap of paper will do. Only you must sign with a drop of blood.

FAUST If this really satisfies you, we'll go through with the tomfoolery.

MEPHISTOPHELES Blood. Blood is special.

Mephistopheles makes it possible for Faust to seduce an innocent young girl named Margarete (or its diminutive, Gretchen). Desirous of making love with Faust in the very bedroom she shares with her mother, Margarete gives her mother a sleeping potion that accidentally kills her. Gretchen's brother, Valentine, learns of his sister's affair, confronts Faust, and challenges him to a duel, but Faust, assisted by Mephistopheles, kills him. The guilt-ridden Margarete then kills the infant fathered by Faust, a crime for which she is put on trial and condemned to death. Faust visits her while she is in prison, but Margarete refuses to flee with him. In the end, she is redeemed and ascends to heaven, but Mephistopheles drags Faust to damnation.

FAUST Day's coming. Darling. Darling.

GRETCHEN Yes, day. The last day. It was to have been my wedding day. Don't tell anyone you were at Gretchen's. Oh my flowers. Well, it's done, We'll meet again, but not at the dance. The crowd's gathering. You can't hear them. The streets, the square won't hold them. The bell calls. The staff is broken. They're seizing hold of me, binding me, dragging me to the block. Everyone feels at his neck the axe blade that's meant for me. The world is silent as the grave.

FAUST I wish I'd never been born.

MEPHISTOPHELES *(appearing outside.)*
Up. Or You're lost. This delay, this chattering's useless. My horses are shivering. It'll soon be light.

GRETCHEN Who is that rising out of the ground? Send him away. What's he doing here in this holy place? He's after me.

FAUST I want you to live.

GRETCHEN God's judgment. I submit to it.

MEPHISTOPHELES *(to Faust)*
Come, or I'll leave the two of you.

GRETCHEN Heavenly father, I'm yours. Save me. Angelic hosts, surround me, preserve me. Faust, I shudder at you.

MEPHISTOPHELES She is doomed.

VOICE *(voice from above)*
She is saved.

MEPHISTOPHELES *(to Faust)*
Come here. *(He disappears with Faust.)*

VOICE *(dying away.)*
Faust, Faust

5 French Romanticism

The development of French Romanticism was impeded by the rationalism of the thinkers of the Enlightenment, by the French Revolution, and by the wars of the Napoleonic era. Consequently, when the French monarchy was restored in 1815, the French were largely still focused on the neoclassical models of the eighteenth century. There was, however, one philosophe who was a precursor of Romanticism. In his novel, *The New Heloise* (1761), Jean Jacques Rousseau (1712–1778) stressed the emotions and championed the freedom of the person who defies the social conventions. In doing so, he helped to establish "the cult of the individual"—a hallmark of the Romantic Movement.

The greatest nineteenth-century French Romantic writer was Victor Hugo (1802–1885). Raised as a monarchist and a traditionalist, Hugo became increasingly liberal during the 1830s and 1840s. By 1848, when Louis Napoleon was elected president of the newly created Second Republic, Hugo was an advocate of democracy. As Louis Napoleon became more and more authoritarian, Hugo began to oppose his regime. When Louis Napoleon made himself Emperor Napoleon III by means of a coup d'etat in 1851, Hugo was forced to go into exile in Belgium, where he remained for nineteen years. Hugo triumphantly returned to France the day after the proclamation of the Third Republic in 1870.

Hugo allowed his political views to shine through in all of his writings. He was a prolific author, writing in every genre, including poetry, drama, and fiction. His first success came in the theater, soon followed by his tremendously successful novel, *The Hunchback of Notre Dame* in 1831. In 1842, he began to write his greatest novel, *Les Misérables* (The Underclass), which he published in exile twenty years later.

Victor Hugo
Les Misérables

Les Misérables is a story that displays Hugo's commitment to political and economic reform in France. The novel not only reflects Hugo's passion for social justice, but it also reveals his concern for the wretched victims of the Industrial Revolution—the *misérables*. During the twentieth century, the novel inspired the long-running Broadway musical, as well as a number of motion pictures. The setting of the novel is the Parisian underworld between the years 1815 and 1832. The protagonist is the ex-convict, Jean Valjean, who has spent nineteen years in prison for stealing a loaf of bread and for attempting several times to escape. After his release, Valjean commits a minor crime, for which he is hunted by Inspector Javert. Valjean finally leaves his life of crime, and, under the assumed name of Madeleine, becomes financially successful as a factory owner. Some time after Valjean becomes mayor of the town, Javert is appointed police inspector there. In the following passage, Javert tells the mayor that another man has been arrested as Jean Valjean.

"Well, what is the matter, Javert?"

Jarvert remained silent for a moment, as if reflecting, and then raised his voice with a sad solemnity, which, however, did not exclude simplicity.

"A culpable deed has been committed, sir."

"What deed?"

"An inferior agent of authority has failed in his respect to a magistrate in the gravest manner. I have come, as is my duty, to bring the fact to your knowledge."

"Who is this agent?" M. Madeleine asked.

"Myself."

"And who is the magistrate who has cause to complain of the agent?"

"You, Monsieur le Maire."

M. Madeleine sat up, and Javert continued, with a stern air and still looking down:

"Monsieur le Maire, I have come to request that you will procure my dismissal from service."

M. Madeleine in his stupefaction opened his mouth, but Javert interrupted him:

"You will say that I could have sent in my resignation, but that is not enough. Such a course is honorable, but I have done wrong, and deserve punishment. I must be dismissed."

And after a pause he added:

"Monsieur le Marie, you were severe to me the other day unjustly, be so to-day justly."

"What is the meaning of all this nonsense?" M. Madeleine exclaimed. "What is the culpable act you have committed? What have you done to me? You accuse yourself; you wish to be removed—"

"Dismissed," said Javert.

"Very good, dismissed. I do not understand it."

"You shall do so, sir."

Javert heaved a deep sigh and continued, still coldly and sadly:

"Six weeks ago, M. le Maire, after the scene about that girl, I was furious, and denounced you."

"Denounced me?"

"To the prefect of police at Paris."

M. Madeleine, who did not laugh much oftener than Javert, burst into a laugh.

"As a mayor who had encroached on the police?"

"As an ex-galley-slave."

The mayor turned livid, but Javert, who had not raised his eyes, continued:

"I thought you were so, and have had these notions for a long time. A resemblance, information you sought at Faverolles, the strength of your loins, the adventure with old Fauchelevent, your skill with firearms, your leg which halts a little—and so on. It was very absurd, but I took you for a man of the name of Jean Valjean."

"What name did you say?"

"Jean Valjean; he is a convict I saw twenty years ago when I was assistant keeper at the Toulon bagne. On leaving the galley, this Valjean, as it appears, robbed a bishop, and then committed a highway robbery on a little Savoyard. For eight years he has been out of the way and could not be found, and I imagined—in a word, I did as I said. Passion decided me, and I denounced you to the prefect."

M. Madeline, who had taken up the charge book again, said with a careless accent:

"And what was the answer you received?"

"That I was mad!"

"Well?"

"They were right."

"It is fortunate that you allow it."

"I must do so, for the real Jean Valjean has been found."

The book M. Madeleine was holding fell from his grasp; he raised his head, looked searchingly at Javert, and said with an indescribable accent:

"Oh!"

His conscience tormented that another man would suffer for his crime, Valjean decides to confess his past, and he is arrested by Javert. He escapes from the town jail, but he must continuously evade Javert, a believer in the harsh penal codes of France who sees Valjean's escape as an insult to justice. Valjean adopts Cosette, an illegitimate child, who grows up to be a beautiful woman. Cosette meets Marius, a former monarchist whose views change so much that he fights in the streets on the barricades during an insurrection in Paris. After the two young people fall in love, Marius thinks about how much he loves Cosette.

For six weeks past Marius had slowly and gradually taken possession of Cosette; it was a perfectly ideal, but profound, possession. As we have explained, in first love men take the soul long before the body; a later date they take the body before the soul, and at times they do not take the soul at all,—the Faublas and Prudhommes add, because there is no such thing, but the sarcasm is fortunately a blasphemy. Marius, then, possessed Cosette in the way that minds possess; but he enveloped her with his entire soul, and jealousy seized her with an incredible conviction. He possessed her touch, her breath, her perfume, the deep flash of her blue eyes, the softness of her skin when he touched her hand, the charming mark which she had on her neck, and all her thoughts. They had agreed never to sleep without dreaming of each other, and had kept their word. He, therefore, possessed all Cosette's dreams. He looked at her incessantly, and sometimes breathed on the short hairs which she had on her neck, and said to himself that there was not one of those hairs which did not belong to him. He contemplated and adored the things she wore, her bows, her cuffs, her gloves, and slippers, like sacred objects of which he was the master. He thought that he was the lord of the small tortoise-shell combs which she had in her hair, and he said to himself, in the confused stammering of dawning voluptuousness, that there was not a seam of her dress, not a mesh of her stockings, not a wrinkle in her bodice, which was not his. By the side of Cosette he felt close to his property, near his creature, who was at once his despot and his slave. It seemed that they had so blended their souls that, if they had wished to take them back, it would have been impossible for them to recognize them. This is mine—no, it is mine—I assure you that you are mistaken. This is really I—what you take for yourself is myself; Marius was something which formed part of Cosette, and Cosette was something that formed part of Marius. Marius felt Cosette live in him; to have Cosette, to possess Cosette, was to him not different from breathing.

When Marius thinks that he has lost Cosette, he joins his radical student friends in an insurrection in Paris. Valjean joins the students, discovers that they have captured Javert, and offers to execute him. Instead, he allows Javert to escape. When Marius is wounded, Valjean saves him by carrying him through the sewers of Paris, only to be arrested by Javert as he emerges from the sewer. Javert, experiencing a change of heart, allows Valjean to go free, then commits suicide for breaching his duty.

Javert retired slowly from the Rue de l'Homme Armé. He walked with drooping head for the first time in his life, and, equally for the first time in his life, with his hands behind his back. Up to that day Javert had only assumed, of Napoleon's two attitudes, the one which expresses resolution, the arms folded on the chest; the one indicating uncertainty, the arms behind the back, was unknown to him. Now a change had taken place, and his whole person, slow and somber, was stamped with anxiety. He buried himself in the silent streets, but followed a certain direction; he went by the shortest road to the Seine, reached the Quai des Ormes, walked along it, passed the Grève, and stopped, a little distance from the Châtelet Square, at the corner of the Pont Notre Dame. The Seine makes there, between that bridge and the Pont au Change on one side, and the Quai de la Mégisserie and the Quai aux Fleurs on the other, a species of square lake traversed by a rapid. This point on the Seine is feared by boatmen; nothing can be more dangerous than this rapid, which just then was contracted and irritated by the stakes of the mill-bridge, since demolished. The two bridges, so close to each other, heighten the danger, for the water hurries formidably through the arches. It rolls in large folds, it is heaped up and piled up; the stream strives to pull away the piles of the bridge with its strong liquid cords. Men who fall in there do not re-appear, and the best swimmers are drowned.

Javert leaned his elbows on the parapet, his chin on his hand, and while his hands mechanically closed on his thick whiskers, he reflected. . . .

One thing had astonished him—Jean Valjean had shown him mercy; and one thing had petrified him—that he, Javert, had shown mercy to Jean Valjean. . . .

Nothing could be seen, but the hostile coldness of the water and the sickly smell of the damp stones could be felt. A ferocious breath rose from this abyss, and the swelling of the river, divined rather than perceived, the tragic muttering of the water, the mournful vastness of the bridge arches, a possible fall into this gloomy vacuum—all this shadow was full of horror.

Javert remained for some moments motionless, gazing at this opening of the darkness, and considered the invisible with an intentness which resembled attention. All at once he took off his hat and placed it on the brink of the quay. A moment after a tall, black figure, which any belated passer-by might have taken at a distance for a ghost, appeared standing on the parapet, stooped toward the Seine, then drew itself up, and fell straight into the darkness. There was a dull plash [splatter], and the shadows alone were in the secret of this obscure form which had appeared beneath the waters.

At the end of the novel, as he lies on his deathbed, Valjean comforts Marius and Cosette.

His face grew pale, and at the same time smiling; life was no longer there, but there was something else. His breath stopped, but his glance expanded; he was a corpse on whom wings could be seen. He made Cosette a sign to approach, and then Marius; it was evidently the last minute of the last hour, and he began speaking to them in so faint a voice that it seemed to come from a distance, and it was as if there were henceforth a wall between them and him.

"Come hither, both of you; I love you dearly. Oh! how pleasant it is to die like this! You, too, love me, my Cosette; I felt certain that you had always a fondness for the poor old man. How kind it was of you to place that pillow at my back! You will weep for me a little, will you not? but not too much, for I do not wish you to feel real sorrow. . . .

Do not weep, my children; I am not going very far; and I shall see you from there; you will only have to look when it is dark, and you will see me smile. . . .

[God] is above. He sees us all, and He knows all that He does amid his great stars. I am going away, my children. Love each other dearly and always, There is no other thing in the world but that; love one another. You will sometimes think of the poor old man who died here. Ah, my Cosette, it is not my fault that I did not see you every day, for it broke my heart. I went as far as the corner of the street, and must have produced a strange effect on the people who saw me pass, for I was like a madman, and even went out without my hat. My children, I can no longer see very clearly. I had several things to say to you, but no matter. Think of me a little. You are blessed beings. I know not what is the matter with me, but I see light. Come hither. I die happy. Let me lay my hands on your beloved heads."

Cosette and Marius fell on their knees, heart-broken and choked with sobs, each under one of Jean Valjean's hands. These august hands did not move again.

He had fallen back, and the light from the two candles illumined him; his white face looked up to heaven, and he let Cosette and Marius cover his hands with kisses.

He was dead.

The night was starless and intensely dark; doubtless some immense angel was standing in the gloom, with outstretched wings, waiting for the soul.

6 The English Gothic Novel

Beginning in the nineteenth century, novels set in faraway times or locales were called "Gothic Romances." Instead of simply referring to the architectural structures of the Middle Ages, "Gothic" now referred to an emotional effect—one imbued with elements of terror, the phantasmagorical, and the supernatural. The theme often had to do with psychological confinement or physical imprisonment. For example, heroines and heroes could be involved in an abusive marriage, a victim of mistaken identity, falsely imprisoned, or held hostage in a dungeon or tower. Therefore, the climax of the Gothic Romance was the liberation of self.

At the turn of the century, German Romantic writers began to employ Gothic buildings or forests to represent humanity's primitive, natural habitat. As other Gothic writers appropriated similar features, consistent religious images and symbols appeared, including temples, graves, churchyards, cathedrals, castles, storms, or mountains. Such Gothic features were often used to represent fallen men and women as victims of their own human nature or to portray them as pawns in the hands of forces beyond their control, either Nature or some supernatural power.

Emily Brontë
Wuthering Heights

Three novels published in 1847 by the Brontë sisters—Charlotte (1816–1855), *Jane Eyre;* Emily (1818–1848), *Wuthering Heights;* and Anne (1820–1849), *Agnes Grey*—exemplify the English Gothic romance novel. Like many of their female contemporaries, the Brontë sisters published under a pseudonym, namely, Currer, Ellis, and Acton Bell. Of the three, *Wuthering Heights,* the only novel Emily Brontë ever published, is arguably the most famous. It is written as a full-blown Gothic Romance—replete with unearthly phantoms and graveyards, but ever-mindful that they represent a transcendent world filled with spiritual meaning. The plot focuses on the disparate pair of Heathcliff, an adopted member of the aristocratic Earnshaw family, and the wildly passionate and headstrong Catherine Earnshaw, who, although attracted to Heathcliff, believes that it would be beneath her to marry an orphaned commoner. Knowing this, Heathcliff departs Wuthering Heights ("wuthering" itself means "stormy") but returns three years later, only to discover that Catherine's brother, Hindley, is now in charge of the estate and that Catherine has married Edgar Linton, an aristocratic gentleman who is deeply dedicated to her. The now successful Heathcliff, driven by vengeance for his perceived mistreatment at the hands of the Earnshaws, seeks to ruin them first by financially ruining Hindley. Through Heathcliff, Brontë creates her own version of the Byronic hero—uncultivated, driven, passionate, and tormented. For example, Nelly Dean (a maid-servant to Catherine) relates how Heathcliff convinces her to carry a letter to Catherine, who is dying from a fever while pregnant with Edgar's child. While Edgar is attending services at the Gimmerton Church, Nelly reads the letter to Catherine just before Heathcliff bursts into her room. The following selection, narrated by Nelly, is drawn from this encounter. It is one of the most memorable scenes in the novel, because it epitomizes Heathcliff's fiery temperament and Catherine's bittersweet love for him.

In the evening, she said, the evening of my visit to the Heights, I knew, as well as if I saw him, that Mr. Heathcliff was about the place; and I shunned going out, because I still carried his letter in my pocket, and didn't want to be threatened or teased any more. I had made up my mind not to give it till my master went somewhere, as I could not guess how its receipt would affect Catherine. The consequence was that it did not reach her before the lapse of three days. The fourth was Sunday, and I brought it into her room after the family were gone to church. There was a man servant left to keep the house with me, and we generally made a practice of locking the doors during the hours of service; but on that occasion the weather was so warm and pleasant that I set them wide open, and, to fulfill my engagement, as I knew who would be coming, I told my companion that the mistress wished very much for some oranges, and he must run over to the village and get a few, to be paid for on the morrow. He departed, and I went upstairs.

Mrs. Linton sat in a loose, white dress, with a light shawl over her shoulders, in the recess of the open window, as usual. Her thick, long hair had been partly removed at the beginning of her illness, and now she wore it simply combed in its natural tresses over her temples and neck. Her appearance was altered, as I had told Heathcliff; but when she was calm, there seemed unearthly beauty in the change. The flash of her eyes had been succeeded by a dreamy and melancholy softness; they no longer gave the impression of looking at the objects around her: they appeared always to gaze beyond, and far beyond—you would have said out of this world. Then the paleness of her face—its haggard aspect having vanished as she recovered flesh—and the peculiar expression arising from her mental state, though painfully suggestive of their causes, added to the touching interest which she awakened; and—invariably to me, I know, and to any person who saw her, I should think—refuted more tangible proofs of convalescence, and stamped her as one doomed to decay.

A book lay spread on the sill before her, and the scarcely perceptible wind fluttered its leaves at intervals. I believe Linton had laid it there: for she never endeavored to divert herself with reading, or occupation of any kind, and he would spend many an hour in trying to entice her attention to some subject which had formerly been her amusement. She was conscious of his aim, and in her better moods endured his efforts placidly, only showing their uselessness by now and then suppressing a wearied sigh, and checking him at last with the saddest of smiles and kisses. At other times, she would turn petulantly away, and hide her face in her hands, or even push him off angrily; and then he took care to let her alone, for he was certain of doing no good.

Gimmerton chapel bells were still ringing; and the full, mellow flow of the beck in the valley came soothingly on the ear. It was a sweet substitute for the yet absent murmur of the summer foliage, which drowned that music about the Grange when the trees were in leaf. At Wuthering Heights it always sounded on quiet days following a great thaw or a season of steady rain. And of Wuthering Heights Catherine was thinking as she listened: that is, if she thought or listened at all; but she had the vague, distant look I mentioned before, which expressed no recognition of material things either by ear or eye.

"There's a letter for you, Mrs. Linton," I said, gently inserting it in one hand that rested on her knee. "You must read it immediately, because it wants an answer. Shall I break the seal?" "Yes," she answered, without altering the direction of her eyes. I opened it—it was very short. "Now," I continued, "read it." She drew away her hand, and let it fall. I replaced it in her lap, and stood waiting till it should please her to glance down; but that movement was so long delayed that at last I resumed:

"Must I read it, ma'am? It is from Mr. Heathcliff."

There was a start and a troubled gleam of recollection, and a struggle to arrange her ideas. She lifted the letter, and seemed to peruse it; and when she came to the signature she sighed; yet still I found she had not gathered its import, for, upon my desiring to hear her reply, she merely pointed to the name, and gazed at me with mournful and questioning eagerness.

"Well, he wishes to see you," said I, guessing her need of an interpreter. "He's in the garden by this time, and impatient to know what answer I shall bring."

As I spoke, I observed a large dog lying on the sunny grass beneath raise its ears as if about to bark, and then smoothing them back, announce, by a wag of the tail, that someone approached whom it did not consider a stranger. Mrs. Linton bent forward, and listened breathlessly. The minute after, a step traversed the hall; the open house was too tempting for Heathcliff to resit [sic] walking in: most likely he supposed that I was inclined to shirk my promise, and so resolved to trust to his own audacity. With straining eagerness Catherine gazed towards the entrance of her chamber. He did not hit the right room directly, she motioned me to admit him, but he found it out ere I could reach the door, and in a stride or two was at her side, and had her grasped in his arms.

He neither spoke nor loosed his hold for some five minutes, during which period he bestowed more kisses than ever he gave in his life before, I daresay: but then my mistress had kissed him first, and I plainly saw that he could hardly bear, for downright agony, to look into her face! The same conviction had stricken him as me, from the instant he beheld her, that there was no prospect of ultimate recovery there—she was fated, sure to die.

"Oh, Cathy! Oh, my life! how can I bear it?" was the first sentence he uttered, in a tone that did not seek to disguise his despair. And now he stared at her so earnestly that I thought the very intensity of his gaze would bring tears into his eyes; but they burned with anguish: they did not melt.

"What now?" said Catherine, leaning back and returning his look with a suddenly clouded brow: her humor was a mere vane for constantly varying caprices. "You and Edgar have broken my heart, Heathcliff! And you both came to bewail the deed to me, as if *you* were the people to be pitied! I shall not pity you, not I. You have killed me—and thriven on it, I think. How strong you are! How many years do you mean to live after I am gone?"

Heathcliff had knelt on one knee to embrace her; he attempted to rise, but she seized his hair, and kept him down.

"I wish I could hold you," she continued bitterly, "till we were both dead! I shouldn't care what you suffered. I care nothing for your sufferings. Why shouldn't *you* suffer? I do! Will you forget me? Will you be happy when I am in the earth? Will you say twenty years hence, 'That's the grave of Catherine Earnshaw. I loved her long ago, and was wretched to lose her; but it is past. I've loved many others since: my children are dearer to me than she was; and a death, I shall not rejoice that I am going to her; I shall be sorry that I must leave them!' Will you say so, Heathcliff?"

"Don't torture me till I am as mad as yourself," cried he, wrenching his head free, and grinding his teeth.

The two, to a cool spectator, made a strange and fearful picture. Well might Catherine deem that heaven would be a land of exile to her, unless with her mortal body she cast away her mortal character also. Her present countenance had a wild vindictiveness in its white cheek, and a bloodless lip and scintillating eye; and she retained in her closed fingers a portion of the locks she had been grasping. As to her companion, while raising himself with one hand, he had taken her arm with the other; and so inadequate was his stock of gentleness to the requirements of her condition, that on his letting go I saw four distinct impressions left blue in the colorless skin.

"Are you possessed with a devil," he pursued savagely, "to talk in that manner to me when you are dying? Do you reflect that all those words will be branded on my memory, and eating deeper eternally after you have left me? You know you lie to say I have killed you: and, Catherine, you know that I could as soon forget you as my existence! Is it not sufficient for your infernal selfishness that, while you are at peace, I shall writhe in the torments of hell?"

"I shall not be at peace," moaned Catherine, recalled to a sense of physical weakness by the violent, unequal throbbing of her heart, which beat visibly and audibly under this excess of agitation. She said nothing further till the paroxysm was over; then she continued, more kindly—

"I'm not wishing you greater torment than I have, Heathcliff. I only wish us never to be parted: and should a word of mine distress you hereafter, think I feel the same distress underground, and for my own sake, forgive me! Come here and kneel down again! You never harmed me in your life. Nay, if you nurse anger, that will be worse to remember than my harsh words! Won't you come here again? Do!"

Heathcliff went to the back of her chair, and leaned over, but not so far as to let her see his face, which was livid with emotion. She bent round to look at him; he would not permit it: turning abruptly, he walked to the fireplace, where he stood, silent, with his back towards us. Mrs. Linton's glance followed him suspiciously: every movement woke a new sentiment in her. After a pause and a prolonged gaze, she resumed; addressing me in accents of indignant disappointment—

"Oh, you see, Nelly, he would not relent a moment to keep me out of the grave. *That* is how I'm loved! Well, never mind. That is not *my* Heathcliff. I shall love mine yet; and take him with me: he's in my soul. And," added she, musingly, "the thing that irks me most is this shattered prison, after all. I'm tired of being enclosed here. I'm wearying to escape into that glorious world, and to be always there: not seeing it dimly through tears, and yearning for it through the walls of an aching heart; but really with it, and in it. Nelly, you think you are better and more fortunate than I; in full health and strength: you are sorry for me—very soon that will be altered. I shall be sorry for *you*. I shall be incomparably beyond and above you all. I *wonder* he won't be near me!" She went on to herself. "I thought he wished it. Heathcliff, dear! you should not be sullen now. Do come to me, Heathcliff."

In her eagerness she rose and supported herself on the arm of the chair. At that earnest appeal he turned to her, looking absolutely desperate. His eyes, wide and wet, at last flashed fiercely on her; his breast heaved convulsively. An instant they held asunder, and then how they met I hardly saw, but Catherine made a spring, and he caught her, and they were locked in an embrace from which I thought my mistress would never be released alive: in fact, to my eyes, she seemed directly insensible. He flung himself into the nearest seat, and on my approaching hurriedly to ascertain if she had fainted, he gnashed at me, and foamed like a mad dog, and gathered her to him with greedy jealousy. I did not feel as if I were in the company of a creature of my own species: it appeared that he would not understand, though I spoke to him; so I stood off, and held my tongue, in great perplexity.

A movement of Catherine's relieved me a little presently: she put up her hand to clasp his neck, and bring her cheek to his as he held her; while he, in return, covering her with frantic caresses, said wildly—

"You teach me now how cruel you've been—cruel and false. *Why* did you despise me? *Why* did you betray your own heart, Cathy? I have not one word of comfort. You deserve this. You have killed yourself. Yes, you may kiss me, and cry; and wring out my kisses and tears: they'll blight you—they'll damn me? What right—answer me—for the poor fancy you felt for Linton? Because misery and degradation, and death, and nothing that God or Satan could inflict would have parted us, *you*, of your own will, did it. I have not broken your heart—*you* have broken it; and in breaking it, you have broken mine. So much the worse for me, that I am strong. Do I want to live? What kind of living will it be when you—oh, God! would *you* like to live with your soul in the grave?"

"Let me alone. Let me alone," sobbed Catherine. "If I have done wrong, I'm dying for it. It is enough! You left me too: but I won't upbraid you! I forgive you. Forgive me!"

"It is hard to forgive, and to look at those eyes, and feel those wasted hands," he answered. "Kiss me again; and don't let me see your eyes! I forgive what you have done to me. I love *my* murderer—but *yours!* How can I?"

They were silent—their faces hid against each other, and washed by each other's tears. At least, I suppose the weeping was on both sides; as it seemed Heathcliff *could* weep on a great occasion like this.

I grew very uncomfortable, meanwhile; for the afternoon wore fast away, the man whom I had sent off returned from his errand, and I could distinguish, by the shine of the western sun up the valley, a concourse thickening outside Gimmerton chapel porch.

"Service is over," I announced. "My master will be here in half an hour."

Heathcliff groaned a curse, and strained Catherine closer: she never moved.

Ere long I perceived a group of the servants passing up the road towards the kitchen wing. Mr. Linton was not far behind; he opened the gate himself and sauntered slowly up, probably enjoying the lovely afternoon that breathed as soft as summer.

"Now he is here," I exclaimed. "For Heaven's sake, hurry down! You'll not meet anyone on the front stairs. Do be quick; and stay among the trees till he is fairly in."

"I must go, Cathy," said Heathcliff, seeking to extricate himself from his companion's arms. "But if I live, I'll see you again before you are asleep. I won't stray five yards from your window."

"You must not go!" she answered, holding him as firmly as her strength allowed. "You *shall* not, I tell you."

"For one hour," he pleaded earnestly.

"Not for one minute," she replied.

"I *must*—Linton will be up immediately," persisted the alarmed intruder.

He would have risen, and unfixed her fingers by the act—she clung fast, grasping: there was mad resolution in her face.

"No!" she shrieked. "Oh, don't, don't go. It is the last time! Edgar will not hurt us. Heathcliff, I shall die! I shall die!"

"Damn the fool! There he is," cried Heathcliff, sinking back into his seat. "Hush, my darling! Hush, hush, Catherine! I'll stay. If he shot me so, I'd expire with a blessing on my lips."

And there they were fast again. I heard my master mounting the stairs—the cold sweat ran from my forehead: I was horrified.

"Are you going to listen to her ravings?" I said passionately. "She does not know what she says. Will you ruin her, because she has not wit to help herself? Get up! You could be free instantly. That is the most diabolical deed that ever you did. We are all done for—master, mistress, and servant."

I wrung my hands, and cried out; and Mr. Linton hastened his step at the noise. In the midst of my agitation, I was sincerely glad to observe that Catherine's arms had fallen relaxed and her head hung down.

"She's fainted or dead," I thought: "so much the better.

Far better that she should be dead, than lingering a burden and a misery maker to all about her."

Edgar sprang to his unbidden guest, blanched with astonishment and rage. What he meant to do, I cannot tell; however, the other stopped all demonstrations, at once, by placing the lifeless-looking form in his arms.

"Look, there!" he said; "unless you be a fiend, help her first—then you shall speak to me!"

He walked into the parlor, and sat down. Mr. Linton summoned me, and with great difficulty, and after resorting to many means, we managed to restore her to sensation; but she was all bewildered; she sighed, and moaned, and knew nobody. Edgar, in his anxiety for her, forgot her hated friend. I did not. I went, at the earliest opportunity, and besought him to depart; affirming that Catherine was better, and he should hear from me in the morning how she passed the night.

"I shall not refuse to go out of doors," he answered; "but I shall stay in the garden: and, Nelly, mind you keep your word tomorrow. I shall be under those larch trees. Mind! or I pay another visit, whether Linton be in or not."

He sent a rapid glance through the half-open door of the chamber, and, ascertaining that what I stated was apparently true, delivered the house of his luckless presence.

Even after Catherine's death (due to fever and giving premature birth to her daughter Cathy), Heathcliff's vengeance on the Earnshaws has yet to run its course. To ruin Edgar Linton, he marries his sister, Isabella, and makes her completely miserable, even referring to her as "a mere slut." Heathcliff then forces Cathy to marry Linton (his son with Isabella) just so he can gain complete control of Thrushcross Grange—the Linton estate. Having nearly exhausted himself in reaping vengeance on the Earnshaws, Heathcliff begins to have supernatural visions about reconciling with Catherine. The Yorkshire settings, which have paralleled the tempestuous relationship between Heathcliff and Catherine throughout, once again serve to enhance the scenes of Heathcliff's visionary ruminations. The brutal, impassioned action of the novel (which astonished Emily's contemporaries) finally ceases with the death of Heathcliff on a *stormy* night in his own room.

7 American Romanticism

By the middle of the nineteenth century, pioneers had pushed the American frontier across the Mississippi River, across the Rocky Mountains, and onto the shores of the Pacific Ocean, and even into the northwestern territory of Alaska. These achievements stirred the Romantic imagination and fostered deep patriotic feelings. Concurrent with the material successes of the United States was the expansion of cultural institutions, including an enhanced appreciation of literature that was indigenous in tradition and character. Even though American literature of the age was characterized as Romantic, it was not intended as a reflection of European culture. Instead, American authors such as Nathaniel Hawthorne, Edgar Allan Poe, and Herman Melville sought to portray the virtue of the American way of life. Moreover, they sought to express the wonder of the new territories and to articulate the hope that the ideals of the Enlightenment, particularly the inevitable progress toward human perfection, could be brought to fruition in the United States.

Nathaniel Hawthorne
The Scarlet Letter

American authors deeply appreciated the various forms that Gothic Romantic literature took, including historical tales, historical novels, and the Gothic Romance. Nathaniel Hawthorne (1804–1864) occupies a significant place, because he developed a unique type of romance novel. At the beginning of his most famous romance, *The Scarlet Letter* (1848), Hawthorne wrote a long, introductory sketch called "The Custom-House," wherein he described a romance as "somewhere between the real world and fairy-land where the Actual and the Imaginary may meet, and each imbue itself with the nature of the other." The novelist, said Hawthorne, must be concerned with atmosphere—"moonlight and sunshine, and the flow of firelight, were just alike in my regard"—and explore the inner conflict of his characters so as "to spiritualize the burden; . . . to seek, resolutely, the true and indestructible value that lay hidden in the petty and wearisome incidents, and ordinary characters."

Hawthorne was also particularly fascinated by what he consistently called "secret sin" and sought "the thoughtful moral" behind the foibles and follies of human existence. Nowhere is this more evident than in the following selection from *The Scarlet Letter* in which the Reverend Dimmesdale is tortured by the secret he bears: He is the father of Hester Prynne's daughter, Pearl, and he is the reason Hester must stand on the "platform of the pillory" for three hours and wear the stigma of the scarlet letter "A" of adultery emblazoned on her clothing for the rest of her life. The chapter opens with the arrival of "a wanderer" in the marketplace dressed in "civilized and savage costume." Later, Hawthorne reveals him to be Hester Prynne's husband, Roger Chillingworth, an English scholar who, unknown to Hester, has been held in captivity by the Indians. During the three hours of her public ignominy, Hester is urged to name the father of Pearl by Governor Bellingham of Massachusetts; John Wilson, "the eldest clergyman of Boston"; and Reverend Dimmesdale himself who would rather have Hester name him as the earthly father of Pearl than try to find the required courage within himself to confess his sin publicly.

III. The Recognition

From this intense consciousness of being the object of severe and universal observation, the wearer of the scarlet letter was at length relieved by discerning, on the outskirts of the crowd, a figure which irresistibly took possession of her thoughts. An Indian, in his native garb, was standing there; but the red men were not so infrequent visitors of the English settlements, that one of them would have attracted any notice from Hester Prynne, at such a time; much less would he have excluded all other objects and ideas from her mind. By the Indian's side, and evidently sustaining a companionship with him, stood a white man, clad in a strange disarray of civilized and savage costume.

He was small in stature, with a furrowed visage, which, as yet, could hardly be termed aged. There was a remarkable intelligence in his features, as of a person who had so cultivated his mental part that it could not fail to mould the physical to itself, and become manifest by unmistakable tokens. Although, by a seemingly careless arrangement of his heterogeneous garb, he had endeavoured to conceal or abate the peculiarity, it was sufficiently evident to Hester Prynne, that one of this man's shoulders rose higher than the other. Again, at the first instant of perceiving that thin visage, and the slight deformity of the figure, she pressed her infant to her bosom, with so convulsive a force that the poor babe uttered another cry of pain. But the mother did not seem to hear it.

At his arrival in the market-place, and some time before she saw him, the stranger had bent his eyes on Hester Prynne. It was carelessly, at first, like a man chiefly accustomed to look inward, and to whom external matters are of little value and import, unless they bear relation to something within his mind. Very soon, however, his look became keen and penetrative. A writhing horror twisted itself across his features, like a snake gliding swiftly over them, and making one little pause, with all its wreathed intervolutions in open sight. His face darkened with some powerful emotion, which, nevertheless, he so instantaneously controlled by an effort of his will, that, save at a single moment, its expression might have passed for calmness. After a brief space, the convulsion grew almost imperceptible, and finally subsided into the depths of his nature. When he found the eyes of Hester Prynne fastened on his own, and saw that she appeared to recognize him, he slowly and calmly raised his finger, made a gesture with it in the air, and laid it on his lips.

Then, touching the shoulder of a townsman who stood next to him, he addressed him in a formal and courteous manner.

"I pray you, good Sir," said he, "who is this woman?—and wherefore is she here set up to public shame?"

"You must needs be a stranger in this region, friend," answered the townsman, looking curiously at the questioner and his savage companion; "else you would surely have heard of Mistress Hester Prynne, and her evil doings. She hath raised a great scandal, I promise you, in godly Master Dimmesdale's church."

"You say truly," replied the other. "I am a stranger, and have been a wanderer, sorely against my will. I have met with grievous mishaps by sea and land, and have been long held in bonds among the heathen-folk, to the southward; and am now brought hither by this Indian, to be redeemed out of my captivity. Will it please you, therefore, to tell me of Hester Prynne's,—have I her name rightly?—of this woman's offences, and what has brought her to yonder scaffold?"

"Truly, friend, and methinks it must gladden your heart, after your troubles and sojourn in the wilderness," said the townsman, "to find yourself, at length, in a land where iniquity is searched out, and punished in the sight of rulers and people; as here in our godly New England. Yonder woman, Sir, you must know, was the wife of a certain learned man, English by birth, but who had long dwelt in Amsterdam, whence, some good time agone, he was minded to cross over and cast in his lot with us of the Massachusetts. To this purpose, he sent his wife before him, remaining himself to look after some necessary affairs. Marry, good Sir, in some two years, or less, that the woman has been a dweller here in Boston, no tidings have come of this learned gentleman,

Master Prynne; and his young wife, look you, being left to her own misguidance—"

"Ah!—aha!—I conceive you," said the stranger, with a bitter smile. "So learned a man as you speak of should have learned this too in his books. And who, by your favor, Sir, may be the father of yonder babe—it is some three or four months old, I should judge—which Mistress Prynne is holding in her arms?"

"Of a truth, friend, that matter remaineth a riddle; and the Daniel[1] who shall expound it is yet a-wanting," answered the townsman. "Madam Hester absolutely refuseth to speak, and the magistrates have laid their heads together in vain. Peradventure the guilty one stands looking on at this sad spectacle, unknown of man, and forgetting that God sees him."

"The learned man," observed the stranger, with another smile, "should come himself to look into the mystery."

"It behooves him well, if he be still in life," responded the townsman. "Now, good Sir, our Massachusetts magistracy, bethinking themselves that this woman is youthful and fair, and doubtless was strongly tempted to her fall;—and that, moreover, as is most likely, her husband may be at the bottom of the sea;—they have not been bold to put in force the extremity of our righteous law against her. The penalty thereof is death. But, in their great mercy and tenderness of heart, they have doomed Mistress Prynne to stand only a space of three hours on the platform of the pillory, and then and thereafter, for the remainder of her natural life, to wear a mark of shame upon her bosom."

"A wise sentence!" remarked the stranger, gravely bowing his head. "Thus she will be a living sermon against sin, until the ignominious letter be engraved upon her tombstone. It irks me, nevertheless, that the partner of her iniquity should not, at least, stand on the scaffold by her side. But he will be known!—he will be known!—he will be known!"

He bowed courteously to the communicative townsman, and, whispering a few words to his Indian attendant, they both made their way through the crowd.

While this passed, Hester Prynne had been standing on her pedestal, still with a fixed gaze towards the stranger; so fixed a gaze, that, at moments of intense absorption, all other objects in the visible world seemed to vanish, leaving only him and her. Such an interview, perhaps, would have been more terrible than even to meet him as she now did, with the hot, mid-day sun burning down upon her face, and lighting up its shame; with the scarlet token of infamy on her breast; with the sin-born infant in her arms; with a whole people, drawn forth as to a festival, staring at the features that should have been seen only in the quiet gleam of the fireside, in the happy shadow of a home, or beneath a matronly veil, at church. Dreadful as it was, she was conscious of a shelter in the presence of these thousand witnesses. It was better to stand thus, with so many betwixt him and her, than to greet

_____
[1]Daniel was a biblical prophet who had visions of the "last days" before the end of the world.

him, face to face, they two alone. She fled for refuge, as it were, to the public exposure, and dreaded the moment when its protection should be withdrawn from her. Involved in these thoughts, she scarcely heard a voice behind her, until it had repeated her name more than once, in a loud and solemn tone, audible to the whole multitude.

"Hearken unto me, Hester Prynne!" said the voice.

It has already been noticed, that directly over the platform on which Hester Prynne stood was a kind of balcony, or open gallery, appended to the meetinghouse. It was the place whence proclamations were wont to be made, amidst an assemblage of the magistracy, with all the ceremonial that attended such public observances in those days. Here, to witness the scene which we are describing, sat Governor Bellingham himself, with four sergeants about his chair, bearing halberds,[2] as a guard of honor. He wore a dark feather in his hat, a border of embroidery on his cloak, and a black velvet tunic beneath; a gentleman advanced in years, and with a hard experience written in his wrinkles. He was not ill fitted to be the head and representative of a community, which owed its origin and progress, and its present state of development, not to the impulses of youth, but to the stern and tempered energies of manhood, and the sombre sagacity of age; accomplishing so much, precisely because it imagined and hoped so little. The other eminent characters, by whom the chief ruler was surrounded, were distinguished by a dignity of mien, belonging to a period when the forms of authority were felt to possess the sacredness of divine institutions. They were, doubtless, good men, just and sage. But, out of the whole human family, it would not have been easy to select the same number of wise and virtuous persons, who should be less capable of sitting in judgment on an erring woman's heart, and disentangling its mesh of good and evil, than the sages of rigid aspect towards whom Hester Prynne now turned her face. She seemed conscious, indeed, that whatever sympathy she might expect lay in the larger and warmer heart of the multitude; for, as she lifted her eyes towards the balcony, the unhappy woman grew pale and trembled.

The voice which had called her attention was that of the reverend and famous John Wilson, the eldest clergyman of Boston, a great scholar, like most of his contemporaries in the profession, and withal a man of kind and genial spirit. This last attribute, however, had been less carefully developed than his intellectual gifts, and was, in truth, rather a matter of shame than self-congratulation with him. There he stood, with a border of grizzled locks beneath his skull-cap; while his gray eyes, accustomed to the shaded light of his study, were winking, like those of Hester's infant, in the unadulterated sunshine. He looked like the darkly engraved portraits

which we see prefixed to old volumes of sermons; and had no more right than one of those portraits would have, to step forth, as he now did, and meddle with a question of human guilt, passion, and anguish.

"Hester Prynne," said the clergyman, "I have striven with my young brother here, under whose preaching of the word you have been privileged to sit,"—here Mr. Wilson laid his hand on the shoulder of a pale young man beside him,—"I have sought, I say, to persuade this godly youth, that he should deal with you, here in the face of Heaven, and before these wise and upright rulers, and in hearing of all the people, as touching the vileness and blackness of your sin. Knowing your natural temper better than I, he could the better judge what arguments to use, whether of tenderness or terror, such as might prevail over your hardness and obstinacy; insomuch that you should no longer hide the name of him who tempted you to this grievous fall. But he opposes to me, (with a young man's oversoftness, albeit wise beyond his years,) that it were wronging the very nature of woman to force her to lay open her heart's secrets in such broad daylight, and in presence of so great a multitude. Truly, as I sought to convince him, the shame lay in the commission of the sin, and not in the showing of it forth. What say you to it, once again, brother Dimmesdale? Must it be thou or I that shall deal with this poor sinner's soul?"

There was a murmur among the dignified and reverend occupants of the balcony; and Governor Bellingham gave expression to its purport, speaking in an authoritative voice, although tempered with respect towards the youthful clergyman whom he addressed.

"Good Master Dimmesdale," said he, "the responsibility of this woman's soul lies greatly with you. It behooves you, therefore, to exhort her to repentance, and to confession, as a proof and consequence thereof."

The directness of this appeal drew the eyes of the whole crowd upon the Reverend Mr. Dimmesdale; a young clergyman, who had come from one of the great English universities, bringing all the learning of the age into our wild forest-land. His eloquence and religious fervor had already given the earnest of high eminence in his profession. He was a person of very striking aspect, with a white, lofty, and impending brow, large, brown, melancholy eyes, and a mouth which, unless when he forcibly compressed it, was apt to be tremulous, expressing both nervous sensibility and a vast power of self-restraint. Notwithstanding his high native gifts and scholar-like attainments, there was an air about this young minister,—an apprehensive, a startled, a half-frightened look,—as of a being who felt himself quite astray and at a loss in the pathway of human existence, and could only be at ease in some seclusion of his own. Therefore, so far as his duties would permit, he trode in the shadowy by-paths, and thus kept himself simple and childlike; coming forth, when occasion was, with a freshness, and fragrance, and dewy purity of thought, which, as many people said, affected them like the speech of an angel.

[2] A halberd was a weapon with a blade sloped like an ax, and a metal spike was mounted at the end of the shaft. It was popular during the fifteenth and sixteenth centuries.

Such was the young man whom the Reverend Mr. Wilson and the Governor had introduced so openly to the public notice, bidding him speak, in the hearing of all men, to that mystery of a woman's soul, so sacred even in its pollution. The trying nature of his position drove the blood from his cheek, and made his lips tremulous.

"Speak to the woman, my brother," said Mr. Wilson. "It is of moment to her soul, and therefore, as the worshipful Governor says, momentous to thine own, in whose charge hers is. Exhort her to confess the truth!"

The Reverend Mr. Dimmesdale bent his head, in silent prayer, as it seemed, and then came forward.

"Hester Prynne," said he, leaning over the balcony, and looking down stedfastly into her eyes, "thou hearest what this good man says, and seest the accountability under which I labor. If thou feelest it to be for thy soul's peace, and that thy earthly punishment will thereby be made more effectual to salvation, I charge thee to speak out the name of thy fellow-sinner and fellow-sufferer! Be not silent from any mistaken pity and tenderness for him; for, believe me, Hester, though he were to step down from a high place, and stand there beside thee, on thy pedestal of shame, yet better were it so, than to hide a guilty heart through life. What can thy silence do for him, except it tempt him—yea, compel him, as it were—to add hypocrisy to sin? Heaven hath granted thee an open ignomiy, that thereby thou mayest work out an open triumph over the evil within thee, and the sorrow without. Take heed how thou deniest to him—who, perchance, hath not the courage to grasp it for himself—the bitter, but wholesome, cup that is now presented to thy lips!"

The young pastor's voice was tremulously sweet, rich, deep, and broken. The feeling that it so evidently manifested, rather than the direct purport of the words, caused it to vibrate within all hearts, and brought the listeners into one accord of sympathy. Even the poor baby, at Hester's bosom, was affected by the same influence; for it directed its hitherto vacant gaze towards Mr. Dimmesdale, and held up its little arms, with a half pleased, half plaintive murmur. So powerful seemed the minister's appeal, that the people could not believe but that Hester Prynne would speak out the guilty name; or else that the guilty one himself, in whatever high or lowly place he stood, would be drawn forth by an inward and inevitable necessity, and compelled to ascend the scaffold.

Hester shook her head.

"Woman, transgress not beyond the limits of Heaven's mercy!" cried the Reverend Mr. Wilson, more harshly than before. "That little babe hath been gifted with a voice, to second and confirm the counsel which thou hast heard. Speak out the name! That, and thy repentance, may avail to take the scarlet letter off thy breast."

"Never!" replied Hester Prynne, looking, not at Mr. Wilson, but into the deep and troubled eyes of the younger clergyman. "It is too deeply branded. Ye cannot take it off. And would that I might endure his agony, as well as mine!"

"Speak, woman!" said another voice, coldly and sternly, proceeding from the crowd about the scaffold. "Speak; and give your child a father!"

"I will not speak!" answered Hester, turning pale as death, but responding to this voice, which she too surely recognized. "And my child must seek a heavenly Father; she shall never know an earthly one!"

"She will not speak!" murmured Mr. Dimmesdale, who, leaning over the balcony, with his hand upon his heart, had awaited the result of his appeal. He now drew back, with a long respiration. "Wondrous strength and generosity of a woman's heart! She will not speak!"

Discerning the impracticable state of the poor culprit's mind, the elder clergyman, who had carefully prepared himself for the occasion, addressed to the multitude a discourse on sin, in all its branches, but with continual reference to the ignominious letter. So forcibly did he dwell upon this symbol, for the hour or more during which his periods were rolling over the people's heads, that it assumed new terrors in their imagination, and seemed to derive its scarlet hue from the flames of the infernal pit. Hester Prynne, meanwhile, kept her place upon the pedestal of shame, with glazed eyes, and an air of weary indifference. She had borne, that morning, all that nature could endure; and as her temperament was not of the order that escapes from too intense suffering by a swoon, her spirit could only shelter itself beneath a stony crust of insensibility, while the faculties of animal life remained entire. In this state, the voice of the preacher thundered remorselessly, but unavailingly, upon her ears. The infant, during the latter portion of her ordeal, pierced the air with its wailings and screams; she strove to hush it, mechanically, but seemed scarcely to sympathize with its trouble. With the same hard demeanour, she was led back to prison, and vanished from the public gaze within its iron-clamped portal. It was whispered, by those who peered after her, that the scarlet letter threw a lurid gleam along the dark passageway of the interior.

Herman Melville
Moby Dick

Herman Melville (1819–1891) was born in New York City and led a comfortable life until his father died in 1832. His mother then became a domineering force in his life as did the dogmatic form of Calvinism she practiced, which Melville was compelled to endure. Throughout his life, Melville was skeptical about organized religion but uncomfortable with the prospect of atheism. In 1839, he enlisted as a deck hand on a merchant ship, and for the next five years, Melville traversed the world; later, he signed on as a seaman on the warship the *United States.* These adventures gave rise to his most famous book—*Moby Dick; or, The Whale*—which many critics argue is the best American novel of the era. As Melville worked and reworked his story of a whaling adventure, he credited Nathaniel Hawthorne for its actual transformation into a compelling masterpiece and dedicated it to him when it appeared in 1851. Melville's rebellion against what he perceives to be a false idea of God is symbolized by Captain Ahab and his quest for "The White Whale." Ahab believes that if he can only "strike through the mask"—penetrate the physical reality of the whale and thus get beyond the superficial—he can know the truth about the whale which leads to truth about God. In his "Cetology [the study of whales] Chapters," Melville meticulously details the attack, death, and processing of each whale—piece by piece—with the hope of discovering some ultimate meaning and truth.

The novel is laden with mystical images of both the demonic and the heavenly. For example, the three chief shipmates represent various opinions about religion and the capacity of human beings. The first mate, Starbuck, is a Christian idealist who bucks the course that Ahab has laid out for his ship. In contrast, Stubb is a self-professed fatalist, who accepts life without critically questioning it. He is cheerful and optimistic, but he fails to grasp the seriousness of Ahab's quest for the White Whale, and it is Stubb who dispassionately abandons the cabin-boy, Pip, at sea, when he is washed overboard. Finally, Flask represents the materialist dolt who never thinks critically about anything, except the task immediately in front of him. Later, when Ahab nails a gold Spanish doubloon to the main mast as a reward for whomever sights the White Whale, Flask can only contemplate buying expensive cigars with it.

The images of evil, however, are less clear-cut. Consider, for example, three of the crew: Queequeg, the Manxman, and Fedallah. Queequeg, a Muslim, is covered in mystical tatoos, and he fashions his own coffin, which ultimately serves as the life raft for the ship's only survivor, Ishmael. The Manxman, from the Isle of Man and hence his name, serves as a prophet figure, much like the biblical prophet Elijah. He interprets omens, which Ahab consistently ignores, that foretell doom for the *Pequod.* Fedallah—a Parsee from India who believes in coequal, coeternal gods of good and evil—is a quiet, obscure figure whom some critics interpret to be the Devil Incarnate, whereas others view him as a disembodied soul.

The symbolic significance of Ahab, and his relationship to the White Whale, is very complex. In a very real sense, Moby Dick represents evil for Ahab, because it is he who is responsible for Ahab's physical deformity—the loss of a leg. Melville, nonetheless, consistently represents Moby Dick as "the White Whale," with the whiteness representing The Good, The True, and The Beautiful of Greek philosophy. If such is the case, then it is Ahab who represents evil, and Moby Dick becomes God's agent of divine vengeance on a sinful humanity when he causes Ahab's death at the end of the novel.

All these symbols come into play in the following chapter, "The Quarter-Deck," narrated by Ishmael. In it, Melville demonstrates Ahab's single-mindedness in pursuing Moby Dick and his ability to motivate everyone in the crew, except Starbuck, to participate in a ritualistic toast (reminiscent of the drinking of the cup in the Christian Eucharist) vowing death to Moby Dick.

CHAPTER 36
The Quarter-Deck

(Enter Ahab: Then, all.)

It was not a great while after the affair of the pipe,[1] that one morning shortly after breakfast, Ahab, as was his wont, ascended the cabin-gangway to the deck. There most sea-captains usually walk at that hour, as country gentlemen, after the same meal, take a few turns in the garden.

Soon his steady, ivory stride was heard, as to and fro he paced his old rounds, upon planks so familiar to his tread, that they were all over dented, like geological stones, with the peculiar mark of his walk. Did you fixedly gaze, too, upon that ribbed and dented brow, there also, you would see still stranger foot-prints—the foot prints of his one unsleeping, ever-pacing thought.

But on the occasion in question, those dents looked deeper, even as his nervous step that morning left a deeper mark. And, so full of his thought was Ahab, that at every uniform turn that he made, now at the main-mast and now at the binnacle, you could almost see that thought turn in him as he turned, and pace in him as he paced; so completely possessing him, indeed, that it all but seemed the inward mould of every outer movement.

"D'ye mark him, Flask?" whispered Stubb; "the chick that's in him pecks the shell. 'Twill soon be out."

The hours wore on;—Ahab now shut up within his cabin; anon, pacing the deck, with the same intense bigotry of purpose[2] in his aspect.

It drew near the close of day. Suddenly he came to a halt by the bulwarks, and inserting his bone leg into the auger-hole there, and with one hand grasping a shroud, he ordered Starbuck to send everybody aft.

"Sir!" said the mate, astonished at an order seldom or never given on ship-board except in some extraordinary case.

"Send everybody aft," repeated Ahab. "Mast-heads, there! come down!"

When the entire ship's company were assembled, and with curious and not wholly unapprehensive faces, were eyeing him, for he looked not unlike the weather horizon when a storm is coming up, Ahab, after rapidly glancing over the

bulwarks, and then darting his eyes among the crew, started from his stand-point; and as though not a soul were nigh him resumed his heavy turns upon the deck. With bent head and half-slouched hat he continued to pace, unmindful of the wondering whispering among the men; till Stubb cautiously whispered to Flask, that Ahab must have summoned them there for the purpose of witnessing a pedestrian feat. But this did not last long. Vehemently pausing, he cried:—

"What do ye do when ye see a whale, men?"

"Sing out for him!" was the impulsive rejoinder from a score of clubbed voices.

"Good!" cried Ahab, with a wild approval in his tones; observing the hearty animation into which his unexpected question had so magnetically thrown them.

"And what do ye next, men?"

"Lower away, and after him!"

"And what tune is it ye pull to, men?"

"A dead whale or a stove boat!"[3]

More and more strangely and fiercely glad and approving, grew the countenance of the old man at every shout; while the mariners began to gaze curiously at each other, as if marvelling how it was that they themselves became so excited at such seemingly purposeless questions.

But, they were all eagerness again, as Ahab, now half-revolving in his pivot-hole, with one band reaching high up a shroud, and tightly, almost convulsively grasping it, addressed them thus:—

"All ye mast-headers have before now heard me give orders about a white whale. Look ye! d'ye see this Spanish ounce of gold?"—holding up a broad bright coin to the sun—"it is a sixteen dollar piece, men,—a doubloon. D'ye see it? Mr. Starbuck, hand me yon top-maul."

While the mate was getting the hammer, Ahab, without speaking, was slowly rubbing the gold piece against the skirts of his jacket, as if to heighten its lustre, and without using any words was meanwhile lowly humming to himself, producing a sound so strangely muffled and inarticulate that it seemed the mechanical humming of the wheels of his vitality in him.

Receiving the top-maul from Starbuck, he advanced towards the main-mast with the hammer uplifted in one hand, exhibiting the gold with the other, and with a high raised voice exclaiming: "Whosoever of ye raises me a white-headed whale with a wrinkled brow and a crooked jaw; whosoever of ye raises me that white-headed whale, with three holes punctured in his starboard fluke—look ye,

---

[1] *Affair of the pipe* refers to an incident in Chapter 30 in which Ahab throws his smoking pipe into the ocean, because he realizes that he no longer enjoys it. This small incident is but one symbol for Ahab's rejection of his connection to the human race. Before the end of the novel, Ahab will throw more objects overboard.

[2] *Bigotry of purpose* means being intent on only one thing.

---

[3] *Stove boat* is a reference to a boat with a hole in it.

whosoever of ye raises me that same white whale, he shall have this gold ounce, my boys!"

"Huzza! Huzza![4]" cried the seamen, as with swinging tarpaulins they hailed the act of nailing the gold to the mast.

"It's a white whale, I say," resumed Ahab, as he threw down the top-maul; "a white whale. Skin your eyes for him, men; look sharp for white water; if ye see but a bubble, sing out."

All this while Tashtego,[5] Daggoo, and Queequeg had looked on with even more intense interest and surprise than the rest, and at the mention of the wrinkled brow and crooked jaw they had started as if each was separately touched by some specific recollection.

"Captain Ahab," said Tashtego, "that white whale must be the same that some call Moby Dick."

"Moby Dick?" shouted Ahab. "Do ye know the white whale then, Tash?"

"Does he fan-tail a little curious, sir, before he goes down?" said the Gay-Header deliberately.

"And has he a curious spout, too," said Daggoo, "very bushy, even for a parmacetty, and mighty quick, Captain Ahab?"

"And he have one, two, tree—oh! good many iron in him hide, too, Captain," cried Queequeg disjointedly, "all twiske-tee betwisk, like him—him—" faltering hard for a word, and screwing his hand round and round as though uncorking a bottle—"like him—him—"

"Corkscrew!" cried Ahab, "aye, Queequeg, the harpoons lie all twisted and wrenched in him; aye, Daggoo, his spout is a big one, like a whole shock of wheat, and white as a pile of our Nantucket wool after the great annual sheep-shearing; aye, Tashtego, and he fan-tails like a split jib in a squall. Death and devils! men, it is Moby Dick ye have seen—Moby Dick—Moby Dick!"

"Captain Ahab," said Starbuck, who, with Stubb and Flask, had thus far been eyeing his superior with increasing surprise, but at last seemed struck with a thought which somewhat explained all the wonder. "Captain Ahab, I have heard of Moby Dick—but it was not Moby Dick that took off thy leg?"

"Who told thee that?" cried Ahab; then pausing, "Aye, Starbuck; aye, my hearties all round; it was Moby Dick that dismasted me; Moby Dick that brought me to this dead stump I stand on now. Aye, aye," he shouted with a terrific, loud, animal sob, like that of a heart-stricken moose; "Aye, aye! it was that accursed white whale that razeed me; made a poor pegging lubber of me for ever and a day!" Then tossing both arms, with measureless imprecations he shouted out: "Aye, aye! and I'll chase him round Good Hope, and round the Horn, and round the Norway Maelstrom, and round perdition's flames before I give him up. And this is what ye have shipped for, men! to chase that white whale on both

sides of land, and over all sides of earth, till he spouts black blood and rolls fin out. What say ye, men, will ye splice hands on it, now? I think ye do look brave."

"Aye, aye!" shouted the harpooneers and seamen, running closer to the excited old man: "A sharp eye for the White Whale; a sharp lance for Moby Dick!"

"God bless ye," he seemed to half sob and half shout. "God bless ye, men. Steward! go draw the great measure of grog. But what's this long face about, Mr. Starbuck; wilt thou not chase the white whale? art not game for Moby Dick?"

"I am game for his crooked jaw, and for the jaws of Death too, Captain Ahab, if it fairly comes in the way of the business we follow; but I came here to hunt whales, not my commander's vengeance. How many barrels will thy vengeance yield thee even if thou gettest it, Captain Ahab? it will not fetch thee much in our Nantucket market."

"Nantucket market! Hoot! But come closer, Starbuck; thou requirest a little lower layer. If money's to be the measurer, man, and the accountants have computed their great counting-house the globe, by girdling it with guineas, one to every three parts of an inch; then, let me tell thee, that my vengeance will fetch a great premium *here!*"

"He smites his chest," whispered Stubb, "what's that for? methinks it rings most vast, but hollow."

"Vengeance on a dumb brute!" cried Starbuck, "that simply smote thee from blindest instinct! Madness! To be enraged with a dumb thing, Captain Ahab, seems blasphemous."

"Hark ye yet again,—the little lower layer. All visible objects, man, are but as pasteboard masks. But in each event—in the living act, the undoubted deed—there, some unknown but still reasoning thing puts forth the mouldings of its features from behind the unreasoning mask. If man will strike, strike through the mask! How can the prisoner reach outside except by thrusting through the wall? To me, the white whale is that wall, shoved near to me. Sometimes I think there's naught beyond. But 'tis enough. He tasks me; he heaps me; I see in him outrageous strength, with an inscrutable malice sinewing it. That inscrutable thing is chiefly what I hate; and be the white whale agent, or be the white whale principal, I will wreak that hate upon him. Talk not to me of blasphemy, man; I'd strike the sun if it insulted me. For could the sun do that, then could I do the other; since there is ever a sort of fair play herein, jealousy presiding over all creations. But not my master, man, is even that fair play. Who's over me? Truth hath no confines. Take off thine eye! more intolerable than fiends' glarings is a doltish stare! So, so; thou reddenest and palest; my heat has melted thee to anger-glow. But look ye, Starbuck, what is said in heat, that thing unsays itself. There are men from whom warm words are small indignity. I meant not to incense thee. Let it go. Look! see yonder Turkish cheeks of spotted tawn—living, breathing pictures painted by the sun. The Pagan leopards—the unrecking and unworshipping things, that live; and seek, and give no reasons for the torrid life they feel! The crew,

---

[4]*Huzza* is an expression of joy.

[5]Tashtego is an American Indian who serves as Stubb's harpooner, and Daggoo, an African, is Flask's harpooner.

man, the crew! Are they not one and all with Ahab, in this matter of the whale? See Stubb! he laughs! See yonder Chilean! he snorts to think of it. Stand up amid the general hurricane, thy one tost sapling cannot, Starbuck! And what is it? Reckon it. 'Tis but to help strike a fin; no wondrous feat for Starbuck. What is it more? From this one poor hunt, then, the best lance out of all Nantucket, surely he will not hang back, when every foremast-hand has clutched a whetstone? Ah! constrainings seize thee; I see! the billow lifts thee! Speak, but speak!—Aye, aye! thy silence, then, *that* voices thee. (*Aside*) Something shot from my dilated nostrils, he has inhaled it in his lungs. Starbuck now is mine; cannot oppose me now, without rebellion."

"God keep me!—keep us all!" murmured Starbuck, lowly.

But in his joy at the enchanted, tacit acquiescence of the mate, Ahab did not hear his foreboding invocation; nor yet the low laugh from the hold; nor yet the presaging vibrations of the winds in the cordage; nor yet the hollow flap of the sails against the masts, as for a moment their hearts sank in. For again Starbuck's downcast eyes lighted up with the stubbornness of life; the subterranean laugh died away; the winds blew on; the sails filled out; the ship heaved and rolled as before. Ah, ye admonitions and warnings! why stay ye not when ye come? But rather are ye predictions than warnings, ye shadows! Yet not so much predictions from without, as verifications of the foregoing things within. For with little external to constrain us, the innermost necessities in our being, these still drive us on,

"The measure! the measure!" cried Ahab.

Receiving the brimming pewter, and turning to the harpooneers, he ordered them to produce their weapons. Then ranging them before him near the capstan, with their harpoons in their hands, while his three mates stood at his side with their lances, and the rest of the ship's company formed a circle round the group; he stood for an instant searchingly eyeing every man of his crew. But those wild eyes met his, as the bloodshot eyes of the prairie wolves meet the eye of their leader, ere he rushes on at their head in the trail of the bison; but, alas! only to fall into the hidden snare of the Indian.

"Drink and pass!" he cried, handing the heavy charged flagon to the nearest seaman. "The crew alone now drink. Round with it, round! Short draughts—long swallows, men; 'tis hot as Satan's[6] hoof. So, so; it goes round excellently. It spiralizes in ye; forks out at the serpent-snapping eye. Well done; almost drained. That way it went, this way it comes. Hand it me—here's a hollow! Men, ye seem the years; so brimming life is gulped and gone. Steward, refill!

"Attend now, my braves. I have mustered ye all round this capstan; and ye mates, flank me with your lances; and ye harpooneers, stand there with your irons; and ye, stout mariners, ring me in, that I may in some sort revive a noble

custom of my fisherman fathers before me. O men, you will yet see that—Ha! boy, come back? bad pennies come not sooner. Hand it me. Why, now, this pewter had run brimming again, wert not thou St. Vitus'[7] imp—away, thou ague!

"Advance, ye mates! Cross your lances full before me. Well done! Let me touch the axis." So saying, with extended arm, he grasped the three level, radiating lances at their crossed centre; while so doing, suddenly and nervously twitched them; meanwhile, glancing intently from Starbuck to Stubb; from Stubb to Flask. It seemed as though, by some nameless, interior volition, he would fain have shocked into them the same fiery emotion accumulated within the Leyden jar[8] of his own magnetic life. The three mates quailed before his strong, sustained, and mystic aspect. Stubb and Flask looked sideways from him; the honest eye of Starbuck fell downright.

"In vain!" cried Ahab; "but, maybe, 'tis well. For did ye three but once take the full-forced shock, then mine own electric thing, *that* had perhaps expired from out me. Perchance, too, it would have dropped ye dead. Perchance ye need it not. Down lances! And now, ye mates, I do appoint ye three cup-bearers to my three pagan kinsmen there—yon three most honorable gentlemen and noblemen, my valiant harpooneers. Disdain the task? What, when the great Pope washes the feet of beggars, using his tiara for ewer? Oh, my sweet cardinals! your own condescension, *that* shall bend ye to it. I do not order ye; ye will it. Cut your seizings and draw the poles, ye harpooneers!"

Silently obeying the order, the three harpooneers now stood with the detached iron part of their harpoons, some three feet long, held, barbs up, before him.

"Stab me not with that keen steel! Cant them; cant them over! know ye not the goblet end? Turn up the socket! So, so; now, ye cup-bearers, advance. The irons! take them; hold them while I fill!" Forthwith, slowly going from one officer to the other, he brimmed the harpoon sockets with the fiery waters from the pewter.

"Now, three to three, ye stand. Commend the murderous chalices! Bestow them, ye who are now made parties to this indissoluble league. Ha! Starbuck! but the deed is done! Yon ratifying sun now waits to sit upon it. Drink, ye harpooneers! drink and swear, ye men that man the deathful whaleboat's bow—Death to Moby Dick! God hunt us all, if we do not hunt Moby Dick to his death!" The long, barbed steel goblets were lifted; and to cries and maledictions against the white whale, the spirits were simultaneously quaffed down with a hiss. Starbuck paled, and turned, and shivered. Once more, and finally, the replenished pewter went the rounds among the frantic crew; when, waving his free hand to them, they all dispersed; and Ahab retired within his cabin.

---

[6]*Satan's hoof* refers to the common understanding that Satan had a cloven foot (like a goat or a deer) as well as horns.

[7]*St. Vitus' imp* refers to a supposed small demon associated with the patron saint who protects sailors from storms.

[8]*Leyden jar* refers to an antiquated device used to store electric energy. Today it is called a capacitor.

15

Realism and Reform

Romanticism dominated European art, literature, and music in the early nineteenth century. Stressing the feelings and the free expression of personality, the Romantic Movement was a reaction against the rationalism of the Enlightenment. In the middle decades of the century, Realism and its close auxiliary Naturalism supplanted Romanticism as the chief norm of cultural expression. Rejecting religious, metaphysical, and Romantic interpretations of reality, Realists aspired to an exact and accurate portrayal of the external world and daily life. Realist and Naturalist writers used the empirical approach—the careful collection, ordering, and interpretation of facts employed in science, which was advancing steadily in the nineteenth century. Among the most important scientific theories formulated was Charles Darwin's theory of evolution, which revolutionized conceptions of time and the origins of the human species.

The principal currents of political thought, Marxism and liberalism, also reacted against Romantic, religious, and metaphysical interpretations of nature and society, focused on the empirical world, and strove for scientific accuracy. This emphasis on objective reality helped to stimulate a growing criticism of social ills, for despite unprecedented material progress, reality was often sordid, somber, and dehumanizing. In the last part of the century, reformers, motivated by an expansive liberalism, revolutionary or evolutionary socialism, or a socially committed Christianity, pressed for the alleviation of social injustice.

1 The Socialist Revolution

After completing a doctorate at the University of Jena in 1841, Karl Marx (1818–1883) edited a newspaper that was suppressed by the Prussian authorities for its radicalism and atheism. He left his native Rhineland for Paris, where he became friendly with Friedrich Engels. Expelled from France at the request of Prussia, Marx went to Brussels. In 1848, Marx and Engels produced for the Communist League the *Communist Manifesto,* advocating the violent overthrow of capitalism and the creation of a socialist society. Marx returned to Prussia and participated in a minor way in the Revolutions of 1848 in Germany. Expelled from Prussia in 1849, he went to England. He spent the rest of his life there, writing and agitating for the cause of socialism.

The *Communist Manifesto* presented a philosophy of history and a theory of society that Marx expanded upon in his later works, particularly *Capital* (1867). In the tradition of the Enlightenment, he maintained that history, like the operations of nature, was governed by scientific law. To understand the past and the present and to predict the essential outlines of the future, said Marx, one must concentrate on economic forces, on how goods are produced and how wealth is distributed. Marx's call for a working-class revolution against capitalism and for the making of a classless society established the ideology of twentieth-century communist revolutionaries.

Karl Marx and Friedrich Engels
Communist Manifesto

In the opening section of the *Manifesto,* the basic premise of the Marxian philosophy of history is advanced: class conflict—the idea that the social order is divided into classes based on conflicting economic interests.

BOURGEOIS AND PROLETARIANS

The history of all hitherto existing society is the history of class struggles.

Freeman and slave, patrician and plebeian [aristocrat and commoner, in the ancient world], lord and serf, guild-master [master craftsman] and journeyman [who worked for a guild-master], in a word, oppressor and oppressed, stood in constant opposition to one another, carried on an uninterrupted, now hidden, now open fight, that each time ended, either in a revolutionary reconstitution of society at large, or in the common ruin of the contending classes.

In the earlier epochs of history we find almost every-where a complicated arrangement of society into various orders, a manifold gradation of social rank. In ancient Rome we have patricians, knights, plebeians, slaves; in the Middle Ages, feudal lords, vassals [landowners pledged to lords], guild-masters, journeymen, apprentices, serfs; in almost all of these classes, again, subordinate gradations.

The modern bourgeois society that has sprouted from the ruins of feudal society, has not done away with class antagonisms. It has but established new forms of struggle in place of the old ones.

Our epoch, the epoch of the bourgeoisie [capitalist class], possesses, however, this distinctive feature; it has simplified the class antagonisms. Society as a whole is more and more splitting up into two great hostile camps, into two great classes directly facing each other: Bourgeoisie and Proletariat [industrial workers].

From the serfs of the middle ages sprang the chartered burghers of the earliest towns. From these burgesses the first elements of the bourgeoisie were developed.

The discovery of America, the rounding of the Cape, opened up fresh ground for the rising bourgeoisie. The East-Indian and Chinese markets, the colonization of America, trade with the colonies, the increase in the means of exchange and in commodities generally, gave to commerce, to navigation, to industry, an impulse never before known, and thereby, to the revolutionary element in the tottering feudal society, a rapid development.

The feudal system of industry, under which industrial production was monopolized by closed guilds, now no longer sufficed for the growing wants of the new market. The manufacturing system took its place. The guildmasters were pushed on one side by the manufacturing middle class; division of labor between the different corporate guilds vanished in the face of division of labor in each single workshop.

Meantime the markets kept ever growing, the demand ever rising. . . . Thereupon steam and machinery revolutionized industrial production. The place of manufacture was taken by the giant, Modern Industry, the place of the industrial middle class, by industrial millionaires, the leaders of whole industrial armies, the modern bourgeois.

Modern Industry has established the world's market, for which the discovery of America paved the way. This market has given an immense development to commerce, to navigation, to communication by land. This development has, in its turn, reacted on the extension of industry; and in proportion, as industry, commerce, navigation, railways extended, in the same proportion, the bourgeoisie developed, increased its capital, and pushed into the background every class handed down from the Middle Ages.

We see, therefore, how the modern bourgeoisie is itself the product of a long course of development, of a series of revolutions in the modes of production and of exchange.

Each step in the development of the bourgeoisie was accompanied by a corresponding political advance of that class. An oppressed class under the sway of the feudal nobility, an armed and self-governing association in the mediaeval commune [town], . . . the bourgeoisie has at last, since the establishment of Modern Industry and of the world's market, conquered for itself, in the modern representative State, exclusive political sway. The executive of the modern State is but a committee for managing the common affairs of the whole bourgeoisie.

The bourgeoisie, historically, has played a most revolutionary part.

The bourgeoisie, wherever it has got the upper hand, has put an end to all feudal, patriarchal, idyllic relations. It has pitilessly torn asunder the motley feudal ties that bound man to his "natural superiors," and has left remaining no other nexus [link] between man and man than naked self-interest, than callous "cash payment." It has drowned the most heavenly ecstasies of religious fervor, of chivalrous enthusiasm, . . . in the icy water of egotistical calculation. It has resolved personal worth into exchange value, and in place of the numberless indefeasible chartered freedoms, has set up that single, unconscionable freedom—Free Trade. In one word, for exploitation, veiled by religious and political illusions, it has substituted naked, shameless, direct, brutal exploitation. . . .

The bourgeoisie, states the *Manifesto,* has subjected nature's forces to human control to an unprece-

dented degree and has replaced feudal organization of agriculture (serfdom) and manufacturing (guild system) with capitalist free competition. But the capitalists cannot control these "gigantic means of production and exchange." Periodically, capitalist society is burdened by severe economic crises; capitalism is afflicted with overproduction—more goods are produced than the market will absorb. In all earlier epochs, which were afflicted with scarcity, the *Manifesto* declares such a condition "would have seemed an absurdity." To deal with the crisis, the capitalists curtail production, thereby intensifying the poverty of the proletariat, who are without work. In capitalist society, the exploited worker suffers from physical poverty—a result of low wages—and spiritual poverty—a result of the monotony, regimentation, and impersonal character of the capitalist factory system. For the proletariat, work is not the satisfaction of a need but a repulsive means for survival. The products they help make bring them no satisfaction; they are alienated from their labor.

In proportion as the bourgeoisie, *i.e.,* capital, is developed, in the same proportion is the proletariat, the modern working class, developed—a class of laborers, who live only so long as they find work, and who find work only so long as their labor increases capital. These laborers, who must sell themselves piecemeal, are a commodity, like every other article of commerce, and are consequently exposed to all the vicissitudes of competition, to all the fluctuations of the market.

Owing to the extensive use of machinery and to division of labor, the work of the proletarians has lost all individual character, and, consequently, all charm for the workman. He becomes an appendage of the machine, and it is only the most simple, most monotonous, and most easily acquired knack, that is required of him. Hence, the cost of production of a workman is restricted, almost entirely, to the means of subsistence that he requires for his maintenance, and for the propagation of his race. But the price of a commodity, and therefore also of labor, is equal to its cost of production. In proportion, therefore, as the repulsiveness of the work increases, the wage decreases. Nay more, in proportion as the use of machinery and division of labor increases, in the same proportion the burden of toil also increases, whether by prolongation of the working hours, by increase of the work exacted in a given time, or by increased speed of the machinery, etc.

Modern industry has converted the little workshop of the patriarchal master into the great factory of the industrial capitalist. Masses of laborers, crowded into the factory, are organized like soldiers. As privates of the industrial army they are placed under the command of a perfect hierarchy of officers and sergeants. Not only are they slaves of the bourgeois class, and of the bourgeois state; they are daily and hourly enslaved by the machine, by the overlooker, and, above all, by the individual bourgeois manufacturer himself. The more openly this despotism proclaims gain to be its end and aim, the more petty, the more hateful and the more embittering it is.

The less the skill and exertion of strength implied in manual labor, in other words, the more modern industry develops, the more is the labor of men superseded by that of women. Differences of age and sex have no longer any distinctive social validity for the working class. All are instruments of labor, more or less expensive to use, according to their age and sex.

No sooner has the laborer received his wages in cash, for the moment escaping exploitation by the manufacturer, than he is set upon by the other portions of the bourgeoisie, the landlord, the shop-keeper, the pawnbroker, etc. . . .

The exploited workers organize to defend their interests against the capitalist oppressors.

But with the development of industry the proletariat not only increases in number; it becomes concentrated in greater masses, its strength grows, and it feels that strength more. The various interests and conditions of life within the ranks of the proletariat are more and more equalized, in proportion as machinery obliterates all distinctions of labor and nearly everywhere reduces wages to the same low level. The growing competition among the bourgeois, and the resulting commercial crises, make the wages of the workers ever more fluctuating. The unceasing improvement of machinery, ever more rapidly developing, makes their livelihood more and more precarious: the collisions between individual workmen and individual bourgeois take more and more the character of collisions between two classes. Thereupon the workers begin to form combinations (trade unions) against the bourgeoisie; they club together in order to keep up the rate of wages; they found permanent associations in order to make provision beforehand for these occasional revolts. Here and there the contest breaks out into riots.

Now and then the workers are victorious, but only for a time. The real fruit of their battles lies, not in the immediate results, but in [their ever-expanding unity]. . . .

This organization of the proletarians into a class, and consequently into a political party, is continually being upset again by the competition between the workers themselves. But it ever rises up again, stronger, firmer, mightier. It compels legislative recognition of particular interests of the workers, by taking advantage of the divisions among the bourgeoisie itself. Thus the ten-hour bill[1] in England was carried. . . .

Increasingly, the proletariat, no longer feeling part of the old society, seeks to destroy it.

---

[1]The Ten Hours Act (1847) provided a ten and a half hour day from 6 A.M. to 6 P.M., with an hour and a half for meals for women and children.

In the conditions of the proletariat, those of the old society at large are already virtually swamped. The proletarian is without property; his relation to his wife and children has no longer anything in common with the bourgeois family relations; modern industrial labor, modern subjection to capital, the same in England as in France, in America as in Germany, has stripped him of every trace of national character. Law, morality, religion, are to him so many bourgeois prejudices, behind which lurk in ambush just as many bourgeois interests.

All the preceding classes that got the upper hand sought to fortify their already acquired status by subjecting society at large to their conditions of appropriation. The proletarians cannot become masters of the productive forces of society, except by abolishing their own previous mode of appropriation, and thereby also every other previous mode of appropriation. They have nothing of their own to secure and to fortify; their mission is to destroy all previous securities for, and insurances of, individual property.

All previous historical movements were movements of minorities, or in the interest of minorities. The proletarian movement is the self-conscious, independent movement of the immense majority, in the interest of the immense majority. The proletariat, the lowest stratum of our present society, cannot stir, cannot raise itself up, without the whole superincumbent [overlying] strata of official society being sprung into the air.

Though not in substance, yet in form, the struggle of the proletariat with the bourgeoisie is at first a national struggle. The proletariat of each country must, of course, first of all settle matters with its own bourgeoisie.

In depicting the most general phases of the development of the proletariat, we traced the more or less veiled civil war, raging within existing society, up to the point where that war breaks out into open revolution, and where the violent overthrow of the bourgeoisie lays the foundation for the sway of the proletariat. . . .

The modern laborer . . . instead of rising with the progress of industry, sinks deeper and deeper below the conditions of existence of his own class. He becomes a pauper, and pauperism develops more rapidly than population and wealth. And here it becomes evident that the bourgeoisie is unfit any longer to be the ruling class in society and to impose its conditions of existence upon society as an overriding law. It is unfit to rule because it is incompetent to assure an existence to its slave within his slavery, because it cannot help letting him sink into such a state that it has to feed him instead of being fed by him. Society can no longer live under this bourgeoisie, in other words its existence is no longer compatible with society.

The essential condition for the existence and for the sway of the bourgeois class, is the formation and augmentation of capital; the condition for capital is wage-labor. Wage-labor rests exclusively on competition between the laborers. The advance of industry, whose involuntary promoter is the bourgeoisie, replaces the isolation of the laborers, due to competition, by their revolutionary combination, due to association. The development of modern industry, therefore, cuts from under its feet the very foundation on which the bourgeoisie produces and appropriates products. What the bourgeoisie therefore produces above all, are its own gravediggers. Its fall and the victory of the proletariat are equally inevitable. . . .

> Communists, says the *Manifesto,* are the most advanced and determined members of working-class parties. Among the aims of the communists are organization of the working class into a revolutionary party, overthrow of bourgeois power and the assumption of political power by the proletariat, and an end to exploitation of one individual by another and the creation of a classless society. These aims will be achieved by the abolition of bourgeois private property (private ownership of the means of production) and the abolition of the bourgeoisie as a class.

The Communists, therefore, are on the one hand, practically, the most advanced and resolute section of the working class parties of every country, that section which pushes forward all others; on the other hand, theoretically, they have over the great mass of the proletariat the advantage of clearly understanding the line of march, the conditions, and the ultimate general results of the proletarian movement.

The immediate aim of the Communists is the same as that of all the other proletarian parties: formation of the proletariat into a class, overthrow of the bourgeois supremacy, conquest of political power by the proletariat. . . .

The distinguishing feature of Communism is not the abolition of property generally, but the abolition of bourgeois property. But modern bourgeois private property is the final and most complete expression of the system of producing and appropriating products, that is based on class antagonisms, on the exploitation of the many by the few.

In this sense the theory of the Communists may be summed up in the single sentence: Abolition of private property. . . .

> One argument leveled against communists by bourgeois critics, says the *Manifesto,* is that the destruction of the bourgeoisie would lead to the disappearance of bourgeois culture, which is "identical with the disappearance of all culture," and the loss of all moral and religious truths. Marx insists that these ethical and religious ideals lauded by the bourgeoisie are not universal truths at all but are common expressions of the ruling class at a particular stage in history.

That culture, the loss of which he [the bourgeois] laments, is for the enormous majority, a mere training to act as a machine.

But don't wrangle with us so long as you [the bour-

geoisie] apply to our [the communists'] intended abolition of bourgeois property, the standard of your bourgeois notions of freedom, culture, law, etc. Your very ideas are but the outgrowth of the conditions of your bourgeois production and bourgeois property, just as your jurisprudence is but the will of your class made into a law for all, a will, whose essential character and direction are determined by the economical conditions of existence of your class.

The selfish misconception that induces you to transform into eternal laws of nature and of reason, the social forms springing from your present mode of production and form of property —historical relations that rise and disappear in the progress of production—this misconception you share with every ruling class that has preceded you. What you see clearly in the case of ancient property, what you admit in the case of feudal property, you are of course forbidden to admit in the case of your own bourgeois form of property. . . .

The charges against Communism made from a religious, a philosophical, and, generally, from an ideological standpoint, are not deserving of serious examination.

Does it require deep intuition to comprehend that man's ideas, views, and conceptions, in one word, man's consciousness changes with every change in the conditions of his material existence, in his social relations and in his social life?

What else does the history of ideas prove than that intellectual production changes its character in proportion as material production is changed? The ruling ideas of each age have ever been the ideas of its ruling class. . . .

. . . The ideas of religious liberty and freedom of conscience merely gave expression to the sway of free competition within the domain of knowledge.

"Undoubtedly," it will be said, "religious, moral, philosophical, and juridical ideas have been modified in the course of historic development. But religion, morality, philosophy, political science, and law, constantly survived this change.

"There are besides, eternal truths, such as Freedom, Justice, etc., that are common to all states of society. But Communism abolishes eternal truths, it abolishes all religion and all morality, instead of constituting them on a new basis; it therefore acts as a contradiction to all past historical experience."

What does this accusation reduce itself to? The history of all past society has consisted in the development of class antagonisms, antagonisms that assumed different forms at different epochs.

But whatever form they may have taken, one fact is common in all past ages, *viz.,* the exploitation of one part of society by the other. No wonder, then, that the social consciousness of past ages, despite all the multiplicity and variety it displays, moves within certain common forms, or general ideas, which cannot completely vanish except with the total disappearance of class antagonisms.

The Communist revolution is the most radical rupture with traditional property relations; no wonder that its development involves the most radical rupture with traditional ideas.

Aroused and united by communist intellectuals, says the *Manifesto*, the proletariat will wrest power from the bourgeoisie and overthrow the capitalist system that has oppressed them. In the new society, people will be fully free.

But let us have done with the bourgeois objections to Communism.

We have seen above that the first step in the revolution by the working class is to raise the proletariat to the position of the ruling class, to win the battle of democracy.

The proletariat will use its political supremacy to wrest, by degrees, all capital from the bourgeoisie; to centralize all instruments of production in the hands of the State, *i.e.,* of the proletariat organized as the ruling class; and to increase the total of productive forces as rapidly as possible. . . .

When, in the course of development, class distinctions have disappeared and all production has been concentrated in the hands of a vast association of the whole nation, the public power will lose its political character. Political power,

properly so called, is merely the organized power of one class for oppressing another. If the proletariat during its contest with the bourgeoisie is compelled, by the force of circumstances, to organize itself as a class, if, by means of a revolution, it makes itself the ruling class, and, as such, sweeps away by force the old conditions of production, then it will, along with these conditions, have swept away the conditions for the existence of class antagonism, and of classes generally, and will thereby have abolished its own supremacy as a class.

In place of the old bourgeois society with its classes and class antagonisms we shall have an association in which the free development of each is the condition for the free development of all. . . .

The Communists disdain to conceal their views and aims. They openly declare that their ends can be attained only by the forcible overthrow of all existing social conditions. Let the ruling classes tremble at a communistic revolution. The proletarians have nothing to lose but their chains. They have a world to win.

Working men of all countries, unite!

2   The Realist Novel

Realism, the dominant movement in art and literature in the mid-nineteenth century, opposed the Romantic veneration of the inner life and the value the Romantics placed on intuition, spontaneity, feeling, and passion. The Romantics often let their imaginations transport them to a presumed idyllic medieval past, and they frequently sought inner solitude amid nature's wonders. Realists, on the other hand, concentrated on the actual world and dealt regularly with social abuses, class divisions, and the ignoble aspects of human behavior. Like scientists, Realist writers and artists empirically investigated the world, and with clinical detachment and meticulous care, they analyzed how people looked, worked, and behaved. This resulted in a body of literature that portrays life as it *is* rather than theorizing about how it *ought* to be.

In the closing decades of the nineteenth century, literary Realism evolved into Naturalism, when writers, reacting to the Realists' emphasis on the commonplace, began to write about the atypical, arguing that it was "real" as well. Instead of writing about the facts of middle-class life, Naturalist writers were drawn to the seamy side of life, including the criminal element. These writers were particularly influenced by scientific determinism and Darwin's theory of evolution. Naturalists tried to demonstrate a causal relationship between human character and the social environment. The belief that the law of cause and effect governed human behavior reflected the immense prestige that Naturalists attached to science.

In analyzing the prose of the Realists and Naturalists, certain basic elements are evident. Character development supersedes the action of the plot, and although characters are affected by their environment, they can also act on it. In addition, the events about which the Realists and Naturalists write are much more plausible than the episodes described by Romantic writers. The structure of the prose is equally believable, with the speech of the characters often reflecting the vernacular of the region in which the action takes place.

Honoré Balzac
Le Père Goriot

Honoré Balzac (1799–1850) was an early Realist who displayed prodigious energy—completing ninety-one novels and short stories in a period of about twenty years. Balzac's depictions of the attitudes and behavior of the middle and upper classes of French society have been praised for their superb insight into people driven by a desire for wealth and status. Balzac indicted such behavior for undermining the moral foundations of French society.

Balzac tried to show how a particular social setting determines a person's behavior. Thus, in *Le Père Goriot* (Old Goriot, 1834), young Eugène de Rastignac loses his integrity when he moves from his small, ancestral country estate to study law in Paris. There, he admires "the carriages which pass along the Champs Elysées and before long he craves a part in the procession." Bitten by the virus that plagues bourgeois Parisian society, Eugène gradually mirrors the covetousness and corruption of those around him.

In the following selection from *Le Père Goriot,* the virile, streetwise, amoral Vautrin tells Eugène that in this fiercely competitive world, people really make their fortune through "the adroitness of corruption. . . . Honesty is of no use." And he devises a scheme for Eugène to make his fortune: Eugène would marry the daughter of a wealthy man and Vautrin would arrange to have her brother killed, making her the only heir.

"I don't blame you for your desires. My boy, everybody hasn't the luck to be ambitious. Ask women which men they seek—the men who have ambition. The ambitious have the strongest bodies, the most iron in their blood, hotter emotions than other men. Women feel happiest and are most beautiful when they are strong, and so they prefer above all other men those who have enormous force, even when they run the risk of having it shatter them. I'm cataloguing your desires because I mean to put a question to you. This is the question. We're as hungry as a wolf; our paws have talons; how are we going to keep the pot boiling? We have first to swallow the law books, that isn't much fun and doesn't teach anything worth knowing! But they have to be dealt with! It can't be helped. We become a lawyer so that we can become the presiding judge at . . . court; we brand poor rascals who are better men than we are in order to prove to the rich that they can sleep quietly in their beds. It's no fun, and it takes a lot of time. To begin with, two years in Paris, hanging around and looking on, but without daring to touch the sweets we want so much. It's very exhausting to be always wanting something and unable to satisfy oneself. If you were thin-blooded, a sort of mollusk, you'd have nothing to fear; but you are as hot-blooded as a lion and your appetite would involve you in a score of foolish acts every day. You'll succumb to this torture—and it's the worst torture there is in God's hell. Let's suppose that you are good, that you drink only milk and compose elegies. Very well, high spirited as you may be, after a lot of trials and privations harsh enough to madden a dog, you'll have to begin by being assistant to some rascal in some dreadful hole of a town where the Government will throw you as your honorarium a thousand francs a year. Why, it's just like setting down a plate of soup before a butcher's mastiff! Go and bark at the thieves, plead the cases of the rich, send the fellows with guts to the guillotine. Many thanks! If you don't have patrons, you can go on rotting in your local court.

"When you're getting on for thirty, you'll be a judge there with twelve hundred francs a year, if you haven't yet thrown your gown into the garbage can. When you're about forty you'll marry some miller's daughter, who has an income of about six thousand francs. Very nice. If you have patrons, you'll be crown-attorney at thirty, with a salary of a thousand crowns, and you'll marry the mayor's daughter. If you go in for some low political tricks, such as reading Villèle for Manuel (there's rhyme, that's enough to pacify your conscience) on some document, by the time you're forty you'll be an attorney-general, and you may even become a member of the Chamber of Deputies. Note, my boy, that we shall have done some tampering with our darling little conscience, that we'll have endured twenty years of tribulations and hidden poverty, and that our sisters will have stayed unmarried. It's my privilege to point out to you, besides, that there only are twenty attorneys-general in France and twenty thousand aspirants to the title, among them some rogues who'd sell their whole family to rise one step. Suppose the profession displeases you; let's see what else there is. Does the Baron de Rastignac want to be an advocate? Very pleasant. You begin with ten years of suffering; you lay out a thousand francs each month; you have an office and a law library; you kiss the robe of a solicitor in order to get briefs; you lick the floor of the Court House. If this turned out well I wouldn't say you were foolish; but just find me in Paris five members of the bar who at fifty make more than fifty thousand francs a year! Bah! Rather than let my soul shrivel in that way I'd be a pirate! And besides, where would you get the money to last the course?

"It isn't very gay, the life I've painted for you. The dowry a wife would bring would help. If you marry there's a stone around your neck; and besides if we marry for money what becomes of our noble feelings, of our sense of honor? You might as well begin your rebellion against social conventions today. It would be nothing to lie down like a snake at a woman's feet, lick her mother's shoes, do things so low they'd disgust a sow, if you found happiness in the end. But you'll be utterly unhappy with a woman you'd have married in this way. It's better to wrestle with men than to match yourself against a woman. Well, there's the battleground of life, my boy. Make your choice. You've already chosen; you've gone to see your cousin de Beauséant, and you've scented luxury at her house. You've gone to the house of the Countess de Restaud, Père Goriot's daughter, and you scented the Parisian woman there. The day you came back from her place one word was graved on your forehead, and I could read it there: it was the word, *Succeed!* Succeed at any cost.

"Bravo, I said to myself, there's a fellow who suits my taste. You had to have money. Where was it to be had? You've taken everything your sisters could give you. It's the way of all brothers to slip away with more or less of their sisters' resources. Those fifteen hundred francs, got together God knows how, in a country where there are more chestnuts than hundred-sous pieces, are going to disappear quicker than a gang of marauding soldiers! And then, when they're gone, what will you do? You'll work? Work, understood as you understand it now, means that when you're old, if you have kept your strength as Poiret has, you'll be able to afford an apartment at Mama Vauquer's in your old age.

"How to make a fortune quickly—that's the problem fifty thousand young fellows in your position are right now trying to solve. You're one unit in that number. you can judge what efforts you'll have to make and how fierce the contest will be. You have to eat one another like so many spiders thrust into a pot, since there aren't fifty thousand good places available. Do you know how a man succeeds here? Either by the flash of genius or the adroitness of corruption. You have to crash into that mass like a cannon ball, or else slip in like a disease. Honesty is of no use. Men will bend beneath the power of genius, hating it, trying to slander it, because it takes all and gives nothing; but in the end they will accept its yoke if genius is stubborn. In a word, they'll worship it on their knees after they've failed to bury it in the mud. Corruption is everywhere; talent is rare. So corruption is the weapon of swarming mediocrity, and wherever you go you feel its edge. You'll see women whose husbands' pay is only six thousand francs a year, and they'll be spending ten on their dress alone. You'll see clerks who make

twelve hundred francs buying property. You'll see women selling their bodies to ride in the carriage of the son of a lord, because then they can drive out to Longchamps in the middle lane. You've seen that poor fool of a Père Goriot forced to meet the note his daughter had endorsed, and her husband has an income of fifty thousand livres. I challenge you to take two steps in Paris without coming upon some devilish machinations. I'd bet my head to a head of that lettuce that you'll commune on a wasp's nest with the first woman who attracts you, no matter if she's wealthy, beautiful and young. They're all up against some law, all at war with their husbands over everything. I'd never end if I had to explain to you all the shabby tricks that are used to get lovers, to get dresses, to hold children, to keep up the household, or just to satisfy vanity, but very seldom for any virtuous end, you may count on that. So the honest man is everyone's enemy. And what do you think an honest man is? In Paris he's the man who keeps silent, who refuses to make a deal. Of course I'm not talking about those poor serfs who exist everywhere to do the world's rough tasks and are never rewarded for their labor—I call them the confraternity of the wooden shoes of God. In them you find virtue in the fine flower of its stupidity, and their mark is utter poverty. I can imagine the horrible disappointment of these worthy folk if God should play a joke on them, a cruel joke, and stay away from the last judgment.

"So if you want to make a fortune in a hurry, you must either be rich already or else give the appearance of being rich. To get rich you have to do things in a big way, otherwise your gains are just small change, and it's all up. If in the hundred occupations which are open to you there are ten men who get rich quick, they're called robbers. Draw your own conclusions. That's the reality of life. It's no prettier than a kitchen; it smells as bad; and you've got to get your hands dirty if you're going to cook anything. The thing is to know how to get them clean again; the whole morality of our age is in that. If I talk to you like this about the world, it's because I've a right to. I know it. Do you suppose that I condemn it? Not at all. That's the way it's always been. Moralists won't ever change it. Man is an imperfect creature. Sometimes he is more of a hypocrite, sometimes less, and ninnies say he's good when he is more, and bad when he's less. I'm not championing the poor against the rich; man is the same at the top, in the middle, at the bottom of the social ladder. In a million of these high-grade cattle there are ten rascals who stand above everything, even above law. I'm one of them.

"And you, if you're really a superior person, plunge right ahead and hold your head high. But you must expect to contend against envy and calumny and mediocrity, against the whole world. Napoleon had to do with a Minister of War, Aubry was the name, who almost sent him out to the colonies. Take stock of yourself! See if you're strong enough to get up every morning with a firmer will than you had the night before. If you are, I'm going to make you a proposition that nobody would refuse. Listen carefully. You see I've got an idea. I mean to go and live a patriarchal life in the midst of a great estate, a hundred thousand acres say, in the southern part of the United States. I mean to be a planter, have slaves, make a nice few millions selling my livestock, my tobacco, my wood, live like a king, doing everything I crave, leading such a life as isn't imagined here where people creep into plaster burrows. I'm a great poet. But I don't write my poems; they are made of feelings and actions. Right now I have fifty thousand francs, and with that sum I could hardly buy forty blacks. I need two hundred thousand because I want two hundred blacks so that I can satisfy my tastes for the patriarchal life. Blacks, you see, they're like new-born children; one can do what one wants with them, without having some prying prosecutor coming along to ask you for explanations. With this black capital, in ten years I'll have three or four million francs. If I succeed, no one will ask: 'Who are you?' I'll be Mr. Four Millions, an American citizen. I'll be fifty, I won't be doddering for a while after that, and I'll have fun in my own way. Here's my question: 'If I get for you a dowry of a million francs, will you give me two hundred thousand?' A commission of twenty per cent. Is that too high? You'll make your sweet little wife fall in love with you, and once you're married, you'll give signs of anxiety and remorse; you'll pretend to be dejected for a fortnight. And one night, after some monkey business, you'll tell your wife between kisses that you owe two hundred thousand francs, and you'll remember to call her darling. The farce is played every day by the most fashionable young fellows. A young woman doesn't close her purse to the man who has taken possession of her heart. Do you fancy that you'll lose by it? Not at all. You'll find a way to make up the two hundred thousand francs in some scheme. With your money and your intelligence, you'll pile up a fortune as large as you could want. Therefore, within six months' time, you'll have made yourself happy, your lovely wife happy and Papa Vautrin happy, not to speak of your family which is perishing with cold all winter because there isn't enough wood. Don't be astonished by what I'm proposing to you, or by what I'm asking of you. Out of sixty splendid marriages in Paris, there are forty-seven that involve some such bargain."

"What do I have to do?" Eugène asked greedily, breaking into Vautrin's discourse.

"Why, scarcely anything," replied Vautrin, with an involuntary flash of joy such as a fisherman feels when a fish tugs at the line. "Listen carefully. The heart of a poor girl who is both unhappy and in poverty is greedier for love than anything else in the world and the smallest particle of love will make it dilate with joy. You have all the trumps in your hand; you're betting in a lottery with knowledge in advance of the number that will win; you're playing the stock market on a sure tip, when you make love to a young girl whom you meet when she is lonely, poor and in despair, and doesn't have any idea of the fortune she's about to have! You're building a marriage on foundations that can't crumble. When this young girl gets her millions she'll shower them on you as if they were only pebbles. Take them, darling! Take them, Adolphe! Alfred! Take

them, Eugène!' That's what she'd say to her Adolphe, or her Alfred, or her Eugène, if he had the wit to make sacrifices for her! What I mean by making sacrifices is selling an old suit to take her to the *Cadran Bleu* for a meal of mushroom pie, and then to spend the evening at the *Ambigu Comique* theatre; pawning your watch to give her a shawl. I'm not thinking of the trickeries of love, the sort of nonsense by which women are so tickled, things like sprinkling drops of water over a letter to imitate tears when you're far away. I'm sure you know all about the special idiom of the passion. Paris, you see, is like a forest in the new world, peopled by twenty different tribes of savages, Illinois and Hurons and so forth, each living on the results of its own particular kind of hunt; you're hunting millions. To get them you have to use snares, and pipes and bait. There are a lot of different ways of hunting. Some hunt for dowries; others for bankruptcies; on one side there's the hunt for consciences; on the other for victims to be sold, bound hand and foot. The man who comes back with his bag well filled is acclaimed, made much of, received by the world of fashion and distinction. We must be fair to this hospitable place; the city you have to deal with is the most complaisant in the world. If the haughty aristocracies of the European capitals won't take into their company the man who has made his million in an infamous way, Paris opens her arms to him, runs to his parties, eats his dinners, and toasts his infamies."

"But where is there such a girl?" asked Eugène.

"She's right here, and she's yours."

"Victorine?"

"That's it!"

"What do you mean?"

"She's already in love with you, already your little Baroness de Rastignac!"

"But she hasn't a penny," Eugène went on in amazement.

"Hasn't she? In a couple of words the whole thing will be perfectly clear to you. Her father is an old scamp who is believed to have killed one of his friends during the Revolution. He's one of those fellows I spoke of who are perfectly indifferent to opinion. He's a banker, the senior partner in the house, Frederic Taillefer and Co. He has an only son, to whom he means to leave his fortune, to the injury of Victorine. As for me, I hate that kind of injustice. I'm like Don Quixote; I like to defend the weak against the strong. If it were God's will to take his son from him, Taillefer would recognize his daughter. He'd want some sort of heir; that's one of the crazy instincts that Nature gives us. He can't have any children now; I know that. Victorine is sweet and a nice girl; she'll wind her father around her finger. He'll have so much affection for her he'll be whirling like a top. She'll be so much moved by your loving her that she won't forget you; she'll marry you. My part in all this is the part of Providence, I'm going to shape God's will. I've a friend for whom I have done a great service, a colonel in the Army of the Loire who has just been given a place in the Royal Guard. He pays attention to what I advise; and he's become an ultraroyalist; he's not one of those idiots who stand by their convictions.

"If there's one more piece of advice I have to give you, my dear fellow, it's not to stand by your convictions any more than by your words. When you're asked to, sell them. A man who boasts that he never changes his convictions is a man who undertakes always to move in a straight line, a ninny who believes in infallibility. There are no such things as principles, there are only events; there are no such things as laws, there are only circumstances; and the superior person unites himself with events and circumstances so that they will serve his interests. If there were fixed principles and laws, nations wouldn't be changing them just as lightly as we change a shirt. A mail isn't required to be better than a whole nation. . . .

"Oh, I know how things go; I know the secrets of a great many men. Enough. I'll have an unshakable conviction the day that I meet three men who agree about the realization of a principle, and I'll wait for a long time for that! You can't find in the courts three judges who have the same opinion about a clause in the law. Let's come back to my friend. He'd put Jesus Christ back on the cross if I told him to. Just one word from Papa Vautrin, and he'll pick a quarrel with that rascal who doesn't send so much as a hundred sous to his poor sister, and . . ."

At this point Vautrin got up, stood like a fencer on guard, and went through the motions of delivering a lunge. "And he'll do it on the quiet," he added.

"How horrible!" exclaimed Eugène. "You're just joking, Monsieur Vautrin?"

"Now, now, don't get excited!" Vautrin went on. "Don't act like a child! Or, if you want, go ahead and get angry, lose your temper! Call me a scoundrel, a rascal, a bandit, only take care you don't call me a deceiver or a spy! Come on, let yourself go. I forgive you; it's natural at your age. I used to be like that. But think the thing over. You'll do something worse one day. You'll make up to some pretty woman and take money from her! You've thought of it! For how are you going to carry out your idea and succeed unless you get paid for loving? Virtue is indivisible, my boy; you either have it or you don't.

Take this idea of repenting for one's sins; it's a pretty system which allow you to feel innocent of a crime just because you've made act of contrition! Seducing a woman in order to set your foot on a certain step in the social ladder, getting the children in a family squabbling among themselves, all the infamous things that are done, behind the door or otherwise, for pleasure or for personal gain, how do they rank as acts of faith, hope and charity ? Why is there a prison sentence of a mere two months for a dandy who in a single night robs a child of half his fortune, and the penitentiary for the poor devil who takes a thousand franc note under aggravating circumstances? That's the way our laws are. There isn't one clause in them that doesn't fall into absurdity. The man in the yellow gloves, the dandy with his deceitful language, committed an act which was a murder though no blood was shed and indeed he left something of his own life behind; the robber opened a door with his jimmy—two deeds of night! The only difference between what I'm proposing to you and what you'll be doing some day is that there's no blood for you to shed in this. How can you believe in any fixed principles in this sort of world? You must learn to despise mankind and to crawl through the holes that are left in the network of the Code [laws]. The secret of large fortunes which have no perceptible explanation is a crime that has been forgotten because it was neatly done."

"Stop, I won't listen to any more of this. You'd make me doubt my own self. Right now, my feelings give me the only guidance I can trust."

"As you wish, my dear boy, I thought you were made of stronger stuff," said Vautrin. "I won't say any more. One last word, though." He looked hard at Eugène. "You know my secret."

"A young man who refuses your proposition will be easily capable of forgetting what it was."

"That's well put. I like that. Another fellow, you know, would not be so scrupulous. Remember what I want to do for you. I give you two weeks. Then you can take it or leave it."

Gustave Flaubert
Madame Bovary

The work often regarded as the quintessential Realist novel is *Madame Bovary: Provincial Customs,* by Gustave Flaubert (1821–1880), which was published serially from October to December in 1856. It tells the story of Emma Bovary, a self-centered wife living in a drab French provincial town, who, interpreting the world from the prism of the romantic stories she reads, yearns for luxury, excitement, and romance. Disillusioned with her marriage to her devoted, hardworking, but dull husband, whom she detests, Emma commits adultery.

In this work, Flaubert strove to remain detached from his characters. Unlike the Romantics, he was not concerned with revealing his own emotions or opinions, but with the accurate depiction of characters, situations, and dialogue. His goal, he said, was a book in which "the personality of the author is *completely* absent." Commenting on the realism of *Madame Bovary,* a contemporary novelist noted that it "represents an obsession with description. Details are counted one by one, all are given equal value, every street, every house, every room, every book, every blade of grass is described in full." Emma's death from self-inflicted poison is also described fully and in great clinical detail. In *Madame Bovary,* Flaubert not only displayed a masterful talent for realism, he also demonstrated a psychologist's ability to probe beneath surface appearance and behavior and reveal inner torment.

The following selection from *Madame Bovary* shows a depressed and distraught Emma who "would ask herself again and again: 'Why—*why*—did I ever marry?'"

Charles's conversation was flat as a sidewalk, a place of passage for the ideas of everyman; they wore drab everyday clothes, and they inspired neither laughter nor dreams. When he had lived in Rouen, he said, he had never had any interest in going to the theatre to see the Parisian company that was acting there. He couldn't swim or fence or fire a pistol; one day he couldn't tell her the meaning of a riding term she had come upon in a novel.

Wasn't it a man's role, though, to know everything? Shouldn't he be expert at all kinds of things, able to initiate you into the intensities of passion, the refinements of life, all the mysteries? *This* man could teach you nothing; he knew nothing, he wished for nothing. He took it for granted that she was content; and she resented his settled calm, his serene dullness, the very happiness she herself brought him. . . .

She wondered whether some different set of circumstances might not have resulted in her meeting some different man; and she tried to picture those imaginary circumstances, the life they would have brought her, the unknown other husband. However she imagined him, he wasn't a bit like Charles. He might have been handsome, witty, distinguished, magnetic—the kind of man her convent schoolmates had doubtless married. What kind of lives were they leading now? Cities, busy streets, buzzing theatres, brilliant balls—such surroundings afforded them unlimited opportunities for deep emotions and exciting sensations. But *her* life was as cold as an attic facing north; and boredom, like a silent spider, was weaving its web in the shadows, in every corner of her heart. She remembered Prize Days, when she had gone up onto the stage to receive her little wreaths. She had been charming, with her braids, her white dress, her prunella-cloth slippers. Gentlemen had leaned over, when she was back in her seat, and paid her compliments; the courtyard had been full of carriages; guests called good-bye to her as they rolled away; the music teacher with his violin case bowed to her as he passed. How far away it all was! How far! . . .

Deep down, all the while, she was waiting for something to happen. Like a sailor in distress, she kept casting desperate glances over the solitary waste of her life, seeking some white sail in the distant mists of the horizon. She had no idea by what wind it would reach her, toward what shore it would bear her, or what kind of craft it would be—tiny boat or towering vessel, laden with heartbreaks or filled to the gunwales

with rapture. But every morning when she awoke she hoped that today would be the day; she listened for every sound, gave sudden starts, was surprised when nothing happened; and then, sadder with each succeeding sunset, she longed for tomorrow.

Spring came again. She found it hard to breathe, the first warm days, when the pear trees were bursting into bloom.

From early in July she began to count on her fingers how many weeks there were till October, thinking that the marquis d'Andervilliers might give another ball at La Vaubyessard. But September passed without letters or visitors.

After the pain of this disappointment had gone, her heart stood empty once more; and then the series of identical days began all over again.

So from now on they were going to continue one after the other like this, always the same, innumerable, bringing nothing! Other people's lives, drab though they might be, held at least the possibility of an event. One unexpected happening often set in motion a whole chain of change: the entire setting of one's life could be transformed. But to her nothing happened. It was God's will. The future was a pitch-black tunnel, ending in a locked door.

She gave up her music: why should she play? Who was there to listen? There wasn't a chance of her ever giving a concert in a short-sleeved velvet gown, skimming butterfly fingers over the ivory keys of a grand piano, feeling the public's ecstatic murmur flow round her like a breeze—so why go through the tedium of practicing? She left her drawing books and her embroidery in a closet. What was the use of anything? What was the use? She loathed sewing.

"I've read everything there is to read," she told herself.

And so she sat—holding the fire tongs in the fire till they glowed red, or watching the falling of the rain.

How depressed she was on Sundays, when the churchbell tolled for vespers! With a dull awareness she listened to the cracked sound as it rang out again and again. Sometimes a cat walking slowly along one of the roofs outside her window arched its back against the pale rays of the sun. The wind blew trails of dust on the highway. Far off somewhere a dog was howling. And the bell would keep on giving its regular, monotonous peals that died away over the countryside.

Madame Bovary has become infatuated with Léon, a young law clerk, who, unlike her husband, shares *her interest in music, poetry, and reading. They are attracted to each other but do not reveal their feelings and there is no sexual intimacy. Eventually Léon leaves the town. Emma's adulterous affair occurs later with someone else.*

The village housewives admired her for her thrift; Charles's patients for her politeness; the poor for her charity.

And all this time she was torn by wild desires, by rage, by hatred. The trim folds of her dress hid a heart in turmoil, and her reticent lips told nothing of the storm. She was in love with Léon, and she sought the solitude that allowed her to revel undisturbed in his image. The sight of his person spoiled the voluptuousness of her musings. She trembled at the sound of his footsteps; then, with him before her, the agitation subsided, and she was left with nothing but a vast bewilderment that turned gradually into sadness.

Léon did not know, when he left her house in despair, that she went immediately to the window and watched him disappear down the street. She worried over his every move, watched every expression that crossed his face; she concocted an elaborate story to have a pretext for visiting his room. The pharmacist's wife seemed to her blessed to sleep under the same roof; and her thoughts came continually to rest on that house, like the pigeons from the Lion d'Or that alighted there to soak their pink feet and white wings in the eaves-trough. But the more aware Emma became of her love the more she repressed it in an effort to conceal it and weaken it. She would have been glad had Léon guessed; and she kept imagining accidents and disasters that would open his eyes. It was indolence, probably, or fear, that held her back, and a feeling of shame. She had kept him at too great a distance, she decided: now it was too late; the occasion was lost. Besides, the pride and pleasure she derived from thinking of herself as "virtuous" and from wearing an air of resignation as she looked at herself in the mirror consoled her a little for the sacrifice she thought she was making.

Her carnal desires, her cravings for money, and the fits of depression engendered by her love gradually merged into a single torment; and instead of trying to put it out of her mind she cherished it, spurring herself on to suffer, never missing an opportunity to do so. A dish poorly served or a door left ajar grated on her nerves; she sighed thinking of the velvet gowns she didn't own, the happiness that eluded her, her unattainable dreams, her entire cramped existence.

What exasperated her was Charles's total unawareness of her ordeal. His conviction that he was making her happy she

took as a stupid insult: such self-righteousness could only mean that he didn't appreciate her. For whose sake, after all, was she being virtuous? Wasn't he the obstacle to every kind of happiness, the cause of all her wretchedness, the sharp-pointed prong of this many-stranded belt that bound her on all sides?

So he became the sole object of her resentment. Her attempts to conquer this feeling served only to strengthen it, for their failure gave her additional cause for despair and deepened her estrangement from her husband. She had moments of revulsion against her own meekness. She reacted to the drabness of her home by indulging in daydreams of luxury, and to matrimonial caresses by adulterous desires. She wished that Charles would beat her: then she would feel more justified in hating him and betraying him out of revenge. Sometimes she was surprised by the horrible possibilities that she imagined; and yet she had to keep smiling, hear herself say time and again that she was happy, pretend to be so, let everyone believe it!

Still, there were times when she could scarcely stomach the hypocrisy. She would be seized with a longing to run off with Léon, escape to some far-off place where they could begin life anew; but at such moments she would shudder, feeling herself at the brink of a terrifying precipice.

"What's the use—he doesn't love me any more," she would decide. What was to become of her? What help could she hope for? What comfort? What relief?

Such a crisis always left her shattered, gasping, prostrate, sobbing to herself, tears streaming down her face.

"Why in the world don't you tell Monsieur?" the maid would ask her, finding her thus distraught.

"It's nerves," Emma would answer. "Don't mention it to him. It would only upset him."

"Ah, yes," Félicité said, one day. "You're just like the daughter of old Guérin, the fisherman at Le Pollet. I knew her at Dieppe before I came to you. She used to be so sad, so terribly sad, that when she stood in her door she made you think of a funeral pall hanging there. It seems it was some kind of a fog in her head that ailed her. The doctors couldn't do anything for her, or the priest either. When it came over her worst, she'd go off by herself along the beach, and sometimes the customs officer would find her stretched out flat on her face on the pebbles and crying, when he made his rounds. It passed off after she was married, they say."

"With me," said Emma, "it was after I was married that it began."

Charles Dickens
Hard Times

In his numerous works, English writer Charles Dickens (1812–1870) depicted in detail the squalor of English industrial cities, the drudgery of factory labor, and the hypocrisy of society that preached Christian morality but permitted these abuses to go on. Dickens recognized that the monotony and stupefying conditions of industrial life crushed the spirit of the workers, curtailing both their imagination and cultural development. Moreover, exploitation of the working class fostered class tensions, because the workers viewed governmental institutions as being impervious to their needs and intent solely on protecting the privileged status of entrepreneurs and business elites. Dickens blamed social institutions for the misery of the downtrodden and maintained that society must be fundamentally changed or it would implode. His works helped to awaken the moral conscience of his day. *Hard Times* (1854), excerpted below, is a harsh indictment of the industrial system and offers a good example of the Realist genre in literature.

It was a town of red brick, or of brick that would have been red if the smoke and ashes had allowed it; but as matters stood it was a town of unnatural red and black like the painted face of a savage. It was a town of machinery and tall chimneys, out of which interminable serpents of smoke trailed themselves for ever and ever, and never got uncoiled. It had a black canal in it, and a river that ran purple with ill-smelling dye, and vast piles of building[s] full of windows where there was a rattling and a trembling all day long, and where the piston of the steam-engine worked monotonously up and down like the head of an elephant in a state of melancholy madness. It contained several large streets all very like one another, and many small streets still more like one another, inhabited by people equally like one another, who all went in and out at the same hours, with the same sound upon the same pavements, to do the same work, and to whom every day was the same as yesterday and tomorrow, and every year the counterpart of the last and the next. . . .

In the hardest working part of Coketown; in the innermost fortifications of that ugly citadel, where Nature was as strongly bricked out as killing airs and gases were bricked in; at the heart of the labyrinth of narrow courts upon courts, and close streets upon streets, which had come into existence piecemeal, every piece in a violent hurry for some one man's purpose, and the whole an unnatural family, shouldering, and trampling, and pressing one another to death; in the last close nook of this great exhausted receiver, where the chimneys, for want of air to make a draught, were built in an immense variety of stunted and crooked shapes, as though every house put out a sign of the kind of people who might be expected to be born in it; among the multitude of Coketown, generically called "the Hands," a race who would have found more favour with some people, if Providence had seen fit to make them only hands, or, like the lower creatures of the seashore, only hands and stomachs—lived a certain Stephen Blackpool, forty years of age. . . .

As Coketown cast ashes not only on its own head but on the neighbourhood's too—after the manner of those pious persons who do penance for their own sins by putting other people into sackcloth—it was customary for those who now and then thirsted for a draught of pure air, which is not absolutely the most wicked among the vanities of life, to get a few miles away by the railroad, and then begin their walk, or their lounge in the fields. . . .

Though the green landscape was blotted here and there with heaps of coal, it was green elsewhere, and there were trees to see, and there were larks singing (though it was Sunday), and there were pleasant scents in the air, and all was over-arched by a bright blue sky. In the distance one way, Coketown showed as a black mist; in another distance hills began to rise; in a third, there was a faint change in the light of the horizon where it shone upon the far-off sea. Under their feet, the grass was fresh; beautiful shadows of branches flickered upon it, and speckled it; hedgerows were luxuriant; everything was at peace. Engines at pits' mouths, and lean old horses that had worn the circle of their daily labour into the ground, were alike quiet; wheels had ceased for a short space to turn; and the great wheel of earth seemed to revolve without the shocks and noises of another time.

Charles Dickens
Nicholas Nickleby

Dickens skillfully creates characters who are concerned only with safeguarding their privileged way of life and ignoring the misery of the working class. These people run the prisons, schools, law courts, and other agencies, both private and governmental, that oppress the poor. In *Nicholas Nickleby,* young Nicholas Nickleby, an idealistic nineteen year old, who, through the efforts of his miserly and conniving uncle, Ralph Nickleby, secures a teaching position at Dotheboys Hall, a dreadful boarding school in Yorkshire. The school is operated by Wackford Squeers who, aided by his heartless wife, tries to squeeze as much profit as he can from the school by depriving the boys of basic necessities. A cruel tyrant, he also brutalizes his charges. In the following passage, Squeers takes Nicholas into the classroom for the first time.

Now, the fact was, that both Mr. and Mrs. Squeers viewed the boys in the light of their proper and natural enemies; or, in other words, they held and considered that their business and profession was to get as much from every boy as could by possibility be screwed out of him. On this point they were both agreed, and behaved in unison accordingly. The only difference between them was, that Mrs. Squeers waged war against the enemy openly and fearlessly, and that Squeers covered his rascality, even at home, with a spice of his habitual deceit; as if he really had a notion of some day or other being able to take himself in, and persuade his own mind that he was a very good fellow.

"But come," said Squeers, interrupting the progress of some thoughts to this effect in the mind of his usher, "let's go to the school-room; and lend me a hand with my school coat, will you?"

Nicholas assisted his master to put on an old fustian shooting-jacket, which he took down from a peg in the passage; and Squeers, arming himself with his cane, led the way across a yard, to a door in the rear of the house.

"There," said the schoolmaster as they stepped in together; "this is our shop, Nickleby!"

It was such a crowded scene, and there were so many objects to attract attention, that, at first, Nicholas stared about him, really without seeing anything at all. By degrees, however, the place resolved itself into a bare and dirty room, with a couple of windows, whereof a tenth part might be of glass, the remainder being stopped up with old copybooks and paper. There were a couple of long old rickety desks, cut and notched, and inked, and damaged, in every possible way; two or three forms; a detached desk for Squeers; and another for his assistant. The ceiling was supported, like that of a barn, by cross beams and rafters; and the walls were so stained and discoloured that it was impossible to tell whether they had ever been touched with paint or whitewash.

But the pupils—the young noblemen! How the last faint traces of hope, the remotest glimmering of any good to be derived from his efforts in this den, faded from the mind of Nicholas as he looked in dismay around! Pale and haggard faces, lank and bony figures, children with the countenances of old men, deformities with irons upon their limbs, boys of stunted growth, and others whose long meagre legs would hardly bear their stooping bodies, all crowded on the view together; there were the bleared eye, the hare-lip, the crooked foot, and every ugliness or distortion that told of unnatural aversion conceived by parents for their offspring, or of young lives which, from the earliest dawn of infancy, had been one horrible endurance of cruelty and neglect. There were little faces which should have been handsome, darkened with the scowl of sullen, dogged suffering; there was childhood with the light of its eye quenched, its beauty gone, and its helplessness alone remaining; there were vicious-faced boys, brooding, with leaden eyes, like malefactors in a jail; and there were young creatures on whom the sins of their frail parents had descended, weeping even for the mercenary nurses they had known, and lonesome even in their loneliness. With every kindly sympathy and affection blasted in its birth, with every young and healthy feeling flogged and starved down, with every revengeful passion that can fester in swollen hearts eating its evil way to their core in silence, what an incipient Hell was breeding here!

And yet this scene, painful as it was, had its grotesque features, which, in a less interested observer than Nicholas, might have provoked a smile. Mrs. Squeers stood at one of the desks, presiding over an immense basin of brimstone and treacle, of which delicious compound she administered a large instalment to each boy in succession: using for the purpose a common wooden spoon, which might have been originally manufactured for some gigantic top, and which widened every young gentleman's mouth considerably: they being all obliged, under heavy corporal penalties, to take in the whole of the bowl at a gasp. In another corner, huddled together for companionship, were the little boys who had arrived on the preceding night, three of them in very large leather breeches, and two in old trousers, a something tighter fit than drawers are usually worn; at no great distance from these was seated the juvenile son and heir of Mr. Squeers—a striking likeness of his father—kicking, with great vigour, under the hands of Smike, who was fitting upon him a pair of new boots that bore a most suspicious resemblance to those which the least of the little boys had worn on the journey down—as the little boy himself seemed to think, for he was regarding the appropriation with a look of most rueful amazement. Besides these, there was a long row of boys waiting, with countenances of no pleasant anticipation, to be treacled; and another file, who had just escaped from the infliction, making a variety of wry mouths indicative of anything but satisfaction. The whole were attired in such motley, ill-sorted, extraordinary garments, as would have been irresistibly ridiculous, but for the foul appearance of dirt, and disease, with which they were associated.

"Now," said Squeers, giving the desk a great rap with his cane, which made half the little boys nearly jump out of their boots, "is that physicking over?"

"Just over," said Mrs. Squeers, choking the last boy in her hurry, and tapping the crown of his head with the wooden spoon to restore him. "Here, you Smike; take away now. Look sharp!"

Smike shuffled out with the basin, and Mrs. Squeers having called up a little boy with a curly head and wiped her hands upon it, hurried out after him into a species of washhouse, where there was a small fire and a large kettle, together with a number of little wooden bowls which were arranged upon a board.

Into these bowls, Mrs. Squeers, assisted by the hungry servant, poured a brown composition which looked like diluted pincushions without the covers, and was called porridge. A minute wedge of brown bread was inserted in each bowl, and when they had eaten their porridge by means of the bread, the boys ate the bread itself, and had finished their breakfast; whereupon Mr. Squeers said, in a solemn voice, "For what we have received, may the Lord make us truly thankful!"—and went away to his own.

Nicholas distended his stomach with a bowl of porridge, for much the same reason which induces some savages to swallow earth—lest they should be inconveniently hungry when there is nothing to eat. Having further disposed of a slice of bread and butter, allotted to him in virtue of his office, he sat himself down to wait for school-time.

He could not but observe how silent and sad the boys all seemed to be. There was none of the noise and clamour of a school-room; none of its boisterous play, or hearty mirth. The children sat crouching and shivering together, and seemed to lack the spirit to move about. The only pupil who evinced the slightest tendency towards locomotion or playfulness was Master Squeers, and as his chief amusement was to tread upon the other boys' toes in his new boots, his flow of spirits was rather disagreeable than otherwise.

After some half-hour's delay, Mr. Squeers reappeared, and the boys took their places and their books, of which latter commodity the average might be about one to eight learners. A few minutes having elapsed, during which Mr.

Squeers looked very profound, as if he had a perfect apprehension of what was inside all the books, and could say every word of their contents by heart if he only chose to take the trouble, that gentleman called up the first class.

Obedient to this summons there ranged themselves in front of the schoolmaster's desk, half-a-dozen scarecrows, out at knees and elbows, one of whom placed a torn and filthy book beneath his learned eye.

"This is the first class in English spelling and philosophy, Nickleby," said Squeers, beckoning Nicholas to stand beside him. "We'll get up a Latin one, and hand that over to you. Now then, where's the first boy?"

"Please, sir, he's cleaning the back parlour window," said the temporary head of the philosophical class.

"So he is, to be sure," rejoined Squeers. "We go upon the practical mode of teaching, Nickleby; the regular education system. C-l-e-a-n, clean, verb active, to make bright, to scour. W-i-n, win, d-e-r, der, winder, a casement. When the boy knows this out of the book, he goes and does it. It's just the same principle as the use of the globes. Where's the second boy?"

"Please, sir, he's weeding the garden," replied a small voice.

"To be sure," said Squeers, by no means disconcerted. "So he is. B-o-t, bot, t-i-n, bottin, n-e-y, ney, bottinney, noun substantive, a knowledge of plants. When he has learned that bottinney means a knowledge of plants, he goes and knows 'em. That's our system, Nickleby; what do you think of it?"

"It's a very useful one, at any rate," answered Nicholas.

"I believe you," rejoined Squeers, not remarking the emphasis of his usher. "Third boy, what's a horse?"

"A beast sir," replied the boy.

"So it is," said Squeers. "Ain't it, Nickleby?"

"I believe there is no doubt of that, sir," answered Nicholas.

"Of course there isn't," said Squeers. "A horse is a quadruped, and quadruped's Latin for beast, as every body that's gone through the grammar, knows, or else where's the use of having grammars at all?"

"Where, indeed!" said Nicholas abstractedly.

"As you're perfect in that," resumed Squeers, turning to the boy, "go and look after *my* horse, and rub him down well, or I'll rub you down. The rest of the class go and draw water up, till somebody tells you to leave off, for it's washing-day tomorrow, and they want the coppers filled."

So saying, he dismissed the first class to their experiments in practical philosophy, and eyed Nicholas with a look, half cunning and half doubtful, as if he were not altogether certain what he might think of him by this time.

"That's the way we do it, Nickleby," he said, after a pause.

Nicholas shrugged his shoulders in a manner that was scarcely perceptible, and said he saw it was.

"And a very good way it is, too," said Squeers. "Now, just take them fourteen little boys and hear them some reading, because, you know, you must begin to be useful. Idling about here, won't do."

Mr. Squeers said this, as if it had suddenly occurred to him, either that he must not say too much to his assistant, or that his assistant did not say enough to him in praise of the establishment. The children were arranged in a semicircle round the new master, and he was soon listening to their dull, drawling, hesitating recital of those stories of engrossing interest which are to be found in the more antiquated spelling books.

In this exciting occupation, the morning lagged heavily on. At one o'clock, the boys, having previously had their appetites thoroughly taken away by stir-about and potatoes, sat down in the kitchen to some hard salt beef, of which Nicholas was graciously permitted to take his portion to his own solitary desk, to eat it there in peace. After this, there was another hour of crouching in the school-room and shivering with cold, and then school began again.

It was Mr. Squeers's custom to call the boys together and make a sort of report, after every half-yearly visit to the metropolis, regarding the relations and friends he had seen, the news he had heard, the letters he had brought down, the bills which had been paid, the accounts which had been left unpaid, and so forth. This solemn proceeding always took place in the afternoon of the day succeeding his return; perhaps, because the boys acquired strength of mind from the suspense of the morning, or, possibly, because Mr. Squeers himself acquired greater sternness and inflexibility from certain warm potations in which he was wont to indulge after his early dinner. Be this as it may, the boys were recalled from house-window, garden, stable, and cow-yard, and the school were assembled in full conclave, when Mr. Squeers, with a small bundle of papers in his hand, and Mrs. S. following with a pair of canes, entered the room and proclaimed silence.

"Let any boy speak a word without leave," said Mr. Squeers mildly, "and I'll take the skin off his back."

This special proclamation had the desired effect, and a death-like silence immediately prevailed, in the midst of which Mr. Squeers went on to say:

"Boys, I've been to London, and have returned to my family and you, as strong and well as ever."

According to half-yearly custom, the boys gave three feeble cheers at this refreshing intelligence. Such cheers! Sighs of extra strength with the chill on.

"I have seen the parents of some boys," continued Squeers, turning over his papers, "and they're so glad to hear how their sons are getting on, that there's no prospect at all of their going away, which of course is a very pleasant thing to reflect upon, for all parties."

Two or three hands went to two or three eyes when Squeers said this, but the greater part of the young gentlemen having no particular parents to speak of, were wholly uninterested in the thing one way or other.

"I have had disappointments to contend against," said Squeers, looking very grim; "Bolder's father was two pound ten short. Where is Bolder?"

"Here he is, please sir," rejoined twenty officious voices. Boys are very like men to be sure.

"Come here, Bolder," said Squeers.

An unhealthy-looking boy, with warts all over his hands, stepped from his place to the master's desk, and raised his eyes imploringly to Squeers's face; his own, quite white from the rapid beating of his heart.

"Bolder," said Squeers, speaking very slowly, for he was considering, as the saying goes, where to have him. "Bolder, if your father thinks that because—why, what's this, sir?"

As Squeers spoke, he caught up the boy's hand by the cuff of his jacket, and surveyed it with an edifying aspect of horror and disgust.

"What do you call this, sir?" demanded the schoolmaster, administering a cut with the cane to expedite the reply.

"I can't help it, indeed, sir," rejoined the boy, crying. "They will come; it's the dirty work I think, sir—at least I don't know what it is, sir, but it's not my fault."

"Bolder," said Squeers, tucking up his wristbands, and moistening the palm of his right hand to get a good grip of the cane, "you are an incorrigible young scoundrel, and as the last thrashing did you no good, we must see what another will do towards beating it out of you."

With this, and wholly disregarding a piteous cry for mercy, Mr. Squeers fell upon the boy and caned him soundly: not leaving off indeed, until his arm was tired out.

"There," said Squeers, when he had quite done; "rub away hard as you like, you won't rub that off in a hurry. Oh! you won't hold that noise, won't you? Put him out, Smike."

The drudge knew better from long experience, than to hesitate about obeying, so he bundled the victim out by a side door, and Mr. Squeers perched himself again on his own stool, supported by Mrs. Squeers, who occupied another at his side.

"Now let us see," said Squeers. "A letter for Cobbey. Stand up, Cobbey."

Another boy stood up, and eyed the letter very hard while Squeers made a mental abstract of the same.

"Oh!" said Squeers: "Cobbey's grandmother is dead, and his uncle John has took to drinking, which is all the news his sister sends, except eighteenpence, which will just pay for that broken square of glass. Mrs. Squeers, my dear, will you take the money?"

The worthy lady pocketed the eighteenpence with a most business-like air, and Squeers passed on to the next boy, as coolly as possible.

"Graymarsh," said Squeers, "he's the next. Stand up, Graymarsh."

Another boy stood up, and the schoolmaster looked over the letter as before.

"Graymarsh's maternal aunt," said Squeers, when he had possessed himself of the contents, "is very glad to hear he's so well and happy, and sends her respectful compliments to Mrs. Squeers, and thinks she must be an angel. She likewise thinks Mr. Squeers is too good for this world; but hopes he may long be spared to carry on the business. Would have sent the two pair of stockings as desired, but is short of money, so forwards a tract instead, and hopes Graymarsh will put his trust in Providence. Hopes, above all, that he will study in everything to please Mr. and Mrs. Squeers, and look upon them as his only friends; and that he will love Master Squeers; and not object to sleeping five in a bed, which no Christian should. Ah!" said Squeers, folding it up, "a delightful letter. Very affecting indeed."

It was affecting in one sense, for Graymarsh's maternal aunt was strongly supposed, by her more intimate friends, to be no other than his maternal parent; Squeers, however, without alluding to this part of the story (which would have sounded immoral before boys), proceeded with the business by calling out "Mobbs," whereupon another boy rose, and Graymarsh resumed his seat.

"Mobbs's step-mother," said Squeers, "took to her bed on hearing that he wouldn't eat fat, and has been very ill ever since. She wishes to know, by an early post, where he expects to go to if he quarrels with his vittles; and with what feelings he could turn up his nose at the cow's liver broth, after his good master had asked a blessing on it. This was told her in the London newspapers—not by Mr. Squeers, for he is too kind and too good to set anybody against anybody—and it has vexed her so much, Mobbs can't think. She is sorry to find he is discontented, which is sinful and horrid, and hopes Mr. Squeers will flog him into a happier state of mind; with this view, she has also stopped his half-penny a week pocket-money, and given a double-bladed knife with a corkscrew in it to the Missionaries, which she had bought on purpose for him."

"A sulky state of feeling," said Squeers, after a terrible pause, during which he had moistened the palm of his right hand again, "won't do. Cheerfulness and contentment must be kept up. Mobbs, come to me!"

Mobbs moved slowly towards the desk, rubbing his eyes in anticipation of good cause for doing so; and he soon afterwards retired by the side door, with as good cause as a boy need have.

Mr. Squeers then proceeded to open a miscellaneous collection of letters; some enclosing money, which Mrs. Squeers "took care of;" and others referring to small articles of apparel, as caps and so forth, all of which the same lady stated to be too large, or too small, and calculated for nobody but young Squeers, who would appear indeed to have had most accommodating limbs, since everything that came into the school fitted him to a nicety. His head, in particular, must have been singularly elastic, for hats and caps of all dimensions were alike to him.

This business despatched, a few slovenly lessons were performed, and Squeers retired to his fireside, leaving Nicholas to take care of the boys in the school-room, which was very cold, and where a meal of bread and cheese was served out shortly after dark.

There was a small stove at that corner of the room which was nearest to the master's desk, and by it Nicholas sat down,

so depressed and self-degraded by the consciousness of his position, that if death could have come upon him at that time he would have been almost happy to meet it. The cruelty of which he had been an unwilling witness, the coarse and ruffianly behaviour of Squeers even in his best moods, the filthy place, the sights and sounds about him, all contributed to this state of feeling; but when he recollected that, being there as an assistant, he actually seemed—no matter what unhappy train of circumstances had brought him to that pass—to be the aider and abettor of a system which filled him with honest disgust and indignation, he loathed himself, and felt, for the moment, as though the mere consciousness of his present situation must, through all time to come, prevent his raising his head again.

But, for the present, his resolve was taken, and the resolution he had formed on the preceding night remained undisturbed. He had written to his mother and sister, announcing the safe conclusion of his journey, and saying as little about Dotheboys Hall, and saying that little as cheerfully, as he possibly could. He hoped that by remaining where he was, he might do some good, even there; at all events, others depended too much on his uncle's favour to admit of his awakening his wrath just then.

One reflection disturbed him far more than any selfish considerations arising out of his own position. This was the probable destination of his sister Kate. His uncle had deceived him, and might he not consign her to some miserable place where her youth and beauty would prove a far greater curse than ugliness and decrepitude? To a caged man, bound hand and foot, this was a terrible idea; but no, he thought, his mother was by; there was the portrait-painter, too—simple enough, but still living in the world, and of it. He was willing to believe that Ralph Nickleby had conceived a personal dislike to himself. Having pretty good reason, by this time, to reciprocate it, he had no great difficulty in arriving at this conclusion, and tried to persuade himself that the feeling extended no farther than between them.

As he was absorbed in these meditations, he all at once encountered the upturned face of Smike, who was on his knees before the stove, picking a few stray cinders from the hearth and planting them on the fire. He had paused to steal a look at Nicholas, and when he saw that he was observed, shrunk back, as if expecting a blow.

"You need not fear me," said Nicholas kindly. "Are you cold?"

"N-n-o."

"You are shivering."

"I am not cold," replied Smike quickly. "I am used to it."

There was such an obvious fear of giving offence in his manner, and he was such a timid, broken-spirited creature, that Nicholas could not help exclaiming, "Poor fellow!"

If he had struck the drudge, he would have slunk away without a word. But, now, he burst into tears.

"Oh dear, oh dear!" he cried, covering his face with his cracked and horny hands. "My heart will break. It will, it will."

"Hush!" said Nicholas, laying his hand upon his shoulder. "Be a man; you are nearly one by years, God help you."

"By years!" cried Smike. "Oh dear, dear, how many of them! How many of them since I was a little child, younger than any that are here now! Where are they all?"

"Whom do you speak of?" inquired Nicholas, wishing to rouse the poor half-witted creature to reason. "Tell me."

"My friends," he replied, "myself—my—oh! what sufferings mine have been!"

"There is always hope," said Nicholas; he knew not what to say.

"No," rejoined the other, "no; none for me. Do you remember the boy that died here?"

"I was not here, you know," said Nicholas gently; "but what of him?"

"Why," replied the youth, drawing closer to his questioner's side, "I was with him at night, and when it was all silent he cried no more for friends he wished to come and sit with him, but began to see faces round his bed that came from home; he said they smiled, and talked to him; and he died at last lifting his head to kiss them. Do you hear?"

"Yes, yes," rejoined Nicholas.

"What faces will smile on me when I die!" cried his companion, shivering. "Who will talk to me in those long nights! They cannot come from home; they would frighten me, if they did, for I don't know what it is, and shouldn't know them. Pain and fear, pain and fear for me, alive or dead. No hope, no hope!"

The bell rang to bed: and the boy, subsiding at the sound into his usual listless state, crept away as if anxious to avoid notice. It was with a heavy heart that Nicholas soon afterwards—no, not retired; there was no retirement there—followed—to his dirty and crowded dormitory.

For years the Squeers have starved and whipped Smike who is really the abandoned son of Ralph Nickleby, Nicholas' uncle, a fact not discovered until after Smike's death. Painfully thin and broken in spirit, Smike flees from the abusive Squeers, but is caught.

Another day came, and Nicholas was scarcely awake when he heard the wheels of a chaise approaching the house. It stopped. The voice of Mrs. Squeers was heard, and in exultation, ordering a glass of spirits for somebody, which was in itself a sufficient sign that something extraordinary had happened. Nicholas hardly dared to look out of the window; but he did so, and the very first object that met his eyes was the wretched Smike: so bedabbled with mud and rain, so haggard and worn and wild, that, but for his garments being such as no scarecrow was ever to wear, he might have been doubtful, even then, of his identity.

"Lift him out," said Squeers, after he had literally feasted his eyes, in silence, upon the culprit. "Bring him in; bring him in!"

"Take care," cried Mrs. Squeers, as her husband proffered his assistance. "We tied his legs under the apron and made 'em fast to the chaise, to prevent his giving us the slip again."

With hands trembling with delight, Squeers unloosened the cord; and Smike, to all appearance more dead than alive, was brought into the house and securely locked up in a cellar, until such time as Mr. Squeers should deem it expedient to operate upon him, in presence of the assembled school.

Upon a hasty consideration of the circumstances, it may be matter of surprise to some persons, that Mr. and Mrs. Squeers should have taken so much trouble to repossess themselves of an incumbrance of which it was their wont to complain so loudly; but their surprise will cease when they are informed that the manifold services of the drudge, if performed by anybody else, would have cost the establishment some ten or twelve shillings per week in the shape of wages; and furthermore, that all runaways were, as a matter of policy, made severe examples of, at Dotheboys Hall, inasmuch as, in consequence of the limited extent of its attractions, there was but little inducement, beyond the powerful impulse of fear, for any pupil, provided with the usual number of legs and the power of using them, to remain.

The news that Smike had been caught and brought back in triumph, ran like wild-fire through the hungry community, and expectation was on tiptoe all the morning. On tiptoe it was destined to remain, however, until afternoon; when Squeers, having refreshed himself with his dinner, and further strengthened himself by an extra libation or so, made his appearance (accompanied by his amiable partner) with a countenance of portentous import, and a fearful instrument of flagellation, strong, supple, wax-ended, and new,—in short, purchased that morning, expressly for the occasion.

"Is every boy here?" asked Squeers, in a tremendous voice.

Every boy was there, but every boy was afraid to speak; so Squeers glared along the lines to assure himself; and every eye drooped, and every head cowered down, as he did so.

"Each boy keep his place," said Squeers, administering his favourite blow to the desk, and regarding with gloomy satisfaction the universal start which it never failed to occasion. "Nickleby! to your desk, sir."

It was remarked by more than one small observer, that there was a very curious and unusual expression in the usher's face; but he took his seat, without opening his lips in reply. Squeers, casting a triumphant glance at his assistant and a look of most comprehensive despotism on the boys, left the room, and shortly afterwards returned, dragging Smike by the collar—or rather by that fragment of his jacket which was nearest the place where his collar would have been, had he boasted such a decoration.

In any other place, the appearance of the wretched, jaded, spiritless object would have occasioned a murmur of compassion and remonstrance. It had some effect, even there; for the lookers-on moved uneasily in their seats; and a few of the boldest ventured to steal looks at each other, expressive of indignation and pity.

They were lost on Squeers, however, whose gaze was fastened on the luckless Smike, as he inquired, according to custom in such cases, whether he had anything to say for himself.

"Nothing, I suppose?" said Squeers, with a diabolical grin.

Smike glanced round, and his eye rested, for an instant, on Nicholas, as if he had expected him to intercede; but his look was riveted on his desk.

"Have you anything to say?" demanded Squeers again: giving his right arm two or three flourishes to try its power and suppleness. "Stand a little out of the way, Mrs. Squeers, my dear; I've hardly got room enough."

"Spare me, sir!" cried Smike.

"Oh! that's all, is it?' said Squeers. "Yes, I'll flog you within an inch of your life, and spare you that."

"Ha, ha, ha," laughed Mrs. Squeers, "that's a good 'un!"

"I was driven to do it," said Smike faintly; and casting another imploring look about him.

"Driven to do it, were you?" said Squeers. "Oh! it wasn't your fault; it was mine, I suppose—eh?"

"A nasty, ungrateful, pig-headed, brutish, obstinate, sneaking dog," exclaimed Mrs. Squeers, taking Smike's head under her arm, and administering a cuff at every epithet; "what does he mean by that?"

"Stand aside, my dear," replied Squeers. "We'll try and find out."

Mrs. Squeers being out of breath with her exertions, complied. Squeers caught the boy firmly in his grip; one desperate cut had fallen on his body—he was wincing from the lash and uttering a scream of pain—it was raised again, and again about to fall—when Nicholas Nickleby suddenly starting up, cried "Stop!" in a voice that made the rafters ring.

"Who cried stop?" said Squeers, turning savagely round.

"I," said Nicholas, stepping forward. "This must not go on."

"Must not go on!" cried Squeers, almost in a shriek.

"No!" thundered Nicholas.

Aghast and stupefied by the boldness of the interference, Squeers released his hold of Smike, and, falling back a pace or two, gazed upon Nicholas with looks that were positively frightful.

"I say must not," repeated Nicholas, nothing daunted; "shall not. I will prevent it."

Squeers continued to gaze upon him, with his eyes starting out of his head; but astonishment had actually, for the moment, bereft him of speech.

"You have disregarded all my quiet interference in the miserable lad's behalf," said Nicholas; "you have returned no answer to the letter in which I begged forgiveness for him, and offered to be responsible that he would remain quietly here. Don't blame me for this public interference. You have brought it upon yourself; not I."

"Sit down, beggar!" screamed Squeers, almost beside himself with rage, and seizing Smike as he spoke.

"Wretch," rejoined Nicholas, fiercely, "touch him at your peril! I will not stand by, and see it done. My blood is up, and I have the strength of ten such men as you. Look to yourself, for by Heaven I will not spare you, if you drive me on!"

"Stand back" cried Squeers, brandishing his weapon.

"I have a long series of insults to avenge," said Nicholas, flushed with passion; "and my indignation is aggravated by the dastardly cruelties practised on helpless infancy in this foul den. Have a care; for if you do raise the devil within me, the consequences shall fall heavily upon your own head!"

He had scarcely spoken, when Squeers, in a violent outbreak of wrath, and with a cry like the howl of a wild beast, spat upon him, and struck him a blow across the face with his instrument of torture, which raised up a bar of livid flesh as it was inflicted. Smarting with the agony of the blow, and concentrating into that one moment all his feelings of rage, scorn, and indignation, Nicholas spring upon him, wrested the weapon from his hand, and pinning him by the throat, beat the ruffian till he roared for mercy.

The boys—with the exception of Master Squeers, who, coming to his father's assistance harassed the enemy in the rear—moved not, hand or foot; but Mrs. Squeers, with many shrieks for aid, hung on to the tail of her partner's coat, and endeavoured to drag him from his infuriated adversary; while Miss Squeers, who had been peeping through the key-hole in expectation of a very different scene, darted in at the very beginning of the attack, and after launching a shower of ink-stands at the usher's head, beat Nicholas to her heart's content: animating herself at every blow, with the recollection of his having refused her proffered love, and thus imparting additional strength to an arm which (as she took after her mother in this respect) was, at no time, one of the weakest.

Nicholas, in the full torrent of his violence, felt the blows no more than if they had been dealt with feathers; but, becoming tired of the noise and uproar, and feeling that his arm grew weak besides, he threw all his remaining strength into half-a-dozen finishing cuts, and flung Squeers from him, with all the force he could muster. The violence of his fall precipitated Mrs. Squeers completely over an adjacent form; and Squeers striking his head against it in his descent, lay at his full length on the ground, stunned and motionless.

Having brought affairs to this happy termination, and ascertained, to his thorough satisfaction, that Squeers was only stunned, and not dead (upon which point he had had some unpleasant doubts at first), Nicholas left his family to restore him, and retired to consider what course he had better adopt. He looked anxiously round for Smike, as he left the room, but he was nowhere to be seen.

After a brief consideration, he packed up a few clothes in a small leathern valise, and, finding that nobody offered to oppose his progress, marched boldly out by the front door, and shortly afterwards, struck into the road which led to Greta Bridge.

3   The Realist Drama

Realism was not restricted to the novel alone. The leading Realist playwright, Henrik Ibsen (1828–1906), a Norwegian, examined with clinical precision the commercial and professional classes, their personal ambitions, business practices, and family relationships. In a period of less than ten years, Ibsen wrote four Realist "problem plays"—*Pillars of Society* (1877), *A Doll's House* (1879), *Ghosts* (1881), and *An Enemy of the People* (1882)—that drew attention to bourgeois pretensions, hypocrisy, and social conventions that thwart individual growth. Thus, Ibsen's characters are typically torn between their sense of duty to others and their own selfish wants. Although Ibsen wrote about profound social issues, he viewed himself as a dramatist relating a piece of reality and not a social reformer agitating for reform.

In *Pillars of Society,* Ibsen portrayed entrepreneurs who, aspiring for wealth and status, not only betray loved ones but also engage in unscrupulous business practices at the expense of their fellow citizens. Thus, the title itself is ironic, for the "pillars of society" are actually corrupt hypocrites.

Ghosts dealt with the theme of a loveless marriage in a bourgeois home. Helene Alving, like Nora (see below), dwells in an oppressive environment; also like Nora, she hides her true feelings and lives an unauthentic existence. Angered by Ibsen's depiction of marital unhappiness, critics accused him of undermining the sanctity of marriage and family life, which they saw as the very foundation of bourgeois society. Adding to their ire and Ibsen's image as a moral subversive was his treatment of the unmentionable, scandalous topic of venereal disease.

Although a comedy, *An Enemy of the People* deals with themes that are crucial to modern democratic society: the failure of the majority to break with inherited ideas and beliefs that do a disservice to society and the ease with which people, driven by self-interest, will close their minds to truth and morality. Dr. Stockmann discovers that the spring water given to guests at a Norwegian spa has been polluted by sewage. Was the infected spring a symbol for a diseased bourgeois society? When Stockmann announces his discovery, town officials and businessmen who profit from the spa conspire to silence him. When he refuses to stay quiet, townspeople attack his house, smash his windows, get him fired, and shun him. However, Stockmann gains inner strength when he stands alone against a hostile society.

Ibsen's plays were often penetrating psychological explorations into the forces, hidden below the surface, that mold a person's character. If he had a message to relate, it was that people should overcome self-deception and be morally honest with themselves.

Henrik Ibsen
A Doll's House

In *A Doll's House,* Ibsen took up a theme that shocked late nineteenth-century bourgeois audiences: a woman leaving her husband and children in search of self-realization. Nora Helmer resents being a submissive and dutiful wife to a husband who does not take her seriously, who treats her like a child, a doll.

In the following selection from *A Doll's House,* Nora tells her husband, Torvald, how she resents being treated like a child and why she is leaving him.

(She sits down at one side of the table.)

HELMER Nora—what is this?—this cold, set face?

NORA Sit down. It will take some time; I have a lot to talk over with you.

HELMER *(sits down at the opposite side of the table)* You alarm me, Nora!—and I don't understand you.

NORA No, that is just it. You don't understand me, and I have never understood you either—before to-night. No, you mustn't interrupt me. You must simply listen to what I say. Torvald, this is a settling of accounts.

HELMER What do you mean by that?

NORA *(after a short silence).* Isn't there one thing that strikes you as strange in our sitting here like this?

HELMER What is that?

NORA We have been married now eight years. Does it not occur to you that this is the first time we two, you and I, husband and wife, have had a serious conversation?

HELMER What do you mean by serious?

NORA In all these eight years—longer than that—from the very beginning of our acquaintance, we have never exchanged a word on any serious subject.

HELMER Was it likely that I would be continually and for ever telling you about worries that you could not help me to bear?

NORA I am not speaking about business matters. I say that we have never sat down in earnest together to try and get at the bottom of anything.

HELMER But, dearest Nora, would it have been any good to you?

NORA That is just it; you have never understood me. I have been greatly wronged, Torvald—first by papa and then by you.

HELMER What! By us two—by us two, who have loved you better than anyone else in the world?

NORA *(shaking her head)* You have never loved me. You have only thought it pleasant to be in love with me.

HELMER Nora, what do I hear you saying?

NORA It is perfectly true, Torvald. When I was at home with papa, he told me his opinion about everything, and so I had the same opinions; and if I differed from him I concealed the fact, because he would not have liked it. He called me his doll-child, and he played with me just as I used to play with my dolls. And when I came to live with you—

HELMER What sort of an expression is that to use about our marriage?

NORA *(undisturbed)* I mean that I was simply transferred from papa's hands into yours. You arranged everything according to your own taste, and so I got the same tastes as you—or else I pretended to, I am really not quite sure which—I think sometimes the one and sometimes the other. When I look back on it, it seems to me as if I had been living here like a poor woman—just from hand to mouth. I have existed merely to perform tricks for you Torvald. But you would have it so. You and papa have committed a great sin against me. It is your fault that I have made nothing of my life.

HELMER How unreasonable and how ungrateful you are, Nora! Have you not been happy here?

NORA No, I have never been happy. I thought I was, but it has never really been so.

HELMER Not—not happy!

NORA No, only merry. And you have always been so kind to me. But our home has been nothing but a playroom. I have been your doll-wife, just as at home I was papa's doll-child; and here the children have been my dolls. I thought it great fun when you played with me, just as they thought it great fun when I played with them. That is what our marriage has been, Torvald.

HELMER There is some truth in what you say—exaggerated and strained as your view of it is. But for the future it shall be different. Playtime shall be over, and lesson-time shall begin.

NORA Whose lessons? Mine, or the children's?

HELMER Both yours and the children's, my darling Nora.

NORA Alas, Torvald, you are not the man to educate me into being a proper wife for you.

HELMER And you can say that!

NORA And I—how am I fitted to bring up the children?

HELMER Nora!

NORA Didn't you say so yourself a little while ago—that you dare not trust me to bring them up?

HELMER In a moment of anger! Why do you pay any heed to that?

NORA Indeed, you were perfectly right. I am not fit for the task. There is another task I must undertake first. I must try and educate myself—you are not the man to help me in that. I must do that for myself. And that is why I am going to leave you now.

HELMER (*springing up*) What do you say?

NORA I must stand quite alone, if I am to understand myself and everything about me. It is for that reason that I cannot remain with you any longer.

HELMER Nora! Nora!

NORA I am going away from here now, at once. I am sure Christine will take me in for the night—

HELMER You are out of your mind! I won't allow it! I forbid you!

NORA It is no use forbidding me anything any longer. I will take with me what belongs to myself. I will take nothing from you, either now or later.

HELMER What sort of madness is this!

NORA To-morrow I shall go home—I mean, to my old home. It will be easiest for me to find something to do there.

HELMER You blind, foolish woman!

NORA I must try and get some sense, Torvald.

HELMER To desert your home, your husband and your children! And you don't consider what people will say!

NORA I cannot consider that at all. I only know that it is necessary for me.

HELMER It's shocking. This is how you would neglect your most sacred duties.

NORA What do you consider my most sacred duties?

HELMER Do I need to tell you that? Are they not your duties to your husband and your children?

NORA I have other duties just as sacred.

HELMER That you have not. What duties could those be?

NORA Duties to myself.

HELMER Before all else, you are a wife and a mother.

NORA I don't believe that any longer. I believe that before all else I am a reasonable human being, just as you are—or, at all events, that I must try and become one. I know quite well, Torvald, that most people would think you right, and that views of that kind are to be found in books; but I can no longer content myself with what most people say, or with what is found in books. I must think over things for myself and get to understand them.

HELMER Can you not understand your place in your own home? Have you not a reliable guide in such matters as that?—have you no religion?

NORA I am afraid, Torvald, I do not exactly know what religion is.

HELMER What are you saying?

NORA I know nothing but what the clergyman said, when I went to be confirmed. He told us that religion was this, and that, and the other. When I am away from all this, and am alone, I will look into that matter too. I will see if what the clergyman said is true, or at all events if it is true for me.

HELMER This is unheard of in a girl of your age! But if religion cannot lead you aright, let me try and awaken your conscience. I suppose you have some moral sense? Or—answer me—am I to think you have none?

NORA I assure you, Torvald, that is not an easy question to answer. I really don't know. The thing perplexes me altogether. I only know that you and I look at it in quite a different light. I am learning, too, that the law is quite another thing from what I supposed; but I find it impossible to convince myself that the law is right. According to it a woman has no right to spare her old dying father, or to save her husband's life. I can't believe that.

HELMER You talk like a child. You don't understand the conditions of the world in which you live.

NORA No, I don't. But now I am going to try. I am going to see if I can make out who is right, the world or I.

HELMER You are ill, Nora; you are delirious; I almost think you are out of your mind.

NORA I have never felt my mind so clear and certain as to-night.

HELMER And is it with a clear and certain mind that you forsake your husband and your children?

NORA Yes, it is.

HELMER Then there is only one possible explanation.

NORA What is that?

HELMER You do not love me any more.

NORA No, that is just it.

HELMER Nora!—and you can say that?

NORA It gives me great pain, Torvald, for you have always been so kind to me, but I cannot help it. I do not love you any more.

HELMER (*regaining his composure*) Is that a clear and certain conviction too?

NORA Yes, absolutely clear and certain. That is the reason I will not stay here any longer.

HELMER And can you tell me what I have done to forfeit your love?

NORA Yes, indeed I can. It was to-night, when the wonderful thing did not happen; then I saw you were not the man I had thought you.

HELMER Explain yourself better—I don't understand you.

NORA I have waited so patiently for eight years; for goodness knows, I knew very well that wonderful things don't happen everyday. Then this horrible misfortune came upon me; and then I felt quite certain that the wonderful thing was going to happen at last. When Krogstad's letter was lying out there, never for a moment did I imagine that you would consent to accept this man's conditions. I was so absolutely certain that you would say to him: Publish the thing to the whole world. And when that was done—

HELMER Yes, what then?—when I had exposed my wife to shame and disgrace?

NORA When that was done, I was so absolutely certain, you would come forward and take everything upon yourself, and say: I am the guilty one.

HELMER Nora——!

NORA You mean that I would never have accepted such a sacrifice on your part? No, of course not. But what would my assurances have been worth against yours? That was the wonderful thing which I hoped for and feared; and it was to prevent that, that I wanted to kill myself.

HELMER I would gladly work night and day for you, Nora—bear sorrow and want for your sake. But no man would sacrifice his honour for the one he loves.

NORA It is a thing hundreds of thousands of women have done.

HELMER Oh, you think and talk like a heedless child.

NORA Maybe. But you neither think nor talk like the man I could bind myself to. As soon as your fear was over—and it was not fear for what threatened me, but for what might happen to you—when the whole thing was past, as far as you were concerned it was exactly as if nothing at all had happened. Exactly as before, I was your little skylark, your doll, which you would in future treat with doubly gentle care, because it was so brittle and fragile. *(Getting up.)* Torvald—it was then it dawned upon me that for eight years I had been living here with a strange man, and had borne him three children——. Oh, I can't bear to think of it! I could tear myself into little bits!

HELMER *(sadly)* I see, I see. An abyss has opened between us—there is no denying it. But, Nora, would it not be possible to fill it up?

NORA As I am now, I am no wife for you

HELMER I have it in me to become a different man.

NORA Perhaps—if your doll is taken away from you.

HELMER But to part!—to part from you! No, no. Nora, I can't understand that idea.

NORA *(going out to the right)* That makes it more certain that it must be done.

(She comes back with her cloak and hat and a small bag which she puts on a chair by the table.)

HELMER Nora, Nora, not now! Wait till to-morrow.

NORA *(putting on her cloak)* I cannot spend the night in a strange man's room.

HELMER But can't we live here like brother and sister——?

NORA *(putting on her hat)* You know very well that would not last long. *(Puts the shawl round her.)* Good-bye, Torvald. I won't see the little ones. I know they are in better hands than mine. As I am now, I can be of no use to them.

HELMER But some day, Nora—some day?

NORA How can I tell? I have no idea what is going to become of me.

HELMER But you are my wife, whatever becomes of you.

NORA Listen, Torvald. I have heard that when a wife deserts her husband's house, as I am doing now, he is legally freed from all obligations towards her. In any case I set you free from all your obligations. You are not to feel yourself bound in the slightest way, any more than I shall. There must be perfect freedom on both sides. See here is your ring back. Give me mine.

HELMER That too?

NORA That too.

HELMER Here it is.

NORA That's right. Now it is all over. I have put the keys here. The maids know all about everything in the house—better than I do. To-morrow, after I have left her, Christine will come here and pack up my own things that I brought with me from home. I will have them sent after me.

HELMER All over! All over!—Nora, shall you never think of me again?

NORA I know I shall often think of you and the children and this house.

HELMER May I write to you, Nora?

NORA No—never. You must not do that.

HELMER But at least let me send you——

NORA Nothing—nothing——

HELMER Let me help you if you are in want.

NORA No. I can receive nothing from a stranger.

HELMER Nora—can I never be anything more than a stranger to you?

NORA (taking her bag) Ah, Torvald, the most wonderful thing of all would have to happen.

HELMER Tell me what that would be!

NORA Both you and I would have to be so changed that——. Oh, Torvald, I don't believe any longer in wonderful things happening.

HELMER But I will believe in it. Tell me? So changed that——?

NORA That our life together would be a real wedlock. Good-bye.

(She goes out through the hall.)

HELMER (sinks down on a chair at the door and buries his face in his hands) Nora! Nora! (looks round, and rises.) Empty. She is gone. (A hope flashes across his mind.) The most wonderful thing of all——?

(The sound of a door shutting is heard from below.)

4 The Golden Age of Russian Literature

In the last part of the nineteenth century, Russian novelists, short story writers, and dramatists produced a rich literary culture that is often referred to as the golden age of Russian literature. Among the literary greats were Ivan Turgenev (1818–1883), Anton Chekov (1860–1904), Leo Tolstoy (1828–1910), and Fyodor Dostoevsky (1821–1881). Demonstrating extraordinary literary skill, these writers provided astute insights into Russian society and, at times, laced their works with political and social criticism.

A true-to-life picture of Russian rural conditions, particularly the brutal life of serfs, was provided by the novelist, dramatist, and short story writer Ivan Turgenev in his book *A Sportsman's Sketches* (1852). In an unpolemical style, Turgenev showed that serfdom not only debased the serfs but also their masters, the rural nobility, who did not recognize serfs as human beings. In 1862, Turgenev published his masterpiece, *Fathers and Sons,* which deals, in part, with the theme of nihilism—the rejection of all values. Personally and artistically, Turgenev was a liberal who stood between the spirit of revolutionary zeal that was overtaking many of his contemporaries and the reactionary government of the tsar.

Anton Chekov was a physician who turned to literature. His major dramas concentrate on the realities, often ugly, of provincial life among dissolute land-owning nobles who squander their money, drink excessively, and do nothing productive to better society. In his last play, *The Cherry Orchard* (1904), Chekov detailed the lives of people who struggle against forces beyond their control. He elucidated, and then impartially analyzed, his characters' inner thoughts and deepest feelings which are illustrated through simple dialogue, using ordinary language.

One of Chekov's friends, Leo Tolstoy, described the tragedies that attended Napoleon's invasion of Russia and the outlook and manners of the Russian nobility in his novel *War and Peace* (1863–1869). More than five hundred people appear in his epic, yet each one has a recognizable personality—a tribute to the author's talent for characterization. Seeking to provide a historically accurate description of the war, Tolstoy examined letters and diaries of participants and spoke with veterans. Even though the work contains several denunciations of war, it also has positive things to say about military life, notably the camaraderie soldiers shared, the self-sacrifice they demonstrated, and the patriotism showed by the Russian people in resisting Napoleon.

In 1844, a number of people who discussed socialist and revolutionary ideas, including the novelist Fydor Dostoevsky, were sentenced to death by the tsar. As they were bound and placed before a firing squad, the tsar's messenger arrived, informing them that the sentence had been commuted to penal servitude. (Actually, the "execution" was merely a charade intended to frighten the group and set an example for those who might hold similar ideas.) Dostoevsky's near-death experience and the five years he spent as a convict in remote Siberia, where he studied the New Testament, deeply affected him. Dostoevsky ultimately abandoned political radicalism, and he placed his faith, instead, in the teachings of the Russian Orthodox Church.

Dostoevsky's fame derives from four major novels: *Crime and Punishment* (1866), *The Idiot* (1868), *The Possessed* (1871), and the *Brothers Karamazov* (1880). In these and other works, he revealed his belief in the need to regenerate Russian spirituality; for him, the truth of Jesus demonstrated by simple Russian peasants was superior to the truth of science heralded by Westerners. He also showed a superb ability to create memorable characters, to probe minds, and to describe vividly and perceptively. He was fascinated by the psychological contradictions inherent within human beings and often stated that he sought to portray the depths of the human soul. Dostoevsky's uniqueness as an author of Russian realistic fiction resulted in the establishment of his own school of literature.

Leo Tolstoy
Anna Karenina

No Russian writer has greater fame outside of his homeland than Leo Tolstoy who is renown, not only as an author, but also as a reformer and religious philosopher. Tolstoy was an aristocrat and former soldier who believed that for a work of literature to be good it must come "singing from the author's soul" and make commonplace feelings procurable by all people. This was what he called "universal art." During his many travels throughout Europe, Tolstoy witnessed the problems that freed serfs faced, and, following their liberation in 1861, he worked actively to set up schools for peasants patterned after those he had encountered during his travels. In 1862, he married Sophie Andreyevna Behrs with whom he had fifteen children. But throughout much of his life, Tolstoy suffered from an inner conflict—he was torn between his natural instincts and his zest for life and his moral responsibility to make life better for those who had less than he did. But by 1877, his inner torment was resolved through a religious conversion. The centerpiece of Tolstoy's faith was not dogma but morality. For him, Jesus was not divine but a genuine ethical person and teacher who set a noble example of loving humanity and repudiating violence and hate, and following Jesus' path was the avenue to personal happiness.

The novel that many critics regard as one of the finest novels ever written is Tolstoy's *Anna Karenina* (1874–1876), his classic story of love and adultery in Russian high society. In it, Tolstoy probes the complexities of marital relationships, including a wife's adultery, the lure of illicit passion, and a woman's place in society. The Russian aristocracy may have had a casual attitude toward marital fidelity, but for Tolstoy a violation of the sacred bond of marriage was a crime that incurred severe punishment. Anna Arkadyevna Karenina is a beautiful woman of the social elite who is married to Alexey Alexandrovich Karenin, an influential governmental official who obsesses over both his money and his social position. The fact that he cares little for Anna's sexual passion or her personal happiness makes her susceptible to the social graces of Count Alexey Kirilich Vronsky—who epitomizes high society on a grand scale. Vronsky loves women and loves flaunting his money. In contrast to the torrid love affair of Anna and Vronsky is the relationship of Princess Catherine Alexandrovna Shtcherbatskaya (known as Kitty) with Konstantin Dmitrich Levin, a man who recognizes (as did Tolstoy) that land is the tie that binds families and societies one to another. It is Levin who serves as Tolstoy's mouthpiece in asserting the simplicity of the pastoral life and his appreciation for the work of the peasants on the land. Tolstoy had no love for industrialization and capitalism, hallmarks of the modern age, and on nearly every page, he provides the reader with illuminating descriptions of the upper classes of Russian society. Much of this is evident in the following passage—an argument between Kitty's parents (Prince and Princess Shtcherbatskaya) over whether she should pin her hopes on Levin (her father's choice) or follow her passion for Vronsky, with whom she is completely enamored (her mother's preference). Moreover, Tolstoy uses the encounter to contrast the marriage customs in England, where free choice was generally favored, and the arranged marriages which predominated in France.

The young Princess Kitty Shtcherbatskaya was eighteen. It was the first winter that she had been out in the world. Her success in society had been greater than that of either of her elder sisters, and greater even than her mother had anticipated. To say nothing of the young men who danced at the Moscow balls being almost all in love with Kitty, two serious suitors had already this first winter made their appearance: Levin, and immediately after his departure, Count Vronsky.

Levin's appearance at the beginning of the winter, his frequent visits, and evident love for Kitty, had led to the first serious conversations between Kitty's parents as to her future, and to disputes between them. The prince was on Levin's side; he said he wished for nothing better for Kitty. The princess for her part, going round the question in the manner peculiar to women, maintained that Kitty was too young, that Levin had done nothing to prove that he had serious intentions, that Kitty felt no great attraction to him, and other side issues; but she did not state the principal point, which was that she looked for a better match for her daughter, and that Levin was not to her liking, and she did not understand him. When Levin had abruptly departed, the princess was delighted, and said to her husband triumphantly: "You see I was right." When Vronsky appeared on the scene, she was still more delighted, confirmed in her opinion that Kitty was to make not simply a good, but a brilliant match.

In the mother's eyes there could be no comparison between Vronsky and Levin. She disliked in Levin his strange and uncompromising opinions and his shyness in society, founded, as she supposed, on his pride and his queer sort of life, as she considered it, absorbed in cattle and peasants. She did not very much like it that he, who was in love with her daughter, had kept coming to the house for six weeks, as though he were waiting for something, inspecting, as though he were

afraid he might be doing them too great an honor by making an offer, and did not realize that a man, who continually visits at a house where there is a young unmarried girl, is bound to make his intentions clear. And suddenly, without doing so, he disappeared. "It's as well he's not attractive enough for Kitty to have fallen in love with him," thought the mother.

Vronsky satisfied all the mother's desires. Very wealthy, clever, of aristocratic family, on the highroad to a brilliant career in the army and at court, and a fascinating man. Nothing better could be wished for.

Vronsky openly flirted with Kitty at balls, danced with her and came continually to the house; consequently there could be no doubt of the seriousness of his intentions. But, in spite of that the mother had spent the whole of that winter in a state of terrible anxiety and agitation.

Princess Shtcherbatskaya had herself been married thirty years ago, her aunt arranging the match. Her husband, about whom everything was well known beforehand, had come, looked at his future bride, and been looked at. The matchmaking aunt had ascertained and communicated their mutual impression. That impression had been favorable. Afterwards, on a day fixed beforehand, the expected offer was made to her parents, and accepted. All had passed very simply and easily. So it seemed, at least, to the princess. But over her own daughters she had felt how far from simple and easy is the business, apparently so commonplace, of marrying off one's daughters. The panics that had been lived through, the thoughts that had been brooded over, the money that had been wasted, and the disputes with her husband over marrying the two older girls, Darya and Natalia! Now, since the youngest had come out, she was going through the same terrors, the same doubts, and still more violent quarrels with her husband than she had over the elder girls. The old prince, like all fathers indeed, was exceedingly punctilious on the score of the honor and reputation of his daughters. He was irrationally jealous over his daughters, especially over Kitty, who was his favorite. At every turn he had scenes with the princess for compromising her daughter. The princess had grown accustomed to this already with her other daughters, but now she felt that there was more ground for the prince's touchiness. She saw that of late years much was changed in the manners of society, that a mother's duties had become still more difficult. She saw that girls of Kitty's age formed some sort of clubs, went to some sort of lectures, mixed freely in men's society; drove about the streets alone, many of them did not curtsey, and, what was the most important thing, all the girls were firmly convinced that to choose their husbands was their own affair, and not their parents'. "Marriages aren't made nowadays as they used to be," was thought and said by all these young girls, and even by their elders. But how marriages were made now, the princess could not learn from any one. The French fashion—of the parents arranging their children's future—was not accepted; it was condemned. The English fashion of the complete independence of girls was also not accepted, and not possible in Russian society. The Russian fashion of matchmaking by the offices of intermediate persons was for some reason considered unseemly; it was ridiculed by every one and by the princess herself. But how girls were to be married, and how parents were to marry them, no one knew. Every one with whom the princess had chanced to discuss the matter said the same thing: "Mercy on us, it's high time in our day to cast off all that old-fashioned business. It's the young people have to marry, and not their parents; and so we ought to leave the young people to arrange it as they choose." It was very easy for any one to say that who had no daughters, but the princess realized that in the process of getting to know each other, her daughter might fall in love, and fall in love with some one who did not care to marry her or who was quite unfit to be her husband. And, however much it was instilled into the princess that in our times young people ought to arrange their lives for themselves, she was unable to believe it, just as she would have been unable to believe that, at any time whatever, the most suitable playthings for children five years old ought to be loaded pistols. And so the princess was more uneasy over Kitty than she had been over her elder sisters.

Although Anna is married to Karenin and has a son with him, she leaves both of them for Vronsky with whom she later has a child. While Vronsky is still able to participate in the social life he has always savored, Anna finds herself shunned by the society that once adored her, and she is jealous of Vronsky's social freedom. This is evident in the following selection in which the aristocratic couple, the Kartasovs, refuse to sit next to the couple—Anna and Yashvin, Anna's escort for the evening—in the adjoining box at the theater. Even though Vronsky goes to Anna following her "hideous" treatment, he begins to feel the pressure of such chronic societal wariness, which compromises his social standing, and his love for Anna begins to wane.

Vronsky for the first time, experienced a feeling of anger against Anna, almost a hatred for her willfully refusing to understand her own position. This feeling was aggravated by his being unable to tell her plainly the cause of his anger. If he had told her directly what he was thinking, he would have said:

"In that dress, with a princess only too well known to every one, to show yourself at the theater is equivalent not merely to acknowledging your position as a fallen woman, but is flinging down a challenge to society, that is to say, cutting yourself off from it forever."

He could not say that to her. "But how can she fail to see it, and what is going on in her?" he said to himself. He felt at the same time that his respect for her was diminished while his sense of her beauty was intensified. . . .

Vronsky went into the theater at half-past eight. The performance was in full swing. The little old box-keeper, recognizing Vronsky as he helped him off with his fur coat, called him "Your Excellency," and suggested he should not take a number but should simply call Fyodor. In the brightly lighted corridor there was no one but the box-opener and two attendants with fur cloaks on their arms listening at the doors. Through the closed doors came the sounds of the discreet *staccato* accompaniment of the orchestra, and a single female voice rendering distinctly a musical phrase. The door opened to let the box-opener slip through, and the phrase, drawing to the end reached Vronsky's hearing clearly. But the doors were closed again at once, and Vronsky did not hear the end of the phrase and the cadence of the accompaniment, though he knew from the thunder of applause that it was over. When he entered the hall, brilliantly lighted with chandeliers and gas jets, the noise was still going on. On the stage the singer, bowing and smiling, with bare shoulders flashing with diamonds, was, with the help of the tenor who had given her his arm, gathering up the bouquets that were flying awkwardly over the footlights. Then she went up to a gentleman with glossy pomaded hair parted down the center, who was stretching across the footlights holding out something to her, and all the public in the stalls as well as in the boxes was in excitement, craning forward, shouting and clapping. The conductor in his high chair assisted in passing the offering, and straightened his white tie. Vronsky walked into the middle of the stalls, and, standing still, began looking about him. That day less than ever was his attention turned upon the familiar, habitual surroundings, the stage, the noise, all the familiar, uninteresting, parti-colored herd of spectators in the packed theater.

There were, as always, the same ladies of some sort with officers of some sort in the back of the boxes; the same gaily dressed women—God knows who—and uniforms and black coats; the same dirty crowd in the upper gallery; and among the crowd, in the boxes and in the front rows, were some forty of the *real* people. And to those oases Vronsky at once directed his attention, and with them he entered at once into relation. . . .

Vronsky had not yet seen Anna. He purposely avoided looking in her direction. But he knew by the direction of people's eyes where she was. . . .

[Vronsky] moved his opera-glass from the stalls and scanned the boxes. Near a lady in a turban and a bald old man, who seemed to wave angrily in the moving opera glass, Vronsky suddenly caught sight of Anna's head, proud, strikingly beautiful, and smiling in the frame of lace. She was in the fifth box, twenty paces from him. She was sitting in front, and slightly turning, was saying something to Yashvin. The setting of her head on her handsome, broad shoulders, and the restrained excitement and brilliance of her eyes and her whole face reminded him of her just as he had seen her at the ball in Moscow. But he felt utterly different towards her beauty now. In his feeling for her now there was no element of mystery, and so her beauty, though it attracted him even more intensely than before, gave him now a sense of injury. She was not looking in his direction, but Vronsky felt that she had seen him already. . . .

In that box on the left were the Kartasovs. Vronsky knew them, and knew that Anna was acquainted with them. Madame Kartasova, a thin little woman, was standing up in her box, and, her back turned upon Anna, she was putting on a mantle that her husband was holding for her. Her face was pale and angry, and she was talking excitedly. Kartasov, a fat, bald man, was continually looking round at Anna, while he attempted to soothe his wife. When the wife had gone out, the husband lingered a long while, and tried to catch Anna's eye, obviously anxious to bow to her. But Anna, with unmistakable intention, avoided noticing him, and talked to Yashvin, whose cropped head was bent down to her. Kartasov went out without making his salutation, and the box was left empty.

Vronsky could not understand exactly what had passed between the Kartasovs and Anna, but he saw that something humiliating for Anna had happened. He knew this both from what he had seen, and most of all from the face of Anna, who, he could see, was taxing every nerve to carry through the part she had taken up. And in maintaining this attitude of external composure she was completely successful. Any one who did not know her and her circle, who had not heard all the utterances of the women expressive of commiseration, indignation, and amazement, that she should show herself in society, and show herself so conspicuously with her lace and her beauty, would have admired the serenity and loveliness of this woman without a suspicion that she was undergoing the sensations of a man in the stocks.

Knowing that something had happened, but not knowing precisely what, Vronsky felt a thrill of agonizing anxiety, and hoping to find out something, he went towards his brother's box. . . .

. . . With rapid steps he went downstairs; he felt that he must do something, but he did not know what. Anger with her for having put herself and him in such a false position, together with pity for her suffering, filled his heart. . . .

Noticing in the next act that her box was empty, Vronsky, rousing indignant "hushes" in the silent audience, went out in the middle of a solo and drove home.

Anna was already at home. When Vronsky went up to her, she was in the same dress as she had worn at the theater. She was sitting in the first armchair against the wall, looking straight before her. She looked at him, and at once resumed her former position.

"Anna," he said.

"You, you are to blame for everything!" she cried, with tears of despair and hatred in her voice, getting up.

"I begged, I implored you not to go; I knew it would be unpleasant. . . ."

"Unpleasant!" she cried—"hideous! As long as I live I shall never forget it. She said it was a disgrace to sit beside me."

"A silly woman's chatter," he said: "but why risk it, why provoke? . . ."

"I hate your calm. You ought not to have brought me to this. If you had loved me . . ."

"Anna! How does the question of my love come in?"

"Oh, if you loved me, as I love, if you were tortured as I am! . . ." she said, looking at him with an expression of terror.

He was sorry for her, and angry notwithstanding. He assured her of his love because he saw that this was the only means of soothing her, and he did not reproach her in words, but in his heart he reproached her.

And the asseverations of his love, which seemed to him so vulgar that he was ashamed to utter them, she drank in eagerly, and gradually became calmer. The next day, completely reconciled, they left for the country.

Anna's deceitful relationship with Count Vronsky ends in the loss of everything Anna cherishes, causing her to commit suicide by throwing herself under a train. Unlike Anna, who seeks life's purpose totally through romantic love, Levin's concern for spiritual development—by discovering "one should live for the soul"—provides him with a vehicle for meaning and happiness, and it enhances his marriage to Kitty.

Fyodor Dostoevsky
Crime and Punishment

Fyodor Dostoevsky's genius was richly demonstrated in *Crime and Punishment,* a gripping psychological thriller that takes place during a stifling summer in St. Petersburg which is swarming with people. With realistic detail, Dostoevsky captures the individuality of his characters and the heartbeat of the city. Raskolnikoff, an impoverished student, and at times, even generous and compassionate, commits murder. Why? He believes that "extraordinary" people have a right to shed blood if the realization of their ideas, which is to the advantage of humanity, requires it:

> It may even be remarked that nearly all these benefactors and teachers of humanity (Solon, Lycurgus, Mohammed, Napoleon, etc.) have been terribly bloodthirsty. Consequently, not only all great men, but all those who by hook or by crook, have raised themselves above the common herd, men who are capable of evolving something new, must, in virtue of their innate power, be undoubtedly criminal, more or less. Otherwise they would not free themselves from trammels; and, as for being bound by them, that they cannot be—their very mission forbidding it.

Does he think committing a murder would prove that he is indeed an extraordinary person, a self-willed Napoleon? ". . . I longed to know if I was vermin, like the majority—or a Man." Does he hope to demonstrate to himself that he has courage?

After the murder, the student's conscience pains him, and, encouraged by Sonia, a religious young prostitute, a tormented Raskolnikoff eventually confesses. The work's greatness lies in Dostoevsky's ingenius treatment of Raskolnikoff's motives for the crime, how he is psychologically affected by the act, and how his agonizing, subconscious struggles compel him to confess.

In the following passage from *Crime and Punishment,* Raskolnikoff explains to Sonia what was on his mind when he planned and executed the murder.

Sonia looked at him quickly.

Again after her first passionate, agonising sympathy for the unhappy man the terrible idea of the murder overwhelmed her. In his changed tone she seemed to hear the murderer speaking. She looked at him bewildered. She knew nothing as yet, why, how, with what object it had been. Now all these questions rushed at once into her mind. And again she could not believe it: "He, he is a murderer! Could it be true?"

"What's the meaning of it? Where am I?" she said in complete bewilderment, as though still unable to recover herself. "How could you, you, a man like you. . . . How could you bring yourself to it? . . . What does it mean?"

"Oh, well—to plunder. Leave off, Sonia," he answered wearily, almost with vexation.

Sonia stood as though struck dumb, but suddenly she cried:

"You were hungry! It was . . . to help your mother? Yes?"

"No, Sonia, no," he muttered, turning away and hanging his head. "I was not so hungry. . . . I certainly did want to help my mother, but . . . that's not the real thing either. . . . Don't torture me, Sonia."

Sonia clasped her hands.

"Could it, could it all be true? Good God, what a truth? Who could believe it? And how could you give away your last farthing and yet rob and murder! Ah," she cried suddenly, "that money you gave Katerina Ivanovna . . . that money. . . . Can that money . . ."

"No, Sonia," he broke in hurriedly, "that money was not it. Don't worry yourself! That money my mother sent me and it came when I was ill, the day I gave it to you. . . . Ruzumihin saw it . . . he received it for me. . . . That money was mine—my own."

Sonia listened to him in bewilderment and did her utmost to comprehend.

"And *that* money. . . . I don't even know really whether there was any money," he added softly, as though reflecting. "I took a purse off her neck, made of chamois leather . . . a purse stuffed full of something . . . but I didn't look in it; I suppose I hadn't time. . . . And the things—chains and trinkets—I buried under a stone with the purse next morning in a yard off the V—— Prospect. They are all there now. . . ."

Sonia strained every nerve to listen.

"Then why . . . why, you said you did it to rob, but you took nothing?" she asked quickly, catching at a straw.

"I don't know. . . . I haven't yet decided whether to take that money or not," he said, musing again; and, seeming to wake up with a start, he gave a brief ironical smile. "Ach, what silly stuff I am talking, eh?"

The thought flashed through Sonia's mind, wasn't he mad? But she dismissed it at once. "No, it was something else." She could make nothing of it, nothing.

"Do you know, Sonia," he said suddenly with conviction, "let me tell you: if I'd simply killed because I was hungry," laying stress on every word and looking enigmatically but sincerely at her, "I should be *happy* now. You must believe that! What would it matter to you," he cried a moment later with a sort of despair, "what would it matter to you if I were to confess that I did wrong! What do you gain by such a stupid triumph over me? Ah, Sonia, was it for that I've come to you today?"

Again Sonia tried to say something, but did not speak.

"I asked you to go with me yesterday because you are all I have left."

"Go where?" asked Sonia timidly.

"Not to steal and not to murder, don't be anxious," he smiled bitterly. "We are so different. . . . And you know, Sonia, it's only now, only this moment that I understand *where* I asked you to go with me yesterday! Yesterday when I said it I did not know where. I asked you for one thing, I came to you for one thing—not to leave me. You won't leave me, Sonia?"

She squeezed his hand.

"And why, why did I tell her? Why did I let her know?" he cried a minute later in despair, looking with infinite anguish at her. "Here you expect an explanation from me, Sonia; you are sitting and waiting for it, I see that. But what can I tell you? You won't understand and will only suffer misery . . . on my account! Well, you are crying and embracing me again. Why do you do it? Because I couldn't bear my burden and have come to throw it on another: you suffer too, and I shall feel better! And can you love such a mean wretch?"

"But aren't you suffering, too?" cried Sonia.

Again a wave of the same feeling surged into his heart, and again for an instant softened it.

"Sonia, I have a bad heart, take note of that. It may explain a great deal. I have come because I am bad. There are men who wouldn't have come. But I am a coward and . . . a mean wretch. But . . . never mind! That's not the point. I must speak now, but I don't know how to begin."

He paused and sank into thought.

"Ach, we are so different," he cried again, "we are not alike. And why, why did I come? I shall never forgive myself that."

"No, no, it was a good thing you came," cried Sonia. "It's better I should know, far better!"

He looked at her with anguish.

"What if it were really that?" he said, as though reaching a conclusion. "Yes, that's what it was! I wanted to become a Napoleon, that is why I killed her. . . . Do you understand now?"

"N-no," Sonia whispered naïvely and timidly. "Only speak, speak, I shall understand, I shall understand *in myself!*" she kept begging him.

"You'll understand? Very well, we shall see!" He paused and was for some time lost in meditation.

"It was like this: I asked myself one day this question—what if Napoleon, for instance, had happened to be in my place, and if he had not had Toulon nor Egypt nor the passage of Mont Blanc to begin his career with, but instead of all those picturesque and monumental things, there had simply been some ridiculous old hag, a pawnbroker, who had to be murdered to get money from her trunk (for his career, you understand). Well, would he have brought himself to that, if there had been no other means? Wouldn't he have felt a pang at its being so far from monumental and . . . and sinful, too? Well, I must tell you that I worried myself fearfully over that 'question' so that I was awfully ashamed when I guessed at last (all of a sudden, somehow) that it would not have given him the least pang, that it would not even have struck him that it was not monumental . . . that he would not have seen that there was anything in it to pause over, and that, if he had had no other way, he would have strangled her in a minute without thinking about it! Well, I too . . . left off thinking about it . . . murdered her, following his example. And that's exactly how it was! Do you think it funny? Yes, Sonia, the funniest thing of all is that perhaps that's just how it was."

Sonia did not think it at all funny.

"You had better tell me straight out . . . without examples," she begged, still more timidly and scarcely audibly.

He turned to her, looked sadly at her and took her hands.

"You are right again, Sonia. Of course that's all nonsense, it's almost all talk! You see, you know of course that my mother has scarcely anything, my sister happened to have a good education and was condemned to drudge as a governess. All their hopes were centered on me. I was a student, but I couldn't help myself at the university and was forced for a time to leave it. Even if I had lingered on like that, in ten or twelve years I might (with luck) hope to be some sort of teacher or clerk with a salary of a thousand roubles" (he repeated it as though it were a lesson) "and by that time my mother would be worn out with grief and anxiety and I could not succeed in keeping her in comfort while my sister . . . well, my sister might well have fared worse! And it's a hard thing to pass everything by all one's life, to turn one's back upon everything, to forget one's mother and decorously accept the insults inflicted on one's sister. Why should one? When one has buried them to burden oneself with others—wife and children—and to leave them again without a farthing? So I resolved to gain possession of the old woman's money and to use it for my first years without worrying my mother, to keep myself at the university and for a little while after leaving it— and to do this all on a broad, thorough scale, so as to build up a completely new career and enter upon a new life of independence. . . . Well . . . that's all. . . . Well, of course in killing the old woman I did wrong. . . . Well, that's enough."

He struggled to the end of his speech in exhaustion and let his head sink.

"Oh, that's not it, that's not it," Sonia cried in distress. "How could one . . . no, that's not right, not right."

"You see yourself that it's not right. But I've spoken truly, it's the truth."

"As though that could be the truth! Good God!"

"I've only killed a louse, Sonia, a useless, loathsome, harmful creature."

"A human being—a louse!"

"I too know it wasn't a louse," he answered, looking strangely at her. "But I am talking nonsense, Sonia," he added. "I've been talking nonsense a long time. . . . That's not it, you are right there. There were quite, quite other causes for it! I haven't talked to anyone for so long, Sonia. . . . My head aches dreadfully now."

His eyes shone with feverish brilliance. He was almost delirious; an uneasy smile strayed on his lips. His terrible exhaustion could be seen through his excitement. Sonia saw how he was suffering. She too was growing dizzy. And he talked so strangely; it seemed somehow comprehensible, but yet . . . "But how, how! Good God!" And she wrung her hands in despair.

"No, Sonia, that's not it," he began again suddenly, raising his head, as though a new and sudden train of thought had struck and as it were roused him—"that's not it! Better . . . imagine—yes, it's certainly better—imagine that I am vain, envious, malicious, base, vindictive and . . . well, perhaps with a tendency to insanity. (Let's have it all out at once! They've talked of madness already, I noticed.) I told you just now I could not keep myself at the university. But do you know what perhaps I might have done? My mother would have sent me what I needed for the fees and I could have earned enough for clothes, boots and food, no doubt. Lessons had turned up at half a rouble. Ruzumihin works! But I turned sulky and wouldn't. (Yes, sulkiness, that's the right word for it!) I sat in my room like a spider. You've been in my den, you've seen it. . . . And do you know, Sonia, that low ceilings and tiny rooms cramp the soul and the mind? Ah, how I hated that garret! And yet I wouldn't go out of it! I wouldn't on purpose! I didn't go out for days together, and I wouldn't work, I wouldn't even eat, I just lay there doing nothing. If Nastasya brought me anything, I ate it, if she didn't, I went all day without; I wouldn't ask, on purpose from sulkiness! At night I had no light, I lay in the dark and I wouldn't earn money for candles. I ought to have studied, but I sold my books; and the dust lies an inch thick on the notebooks on my table. I preferred lying still and thinking. And I kept thinking. . . . And I had dreams all the time, strange dreams of all sorts, no need to describe! Only then I began to fancy that. . . . No, that's not it! Again I am telling you wrong! You see I kept asking myself then: why am I so stupid that if others are stupid—and I know they are—yet I won't be wiser? Then I saw, Sonia, that if one waits for every one to get wiser it will take too long. . . . Afterwards I understood that that would never come to pass, that men won't change and that nobody can alter it and that it's not worth wasting effort over it. Yes, that's so. That's the law of their nature, Sonia, . . . that's so! . . . And I know now, Sonia,

that whoever is strong in mind and spirit will have power over them. Anyone who is greatly daring is right in their eyes. He who despises most things will be a lawgiver among them and he who dares most of all will be most in the right! So it has been till now and so it will always be. A man must be blind not to see it!"

Though Raskolnikov looked at Sonia as he said this, he no longer cared whether she understood or not. The fever had complete hold of him; he was in a sort of gloomy ecstasy (he certainly had been too long without talking to anyone). Sonia felt that his gloomy creed had become his faith and code.

"I divined them, Sonia," he went on eagerly, "that power is only vouchsafed to the man who dares to stoop and pick it up. There is only one thing, one thing needful: one has only to dare! Then for the first time in my life an idea took shape in my mind which no one had ever thought of before me, no one! I saw clear as daylight how strange it is that not a single person living in this mad world has had the daring to go straight for it all and send it flying to the devil! I . . . I wanted *to have the daring* . . . and I killed her. I only wanted to have the daring, Sonia! That was the whole cause of it!"

"Oh hush, hush," cried Sonia, clasping her hands. "You turned away from God and God has smitten you, has given you over to the devil!"

"Then, Sonia, when I used to lie there in the dark and all this became clear to me, was it a temptation of the devil, eh?"

"Hush, don't laugh, blasphemer! You don't understand, you don't understand! Oh God! He won't understand!"

"Hush, Sonia! I am not laughing. I know myself that it was the devil leading me. Hush, Sonia, hush!" he repeated with gloomy insistence. "I know it all, I have thought it all over and over and whispered it all over to myself, lying there in the dark. . . . I've argued it all over with myself, every point of it, and I know it all, all! And how sick, how sick I was then of going over it all! I have kept wanting to forget it and make a new beginning, Sonia, and leave off thinking. And you don't suppose that I went into it headlong like a fool? I went into it like a wise man, and that was just my destruction. And you mustn't suppose that I didn't know, for instance, that if I began to question myself whether I had the right to gain power—I certainly hadn't the right—or that if I asked myself whether a human being is a louse it proved that it wasn't so for me, though it might be for a man who would go straight to his goal without asking questions. . . . If I worried myself all those days, wondering whether Napoleon would have done it or not, I felt clearly of course that I wasn't Napoleon. I had to endure all the agony of that battle of ideas, Sonia, and I longed to throw it off: I wanted to murder without casuistry, to murder for my own sake, for myself alone! I didn't want to lie about it even to myself. It wasn't to help my mother I did the murder—that's nonsense—I didn't do the murder to gain wealth and power and to become a benefactor of mankind. Nonsense! I simply did it; I did the murder for myself, for myself alone, and whether I became a benefactor to others, or spent my life like a spider catching men in my web and sucking the life out of men, I couldn't have cared at that moment. . . . And it was not the money I wanted, Sonia, when I did it. It was not so much the money I wanted, but something else. . . . I know it all now. . . . Understand me! Perhaps I should never have committed a murder again. I wanted to find out something else; it was something else led me on. I wanted to find out then and quickly whether I was a louse like everybody else or a man. Whether I can step over barriers or not, whether I dare stoop to pick up or not, whether I am a trembling creature or whether I have the *right* . . ."

"To kill? Have the right to kill?" Sonia clasped her hands.

"Ach, Sonia!" he cried irritably and seemed about to make some retort, but was contemptuously silent. "Don't interrupt me, Sonia. I want to prove one thing only, that the devil led me on then and he has shown me since that I had not the right to take that path, because I am just such a louse as all the rest. He was mocking me and here I've come to you now! Welcome your guest! If I were not a louse, should I have come to you? Listen: when I went then to the old woman's I only went to *try*. . . . You may be sure of that!"

"And you murdered her!"

"But how did I murder her? Is that how men do murders? Do men go to commit a murder as I went then? I will tell you some day how I went! Did I murder the old woman? I murdered myself, not her! I crushed myself once for all, for ever. . . . But it was the devil that killed that old woman, not I. Enough, enough, Sonia, enough! Let me be!" he cried in a sudden spasm of agony, "let me be!"

He leaned his elbows on his knees and squeezed his head in his hands as in a vice.

"What suffering!" A wail of anguish broke from Sonia.

"Well, what am I to do now?" he asked, suddenly raising his head and looking at her with a face hideously distorted by despair.

"What are you to do?" she cried, jumping up, and her eyes that had been full of tears suddenly began to shine. "Stand up!" (She seized him by the shoulder, he got up, looking at her almost bewildered.) "Go at once, this very minute, stand at the cross-roads, bow down, first kiss the earth which you have defiled and then bow down to all the world and say to all men aloud, 'I am a murderer!' The God will send you life again. Will you go, will you go?" she asked him, trembling all over, snatching his two hands, squeezing them in hers and gazing at him with eyes full of fire.

He was amazed at her sudden ecstasy.

"You mean Siberia, Sonia? I must give myself up?" he asked gloomily.

"Suffer and expiate your sin by it, that's what you must do."

"No! I am not going to them, Sonia!"

"But how will you go on living? What will you live for?" cried Sonia, "how is it possible now? Why, how can you talk to your mother? (Oh, what will become of them now!) But what am I saying? You have abandoned your mother and your sister already. He has abandoned them already! Oh God!" she cried, "why, he knows it all himself. How, how can he live by himself! What will become of you now?"

"Don't be a child, Sonia," he said softly. "What wrong

have I done them? Why should I go to them? What should I say to them? That's only a phantom. . . . They destroy men by millions themselves and look on it as a virtue. They are knaves and scoundrels, Sonia! I am not going to them. And what should I say to them—that I murdered her, but did not dare to take the money and hid it under a stone?" he added with a bitter smile. "Why, they would laugh at me, and would call me a fool for not getting it. A coward and a fool! They wouldn't understand and they don't deserve to understand. Why should I go to them? I won't. Don't be a child, Sonia. . . ."

"It will be too much for you to bear, too much!" she repeated holding out her hands in despairing supplication.

"Perhaps I've been unfair to myself," he observed gloomily, pondering, "perhaps after all I am a man and not a louse and I've been in too great a hurry to condemn myself. I'll make another fight for it."

A haughty smile appeared on his lips.

"What a burden to bear! And your whole life, your whole life!"

"I shall get used to it," he said grimly and thoughtfully. "Listen," he began a minute later, "stop crying, it's time to talk of the facts: I've come to tell you that the police are after me, on my track. . . ."

"Ach!" Sonia cried in terror.

"Well, why do you cry out? You want me to go to Siberia and now you are frightened? But let me tell you: I shall not give myself up. I shall make a struggle for it and they won't do anything to me. They've no real evidence. Yesterday I was in great danger and believed I was lost; but to-day things are going better. All the facts they know can be explained two ways, that's to say I can turn their accusations to my credit, do you understand? And I shall, for I've learnt my lesson. But they will certainly arrest me. If it had not been for something that happened, they would have done so to-day for certain; perhaps even now they will arrest me to-day. . . . But that's no matter, Sonia; they'll let me out again . . . for there isn't any real proof against me, and there won't be, I give you my word for it. And they can't convict a man on what they have against me. Enough. . . . I only tell you that you may know. . . . I will try to manage somehow to put it to my mother and sister so that they won't be frightened. . . . My sister's future is secure, however, now, I believe . . . and my mother's must be too. . . . Well, that's all. Be careful, though. Will you come and see me in prison when I am there?"

"Oh, I will, I will."

They sat side by side, both mournful and dejected, as though they had been cast up by the tempest alone on some deserted shore. He looked at Sonia and felt how great was her love for him, and strange to say he felt it suddenly burdensome and painful to be so loved. Yes, it was a strange and awful sensation! On his way to see Sonia he had felt that all his hopes rested on her; he expected to be rid of at least part of his suffering, and now, when all her heart turned towards him, he suddenly felt that he was immeasurably unhappier than before.

"Sonia," he said, "you'd better not come and see me when I am in prison."

Sonia did not answer, she was crying. Several minutes passed.

"Have you a cross on you?" she asked, as though suddenly thinking of it.

He did not at first understand the question.

"No, of course not. Here, take this one, of cypress wood. I have another, a copper one that belonged to Lizaveta. I changed with Lizaveta: she gave me her cross and I gave her my little ikon. I will wear Lizaveta's now and give you this. Take it . . .

it's mine! It's mine, you know," she begged him. "We will go to suffer together, and together we will bear our cross!"

"Give it me," said Raskolnikov.

He did not want to hurt her feelings. But immediately he drew back the hand he held out for the cross.

"Not now, Sonia. Better later," he added to comfort her.

"Yes, yes, better," she repeated with conviction, "when you go to meet your suffering, then put it on. You will come to me, I'll put it on you, we will pray and go together."

Fyodor Dostoyevsky
Notes from Underground

Because he perceived human beings as inherently depraved, irrational, and rebellious and probed the unconscious mind, Dostoevsky was also a forerunner of the modernist movement in thought and culture (see Chapter 16). The work that best links Dostoevsky to the modernist movement is *Notes from Underground* (1864). In this work, the narrator (the Underground Man) rebels against the efforts of rationalists, humanists, liberals, and socialists to define human nature according to universal principles and to reform society so as to promote greater happiness. He rebels against science and reason, against the entire liberal and socialist vision. He does so in the name of human subjectivity: the uncontainable, irrepressible, whimsical, and foolish human will. Human nature, says the Underground Man, is too volatile, too diversified to be schematized by the theoretical mind.

For the Underground Man, there are no absolute and timeless truths that precede the individual and to which the individual should conform. There is only a terrifying world of naked wills vying with one another. In such a world, people do not necessarily seek happiness, prosperity, and peace—all that is good for them, according to "enlightened" thinkers. To the rationalist who aims to eliminate suffering and deprivation, Dostoevsky replies that some people freely choose suffering and depravity because it gratifies them—for some, "even in a toothache there is enjoyment"—and they are repelled by wealth, peace, security, and happiness. If Dostoevsky is right, if individuals do not act out of enlightened self-interest, if they are driven by instinctual cravings that resist reason's appeals, then what hope is there for a social planner wishing to create the "good" society?

In rejecting external security and liberal and socialist concepts of progress—in aspiring to assert his own individuality even if this means acting against his own best interests—the Underground Man demonstrates that a powerful element of irrationality underlies human nature, an element that reason can neither understand nor justify. In succeeding decades, philosophers, social theorists, and literary figures would become preoccupied with this theme.

In the first part of *Notes from Underground,* the Underground Man addresses an imaginary audience. In a long monologue, he expresses a revulsion for the liberal-rationalist assertion that with increased enlightenment, people would "become good and noble," that they would realize it was to their advantage to pursue "prosperity, wealth, [political] freedom, peace." The Underground Man argues that the individual's principal concern is not happiness or security but a free and unfettered will.

. . . Oh, tell me, who first declared, who first proclaimed, that man only does nasty things because he does not know his own real interests; and that if he were enlightened, if his eyes were opened to his real normal interests, man would at once cease to do nasty things, would at once become good and noble because, being enlightened and understanding his real advantage, he would see his own advantage in the good and nothing else, and we all know that not a single man can knowingly act to his own disadvantage. Consequently, so to say, he would begin doing good through necessity. Oh! the babe! Oh, the pure, innocent child! Why, in the first place, when in all these thousands of years has there ever been a time when man has acted only for his own advantage? What is to be done with the millions of facts that bear witness that men, *knowingly,* that is, fully understanding their real advantages, have left them in the background and have rushed headlong on another path, to risk, to chance, compelled to this course by nobody and by nothing, but, as it were, precisely because they did not want the beaten track, and stubbornly, willfully, went off on another difficult, absurd way seeking it almost in the darkness. After all, it means that this stubbornness and willfulness were more pleasant to them than any advantage. Advantage! What is advantage? And will you take it upon yourself to define with perfect accuracy in exactly what the advantage of man consists of? And what if it so happens that a man's advantage *sometimes* not only may, but even must, consist exactly in his desiring under certain conditions what is harmful to himself and not what is advantageous. . . . After all, you, [imaginary] gentlemen, so far as I know, have taken your whole register of human advantages from the average of statistical figures and scientific-economic formulas. After all, your advantages are prosperity, wealth, freedom, peace—and so on, and so on. So that a man who, for instance, would openly and knowingly oppose that whole list would, to your thinking, and indeed to mine too, of course, be an obscurantist [one who prevents enlightenment] or an absolute madman, would he not? But, after all, here is something amazing: why does it happen that all these statisticians, sages and lovers of humanity, when they calculate human advantages invariably leave one out! . . .

. . . The fact is, gentlemen, it seems that something that is dearer to almost every man than his greatest advantages must really exist, or (not to be illogical) there is one most advantageous advantage (the very one omitted of which we spoke just now) which is more important and more advantageous than all other advantages, for which, if necessary, a man is ready to act in opposition to all laws, that is, in opposition to reason, honor, peace, prosperity—in short, in opposition to all those wonderful and useful things if only he can attain that fundamental, most advantageous advantage which is dearer to him than all. . . .

. . . Why, one may choose what is contrary to one's own interests, and sometimes one *positively ought* (that is my idea). One's own free unfettered choice, one's own fancy, however wild it may be, one's own fancy worked up at times to frenzy—why that is that very "most advantageous advantage" which we have overlooked, which comes under no classification and through which all systems and theories are continually being sent to the devil. And how do these sages know that man must necessarily need a rationally advantageous choice? What man needs is simply *independent* choice, whatever that independence may cost and wherever it may lead. Well, choice, after all, the devil only knows. . . .

Life is more than reasoning, more than "simply extracting square roots," declares the Underground Man. The will, which is "a manifestation of all life," is more precious than reason. Simply to have their own way, human beings will do something stupid, self-destructive, irrational. Reason constitutes only a small part of the human personality.

. . . You see, gentlemen, reason, gentlemen, is an excellent thing, there is no disputing that, but reason is only reason and can only satisfy man's rational faculty, while will is a manifestation of all life, that is, of all human life including reason as well as all impulses. And although our life, in this manifestation of it, is often worthless, yet it is life nevertheless and not simply extracting square roots. After all, here I, for instance, quite naturally want to live, in order to satisfy all my faculties for life, and not simply my rational faculty, that is, not simply one-twentieth of all my faculties for life. What does reason know? Reason only knows what it has succeeded in learning (some things it will perhaps never learn; while this is nevertheless no comfort, why not say so frankly?) and human nature acts as a whole, with everything that is in it, consciously or unconsciously, and, even if it goes wrong, it lives. I suspect, gentlemen, that you are looking at me with compassion; you repeat to me that an enlightened and developed man, such, in short, as the future man will be, cannot knowingly desire anything disadvantageous to himself, that this can be proved mathematically. I thoroughly agree, it really can—by mathematics. But I repeat for the hundreth time, there is one case, one only, when man may purposely, consciously, desire what is injurious to himself, what is stupid, very stupid—simply in order *to have the right* to desire for himself even what is very stupid and not to be bound by an obligation to desire only what is rational. After all, this very stupid thing, after all, this caprice of ours, may really be more advantageous for us, gentlemen, than anything else on earth, especially in some cases. And in particular it may be more advantageous than any advantages even when it does us obvious harm, and contradicts the soundest conclusions of our reason about our advantage—because in any case it preserves for us what is most precious and most important—that is, our personality, our individuality. Some, you see, maintain that this really is the most precious thing for man; desire can, of course, if it desires, be in agreement with reason; particularly if it does not abuse this practice but does so in moderation, it is both useful and sometimes even praiseworthy. But very of-

Fyodor Dostoyevsky • *Notes from Underground* **175**

ten, and even most often, desire completely and stubbornly opposes reason, and . . . and . . . and do you know that that, too, is useful and sometimes even praiseworthy?

To intellectuals who want to "cure men of their old habits and reform their will in accordance with science and common sense," the Underground Man asks: Is it possible or even desirable to reform human beings? Perhaps they prefer uncertainty and caprice, chaos and destruction, or just living in their own way. How else do they preserve their uniqueness?

. . . In short, one may say anything about the history of the world—anything that might enter the most disordered imagination. The only thing one cannot say is that it is rational. The very word sticks in one's throat. And, indeed, this is even the kind of thing that continually happens. After all, there are continually turning up in life moral and rational people, sages, and lovers of humanity, who make it their goal for life to live as morally and rationally as possible, to be, so to speak, a light to their neighbors, simply in order to show them that it is really possible to live morally and rationally in this world. And so what? We all know that those very people sooner or later toward the end of their lives have been false to themselves, playing some trick, often a most indecent one. Now I ask you: What can one expect from man since he is a creature endowed with such strange qualities? Shower upon him every earthly blessing, drown him in bliss so that nothing but bubbles would dance on the surface of his bliss, as on a sea; give him such economic prosperity that he would have nothing else to do but sleep, eat cakes and busy himself with ensuring the continuation of world history and even then man, out of sheer ingratitude, sheer libel, would play you some loathsome trick. He would even risk his cakes and would deliberately desire the most fatal rubbish, the most uneconomical absurdity, simply to introduce into all this positive rationality his fatal fantastic element. It is just his fantastic dreams, his vulgar folly, that he will desire to retain, simply in order to prove to himself (as though that were so necessary) that men still are men and not piano keys, which even if played by the laws of nature themselves threaten to be controlled so completely that soon one will be able to desire nothing but by the calendar. And, after all, that is not all: even if man really were nothing but a piano key, even if this were proved to him by natural science and mathematics, even then he would not become reasonable, but would purposely do something perverse out of sheer ingratitude, simply to have his own way. And if he does not find any means he will devise destruction and chaos, will devise sufferings of all

sorts, and will thereby have his own way. He will launch a curse upon the world . . . [to] convince himself that he is a man and not a piano key! If you say that all this, too, can be calculated and tabulated, chaos and darkness and curses, so that the mere possibility of calculating it all beforehand would stop it all, and reason would reassert itself—then man would purposely go mad in order to be rid of reason and have his own way! I believe in that, I vouch for it, because, after all, the whole work of man seems really to consist in nothing but proving to himself continually that he is a man and not an organ stop. It may be at the cost of his skin! But he has proved it; he may become a caveman, but he will have proved it. And after that can one help sinning, rejoicing that it has not yet come, and that desire still depends on the devil knows what! . . .

. . . Gentlemen, I am tormented by questions; answer them for me. Now you, for instance, want to cure men of their old habits and reform their will in accordance with science and common sense. But how do you know, not only that it is possible, but also that it is *desirable,* to reform man in that way? And what leads you to the conclusion that it is so *necessary* to reform man's desires? In short, how do you know that such a reformation will really be advantageous to man? And go to the heart of the matter, why are you *so sure* of your conviction that not to act against his real normal advantages guaranteed by the conclusions of reason and arithmetic is always advantageous for man and must be a law for all mankind? . . .

And why are you so firmly, so triumphantly convinced that only the normal and the positive—in short, only prosperity—is to the advantage of man? Is not reason mistaken about advantage? After all, perhaps man likes something besides prosperity? Perhaps he likes suffering just as much? Perhaps suffering is just as great an advantage to him as prosperity. Man is sometimes fearfully, passionately in love with suffering and that is a fact. There is no need to appeal to universal history to prove that; only ask yourself, if only you are a man and have lived at all. As far as my own personal opinion is concerned, to care only for prosperity seems to me somehow even ill-bred. Whether its good or bad, it is sometimes very pleasant to smash things, too. After all, I do not really insist on suffering or on prosperity either. I insist on my caprice, and its being guaranteed to me when necessary. Suffering would be out of place in vaudevilles, for instance; I know that. In the crystal palace [utopia] it is even unthinkable; suffering means doubt, means negation, and what would be the good of a crystal palace if there could be any doubt about it? And yet I am sure man will never renounce real suffering, that is, destruction and chaos.

5 American Realism

Like their European counterparts, American authors also rejected Romantic sentimentality in literature. They set their novels, short stories, and poems in recognizable American locales, even capturing the essence of "local color" in both dialect and dialogue. Like Charles Dickens, American Realists often portrayed the bleak realities of mundane life in the city and illustrated the breakdown of traditional systems of morality. The general public was enticed by the Realist authors, because they could see themselves as the characters in the books. Were they not also engaged in real-life struggles with themselves, with society, with the environment, and with governmental institutions?

Mark Twain
The Adventures of Huckleberry Finn

Portraying true-to-life characters, situations, and dialogue, the journalist, philosopher, humorist, and novelist Samuel Langhorne Clemens (1835–1910), better known as Mark Twain (a term used by riverboat pilots meaning "two fathoms"), exemplified American Realism. Twain's boyhood in Hannibal, Missouri, on the Mississippi River, is evident in his most famous novel—*The Adventures of Huckleberry Finn* (1884). Following the Civil War, Southerners introduced "Jim Crow" laws that curtailed the freedom of former slaves and legalized new forms of oppression. Twain chose to write an antislavery novel twenty years after the Civil War had ended, because in his eyes, Jim Crow was as insidious as slavery. Racism and slavery are the dominant themes of *Huck Finn,* which centers on the relationship between Huck Finn and the runaway slave Jim. Their adventures together and with young Tom Sawyer, the principal character in Twain's previous novel, allow Twain to explore the issue of child abuse and the social and moral development of two young boys. On March 17, 1885, *Huck Finn* was banned from the Concord, Massachusetts, public library. The directors of the library declared that the book was better suited for the slums than for intelligent, respectable people. They based their decision primarily on the dialect that Huck employs throughout his narration, but they also considered Huck Finn and Tom Sawyer to be unsatisfactory role models. Twain, nonetheless, predicted that his banned book would sell an additional twenty-five thousand copies (he was right).

Huck Finn, the protagonist and narrator of the novel, is the thirteen-year-old son of Pap, the town drunk, who beats him regularly. Huck, therefore, is compelled to survive by his own initiative. When Huck goes to live with the Widow Douglas and her sister Miss Watson, they effectively "civilize" him by teaching him manners and cleanliness and by sending him to church and to school. Pap, however, kidnaps Huck, and imprisons him in a cabin on the Mississippi River. To free himself from Pap, Huck escapes and fakes his own death. But while he is hiding out waiting for the commotion over his death to subside, he meets Jim, one of Miss Watson's slaves, who is fleeing the plantation, because he has overheard her say that she intends to sell him. Huck and Jim live contentedly on an island in the river, until Huck learns that people on shore believe that Jim is holed up on the island, and they issue a reward for his capture. Jim and Huck then decide to flee up the Ohio River and into the "free states" of the North where slavery is illegal. Throughout their adventures together, Huck is continually faced with the moral choice of whether to hand Jim over to the authorities because he is someone else's "property."

Jim and Huck subsequently team up with a pair of con artists, the Duke and the Dauphin (who calls himself "king"), pretenders to the French throne. In the chapter that follows, "You Can't Pray a Lie," Huck reflects on the southern scene, as well as the deceptions played out by the Duke and the Dauphin, including fake dance lessons and elocution studies. When Huck learns that they have sold Jim to a local farmer named Silas Phelps, he reflects on the moral consequences of both his actions and those of the Duke and the Dauphin. Ultimately, Huck makes the conscientious choice to free his friend Jim with the help of Tom Sawyer.

You Can't Pray a Lie

We dasn't stop again at any town for days and days; kept right along down the river. We was down south in the warm weather now, and a mighty long ways from home. We begun to come to trees with Spanish moss on them, hanging down from the limbs like long, gray beards. It was the first I ever see it growing, and it made the woods look solemn and dismal. So now the frauds reckoned they was out of danger, and they begun to work the villages again.

First they done a lecture on temperance; but they didn't make enough for them both to get drunk on. Then in another village they started a dancing school; but they didn't know no more how to dance than a kangaroo does; so the first prance they made the general public jumped in and pranced them out of town. Another time they tried to go at yellocution; but they didn't yellocute long till the audience got up and give them a solid good cussing, and made them skip out. They tackled missionarying, and mesmerizing, and doctoring, and telling fortunes, and a little of everything; but they couldn't seem to have no luck. So at last they got just about dead broke, and laid around the raft as she floated along, thinking and thinking, and never saying nothing, by the half a day at a time, and dreadful blue and desperate.

And at last they took a change and begun to lay their heads together in the wigwam and talk low and confidential two or three hours at a time. Jim and me got uneasy. We didn't like the look of it. We judged they was studying up some kind of worse deviltry than ever. We turned it over and over, and at last we made up our minds they was going to break into somebody's house or store, or was going into the counterfeit-money business, or something. So then we was pretty scared, and made up an agreement that we wouldn't have nothing in the world to do with such actions, and if we ever got the least show we would give them the cold shake and clear out and leave them behind. Well, early one morning we hid the raft in a good, safe place about two mile below a little bit of a shabby village named Pikesville, and the king he went ashore and told us all to stay hid whilst he went up to town and smelt around to see if anybody had got any wind of the "Royal Nonesuch" there yet. ("House to rob, you *mean*," says I to myself; "and when you get through robbing

it you'll come back here and wonder what has become of me and Jim and the raft—and you'll have to take it out in wondering.") And he said if he warn't back by midday the duke and me would know it was all right, and we was to come along.

So we stayed where we was. The duke he fretted and sweated around, and was in a mighty sour way. He scolded us for everything, and we couldn't seem to do nothing right; he found fault with every little thing. Something was a-brewing, sure. I was good and glad when midday come and no king; we could have a change, anyway—and maybe a chance for *the* chance on top of it. So me and the duke went up to the village, and hunted around there for the king, and by and by we found him in the back room of a little low doggery, very tight, and a lot of loafers bullyragging him for sport, and he a-cussing and a-threatening with all his might and so tight he couldn't walk, and couldn't do nothing to them. The duke he begun to abuse him for an old fool, and the king begun to sass back, and the minute they was fairly at it I lit out and shook the reefs out of my hind legs, and spun down the river road like a deer, for I see our chance; and I made up my mind that it would be a long day before they ever see me and Jim again. I got down there all out of breath but loaded up with joy, and sung out:

"Set her loose, Jim; we're all right now!"

But there warn't no answer, and nobody come out of the wigwam. Jim was gone! I set up a shout—and then another—and then another one; and run this way and that in the woods, whooping and screeching; but it warn't no use—old Jim was gone. Then I set down and cried; I couldn't help it. but I couldn't set still long. Pretty soon I went out on the road, trying to think what I better do, and I run across a boy walking, and asked him if he'd seen a strange nigger dressed so and so, and he says:

"Yes."

"Whereabouts?" says I.

"Down to Silas Phelps's place, two mile below here. He's a runaway nigger, and they've got him. Was you looking for him?"

"You bet I ain't! I run across him in the woods about an

hour or two ago, and he said if I hollered he'd cut my livers out—and told me to lay down and stay where I was; and I done it. Been there ever since; afeared to come out."

"Well," he says, "you needn't be afeared no more, becuz they've got him. He run off f'm down South, som'ers."

"It's a good job they got him."

"Well, I *reckon!* There's two hundred dollars' reward on him. Its like picking up money out'n the road."

"Yes, it is—and *I* could 'a' had it if I'd been big enough; I see him first. Who nailed him?"

"It was an old fellow—a stranger—and he sold out his chance in him for forty dollars, becuz he's got to go up the river and can't wait. Think o' that, now! You bet *I'd* wait, if it was seven year."

"That's me, every time," says I. "But maybe his chance ain't worth no more than that, if he'll sell it so cheap. Maybe, there's something ain't straight about it."

"But it *is*, though—straight as a string. I see the handbill myself. It tells all about him, to a dot—paints him like a picture, and tells the plantation he's frum, below Newr*leans*. No-sirree-*bob*, they ain't no trouble 'bout *that* speculation, you bet you. Say, gimme a chaw tobacker, won't ye?"

I didn't have none, so he left. I went to the raft, and set down in the wigwam to think. But I couldn't come to nothing. I thought till I wore my head sore, but I couldn't see no way out of the trouble. After all this long journey, and after all we'd done for them scoundrels, here it was all come to nothing, everything all busted up and ruined, because they could have the heart to serve Jim such a trick as that, and make him a slave again all his life, and amongst strangers, too, for forty dirty dollars.

Once I said to myself it would be a thousand times better for Jim to be a slave at home where his family was, as long as he'd *got* to be a slave, and so I'd better write a letter to Tom Sawyer and tell him to tell Miss Watson where he was. But I soon give up that notion for two things: she'd be mad and disgusted at his rascality and ungratefulness for leaving her, and so she'd sell him straight down the river again; and if she didn't, everybody naturally despises an ungrateful nigger, and they'd make Jim feel it all the time, and so he'd feel ornery and disgraced. And then think of *me!* It would get all around that Huck Finn helped a nigger to get his freedom; and if I was ever to see anybody from that town again I'd be ready to get down and lick his boots for shame. That's just the way: a person does a low-down thing, and then he don't want to take no consequences of it. Thinks as long as he can hide, it ain't no disgrace. That was my fix exactly. The more I studied about this the more my conscience went to grinding me, and the more wicked and low-down and ornery I got to feeling. And at last, when it hit me all of a sudden that here was the plain hand of Providence slapping me in the face and letting me know my wickedness was being watched all the time from up there in heaven, whilst I was stealing a poor old woman's nigger that hadn't ever done me no harm, and now was showing me there's One that's always on the lookout, and ain't a-going to allow no such miserable doings to go only just so fur and no further, I most dropped in my

tracks I was so scared. Well, I tried the best I could to kinder soften it up somehow for myself by saying I was brung up wicked, and so I warn't so much to blame; but something inside of me kept saying, "There was the Sunday school, you could 'a' gone to it; and if you'd 'a' done it they'd 'a' learnt you there that people that acts as I'd been acting about that nigger goes to everlasting fire."

It made me shiver. And I about made up my mind to pray, and see if I couldn't try to quit being the kind of a boy I was and be better. So I kneeled down. But the words wouldn't come. Why wouldn't they? It warn't no use to try and hide it from Him. Nor from *me*, neither. I knowed very well why they wouldn't come. It was because my heart warn't right; it was because I warn't square; it was because I was playing double. I was letting *on* to give up sin, but away inside of me I was holding on to the biggest one of all. I was trying to make my mouth *say* I would do the right thing and the clean thing, and go and write to that nigger's owner and tell where he was; but deep down in me I knowed it was a lie, and He knowed it. You can't pray a lie—I found that out.

So I was full of trouble, full as I could be; and didn't know what to do. At last I had an idea; and I says, I'll go and write the letter—and *then* see if I can pray. Why, it was astonishing, the way I felt as light as a feather right straight off, and my troubles all gone. So I got a piece of paper and a pencil, all glad and excited, and set down and wrote:

Miss Watson, your runaway nigger Jim is down here two mile below Pikesville, and Mr. Phelps has got him and he will give him up for the reward if you send.

HUCK FINN

I felt good and all washed clean of sin for the first time I had ever felt so in my life, and I knowed I could pray now. But I didn't do it straight off, but laid the paper down and set there thinking—thinking how good it was all this happened so, and how near I come to being lost and going to hell. And went on thinking. And got to thinking over our trip down the river; and I see Jim before me all the time: in the day and in the nighttime, sometimes moonlight, sometimes storms, and we a-floating along, talking and singing and laughing. But somehow I couldn't seem to strike no places to harden me against him, but only the other kind. I'd see him standing my watch on top of his'n, 'stead of calling me, so I could go on sleeping; and see him how glad he was when I come back out of the fog; and when I come to him again in the swamp, up there where the feud was; and such-like times; and would always call me honey, and pet me, and do everything he could think of for me, and how good he always was; and at last I struck the time I saved him by telling the men we had small-pox aboard, and he was so grateful, and said I was the best friend old Jim ever had in the world, and the *only* one he's got now; and then I happened to look around and see that paper.

It was a close place. I took it up, and held it in my hand. I was a-trembling, because I'd got to decide, forever, betwixt two things, and I knowed it. I studied a minute, sort of holding my breath, and then says to myself:

"All right, then, I'll *go* to hell"—and tore it up.

It was awful thoughts and awful words, but they was said. And I let them stay said; and never thought no more about reforming. I shoved the whole thing out of my head, and said I would take up wickedness again, which was in my line, being brung up to it, and the other warn't. And for a starter I would go to work and steal Jim out of slavery again; and if I could think up anything worse, I would do that, too; because as long as I was in, and in for good, I might as well go the whole hog.

Then I set to thinking over how to get at it, and turned over some considerable many ways in my mind; and at last fixed up a plan that suited me. So then I took the bearings of a woody island that was down the river a piece, and as soon as it was fairly dark I crept out with my raft and went for it, and hid it there, and then turned in. I slept the night through, and got up before it was light, and had my breakfast, and put on my store clothes, and tied up some others and one thing or another in a bundle, and took the canoe and cleared for shore. I landed below where I judged was Phelps's place, and hid my bundle in the woods, and then filled up the canoe with water, and loaded rocks into her and sunk her where I could find her again when I wanted her, about a quarter of a mile below a little steam sawmill that was on the bank.

Then I struck up the road, and when I passed the mill I see a sign on it, "Phelps's Sawmill," and when I come to the farm houses, two or three hundred yards further along, I kept my eyes peeled, but didn't see nobody around, though it was good daylight now. But I didn't mind, because I didn't want to see nobody just yet—I only wanted to get the lay of the land. According to my plan, I was going to turn up there from the village, not from below. So I just took a look, and shoved along, straight for town. Well, the very first man I see when I got there was the duke. He was sticking up a bill for the "Royal Nonesuch"—three-night performance—like that other time. *They* had the cheek, them frauds! I was right on him before I could shirk. He looked astonished, and says;

"Hel-*lo!* Where'd *you* come from?" Then he says, kind of glad and eager, "Where's the raft?—got her in a good place?"

I says:

"Why, that's just what I was going to ask your grace."

Then he didn't look so joyful, and says:

"What was your idea for asking *me?*" he says.

"Well," I says, "when I see the king in that doggery yesterday I says to myself, we can't get him home for hours, till he's soberer; so I went a-loafing around town to put in the time and wait. A man up and offered me ten cents to help him pull a skiff over the river and back to fetch a sheep, and so I went along; but when we was dragging him to the boat, and the man left me a-holt of the rope and went behind him to shove him along, he was too strong for me and jerked loose and ran, and we after him. We didn't have no dog, and so we had to chase him all over the country till we tired him out. We never got him till dark; then we fetched him over, and I started down for the raft. When I got there and see it was gone, I says to myself, 'They've got into trouble and had to leave; and they've

took my nigger, which is the only nigger I've got in the world, and now I'm in a strange country, and ain't got no property no more, nor nothing, and no way to make my living'; so I set down and cried. I slept in the woods all night. But what *did* become of the raft, then?—and Jim—poor Jim!"

"Blamed if *I* know—that is, what's become of the raft. That old fool had made a trade and got forty dollars, and when we found him in the doggery the loafers had matched half-dollars with him and got every cent but what he'd spent for whisky; and when I got him home late last night and found the raft gone, we said, 'That little rascal has stole our raft and shook us, and run off down the river.'"

"I wouldn't shake my *nigger,* would I?—the only nigger I had in the world, and the only property."

"We never thought of that. Fact is, I reckon we'd come to consider him *our* nigger; yes, we did consider him so—goodness knows we had trouble enough for him. So when we see the raft was gone and we flat broke, there warn't anything for it but to try the 'Royal Nonesuch' another shake. And I've pegged along ever since, dry as a powder-horn. Where's that ten cents? Give it here."

I had considerable money, so I give him ten cents, but begged him to spend it for something to eat, and give me some, because it was all the money I had, and I hadn't had nothing to eat since yesterday. He never said nothing. The next minute he whirls on me and says:

"Do you reckon that nigger would blow on us? We'd skin him if he done that!"

"How can he blow? Hain't he run off?"

"No! That old fool sold him, and never divided with me, and the moneys gone."

"*Sold* him?" I says, and begun to cry; "why, he was *my* nigger, and that was my money. Where is he?—I want my nigger."

"Well, you can't *get* your nigger, that's all—so dry up your blubbering. Looky here—do you think *you'd* venture to blow on us? Blamed if I think I'd trust you—"

He stopped, but I never see the duke look so ugly out of his eyes before. I went on a-whimpering, and says:

"I don't want to blow on nobody; and I ain't got no time to blow, nohow; I got to turn out and find my nigger."

He looked kinder bothered, and stood there with his bills fluttering on his arm, thinking, and wrinkling up his forehead. At last he says:

"I'll tell you something. We got to be here three days. If you'll promise you won't blow, and won't let the nigger blow, I'll tell you where to find him."

So I promised, and he says:

"A farmer by the name of Silas Ph—" and then he stopped. You see, he started to tell me the truth; but when he stopped that way, and begun to study and think again, I reckoned he was changing his mind. And so he was. He wouldn't trust me; he wanted to make sure of having me out of the way the whole three days. So pretty soon he says:

"The man that bought him is named Abram Foster—Abram G. Foster—and he lives forty mile back here in the country, on the road to Lafayette."

"All right," I says, "I can walk it in three days. And I'll start this very afternoon."

"No you won't, you'll start *now;* and don't you lose any time about it, neither, nor do any gabbling by the way. Just keep a tight tongue in your head and move right along, and then you won't get into trouble with *us,* d'ye hear?"

That was the order I wanted, and that was the one I played for. I wanted to be left free to work my plans.

"So clear out," he says; "and you can tell Mr. Foster whatever you want to. Maybe you can get him to believe that Jim *is* your nigger—some idiots don't require documents—leastways I've heard there's such down South here. And when you tell him the handbill and the reward's bogus, maybe he'll believe you when you explain to him what the idea was for getting 'em out. Go 'long now, and tell him anything you want to; but mind you don't work your jaw *between* here and there."

So I left, and struck for the back country. I didn't look around, but I kinder felt like he was watching me. But I knowed I could tire him out at that. I went straight out in the country as much as a mile before I stopped; then I doubled back through the woods towards Phelps's. I reckoned I better start in on my plan straight off without fooling around, because I wanted to stop Jim's mouth till these fellows could get away. I didn't want no trouble with their kind. I'd seen all I wanted to of them, and wanted to get entirely shut of them.

In executing Tom's elaborate scheme to free Jim, Tom is shot in the leg, and Jim sacrifices his own freedom to help Tom. The novel ends with the discovery of the deaths of Pap and Miss Watson who, two months before her death, made an amendment to her will legally freeing Jim.

Walt Whitman
Leaves of Grass

In his book of poetry called *Leaves of Grass,* first published in 1855, Walt Whitman (1819–1892) expressed himself on many issues, sometimes using complex extended metaphors (such as the sea or ocean). Whitman was a multifarious, free-spirited individual. He loved democracy, nature, metaphysics, and philosophy, and he was an advocate of toleration, proportion, and moderation—all of which is evident somewhere in the wide-ranging subject matter of the poems contained in *Leaves of Grass.* Upon receiving a copy of *Leaves of Grass* from Whitman, Ralph Waldo Emerson—poet, philosopher, and essayist—wrote to him, saying, "I greet you at the beginning of a great career." Whitman, however, never wrote another book and struggled to support himself throughout most of his life. In 1881, James R. Osgood (1836–1892),[1] Whitman's publisher, released the sixth edition of *Leaves of Grass,* but he was compelled to withdraw it a year later, because Boston's district attorney claimed that it violated the city's statutes regarding obscene literature. However, when a Philadelphia publisher issued the book, sales soared, and Whitman's fame grew. Thus, the term "banned in Boston" became an emblem of distinction, instead of a mark of shame, virtually ensuring that a book would have huge sales.

Distressed by the loss of 600,000 lives during the Civil War (1861–1865), during which Whitman served as a nurse, he published a series of poems called *Drum-Taps,* including the one that follows—"Beat! Beat! Drums!"—that deals with the chaos caused by war. This poem, and the others comprising *Drum-Taps,* were included in later editions of *Leaves of Grass.*

---

[1] In 1880, Osgood dissolved his partnership with Henry Oscar Houghton (1823–1895). Most of Osgood's titles were appropriated by the newly formed Houghton Mifflin & Company—the publishers of this literary reader.

BEAT! BEAT! DRUMS!

Beat! beat! drums!—blow! bugles! blow!
Through the windows—through doors—burst like a
    ruthless force,
Into the solemn church, and scatter the congregation,
Into the school where the scholar is studying,
Leave not the bridegroom quiet—no happiness must
    he have now with his bride,
Nor the peaceful farmer any peace, ploughing his
    field or gathering his grain,
So fierce you whirr and pound you drums—so shrill
    you bugles blow.

Beat! beat! drums!—blow! bugles! blow!
Over the traffic of cities—over the rumble of wheels in the
    streets;
Are beds prepared for sleepers at night in the houses?
    no sleepers must sleep in those beds,
No bargainers' bargains by day—no brokers or specula-
    tors—would they continue?
Would the talkers be talking? would the singer attempt to
    sing?
Would the lawyer rise in the court to state his case
    before the judge?
Then rattle quicker, heavier drums—you bugles wilder
    blow.

Beat! beat! drums!—blow! bugles! blow!
Make no parley—stop for no expostulation,
Mind not the timid—mind not the weeper or
    prayer,
Mind not the old man beseeching the young man,
Let not the child's voice be heard, nor the mother's
    entreaties,
Make even the trestles to shake the dead where they
    lie awaiting the hearses,
So strong you thump O terrible drums—so loud you
    bugles blow.

O CAPTAIN! MY CAPTAIN!

Following the assassination of the sixteenth president
of the United States, Abraham Lincoln (1809–1865),
Whitman composed a series of poems called *Memories of President Lincoln*, which were later included
in *Leaves of Grass*. One of the most poignant—
"O Capain, My Captain!"—soon became a
mainstay for memorization by schoolchildren.

O Captain! my Captain! our fearful trip is done,
The ship has weather'd every rack, the prize we sought is won,
The port is near, the bells I hear, the people all exulting,
While follow eyes the steady keel, the vessel grim and daring:
      But O heart! heart! heart!
        O the bleeding drops of red,
           Where on the deck my Captain lies,
           Fallen cold and dead.

O Captain! my Captain! rise up and hear the bells;
Rise up—for you the flag is flung—for you the bugle trills,
For you bouquets and ribbon'd wreaths—for you the
    shores a-crowding,
For you they call, the swaying mass, their eager faces turning;
      Here Captain! dear father!
        The arm beneath your head!
           It is some dream that on the deck,
           You've fallen cold and dead.

My Captain does not answer, his lips are pale and still,
My father does not feel my arm, he has no pulse nor will,
The ship is anchor'd safe and sound, its voyage closed
    and done,
From fearful trip the victor ship comes in with object won;
      Exult O shores, and ring O bells!
        But I with mournful tread,
           Walk the deck my Captain lies,
           Fallen cold and dead.

Emily Dickinson
SELECTED POEMS

Along with Walt Whitman, Emily Dickinson (1830–1886) is credited with defining an American voice in poetry. But unlike Whitman, Dickinson led a very solitary life in Amherst, Massachusetts, where she was born, raised, and died. She was influenced more by her Puritanical upbringing and her reading of the seventeenth-century English poets, as well as the Victorian ones, than by the political and social upheavals that swirled around her. Her poetry is deeply personal and intimately introspective, often reflecting her loneliness and thoughts about death. Although she was a prolific poet, Dickinson was not publicly recognized in her own lifetime because all of her poems were published posthumously—the first volume appearing in 1890 and the last one in 1955. The first two poems reflect Dickinson's love of reading and how she viewed it as a vehicle for traversing the world and enlightening her soul—without ever leaving home.

1263

There is no Frigate like a Book
To take us Lands away
Nor any Coursers[1] like a Page
Of prancing Poetry—
This Traverse may the poorest take
Without oppress of Toll—
How frugal is the Chariot
That bears the Human soul.

1052

I never saw a Moor—
I never saw the Sea—
Yet know I how the Heather looks
And what a Billow be.

I never spoke with God
Nor visited in Heaven—
Yet certain am I of the spot
As if the Checks[2] were given—

In the next two poems, Dickinson reflects on that most melancholy of all subjects—Death. In the first one she imagines being alone to die, after all the mourners are gone, with only a fly to keep her company.

465

I heard a Fly buzz—when I died—
The Stillness in the Room

Was like the Stillness in the Air—
Between the Heaves of Storm—

The Eyes around—had wrung them dry—
And Breaths were gathering firm

For that last Onset—when the King
Be witnessed—in the Room—

I willed my Keepsakes—Signed away
What portion of me be
Assignable—and then it was
There interposed a Fly—

With Blue—uncertain stumbling Buzz—
Between the light—and me—
And then the Windows failed—and then
I could not see to see—

In the following poem, Dickinson likens Death to a quiet, secure place where those who are weary and have been wandering find repose.

1065

Let down the Bars, Oh Death—
The tired Flocks come in
Whose bleating ceases to repeat
Whose wandering is done—

Thine is the stillest night
Thine the securest Fold
Too near Thou art for seeking Thee
Too tender, to be told.

---

[1]A courser is a swift horse.
[2]"Checks," in this instance, refers to verification marks.

16

Modern Consciousness

The closing decades of the nineteenth century and the opening of the twentieth witnessed a crisis in Western thought. Rejecting the Enlightenment belief in the essential rationality of human beings, thinkers such as Friedrich Nietzsche and Sigmund Freud stressed the immense power of the nonrational in individual and social life. They held that subconscious drives, impulses, and instincts lay at the core of human nature, that people were moved more by religious-mythic images and symbols than by logical thought, that feelings determine human conduct more than reason does. This new image of the individual led to unsettling conclusions. If human beings are not fundamentally rational, then what are the prospects of resolving the immense problems of modern industrial civilization? Although most thinkers shared the Enlightenment's visions of humanity's future progress, doubters were also heard.

The crisis of thought also found expression in art and literature. Artists like Pablo Picasso and writers like Franz Kafka exhibited a growing fascination with the nonrational—with dreams, fantasies, sexual conflicts, and guilt, with tortured, fragmented, and dislocated inner lives. In the process, they rejected traditional aesthetic standards established during the Renaissance and the Enlightenment and experimented with new forms of artistic and literary representation.

These developments in thought and culture produced insights into human nature and society and opened up new possibilities in art and literature. But such changes also contributed to the disorientation and insecurity that characterized the twentieth century.

1   The Overman and the Will to Power

Few modern thinkers have aroused more controversy than the German philosopher Friedrich Nietzsche (1844–1900). Although scholars pay tribute to Nietzsche's originality and genius, they are often in sharp disagreement over the meaning and influence of his work. Nietzsche was a relentless critic of modern society. He attacked democracy, universal suffrage, equality, and socialism for suppressing a higher type of human existence. Nietzsche was also critical of the Western rational tradition. The theoretical outlook, the excessive intellectualizing of philosophers, he said, smothers the will, thereby stifling creativity and nobility; reason also falsifies life through the claim that it allows apprehension of universal truth. Nietzsche was not opposed to the critical use of the intellect, but like the Romantics, he focused on the immense vitality of the emotions. He also held that life is a senseless flux devoid of any overarching purpose. There are no moral values revealed by God. Indeed, Nietzsche proclaimed that God is dead. Nor are values and certainties woven into the fabric of nature that can be apprehended by reason—the "natural rights of man," for example. All the values taught by Christian and bourgeois thinkers are without foundation, said Nietzsche. There is only naked man living in a godless and absurd world.

Nietzsche called for the emergence of the *overman* or *higherman,* a higher type of man who asserts his will, gives order to chaotic passions, makes great demands on himself, and lives life with a fierce joy. The overman aspires to self-perfection. Without fear or guilt, he creates his own values and defines his own life. In this way, he overcomes nihilism—the belief that there is nothing of ultimate value. It is such rare individuals, the highest specimens of humanity, that concern Nietzsche, not the herdlike masses.

The overman grasps the central reality of human existence—that people instinctively, uncompromisingly, ceaselessly, strive for power. The will to exert power is the determining factor in domestic politics, personal relations, and international affairs. Life is a contest in which the enhancement of power is the ultimate purpose of our actions; it brings supreme enjoyment: "the love of power is the demon of men. Let them have everything—health, food, a place to live, entertainment—they are and remain unhappy and low-spirited: for the demon waits and waits and will be satisfied. Take everything from them and satisfy this and they are almost happy—as happy as men and demons can be."

Friedrich Nietzsche
The Will to Power, The Antichrist, and The Gay Science

Three of Nietzsche's works—*The Will to Power, The Antichrist,* and *The Gay Science*—are represented in the following readings. First published in 1901, one year after Nietzsche's death, *The Will to Power* consists of the author's notes written in the years 1883 to 1888. The following passages from this work show Nietzsche's contempt for democracy and socialism and proclaim the will to power.

THE WILL TO POWER
720 (1886–1887)

The most fearful and fundamental desire in man, his drive for power—this drive is called "freedom"—must be held in check the longest. This is why ethics . . . has hitherto aimed at holding the desire for power in check: it disparages the tyrannical individual and with its glorification of social welfare and patriotism emphasizes the power-instinct of the herd.

728 (March–June 1888)

. . . A society that definitely and *instinctively* gives up war and conquest is in decline: it is ripe for democracy and the rule of shopkeepers—In most cases, to be sure, assurances of peace are merely narcotics.

751 (March–June 1888)

"The will to power" is so hated in democratic ages that their entire psychology seems directed toward belittling and defaming it. . . .

752 (1884)

. . . Democracy represents the disbelief in great human beings and an elite society: "Everyone is equal to everyone else." "At bottom we are one and all self-seeking cattle and mob."

753 (1885)

I am opposed to 1. socialism, because it dreams quite naively of "the good, true, and beautiful" and of "equal rights" (—anarchism also desires the same ideal, but in a more brutal fashion); 2. parliamentary government and the press, because these are the means by which the herd animal becomes master.

762 (1885)

European democracy represents a release of forces only to a very small degree. It is above all a release of laziness, of weariness, of *weakness.*

765 (Jan.–Fall 1888)

. . . Another Christian concept, no less crazy, has passed even more deeply into the tissue of modernity: the concept of the "equality of souls before God." This concept furnishes the prototype of all theories of equal rights: mankind was first taught to stammer the proposition of equality in a religious context, and only later was it made into morality: no wonder that man ended by taking it seriously, taking it practically!—

that is to say, politically, democratically, socialistically, in the spirit of the pessimism of indignation.

854 (1884)

In the age of *suffrage universal,* i.e., when everyone may sit in judgment on everyone and everything, I feel impelled to reestablish *order of rank.*

855 (Spring–Fall 1887)

What determines rank, sets off rank, is only quanta of power, and nothing else.

857 (Jan.–Fall 1888)

I distinguish between a type of ascending life and another type of decay, disintegration, weakness. Is it credible that the question of the relative rank of these two types still needs to be posed?

858 (Nov. 1887–March 1888)

What determines your rank is the quantum of power you are: the rest is cowardice.

861 (1884)

A declaration of war on the masses by *higher men* is needed! Everywhere the mediocre are combining in order to make themselves master! Everything that makes soft and effeminate, that serves the ends of the "people" or the "feminine," works in favor of *suffrage universel,* i.e., the dominion of *inferior* men. But we should take reprisal and bring this whole affair (which in Europe commenced with Christianity) to light and to the bar of judgment.

862 (1884)

A doctrine is needed powerful enough to work as a breeding agent: strengthening the strong, paralyzing and destructive for the world-weary.

The annihilation of the decaying races. Decay of Europe.—The annihilation of slavish evaluations.—Dominion over the earth as a means of producing a higher type.—The annihilation of the tartuffery [hypocrisy] called "morality." . . . The annihilation of *suffrage universel;* i.e., the system through which the lowest natures prescribe themselves as laws for the higher.—The annihilation of mediocrity and its acceptance, (The onesided, individuals—peoples; to strive for fullness of nature through the pairing of opposites: race mixture to this end).—The new courage—no *a priori* [innate and universal] truths (such truths were sought by those accustomed to faith!), but a *free* subordination to a ruling idea that has its time: e.g., time as a property of space, etc.

870 (1884)

The root of all evil: that the slavish morality of meekness, chastity, selflessness, absolute obedience, has triumphed—ruling natures were thus condemned (1) to hypocrisy, (2) to torments of conscience—creative natures felt like rebels against God, uncertain and inhibited by eternal values. . . .

In summa: the best things have been slandered because the weak or the immoderate swine have cast a bad light on them—and the best men have remained hidden—and have often misunderstood themselves.

874 (1884)

The degeneration of the rulers and the ruling classes has been the cause of the greatest mischief in history! Without the Roman Caesars and Roman society, the insanity of Christianity would never have come to power.

When lesser men begin to doubt whether higher men exist, then the danger is great! And one ends by discovering that there is *virtue* also among the lowly and subjugated, the poor in spirit, and that *before God* men are equal—which has so far been the . . . [height] of nonsense on earth! For ultimately, the higher men measured themselves according to the standard of virtue of slaves—found they were "proud," etc., found all their higher qualities reprehensible.

997 (1884)

I teach: that there are higher and lower men, and that a single individual can under certain circumstances justify the existence of whole millennia—that is, a full, rich, great, whole human being in relation to countless incomplete fragmentary men.

998 (1884)

The highest men live beyond the rulers, freed from all bonds; and in the rulers they have their instruments.

999 (1884)

Order of rank: He who *determines* values and directs the will of millennia by giving direction to the highest natures is the *highest* man.

1001 (1884)

Not "mankind" but *overman* is the goal!

1067 (1885)

. . . *This world is the will to power—and nothing besides!* And you yourselves are also this will to power—and nothing besides!

Nietzsche regarded Christianity as a life-denying religion that appeals to the masses. Fearful and resentful of their betters, he said, the masses espouse a faith that preaches equality and compassion. He maintained that Christianity has "waged a war to the death against (the) higher type of man." The following passages are from *The Antichrist,* written in 1888.

THE ANTICHRIST

2. What is good?—All that heightens the feeling of power, the will to power, power itself in man.

What is bad?—All that proceeds from weakness.

What is happiness?—The feeling that power *increases*—that a resistance is overcome.

Not contentment, but more power; *not* peace at all, but war; *not* virtue, but proficiency (virtue in the Renaissance style, *virtù,* virtue free of moralic acid).

The weak and ill-constituted shall perish: first principle of *our* philanthropy. And one shall help them to do so.

What is more harmful than any vice?—Active sympathy for the ill-constituted and weak—Christianity. . . .

3. The problem I raise here is not what ought to succeed mankind in the sequence of species (—the human being is an *end*—): but what type of human being one ought to *breed,* ought to *will,* as more valuable, more worthy of life, more certain of the future.

This more valuable type has existed often enough already: but as a lucky accident, as an exception, never as *willed.* He has rather been the most feared, he has hitherto been virtually *the* thing to be feared—and out of fear the reverse type has been willed, bred, *achieved:* the domestic animal, the herd animal, the sick animal man—the Christian. . . .

5. One should not embellish or dress up Christianity: it has waged *a war to the death* against this *higher* type of man, it has excommunicated all the fundamental instincts of this type, it has distilled evil, the *Evil One,* out of these instincts—the strong human being as the type of reprehensibility, as the "outcast." Christianity has taken the side of everything weak, base, ill-constituted, it has made an ideal out of *opposition* to the preservative instincts of strong life; it has depraved the reason even of the intellectually strongest natures by teaching men to feel the supreme values of intellectuality as sinful, as misleading, as *temptations.* The most deplorable example: the depraving of Pascal,[1] who believed his reason had been depraved by original sin while it had only been depraved by his Christianity! . . .

7. Christianity is called the religion of *pity.*—Pity stands in antithesis to the tonic emotions which enhance the en-

---

[1] Blaise Pascal (1623–1662) was a French mathematician, philosopher, and eloquent defender of the Christian faith.

ergy of the feeling of life: it has a depressive effect. One loses force when one pities. . . .

15. In Christianity neither morality nor religion come into contact with reality at any point. Nothing but imaginary *causes* ("God," "soul," ego," "spirit," "free will"—or "unfree will"): nothing but imaginary *effects* ("sin," "redemption," "grace," "punishment," "forgiveness of sins"). . . .

18. The Christian conception of God—God as God of the sick, God as spider, God as spirit—is one of the most corrupt conceptions of God arrived at on earth: perhaps it even represents the low-water mark in the descending development of the God type. God degenerated to the *contradiction of life,* instead of being its transfiguration and eternal *Yes!* In God a declaration of hostility towards life, nature, the will to life! God the formula for every calumny of "this world," for every lie about "the next world"! In God, nothingness deified, the will to nothingness sanctified! . . .

21. In Christianity the instincts of the subjugated and oppressed come into the foreground: it is the lowest classes which seek their salvation in it. . . .

43. The poison of the doctrine *"equal* rights for all"—this has been more thoroughly sowed by Christianity than by anything else; from the most secret recesses of base instincts, Christianity has waged a war to the death against every feeling of reverence and distance between man and man, against, that is, the *precondition* of every elevation, every increase in culture—it has forged out of the [resentment] of the masses its *chief weapon* against *us,* against everything noble—joyful, high-spirited on earth, against our happiness on earth. . . . "Immortality" granted to every Peter and Paul has been the greatest and most malicious outrage on *noble* mankind ever committed.—*And* let us not underestimate the fatality that has crept out of Christianity even into politics! No one any longer possesses today the courage to claim special privileges or the right to rule, the courage to feel a sense of reverence towards himself and towards his equals—the courage for a *pathos of distance.* . . . Our politics is *morbid* from this lack of courage!—The aristocratic outlook has been undermined most deeply by the lie of equality of souls; and if the belief in the "prerogative of the majority" makes revolutions and *will continue to make them*—it is Christianity, let there be no doubt about it, *Christian* value judgement which translates every revolution into mere blood and crime! Christianity is a revolt of everything that crawls along the ground directed against that which is *elevated:* the Gospel of the "lowly" *makes* low. . . .

THE GAY SCIENCE

Nietzsche's unqualified atheism is made clear in his famous dictum "God is dead." He proclaimed the death of God for the first time in the following passage from *The Gay Science* (1882).

The madman.—Have you not heard of that madman who lit a lantern in the bright morning hours, ran to the market place, and cried incessantly: "I seek God! I seek God!"—As many of those who did not believe in God were standing around just then, he provoked much laughter. Has he got lost? asked one. Did he lose his way like a child? asked another. Or is he hiding? Is he afraid of us? Has he gone on a voyage? emigrated?—Thus they yelled and laughed.

The madman jumped into their midst and pierced them with his eyes. "Whither is God?" he cried; "I will tell you. *We have killed him*—you and I. All of us are his murderers. But how did we do this? How could we drink up the sea? Who gave us the sponge to wipe away the entire horizon? What were we doing when we unchained this earth from its sun? Whither is it moving now? Whither are we moving? Away from all suns? Are we not plunging continually? Backward, sideward, forward, in all directions? Is there still any up or down? Are we not straying as through an infinite nothing? Do we not feel the breath of empty space? Has it not become colder? Is not night continually closing in on us? Do we not need to light lanterns in the morning? Do we hear nothing as yet of the noise of the gravediggers who are burying God? Do we smell nothing as yet of the divine decomposition? Gods, too, decompose. God is dead. God remains dead. And we have killed him.

"How shall we comfort ourselves, the murderers of all murderers? What was holiest and mightiest of all that the world has yet owned has bled to death under our knives: who will wipe this blood off us? What water is there for us to clean ourselves? What festivals of atonement, what sacred games shall we have to invent? Is not the greatness of this deed too great for us? Must we ourselves not become gods simply to appear worthy of it? There has never been a greater deed: and whoever is born after us—for the sake of this deed he will belong to a higher history than all history hitherto."

Here the madman fell silent and looked again at his listeners; and they, too, were silent and stared at him in astonishment. At last he threw his lantern on the ground, and it broke into pieces and went out. "I have come too early," he said then; "my time is not yet. This tremendous event is still on its way, still wandering; it has not yet reached the ears of men. Lightning and thunder require time; the light of the stars requires time; deeds, though done, still require time to be seen and heard. This deed is still more distant from them than the most distant stars—*and yet they have done it themselves.*"

It has been related further that on the same day the madman forced his way into several churches and there struck up his *requiem aeternam deo* [funeral Mass for the eternal God]. Led out and called to account, he is said always to have replied nothing but: "What after all are these churches now if they are not the tombs and sepulchers of God."

2   The Unconscious Mind

The outlook of the Enlightenment, which stressed science, political freedom, the rational reform of society, and the certainty of progress, was the dominant intellectual current in the late nineteenth century. However, in the closing decades of the century, several thinkers challenged the Enlightenment outlook. In particular, they maintained that people are not fundamentally rational, that below surface rationality lie impulses, instincts, and drives that constitute a deeper reality. A powerful challenge to the rational-scientific tradition of the Enlightenment came from Sigmund Freud.

After graduating from medical school in Vienna, Sigmund Freud (1856–1939), the founder of psychoanalysis, specialized in the treatment of nervous disorders. By encouraging his patients to speak to him about their troubles, Freud was able to probe deeper into their minds. These investigations led him to conclude that childhood fears and experiences, often sexual in nature, accounted for neuroses—hysteria, anxiety, depression, obsessions, and so on. So threatening and painful were these childhood emotions and experiences that his patients banished them from conscious memory to the realm of the unconscious. To understand and treat neurotic behavior, Freud said it is necessary to look behind overt symptoms and bring to the surface emotionally charged experiences and fears—childhood traumas—that lie buried in the unconscious. Freud probed the unconscious by urging his patients to say whatever came to their minds. This procedure, called free association, rests on the premise that spontaneous and uninhibited talk reveals a person's underlying preoccupations, his or her inner world. A second avenue to the unconscious is the analysis of dreams; an individual's dreams, said Freud, reveal his or her secret wishes.

Sigmund Freud
The Unconscious, Psychoanalysis, and *Civilization and Its Discontents*

Readings from three works of Freud are included: *A Note on the Unconscious in Psychoanalysis, Five Lectures on Psychoanalysis,* and *Civilization and Its Discontents.* Freud's scientific investigation of psychic development led him to conclude that powerful mental processes hidden from consciousness govern human behavior more than reason does. His exploration of the unconscious produced a new image of the human being that has had a profound impact on twentieth-century thought. In the following excerpt from *A Note on the Unconscious in Psychoanalysis* (1912), Freud defined the term *unconscious.*

A NOTE ON THE UNCONSCIOUS IN PSYCHOANALYSIS

I wish to expound in a few words and as plainly as possible what the term "unconscious" has come to mean in psychoanalysis and in psychoanalysis alone. . . .

. . . The well-known experiment, . . . of the "post-hypnotic suggestion" teaches us to insist upon the importance of the distinction between *conscious* and *unconscious* and seems to increase its value.

In this experiment, as performed by Bernheim,[1] a person is put into a hypnotic state and is subsequently aroused. While he was in the hypnotic state, under the influence of the physician, he was ordered to execute a certain action at a certain fixed moment after his awakening, say half an hour later. He awakes, and seems fully conscious and in his ordinary condition; he has no recollection of his hypnotic state, and yet at the prearranged moment there rushes into his mind the impulse to do such and such a thing, and he does it consciously, though not knowing why. It seems impossible to give any other description of the phenomenon than to say that the order has been present in the mind of the person in a condition of latency, or had been present unconsciously, until the given moment came, and then had become conscious. But not the whole of it emerged into consciousness: only the conception of the act to be executed. All the other ideas associated with this conception—the order, the influence of the physician, the recollection of the hypnotic state, remained unconscious even then. . . .

The mind of the hysterical patient is full of active yet unconscious ideas; all her symptoms proceed from such ideas. It is in fact the most striking character of the hysterical mind to be ruled by them. If the hysterical woman vomits, she may do so from the idea of being pregnant. She has, however, no knowledge of this idea, although it can easily be detected in her mind, and made conscious to her, by one of the technical procedures of psychoanalysis. If she is executing the jerks and movements constituting her "fit," she does not even consciously represent to herself the intended actions, and she may perceive those actions with the detached feelings of an onlooker. Nevertheless analysis will show that she was acting her part in the dramatic reproduction of some incident in her life, the memory of which was unconsciously active during the attack. The same preponderance of active unconscious ideas is revealed by analysis as the essential fact in the psychology of all other forms of neurosis. . . .

. . . The term *unconscious* . . . designates . . . ideas with a certain dynamic character, ideas keeping apart from consciousness in spite of their intensity and activity.

---

[1]Hippolyte Bernheim (1840–1919), a French physician, used hypnosis in the treatment of his patients and published a successful book on the subject.

This passage from a lecture given in 1909 describes Freud's attempt to penetrate the world of the unconscious.

FIVE LECTURES ON PSYCHOANALYSIS

. . . At first, I must confess, this seemed a senseless and hopeless undertaking. I was set the task of learning from the patient something that I did not know and that he did not know himself. How could one hope to elicit it? But there came to my help a recollection of a most remarkable and instructive experiment which I had witnessed when I was with Bernheim at Nancy [in 1889]. Bernheim showed us that people whom he had put into a state of hypnotic somnambulism [a hypnotically induced condition of sleep in which acts are performed], and who had had all kinds of experiences while they were in that state, only *appeared* to have lost the memory of what they had experienced during somnambulism; it was possible to revive these memories in their normal state. It is true that, when he questioned them about their somnambulistic experiences, they began by maintaining that they knew nothing about them; but if he refused to give way, and insisted, and assured them that they *did* know about them, the forgotten experiences always reappeared.

So I did the same thing with my patients. When I reached a point with them at which they maintained that they knew nothing more, I assured them that they *did* know it all the same, and that they had only to say it; and I ventured to declare that the right memory would occur to them at the moment at which I laid my hand on their forehead. In that way I succeeded, without using hypnosis, in obtaining from the patients whatever was required for establishing the connection between the pathogenic [capable of causing disease] scenes they had forgotten and the symptoms left over from those scenes. But it was a laborious procedure, and in the long run an exhausting one; and it was unsuited to serve as a permanent technique.

I did not abandon it, however, before the observations I made during my use of it afforded me decisive evidence. I found confirmation of the fact that the forgotten memories were not lost. They were in the patient's possession and were ready to emerge in association to what was still known by him; but there was some force that prevented them from becoming conscious and compelled them to remain unconscious. The existence of this force could be assumed with certainty, since one became aware of an effort corresponding to it if, in opposition to it, one tried to introduce the unconscious memories into the patient's consciousness. The force which was maintaining the pathological condition became apparent in the form of *resistance* on the part of the patient.

It was on this idea of resistance, then, that I based my view of the course of psychical events in hysteria. In order to effect a recovery, it had proved necessary to remove these resistances. Starting out from the mechanism of cure, it now became possible to construct quite definite ideas of the origin of the illness. The same forces which, in the form of resistance, were now offering opposition to the forgotten material's being made conscious, must formerly have brought about the forgetting and must have pushed the pathogenic experiences in question out of consciousness. I gave the name of *"repression"* to this hypothetical process, and I considered that it was proved by the undeniable existence of resistance.

The further question could then be raised as to what these forces were and what the determinants were of the repression in which we now recognized the pathogenic mechanism of hysteria. A comparative study of the pathogenic situations which we had come to know through the cathartic procedure made it possible to answer this question. All these experiences had involved the emergence of a wishful impulse which was in sharp contrast to the subject's other wishes and which proved incompatible with the ethical and aesthetic standards of his personality. There had been a short conflict, and the end of this internal struggle was that the idea which had appeared before consciousness as the vehicle of this irreconcilable wish fell a victim to repression, was pushed out of consciousness with all its attached memories, and was forgotten. Thus the incompatibility of the wish in question with the patient's ego was the motive for the repression; the subject's ethical and other standards were the repressing forces. An acceptance of the incompatible wishful impulse or a prolongation of the conflict would have produced a high degree of unpleasure; this unpleasure was avoided by means of repression, which was thus revealed as one of the devices serving to protect the mental personality.

To take the place of a number of instances, I will relate a single one of my cases, in which the determinants and advantages of repression are sufficiently evident. For my present purpose I shall have once again to abridge the case history and omit some important underlying material. The patient was a girl, who had lost her beloved father after she had taken a share in nursing him—a situation analogous to that of Breuer's[2] patient. Soon afterwards her elder sister married, and her new brother-in-law aroused in her a peculiar feeling of sympathy which was easily masked under a disguise of family affection. Not long afterwards her sister fell ill and died, in the absence of the patient and her mother. They were summoned in all haste without being given any definite information of the tragic event. When the girl reached the bedside of her dead sister, there came to her for a brief moment an idea that might be expressed in these words: "Now he is free and can marry me." We may assume with certainty that this idea, which betrayed to her consciousness the intense love for her brother-in-law of which she had not herself been

conscious, was surrendered to repression a moment later, owing to the revolt of her feelings. The girl fell ill with severe hysterical symptoms, and while she was under my treatment it turned out that she had completely forgotten the scene by her sister's bedside and the odious egoistic impulse that had emerged in her. She remembered it during the treatment and reproduced the pathogenic moment with signs of the most violent emotion, and, as a result of the treatment, she became healthy once more.

In the tradition of the Enlightenment philosophes, Freud valued reason and science, but he did not share the philosophes' confidence in human goodness and humanity's capacity for future progress. In *Civilization and Its Discontents* (1930), Freud posited the frightening theory that human beings are driven by an inherent aggressiveness that threatens civilized life—that civilization is fighting a losing battle with our aggressive instincts. Although Freud's pessimism was no doubt influenced by the tragedy of World War I, many ideas expressed in *Civilization and Its Discontents* derived from views that he had formulated decades earlier.

CIVILIZATION AND ITS DISCONTENTS

The element of truth behind all this, which people are so ready to disavow, is that men are not gentle creatures who want to be loved, and who at most can defend themselves if they are attacked; they are, on the contrary, creatures among whose instinctual endowments is to be reckoned a powerful share of aggressiveness. As a result, their neighbour is for them not only a potential helper or sexual object, but also someone who tempts them to satisfy their aggressiveness on him, to exploit his capacity for work without compensation, to use him sexually without his consent, to seize his possessions, to humiliate him, to cause him pain, to torture and to kill him. *Homo homini lupus*. [Man is wolf to man.] Who, in the face of all his experience of life and of history, will have the courage to dispute this assertion? As a rule this cruel aggressiveness waits for some provocation or puts itself at the service of some other purpose, whose goal might also have been reached by milder measures. In circumstances that are favourable to it, when the mental counterforces which ordinarily inhibit it are out of action, it also manifests itself spontaneously and reveals man as a savage beast to whom consideration towards his own kind is something alien. Anyone who calls to mind the atrocities committed during the racial migrations or the invasions of the Huns, or by the people known as Mongols under Jenghiz Khan and Tamerlane, or at the capture of Jerusalem by the pious Crusaders, or even, indeed, the horrors of the recent World War—anyone

---

[2]Joseph Breuer (1842–1925) was an Austrian physician and Freud's early collaborator.

who calls these things to mind will have to bow humbly before the truth of this view.

The existence of this inclination to aggression, which we can detect in ourselves and justly assume to be present in others, is the factor which disturbs our relations with our neighbour and which forces civilization into such a high expenditure [of energy]. In consequence of this primary mutual hostility of human beings, civilized society is perpetually threatened with disintegration. The interest of work in common would not hold it together; instinctual passions are stronger than reasonable interests. Civilization has to use its utmost efforts in order to set limits to man's aggressive instincts and to hold the manifestations of them in check by psychical reaction-formations. Hence, therefore, the use of methods intended to incite people into identifications and aim-inhibited relationships of love, hence the restriction upon sexual life, and hence too the ideal's commandment to love one's neighbour as oneself—a commandment which is really justified by the fact that nothing else runs so strongly counter to the original nature of man. In spite of every effort, these endeavours of civilization have not so far achieved very much. It hopes to prevent the crudest excesses of brutal violence by itself assuming the right to use violence against criminals, but the law is not able to lay hold of the more cautious and refined manifestations of human aggressiveness. The time comes when each one of us has to give up as illusions the expectations which, in his youth, he pinned upon his fellowmen, and when he may learn how much difficulty and pain has been added to his life by their ill-will. At the same time, it would be unfair to reproach civilization with trying to eliminate strife and competition from human activity. These things are undoubtedly indispensable. But opposition is not necessarily enmity; it is merely misused and made an *occasion* for enmity.

The communists believe that they have found the path to deliverance from our evils. According to them, man is wholly good and is well-disposed to his neighbour; but the institution of private property has corrupted his nature. The ownership of private wealth gives the individual power, and with it the temptation to ill-treat his neighbour; while the man who is excluded from possession is bound to rebel in hostility against his oppressor. If private property were abol-

ished, all wealth held in common, and everyone allowed to share in the enjoyment of it, ill-will and hostility would disappear among men. Since everyone's needs would be satisfied, no one would have any reason to regard another as his enemy; all would willingly undertake the work that was necessary. I have no concern with any economic criticisms of the communist system. . . . But I am able to recognize that the psychological premises on which the system is based are an untenable illusion. In abolishing private property we deprive the human love of aggression of one of its instruments, certainly a strong one, though certainly not the strongest; but we have in no way altered the differences in power and influence which are misused by aggressiveness, nor have we altered anything in its nature. Aggressiveness was not created by property. It reigned almost without limit in primitive times, when property was still very scanty, and it already shows itself in the nursery almost before property has given up its primal, anal form; it forms the basis of every relation of affection and love among people (with the single exception, perhaps, of the mother's relation to her male child). If we do away with personal rights over material wealth, there still remains prerogative in the field of sexual relationships, which is bound to become the source of the strongest dislike and the most violent hostility among men who in other respects are on an equal footing. If we were to remove this factor, too, by allowing complete freedom of sexual life and thus abolishing the family, the germ-cell of civilization, we cannot, it is true, easily foresee what new paths the development of civilization could take; but one thing we can expect, and that is that this indestructible feature of human nature will follow it there.

It is clearly not easy for men to give up the satisfaction of this inclination to aggression. They do not feel comfortable without it. . . .

If civilization imposes such great sacrifices not only on man's sexuality but on his aggressivity, we can understand better why it is hard for him to be happy in that civilization. . . .

In all that follows I adopt the standpoint, therefore, that the inclination to aggression is an original, self-subsisting instinctual disposition in man, and I return to my view that it constitutes the greatest impediment to civilization.

3 Human Irrationality in the Modernist Novel

At the same time that Nietzsche, Freud, and other thinkers were breaking with the Enlightenment view of human nature and society, artists and writers were rebelling against traditional forms of artistic and literary expression that had governed European cultural life since the Renaissance. Rejecting both Classical and Realist models, they subordinated form and objective reality to the inner life—to feelings, imagination, and the creative process. These avant-garde writers and artists found new and creative ways to express those explosive forces within the human psyche that increasingly had become the subject of contemporary thinkers. Their experimentations produced a great cultural revolution called *Modernism,* which still profoundly influences the arts. In some ways, Modernism was a continuation of the Romantic Movement, which had dominated European culture in the early nineteenth century. Both movements subjected to searching criticism cultural styles that had been formulated during the Renaissance and had roots in ancient Greece.

Even more than Romanticism, Modernism aspired to an intense introspection—a heightened awareness of self—and saw the intellect as a barrier to the free expression of elemental human emotions. Modernist artists and writers abandoned conventional literary and artistic models and experimented with new modes of expression. They liberated the imagination from the restrictions of conventional forms and enabled their audience, readers and viewers alike, to share in the process of creation, often unconscious, and to discover fresh insights into objects, sounds, people, and social conditions. They believed that there were further discoveries to be made in the arts, further possibilities of expression, that past masters had not realized.

Like Freud, Modernist artists and writers probed beyond surface appearances for a more profound reality—impulses, instincts, and drives—hidden in the human psyche. Writers such as Marcel Proust, August Strindberg, D. H. Lawrence, and Franz Kafka explored the inner life of the individual and the psychopathology of human relations in order to lay bare the self. They dealt with the predicament of men and women who rejected the values and customs of their day, and they depicted the anguish of people burdened by guilt, torn by internal conflicts, and driven by an inner self-destructiveness. Besides showing the overwhelming might of the irrational and the seductive power of the primitive, they also broke the silence about sex that had prevailed in Victorian literature.

Joseph Conrad
Heart of Darkness

Behavior driven by the unconscious and the human being's capacity to act irrationally and cruelly—the dark side of human nature, which was the subject of Freud's investigations—intrigued many modernist writers, including British novelist Joseph Conrad (1857–1924), born Jozel Tendor Konrad Korzeniowski. In 1862, when Conrad was not yet five years old, his father, who had participated in an insurrection to liberate Poland from Russian rule, was exiled to northern Russia. In this harsh environment, his mother died of tuberculosis in 1865. His father, who translated the works of French and English authors into Polish, which the precocious young Conrad read voraciously, made the difficult decision to place his only child in the care of Joseph's maternal uncle in Poland, where he attended school. Joseph lost his father when he was twelve, and five years later, he left school to become an apprentice seaman on a French merchant ship. In 1878, speaking only a few words of English, he joined the British merchant navy.

During his twenty years at sea, Conrad visited exotic lands and experienced danger. These adventures found literary expression in Conrad's novels and short stories, including *An Outcast of the Islands* (1896), *Lord Jim* (1900), *Heart of Darkness* (1902), *Nostromo* (1904), and *The Secret Agent* (1907). But Conrad was far more than a masterful renderer of adventure stories. His reputation as one of England's finest novelists derives from both his compelling prose and his creative exploration of human depravity, a phenomenon to which he seemed irresistibly drawn. In 1891, after a four-month stay in the Congo Free State, a land notoriously exploited and brutalized by agents of the Belgian King Leopold, Conrad suffered psychological trauma. His experiences in the heart of Africa led him to write his most compelling work, *Heart of Darkness.*

The two principal characters in the work are Kurtz, a company agent who runs a very successful ivory trading post deep in the Congo, and Marlow, a riverboat pilot, who is repelled by the cruelty inflicted on Africans by the company's agents. Marlow, who narrates his experiences, pilots a steamer upriver to Kurtz's station. Slowly he learns about Kurtz from the other agents of the company, including those accompanying him, and from a young Russian devoted to Kurtz, whom Marlow spots on the shore near Kurtz's post. Marlow finds out that not only is Kurtz a poet, musician, and painter with politically progressive views, but that when he first came to Africa, Kurtz was imbued with humanitarian sentiments. One company employee describes him as "an emissary of pity and science and progress" who intended to bring enlightenment to "savage" Africans. But in the primeval African jungle, his other self, long repressed by European values, comes to the fore. Kurtz becomes a depraved tyrant, who decorates the fence poles around his house with human heads. The charismatic Kurtz has made disciples of the villagers, who view him as a godlike figure; they heed his every word and, at his command, launch murderous raids against nearby villages for more ivory. Kurtz engages in mysterious ceremonies—Conrad leaves the nature of these ceremonies to the reader's imagination, but it is likely that they are human sacrifices—which contribute to his uncanny power over the Africans.

Although shriveled by disease, Kurtz is reluctant to return with Marlow, but eventually relents. As the ship travels down the river, Marlow engages Kurtz in long conversations. During one of these talks, Kurtz senses that death is imminent, and suddenly gripped by "craven terror," he blurts out: "The horror! The horror!" He dies later that evening. Here, too, as in the case of the ceremonies, Conrad relies on the reader to determine the meaning of Kurtz's agonizing cry.

There now exists a rich body of commentary analyzing the layers of meaning in Conrad's work. One obvious interpretation is that Conrad intended to write an indictment of imperialism, for *Heart of Darkness* expressed his revulsion of avaricious European imperialists who, in their quest for riches, plundered and destroyed African villages and impressed the natives into forced labor. Their greed, callousness, and brutality belied the altruism that they claimed was their motivation for coming to Africa.

Most commentators also regard *Heart of Darkness* as a tale of moral deterioration: The forbidding jungle environment, far from the restraints of European civilization, and the repulsive scramble for riches disfigure Kurtz, who is transformed into a sadist driven by dark urges no longer buried within his unconscious. The wilderness "whispered to him things about himself which he did not know, things of which he had no conception till he took counsel with this great solitude—and the whisper had proved irresistibly fascinating." When the dying Kurtz cries out: "The horror! The horror!" in "that supreme moment of complete knowledge," was he referring to his own moral collapse? Thus "darkness" refers not only to the jungle interior, but also to the destructive tendencies that are at the core of human nature. Marlow's travels into the dark interior of Africa in search of Kurtz can be seen as a descent into the dark interior of the unconscious. Civilization, as Freud maintained, is very fragile; only a thin barrier separates it from barbarism. Given the right circumstances, all human beings are capable of the moral disfigurement experienced by Kurtz.

In the following excerpt from *Heart of Darkness,* Marlow, an experienced seaman, sets out upstream on a steamer in order to relieve Kurtz at the Inner

Station. The journey is filled with symbolic meaning. Marlowe is not only penetrating a primeval forest, but he is also returning to humanity's primitive, barbaric past, particularly the inner darkness of the human heart which is capable of savage behavior. Marlow, like Freud, understands the importance of resisting this descent to savagery.

". . . I don't pretend to say that steamboat floated all the time. More than once she had to wade for a bit, with twenty cannibals splashing around and pushing. We had enlisted some of these chaps on the way for a crew. Fine fellows—cannibals—in their place. They were men one could work with, and I am grateful to them. And, after all, they did not eat each other before my face: they had brought along a provision of hippo meat which went rotten, and made the mystery of the wilderness stink in my nostrils. Phoo! I can sniff it now. I had the manager on board and three or four pilgrims with their staves—all complete. Sometimes we came upon a station close by the bank, clinging to the skirts of the unknown, and the white men rushing out of a tumbledown hovel, with great gestures of joy and surprise and welcome, seemed very strange—had the appearance of being held there captive by a spell. The word ivory would ring in the air for a while—and on we went again into the silence, along empty reaches, round the still bends, between the high walls of our winding way, reverberating in hollow claps the ponderous beat of the stern wheel. Trees, trees, millions of trees, massive, immense, running up high; and at their foot, hugging the bank against the stream, crept the little begrimed steamboat, like a sluggish beetle crawling on the floor of a lofty portico. It made you feel very small, very lost, and yet it was not altogether depressing, that feeling. After all, if you were small, the grimy beetle crawled on—which was just what you wanted it to do. Where the pilgrims imagined it crawled to I don't know. To some place where they expected to get something, I bet! For me it crawled towards Kurtz—exclusively; but when the steam pipes started leaking we crawled very slow. The reaches opened before us and closed behind, as if the forest had stepped leisurely across the water to bar the way for our return. We penetrated deeper and deeper into the heart of darkness. It was quiet there. At night sometimes the roll of drums behind the curtain of trees would run up the river and remain sustained faintly, as if hovering in the air high over our heads, till the first break of day. Whether it meant war, peace, or prayer we could not tell. The dawns were heralded by the descent of a chill stillness; the woodcutters slept, their fires burned low; the snapping of a twig would make you start. We were wanderers on prehistoric earth, on an earth that wore the aspect of an unknown planet. We could have fancied ourselves the first of men taking possession of an accursed inheritance, to be subdued at the cost of profound anguish and of excessive toil. But suddenly, as we struggled round a bend, there would be a glimpse of rush walls, of peaked grass roofs, a burst of yells, a whirl of black limbs, a mass of hands clapping, of feet stamping, of bodies swaying, of eyes rolling, under the droop of heavy and motionless fo-

liage. The steamer toiled along slowly on the edge of a black and incomprehensible frenzy. The prehistoric man was cursing us, praying to us, welcoming us—who could tell? We were cut off from the comprehension of our surroundings; we glided past like phantoms, wondering and secretly appalled, as sane men would be before an enthusiastic outbreak in a madhouse. We could not understand because we were too far and could not remember, because we were traveling in the night of first ages, of those ages that are gone, leaving hardly a sign—and no memories.

"The earth seemed unearthly. We are accustomed to look upon the shackled form of a conquered monster, but there—there you could look at a thing monstrous and free. It was unearthly, and the men were—No, they were not inhuman. Well, you know, that was the worst of it—this suspicion of their not being inhuman. It would come slowly to one. They howled and leaped, and spun, and made horrid faces; but what thrilled you was just the thought of their humanity—like yours—the thought of your remote kinship with this wild and passionate uproar. Ugly. Yes, it was ugly enough; but if you were man enough you would admit to yourself that there was in you just the faintest trace of a response to the terrible frankness of that noise, a dim suspicion of there being a meaning in it which you—you so remote from the night of first ages—could comprehend. And why not? The mind of man is capable of anything—because everything is in it, all the past as well as all the future. What was there after all? Joy, fear, sorrow, devotion, valor, rage—who can tell? but truth—truth stripped of its cloak of time. Let the fool gape and shudder—the man knows, and can look on without a wink. But he must at least be as much of a man as these on the shore. He must meet that truth with his own true stuff—with his own inborn strength."

It is this lure of savage reversion, symbolized by the wilderness, which has overwhelmed Kurtz. Far from the restraints of European civilization, Kurtz is claimed by the powers of darkness. The manager of the Central Station, who is onboard the steamer, fills Marlow in on Kurtz's background and doings.

". . . The wilderness had patted him on the head, and, behold, it was like a ball—an ivory ball; it had caressed him, and—lo!—he had withered; it had taken him, loved him, embraced him, got into his veins, consumed his flesh, and sealed his soul to its own by the inconceivable ceremonies of some devilish initiation. He was its spoiled and pampered favorite. Ivory? I should think so. Heaps of it, stacks of it. The old mud shanty was bursting with it. You would think there was not a single tusk left either above or below the ground in the whole country. 'Mostly fossil,' the manager had remarked, disparagingly. It was no more fossil than I am; but they call it fossil when it is dug up. It appears these niggers do bury the tusks sometimes—but evidently they couldn't bury this parcel deep enough to save the gifted Mr. Kurtz from his fate. We filled the steamboat with it, and had to pile a lot on the deck. Thus he could see and enjoy as long as he could see, because the appreciation of his favor had remained with him to the last. You should have heard him say, 'My ivory.' Oh yes, I heard him. 'My Intended, my ivory, my station, my river, my—' everything belonged to him. It made me hold my breath in expectation of hearing the wilderness burst into a prodigious peal of laughter that would shake the fixed stars in their places. Everything belonged to him—but that was a trifle. The thing was to know what he belonged to, how many powers of darkness claimed him for their own. That was the reflection that made you creepy all over. It was impossible—it was not good for one either—trying to imagine. He had taken a high seat amongst the devils of the land—I mean literally. You can't understand. How could you?—with solid pavement under your feet, surrounded by kind neighbors ready to cheer you or to fall on you, stepping delicately between the butcher and the policeman, in the holy terror of scandal and gallows and lunatic asylums—how can you imagine what particular region of the first ages a man's untrammeled feet may take him into by the way of solitude—utter solitude without a policeman—by the way of silence—utter silence, where no warning voice of a kind neighbor can be heard whispering of public opinion? These little things make all the great difference. When they are gone you must fall back upon your own innate strength, upon your own capacity for faithfulness. . . .

"... The original Kurtz had been educated partly in England, and—as he was good enough to say himself—his sympathies were in the right place. His mother was half-English, his father was half-French. All Europe contributed to the making of Kurtz; and by and by I learned that, most appropriately, the International Society for the Suppression of Savage Customs had intrusted him with the making of a report, for its future guidance. And he had written it, too. I've seen it. I've read it. It was eloquent, vibrating with eloquence, but too high-strung, I think. Seventeen pages of close writing he had found time for! But this must have been before his—let us say—nerves, went wrong, and caused him to preside at certain midnight dances ending with unspeakable rites, which—as far as I reluctantly gathered from what I heard at various times—were offered up to him—do you understand?—to Mr. Kurtz himself. But it was a beautiful piece of writing. The opening paragraph, however, in the light of later information, strikes me now as ominous. He began with the argument that we whites, from the point of development we had arrived at, 'must necessarily appear to them [savages] in the nature of supernatural beings—we approach them with the might as of a deity,' and so on, and so on. 'By the

simple exercise of our will we can exert a power for good practically unbounded,' etc., etc. From that point he soared and took me with him. The peroration was magnificent, though difficult to remember, you know. It gave me the notion of an exotic Immensity ruled by an august Benevolence. It made me tingle with enthusiasm. This was the unbounded power of eloquence—of words—of burning noble words. There were no practical hints to interrupt the magic current of phrases, unless a kind of note at the foot of the last page, scrawled evidently much later, in an unsteady hand, may be regarded as the exposition of a method. It was very simple, and at the end of that moving appeal to every altruistic sentiment it blazed at you, luminous and terrifying, like a flash of lightning in a serene sky: 'Exterminate all the brutes!' "

As the steamer approaches the Inner station, Marlow spots a white man on the shore who greets them. He turns out to be a young and strange Russian adventurer very much devoted to Kurtz. Accompanied by the Russian, Marlow heads for Kurtz's house. When he is within distance, he peers into his field glasses.

"... I directed my glass to the house. There were no signs of life, but there was the ruined roof, the long mud wall peeping above the grass, with three little square window holes, no two of the same size; all this brought within reach of my hand, as it were. And then I made a brusque movement, and one of the remaining posts of that vanished fence leaped up in the field of my glass. You remember I told you I had been struck at the distance by certain attempts at ornamentation, rather remarkable in the ruinous aspect of the place. Now I had suddenly a nearer view, and its first result was to make me throw my head back as if before a blow. Then I went carefully from post to post with my glass, and I saw my mistake. These round knobs were not ornamental but symbolic; they were expressive and puzzling, striking and disturbing—food for thought and also for the vultures if there had been any looking down from the sky; but at all events for such ants as were industrious enough to ascend the pole. They would have been even more impressive, those heads on the stakes, if their faces had not been turned to the house. Only one, the first I had made out, was facing my way. I was not so shocked as you may think. The start back I had given was really nothing but a movement of surprise. I had expected to see a knob of wood there, you know. I returned deliberately to the first I had seen—and there it was, black, dried, sunken, with closed eyelids, a head that seemed to sleep at the top of that pole, and, with the shrunken dry lips showing a narrow white line of the teeth, was smiling, too, smiling continuously at some endless and jocose dream of that eternal slumber.

"I am not disclosing any trade secrets. In fact, the manager said afterwards that Mr. Kurtz's methods had ruined the district. I have no opinion on that point, but I want you clearly to understand that there was nothing exactly profitable in these heads being there. They only showed that Mr. Kurtz lacked restraint in the gratification of his various lusts, that there was something wanting in him—some small matter which, when the pressing need arose, could not be found under his magnificent eloquence. Whether he knew of this deficiency himself I can't say. I think the knowledge came to him at last—only at the very last. But the wilderness had found him out early, and had taken on him a terrible vengeance for the fantastic invasion. I think it had whispered to him things about himself which he did not know, things of which he had no conception till he took counsel with this great solitude—and the whisper had proved irresistibly fascinating. It echoed loudly within him because he was hollow at the core. . . . I put down the glass, and the head that had appeared near enough to be spoken to seemed at once to have leaped away from me into inaccessible distance.

"The admirer of Mr. Kurtz was a bit crestfallen. In a hurried, indistinct voice he began to assure me he had not dared to take these—say, symbols—down. He was not afraid of the natives; they would not stir till Mr. Kurtz gave the word. His ascendancy was extraordinary. The camps of these people surrounded the place, and the chiefs came every day to see him.

They would crawl. . . . 'I don't want to know anything of the ceremonies used when approaching Mr. Kurtz,' I shouted. Curious, this feeling that came over me that such details would be more intolerable than those heads drying on the stakes under Mr. Kurtz's windows. After all, that was only a savage sight, while I seemed at one bound to have been transported into some lightless region of subtle horrors, where pure, uncomplicated savagery was a positive relief, being something that had a right to exist—obviously—in the sunshine. The young man looked at me with surprise. I suppose it did not occur to him that Mr. Kurtz was no idol of mine. He forgot I hadn't heard any of these splendid monologues on, what was it? On love, justice, conduct of life—or whatnot. If it had come to crawling before Mr. Kurtz, he crawled as much as the veriest savage of them all. I had no idea of the conditions, he said: these heads were the heads of rebels. I shocked him excessively by laughing. Rebels! What would be the next definition I was to hear? There had been enemies, criminals, workers—and these were rebels. Those rebellious heads looked very subdued to me on their sticks. 'You don't know how such a life tries a man like Kurtz,' cried Kurtz's last disciple."

Franz Kafka
The Trial

The Modernist concern with human irrationality was captured brilliantly by Franz Kafka (1883–1924), whose major novels, *The Trial* and *The Castle*, were published after his death and did not receive recognition until after World War II. Yet perhaps better than any other novelist of his generation, Kafka grasped the dilemma of the modern age. There is no apparent order or stability in Kafka's world. Human beings strive to make sense out of life, but everywhere ordinary occurrences thwart them. They are caught in a bureaucratic web that they cannot control; they live in a nightmare society dominated by oppressive, cruel, and corrupt officials and amoral torturers. In Kafka's world, cruelty and injustice are accepted facts of existence, power is exercised without limits, and victims cooperate in their own destruction. Traditional values and ordinary logic do not operate. Our world, thought to be secure, stale, and purposeful, easily falls apart.

Kafka understood the intense anxiety that torments modern people. In *The Trial* (1925), for example, an ordinary man who has no consciousness of wrongdoing is arrested. "K. lived in a country with a legal constitution, there was universal peace, all the laws were in force; who dared seize him in his own dwelling?" Josef K. is never told the reason for his arrest, and he is eventually executed, a victim of institutional evil that breaks and destroys him "like a dog." In these observations, Kafka anticipated the emerging totalitarian state. (Kafka's three sisters perished in the Holocaust.)

A German-speaking Jew in the alien Slav environment of Czechoslovakia, Kafka died of tuberculosis at an early age. In voicing his own deep anxieties,

Kafka expressed the feelings of alienation and isolation that characterize the modern individual. He explored life's dreads and absurdities, offering no solutions or consolation. In Kafka's works, people are defeated and unable to comprehend the irrational forces that contribute to their destruction. Although the mind yearns for coherence, Kafka tells us that uncertainty, if not chaos, governs human relationships. We can be sure neither of our own identities nor of the world we encounter, for human beings are the playthings of unfathomable forces, too irrational to master.

A brooding pessimism about the human condition pervades Kafka's work. One reason for the intensified interest in Kafka after World War II, observes Angel Flores, "is that the European world of the late 30s and 40s with its betrayals and concentration camps, its resulting cruelties and indignities, bore a remarkable resemblance to the world depicted by Kafka in the opening decades of the century. History seems to have imitated the nightmarish background evoked by the dreamer of Prague."

. . . [T]he proceedings were not only kept secret from the general public, but from the accused as well. Of course only so far as this was possible, but it had proved possible to a very great extent. For even the accused had no access to the Court records, and to guess from the course of all interrogation what documents the Court had up its sleeve was very difficult, particularly for an accused person, who was himself implicated and had all sorts of worries to distract him. Now here was where defending counsel stepped in. Generally speaking, he was not allowed to be present during the examination, consequently he had to cross-question the accused immediately after an interrogation, if possible at the very door of the Court of Inquiry, and piece together from the usually confused reports he got anything that might be of use for the Defense. But even that was not the most important thing, for one could not elicit very much in that way, though of course here as elsewhere a capable man could elicit more than others. The most important thing was counsel's personal connection with officials of the Court; in that lay the chief value of the Defense. Now K. must have discovered from experience that the very lowest grade of the Court organization was by no means perfect and contained venal and corrupt elements, whereby to some extent a breach was made in the watertight system of justice. This was where most of the petty lawyers tried to push their way in, by bribing and listening to gossip, in fact there had actually been cases of purloining documents, at least in former times. It was not to be gainsaid that these methods could achieve for the moment surprisingly favorable results for the accused, on which the petty lawyers prided themselves, spreading them out as a lure for new clients, but they had no effect on the further progress of the case, or only a bad effect. Nothing was of any real value but respectable personal connections with the higher officials, that was to say higher officials of subordinate rank, naturally. Only through these could the course of the proceedings be influenced, imperceptibly at first, perhaps, but more and more strongly as the case went on. Of course very few lawyers had such connections, and here K.'s choice had been a very fortunate one. Perhaps only one or two other lawyers could boast of the same connections as Dr. Huld. These did not worry their heads about the mob in the lawyers' room and had nothing whatever to do with them. But their relations with the Court officials were all the more intimate. It was not even necessary that Dr. Huld should always attend the Court, wait in the Anteroom of the Examining Magistrates till they chose to appear, and be dependent on their moods for earning perhaps a delusive success or not even that. No, as K. had himself seen, the officials, and very high ones among them, visited Dr. Huld of their own accord, voluntarily providing information with great frankness or at least in broad enough hints, discussing the next turn of the various cases; more, even sometimes letting themselves be persuaded to a new point of view. Certainly one should not rely too much on their readiness to be persuaded, for definitely as they might declare themselves for a new standpoint favorable to the Defense, they might well go straight to their offices and issue a statement in the directly contrary sense, a verdict far more severe on the accused than the original intention which they claimed to have renounced completely. Against that, of course, there was no remedy, for what they said to you in private was simply said to you in private and could not be followed up in public, even if the Defense were not obliged for other reasons to do its utmost to retain the favor of these gentlemen. . . .

Dr. Huld recounts the relationship between overworked and irritated officials in the judiciary system and the lawyers for the defense. Restricted to working on only one stage of the judicial process, these officials have no comprehension of the proceedings of the court as the case unfolds. They are no more than cogs in an unfathomable bureaucratic process.

The ranks of officials in this judiciary system mounted endlessly, so that not even the initiated could survey the hierarchy as a whole. And the proceedings of the Courts were generally kept secret from subordinate officials, consequently they could hardly ever quite follow in their further progress the cases on which they had worked; any particular case thus appeared in their circle of jurisdiction often without their knowing whence it came, and passed from it they knew not whither. Thus the knowledge derived from a study of the various single stages of the case, the final verdict and the reasons for that verdict lay beyond the reach of these officials. They were forced to restrict themselves to that stage of the case which was prescribed for them by the Law, and as for what followed, in other words the results of their own work, they generally knew less about it than the Defense, which as a rule remained in touch with the accused almost to the end of the case. So in that respect, too, they could learn much that was worth knowing from the Defense. Should it surprise K., then, keeping all this in mind, to find that the officials lived in a state of irritability which sometimes expressed itself in offensive ways when they dealt with their clients? That was the universal experience. All the officials were in a constant state of irritation, even when they appeared calm. Naturally the petty lawyers were most liable to suffer from it. The following story, for example, was current, and it had all the appearance of truth. An old official, a well-meaning, quiet man, had a difficult case in hand which had been greatly complicated by the lawyer's petitions, and he had studied it continuously for a whole day and night—the officials were really more conscientious than anyone else. Well, toward morning, after twenty-four hours of work with probably very little result, he went to the entrance door, hid himself behind it, and flung down the stairs every lawyer who tried to enter. The lawyers gathered down below on the landing and took counsel what they should do; on the one hand they had no real claim to be admitted and consequently could hardly take any legal action against the official, and also, as already mentioned, they had to guard against antagonizing the body of officials. But on the other hand every day they spent away from the Court was a day lost to them, and so a great deal depended on their getting in. At last they all agreed that the best thing to do was to tire out the old gentleman. One lawyer after another was sent rushing upstairs to offer the greatest possible show of passive resistance and let himself be thrown down again into the arms of his colleagues. That lasted for about an hour, then the old gentleman—who was exhausted in any case by his work overnight—really grew tired and went back to his office. The lawyers down below would not believe it at first and sent one of their number up to peep behind the door and assure himself that the place was actually vacant. Only then were they able to enter, and probably they did not dare even to grumble. For although the pettiest lawyer might be to some extent capable of analyzing the state of things in the Court, it never occurred to the lawyers that they should suggest or insist on any improvements in the system, while—and this was very characteristic—almost every accused man, even quite simple people among them, discovered from the earliest stages a passion for suggesting reforms which often wasted time and energy that could have been better employed in other directions. The only sensible thing was to adapt oneself to existing conditions. Even if it were possible to alter a detail for the better here or there—but it was simple madness to think of it—any benefit arising from that would profit clients in the future only, while one's own interests would be immeasurably injured by attracting the attention of the ever-vengeful officials. Anything rather than that! One must lie low, no matter how much it went against the grain, and try to understand that this great organization remained, so to speak, in a state of delicate balance, and that if someone took it upon himself to alter the disposition of things around him, he ran the risk of losing his footing and falling to destruction, while the organization would simply right itself by some compensating reaction in another part of its machinery—since everything interlocked—and remain unchanged, unless, indeed, which was very probable, it became still more rigid, more vigilant, severer, and more ruthless.

K. is referred to Titorelli, an artist who paints portraits of the judges, a position that gives him access to judges and an insider's understanding of the judicial process, which Titorelli explains to K. Judicial procedures are not designed to attain justice, for "the Court procedure is impervious to proof." Innocents are swept up in a bureaucratic nightmare that dooms them.

"Are you innocent?" he asked. "Yes," said K. The answering of this question gave him a feeling of real pleasure, particularly as he was addressing a private individual and therefore need fear no consequences. Nobody else had yet asked him such a frank question. To savor his elation to the full, he added: "I am completely innocent." "I see," said the painter, bending his head as if in thought. Suddenly he raised it again and said: "If you are innocent, then the matter is quite simple." K.'s eyes darkened, this man who said he was in the confidence of the Court was talking like an ignorant child. "My innocence doesn't make the matter any simpler," said K. But after all he could not help smiling, and then he slowly shook his head. "I have to fight against countless subtleties in which the Court indulges. And in the end, out of nothing at all, an enormous fabric of guilt will be conjured up." "Yes, yes, of course," said the painter, as if K. were needlessly interrupting the thread of his ideas. "But you're innocent all the same?" "Why, yes," said K. "That's the main thing," said the painter. He was not to be moved by argument, yet in spite of his decisiveness it was not clear whether he spoke out of conviction or out of mere indifference. K. wanted first to be sure of this, so he said: "You know the Court much better than I do, I feel certain, I don't know much more about it than what I've heard from all sorts and conditions of people. But they all agree on one thing, that charges are never made frivolously, and that the Court, once it has brought a charge against someone, is firmly convinced of the guilt of the accused and can be dislodged from that conviction only with the greatest difficulty." "The greatest difficulty?" cried the painter, flinging one hand in the air. "The Court can never be dislodged from that conviction. If I were to paint all the Judges in a row on one canvas and you were to plead your case before it, you would have more hope of success than before the actual Court." "I see," said K. to himself, forgetting that he merely wished to pump the painter. . . .

"You don't seem to have any general idea of the Court yet," said the painter, stretching his legs wide in front of him and tapping with his shoes on the floor. "But since you're innocent you won't need it anyhow. I shall get you off all by myself." "How can you do that?" asked K. "For you told me yourself a few minutes ago that the Court was quite impervious to proof." "Impervious only to proof which one brings before the Court," said the painter, raising one finger as if K. had failed to perceive a fine distinction. "But it is quite a different matter with one's efforts behind the scenes; that is, in the consulting-rooms, in the lobbies or, for example, in this very studio." What the painter now said no longer seemed incredible to K., indeed it agreed in the main with what he had heard from other people. More, it was actually hopeful in a high degree. If a judge could really be so easily influenced by personal connections as the lawyer insisted, then the painter's connections with these vain functionaries were especially important and certainly not to be undervalued. That made the painter an excellent recruit to the ring of helpers which K. was gradually gathering round him. . . .

Titorelli drew his chair closer to the bed and continued in a low voice: "I forgot to ask you first what sort of acquittal you want. There are three possibilities, that is, definite acquittal, ostensible acquittal, and indefinite postponement. Definite acquittal is, of course, the best, but I haven't the slightest influence on that kind of verdict. As far as I know, there is no single person who could influence the verdict of definite acquittal. The only deciding factor seems to be the innocence of the accused. Since you're innocent, of course it would be possible for you to ground your case on your innocence alone. But then you would require neither my help nor help from anyone."

This lucid explanation took K. aback at first, but he replied in the same subdued voice as the painter: "It seems to me that you're contradicting yourself." "In what way?" asked the painter patiently, leaning back with a smile. The smile awoke in K. a suspicion that he was now about to expose contradictions not so much in the painter's statements as in the Court procedure itself. However, he did not retreat, but went on: "You made the assertion earlier that the Court is impervious to proof, later you qualified that assertion by confining it to the public sessions of the Court, and now you actually say that an innocent man requires no help before the Court. That alone implies a contradiction. But, in addition, you said at first that the Judges can be moved by personal intervention, and now you deny that definite acquittal, as you call it,

can ever be achieved by personal intervention. In that lies the second contradiction!" "These contradictions are easy to explain," said the painter. "We must distinguish between two things: what is written in the Law, and what I have discovered through personal experience; you must not confuse the two. In the code of the Law, which admittedly I have not read, it is of course laid down on the one hand that the innocent shall be acquitted, but it is not stated on the other hand that the Judges are open to influence. Now, my experience is diametrically opposed to that. I have not met one case of definite acquittal, and I have met many cases of influential intervention. It is possible, of course, that in all the cases known to me there was none in which the accused was really innocent. But is not that improbable? Among so many cases no single case of innocence? Even as a child I used to listen carefully to my father when he spoke of cases he had heard about; the Judges, too, who came to his studio were always telling stories about the Court, in our circle it is in fact the sole topic of discussion; no sooner did I get the chance to attend the Court myself than I took full advantage of it; I have listened to countless cases in their most crucial stages, and followed them as far as they could be followed, and yet—I must admit it—I have never encountered one case of definite acquittal." "Not one case of acquittal, then," said K. as if he were speaking to himself and his hopes, "but that merely confirms the opinion that I have already formed of this Court. It is a pointless institution from any point of view. A single executioner could do all that is needed." "You mustn't generalize," said the painter in displeasure. "I have only quoted my own experience." "That's quite enough," said K. "Or have you ever heard of acquittals in earlier times?" "Such acquittals," replied the painter, "are said to have occurred. Only it is very difficult to prove the fact. The final decisions of the Court are never recorded, even the Judges can't get hold of them, consequently we have only legendary accounts of ancient cases. These legends certainly provide instances of acquittal; actually the majority of them are about acquittals, they can be believed, but they cannot be proved. All the same, they shouldn't be entirely left out of account, they must have an element of truth in them, and besides they are very beautiful. I myself have painted several pictures founded on such legends." "Mere legends cannot alter my opinion," said K., "and I fancy that one cannot appeal to such legends before the Court?" The painter laughed. "No, one can't do that," he said. "Then there's no use talking about them," said K., willing for the time being to accept the painter's opinions, even where they seemed improbable or contradicted other reports he had heard. He had no time now to inquire into the truth of all the painter said, much less contradict it, the utmost he could hope to do was to get the man to help him in some way, even should the help prove inconclusive. Accordingly he said: "Let us leave definite acquittal out of account, then; you mentioned two other possibilities as well." "Ostensible acquittal and postponement. These are the only possibilities," said the painter. . . .

First, then, let us take ostensible acquittal. If you decide on that, I shall write down on a sheet of paper an affidavit of innocence. The text for such an affidavit has been handed down to me by my father and is unassailable. Then with this affidavit I shall make a round of the Judges I know, beginning, let us say, with the Judge I am painting now, when he comes for his sitting tonight. I shall lay the affidavit before him, explain to him that you are innocent, and guarantee your innocence myself. And that is not merely a formal guarantee but a real and binding one." In the eyes of the painter there was a faint suggestion of reproach that K. should lay upon him the burden of such a responsibility. "That would be very kind of you," said K. "And the Judge would believe you and yet not give me a definite acquittal?" "As I have already explained," replied the painter. "Besides, it is not in the least certain that every Judge will believe me; some Judges, for instance, will ask to see you in person. And then I should have to take you with me to call on them. Though when that happens the battle is already half won, particularly as I should tell you beforehand, of course, exactly what line to take with each Judge. The real difficulty comes with the Judges who turn away at the start—and that's sure to happen too. I shall go on petitioning them, of course, but we shall have to do without them, though one can afford to do that, since dissent by individual Judges cannot affect the result. Well then, if I get a sufficient number of Judges to subscribe to the affidavit, I shall then deliver it to the Judge who is actually conducting your trial. Possibly I may have secured his signature too, then everything will be settled fairly soon, a little sooner than usual. Generally speaking, there should be no difficulties worth mentioning after that, the accused at this stage feels supremely confident. Indeed it's remarkable, but true, that people's confidence mounts higher at this stage than after their acquittal. There's no need for them to do much more. The Judge is covered by the guarantees of the other Judges subscribing to the affidavit, and so he can grant an acquittal with an easy mind, and though some formalities will remain to be settled, he will undoubtedly grant the acquittal to please me and his other friends. Then you can walk out of the Court a free man." "So then I'm free," said K. doubtfully. "Yes," said the painter, "but only ostensibly free, or more exactly, provisionally free. For the Judges of the lowest grade, to whom my acquaintances belong, haven't the power to grant a final acquittal, that power is reserved for the highest Court of all, which is quite inaccessible to you, to me, and to all of us. What the prospects are up there we do not know and, I may say in passing, do not even want to know. The great privilege, then, of absolving from guilt our Judges do not possess, but they do have the right to take the burden of the charge off your shoulders. That is to say, when you are acquitted in this fashion the charge is lifted from your shoulders, for the time being, but it continues to hover above you and can, as soon as an order comes from on high, be laid upon you again. As my connection with the Court is such a close one, I can also tell you how in the regulations of the Law Court offices the distinction between definite and ostensible acquittal is made manifest. In definite acquittal the documents relating to the case are said to be completely annulled, they simply vanish from sight, not only the charge but also the records of the case and even the acquittal are destroyed, everything is destroyed. That's not the case with ostensible acquittal. The documents remain as they were, except that the affidavit is added to them and a record of the acquittal and the grounds for granting it. The whole dossier continues to circulate, as the regular official routine demands, passing on to the higher Courts, being referred to the lower ones again, and thus swinging backwards and forwards with greater or smaller oscillations, longer or shorter delays. These peregrinations are incalculable. A detached observer might sometimes fancy that the whole case had been forgotten, the documents lost, and the acquittal made absolute. No one really acquainted with the Court could think such a thing. No document is ever lost, the Court never forgets anything. One day—quite unexpectedly—some Judge will take up the documents and look at them attentively, recognize that in this case the charge is still valid, and order an immediate arrest. I have been speaking on the assumption that a long time elapses between the ostensible acquittal and the new arrest; that is possible and I have known of such cases, but it is just as possible for the acquitted man to go straight home from the Court and find officers already waiting to arrest him again. Then, of course, all his freedom is at an end." "And the case begins all over again?" asked K. almost incredulously. "Certainly," said the painter. "The case begins all over again, but again it is possible, just as before, to secure an ostensible acquittal. One must again apply all one's energies to the case and never give in." These last words were probably uttered because he noticed that K. was looking somewhat collapsed. "But," said K., as if he wanted to forestall any more revelations, "isn't the engineering of a second acquittal more difficult than the first?" "On that point," said the painter, "one can say nothing with certainty. You mean, I take it, that the second arrest might influence the Judges against the accused? That is not so. Even while they are pronouncing the first acquittal the Judges foresee the possibility of the new arrest. Such a consideration, therefore, hardly comes into question. But it may happen, for hundreds of reasons, that the Judges are in a different frame of mind about the case, even from a legal viewpoint, and one's efforts to obtain a second acquittal must consequently be adapted to the changed circumstances, and in general must be every whit as energetic as those that secured the first one." "But this second acquittal isn't final either," said K., turning away his head in repudiation. "Of course not," said the painter. "The second acquittal is followed by the third arrest, the third acquittal by the fourth arrest, and so on. That is implied in the very conception of ostensible acquittal." K. said nothing. "Ostensible acquittal doesn't seem to appeal to you," said the painter. "Perhaps postponement would suit you better. Shall I explain to you how postponement works?" K. nodded. The painter was lolling back in his chair, his nightshirt gaped open, he had thrust one hand inside it and was lightly fingering his breast. "Postponement," he said, gazing in front of him for a moment as if seeking a completely accurate explanation, "postponement consists in preventing the case from ever getting any further than its first stages. To achieve that it is necessary for the accused and his agent, but more particularly his agent, to remain continuously in personal touch with the Court. Let me point out again that this does not demand such intense concentration of ones energies as an ostensible acquittal, yet on the other hand it does require far greater vigilance. You daren't let the case out of your sight, you visit the Judge at regular intervals as well as in emergencies and must do all that is in your power to keep him friendly; if you don't know the Judge personally, then you must try to influence him through other Judges whom you do know, but without giving up your efforts to secure a personal interview. If you neglect none of these things, then you can assume with fair certainty that the case will never pass beyond its first stages. Not that the proceedings are quashed, but the accused is almost as likely to escape sentence as if he were free. As against ostensible acquittal postponement has this advantage, that the future of the accused is less uncertain, he is secured from the terrors of sudden arrest and doesn't need to fear having to undergo—perhaps at a most inconvenient moment—the strain and agitation which are inevitable in the achievement of ostensible acquittal. Though postponement, too, has certain drawbacks for the accused, and these must not be minimized. In saying this I am not thinking of the fact that the accused is never free; he isn't free either, in any real sense, after the ostensible acquittal. There are other drawbacks. The case can't be held up indefinitely without at least some plausible grounds being provided. So as a matter of form a certain activity must be shown from time to time, various measures have to be taken, the accused is questioned, evidence is collected, and so on. For the case must be kept going all the time, although only in the small circle to which it has been artificially restricted. This naturally involves the accused in occasional unpleasantness, but you must not think of it as being too unpleasant. For it's all a formality, the interrogations, for instance, are only short ones; if you have neither the time nor the inclination to go, you can excuse yourself; with some Judges you can even plan your interviews a long time ahead, all that it amounts to is a formal recognition of your status as an accused man by regular appearances before your Judge." Already while these last words were being spoken K. had taken his jacket across his arm and got up. . . . "Are you going already?" asked the painter, who had also got up. "I'm sure it's the air here that is driving you away. I'm sorry about it. I had a great deal more to tell you. I have had to express myself very briefly. But I hope my statements were lucid enough." "Oh, yes," said K., whose head was aching with the strain of forcing himself to listen. In spite of K.'s confirmation, the painter went on to sum up the matter again, as if to give him a last word of comfort: "Both methods have this in common, that they prevent the accused from coming up for sentence." "But they also prevent an actual acquittal," said K. in a low voice, as if embarrassed by his own perspicacity. "You have grasped the kernel of the matter," said the painter quickly.

4 The Stream of Consciousness Novel

Modernist writers abandoned the efforts of the Realists and the Naturalists to produce a clinical and objective description of the external world; instead, they probed subjective views and visions and the inner world of the unconscious. Recoiling from a middle-class, industrial civilization, which prized rationalism, organization, clarity, stability, and definite norms and values, Modernist writers were fascinated by the bizarre, the mysterious, the unpredictable, the primitive, the irrational, and the formless. They attempted to represent ideas, emotions, and sensations in a uniquely personal way, free of rules and customary conventions. Writers, for example, experimented with new techniques to convey the intense struggle between the conscious and the unconscious and to explore the aberrations and complexities of human personality and the irrationality of human behavior. In particular, they devised a new way, the stream of consciousness, to exhibit the mind's every level—both conscious reflection and unconscious strivings—and to capture how thought is punctuated by spontaneous outbursts, disconnected assertions, random memories, hidden desires, and persistent fantasies.

Instead of presenting the plot, characters, and descriptive narration in the conventional linear way, stream of consciousness technique relates the action though images and symbols that are conjured up in the mind of one or more of the characters. What matters most is not the articulation of ordered, verbalized thoughts, but rather the psychological state of each character. Often a third-person, the omniscient narrator, describes everything about each of the characters, how they think, what they feel, and why they do what they do. Omniscient narrators often express themselves in the form of soliloquies whereby, talking only to themselves, they reveal to the reader not only the character's innermost thoughts but their own as well. The introspective turn in the novel is also expressed through "interior monologue," in which a character's meandering and disconnected comments progressively penetrate deeper into the unconscious, disclosing buried fears and torments.

Modernist writers also made use of symbols, attributing a larger meaning to particular phenomena and events. All the elements of the novel—the actions of characters and the ways in which they are presented—have symbolic meanings. These particularities convey larger implications about the human condition. A bird in a cage can represent entrapment and a bird spreading its wings symbolizes self-actualization. A fog can stand for confusion, a jungle for primal instincts, and taking off one's clothes can symbolize the shunning of societal norms that stifle self-expression. The moon can represent not only the mythic power of the universe but also romantic and sexual notions of love. Bodies of water, particularly the ocean, represent escape and freedom, as does sleep, which often precedes moments of self-realization.

Virginia Woolf
Mrs. Dalloway

Virginia Woolf (1882–1941) drew heavily upon personal experience in writing her novels, particularly the emotional travail that led to at least three mental breakdowns. For her first great novel, *Mrs. Dalloway,* Woolf called upon her life experiences to give definition to the character of her protagonist—Clarissa Dalloway, the middle-aged, upper-crust wife of Richard Dalloway, a member of Parliament who is frustrated by his inability to accede to a Cabinet post. The events of Woolf's *Mrs. Dalloway* take up only one day, in the middle of June, during the 1920s.

The action centers on an evening dinner party to be hosted by Mrs. Dalloway who, as she prepares for her party, reminiscences about her past, including a lover, the commoner Peter Walsh, whom she had rejected so that she could marry Richard Dalloway, a member of the upper echelons of society. Spurned by Mrs. Dalloway, Peter travels to India, returns unexpectedly, and drops by Clarissa's house. When their uneasy conversation is interrupted by Mrs. Dalloway's daughter, Peter goes to a nearby park to reflect on their past. Later that evening, he attends Mrs. Dalloway's party.

Parallel to Clarissa's interior monologue are the thoughts of Septimus Warren Smith, a World War I veteran suffering from shell shock, whose suicide has a profound effect on Clarrisa when she learns of it at her dinner party. Before the war, Septimus loved Shakespeare and wanted to be a poet; now, however, he fears that life has no meaning, and he hears voices and "talks" to his dead friend, Evans, a casualty of the war. In the following selection, while he and his wife Lucrezia stroll in a park, Septimus discusses the merits of suicide as a way to bring an end to suffering.

Lucrezia Warren Smith was saying to herself, It's wicked; why should I suffer? she was asking, as she walked down the broad path. No; I can't stand it any longer, she was saying, having left Septimus, who wasn't Septimus any longer, to say hard, cruel, wicked things, to talk to himself, to talk to a dead man [Evans], on the seat over there; when the child ran full tilt into her, fell flat, and burst out crying.

That was comforting rather. She stood her upright, dusted her frock, kissed her.

But for herself she had done nothing wrong; she had loved Septimus; she had been happy; she had had a beautiful home, and there her sisters lived still, making hats. Why should *she* suffer?

The child ran straight back to its nurse, and Rezia saw her scolded, comforted, taken up by the nurse who put down her knitting, and the kind-looking man gave her his watch to blow open to comfort her—but why should *she* be exposed? . . . Why tortured? Why? . . .

To be rocked by this malignant torturer was her lot. But why? She was like a bird sheltering under the thin hollow of a leaf, who blinks at the sun when the leaf moves; starts at the crack of a dry twig. She was exposed; she was surrounded by the enormous trees, vast clouds of an indifferent world, exposed; tortured; and why should she suffer? Why?

She frowned; she stamped her foot. She must go back again to Septimus since it was almost time for them to be going to Sir William Bradshaw. She must go back and tell him, go back to him sitting there on the green chair under the tree, talking to himself, or to that dead man Evans, whom she had only seen once for a moment in the shop. He had seemed a nice quiet man; a great friend of Septimus's, and he had been killed in the War. But such things happen to every one. Every one has friends who were killed in the War. Every one gives up something when they marry. She had given up her home. She had come to live here, in this awful city. But Septimus let himself think about horrible things, as she could too, if she tried. He had grown stranger and stranger. He said people were talking behind the bedroom walls. . . . He saw things too—he had seen an old woman's head in the middle of a fern. Yet he could be happy when he chose. They went to Hampton Court on top of a bus, and they were perfectly happy. All the little red and yellow flowers were out on the grass, like floating lamps he said, and talked and chattered and laughed, making up stories. Suddenly he said, "Now we will kill ourselves," when they were standing by the river, and he looked at it with a look which she had seen in his eyes when a train went by, or an omnibus—a look as if something fascinated him; and she felt he was going from her and she caught him by the arm. But going home he was perfectly quiet—perfectly reasonable. He would argue with her about killing themselves; and explain how wicked people were; how he could see them making up lies as they passed in the street. He knew all their thoughts, he said; he knew everything. He knew the meaning of the world, he said.

Then when they got back he could hardly walk. He lay on the sofa and made her hold his hand to prevent him from falling down, down, he cried, into the flames! and saw faces laughing at him, calling him horrible disgusting names, from the walls and hands pointing round the screen. Yet they were quite alone. But he began to talk aloud, answering people, arguing, laughing, crying, getting very excited and making her write things down. Perfect nonsense it was; about death. . . . She could stand it no longer. She would go back.

She was close to him now, could see him staring at the sky, muttering, clasping his hands. Yet Dr. Holmes said there was nothing the matter with him. What, then, had happened—why had he gone, then, why, when she sat by him, did he start, frown at her, move away, and point at her hand, take her hand, look at it terrified?

Was it that she had taken off her wedding ring? "My hand has gown so thin," she said; "I have put it in my purse," she told him.

He dropped her hand. Their marriage was over, he thought, with agony, with relief. The rope was cut; he mounted; he was free, as it was decreed that he, Septimus, the lord of men, should be free; alone (since his wife had thrown away her wedding ring; since she had left him), he, Septimus, was alone, called forth in advance of the mass of men to hear the truth, to learn the meaning, which now at last, after all the toils of civilisation—Greeks, Romans, Shakespeare, Darwin, and now himself—was to be given whole to . . . "To whom?" he asked aloud, "To the Prime Minister," the voices which rustled above his head replied. The supreme secret must be told to the Cabinet; first, that trees are alive; next, there is no crime; next, love, universal love, he muttered, gasping, trembling, painfully drawing out these profound truths which needed, so deep were they, so difficult, an immense effort to speak out, but the world was entirely changed by them for ever.

No crime; love; he repeated, fumbling for his card and pencil, when a Skye terrier sniffed his trousers and he started in an agony of fear. It was turning into a man! He could not watch it happen! It was horrible, terrible to see a dog become a man! At once the dog trotted away.

Heaven was divinely merciful, infinitely benignant. It spared him, pardoned his weakness. But what was the scientific explanation (for one must be scientific above all things)? Why could he see through bodies, see into the future, when dogs will become men? It was the heat wave presumably, operating upon a brain made sensitive by eons of evolution. Scientifically speaking, the flesh was melted off the world. His body was macerated [emaciated] until only the nerve fibres were left. It was spread like a veil upon a rock.

He lay back in his chair, exhausted but upheld. He lay resting, waiting, before he again interpreted, with effort, with agony, to mankind. He lay very high, on the back of the world. The earth thrilled beneath him. Red flowers grew through his flesh; their stiff leaves rustled by his head. Music began clanging against the rocks up here. It is a motor horn down in the street, he muttered; but up here it cautioned from rock to rock, divided, met in shocks of sound which rose in smooth columns (that music should be visible was a discovery) and became an anthem, an anthem twined round now by a shepherd boy's piping (That's an old man playing a penny whistle by the public-house, he muttered) which, as the boy stood still, came bubbling from his pipe, and then, as he climbed higher, made its exquisite plaint while the traffic passed beneath. This boy's elegy is played among the traffic, thought Septimus. Now he withdraws up into the snows, and roses hang about him—the thick red roses which grow on my bedroom wall, he reminded himself. The music stopped. He has his penny, he reasoned it out, and has gone on to the next public-house.

But he himself remained high on his rock, like a drowned sailor on a rock. I leant over the edge of the boat and fell down, he thought. I went under the sea. I have been dead, and yet am now alive, but let me rest still, he begged (he was talking to himself again—it was awful, awful!); and as, before waking, the voices of birds and the sound of wheels chime and chatter in a queer harmony, grow louder and louder, and the sleeper feels himself drawing to the shores of life, so he felt himself drawing towards life, the sun growing hotter, cries sounding louder, something tremendous about to happen.

He had only to open his eyes; but a weight was on them; a fear. He strained; he pushed; he looked; he saw Regent's Park before him. Long streamers of sunlight fawned at his feet. The trees waved, brandished. We welcome, the world seemed to say; we accept; we create. Beauty, the world seemed to say. And as if to prove it (scientifically) wherever he looked, at the houses, at the railings, at the antelopes stretching over the palings, beauty sprang instantly. To watch a leaf quivering in the rush of air was an exquisite joy. Up in the sky swallows swooping, swerving, flinging themselves in and out, round and round, yet always with perfect control as if elastics held them; and the flies rising and falling; and the sun spotting now this leaf, now that, in mockery, dazzling it with soft gold in pure good temper; and now and again some chime (it might be a motor horn) tinkling divinely on the grass stalks—all of this, calm and reasonable as it was, made out of ordinary things as it was, was the truth now; beauty, that was the truth now. Beauty was everywhere.

"It is time," said Rezia.

The word "time" split its husk; poured its riches over him; and from his lips fell like shells, like shavings from a plane, without his making them, hard, white, imperishable, words, and flew to attach themselves to their places in an ode to Time; an immortal ode to Time. He sang. Evans answered from behind the tree. The dead were in Thessaly, Evans sang, among the orchids. There they waited till the War was over, and now the dead, now Evans himself—

"For God's sake don't come!" Septimus cried out. For he could not look upon the dead.

But the branches parted. A man in grey was actually walking towards them. It was Evans! But no mud was on him; no wounds; he was not changed. I must tell the whole world, Septimus cried, raising his hand (as the dead man in the grey suit came nearer), raising his hand like some colossal figure who has lamented the fate of man for ages in the desert alone with his hands pressed to his forehead, furrows of despair on his cheeks, and now sees light on the desert's edge which broadens and strikes the iron-black figure (and Septimus half rose from his chair), and with legions of men prostrate behind him he, the giant mourner, receives for one moment on his face the whole—

"But I am so unhappy, Septimus," said Rezia, trying to make him sit down.

The millions lamented; for ages they had sorrowed. He would turn round, he would tell them in a few moments, only a few moments more, of this relief, of this joy, of this astonishing revelation—

"The time, Septimus," Rezia repeated. "What is the time?"

He was talking, he was starting, this man must notice him. He was looking at them.

"I will tell you the time," said Septimus, very slowly, very drowsily, smiling mysteriously at the dead man in the grey suit. As he sat smiling, the quarter struck—the quarter to twelve.

When Lucrezia can no longer withstand her husband's mental affliction, she arranges for him to visit the eminent doctor, Sir William Bradshaw, who specializes in "nerve cases." But Dr. Bradshaw treats Septimus callously, even suggesting that his affliction is nothing more than a reflection of his inability to place things in their proper perspective. He advises Septimus to go to a sanatorium in the country to rest, but while the couple awaits the arrival of the attendants who will take him there, Septimus commits suicide by jumping out of a window. During her party later that evening, Mrs. Dalloway worries about whether everyone is having a good time. Adding to her concern is the late arrival of Sir William Bradshaw who, upon his arrival, announces that one of his patients, a young veteran, has committed suicide. In the following selection, one of the most compelling passages in the novel, Mrs. Dalloway reflects on Septimus' suicide, which she attributes to a society peopled with insensitive curs, like Bradshaw.

What business had the Bradshaws to talk of death at her party? A young man had killed himself. And they talked of it at her party—the Bradshaws talked of death. He had killed himself—but how? Always her body went through it, when she was told, first, suddenly, of an accident; her dress flamed, her body burnt. He had thrown himself from a window. Up had flashed the ground; through him, blundering, bruising, went the rusty spikes. There he lay with a thud, thud, thud in his brain, and then a suffocation of blackness. So she saw it. But why had he done it? And the Bradshaws talked of it at her party! . . .

. . . A thing there was that mattered; a thing, wreathed about with chatter, defaced, obscured in her own life, let drop every day in corruption, lies, chatter. This he had preserved. Death was defiance. Death was an attempt to communicate, people feeling the impossibility of reaching the centre which, mystically, evaded them; closeness drew apart; rapture faded; one was alone. There was an embrace in death.

But this young man who had killed himself—had he plunged holding his treasure? "If it were now to die, 'twere now to be most happy," she had said to herself once, coming down, in white.

Or there were the poets and thinkers. Suppose he had had that passion, and had gone to Sir William Bradshaw, a great doctor, yet to her obscurely evil, without sex or lust, ex-tremely polite to women, but capable of some indescribable outrage—forcing your soul, that was it—if this young man had gone to him, and Sir William had impressed him, like that, with his power, might he not then have said (indeed she felt it now), Life is made intolerable; they make life intolerable, men like that?

Then (she had felt it only this morning) there was the terror; the overwhelming incapacity, one's parents giving it into one's hands, this life, to be lived to the end, to be walked with serenely; there was in the depths of her heart an awful fear. Even now, quite often if Richard had not been there reading the *Times,* so that she could crouch like a bird and gradually revive, send roaring up that immeasurable delight, rubbing stick to stick, one thing with another, she must have perished. She had escaped. But that young man had killed himself.

The novel concludes with Clarissa pondering her own "suicide" when she allowed herself to give up the possibility of a loving marriage with Peter Walsh, thus losing her unique identity as "Clarissa," only to become the snobbish "Mrs. Richard Dalloway."

William Faulkner
The Sound and the Fury

One of the greatest American novelists and short story writers was William Faulkner (1897–1962), whose novel cycle about the fictional Yoknapatawpha County, in Mississippi, earned him the Nobel Prize for literature in 1949. This novel cycle is viewed as both a legend of American life in the South and as a drama of human fortune. In slightly over one decade (from 1929–1942), Faulkner achieved greatness as an author, in spite of never having graduated from either high school or college and growing up in one of the poorest states in the nation during the Great Depression. Faulkner was born in New Albany, Mississippi, and was raised in Oxford, Mississippi, by a black woman named Caroline Barr, for whom he had a great deal of respect and admiration. Faulkner recalled that Aunt Callie (as he called her) encouraged him to tell the truth, to avoid wastefulness, and to be considerate of others, especially the weak and the elderly. She inspired the character of Dilsey Gibson in *The Sound and the Fury* (1929)—the omniscient narrator of the fourth section of the novel—as well as Mollie Beauchamp in *Go Down, Moses* (1942). Such characterizations ultimately compelled Faulkner to become a beleaguered spokesperson for the white liberal position regarding racial tensions in the South.

Faulkner considered *The Sound and the Fury* to be the best novel he ever wrote, and many critics continue to agree. By focusing on the promiscuous behavior of Candace "Caddy" Compson, the novel traces the demise of the Compson family once the most prominent family in Jackson, Mississippi; the family is a compelling symbol for the death of the "Old" South of pre–Civil War days. Faulkner, using stream of consciousness technique, tells her story through the eyes of her three brothers: Benjamin, Quentin, and Jason. To help the reader follow the shifting time sequences, Faulkner once considered having the publisher use different colors of ink to indicate a change in time, but he abandoned the idea, because it was too expensive. Instead, to indicate a shift in time, he put much of Benjy's section of the narrative in italics. But Benjy's narrative is still, by far, the most challenging, because the thirty-three-year-old Benjy has a severe mental disability and is unable to care for himself properly. The character of Benjy also gives rise to the title of the novel, which Faulkner borrowed from Shakespeare's tragedy, *Macbeth,* to describe the passage of time (even though Benjy has no sense of time) and the perceived meaninglessness of human existence:

> To-morrow, and to-morrow, and to-morrow
> Creeps in this petty pace from day to day
> To the last syllable of recorded time;
> And all our yesterdays have lighted fools
> The way to dusty. Death. Out, out, brief candle!
> Life's but a walking shadow, a poor player
> That struts and frets his hour upon the stage
> And then is heard no more. It is a tale
> Told by an idiot, full of sound and fury,
> Signifying nothing.
> (MACBETH, ACT 5, SCENE 5, LINES 19–28)

Indeed, *The Sound and the Fury* is a "tale told by an idiot," in this case Benjy Compson, whose thought processes skip backward and forward in time, as he relives events of the past, even while living in the present. Moreover, the Benjy narrative serves as a microcosm for the themes of the entire novel; Faulkner uses Benjy's mental deficiency as a symbol to foreshadow the demise of the Compson family. The section takes place on the day before Easter Sunday (April 7, 1928), which also happens to be Benjy's thirty-third birthday.[1] Readers are, however, initially confused by the black servants' references to him as "Maury," until they find out that his name was changed to Benjy in 1900 (another of his recollections) when his family discovered that he was severely mentally disabled. The passage excerpted below reveals Benjy's recollection of an incident in 1898, when he was three years old, that had a powerful effect on him. It also serves to foreshadow the sullying of the Compson name by Caddy's promiscuity. The participants in the scene are Luster, Dilsey's grandson, who is half the age of Benjy but who, nonetheless, serves as his caretaker; Versh, Dilsey's son; and Roskus, Dilsey's husband. The episode begins in the present on a golf course—"Benjy's pasture," which was once part of the Compson estate. But as soon as the golfers call for their caddie, Benjy starts to moan and is mentally transported back in time as he remembers his sister, Caddy, how she fell down in the "branch" (stream), and got her drawers all muddied (a symbol for the loss of her virginity), how the children tried to figure out a way to keep the "dirty" fact a secret from their parents, and how Luster was preoccupied with searching for his quarter, so that he could go to the minstrel show.

"Did a ball come down here."

"It ought to be in the water. Didn't any of you boys see it or hear it."

"Aint heard nothing come down here." Luster said. "Heard something hit that tree up yonder. Dont know which way it went."

They looked in the branch.

"Hell. Look along the branch. It came down here. I saw it."

They looked along the branch. Then they went back up the hill.

"Have you got that ball." the boy said.

---

[1] Many critics view Benjy as a Christ figure. They cite the fact that he, like Jesus, is thirty-three years old and that his life has been filled with patient suffering.

"What I want with it." Luster said. "I aint seen no ball."

The boy got in the water. He went on. He turned and looked at Luster again. He went on down the branch.

The man said "Caddie" up the hill. The boy got out of the water and went up the hill.

"Now, just listen at you." Luster said. "Hush up."

"What he moaning about now."

"Lawd knows." Luster said. "He just starts like that. He been at it all morning. Cause it his birthday, I reckon."

"How old he."

He thirty-three." Luster said. "Thirty-three this morning."

"You mean, he been three years old thirty years."

"I going by what mammy say." Luster said. "I dont know. We going to have thirty-three candles on a cake, anyway. Little cake. Wont hardly hold them. Hush up. Come on back here." He came and caught my arm. "You old loony." he said. "You want me to whip you."

"I bet you will."

"I is done it. Hush, now." Luster said. "Aint I told you you cant go up there. They'll knock your head clean off with one of them balls. Come on, here." He pulled me back. "Sit down." I sat down and he took off my shoes and rolled up my trousers. "Now, git in that water and play and see can you stop that slobbering and moaning."

Benjy's mind drifts back to when he was very young.

I hushed and got in the water *and Roskus came and said to come to supper and Caddy said,*

It's not supper time yet. I'm not going.

She was wet. We were playing in the branch and Caddy squatted down and got her dress wet and Versh said,

"Your mommer going to whip you for getting your dress wet."

"She's not going to do any such thing." Caddy said.

"How do you know." Quentin said.

"That's all right how I know." Caddy said. "How do you know."

"She said she was." Quentin said. "Besides, I'm older than you."

"I'm seven years old." Caddy said, "I guess I know."

"I'm older than that." Quentin said. "I go to school. Dont I, Versh."

"I'm going to school next year." Caddy said, "When it comes. Aint I, Versh."

"You know she whip you when you get your dress wet." Versh said.

"It's not wet." Caddy said. She stood up in the water and looked at her dress. "I'll take it off." she said. "Then it'll dry."

"I bet you wont." Quentin said.

"I bet I will." Caddy said.

"I bet you better not." Quentin said.

Caddy came to Versh and me and turned her back.

"Unbutton it, Versh." she said.

"Dont you do it, Versh." Quentin said.

"Taint none of my dress." Versh said.

"You unbutton it, Versh." Caddy said, "Or I'll tell Dilsey what you did yesterday." So Versh unbuttoned it.

"You just take your dress off." Quentin said. Caddy took her dress off and threw it on the bank. Then she didn't have on anything but her bodice and drawers, and Quentin slapped her and she slipped and fell down in the water. When she got up she began to splash water on Quentin, and Quentin splashed water on Caddy. Some of it splashed on Versh and me and Versh picked me up and put me on the bank. He said he was going to tell on Caddy and Quentin, and then Quentin and Caddy began to splash water at Versh. He got behind a bush.

"I'm going to tell mammy on you all." Versh said.

Quentin climbed up the bank and tried to catch Versh, but Versh ran away and Quentin couldn't. When Quentin came back Versh stopped and hollered that he was going to tell. Caddy told him that if he wouldn't tell, they'd let him come back. So Versh said he wouldn't, and they let him.

"Now I guess you're satisfied." Quentin said, "We'll both get whipped now."

"I dont care." Caddy said. "I'll run away."

"Yes you will." Quentin said.

"I'll run away and never come back." Caddy said. I began to cry. Caddy turned around and said "Hush." So I hushed. Then they played in the branch. Jason was playing too. He was by himself further down the branch. Versh came around the bush and lifted me down into the water again. Caddy was all wet and muddy behind, and I started to cry and she came and squatted in the water.

"Hush now." she said. "I'm not going to run away." So I hushed. Caddy smelled like trees in the rain.

What is the matter with you, Luster said. Cant you get done with that moaning and play in the branch like folks.

Whyn't you take him on home. Didn't they told you not to take him off the place.

He still think they own this pasture, Luster said. Cant nobody see down here front the house, noways.

We can. And folks dont like to look at a loony. Taint no luck in it.

Roskus came and said to come to supper and Caddy said it wasn't supper time yet.

"Yes tis." Roskus said. "Dilsey say for you all to come on to the house. Bring them on, Versh." He went up the hill, where the cow was lowing.

"Maybe we'll be dry by the time we get to the house." Quentin said.

"It was all your fault." Caddy said. "I hope we do get whipped." She put her dress on and Versh buttoned it.

"They wont know you got wet." Versh said. "It dont show on you. Less me and Jason tells."

"Are you going to tell, Jason." Caddy said.

"Tell on who." Jason said.

"He wont tell." Quentin said. "Will you, Jason."

"I bet he does tell." Caddy said. "He'll tell Damuddy."[2]

"He cant tell her." Quentin said. "She's sick. If we walk slow it'll be too dark for them to see."

"I dont care whether they see or not." Caddy said. "I'm going to tell, myself. You carry him up the hill, Versh."

"Jason wont tell." Quentin said. "You remember that bow and arrow I made you, Jason."

"It's broke now." Jason said.

"Let him tell." Caddy said. "I dont give a cuss. Carry Maury tip the hill, Versh." Versh squatted and I got on his back.

See you all at the show tonight, Luster said. Come on, here. We got to find that quarter.

Caddy is a mother figure to Benjy, as she provided order, comfort, and affection to him when he was still young. Consequently, he loves her very much and is deeply devoted to her, but when she becomes involved in an ill-fated marriage, Benjy loses her and the event plunges him into emotional chaos. In the following passage, Benjy reflects on this loss of Caddy. He remembers drinking "sassparilluh" with T.P. (one of Dilsey's sons who helps take care of him) and about how T.P. told him to "hush" so that their parents would not discover them. Most important, Benjy reflects on his memories of Christmas 1905 when Caddy used perfume for the first time and did not "smell like trees." She was, however, able to go to the bathroom and wash the smell away. When Caddy becomes sexually active, Benjy associates her promiscuous behavior with her not smelling like trees. Later, Benjy tries to push her into the bathroom, hoping to wash away her "sins" of promiscuity—another link to the scene at the branch in 1898. Benjy thus associates his sister's virginity to the smell of trees and her promiscuity to her using perfume and not smelling like trees.

Then I saw Caddy, with flowers in her hair, and a long veil like shining wind. Caddy. Caddy

"Hush." T.P. said, "They going to hear you. Get down quick." He pulled me. Caddy. I clawed my hands against the wall Caddy. T.P. pulled me.

"Hush." he said, "Hush. Come on here quick." He pulled me on. Caddy "Hush up, Benjy. You want them to hear you. Come on, les drink some more sassprilluh, then we can come back if you hush. We better get one more bottle or we both be hollering. We can say Dan drunk it. Mr Quentin always saying he so smart, we can say he sassprilluh dog, too."

The moonlight came down the cellar stairs. We drank some more sassprilluh.

"You know what I wish." T.P. said. "I wish a bear would walk in that cellar door. You know what I do. I walk right up

to him and spit in he eye. Gimme that bottle to stop my mouth before I holler."

T.P. fell down. He began to laugh, and the cellar door and the moonlight jumped away and something hit me.

"Hush up." T.P. said, trying not to laugh, "Lawd, they'll all hear us. Get up." T.P. said, "Get up, Benjy, quick." He was thrashing about and laughing and I tried to get up. The cellar steps ran up the hill in the moonlight and T.P. fell up the hill, into the moonlight, and I ran against the fence and T.P. ran behind me saying "Hush up hush up" Then he fell into the flowers, laughing, and I ran into the box. But when I tried to climb onto it it jumped away and hit me on the back of the head and my throat made a sound. It made the sound again and I stopped trying to get up, and it made the sound again and I began to cry. But throat kept on making the sound while T.P. was pulling me. It kept on making it and I couldn't tell if I was crying or not, and T.P. fell down on top of me, laughing, and it kept on making the sound and Quentin kicked T.P. and Caddy put her arms around me, and her shining veil, and I couldn't smell trees anymore and I began to cry.

Benjy, Caddy said, Benjy. She put her arms around me again, but I went away. "What is it, Benjy." she said, "Is it this hat." She took her hat off and came again, and I went away.

"Benjy." she said, "What is it, Benjy. What has Caddy done."

"He dont like that prissy dress." Jason said. "You think you're grown up, dont you. You think you're better than anybody else, dont you. Prissy."

"You shut your mouth." Caddy said, "You dirty little beast. Benjy."

"Just because you are fourteen, you think you're grown up, dont you." Jason said. "You think you're something. Dont you."

"Hush, Benjy." Caddy said. "You'll disturb Mother. Hush."

But I didn't hush, and when she went away I followed, and she stopped on the stairs and waited and I stopped too.

"What is it, Benjy." Caddy said, "Tell Caddy. She'll do it. Try."

"Candace." Mother said.

"Yessum." Caddy said.

"Why are you teasing him." Mother said. "Bring him here."

We went to Mother's room, where she was lying with the sickness on a cloth on her head.

"What is the matter now." Mother said. "Benjamin."

"Benjy." Caddy said. She came again, but I went away.

"You must have done something to him." Mother said. "Why wont you let him alone, so I can have some peace. Give him the box and please go on and let him alone."

Caddy got the box and set it on the floor and opened it. It was full of stars. When I was still, they were still. When I moved, they glinted and sparkled. I hushed.

Then I heard Caddy walking and I began again.

"Benjamin." Mother said, "Come here." I went to the door. "You, Benjamin." Mother said.

"What is it now." Father said, "Where are you going."

"Take him downstairs and get someone to watch him, Jason." Mother said. "You know I'm ill, yet you"

Father shut the door behind us.

"T.P." he said.

"Sir." T.P. said downstairs.

"Benjy's coming down." Father said. "Go with T.P."

I went to the bathroom door. I could hear the water.

"Benjy." T.P. said downstairs.

I could hear the water. I listened to it.

"Benjy." T.P. said downstairs.

I listened to the water.

I couldn't hear the water, and Caddy opened the door.

"Why, Benjy." she said. She looked at me and I went and she put her arms around me. "Did you find Caddy again." she said. "Did you think Caddy had run away." Caddy smelled like trees.

We went to Caddy's room. She sat down at the mirror. She stopped her hands and looked at me.

"Why, Benjy. What is it." she said. "You mustn't cry. Caddy's not going away. See here." she said. She took up the bottle and took the stopper out and held it to my nose. "Sweet. Smell. Good."

I went away and I didn't hush, and she held the bottle in her hand, looking at me.

"Oh." she said. She put the bottle down and came and put her arms around me. "So that was it. And you were trying to tell Caddy and you couldn't tell her. You wanted to,

but you couldn't, could you. Of course Caddy wont. Of course Caddy wont. Just wait till I dress."

Caddy dressed and took up the bottle again and we went down to the kitchen.

"Dilsey." Caddy said, "Benjy's got a present for you." She stooped down and put the bottle in my hand. "Hold it out to Dilsey, now." Caddy held my hand out and Dilsey took the bottle.

"Well I'll declare." Dilsey said, "If my baby aint give Dilsey a bottle of perfume. Just look here, Roskus."

Caddy smelled like trees. "We dont like perfume ourselves." Caddy said.

She smelled like trees.

Benjy often stood at the iron gate, waiting for Caddy to come home from school, and he continued to do so even after she was gone. But when he chased some girls to tell them how much he missed Caddy, the Compsons had him castrated in the false belief that Benjy was trying to sexually molest the girls. Benjy's castration serves as another symbol for the death of the Compson family line, and many of his reflections deal with death—of his grandmother Damuddy, his father, their servant Roskus, their horse Nancy, and the suicide of his brother Quentin. Each death symbolically augments the demise of the Compsons. Benjy's section concludes with a final reference to Caddy's soiled drawers and how Dilsey will not have time to bathe Caddy until morning.

5 Sex Outside of the Victorian Closet

The Victorian Age is generally regarded as prudish and sexually repressive; well-bred Victorians were expected to resist sexual temptation. Victorians assumed that "decent" women had no sexual appetites and that men represented a sinful, lustful, and fallen humanity who preyed on women. Women came to be portrayed in one of two ways—either as insatiable sexual harlots or as chaste and frigid innocents. But an American female writer, Kate Chopin, and a British male writer, D. H. Lawrence, put an end to such stereotypical characterizations. In their novels they created portraits of women who fight to end their subjugation to men and are vibrant and sexually responsive.

Kate Chopin
The Awakening

After her husband's death in 1882, Kate Chopin (1850–1904), with her six children, moved back to St. Louis, the city of her birth, and began a career as a celebrated "local color" writer. In 1889, Chopin published her first novel which was a failure, but it did establish the theme for which Chopin is best known—a submissive woman struggling to end her subjugation to a man. In 1899, Chopin dealt with the theme of female oppression and a woman's need to feel emotionally and sexually fulfilled in her "scandalous" second (and final) novel *The Awakening.* The novel opens in the city of New Orleans with the image of a caged parrot endlessly repeating "*Allez vous-en! Allez vous-en!* That's all right!" to symbolize the entrapment of the novel's protagonist, Mrs. Edna Pontellier. Edna feels confined by her roles—as mother to Raoul and Ètienne, and as wife to Léonce, who is twelve years her senior and views her as "a valuable piece of personal property." While vacationing with Léonce at Grand Isle, Edna makes the acquaintance of Madame Lebrun's son, Robert (two years her junior), with whom she eventually enters into an adulterous relationship.

In the following passage, using symbols of the sea, Chopin documents the emerging passion of Edna for Robert as she awakens to herself as a sexual being. When Robert invites her to go swimming, Edna resists, for she is a weak swimmer, but she is lured by the sea's "sonorous murmur" and Robert's insistence, which is laden with sexual overtones.

Mrs. Pontellier had brought her sketching materials, which she sometimes dabbled with in an unprofessional way. She liked the dabbling. She felt in it satisfaction of a kind which no other employment afforded her.

She had long wished to try herself on Madame Ratignolle.[1] Never had that lady seemed a more tempting subject than at that moment, seated there like some sensuous Madonna, with the gleam of the fading day enriching her splendid color.

Robert crossed over and seated himself upon the step below Mrs. Pontellier, that he might watch her work. She handled her brushes with a certain ease and freedom which came, not from long and close acquaintance with them, but from a natural aptitude. Robert followed her work with close attention, giving forth little ejaculatory expressions of appreciation in French, which he addressed to Madame Ratignolle.

"*Mais ce n'est pas mal! Elle s'y connait, elle a de la force, oui.*"[2]

During his oblivious attention he once quietly rested his head against Mrs. Pontellier's arm. As gently she repulsed him. Once again he repeated the offense. She could not but believe it to be thoughtlessness on his part, yet that was no reason she should submit to it. She did not remonstrate, except again to repulse him quietly but firmly. He offered no apology.

The picture completed bore no resemblance to Madame Ratignolle. She was greatly disappointed to find that it did not look like her. But it was a fair enough piece of work, and in many respects satisfying.

Mrs. Pontellier evidently did not think so. After surveying the sketch critically she drew a broad smudge of paint across its surface, and crumpled the paper between her hands.

The youngsters came tumbling up the steps, the quadroon following at the respectful distance which they required her to observe. Mrs. Pontellier made them carry her paints and things into the house. She sought to detain them for a little talk and some pleasantry. But they were greatly in earnest. They had only come to investigate the contents of the bonbon box. They accepted without murmuring what she chose to give them, each holding out two chubby hands scoop-like, in the vain hope that they might be filled; and then away they went.

The sun was low in the West, and the breeze soft and languorous that came up from the south, charged with the seductive odor of the sea. Children, freshly befurbeloved [adorned], were gathering for their games under the oaks. Their voices were high and penetrating.

Madame Ratignolle folded her sewing, placing thimble, scissors and thread all neatly together in the roll, which she pinned securely. She complained of faintness. Mrs. Pontellier flew for the cologne water and a fan. She bathed Madame Ratignolle's face with cologne, while Robert plied the fan with unnecessary vigor.

The spell was soon over, and Mrs. Pontellier could not help wondering if there were not a little imagination responsible for its origin, for the rose tint had never faded from her friend's face.

She stood watching the fair woman walk down the long line of galleries[3] with the grace and majesty which queens are sometimes supposed to possess. Her little ones ran to meet her. Two of them clung about her white skirts, the third she took from its nurse and with a thousand endearments bore it along in her own fond, encircling arms. Though, as

---

[1]Madame Adèle Ratignolle is one of Edna's closest friends. She represents the Victorian ideal of the proper role of women in society. She is a married Creole woman who exudes a sense of grace, elegance, and charm—all the while she is a devoted mother and wife.

[2]"But it's not bad. She knows what she's doing, she has ability, hasn't she?"

---

[3]Galleries are verandas or balconies.

ever[y]body well knew, the doctor had forbidden her to lift so much as a pin!

"Are you going bathing?" asked Robert of Mrs. Pontellier. It was not so much a question as a reminder

"Oh, no," she answered, with a tone of indecision. "I'm tired; I think not." Her glance wandered from his face away toward the Gulf, whose sonorous murmur reached her like a loving but imperative entreaty.

"Oh, come," he insisted. "You mustn't miss your bath. Come on. The water must be delicious; it will not hurt you. Come."

He reached up for her big, rough straw hat that hung on a peg outside the door, and put it on her head. They descended the steps, and walked away together toward the beach. The sun was low in the west and the breeze was soft and warm.

VI

Edna Pontellier could not have told why, wishing to go to the beach with Robert, she should in the first place have declined, and in the second place have followed in obedience to one of the two contradictory impulses which impelled her.

A certain light was beginning to dawn dimly within her—the light which, showing the way, forbids it.

At that early period it served but to bewilder her. It moved her to dreams, to thoughtfulness, to the shadowy anguish which had overcome her the midnight when she had abandoned herself to tears.

In short, Mrs. Pontellier was beginning to realize her position in the universe, as a human being, and to recognize her relations as an individual to the world within and about her. This may seem like a ponderous weight of wisdom to descend upon the soul of a young woman of twenty-eight—perhaps more wisdom than the Holy Ghost is usually pleased to vouchsafe to any woman.

But the beginning of things, of a world especially, is necessarily vague, tangled, chaotic, and exceedingly disturbing. How few of us ever emerge from such beginning! How many souls perish in its tumult!

The voice of the sea is seductive; never ceasing, whispering, clamoring, murmuring, inviting the soul to wander for a spell in abysses of solitude: to lose itself in mazes of inward contemplation.

The voice of the sea speaks to the soul. The touch of the sea is sensuous, enfolding the body in its soft, close embrace.

Following her first summer visit to Grand Isle, Edna's awakening to her sexual self cuts against the grain of her identity as "Mrs. Pontellier" and mother of her children. She has come to value her freedom, art, and music. Consequently, she seeks to become an independent female artist and enters into an adulterous affair with Alcée Arobin, a gigolo in New

Orleans. By the end of the novel, however, Robert has permanently left her, and a despondent Edna decides to free herself from her societal entrapment by drowning herself. As she walks on the beach, she hears the sea seductively beckoning her. She sheds all of her clothing—symbolic of her freeing herself from the confinement of societal norms—and steps into the open air. She finally enters the sea, embracing it as she would a lover, drowning herself in its passion.

Edna walked on down to the beach rather mechanically, not noticing anything special except that the sun was hot. She was not dwelling upon any particular train of thought. She had done all the thinking which was necessary after Robert went away, when she lay awake upon the sofa till morning.

She had said over and over to herself: "Today it is Arobin; tomorrow it will be some one else. It makes no difference to me, it doesn't matter about Léonce Pontellier—but Raoul and Étienne!" She understood now clearly what she had meant long ago when she said to Adèle Ratignolle that she would give up the unessential, but she would never sacrifice herself for her children.

Despondency had come upon her there in the wakeful night, and had never lifted. There was no one thing in the world that she desired. There was no human being whom she wanted near her except Robert; and she even realized that the day would come when he, too, and the thought of him would melt out of her existence, leaving her alone. The children appeared before her like antagonists who had overcome her, who had overpowered and sought to drag her into the soul's slavery for the rest of her days. But she knew a way to elude them. She was not thinking of these things when she walked down to the beach.

The water of the Gulf stretched out before her, gleaming with the million lights of the sun. The voice of the sea is seductive, never ceasing, whispering, clamoring, murmuring, inviting the soul to wander in abysses of solitude. All along the white beach, up and down, there was no living thing in sight. A bird with a broken wing was beating the air above, reeling, fluttering, circling disabled down, down to the water.

Edna had found her old bathing suit still hanging, faded, upon its accustomed peg.

She put it on, leaving her clothing in the bath house. But when she was there beside the sea, absolutely alone, she cast the unpleasant, pricking garments from her, and for the first time in her life she stood naked in the open air, at the mercy of the sun, the breeze that beat upon her, and the waves that invited her.

How strange and awful it seemed to stand naked under the sky! how delicious! She felt like some new-born creature, opening its eyes in a familiar world that it had never known.

The foamy wavelets curled up to her white feet, and coiled like serpents about her ankles. She walked out. The water was chill, but she walked on. The water was deep, but she lifted her white body and reached out with a long, sweeping stroke. The touch of the sea is sensuous, enfolding the body in its soft, close embrace.

She went on and on. She remembered the night she swam far out, and recalled the terror that seized her at the fear of being unable to regain the shore. She did not look back now, but went on and on, thinking of the bluegrass meadow that she had traversed when a little child, believing that it had no beginning and no end.

Her arms and legs were growing tired.

She thought of Léonce and the children. They were a part of her life. But they need not have thought that they could possess her, body and soul. How Mademoiselle Reisz[4] would have laughed, perhaps sneered, if she knew! "And you call yourself an artist! What pretensions, Madame! The artist must possess the courageous soul that dares and defies."

Exhaustion was pressing upon and overpowering her. "Good-by—because, I love you." He did not know; he did not understand. He would never understand. Perhaps Doctor Mandelet[5] would have understood if she had seen him—but it was too late; the shore was far behind her, and her strength was gone.

She looked into the distance, and the old terror flamed up for an instant, then sank again. Edna heard her father's voice and her sister Margaret's. She heard the barking of an old dog that was chained to the sycamore tree. The spurs of the cavalry officer clanged as he walked across the porch. There was the hum of bees, and the musky odor of pinks filled the air.

---

[4]Mademoiselle Reisz epitomizes everything that Edna would like to be. She is an unmarried, self-sufficient woman who is an accomplished pianist. It is she who inspires Edna to take her painting seriously.

[5]Doctor Mandelet is Edna's personal physician who worries about her passionate, socially unacceptable, transformation; and he urges her to become a devoted wife and mother again.

D. H. Lawrence
Lady Chatterley's Lover

David Herbert Lawrence (1885–1930), the son of an illiterate British coal miner whose bawdy drunkenness conflicted severely with his wife's gentility, was one of the most important, yet controversial, novelists of the twentieth century.

Lawrence was saddened and angered by the consequences of industrial society: the deterioration of nature, tedious, regimented work divorced from personal satisfaction, and a life-denying quest for wealth and possessions at the expense of humanitarian concerns. Thus, in *Women in Love* (1921), the new owner of the family coal mine, determined to utilize modern management techniques in order to extract greater wealth from the business, dismisses the human needs of the workers:

Suddenly he had conceived the pure instrumentality of mankind. There had been so much humanitarianism, so much talk of sufferings and feelings. It was ridiculous. The sufferings and feelings of individuals did not matter in the least. . . . What mattered was the pure instrumentality of the individual. As a man as of a knife: does it cut well? Nothing else mattered.

Everything in the world has its function and is good or not good in so far as it fulfills this function. . . . Was a miner a good miner? Then he was complete.

Lawrence looked back longingly on preindustrial England and wanted people to reorient their thinking away from moneymaking and suppression of the instincts.

Lawrence's affirmation of sexual passion as both necessary and beneficial for a fulfilling life led him to rail against cultural norms, including puritanical attitudes that stifled human sexuality and disfigured it with shame and guilt. His feelings about sex were poignantly expressed in his highly erotic novel, *Lady Chatterley's Lover* (1928). Because of its use of four-letter words and intimate descriptions of sexual activity, Lawrence was forced to publish it in Italy. An unexpurgated version was not released in Britain until 1960, after a celebrated trial.

Lady Chatterley, married to Sir Clifford, who considers sex distasteful, has an affair with the gamekeeper, Mellors, a commoner who exudes sexuality and whose passionate lovemaking is deeply tender.

In the following passage from *Lady Chatterley's Lover*, Mellors tells Lady Chatterley that modern industrial-capitalist society has taken the joy out of life, that it is necessary for human beings to rediscover the virtue of passion.

"Let's live for summat else. Let's not live ter make money, neither for us-selves not for anybody else. Now we're forced to. We're forced to make a bit for us-selves, an' a fair lot for th' bosses. Let's stop it! Bit by bit, let's stop it. We needn't rant an' rave. Bit by bit, let's drop the whole industrial life an' go back. The least little bit o' money'll do. For everybody, me an' you, bosses an' masters, even th' king. The least little bit o' money'll really do. Just make up your mind to it, an' you've got out o' th' mess." He paused, then went on:

"An' I'd tell 'em: Look! Look at Joe! He moves lovely! Look how he moves, alive and aware. He's beautiful! An' look at Jonah! He's clumsy, he's ugly, because he's niver willin' to rouse himself. I'd tell 'em: Look! look at yourselves! one shoulder higher than t'other, legs twisted, feet all lumps! What have yer done ter yerselves, wi' the blasted work? Spoilt yerselves. No need to work that much. Take yer clothes off an' look at yourselves. Yer ought ter be alive an' beautiful, an' yer ugly an' half dead. So I'd tell 'em. An' I'd get my men to wear different clothes: 'appen close red trousers, bright red, an' little short white jackets. Why, if men had red, fine legs, that alone would change them in a month. They'd begin to be men again, to be men! An' the women could dress as they liked. Because if once the men walked with legs close bright scarlet, and buttocks nice and showing scarlet under a little white jacket: then the women 'ud begin to be women. It's because th' men *aren't* men, that th' women have to be.—An in time pull down Tevershall and build a few beautiful buildings, that would hold us all. An' clean the country up again. An' not have many children, because the world is overcrowded.

But I wouldn't preach to the men: only strip 'em an' say: "Look at yourselves! That's workin' for money!—Hark at yourselves! That's working for money. You've been working for money! Look at Tevershall! It's horrible. That's because it was built while you was working for money. Look at your girls! They don't care about you, you don't care about them. It's because you've spent your time working an' caring for money. You can't talk nor move nor live, you can't properly be with a woman. You're not alive. Look at yourselves!"

There fell a complete silence. Connie was half listening, and threading in the hair at the root of his belly a few forget-me-nots that she had gathered on the way to the hut. Outside, the world had gone still, and a little icy.

"You've got four kinds of hair," she said to him. "On your chest it's nearly black, and your hair isn't dark on your head: but your mustache is hard and dark red, and your hair here, your love-hair, is like a little bush of bright red-gold mistletoe. It's the loveliest of all!"

He looked down and saw the milky bits of forget-me-nots in the hair on his groin.

"Ay! That's where to put forget-me-nots, in the man-hair, or the maiden-hair. But don't you care about the future?"

She looked up at him.

"Oh, I do, terribly!" she said.

"Because when I feel the human world is doomed, has doomed itself by its own mingy beastliness, then I feel the Colonies aren't far enough. The moon wouldn't be far enough, because even there you could look back and see the earth, dirty, beastly, unsavory among all the stars: made foul by men. Then I feel I've swallowed gall, and it's eating my inside out, and nowhere's far enough away to get away. But when I get a turn, I forget it all again. Though it's a shame, what's been done to people these last hundred years: men turned into nothing but labour-insects, and all their manhood taken away, and all their real life. I'd wipe the machines off the face of the earth again, and end the industrial epoch absolutely, like a black mistake. But since I can't, an' nobody can, I'd better hold my peace, an' try an' live my own life: if I've got one to live, which I rather doubt."

The thunder had ceased outside, but the rain which had abated, suddenly came striking down, with a last blench of lightning and mutter of departing storm. Connie was uneasy. He had talked so long now, and he was really talking to himself, not to her. Despair seemed to come down on him completely, and she was feeling happy, she hated despair. She knew her leaving him, which he had only just realised inside himself, had plunged him back into this mood. And she triumphed a little.

She opened the door and looked at the straight heavy rain, like a steel curtain, and had a sudden desire to rush out into it, to rush away. She got up, and began swiftly pulling off her stockings, then her dress and underclothing, and he held his breath. Her pointed keen animal breasts tipped and stirred as she moved. She was ivory-coloured in the greenish light. She slipped on her rubber shoes again and ran out with a wild little laugh, holding up her breasts to the heavy rain and spreading her arms, and running blurred in the rain with the eurythmic dance-movements she had learned so long ago in Dresden. It was a strange pallid figure lifting and falling, bending so the rain beat and glistened on the full haunches, swaying up again and coming belly-forward through the rain, then stooping again so that only the full loins and buttocks were offered in a kind of homage towards him, repeating a wild obeisance.

He laughed wryly, and threw off his clothes. It was too much. He jumped out, naked and white, with a little shiver, into the hard slanting rain. Flossie sprang before him with a frantic little bark. Connie, her hair all wet and sticking to her head, turned her hot face and saw him. Her blue eyes blazed with excitement as she turned and ran fast, with a strange charging movement, out of the clearing and down the path, the wet boughs whipping her. She ran, and he saw nothing but the round wet head, the wet back leaning forward in flight, the rounded buttocks twinkling: a wonderful cowering female nakedness in flight.

She was nearly at the wide riding when he came up and flung his naked arm round her soft, naked-wet middle. She gave a shriek and straightened herself, and the heap of her soft, chill flesh came up against his body. He pressed it all up against him, madly, the heap of soft, chilled female flesh that became quickly warm as flame, in contact. The rain streamed on them till they smoked. He gathered her lovely, heavy posteriors one in each hand and pressed them in towards him in a frenzy, quivering motionless in the rain. Then suddenly he tipped her up and fell with her on the path, in the roaring silence of the rain, and short and sharp, he took her, short and sharp and finished, like an animal.

He got up in an instant, wiping the rain from his eyes.

"Come in," he said, and they started running back to the hut. He ran straight and swift: he didn't like the rain. But she came slower, gathering forget-me-nots and campion and bluebells, running a few steps and watching him fleeting away from her.

When she came with her flowers, panting to the hut, he had already started a fire, and the twigs were crackling. Her sharp breasts rose and fell, her hair was plastered down with rain, her face was flushed ruddy and her body glistened and trickled. Wide-eyed and breathless, with a small wet head and full, trickling, naïve haunches, she looked another creature.

He took the old sheet and rubbed her down, she standing like a child. Then he rubbed himself, having shut the door of the hut. The fire was blazing up. She ducked her head in the other end of the sheet, and rubbed her wet hair.

"We're drying ourselves together on the same towel, we shall quarrel!" he said.

She looked up for a moment, her hair all odds and ends.

"No!" she said, her eyes wide. "It's not a towel, it's a sheet."

And she went on busily rubbing her head, while he busily rubbed his.

Still panting with their exertions, each wrapped in an army blanket, but the front of the body open to the fire, they sat on a log side by side before the blaze, to get quiet. Connie hated the feel of the blanket against her skin. But now the sheet was all wet.

She dropped her blanket and kneeled on the clay hearth, holding her head to the fire, and shaking her hair to dry it.

He watched the beautiful curving drop of her haunches. That fascinated him to-day. How it sloped with a rich down-slope to the heavy roundness of her buttocks! And in between, folded in the secret warmth, the secret entrances!

He stroked her tail with his hand, long and subtly taking in the curves and the globe-fulness.

"Tha's got such a nice tail on thee," he said, in the throaty caressive dialect. "Tha's got the nicest arse of anybody. It's the nicest, nicest woman's arse as is! An' ivry bit of it is woman, woman sure as nuts. Tha'rt not one o' them buttonarsed lasses as should be lads, are ter! Tha's got a real soft sloping bottom on thee, as a man loves in 'is guts. It's a bottom as could hold the world up, it is!"

All the while he spoke he exquisitely stroked the rounded tail, till it seem[e]d as if a slippery sort of fire came from it into his hands. And his finger-tips touched the two secret openings to her body, time after time, with a soft little brush of fire.

Sir Clifford, who is unaware of his wife's affair, tells Lady Chatterley with approval about a scientific-religious book he is reading in which the author maintains: "The universe shows us two aspects: on one side it is physically wasting, on the other it is spiritually ascending." Lady Chatterley, still fresh from her immensely satisfying lovemaking with Mellors, replies:

"What silly hocus-pocus! As if his little conceited consciousness could know what was happening as slowly as all that! It only means *he's* a physical failure on the earth, so he wants to make the whole universe a physical failure. Priggish little impertinence!"

"Oh but listen! Don't interrupt the great man's solemn words!—The present type of order in the world has risen from an unimaginable past, and will find its grave in an unimaginable future. There remains the inexhaustive realm of abstract forms, and creativity with its shifting character ever determined afresh by its own creatures, and God, upon whose wisdom all forms of order depend.—There, that's how he winds up!"

Connie sat listening contemptuously.

"He's spiritually blown out," she said. "What a lot of stuff! Unimaginables, and types of order in graves, and realms of abstract forms, and creativity with a shifty character, and God mixed up with forms of order! Why it's idiotic!"

"I must say, it is a little vaguely conglomerate, a mixture of gases, so to speak," said Clifford. "Still, I think there is something in the idea that the universe is physically wasting and spiritually ascending."

"Do you? Then let it ascend, so long as it leaves me safely and solidly physically here below."

"Do you like your physique?" he asked.

"I love it!" And through her mind went the words: It's the nicest, nicest woman's arse as is!

"But that is really rather extraordinary, because there's no denying it's an encumbrance. But then I suppose a woman doesn't take a supreme pleasure in the life of the mind."

"Supreme pleasure?" she said, looking up at him. "Is that sort of idiocy the supreme pleasure of the life of the mind? no thank you! Give me the body. I believe the life of the body is a greater reality than the life of the mind: when the body is really wakened to life. But so many people, like your famous wind-machine, have only got minds tacked on to their physical corpses."

He looked at her in wonder.

"The life of the body," he said, "is just the life of the animals."

"And that's better than the life of professional corpses. But it's not true! The human body is only just coming to real life. With the Greeks it gave a lovely flicker, then Plato and Aristotle killed it, and Jesus finished it off. But now the body is coming really to life, it is really rising from the tomb. And it will be a lovely, lovely life in the lovely universe, the life of the human body."

"My dear, you speak as if you were ushering it all in! True, you are going away on a holiday: but don't please be quite so indecently elated about it. Believe me, whatever God there is is slowly eliminating the guts and alimentary system from the human being, to evolve a higher, more spiritual being."

"Why should I believe you, Clifford, when I feel that whatever God there is has at last wakened up in my guts, as you call them, and is rippling so happily there, like dawn. Why should I believe you, when I feel so very much the contrary?"

Before departing on a vacation abroad, Lady Chatterley determines to have one more sexual encounter with Mellors.

It was a night of sensual passion, in which she was a little startled and almost unwilling: yet pierced again with piercing thrills of sensuality, different, sharper, more terrible than the thrills of tenderness, but, at the moment, more desirable. Though a little frightened, she let him have his way, and the reckless, shameless sensuality shook her to her foundations, stripped her to the very last, and made a different woman of her. It was not really love. It was not voluptuousness. It was sensuality sharp and searing as fire, burning the soul to tinder.

Burning out the shames, the deepest, oldest shames, in the most secret places. It cost her an effort to let him have his way and his will of her. She had to be a passive, consenting thing, like a slave, a physical slave. Yet the passion licked round her, consuming, and when the sensual flame of it pressed through her bowels and breast, she really thought she was dying: yet a poignant, marvellous death.

She had often wondered what Abélard meant, when he said that in their year of love he and Heloïse had passed through all the stages and refinements of passion. The same

thing, a thousand years ago: ten thousand years ago! The same on the Greek vases, everywhere! The refinements of passion, the extravagances of sensuality! And necessary, forever necessary, to burn out false shames and smelt out the heaviest ore of the body into purity. With the fire of sheer sensuality.

In the short summer night she learnt so much. She would have thought a woman would have died of shame. Instead of which, the shame died. Shame, with [which] is fear: the deep organic shame, the old, old physical fear which crouches in the bodily tools of us, and can only be eased away by the sensual fire, at last it was roused up and routed by the phallic hunt of the man, and she became to the very heart of the jungle of herself. She felt, now, she had come to the real bed-rock of her nature, and was essentially shameless. She was her sensual self, naked and unashamed. She felt a triumph, almost a vainglory. So! That was how it was! That was life! That was how oneself really was! There was nothing left to disguise or be ashamed of. She shared her ultimate nakedness with a man, another being.

And what a reckless devil the man was! really like a devil! One had to be strong to bear him. But it took some getting at, the core of the physical jungle, the last and deepest recess of organic shame. The phallus alone could explore it. And how he had pressed in on her!

And how, in fear, she had hated it. But how she had really wanted it! She knew now. At the bottom of her soul, fundamentally, she had needed this phallic hunting out, she had secretly wanted it, and she had believed that she would never get it. Now suddenly there it was, and a man was sharing her last and final nakedness, she was shameless.

What liars poets and everybody were! They made one think one wanted sentiment. When what one supremely wanted was this piercing, consuming, rather awful sensuality. To find a man who dared do it, without shame or sin or final misgiving! If he had been ashamed afterwards, and made one feel ashamed, how awful! What a pity most men are so doggy, a bit shameful, like Clifford! Like Michaelis even! Both sensually a bit doggy and humiliating. The supreme pleasure of the mind! And what is that to a woman? What is it, really, to the man either! He becomes merely messy and doggy, even in his mind. It needs sheer sensuality even to purify and quicken the mind. Sheer fiery sensuality, not messiness.

Ah God, how rare a thing a man is! They are all dogs that trot and sniff and copulate. To have found a man who was not afraid and not ashamed! She looked at him now, sleeping so like a wild animal asleep, gone, gone in the remoteness of it. She nestled down, not to be away from him.

Till his rousing waked her completely. He was sitting up in bed, looking down at her. She saw her own nakedness in his eyes, immediate knowledge of her. And the fluid, male knowledge of herself seemed to flow to her from his eyes and wrap her voluptuously. Oh, how voluptuous and lovely it was to have limbs and body half-asleep, heavy and suffused with passion.

"Is it time to wake up?" she said.

"Half-past six." . . .

. . . He got up and threw off his pyjamas, and rubbed himself with a towel. When the human being is full of courage and full of life, how beautiful it is! So she thought, as she watched him in silence.

"Draw the curtain, will you?"

The sun was shining already on the tender green leaves of morning, and the wood stood bluey-fresh, in the nearness. She sat up in bed, looking dreamily out through the dormer window, her naked arms pushing her naked breasts together. He was dressing himself. She was half-dreaming of life, a life together with him: just a life.

He was going, fleeing from her dangerous, crouching nakedness.

"Have I lost my nightie altogether?" she said.

He pushed his hand down in the bed, and pulled out the bit of flimsy silk.

"I knowed I felt silk at my ankles," he said.

But the night-dress was slit almost in two.

"Never mind!" she said. "It belongs here, really. I'll leave it."

"Ay, leave it, I can put it between my legs at night, for company."

6 The Problem Play

Henrik Ibsen had introduced the problem play that dealt with contemporary social problems, including marital discord, capitalist greed and corruption, and the clash of generations. He also introduced poignant discussions in which the principal characters aired their views. Modernist playwrights, including the prolific Irish dramatist George Bernard Shaw (1856–1950), continued in the directions pioneered by Ibsen. Shaw's plays are distinguished by brilliant intellectual discussions around themes that reveal the dramatist's own political and ideological convictions and his moral passion to remedy injustice. (At the time, critics protested that didactic discussions have little dramatic appeal; they cannot hold an audience's interest, but for the most part, Shaw made them work.)

Shaw was a democratic socialist committed to the cause of social justice for the poor. He also denounced munitions manufacturers, imperialism, and the pursuit of military glory and was concerned with the preservation of personal integrity in a society that demanded conformity to tradition and acquiescence to authority. Shaw used drama as a vehicle for his ideas; he believed that drama was a way of compelling the public to rethink its morals, of influencing and converting minds. His plays, even the comedies, are replete with challenging, often significant, philosophical ideas, penetrating dialectical exchanges between articulate individuals who hold conflicting views, and critical analyses of current issues. For example, in an early play, *Widower's Houses* (1892), he posed the question: Should a bridegroom accept a dowry from his fiancé's father, a slumlord, who had obtained his wealth and middle-class respectability by shamelessly exploiting the poor?

George Bernard Shaw
Mrs. Warren's Profession

In several plays, Shaw's principal characters are strong-willed women striving to overcome enormous obstacles. Thus in *Pygmalion* (1912)—the basis for the Broadway and Hollywood hit, *My Fair Lady*—Eliza Doolittle demonstrates that she has become a self-confident woman capable of turning the tables on her arrogant mentor. In *Saint Joan* (1924), Shaw's most famous play, Joan of Arc is a strong-willed woman determined to do what God had commanded her through her voices despite the threat of being burned at the stake by the Inquisition. In *Mrs. Warren's Profession* (originally 1893, but censored until 1924), Shaw deals with prostitution, which was not considered a proper topic for polite Victorian society. At a young age, Mrs. Warren decides that selling her body is preferable to toiling long hours for starvation wages in a factory. In time, Mrs. Warren becomes a successful businesswoman, managing several brothels and able to provide her daughter with a good education and a comfortable bourgeois life style. Shaw, the social reformer, does not view Mrs. Warren as an immoral woman worthy of condemnation. Rather he condemns society for driving women to use their sexuality in order to advance themselves, if not to survive. Both of Mrs. Warren's stepsisters made proper choices, yet one died of lead poisoning and the other's alcoholic husband's meager wage could not support her three children. Mrs. Warren resolved to make a wiser choice.

The high point of the drama comes when the daughter discovers the mother's profession. Excerpts from this scene follow.

Mrs Warren ...D'you know what your gran'mother was?

Vivie No.

Mrs Warren No, you dont. I do. She called herself a widow and had a fried-fish shop down by the Mint, and kept herself and four daughters out of it. Two of us were sisters: that was me and Liz; and we were both good-looking and well made. I suppose our father was a well-fed man: mother pretended he was a gentleman; but I dont know. The other two were only half sisters: undersized, ugly, starved looking, hard working, honest poor creatures: Liz and I would have half-murdered them if mother hadnt half-murdered us to keep our hands off them. They were the respectable ones. Well, what did they get by their respectability? I'll tell you. One of them worked in a white-lead factory twelve hours a day for nine shillings a week until she died of lead poisoning. She only expected to get her hands a little paralyzed; but she died. The other was always held up to us as a model because she married a Government laborer in the Deptford victualling yard, and kept his room and the three children neat and tidy on eighteen shillings a week—until he took to drink. That was worth being respectable for, wasnt it?

Vivie (*now thoughtfully attentive*) Did you and your sister think so?

Mrs Warren Liz didnt, I can tell you: she had more spirit. We both went to a church school—that was part of the ladylike airs we gave ourselves to be superior to the children that know nothing and went nowhere—and we stayed there until Liz went out one night and never came back. I know the schoolmistress thought I'd soon follow her example; for the clergyman was always warning me that Lizzie'd end by jumping off Waterloo Bridge. Poor fool: that was all he knew about it! But I was more afraid of the whitelead factory than I was of the river; and so would you

have been in my place. That clergyman got me a situation as scullery maid in a temperance restaurant where they sent out for anything you liked. Then I was waitress; and then I went to the bar at Waterloo station: fourteen hours a day serving drinks and washing glasses for four shillings a week and my board. That was considered a great promotion for me. Well, one cold, wretched night, when I was so tired I could hardly keep myself awake, who should come up for a half of Scotch but Lizzie, in a long fur cloak, elegant and comfortable, with a lot of sovereigns in her purse.

Vivie (*grimly*) My aunt Lizzie!

Mrs Warren Yes; and a very good aunt to have, too. She's living down at Winchester now, close to the cathedral, one of the most respectable ladies there. Chaperones girls at the county ball, if you please. No river for Liz, thank you! You remind me of Liz a little: she was a first-rate business woman—saved money from the beginning—never let herself look too like what she was—never lost her head or threw away a chance. When she saw I'd grown up good-looking she said to me across the bar "What are you doing there, you little fool? wearing out your health and your appearance for other people's profit!" Liz was saving money then to take a house for herself in Brussels; and she thought we two could save faster than one. So she lent me some money and gave me a start; and I saved steadily and first paid her back, and then went into business with her as her partner. Why shouldnt I have done it? The home in Brussels was real high class: a much better place for a woman to be in than the factory where Anne Jane got poisoned. None of our girls were ever treated as I was treated in the scullery of that temperance place, or at the Waterloo bar, or at home. Would you have had me stay in them and become a worn out old drudge before I was forty?

Vivie (*intensely interested by this time*) No; but why did you choose that business? Saving money and good management will succeed in any business.

MRS WARREN Yes, saving money. But where can a woman get the money to save in any other business? Could you save out of four shillings a week and keep yourself dressed as well? Not you. Of course, if youre a plain woman and cant earn anything more; or if you have a turn for music, or the stage, or newspaper-writing: thats different. But neither Liz nor I had any turn for such things: all we had was our appearance and our turn for pleasing men. Do you think we were such fools as to let other people trade in our good looks by employing us as shopgirls, or barmaids, or waitresses, when we could trade in them ourselves and get all the profits instead of starvation wages? Not likely.

VIVIE You were certainly quite justified—from the business point of view.

MRS WARREN Yes; or any other point of view. What is any respectable girl brought up to do but to catch some rich man's fancy and get the benefit of his money by marrying him?—as if a marriage ceremony could make any difference in the right or wrong of the thing! Oh, the hypocrisy of the world makes me sick! Liz and I had to work and save and calculate just like other people; elseways we should be as poor as any good-for-nothing drunken waster of a woman that thinks her luck will last for ever. (*With great energy*) I despise such people: theyve no character; and if theres a thing I hate in a woman, its want of character.

VIVIE Come now, mother: frankly! Isnt it part of what you call character in a woman that she should greatly dislike such a way of making money?

MRS WARREN Why, of course. Everybody dislikes having to work and make money; but they have to do it all the same. I'm sure Ive often pitied a pool girl, tired out and in low spirits, having to try to please some man that she doesnt care two straws for—some half-drunken fool that thinks he's making himself agreeable when he's teasing and worrying and disgusting a woman so that hardly any money could pay her for putting up with it. But she has to bear with disagreeables and take the rough with the smooth, just like a nurse in a hospital or anyone else. It's not work that any woman would do for pleasure, goodness knows; though to hear the pious people talk you would suppose it was a bed of roses.

VIVIE Still, you consider it worth while. It pays.

MRS WARREN Of course it's worth while to a poor girl, if she can resist temptation and is good-looking and well conducted and sensible. It's far better than any other employment open to her. I always thought that oughtnt to be. It cant be right, Vivie, that there shouldnt be better opportunities for women. I stick to that: it's wrong. But it's so, right or wrong; and a girl must make the best of it. But of course it's not worth while for a lady. If you took to it youd be a fool; but I should have been a fool if I'd taken to anything else.

VIVIE (*more and more deeply moved*) Mother: suppose we were both as poor as you were in those wretched old days, are you quite sure that you wouldnt advise me to try the Waterloo bar, or marry a laborer, or even go into the factory?

MRS WARREN (*indignantly*) Of course not. What sort of mother do you take me for! How could you keep your self-respect in such starvation and slavery? And whats a woman worth? whats life worth? without self-respect? Why am I independent and able to give my daughter a first-rate education, when other women that had just as good opportunities are in the gutter? Because I always knew how to respect myself and control myself. Why is Liz looked up to in a cathedral town? The same reason. Where would we be now if we'd minded the clergyman's foolishness? Scrubbing floors for one and sixpence a day and nothing to look forward to but the workhouse infirmary. Dont you be led astray by people who dont know the world, my girl. The only way for a woman to provide for herself decently is for her to be good to some man that can afford to be good to her. If she's in his own station of life, let her make him marry her; but if she's far beneath him she cant expect it: why should she? it wouldnt be for her own happiness. Ask any lady in London society that has daughters; and she'll tell you the same, except that I tell you straight and she'll tell you crooked. Thats all the difference.

VIVIE (*fascinated, gazing at her*) My dear mother: you are a wonderful woman: you are stronger than all England. And are you really and truly not one wee bit doubtful—or—or—ashamed ?

MRS WARREN Well, of course, dearie, it's only good manners to be ashamed of it: it's expected from a woman. Women have to pretend to feel a great deal that they dont feel. Liz used to be angry with me for plumping out the truth about it. She used to say that when every woman could learn enough from what was going on in the world before her eyes, there was no need to talk about it to her. But then Liz was such a perfect lady! She had the true instinct of it; while I was always a bit of a vulgarian. I used to be so pleased when you sent me your photos to see that you were growing up like Liz: youve just her ladylike, determined way. But I cant stand saying one thing when everyone knows I mean another. Whats the use in such hypocrisy? If people arrange the world that way for women, theres no good pretending it's arranged the other way. No: I never was a bit ashamed really. I consider I had a right to be proud of how we managed everything so respectably, and never had a word against us, and how the girls were so well taken care of. Some of them did very well: one of them married an ambassador. But of course now I darent talk about such things: whatever would they think of us! (*She yawns.*) Oh dear! I do believe I'm getting sleepy after all. (*She stretches herself lazily, thoroughly relieved by her explosion, and placidly ready for her night's rest.*)

VIVIE I believe it is I who will not be able to sleep now. (*She goes to the dresser and lights the candle. Then she extinguishes the lamp, darkening the room a good deal*). Better let in some fresh air before locking up. (*She opens the cottage door, and finds that it is broad moonlight.*) What a beautiful night! Look! (*She draws aside the curtains of the window. The landscape is seen bathed in the radiance of the harvest moon rising over Blackdown.*)

MRS WARREN (*with a perfunctory glance at the scene*) Yes, dear; but take care you dont catch your death of cold from the night air.

VIVIE (*contemptuously*) Nonsense.

MRS WARREN (*querulously*) Oh yes: everything I say is nonsense, according to you.

VIVIE (*turning to her quickly*) No: really that is not so, mother. You have got completely the better of me tonight, though I intended it to be the other way. Let us be good friends now.

MRS WARREN (*shaking her head little ruefully*) So it has been the other way. But I suppose I must give in to it. I always got the worst of it from Liz; and now I suppose it'll be the same with you.

VIVIE Well, never mind. Come: goodnight, dear old mother. (*She takes her mother in her arms*).

MRS WARREN (*fondly*) I brought you up well, didnt I, dearie ?

VIVIE You did.

MRS WARREN And youll be good to your poor old mother for it, wont you?

VIVIE I will, dear. (*Kissing her*) Goodnight.

MRS WARREN (*with unction*) Blessings on my own dearie darling! a mother's blessing!

(*She embraces her daughter protectingly, instinctively looking upward for divine sanction.*)

7 Modern Art and the Questioning of Western Values

New trends in art that emerged during the late nineteenth and the early twentieth centuries resulted in Modern art. Beginning with the Postimpressionists of the 1880s and 1890s (such as Paul Cézanne, Paul Gauguin, and Vincent van Gogh), artists began to turn away from standards that had ruled art since the Renaissance, increasingly repudiating the idea of depicting an object as it appears to the eye. Then, in the years just prior to World War I, Henri Matisse, Vassily Kandinsky, and others further obscured the physical world from their paintings and expressed their private inner experiences. But it was Pablo Picasso's *The Young Ladies of Avignon* of 1907, the first cubist painting, that broke all of the established rules. These innovators repudiated Western aesthetic standards that were based on the conviction that the universe embodied an inherent mathematical order. Modernist artists acknowledged no objective reality; reality is what the viewer perceives it to be through the prism of the imagination. An abstract form will reveal a deeper reality than will a depiction of physical reality.

Although these innovators questioned Western artistic values, they did not repudiate Enlightenment values. But many artists and literary figures who followed them regarded the Enlightenment belief in human goodness, reason, and the progress of humanity as expressions of naive optimism. Three movements in particular—Futurism, Dada, and Surrealism—manifest this loss of faith in Western values. Futurism, launched prior to World War I, glorified the irrational and abhored what it considered to be the cultural decadence of the West. "The Great War," World War I, led to art and literary movements that intensified this critique of Western values. Dada, which came into existence during the war, embraced nihilism and a contempt for Europe's moral and intellectual values. Following the war, Surrealism focused on the importance of the unconscious to reach a higher reality. Following are excerpts from three manifestos espousing the ideas of these movements.

Filippo Tommaso Marinetti
Manifesto of Futurism

On February 20, 1909, the Paris newspaper *Le Figaro* published a manifesto by the Italian poet, Filippo Tommaso Marinetti (1876–1944), proclaiming the emergence of a new literary movement called Futurism. The movement appealed to young Italian artists and writers who were repulsed by bourgeois materialism and by what they considered to be Italy's political weakness and cultural decadence. The most prominent Futurist artists—Umberto Coccioni, Carlo Carrá, and Luigi Russolo—sought to depict the dynamism—the speed and power—of modern urban life and modern industry. The historical significance of Futurist artists and poets lay less in the aesthetic merit of their works (which in some cases was considerable) and more in their rejection of the Western liberal-humanist tradition and their espousal of action and the primordial. To this extent they were symptomatic of a mindset that welcomed World War I and embraced fascism after the war. Marinetti himself was a staunch Italian nationalist who served Mussolini's fascist state. Excerpted below is the *Manifesto of Futurism* written by Marinetti in 1909.

1. We intend to sing the love of danger, the habit of energy and fearlessness.

2. Courage, audacity, and revolt will be essential elements of our poetry.

3. Up to now literature has exalted a pensive immobility, ecstasy, and sleep. We intend to exalt aggressive action, a feverish insomnia, the racer's stride, the mortal leap, the punch and the slap.

4. We say that the world's magnificence has been enriched by a new beauty; the beauty of speed. A racing car whose hood is adorned with great pipes, like serpents of explosive breath—a roaring car that seems to ride on grapeshot—is more beautiful than the *Victory of Samothrace.*

5. We want to hymn the man at the wheel, who hurls the lance of his spirit across the Earth, along the circle of its orbit.

6. The poet must spend himself with ardor, splendor, and generosity, to swell the enthusiastic fervor of the primordial elements.

7. Except in struggle, there is no more beauty. No work without an aggressive character can be a masterpiece. Poetry must be conceived as a violent attack on unknown forces, to reduce and prostate them before man.

8. We stand on the last promontory of the centuries.... Why should we look back, when what we want is to break down the mysterious doors of the Impossible? Time and Space died yesterday. We already live in the absolute, because we have created eternal, omnipresent speed.

9. We will glorify war—the world's only hygiene—militarism, patriotism, the destructive gesture of freedom-bringers, beautiful ideas worth dying for, and scorn for woman.

10. We will destroy the museums, libraries, academies of every kind, will fight moralism, feminism, every opportunistic or utilitarian cowardice.

11. We will sing of great crowds excited by work, by pleasure, and by riot; we will sing of the multicolored polyphonic tides of revolution in the modern capitals; we will sing of the vibrant nightly fervor of arsenals and shipyards blazing with violent electric moons; greedy railway stations that devour smoke-plumed serpents; factories hung on clouds by the crooked lines of their smoke; bridges that stride the rivers like giant gymnasts, flashing in the sun with a glitter of knives; adventurous steamers that sniff the horizon; deep-chested locomotives whose wheels paw the tracks like the hooves of enormous steel horses bridled by tubing; and the sleek flight of planes whose propellers chatter in the wind like banners and seem to cheer like an enthusiastic crowd.

It is from Italy that we launch through the world this violently upsetting, incendiary manifesto of ours. With it, today, we establish *Futurism* because we want to free this land from its smelly gangrene of professors, archaeologists, ciceroni, and antiquarians. For too long has Italy been a dealer in secondhand clothes. We mean to free her from the numberless museums that cover her like so many graveyards.

Museums: cemeteries! . . . Identical, surely, in the sinister promiscuity of so many bodies unknown to one another.

Museums: public dormitories where one lies forever beside hated or unknown beings. Museums; absurd abattoirs of painters and sculptors ferociously macerating each other with color-blows and line-blows, the length of the fought-over walls!

That one should make an annual pilgrimage, just as one goes to the graveyard on All Souls' Day—that I grant. That once a year one should leave a floral tribute beneath the *Gioconda* [Mona Lisa], I grant you that. . . . But I don't admit that our sorrows, our fragile courage, our morbid restlessness should be given a daily conducted tour through the museums. Why poison ourselves? Why rot?

And what is there to see in an old picture except the laborious contortions of an artist throwing himself against the barriers that thwart his desire to express his dream completely? . . . Admiring an old picture is the same as pouring our sensibility into a funerary urn instead of hurling it far off, in violent spasms of action and creation.

Do you, then, wish to waste all your best powers in this eternal and futile worship of the past, from which you emerge fatally exhausted, shrunken, beaten down?

In truth I tell you that daily visits to museums, libraries, and academies (cemeteries of empty exertion, calvaries of crucified dreams, registries of aborted beginnings!) is, for artists, as damaging as the prolonged supervision by parents of certain young people drunk with their talent and their ambitious wills. When the future is barred to them, the admirable past may be a solace for the ills of the moribund, the sickly, the prisoner. . . . But we want no part of it, the past, we the young and strong *Futurists!*

So let them come, the gay incendiaries with charred fingers! Here they are! Here they are! . . . Come on! set fire to the library shelves! Turn aside the canals to flood the museums! . . . Oh, the joy of seeing the glorious old canvases bobbing adrift on those waters, discolored and shredded! . . . Take up your pickaxes, your axes and hammers, and wreck, wreck the venerable cities, pitilessly!

The oldest of us is thirty: so we have at least a decade for finishing our work. When we are forty, other younger and stronger men will probably throw us in the wastebasket like useless manuscripts—we want it to happen!

They will come against us, our successors, will come from far away, from every quarter, dancing to the winged cadence of their first songs, flexing the hooked claws of predators, sniffing doglike at the academy doors the strong odor of our decaying minds, which already will have been promised to the literary catacombs.

But we won't be there. . . . At last they'll find us—one winter's night—in open country, beneath a sad roof drummed by a monotonous rain. They'll see us crouched beside our trembling airplanes in the act of warming our hands at the poor little blaze that our books of today will give out when they take fire from the flight of our images.

They'll storm around us, panting with scorn and anguish, and all of them, exasperated by our proud daring, will hurtle to kill us, driven by hatred: the more implacable it is, the more their hearts will be drunk with love and admiration for us.

Injustice, strong and sane, will break out radiantly in their eyes.

Art, in fact, can be nothing but violence, cruelty, and injustice.

The oldest of us is thirty: even so we have already scattered treasures, a thousand treasures of force, love, courage, astuteness, and raw will power; have thrown them impatiently away, with fury, carelessly, unhesitatingly, breathless and unresting . . . Look at us! We are still untired! Our hearts know no weariness because they are fed with fire, hatred, and speed! . . . Does that amaze you? It should, because you can never remember having lived! Erect on the summit of the world, once again we hurl our defiance at the stars!

You have objections?—Enough! Enough! We know them . . . we've understood! . . . Our fine deceitful intelligence tells us that we are the revival and extension of our ancestors—perhaps! . . . If only it were so!—But who cares? We don't want to understand! . . . Woe to anyone who says those infamous words to us again!

Lift up your heads!

Erect on the summit of the world, once again we hurl defiance to the stars!

Tristan Tzara
Dada

One example of the intellectual disorientation fostered by World War I was the Dadaist Movement, which arose in 1916 in Zurich, Switzerland. The artists and writers who founded Dada intended to express their contempt for the war and the civilization that produced it. The movement spread from neutral

Switzerland to Germany and Paris, attracting disillusioned intellectuals. Rejecting God, reason, and traditional standards of culture, Dadaists viewed life as absurd and nonsensical (Dada itself is a nonsense term). Tristan Tzara (1896–1945), a Romanian-French poet and essayist, one of the founders of Dada and its chief spokesman, expressed this revulsion for the Western tradition in a series of manifestos. Below are excerpts from a lecture Tzara gave in 1922.

I know that you have come here today to hear explanations. Well, don't expect to hear any explanations about Dada. You explain to me why you exist. You haven't the faintest idea. You will say: I exist to make my children happy. But in your hearts you know that isn't so. You will say: I exist to guard my country against barbarian invasions. That's a fine reason. You will say: I exist because God wills. That's a fairy tale for children. You will never be able to tell me why you exist but you will always be ready to maintain a serious attitude about life. You will never understand that life is a pun, for you will never be alone enough to reject hatred, judgments, all these things that require such an effort, in favor of a calm and level state of mind that makes everything equal and without importance. . . .

These observations of everyday conditions have led us to a realization which constitutes our minimum basis of agreement, aside from the sympathy which binds us and which is inexplicable. It would not have been possible for us to found our agreement on principles. For everything is relative. What are the Beautiful, the Good, Art, Freedom? Words that have a different meaning for every individual. Words with the pretension of creating agreement among all, and that is why they are written with capital letters. Words which have not the moral value and objective force that people have grown accustomed to finding in them. Their meaning changes from one individual, one epoch, one country to the next. Men are different. It is diversity that makes life interesting. There is no common basis in men's minds. The unconscious is inexhaustible and uncontrollable. Its force surpasses us. It is as mysterious as the last particle of a brain cell. Even if we knew it, we could not reconstruct it.

What good did the theories of the philosophers do us? Did they help us to take a single step forward or backward? What is forward, what is backward? Did they alter our forms of contentment? We are. We argue, we dispute, we get excited. The rest is sauce. Sometimes pleasant, sometimes mixed with a limitless boredom, a swamp dotted with tufts of dying shrubs.

We have had enough of the intelligent movements that have stretched beyond measure our credulity in the benefits of science. What we want now is spontaneity. Not because it is better or more beautiful than anything else. But because everything that issues freely from ourselves, without the intervention of speculative ideas, represents us. We must intensify this quantity of life that readily spends itself in every quarter. Art is not the most precious manifestation of life. Art has not the celestial and universal value that people like to attribute to it. Life is far more interesting. Dada knows the correct measure that should be given to art: with subtle, perfidious methods, Dada introduces it into daily life. And vice versa. In art, Dada reduces everything to an initial simplicity, growing always more relative. It mingles its caprices with the chaotic wind of creation and the barbaric dances of savage tribes. It wants logic reduced to a personal minimum. . . . The absurd has no terrors for me, for from a more exalted point of view everything in life seems absurd to me. . . . The Beautiful and the True in art do not exist; what interests me is the intensity of a personality transposed directly, clearly into the work; the man and his vitality; the angle from which he regards the elements and in what manner he knows how to gather sensation, emotion, into a lacework of words and sentiments. . . .

We are often told that we are incoherent, but into this word people try to put an insult that it is rather hard for me to fathom. Everything is incoherent. The gentleman who decides to take a bath but goes to the movies instead. The one who wants to be quiet but says things that haven't even entered his head. Another who has a precise idea on some subject but succeeds only in expressing the opposite in words which for him are a poor translation. There is no logic. Only relative necessities discovered *a posteriori* [after the fact], valid not in any exact sense but only as explanations.

The acts of life have no beginning or end. Everything happens in a completely idiotic way. That is why everything is alike. Simplicity is called Dada.

Any attempt to conciliate an inexplicable momentary state with logic strikes me as a boring kind of game. The convention of the spoken language is ample and adequate for us, but for our solitude, for our intimate games and our literature we no longer need it.

The beginnings of Dada were not the beginnings of an art, but of a disgust. Disgust with the magnificence of philosophers who for 3000 years have been explaining everything to us (what for?), disgust with the pretensions of these artists-God's-representatives-on-earth, disgust with passion and with real pathological wickedness where it was not worth the bother; disgust with a false form of domination and restriction *en masse,* that accentuates rather than appeases man's instinct of domination, disgust with all the catalogued categories, with the false prophets who are nothing but a front for the interests of money, pride disease, disgust with the lieutenants of a mercantile art made to order according to a few infantile laws, disgust with the divorce of good and evil, the beautiful and the ugly (for why is it more estimable to be red rather than green, to the left rather than the right, to be large or small?). Disgust finally with the Jesuitical dialectic which can explain everything and fill people's minds with oblique and obtuse ideas without any physiological basis or ethnic roots, all this by means of blinding artifice and ignoble charlatan's promises.

As Dada marches it continuously destroys, not in extension but in itself. From all these disgusts, may I add, it draws no conclusion, no pride, no benefit. It has even stopped combating anything, in the realization that it's no use, that all this doesn't matter. What interests a Dadaist is his own mode of life. But here we approach the great secret.

Dada is a state of mind. That is why it transforms itself according to races and events. Dada applies itself to everything, and yet it is nothing, it is the point where the yes and the no and all the opposites meet, not solemnly in the castles of human philosophies, but very simply at street corners, like dogs and grasshoppers.

Like everything in life, Dada is useless.

Dada is without pretension, as life should be.

Perhaps you will understand me better when I tell you that Dada is a virgin microbe that penetrates with the insistence of air into all the spaces that reason has not been able to fill with words or conventions.

André Breton
Manifestoes of Surrealism

The principal spokesman for Surrealism was the French poet, André Breton, who published his *Manifesto of Surrealism* in 1924, and then, in 1930 his *Second Manifesto of Surrealism.* Breton shared Dada's contempt for reason, but Surrealism was a less negative movement. Surrealists stressed fantasy and made use of Freudian insights and symbols in their writings and art as they sought to reproduce the raw state of the unconscious and to arrive at truths beyond reason's grasp. Breton urged writers to penetrate the interior of the mind by writing quickly and without thought. Writing should flow automatically from the unconscious not from the intellect. He urged artists to live their dreams, to portray the world of fantasy and hallucination, the marvelous and the spontaneous. By breaking through the constraints of rationality, writers and artists could reach "the liberation of the mind," that is, a higher reality, a "surreality." Important Surrealist artists were Max Ernst, Joan Miró, Salvador Dali, and Alberto Giacometti. Surrealism's emphasis on the significance of the unconscious for creativity had an important influence on the artists who introduced Abstract Expressionism in the United States after World War II. The following excerpts are from Breton's manifestoes of Surrealism.

We are still living under the reign of logic: this, of course, is what I have been driving at. But in this day and age logical methods are applicable only to solving problems of secondary interest. The absolute rationalism that is still in vogue allows us to consider only facts relating directly to our experience! . . .

Under the pretense of civilization and progress, we have managed to banish from the mind everything that may rightly or wrongly be termed superstition, or fancy; forbidden is any kind of search for truth which is not in conformance with accepted practices. It was, apparently, by pure chance that a part of our mental world which we pretended not to be concerned with any longer—and, in my opinion by far the most important part—has been brought back to light. For this we must give thanks to the discoveries of Sigmund Freud. On the basis of these discoveries a current of opinion is finally forming by means of which the human explorer will be able to carry his investigations much further, authorized as he will henceforth be not to confine himself solely to the most summary realities. The imagination is perhaps on the point of reasserting itself, of reclaiming its rights. If the depths of our mind contain within it strange forces capable of augmenting those on the surface, or of waging a victorious battle against them, there is every reason to seize them—first to seize them, then, if need be, to submit them to the control of our reason. The analysts themselves have everything to gain by it. But it is worth noting that no means has been designated a priori for carrying out this undertaking, that until further notice it can be construed to be the province of poets as well as scholars, and that its success is not dependent upon the more or less capricious paths that will be followed.

Freud very rightly brought his critical faculties to bear upon the dream. It is, in fact, inadmissible that this considerable portion of psychic activity (since, at least from man's birth until his death, thought offers no solution of continuity, the sum of the moments of dream, from the point of view of time, and taking into consideration only the time of pure dreaming, that is the dreams of sleep, is not inferior to the sum of the moments of reality, or, to be more precisely limiting, the moments of waking) has still today been so grossly neglected. I have always been amazed at the way an ordinary observer lends so much more credence and attaches so much more importance to waking events than to those occurring in dreams. It is because man, when he ceases to sleep, is above all the plaything of his memory, and in its normal state memory takes pleasure in weakly retracing for him the circumstances of the dream, in stripping it of any real importance, and in dismissing the only *determinant* from the point where he thinks he has left it a few hours before: this firm hope, this concern. He is under the impression of continuing something that is worthwhile. Thus the dream finds itself reduced to a mere parenthesis, as is the night. And, like the night, dreams generally contribute little to furthering our understanding. . . .

Those who might dispute our right to employ the term SURREALISM in the very special sense that we understand it are being extremely dishonest, for there can be no doubt that this word had no currency before we came along. Therefore, I am defining it once and for all:

SURREALISM, *n.* Psychic automatism in its pure state, by which one proposes to express—verballly, by means of the written word, or in any other manner—the actual functioning of thought. Dictated by thought, in the absence of any control exercised by reason, exempt from any aesthetic or moral concern.

ENCYCLOPEDIA. *Philosophy.* Surrealism is based on the belief in the superior reality of certain forms of previously neglected associations, in the omnipotence of dream, in the disinterested play of thought. It tends to ruin once and for all other psychic mechanisms and to substitute itself for them in solving all the principal problems of life. . . .

Surrealism, such as I conceive of it, asserts our complete *nonconformism* clearly enough so that there can be no question of translating it, at the trial of the real world, as evidence for the defense. It could, on the contrary, only serve to justify the complete state of distraction which we hope to achieve here below. . . . This world is only very relatively in tune with thought, and incidents of this kind are only the most obvious episodes of a war in which I am proud to be participating. Surrealism is the "invisible ray" which will one day enable us to win out over our opponents. "You are no longer trembling, carcass." This summer the roses wood are blue; the wood is of glass. The earth, draped in its verdant cloak, makes as little impression upon me as a ghost. It is living and ceasing to live that are imaginary solutions. Existence is elsewhere. . . .

[I]t is worthwhile to know just what kind of moral virtues Surrealism lays claim to, since, moreover, it plunges its roots into life and, no doubt not by chance, into *the life of this period,* seeing that I laden this life with anecdotes like the sky, the sound of a watch, the cold, a malaise, that is, I begin to speak about it in a vulgar manner. To think these things, to hold any rung whatever of this weather-beaten ladder—none of us is beyond such things until he has passed through the last stage of asceticism. It is in fact from the disgusting cauldron of these meaningless mental images that the desire to proceed beyond the insufficient, the absurd, distinction between the beautiful and the ugly, true and false, good and evil, is born and sustained. And, as it is the degree of resistance that this choice idea meets with which determines the more or less certain flight of the mind toward a world at last inhabitable, one can understand why Surrealism was not afraid to make for itself a tenet of total revolt, complete insubordination, of sabotage according to rule, and why it still expects nothing save from violence. The simplest Surrealist act consists of dashing down into the street, pistol in hand, and firing blindly, as fast as you can pull the trigger, into the crowd. Anyone who, at least once in his life, has not dreamed of thus putting an end to the petty system of debasement and cretinization in effect has a well-defined place in that crowd, with his belly at barrel level.

PART V

MODERNISM AND BEYOND

CHAPTER

17

World War I and Its Aftermath

To many Europeans, the opening years of the twentieth century seemed full of promise. Advances in science and technology, the rising standard of living, the expansion of education, and the absence of wars between the Great Powers since the Franco-Prussian War (1870–1871) all contributed to a general feeling of optimism. Yet these accomplishments hid disruptive forces that were propelling Europe toward a cataclysm. On June 28, 1914, Archduke Francis Ferdinand, heir to the throne of Austria-Hungary, was assassinated by Gavrilo Princip, a young Serbian nationalist (and Austrian subject), at Sarajevo in the Austrian province of Bosnia, inhabited largely by South Slavs. The assassination triggered those explosive forces that lay below the surface of European life, and six weeks later, Europe was engulfed in a general war that altered the course of Western civilization.

Belligerent, irrational, and extreme nationalism was a principal cause of World War I. Placing their country above everything, nationalists in various countries fomented hatred of other nationalities and called for the expansion of their nation's borders—attitudes that fostered belligerence in foreign relations. Wedded to nationalism was a militaristic view that regarded war as heroic and as the highest expression of individual and national life.

Yet Europe might have avoided the world war had the nations not been divided into hostile alliance systems. By 1907, the Triple Alliance of Germany, Austria-Hungary, and Italy confronted the loosely organized Triple Entente of France, Russia, and Great Britain. What German chancellor Otto von Bismarck said in 1879 was just as true in 1914: "The great powers of our time are like travellers, unknown to one another, whom chance has brought together in a carriage. They watch each other, and when one of them puts his hand into his pocket, his neighbor gets ready his own revolver in order to be able to fire the first shot."

A danger inherent in an alliance is that a country, knowing that it has the support of allies, may pursue an aggressive foreign policy and may be less likely to compromise during a crisis; also, a war between two states may well draw in the other allied powers. These dangers materialized in 1914.

In the diplomatic furor of July and early August 1914, following the assassination of Francis Ferdinand, several patterns emerged. Austria-Hungary, a multinational empire dominated by Germans and Hungarians, feared the nationalist aspirations of its Slavic minorities. The nationalist yearnings of neighboring Serbia aggravated Austria-Hungary's problems, for the Serbs, a South Slav people, wanted to create a Greater Serbia by uniting with South Slavs of Austria-Hungary. If Slavic nationalism gained in intensity, the Austro-Hungarian (or Hapsburg) Empire would be broken into states based on nationality. Austria-Hungary decided to use the assassination as justification for crushing Serbia.

The system of alliances escalated the tensions between Austria-Hungary and Serbia into a general European war. Germany saw itself threatened by the Triple Entente (a conviction based more on paranoia than on objective fact) and regarded Austria-Hungary as its only reliable ally. Holding that at all costs its ally must be kept strong, German officials supported Austria-Hungary's decision to crush Serbia. Fearing that Germany and Austria-Hungary aimed to extend their power into southeastern Europe, Russia would not permit the destruction of Serbia. With the support of France, Russia began to mobilize, and when it moved to full mobilization, Germany declared war. As German battle plans, drawn up years before, called for a war with both France and Russia, France was drawn into the conflict; Germany's invasion of neutral Belgium brought Great Britain into the war.

Most European statesmen and military men believed the war would be over in a few months. Virtually no one anticipated that it would last more than four years and that the casualties would number in the millions.

World War I was a turning point in Western history. In Russia, it led to the downfall of the tsarist autocracy and the rise of the Soviet state. The war created unsettling conditions that led to the emergence of fascist movements in Italy and Germany, and it shattered, perhaps forever, the Enlightenment belief in the inevitable and perpetual progress of Western civilization.

1 Trench Warfare

In 1914, the young men of European nations marched off to war believing that they were embarking on a glorious and chivalrous adventure. They were eager to serve their countries, to demonstrate personal valor, and to experience life at its most intense moments. But in the trenches, where unseen enemies fired machine guns and artillery that killed indiscriminately and relentlessly, this romantic illusion about combat disintegrated.

Siegfried Sassoon
"Base Details" and "Aftermath"

Front-line soldiers often looked with contempt on generals who, from a safe distance, ordered massive assaults against enemy lines protected by barbed wire and machine guns. Such attacks could cost the lives of tens of thousands of soldiers in just a few days. Siegfried Sassoon (1886–1967), a British poet who served at the front for much of the war and earned a Military Cross for bravery, expressed his contempt for callous generals who, from a safe distance, ordered massive assaults against well-defended enemy lines. In "Base Details," printed below, Sassoon draws a sharp distinction between the "glum heroes" at the front and their "bald," "short of breath," "puffy" generals.

BASE DETAILS

If I were fierce, and bald, and short of breath,
I'd live with scarlet Majors at the Base,
And speed glum heroes up the line to death.
You'd see me with my puffy petulant face,
Guzzling and gulping in the best hotel,
Reading the Roll of Honor. "Poor young chap,"
I'd say—"I used to know his father well;
Yes, we've lost heavily in this last scrap."
And when the war is done and youth stone
    dead,
I'd toddle safely home and die—in bed.

AFTERMATH

After the war Sassoon wrote "Aftermath," in which he
urges veterans to "swear by the slain of the War that
you'll never forget."

Do you remember the rats; and the stench
Of corpses rotting in front of the front-line
    trench—
And dawn coming, dirty-white, and chill with a
    hopeless rain?
Do you ever stop and ask, 'Is it all going to happen again?'

Do you remember that hour of din before the
    attack—
And the anger, the blind compassion that
    seized and shook you then
As you peered at the doomed and haggard
    faces of your men?
Do you remember the stretcher-cases lurching
    back
With dying eyes and lolling heads—those ashen-grey
Masks of the lads who once were keen and kind
    and gay?

Have you forgotten yet? . . .
Look up, and swear by the green of the spring
    that you'll never forget.

Wilfred Owen
"Disabled"

Wilfred Owen (1893–1918), another British poet, volunteered for duty in 1915. At the Battle of the Somme, he sustained shell shock, and he was sent to a hospital in Britain. In 1918, he returned to the front and was awarded the Military Cross; he died one week before the Armistice. In the following poem, "Disabled," Owen portrays the enduring misery of war.

He sat in a wheeled chair, waiting for dark,
And shivered in his ghastly suit of gray,
Legless, sewn short at elbow. Through the
    park
Voices of boys rang saddening like a hymn,
Voices of play and pleasure after day,
Till gathering sleep mothered them from him.

About this time Town used to swing so gay
When glow-lamps budded in the light blue
    trees,
And girls glanced lovelier as the air grew
    dim,—
In the old times, before he threw away his
    knees. . . .

He asked to join. He didn't have to beg;
Smiling they wrote his lie: aged nineteen
    years.

Germans he scarcely thought of; all their guilt,
And Austria's, did not move him. And no fears
Of Fear came yet. He thought of jeweled hilts
For daggers in plaid socks; of smart salutes;
And care of arms; and leave; and pay arrears;
*Esprit de corps,** and hints for young recruits.
And soon, he was drafted out with drums and cheers. . . .

Now, he will spend a few sick years in
    Institutes,
And do what things the rules consider wise,
And take whatever pity they may dole.
Tonight he noticed how the women's eyes
Passed from him to the strong men that were
    whole.
How cold and late it is! Why don't they come
And put him into bed? Why don't they come?

*Esprit de corps: group spirit.

Erich Maria Remarque
All Quiet on the Western Front

The following reading is taken from Erich Maria Remarque's novel *All Quiet on the Western Front* (1929), the most famous literary work to emerge from World War I. A veteran of the trenches himself, Remarque (1898–1970) graphically described the slaughter that robbed Europe of its young men. His narrator is a young German soldier.

We wake up in the middle of the night. The earth booms. Heavy fire is falling on us. We crouch into corners. We distinguish shells of every calibre.

Each man lays hold of his things and looks again every minute to reassure himself that they are still there. The dug-out heaves, the night roars and flashes. We look at each other in the momentary flashes of light, and with pale faces and pressed lips shake our heads.

Every man is aware of the heavy shells tearing down the parapet, rooting up the embankment and demolishing the upper layers of concrete. When a shell lands in the trench we note how the hollow, furious blast is like a blow from the paw of a raging beast of prey. Already by morning a few of the recruits are green and vomiting. They are too inexperienced. . . .

The bombardment does not diminish. It is falling in the rear too. As far as one can see spout fountains of mud and iron. A wide belt is being raked.

The attack does not come, but the bombardment continues. We are gradually benumbed. Hardly a man speaks. We cannot make ourselves understood.

Our trench is almost gone, At many places it is only eighteen inches high, it is broken by holes, and craters, and mountains of earth. A shell lands square in front of our post. At once it is dark. We are buried and must dig ourselves out. . . .

Towards morning, while it is still dark, there is some excitement. Through the entrance rushes in a swarm of fleeing rats that try to storm the walls. Torches light up the confusion. Everyone yells and curses and slaughters. The madness and despair of many hours unloads itself in this outburst. Faces are distorted, arms strike out, the beasts scream; we just stop in time to avoid attacking one another. . . .

Suddenly it howls and flashes terrifically, the dug-out cracks in all its joints under a direct hit, fortunately only a light one that the concrete blocks are able to withstand. It rings metallically, the walls reel, rifles, helmets, earth, mud, and dust fly everywhere. Sulphur fumes pour in.

If we were in one of those light dug-outs that they have been building lately instead of this deeper one, none of us would be alive.

But the effect is bad enough even so. The recruit starts to rave again and two others follow suit. One jumps up and rushes out, we have trouble with the other two. I start after the one who escapes and wonder whether to shoot him in the leg—then it shrieks again, I fling myself down and when I stand up the wall of the trench is plastered with smoking splinters, lumps of flesh, and bits of uniform. I scramble back.

The first recruit seems actually to have gone insane. He butts his head against the wall like a goat. We must try to-night to take him to the rear. Meanwhile we bind him, but in such a way that in case of attack he can be released at once. . . .

Suddenly the nearer explosions cease. The shelling continues but it has lifted and falls behind us, our trench is free. We seize the hand-grenades, pitch them out in front of the dug-out and jump after them. The bombardment has stopped and a heavy barrage now falls behind us. The attack has come.

No one would believe that in this howling waste there could still be men; but steel helmets now appear on all sides out of the trench, and fifty yards from us a machine-gun is already in position and barking.

The wire entanglements are torn to pieces. Yet they offer some obstacle. We see the storm-troops coming. Our artillery opens fire. Machine-guns rattle, rifles crack. The charge works its way across. Haie and Kropp begin with the hand-grenades. They throw as fast as they can, others pass them, the handles with the strings already pulled. Haie throws seventy-five yards, Kropp sixty, it has been measured, the distance is important. The enemy as they run cannot do much before they are within forty yards.

We recognize the smooth distorted faces, the helmets: they are French. They have already suffered heavily when they reach the remnants of the barbed wire entanglements. A whole line has gone down before our machine-guns; then we have a lot of stoppages and they come nearer.

I see one of them, his face upturned, fall into a wire cradle. His body collapses, his hands remain suspended as though he were praying. Then his body drops clean away and only his hands with the stumps of his arms, shot off, now hang in the wire.

The moment we are about to retreat three faces rise up from the ground in front of us. Under one of the helmets a dark pointed beard and two eyes that are fastened on me. I raise my hand, but I cannot throw into those strange eyes; for one mad moment the whole slaughter whirls like a circus round me, and these two eyes alone are motionless; then the head rises up, a hand, a movement, and my hand-grenade flies through the air and into him.

We make for the rear, pull wire cradles into the trench and leave bombs behind us with the strings pulled, which ensures us a fiery retreat. The machine-guns are already firing from the next position.

We have become wild beasts. We do not fight, we defend ourselves against annihilation. It is not against men that we fling our bombs, what do we know of men in this moment when Death is hunting us down—now, for the first time in three days we can see his face, now for the first time in three days we can oppose him; we feel a mad anger. No longer do we lie helpless, waiting on the scaffold, we can destroy and kill, to save ourselves, to save ourselves and to be revenged.

We crouch behind every corner, behind every barrier of barbed wire, and hurl heaps of explosives at the feet of the advancing enemy before we run. The blast of the hand-grenades impinges powerfully on our arms and legs; crouching like cats we run on, overwhelmed by this wave that bears us along, that fills us with ferocity, turns us into thugs, into murderers, into God only knows what devils; this wave that multiplies our strength with fear and madness and greed of life, seeking and fighting for nothing but our deliverance. If your own father came over with them you would not hesitate to fling a bomb at him.

The forward trenches have been abandoned. Are they still trenches? They are blown to pieces, annihilated—there are only broken bits of trenches, holes linked by cracks, nests of craters, that is all. But the enemy's casualties increase. They did not count on so much resistance.

It is nearly noon. The sun blazes hotly, the sweat stings in our eyes, we wipe it off on our sleeves and often blood with it. At last we reach a trench that is in a somewhat better condition. It is manned and ready for the counterattack, it receives us. Our guns open in full blast and cut off the enemy attack.

The lines behind us stop. They can advance no farther. The attack is crushed by our artillery. We watch. The fire lifts a hundred yards and we break forward. Beside me a lance-corporal has his head torn off. He runs a few steps more while the blood spouts from his neck like a fountain.

It does not come quite to hand-to-hand fighting; they are driven back. We arrive once again at our shattered trench and pass on beyond it. . . .

We have lost all feeling for one another. We can hardly control ourselves when our glance lights on the form of some other man. We are insensible, dead men, who through some trick, some dreadful magic, are still able to run and to kill.

A young Frenchman lags behind, he is overtaken, he puts up his hands, in one he still holds his revolver—does he mean to shoot or to give himself up!—a blow from a spade cleaves through his face. A second sees it and tries to run farther; a bayonet jabs into his back. He leaps in the air, his arms thrown wide, his mouth wide open, yelling; he staggers, in his back the bayonet quivers. A third throws away his rifle, cowers down with his hands before his eyes. He is left behind with a few other prisoners to carry off the wounded.

Suddenly in the pursuit we reach the enemy line.

We are so close on the heels of our retreating enemies that we reach it almost at the same time as they. In this way we suffer few casualties. A machine-gun barks, but is silenced with a bomb. Nevertheless, the couple of seconds has sufficed to give us five stomach wounds. With the butt of his rifle Kat smashes to pulp the face of one of the unwounded machine-gunners. We bayonet the others before they have time to get out their bombs. Then thirstily we drink the water they have for cooling the gun.

Everywhere wire-cutters are snapping, planks are thrown across the entanglements, we jump through the narrow entrances into the trenches. Haie strikes his spade into the neck of a gigantic Frenchman and throws the first hand-grenade; we duck behind a breastwork for a few seconds, then the straight bit of trench ahead of us is empty. The next throw whizzes obliquely over the corner and clears a passage; as we run past we toss handfuls down into the dug-outs, the earth shudders, it crashes, smokes and groans, we stumble over slippery lumps of flesh, over yielding bodies; I fall into an open belly on which lies a clean, new officer's cap.

The fight ceases. We lose touch with the enemy. We cannot stay here long but must retire under cover of our artillery to our own position. No sooner do we know this than we dive into the nearest dug-outs, and with the utmost haste seize on whatever provisions we can see, especially the tins of corned beef and butter, before we clear out.

We get back pretty well. There is no further attack by the enemy. We lie for an hour panting and resting before anyone speaks. We are so completely played out that in spite of our great hunger we do not think of the provisions. Then gradually we become something like men again.

2   American Expatriates: Stein and Hemingway

Between 1900 and 1930, Paris was the center of the avant-garde world. Parisian culture attracted authors and artists from all over Europe, and, especially from America. One of the earliest of the American expatriates was Gertrude Stein, who settled in Paris on the Left Bank of the Seine River. Other famous Americans came to live in Paris during the 1920s, including Ernest Hemingway. The stock market crash of 1929 and the resulting depression forced most of the Americans to return to the United States, although some remained in Paris until the outbreak of World War II.

Gertrude Stein
The Autobiography of Alice B. Toklas

In 1903, the author Gertrude Stein (1874–1946) settled in an apartment at 27 Rue de Fleurus. Stein was one of the first to collect the works of Matisse, Picasso, and Braque, and the apartment—frequented by avant-garde painters and literary figures—soon became a private art gallery. Stein's secretary and companion, Alice B. Toklas, arrived in Paris in 1907. In describing her abstract style of writing, Stein declared that it was the literary equivalent of Cubism. Nonetheless, her most famous book, *The Autobiography of Alice B. Toklas* (1933), was written in a more traditional, conversational style. The voice of Toklas narrates the story, but the book actually details the life of Stein herself during the time she lived in Paris, up until 1932. The first portion of the book describes the social gatherings on Saturday evenings at 27 Rue de Fleurus, which came to be known as Gertrude Stein's Salon. The following excerpt describes Stein's friendship with the artists and the beginnings of the Saturday evening gatherings.

The friendship with the Matisses grew apace. Matisse at that time was at work at his first big decoration, *Le Bonheur de Vivre* [The Joy of Life]. He was making small and larger and very large studies for it. It was in this picture that Matisse first clearly realised his intention of deforming the drawing of the human body in order to harmonise and intensify the colour values of all the simple colours mixed only with white. He used his distorted drawing as a dissonance is used in music or as vinegar or lemons are used in cooking or egg shells in coffee to clarify. I do inevitably take my comparisons from the kitchen because I like food and cooking and know something about it. However this was the idea. Cézanne had come to his unfinishedness and distortion of necessity, Matisse did it by intention.

Little by little people began to come to the rue de Fleurus to see the Matisses and the Cézannes, Matisse brought people, everybody brought somebody, and they came at any time and it began to be a nuisance, and it was in this way that Saturday evenings began. It was also at this time that Gertrude Stein got into the habit of writing at night. It was

only after eleven o'clock that she could be sure that no one would knock at the studio door. She was at that time planning her long book, The Making of Americans, she was struggling with her sentences, those long sentences that had to be so exactly carried out. Sentences not only words but sentences and always sentences have been Gertrude Stein's life long passion. And so she had then and indeed it lasted pretty well to the war, which broke down so many habits, she had then the habit of beginning her work at eleven o'clock at night and working until the dawn. She said she always tried to stop before the dawn was too clear and the birds were too lively because it is a disagreeable sensation to go to bed then. There were birds in many trees behind high walls in those days, now there are fewer. But often the birds and the dawn caught her and she stood in the court waiting to get used to it before she went to bed. She had the habit then of sleeping until noon and the beating of the rugs into the court, because everybody did that in those days, even her household did, was one of her most poignant irritations.

So the Saturday evenings began.

Stein was acquainted with many of the artists who were in Paris at the time, but no friendship was closer than the one she had with Picasso. In the following excerpts, she tells how both Picasso and Matisse were influenced by African art; then she relates her belief that only Spaniards could be Cubists.

At that time negro sculpture had been well known to curio hunters but not to artists. Who first recognised its potential value for the modern artist I am sure I do not know. Perhaps it was Maillol who came from the Perpignan region and knew Matisse in the south and called his attention to it. There is a tradition that it was Derain. It is also very possible that it was Matisse himself because for many years there was a curio-dealer in the rue de Rennes who always had a great many things of this kind in his window and Matisse often went up the rue de Rennes to go to one of the sketch classes.

In any case it was Matisse who first was influenced, not so much in his painting but in his sculpture, by the african statues and it was Matisse who drew Picasso's attention to it just after Picasso had finished painting Gertrude Stein's portrait.

The effect of this african art upon Matisse and Picasso was entirely different. Matisse through it was affected more in his imagination than in his vision. Picasso more in his vision than in his imagination. Strangely enough it is only very much later in his life that this influence has affected his imagination and that may be through its having been re-enforced by the Orientalism of the russians when he came in contact with that through Diaghilev and the russian ballet.

In these early days when he created cubism the effect of the african art was purely upon his vision and his forms, his imagination remained purely spanish. The spanish quality of ritual and abstraction had been indeed stimulated by his painting the portrait of Gertrude Stein. . . .

Gertrude Stein always says that cubism is a purely spanish conception and only spaniards can be cubists and that the only real cubism is that of Picasso and Juan Gris. Picasso created it and Juan Gris permeated it with his clarity and his exaltation. To understand this one has only to read the life and death of Juan Gris by Gertrude Stein, written upon the death of one of her two dearest friends, Picasso and Juan Gris, both spaniards. . . .

We were very much struck, the first time Gertrude Stein and I went to Spain, which was a year or so after the beginning of cubism, to see how naturally cubism was made in Spain. In the shops in Barcelona instead of post cards they had square little frames and inside it was placed a cigar, a real one, a pipe, a bit of handkerchief etcetera, all absolutely the arrangement of many a cubist picture and helped out by cut paper representing other objects. That is the modern note that in Spain had been done for centuries.

Ernest Hemingway
The Sun Also Rises

In 1921, the young Ernest Hemingway (1899–1961) and his wife Hadley Richardson traveled to Paris, where they lived for the next five years. Soon after their arrival, Hemingway met Gertrude Stein, who, in a conversation with him, coined the phrase "You are all a lost generation." Stein used the phrase to describe the generation that served in World War I, men who were unable to adjust to life after the war. Soon, however, it came to refer to all the expatriates from America, especially authors and artists. In 1926, Hemingway used Stein's sentence, along with a passage from Ecclesiastes (1:4–7), as the epigraph to his first novel. He appropriated the title of the novel, *The Sun Also Rises,* from the same Ecclesiastes passage:

One generation passeth away, and another generation cometh; but the earth abideth forever. . . . The sun also ariseth, and the sun goeth down, and hasteth to the place where he arose. . . . The wind goeth toward the south, and turneth about unto the north; it whirleth about continually, and the wind returneth again according to his circuits. . . . All the rivers run into the sea; yet the sea is not full; unto the place from whence the rivers come, thither they return again.

The Sun Also Rises brought Hemingway an international reputation, Like a journalist reporting a story, Hemingway relates what he has to say as simply as possible. His writing is free of stylistic devices—metaphors, similes, image-signs—and he rarely uses adjectives and adverbs to modify his carefully chosen nouns and verbs. Hemingway's direct, clipped, bare, and hard prose style continues to exert an incalculable influence on modern writers. "Hemingway as much as any other man has put the raw language of the street, the poolroom, the barracks and the brothel into modern literature."

The narrator of the novel is the journalist Jake Barnes, a veteran of World War I, whose unnamed injury has left him impotent. Jake is in love with Brett Ashley, whom he met in England while recovering from his war wound. Although Brett also loves Jake, she is unwilling to live without sex and plans to marry Mike Campbell, a hard-drinking Scottish war veteran. Robert Cohn, an American Jewish author who lives in Paris, also falls in love with Brett and she has an affair with him. When Bill Gorton, Jake's friend, arrives from America, he and Jake decide to travel to Spain to fish and then to attend the fiesta in Pamplona. Early their first morning in Spain, Jake goes out to dig for worms while Bill sleeps. In the following passage, he has just returned to their room.

"I saw you out of the window," he said. "Didn't want to interrupt you. What were you doing? Burying your money?"

"You lazy bum!"

"Been working for the common good? Splendid. I want you to do that every morning."

"Come on," I said. "Get up."

"What? Get up? I never get up."

He climbed into bed and pulled the sheet up to his chin.

"Try and argue me into getting up."

I went on looking for the tackle and putting it all together in the tackle-bag.

"Aren't you interested?" Bill asked.

"I'm going down and eat."

"Eat? Why didn't you say eat? I thought you just wanted me to get up for fun. Eat? Fine. Now you're reasonable. You go out and dig some more worms and I'll be right down."

"Oh, go to hell!"

"Work for the good of all." Bill stepped into his underclothes. "Show irony and pity."

I started out of the room with the tackle-bag, the nets, and the rod-case.

"Hey! come back!"

I put my head in the door.

"Aren't you going to show a little irony and pity?"

I thumbed my nose.

"That's not irony."

As I went down-stairs I heard Bill singing, "Irony and Pity. When you're feeling . . . oh, Give them Irony and Give them pity. Oh, give them Irony. When they're feeling . . . Just a little irony. Just a little pity . . ." He kept on singing until he came down-stairs. The tune was: "The Bells are Ringing for Me and my Gal." I was reading a week-old Spanish paper.

"What's all this irony and pity?"

"What? Don't you know about Irony and Pity?"

"No. Who got it up?" . . .

"There you go. And you claim you want to be a writer, too. You're only a newspaper man. An expatriated newspaper man. You ought to be ironical the minute you get out of bed. You ought to wake up with your mouth full of pity."

"Go on," I said. "Who did you get this stuff from?"

"Everybody. Don't you read? Don't you ever see anybody? You know what you are? You're an expatriate. Why don't you live in New York? Then you'd know these things. What do you want me to do? Come over here and tell you every year?"

"Take some more coffee," I said.

"Good. Coffee is good for you. It's the caffeine, in it. Caffeine, we are here. Caffeine puts a man on her horse and a woman in his grave. You know what's the trouble with you? You're an expatriate. One of the worst type. Haven't you heard that? Nobody that ever left their own country ever wrote anything worth printing. Not even in the newspapers."

He drank the coffee.

"You're an expatriate. You've lost touch with the soil. You get precious. Fake European standards have ruined you. You drink yourself to death. You become obsessed by sex. You spend all your time talking, not working. You are an expatriate, see? You hang around cafés."

"It sounds like a swell life," I said. "When do I work?"

"You don't work. One group claims women support you. Another group claims you're impotent."

"No," I said. "I just had an accident."

Alcohol had a particular allure for many of the expatriates, perhaps partially because of Prohibition at home. Some were so inclined toward self-destruction that they seemed determined to earn ownership of the label "the lost generation" as Hemingway suggests in the following passage. Jake and Bill are in a cafe in Pamplona during the evening after the bullfight at the end of the fiesta.

We had another absinthe.

"When do you go back?" I asked.

"To-morrow."

After a little while Bill said; "Well, it was a swell fiesta."

"Yes," I said; "something doing all the time."

"You wouldn't believe it. It's like a wonderful nightmare."

"Sure," I said. "I'd believe anything. Including nightmares."

"What's the matter? Feel low?"

"Low as hell."

"Have another absinthe. Here, waiter! Another absinthe for this señor."

"I feel like hell," I said.

"Drink that," said Bill. "Drink it slow."

It was beginning to get dark. The fiesta was going on. I began to feel drunk but I did not feel any better.

"How do you feel?"

"I feel like hell."

"Have another?"

"It won't do any good."

"Try it. You can't tell; maybe this is the one that gets it. Hey, waiter! Another absinthe for this señor!"

I poured the water directly into it and stirred it instead of letting it drip. Bill put in a lump of ice. I stirred the ice around with a spoon in the brownish, cloudy mixture.

"How is it?"

"Fine."

"Don't drink it fast that way. It will make you sick."

I set down the glass. I had not meant to drink it fast.

"I feel tight."

"You ought to."

"That's what you wanted, wasn't it?"

"Sure. Get tight. Get over your damn depression."

"Well, I'm tight. Is that what you want?"

"Sit down."

"I won't sit down," I said. "I'm going over to the hotel."

I was very drunk. I was drunker than I ever remembered having been. At the hotel I went up-stairs. Brett's door was open. I put my head in the room. Mike was sitting on the bed. He waved a bottle.

"Jake," he said. "Come in, Jake."

I went in and sat down. The room was unstable unless I looked at some fixed point.

"Brett, you know. She's gone off with the bull-fighter chap."

"No."

"Yes. She looked for you to say good-bye. They went on the seven o'clock train."

"Did they?"

"Bad thing to do," Mike said. "She shouldn't have done it."

"No."

"Have a drink? Wait while I ring for some beer."

"I'm drunk," I said. "I'm going in and lie down."

"Are you blind? I was blind myself."

"Yes," I said, "I'm blind."

"Well, bung-o." Mike said. "Get some sleep, old Jake."

I went out the door and into my own room and lay on the bed. The bed went sailing off and I sat up in bed and looked at the wall to make it stop. Outside in the square the fiesta was going on. It did not mean anything. Later Bill and Mike came in to get me to go down and eat with them. I pretended to be asleep.

"He's asleep. Better let him alone."

"He's blind as a tick," Mike said. They went out.

I got up and went to the balcony and looked out at the dancing in the square. The world was not wheeling any more. It was just very clear and bright and inclined to blur at the edges. I washed, brushed my hair. I looked strange to myself in the glass, and went down-stairs to the dining-room.

"Here he is!" said Bill. "Good old Jake! I knew you wouldn't pass out."

"Hello, you old drunk," Mike said.

"I got hungry and woke up."

"Eat some soup," Bill said.

The three of us sat at the table, and it seemed as though about six people were missing.

3 Modernist Poetry

During the early decades of the twentieth century, T. S. Eliot, along with Ezra Pound (1885–1972), is credited with starting a "poetic revolution" that transformed the rhyme, diction, and verse of traditional poetic norms. Along with Eliot, William Butler Yeats struggled to find a metaphor for the fear, anxiety, disillusionment, despair, and spiritual desolation of the "lost generation."

The new poetry, like the avant-garde art of the period, was fragmented, disconnected, introspective, and peered into the unconscious. It often dealt with the psyche of the quintessential modern person—neurotic and emotionally disturbed as in T. S.

Eliot's *The Hollow Men.* Conversely, it confronted an impending catastrophic event, as in William Butler Yeats' *Second Coming;* or it considered matters such as old age, as in his *Sailing to Byzantium.*

T. S. Eliot
"The Hollow Men"

Thomas Stearns Eliot (1888–1965) was born in St. Louis and educated at Harvard University. Eliot was in London when World War I broke out, and he remained in England for most of his adult life. In 1914, he met Ezra Pound, who became his friend and mentor. Eliot published his first book of poems, which included the famous *Love Song of J. Alfred Prufrock.* His first major work, *The Waste Land* (1922), made him a leading Modernist poet, along with Pound. The third work that established Eliot as the voice of Modernist poetry was "The Hollow Men," published in 1925. Eliot's early poetry is characterized by chaotic imagery and fragmentation, and it often contains more than a single speaker's voice. It also is distinguished by Eliot's apparent feelings about the meaningless of existence in the years following World War I. However, in 1927, Eliot publicly embraced Anglo-Catholicism, thereby rejecting the Unitarianism of his upbringing; his poetry evidenced a more positive and spiritual dimension after this conversion.

Eliot's "The Hollow Men" contains a two-part epigraph. The first part "Mistah Kurtz—he dead," is from Joseph Conrad's novel *Heart of Darkness* (see page 192). The second part of the epigraph, "A penny for the Old Guy," pertains to the English celebration of Guy Fawkes Day, which commemorates the aborted attempt by Guy Fawkes, in 1605, to blow up a government building and kill King James I. On November 5, when effigies of the traitor are burned, the children call out "a penny for the old guy," hoping to pay for their straw figures of Fawkes. Then, in the first lines of the poem, Eliot identifies the hollow men with straw men, thus establishing the tone of emptiness and despair. The hollow men are empty; they are the walking dead (Mistah Kurtz—he dead); they live in "a dead land." The final part of the poem begins with a parody of the familiar nursery rhyme, "Here we go around the mulberry bush," but instead substitutes the prickly pear cactus. This extends the desert imagery of the third section, and gives a sense of a childish dance gone awry. Then, the Shadow—a paralysis or an inability to act—always falls between good intentions and a beneficial result, indicating that the hollow men are not able to connect vision with reality. The poem ends with a grim echo of the "mulberry bush," warning that the world will not end with a "bang" (great catastrophe) but rather with a "whimper" because of the complacency and indifference of "The Hollow Men."

Mistah Kurtz—he dead.
   A penny for the Old Guy

I

We are the hollow men
We are the stuffed men
Leaning together
Headpiece filled with straw. Alas!
Our dried voices, when
We whisper together

Are quiet and meaningless
As wind in dry grass
Or rats' feet over broken glass
In our dry cellar

   Shape without form, shade without colour,
Paralysed force, gesture without motion;

   Those who have crossed
With direct eyes, to death's other Kingdom
Remember us—if at all—not as lost

Violent souls, but only
As the hollow men
The stuffed men.

II

Eyes I dare not meet in dreams
In death's dream kingdom
These do not appear:
There, the eyes are
Sunlight on a broken column
There, is a tree swinging
And voices are
In the wind's singing
More distant and more solemn
Than a fading star.

Let me be no nearer
In death's dream kingdom
Let me also wear
Such deliberate disguises
Rat's coat, crowskin, crossed staves
In a field
Behaving as the wind behaves
No nearer—

Not that final meeting
In the twilight kingdom.

III

This is the dead land
This is cactus land
Here the stone images
Are raised, here they receive
The supplication of a dead man's hand
Under the twinkle of a fading star.

Is it like this
In death's other kingdom
Waking alone
At the hour when we are
Trembling with tenderness
Lips that would kiss
Form prayers to broken stone.

IV

The eyes are not here
There are no eyes here
In this valley of dying stars
In this hollow valley
This broken jaw of our lost kingdoms

In this last of meeting places
We grope together
And avoid speech
Gathered on this beach of the tumid river

Sightless, unless
The eyes reappear
As the perpetual star
Multifoliate rose
Of death's twilight kingdom
The hope only
Of empty men.

V

*Here we go round the prickly pear
Prickly pear prickly pear
Here we go round the prickly pear
At five o'clock in the morning.*

Between the idea
And the reality
Between the motion
And the act
Falls the Shadow
                    For Thine is the Kingdom

Between the conception
And the creation
Between the emotion
And the response
Falls the Shadow
                    Life is very long

Between the desire
And the spasm
Between the potency
And the existence
Between the essence
And the descent
Falls the Shadow
                    For Thine is the Kingdom
For Thine is
Life is
For Thine is the

*This is the way the world ends
This is the way the world ends
This is the way the world ends
Not with a bang but a whimper.*

William Butler Yeats
"The Second Coming" and "Sailing to Byzantium"

The poet William Butler Yeats (1865–1939) is generally considered to be the greatest Irish poet, and he has often been called the greatest poet of the twentieth century. He was born in Dublin, the son of an Irish-English father and an Irish mother. After spending much of his childhood in London, he settled in Ireland where he immersed himself in Irish folklore and tradition. Yeats was awarded the Nobel Prize in Literature in 1923 "for his always inspired poetry, which in a highly artistic form gives expression to the spirit of a whole nation." Another important influence on his poetry was Maud Gonne (1865–1953), the Irish patriot and revolutionary with whom he was close but whom he never married. Although Yeats never abandoned traditional verse forms, his poems are filled with Modern images, or word pictures, such as those in his poem "The Second Coming." It was written in January 1919, just as the peace conference ending World War I was getting underway in Paris.

The terrifying images in the poem express Yeats' dread of what the future might hold after the horror of World War I. The reference to "the widening gyre" in the opening line of the poem reflects a facet of Yeats' belief in a cyclical theory of history. Each new age, or gyre, lasts two thousand years and begins and ends with an apocalyptic event. Nonetheless, this is not the new age promised with the Christian teaching about the Second Coming of Christ, predicted in Matthew 24; nor is the beast a reference to the beast of the Apocalypse of Revelation 13. This "rough beast" is a different sort of deity, who will take advantage of the anarchy of the day. The "Spiritus Mundi" is, for Yeats, the subconscious mind of the human race in which all humans participate. Literally, this "spirit of the world" is the source of all images for the poet.

THE SECOND COMING

Turning and turning in the widening gyre
The falcon cannot hear the falconer;
Things fall apart; the centre cannot hold;
Mere anarchy is loosed upon the world,
The blood-dimmed tide is loosed, and everywhere
The ceremony of innocence is drowned;
The best lack all convictions, while the worst
Are full of passionate intensity.

Surely some revelation is at hand;
Surely the Second Coming is at hand.
The Second Coming! Hardly are those words out
When a vast image out of Spiritus Mundi
Troubles my sight: somewhere in sands of the desert
A shape with lion body and the head of a man,
A gaze blank and pitiless as the sun,
Is moving its slow thighs, while all about it
Reel shadows of the indignant desert birds.
The darkness drops again; but now I know
That twenty centuries of stony sleep

Were vexed to nightmare by a rocking cradle,
And what rough beast, its hour come round at last,
Slouches towards Bethlehem to be born?

SAILING TO BYZANTIUM

In 1926 at the age of sixty-one, Yeats wrote "Sailing to Byzantium," in which he not only came to grips with his apprehensions about becoming an old man, but also affirmed his belief in the immortality of his soul or spirit. Byzantium (also Constantinople, and today Istanbul) was, for Yeats, a holy land, a paradise akin to heaven, especially during the reign of the Emperor Justinian (527–565). Although Yeats never actually traveled to Byzantium, he had visited Ravenna, Italy, where he learned about Byzantine art and architecture. The first stanza of the poem describes the temporal, sensual present time, where real birds sing. In the second stanza, there is no singing school for the old man, so he escapes, sailing from the present to Byzantium. In the third stanza, he appeals to the sages of God to be "the singing-masters of my soul" and to take his heart away from this "dying animal" and gather him into "the artifice of eternity." When he is finally free from his body, he hopes to take on the form of a golden bird singing on a golden bough about past, present, and future, all as a single occurrence.

I

That is no country for old men. The young
In one another's arms, birds in their trees
—Those dying generations—at their song,
The salmon-falls, the mackerel-crowded seas,
Fish, flesh, or fowl, commend all summer long
Whatever is begotten, born, and dies.
Caught in that sensual music all neglect
Monuments of unageing intellect.

II

An aged man is but a paltry thing,
A tattered coat upon a stick, unless
Soul clap its hands and sing, and louder sing
For every tatter in its mortal dress,

Nor is there singing school but studying
Monuments of its own magnificence;
And therefore I have sailed the seas and come
To the holy city of Byzantium.

III

O sages standing in God's holy fire
As in the gold mosaic of a wall,
Come from the holy fire, perne [spinning] in a gyre,
And be the singing-masters of my soul.
Consume my heart away; sick with desire
And fastened to a dying animal
It knows not what it is; and gather me
Into the artifice of eternity.

IV

Once out of nature I shall never take
My bodily form from any natural thing,
But such a form as Grecian goldsmiths make
Of hammered gold and gold enamelling
To keep a drowsy Emperor awake;
Or set upon a golden bough to sing
To lords and ladies of Byzantium
Of what is past, or passing, or to come.

4 Modernist Drama

Poets, novelists, and playwrights continued to experiment with ways to express the intense struggle between the conscious and the unconscious and to explore the aberrations and complexities of human personality and the irrationality of human behavior. Expressionist writers concerned themselves with the inner reality of the mind, with the hidden self that was often revealed in fantasies, dreams, and hallucinations. They portrayed frenzied and irrational behavior that gave expression to intense, subjective feelings. To dramatize this behavior, dramatists and novelists punctuated dialogue with nervous and explosive outbursts. Reacting against Realism and Naturalism, which aspired to an accurate and objective depiction of external reality and human behavior, Expressionist writers deliberately distorted shapes and movements.

Although Expressionism as a movement died out by the mid-1920s, its techniques, assimilated by playwrights, became a permanent part of drama. Social questions were another concern of dramatists in the period between the two world wars. Liberal and Marxist playwrights focused on the plight of the poor and the misbehavior of capitalists. Among the leading playwrights of this generation was Eugene O'Neill.

Eugene Gladstone O'Neill (1888–1953), considered by many to be America's finest dramatist, grew up in a troubled household; the love-hate that consumed relationships among his father, a prominent actor; his morphine addicted mother; his alcoholic brother; and himself were dramatized in his plays, particularly in the autobiographical *Long Day's Journey into Night,* published posthumously, in 1956.

After being expelled for misbehavior from Princeton at the end of his freshman year, O'Neill worked at various jobs, including as a gold prospector in Honduras, a seaman, and a reporter before he decided to become a playwright. O'Neill established himself in the 1920s as a major dramatist with more than a dozen plays, including *The Emperor Jones* (1920), *The Hairy Ape* (1922), and *Strange Interlude* (1928).

The Emperor Jones, which depicts a man coming apart emotionally, is an experiment in depth psychology. It shows how easily our rational faculties break down, and at such times, the unconscious, a storehouse of primitive feelings shared collectively by all human beings, takes control of us. Influenced by Expressionism, O'Neill sought to penetrate the mind's deepest recesses.

Eugene O'Neill
The Hairy Ape

The Hairy Ape deals with alienation, a crucial concern in modern urban and industrial society. Yank, the principal character, toils as a stoker fueling the furnaces in the bowels of a transatlantic liner. The stokers are all hard-drinking, hairy-chested, long-armed, powerful men. All of them fear and respect Yank for his superior strength. A passenger on the ship, Mildred, a wealthy and attractive young woman of twenty, who had done social work in the slums of the East Side of New York, visits the stokehole "anxious . . . {to} investigate how the other half lives and works on ships." Accompanied by two engineers. Mildred, wearing a white dress, enters the blazing hot stokehole, where the men, stripped to the waist, rhythmically shovel coal into the fiery furnace.

SCENE III

The stokehole. In the rear, the dimly outlined bulks of the furnaces and boilers. High overhead one hanging electric bulb sheds just enough light through the murky air laden with coal dust to pile up masses of shadows everywhere. A line of men, stripped to the waist, is before the furnace doors. They bend over, looking neither to right nor left, handling their shovels as if they were part of their bodies, with a strange, awkward, swinging rhythm. They use the shovels to throw open the furnace doors. Then from these fiery round holes in the black a flood of terrific light and heat pours full upon the men who are outlined in silhouette in the crouching, inhuman attitudes of chained gorillas. The men shovel with a rhythmic motion, swinging as on a pivot from the coal which lies in heaps on the floor behind to hurl it into the flaming mouths before them. There is a tumult of noise—the brazen clang of the furnace doors as they are flung open or slammed shut, the grating, teeth-gritting grind of steel against steel, and of crunching coal. This clash of sounds stuns one's ears with its rending dissonance. But there is order in it, rhythm, a mechanically regulated recurrence, a tempo. And rising above all, making the air hum with the quiver of liberated energy, the roar of leaping flames in the furnaces, the monotonous throbbing beat of the engines.

As the curtain rises, the furnace doors are shut. The Men are taking a breathing spell. One or two are arranging the coal behind them, pulling it into more accessible heaps. The others can be dimly made out leaning on their shovels in relaxed attitudes of exhaustion.

PADDY (*From somewhere in the line —plaintively*) Yerra, will this divil's own watch nivir end? Me back is broke. I'm destroyed entirely.

YANK (*From the center of the line—with exuberant scorn*) Aw, yuh make me sick! Lie down and croak, why don't yuh? Always beefin', dat's you! Say, dis is a cinch! Dis was made for me! It's my meat, get me! (*A whistle is blown—a thin, shrill note from somewhere overhead in the darkness.* Yank *curses without resentment*) Dere's de damn engineer crackin de whip. He tinks we're loafin'.

PADDY (*Vindictively*) God stiffen him!

YANK (*In an exultant tone of command*) Come on, youse guys! Git into de game! She's gittin' hungry! Pile some grub in her. Trow it into her belly! Come on now, all of youse! Open her up!

(*At this last all the* Men, *who have followed his movements of getting into position, throw open their furnace doors with a deafening clang. The fiery light floods over their shoulders as they bend round for the coal. Rivulets of sooty sweat have traced maps on their backs. The enlarged muscles form bunches of high light and shadow*)

YANK (*Chanting a count as he shovels without seeming effort*) One-two-three——(*His voice rising exultantly in the joy of battle*) Dat's de stuff? Let her have it! All togedder now! Sling it into her! Let her ride! Shoot de piece now! Call de toin on her! Drive her into it! Feel her move! Watch her smoke! Speed, dat's her middle name! Give her coal, youse guys! Coal, dat's her booze! Drink it up, baby! Let's see yuh sprint! Dig in and gain a lap! Dere she go-o-es.

(*This last in the chanting formula of the gallery gods at the six day bike race. He slams his furnace door shut. The others do likewise with as much unison as their wearied bodies will permit. The effect is of one fiery eye after another being blotted out with a series of accompanying bangs*)

PADDY (*Groaning*) Me back is broke. I'm bate out—bate——

(*There is a pause. Then the inexorable whistle sounds again from the dim regions above the electric light. There is a growl of cursing rage from all sides*)

YANK (*Shaking his fist upward—contemptuously*) Take it easy dare, you! Who d'yuh tink's runnin' dis game, me or you? When I git ready, we move, not before! When I git ready, get me!

VOICES (*Approvingly*) That's the stuff! Yank tal him, py golly!
Yank ain't affeerd.
Goot poy, Yank!
Give him hell!
Tell 'im 'e's a bloody swine!
Bloody slave-driver!

YANK (*Contemptuously*) He ain't got no noive. He's yellow, get me? All de engineers is yellow. Dey got streaks a mile wide. Aw, to hell wit him! Let's move, youse guys. We had a rest. Come on, she needs it! Give her pep! It ain't for him. Him and his whistle, dey don't belong. But we belong, see! We gotter feed de baby! Come on!

(*He turns and flings his furnace door open. They all follow his lead. At this instant the Second and Fourth Engineers enter from the darkness on the left with Mildred between them. She starts, turns paler, her pose is crumbling, she shivers with fright in spite of the blazing heat, but forces herself to leave the Engineers and take a few steps nearer the men. She is right behind Yank. All this happens quickly while the men have their backs turned*)

YANK Come on, youse guys!

(*He is turning to get coal when the whistle sounds again in a peremptory, irritating note. This drives Yank into a sudden fury. While the other Men have turned full around and stopped dumbfounded by the spectacle of Mildred standing there in her white dress, Yank does not turn far enough to see her. Besides, his head is thrown back, he blinks upward through the murk trying to find the owner of the whistle, he brandishes his shovel murderously over his head in one hand, pounding on his chest, gorilla-like, with the other, shouting*)

YANK Toin off dat whistle! Come down outa dare, yuh yellow, brass-buttoned, Belfast bum, yuh! Come down and I'll knock yer brains out! Yuh lousy, stinkin', yellow mut of a Catholic-moiderin' bastard! Come down and I'll moider yuh! Pullin' dat whistle on me, huh? I'll show yuh! I'll crash yer skull in! I'll drive yer teet' down yer troat! I'll slam yer nose trou de back of yer head! I'll cut yer guts out for a nickel, yuh lousy boob, yuh dirty, crummy, muck-eatin' son of a——

(*Suddenly he becomes conscious of all the other Men staring at something directly behind his back. He whirls defensively with a snarling, murderous growl, crouching to spring, his lips drawn back over his teeth, his small eyes gleaming ferociously. He sees Mildred, like a white apparition in the full light from the open furnace doors. He glares into her eyes, turned to stone. As for her, during his speech she has listened, paralyzed with horror, terror, her whole personality crushed, beaten in, collapsed, by the terrific impact of this unknown, abysmal brutality, naked and shameless. As she looks at his gorilla face, as his eyes bore into hers, she utters a low, choking cry and shrinks away from him, putting both hands up before her eyes to shut out the sight of his face, to protect her own. This startles Yank to a reaction. His mouth falls open, his eyes grow bewildered*)

MILDRED (*About to faint—to the Engineers, who now have her one by each arm—whimperingly*) Take me away! Oh, the filthy beast!

(*She faints. They carry her quickly back, disappearing in the darkness at the left, rear. An iron door clangs shut. Rage and bewildered fury rush back on Yank. He feels himself insulted in some unknown fashion in the very heart of his pride. He roars*)

YANK God damn yuh!

(*And hurls his shovel after them at the door which has just closed. It hits the steel bulkhead with a clang and falls clattering on the steel floor. From overhead the whistle sounds again in a long, angry, insistent command*)

CURTAIN

SCENE IV

The firemen's forecastle. *Yank's* watch has just come off duty and had dinner. Their faces and bodies shine from a soup and water scrubbing but around their eyes, where a hasty dousing does not touch, the coal dust sticks like black make-up, giving them a queer, sinister expression.

Yank has not washed either face or body. He stands out in contrast to them, a blackened, brooding figure. He is seated forward on a bench in the exact attitude of Rodin's "The Thinker," The others, most of them smoking pipes, are staring at *Yank* half-apprehensively, as if fearing an outburst; half-amusedly, as if they saw a joke somewhere that tickled them.

VOICES He ain't ate nothin'.
Py golly, a fallar gat to gat grub in him.

Divil a lie.
Yank feeda da fire, no feeda da face.
Ha-ha.
He ain't even washed hisself.
He's forgot.
Hey, Yank, you forgot to wash.

YANK (*Sullenly*) Forgot nothin'! To hell wit washin'.

VOICES I'll stick to you.
It'll get under your skin.
Give yer the bleedin' itch, that's wot.
It makes spots on you—like a leopard.
Like a piebald nigger, you mean.
Better wash up, Yank.
You sleep better,
Wash up, Yank.
Wash up! Wash up!

YANK (*Resentfully*) Aw say, youse guys. Lemme alone. Can't youse see I'm tryin to tink?

ALL (*Repeating the word after him, as one, with cynical mockery*) Think!
(*The word has a brazen, metallic quality as if their throats were phonograph horns. It is followed by a chorus of hard, barking laughter*)

YANK (*Springing to his feet and glaring at them belligerently*) Yes, tink! Tink, dat's what I said! What about it?
(*They are silent, puzzled by his sudden resentment at what used to be one of his jokes. Yank sits down again in the same attitude of "The Thinker"*)

VOICES Leave him alone.
He's got a grouch on.
Why wouldn't he?

PADDY (*With a wink at the others*) Sure I knows what's the matther. 'Tis aisy to see. He's fallen in love, I'm telling you.

ALL (*Repeating the word after him, as one, with cynical mockery*) Love!
(*The word has a brazen metallic quality as if their throats were phonograph horns. It is followed by a chorus of hard, barking laughter*)

YANK (*With a contemptuous snort*) Love, hell! Hate, dat's what. I've fallen in hate, get me?

PADDY (*Philosophically*) 'Twould take a wise man to tell one from the other. (*With a bitter, ironical scorn, increasing as he goes on*) But I'm telling you it's love that's in it. Sure what else but love for us poor bastes in the stoke-hole would be bringing a fine lady, dressed like a white quane, down a mile of ladders and steps to be havin' a look at us?
(*A growl of anger goes up from all sides*)

LONG (*Jumping on a bench—hecticly*) Hinsultin' us! Hinsultin' us, the bloody cow! And them bloody engineers! What right 'as they got to be exhibitin' us 's if we was bleedin' monkeys in a menagerie? Did we sign for hinsults to our dignity as 'onest workers? Is that in the ship's articles? You kin bloody well bet it ain't! But I knows why they done it. I arsked a deck steward 'oo she was and 'e told me. 'Er old man's a bleedin' millionaire, a bloody Capitalist! 'E's got enuf bloody gold to sink this bleedin' ship! 'E makes arf the bloody steel in the world! 'E owns this bloody boat! And you and me, Comrades, we're 'is slaves! And the skipper and mates and engineers, they're 'is slaves! And she's 'is bloody daughter and we're all 'er slaves, too! And she gives 'er orders as 'ow she wants to see the bloody animals below decks and down they takes 'er!
(*There here is a roar of rage from all sides*)

YANK (*Blinking at him bewilderedly*) Say! Wait a moment! Is all dat straight goods?

LONG Straight as string! The bleedin' steward as waits on 'em, 'e told me about 'er. And what're we goin' ter do, I arsks yet? 'Ave we got ter swaller 'er hinsults like dogs? It ain't in the ship's articles. I tell yer we got a case. We kin go to law——

YANK (*With abysmal contempt*) Hell! Law!

ALL (*Repeating the word after him, as one, with cynical mockery*) Law!
(*The word has a brazen metallic quality as if their throats were phonograph horns. It is followed by a chorus of hard, barking laughter*)

LONG (*Feeling the ground slipping from under his feet—desperately*) As voters and citizens we kin force the bloody governments——

YANK (*With abysmal contempt*) Hell! Governments!

ALL (*Repeating the word after him, as one, with cynical mockery*) Governments!
(*The word has a brazen metallic quality as if their throats were phonograph horns. It is followed by a chorus of hard, barking laughter*)

LONG (*Hysterically*) We're free and equal in the sight at God——

YANK (*With abysmal contempt*) Hell! God!

ALL (*Repeating the word after him, as one, with cynical mockery*) God!
(*The word has a brazen metallic quality as it their throats were phonograph horns. It is followed by a chorus of hard, barking, laughter*)

YANK (*Witheringly*) Aw, join de Salvation Army!

ALL Sit down! Shut up! Damn fool! Sea-lawyer! (Long *slinks back out of sight*)

PADDY (*Continuing the trend of his thoughts as if he had never been interrupted—bitterly*) And there she was standing behind us, and the Second pointing at us like a man you'd hear in a circus would be saying: In this cage is a queerer kind of baboon than ever you'd find in darkest Africy. We roast them in their own sweat—and be damned if you won't hear some of thim saying they like it! (*He glances scornfully at* Yank)

YANK (*With a bewildered uncertain growl*) Aw!

PADDY And there was Yank roarin' curses and turning round wid his shovel to brain her—and she looked at him, and him at her——

YANK (*Slowly*) She was all white. I tought she was a ghost. Sure.

PADDY (*With heavy, biting sarcasm*) 'Twas love at first sight, divil a doubt of it! If you'd seen the endearin' look on her pale mug when she shriveled away with her hands over her eyes to shut out the sight of him! Sure, 'twas as if she'd seen a great hairy ape escaped from the Zoo!

YANK (*Stung—with a growl of rage*) Aw!

PADDY And the loving way Yank heaved his shovel at the skull at her, only she was out the door! (*A grin breaking over his face*) 'Twas touching, I'm telling you! It put the touch of home, swate home in the stokehole.

(*There is a roar of laughter from all*)

YANK (*Glaring at* Paddy *menacingly*) Aw, choke dat off, see!

PADDY (*Not heeding him—to the others*) And her grabbin' at the Second's arm for protection. (*With a grotesque imitation of a woman's voice*) Kiss me, Engineer dear, for it's dark down here and me old man's in Wall Street making money; Hug me tight, darlin', for I'm afeerd in the dark and me mother's on deck makin' eyes at the skipper!

(*Another roar of laughter*)

YANK (*Threateningly*) Say! What yuh tryin' to do, kid me, yuh old Harp?

PADDY Divil a bit! Ain't I wishin' myself you'd brained her?

YANK (*Fiercely*) I'll brain her! I'll brain her yet, wait 'n' see! (*Coming over to* Paddy—*slowly*) Say, is dat what she called me—a hairy ape?

PADDY She looked it at you if she didn't say the word itself.

YANK (*Grinning horribly*) Hairy ape, huh? Sure! Dat's de way she looked at me, aw right. Hairy ape! So dat's me, huh? (*Bursting into rage—as if she were still in front of him*) Yuh skinny tart! Yuh white-faced bum, yuh! I'll show yuh who's a ape! (*Turning to the others, bewilderment seizing him again*) Say, youse guys. I was bawlin' him out for pullin' de whistle on us. You heard me. And den I seen youse lookin' at somep'n and I tought he'd sneaked down to come up in

back of me, and I hopped round to knock him dead wit de shovel. And dere she was wit de light on her! Christ, yuh coulda pushed me over wit a finger! I was scared, get me? Sure! I tought she was a ghost, see? She was all in white like dey wrap around stiffs. You seen her. Kin yuh blame me? She didn't belong, dat's what. And den when I come to and seen it was a real skoit and seen de way she was lookin' at me—like Paddy said—Christ, I was sore, get me? I don't stand for dat stuff from nobody. And I flung de shovel—on'y she'd beat it. (*Furiously*) I wished it'd banged her! I wished it'd knocked her block off!

LONG And be 'anged for murder or 'lectrocuted? She ain't bleedin' well worth it.

YANK I don't give a damn what! I'd be square wit her, wouldn't I? Tink I wanter let her put somep'n over on me? Tink I'm goin' to let her git away wit dat stuff? Yuh don't know me! No one ain't never put nothin' over on me and got away wit it, see!—not dat kind of stuff—no guy and no skoit neither! I'll fix her! Maybe she'll come down again——

VOICE No chance, Yank. You scared her out of a year's growth.

YANK I scared her? Why de hell should I scare her? Who de hell is she? Ain't she de same as me? Hairy ape, huh? (*With his old confident bravado*) I'll show her I'm better'n her, if she on'y knew it. I belong and she don't, see! I move and she's dead! Twenty-five knots a hour, dat's me! Dat carries her but I make dat. She's on'y baggage. Sure! (*Again bewilderedly*) But, Christ, she was funny lookin'! Did yuh pipe her hands? White and skinny. Yuh could see de bones through 'em. And her mush, dat was dead white, too. And her eyes, dey was like dey'd seen a ghost. Me, dat was! Sure! Hairy ape! Ghost, huh? Lack at dat arm! (*He extends his right arm, swelling out the great muscles*) I coulda took her wit dat, wit just my little finger even, and broke her in two. (*Again bewilderedly*) Say, who is dat skoit, huh? What is she? What's she come from? Who made her? Who give her de noive to look at me like dat? Dis ting's got my goat right. I don't get her. She's new to me. What does a skoit like her mean, huh? She don't belong, get me! I can't see her. (*With growing anger*) But one ting I'm wise to, aw right, aw right! Youse all kin bet your shoits I'll git even wit her. I'll show her if she tinks she— She grinds de organ and I'm on de string, huh? I'll fix her! Let her come down again and I'll fling her in de furnace! She'll move den! She won't shiver at nothin', den! Speed, dat'll be her! She'll belong den! (*He grins horribly*)

PADDY She'll never come. She's had her bellyfull, I'm telling you. She'll be in bed now, I'm thinking, wid ten doctors and nurses feedin' her salts to clean the fear out of her.

YANK (*Enraged*) Yuh tink I made her sick too, do yuh? Just lookin' at me, huh? Hairy ape, huh? (*In a frenzy of rage*) I'll fix her! I'll tell her where to git off! She'll git down on her knees and take it back or I'll bust de face offen her! (*Shaking one fist upward and beating on his chest with the other*) I'll find yuh! I'm comin', d'yuh hear? I'll fix yuh, God damn yuh! (*He makes a rush for the door*)

VOICES Stop him! He'll get shot!
He'll murder her!
Trip him up!
Hold him!
He's gone crazy!
Gott, he's strong!
Hold him down!
Look out for a kick!
Pin his arms!
(*They have all piled on him and, after a fierce struggle, by sheer weight of numbers have borne him to the floor just inside the door*)

PADDY (*Who has remained detached*) Kape him down till he's cooled off. (*Scornfully*) Yerra, Yank, you're a great fool. Is it payin' attention at all you are to the like of that skinny sow widout one drop of rale blood in her?

YANK (*Frenziedly, from the bottom of the heap*) She done me doit! She done me doit, didn't she? I'll git square wit her! I'll get her some way! Git offen me, youse guys! Lemme up! I'll show her who's a ape!

CURTAIN

SCENE V

Three weeks later. A corner of Fifth Avenue in the Fifties on a fine Sunday morning. A general atmosphere of clean, well-tidied, wide street; a flood of mellow, tempered sunshine; gentle, genteel breezes. In the rear, the show windows of two shops, a jewelry establishment on the corner, a furrier's next to it. Here the adornments of extreme wealth are tantalizingly displayed. The jeweler's window is gaudy with glittering diamonds, emeralds, rubies, pearls, etc., fashioned in ornate tiaras, crowns, necklaces, collars, etc. From each piece hangs an enormous tag from which a dollar sign and numerals in intermittent electric lights wink out the incredible prices. The same in the furrier's. Rich furs of all varieties hang there bathed in a downpour of artificial light. The general effect is of a background of magnificence cheapened and made grotesque by commercialism, a background in tawdry disharmony with the clear light and sunshine on the street itself.

Up the side street *Yank* and *Long* come swaggering. *Long* is dressed in shore clothes, wears a black Windsor tie, cloth cap. *Yank* is in his dirty dungarees. A fireman's cap with black peak is cocked defiantly on the side of his head. He has not shaved for days and around his fierce, resentful eyes—as around those of *Long* to a lesser degree—the black smudge of coal dust still sticks like make-up. They

hesitate and stand together on the corner, swaggering, looking about them with a forced, defiant contempt.

LONG (*Indicating it all with an oratorical gesture*) Well, 'ere we are. Fif' Avenoo. This 'ere's their bleedin' private lane, as yer might say. (*Bitterly*) We're trespassers 'ere. Proletarians keep orf the grass!

YANK (*Dully*) I don't see no grass, yuh boob. (*Staring at the sidewalk*) Clean, ain't it? Yuh could eat a fried egg offen it. The white wings got some job sweepin' dis up. (*Looking up and down the avenue—surlily*) Where's all de white-collar stiffs yuh said was here—and de skoits—her kind?

LONG In church, blarst 'em! Arskin' Jesus to give 'em more money.

YANK Choich, huh? I useter go to choich onct—sure—when I was a kid. Me old man and woman, dey made me. Dey never went demselves, dough. Always got too big a head on Sunday mornin', dat was dem. (*With a grin*) Dey was scrappers for fair, bot' of dem. On Satiday nights when dey bot' got a skinful dey could put up a bout oughter been staged at de Garden. When dey got trough dere wasn't a chair or table wit a leg under it. Or else dey bot' jumped on me for somep'n. Dat was where I loined to take punishment. (*With a grin and a swagger*) I'm a chip offen de old block, get me? . . .

LONG (*Excitedly*) Church is out. 'Ere they come, the bleedin' swine. (*After a glance at* Yank's *lowering face—uneasily*) Easy goes, Comrade. Keep yer bloomin' temper. Remember force defeats itself. It ain't our weapon. We must impress our demands through peaceful means—the votes of the on-marching proletarians of the bloody world!

YANK (*With abysmal contempt*) Votes, hell! Votes is a joke, see? Votes for women! Let dem do it!

LONG (*Still more uneasily*) Calm, now. Treat 'em wiv the proper contempt. Observe the bieedin' parasites but 'old yer 'orses.

YANK (*Angrily*) Git away from me! Yuh're yellow, dat's what. Force, dat's me! De punch, dat's me every time, see! (*The* Crowd *from church enter from the right, sauntering slowly and affectedly, their heads held stiffly up, looking neither to right nor left, talking in toneless, simpering voices. The* Women *are rouged, calcimined, dyed, overdressed to the nth degree. The* Men *are in Prince Alberts, high hats, spats, canes, etc. A procession of gaudy marionettes, yet with something of the relentless horror of Frankensteins in their detached, mechanical unawareness*)

VOICES Dear Doctor Caiaphas! He is so sincere! What was the sermon? I dozed off.
About the radicals, my dear—and the false doctrines that are being preached.
We must organize a hundred per cent American bazaar.
And let everyone contribute one one-hundredth per cent of their income tax.

What an original idea!

We can devote the proceeds to rehabilitating the veil of the temple.

But that has been done so many times.

YANK (*Glaring from one to the other of them—with an insulting snort of scorn*) Huh! Huh!
(*Without seeming to see him, they make wide detours to avoid the spot where he stands in the middle of the sidewalk*)

LONG (*Frightenedly*) Keep yer bloomin' mouth shut, I tells yer.

YANK (*Viciously*) G'wan! Tell it to Sweeney! (*He swaggers away and deliberately lurches into a top-hatted* Gentleman, *then glares at him pugnaciously*) Say, who d'yuh tink yuh're bumpin'? Tink yuh own do oith?

GENTLEMAN (*Coldly and affectedly*) I beg your pardon. (*He has not looked at Yank and passes on without a glance, leaving him bewildered*)

LONG (*Rushing up and grabbing* Yank's *arm*) 'Ere! Come away! This wasn't what I meant. Yer'll ave the bloody coppers down on us.

YANK (*Savagely—giving him a push that sends him sprawling*) G'wan!

LONG (*Picks himself up—hysterically*) I'll pop orf then. This ain't what I meant. And whatever 'appens, yet can't blame me. (*He slinks off left*)

YANK T' hell wit youse! (*He approaches a* Lady—*with a vicious grin and a smirking wink*) Hello, Kiddo. How's every little ting? Got anything on for tonight? I know an old boiler down to de docks we kin crawl into. (*The* Lady *stalks by without a look, without a change of pace.* Yank *turns to others—insultingly*) Holy smokes, what a mug! Go hide yuhself before de horses shy at yuh. Gee, pipe de heinie on dat one! Say, youse, yuh look like de stoin of a ferryboat. Paint and powder! All dolled up to kill! Yuh look like stiffs laid out for de boneyard! Aw, g'wan, de lot of youse! Yuh give me de eye-ache. Yuh don't belong, get me! Look at me, why don't youse dare? I belong, dat's me! (*Pointing to a sky-scraper across the street which is in process of construction—with bravado*) See dat building goin', up dere? See de steel work? Steel, dat's me! Youse guys live on it and tink yuh're somep'n. But I'm *in* it, see! I'm de hoistin' engine dat makes it go up! I'm it—de inside and bottom of it! Sure! I'm steel and steam and smoke and de rest of it! It moves—speed—twenty-five stories up—and me at de top and bottom—movin'! Youse simps don't move. Yuh're on'y dolls I winds up to see 'm spin. Yuh're de garbage, get me—de leavins—de ashes we dump over de side! Now, what 'a' yuh gotta say? (*But as they seem neither to see nor hear him, he flies into a fury*) Bums! Pigs! Tarts! Bitches! (*He turns in a rage on the* Men, *bumping viciously into them but not jarring them the least bit. Rather it is he who recoils after*

each collision. He keeps growling) Git off de oith! G'wan, yuh bum! Look where yuh're goin', can't yuh? Git outa here! Fight, why don't yuh? Put up yer mits! Don't be a dog! Fight or I'll knock yuh dead! (*But, without seeming to see him, they all answer with mechanical affected politeness:*) I beg your pardon.
(*Then, at a cry from one of the* Women, *they all scurry to the furrier's window*)

THE WOMAN (*Ecstatically, with a gasp of delight*) Monkey fur! (*The whole crowd of* Men *and* Women *chorus after her in the same tone of affected delight*) Monkey fur!

YANK (*With a jerk of his head back on his shoulders, as if he had received a punch full in the face—raging*) I see yuh, all in white! I see yuh, yuh white-faced tart, yuh! Hairy ape, huh? I'll hairy ape yuh!
(*He bends down and grips at the street curbing as if to pluck it out and hurl it. Foiled in this, snarling with passion, he leaps to the lamppost on the corner and tries to pull it up for a club. Just at that moment a bus is heard rumbling up. A fat, high-hatted, spatted* Gentleman *runs out from the side street. He calls out plaintively:*)

GENTLEMAN Bus! Bus! Stop there! (*And runs full tilt into the bending, straining* Yank, *who is bowled off his balance*)

YANK (*Seeing a fight—with a roar of joy as he springs to his feet*) At last! Bus, huh? I'll bust yuh! (*He lets drive a terrific swing, his fist landing full on the fat* Gentleman's *face. But the* Gentleman *stands unmoved as if nothing had happened*)

GENTLEMAN I beg your pardon. (*Then irritably*) You have made me lose my bus. (*He claps his hands and begins to scream:*) Officer! Officer!
(*Many police whistles shrill out on the instant and a whole platoon of* Policemen *rush in on Yank from all sides. He tries to fight but is clubbed to the pavement and fallen upon. The* Crowd *at the window have not moved or noticed this disturbance. The clanging gong of the patrol wagon approaches with a clamoring din*)

The upper classes view Yank as a primitive manbeast and totally ignore him. Even a labor union, which fights for workers like Yank, rejects him. When Yank wants to blow up the steel works owned by Mildred's father, the union official regards him as a "dirty spy, a rotten agent provacator" and tells him to "go back and tell whatever skunk is paying you blood-money for betraying your brothers that he's wasting his coin. And tell him that all he'll ever get on us, or ever has got, is just his own sneaking plots that he's framed up to put us in jail." Several husky men kick and throw Yank sprawling into the middle of the cobbled street. Sitting like Rodin's sculpture "The Thinker," a brooding Yank mutters bitterly: "so dem boids don't tink I belong, neider."

SCENE VIII

Twilight of the next day. The monkey house at the Zoo. One spot of clear gray light falls on the front of one cage so that the interior can be seen. The other cages are vague, shrouded in shadow from which chatterings pitched in a conversational tone can be heard. On the one cage a sign from which the word "gorilla" stands out. The gigantic Animal himself is seen squatting on his haunches on a bench in much the same attitude as Rodin's "Thinker." Yank enters from the left. Immediately a chorus of angry chattering and screeching breaks out, The Gorilla turns his eyes but makes no sound or move.

YANK (*With a hard, bitter laugh*) Welcome to your city, huh? Hail, hail, de gang's all here! (*At the sound of his voice the chattering dies away into an attentive silence. Yank walks up to the Gorilla's cage and, leaning over the railing, stares in at its occupant, who stares back at him, silent and motionless. There is a pause of dead stillness. Then Yank begins to talk in a friendly confidential tone, half-mockingly, but with a deep undercurrent of sympathy*) Say, yuh're some hard-lookin' guy, ain't yuh? I seen lots of tough nuts dat de gang called gorillas, but yuh're de foist real one I ever seen. Some chest yuh got, and shoulders, and dem arms and mits! I bet yuh got a punch in eider fist dat'd knock 'em all silly! (*This with genuine admiration. The Gorilla, as if he understood, stands upright, swelling out his chest and pounding on it with his fist. Yank grins sympathetically*) Sure, I get yuh. Yuh challenge de whole woild, huh? Yuh got what I was sayin' even if yuh muffed de woids. (*Then bitterness creeping in*) And why wouldn't yuh get me? Ain't we both members of de same club—de Hairy Apes? (*They stare at each other—a pause—then Yank goes on slowly and bitterly*) So yuh're what she seen when she looked at me, de white-faced tart! I was you to her, get me? On'y outa de cage—broke out—free to moider her, see? Sure! Dat's what she tought. She wasn't wise dat I was in a cage, too—worser'n yours—sure—a damn sight—'cause you got some chanct to bust loose—but me— (*He grows confused*) Aw, hell! It's wrong, ain't it? (*A pause*) I s'pose yuh wanter know what I'm doin' here, huh? I been warmin' a bench down to de Battery—ever since last night. Sure. I seen de sun come up. Dat was pretty, too—all red and pink and green. I was lookin' at de skyscrapers—steel—and all de ships comin' in, sailin' out, all over de oith—and dey was steel, too. De sun was warm, dey wasn't no clouds, and dere was a breeze blowin'. Sure, it was great stuff. I got it aw right—what Paddy said about dat bein' de right dope—on'y I couldn't get *in* it, see? I couldn't belong in dat. It was over my head. And I kept tinkin'—and den I beat it up here to see what youse was like. And I waited till dey was all gone to git yuh alone. Say, how d'yuh feel sittin' in dat pen all de time, havin' to stand for 'em comin' and starin' at yuh—de

white-faced, skinny tarts and de boobs what marry 'em—makin' fun of yuh, laughin' at yuh, gittin' scared of yuh—damn 'em! (*He pounds on the rail with his fist. The Gorilla rattles the bars of his cage and snarls. All the other monkeys set up an angry chattering in the darkness. Yank goes on excitedly*) Sure! Dat's de way it hits me, too. On'y yuh're lucky, see? Yuh don't belong wit 'em and yuh know it. But me, I belong wit 'em—but I don't, see? Dey don't belong wit me, dat's what. Get me? Tinkin' is hard— (*He passes one hand across his forehead with a painful gesture. The Gorilla growls impatiently. Yank goes on gropingly*) It's dis way, what I'm drivin' at. Youse can sit and dope dream in de past, green woods, de jungle, and de rest of it. Den yuh belong and dey don't. Den yuh kin laugh at 'em, see? Yuh're de champ of de woild. But me—I ain't got no past to tink in, nor nothin' dat's comin', on'y what's now—and dat don't belong. Sure, you're de best off! Yuh can't tink, can yuh? Yuh can't talk neider. But I kin make a bluff at talkin' and tinkin'—a'most git away wit it—a'most!—and dat's where de joker comes in. (*He laughs*) I ain't on oith and I ain't in heaven, get me? I'm in de middle tryin' to separate 'em, takin' all de woist punches from bot' of 'em. Maybe dat's what dey call hell, huh? But you, yuh're at de bottom. You belong! Sure! Yuh're de on'y one in de woild dat does, yuh lucky stiff! (*The Gorilla growls proudly*) And dat's why dey getter put yuh in a cage, see? (*The Gorilla roars angrily*) Sure! Yuh get me. It beats it when you try to tink it or talk it—it's way down—deep—behind—you 'n' me we feel it. Sure! Bot' members of dis club! (*He laughs—then in a savage tone*) What de hell! T'hell wit it! A little action, dat's our meat! Dat belongs! Knock 'em down and keep bustin' 'em till dey croaks yuh wit a gat—wit steel! Sure? Are yuh game? Dey've looked at youse, ain't dey—in a cage? Wanter git even? Wanter wind up like a sport 'stead of croakin' slow in dere? (*The Gorilla roars an emphatic affirmative. Yank goes on with a sort of furious exaltation*) Sure! Yuh're reg'lar. Yuh'll stick to de finish! Me 'n' you, huh?—bot' members of this club! We'll put up one last star bout dat'll knock 'em offen deir seats! Dey'll have to make de cages stronger after we're trou! (*The Gorilla is straining at his bars, growling, hopping from one foot to the other. Yank takes a jimmy from under his coat and forces the lock on the cage door. He throws this open*) Pardon from de governor! Step out and shake hands! I'll take yuh for walk down Fif' Avenoo. We'll knock 'em offen de oith and croak wit de band playin'. Come on, Brother. (*The Gorilla scrambles gingerly out of his cage. Goes to Yank and stands looking at him. Yank keeps his mocking tone—holds out his hand*) Shake—de secret grip of our order. (*Something, the tune of mockery, perhaps, suddenly enrages the Animal. With a spring he wraps his huge arms around Yank in a murderous hug. There is a crackling snap of crushed ribs—a gasping cry, still mocking, from Yank*) Hey, I didn't say kiss me! (*The Gorilla lets the crushed body slip to the floor; stands over it uncertainly, considering; then picks it up, throws it in the cage, shuts the door, and shuffles off menacingly into the darkness at left. A great uproar of frightened chattering and whimpering comes from the other cages. Then* Yank *moves, groaning, opening his eyes, and there is silence. He mutters painfully:*) Say—dey oughter match him—wit Zybszko. He got me, aw right. I'm trou. Even him didn't tink I belonged. (*Then, with sudden passionate despair*) Christ, where do I get off at? Where do I fit in? (*Checking himself as suddenly*) Aw, what de hell! No squawkin', see! No quittin', get me! Croak wit your boots on! (*He grabs hold of the bars*

of the cage and hauls himself painfully to his feet—looks around him bewilderedly—forces a mocking laugh) In de cage, huh? (*In the strident tones of a circus barker*) Ladies and gents, step forward and take a slant at de one and only—(*His voice weakening*) one and original—Hairy Ape from de wilds of—

> (*He slips in a heap on the floor and dies. The monkeys set up a chattering, whimpering wail. And, perhaps, the Hairy Ape at last belongs*)

CURTAIN

5 The Harlem Renaissance

During and immediately after World War I, in the so-called Great Migration, some 450,000 blacks moved from the rural South to northern cities to work in factories. Many of these blacks were sharecroppers eager to escape the vicious cycle of poverty, landlessness, and debt to unscrupulous landowners; or they were fleeing southern racism, which subjected them to humiliation and violence. But the North was no "Promised Land," as some northern black newspapers touted it, for blacks were segregated into ghettos and victims of white bigotry. In 1919, race riots broke out in thirty-six cities; the worst was Chicago where a riot lasted for three weeks and thirty-eight people died. Nevertheless, the Great Migration was a benefit to blacks. A new urbanized middle class emerged, and blacks became more organized in their struggle to end racial injustice and more determined to take their rightful place as Americans of African descent. Migration to northern urban centers also stimulated intellectual and artistic pursuits among blacks. Nowhere was this more evident than in the Harlem district of New York City, which witnessed a cultural explosion.

Popular histories of the Harlem Renaissance conveniently tend to choose the year 1920 to mark the beginning of the period. Others point to March 1924 when a formal dinner was held at New York's Civic Club to celebrate the publication of Jessie Fauset's *There Is Confusion,* the first novel published by the movement. Whenever it may have begun, the Harlem Renaissance is generally recognized for the prose and poetry of African-American writers, but it also included a number of artists and jazz musicians. For example, the Cotton Club, in Harlem, which opened in the fall of 1923, brought international attention to America's jazz music, and it became the home to accomplished musicians, including the legendary Edward Kennedy "Duke" Ellington (1899–1974). Moreover, African-American art was finally being taken seriously, and for the first time ever, the artists themselves were speaking out loud about what it was like to be an African-American living in the United States. Unfortunately, with the advent of the Great Depression in the early 1930s, the Harlem Renaissance virtually ended.

Langston Hughes
"The Negro Speaks of Rivers" and "The Weary Blues"

In the first volume of his autobiography, *The Big Sea* (1940), Langston Hughes (1902–1967) is credited with defining the essence of the Harlem Renaissance from the literary perspective. Blues forms, the language of the street, and jazz rhythms are all an integral part of his poetry. Hughes was born in Joplin, Missouri, raised in Lawrence, Kansas, by his grandmother, and graduated from high school in Cleveland, Ohio. During his high school years, Hughes demonstrated a talent for writing (publishing his first poems in the *Central High Monthly*), and an English teacher introduced him to the poetry of Walt Whitman and Carl Sandburg, which influenced his early style. Following graduation, Hughes traveled to Mexico to reunite with his father in the hope that his father would pay for his college education at Columbia University in New York. While on the train, reflecting on his life experiences up to the age of seventeen, Hughes penned one of his most famous poems, "The Negro Speaks of Rivers" which is quoted below.

He dedicated the poem to W. E. B. DuBois (1868–1963), who wrote *The Souls of Black Folk* (1903), which enabled Negroes, as he called them, to see that America belonged as much to them as it did to white people. Hughes uses the river as a metaphor for the source of all life. He traces the history of black people to a time before slavery and condenses human history from approximately 3000 B.C. until his own age. He refers to the Euphrates River, in ancient Mesopotamia, where civilization was born; the Congo River in Central Africa, the ancestral home of African-Americans; and the Nile River, which runs through Egypt where, in ancient times, its people had contact with black lands to the south. As he ponders the Mississippi River, Hughes thinks of Abraham Lincoln's *Emancipation Proclamation,* which freed the slaves in the United States and metaphorically changed the soul of black slaves from "muddy" to "golden" just like the river during a sunset. The final reference to his soul growing "deep like the rivers" indicates the durability of the human soul, as well as the force of human history including the pain caused by slavery and racism.

THE NEGRO SPEAKS OF RIVERS

I've known rivers:
I've known rivers ancient as the world and older than the
  flow of human blood in human veins.

My soul has grown deep like the rivers.

I bathed in the Euphrates when dawns were young.
I built my hut near the Congo and it lulled me to sleep.
I looked upon the Nile and raised the pyramids above it.
I heard the singing of the Mississippi when Abe Lincoln
  went down to New Orleans, and I've seen its muddy
  bosom turn all golden in the sunset.

I've known rivers:
Ancient, dusky rivers.

My soul has grown deep like the rivers

THE WEARY BLUES

Hughes left Columbia University after only one year to become deeply involved in the arts in the New York Harlem community. In 1925, his poem "The Weary Blues," quoted below, won the poetry prize in *Opportunity Magazine* and jump-started Hughes' literary career. Hughes acknowledged that he was referencing blues music (which he first heard in Lawrence, Kansas, as a young boy) as a way to heighten the "melancholy tone" of "a black man's soul." The poem also inspired the title of his first volume of poetry, which was published in 1926. Phrases such as "syncopated tune," "mellow croon," and "swaying to and fro" evoke an image of a blues performer playing his instrument. Moreover, the poem suggests an intimate relationship between the performer and his song. Playing the blues helps the singer maintain his identity, and by extension, it helps all blacks preserve their collective identity.

Droning a drowsy syncopated tune,
Rocking back and forth to a mellow croon,
    I heard a Negro play.
Down on Lenox Avenue the other night
By the pale dull pallor of an old gas light
    He did a lazy sway. . . .
    He did a lazy sway. . . .
To the tune o'those Weary Blues.
With his ebony hands on each ivory key
He made that poor piano moan with melody.
    O Blues!
Swaying to and fro on his rickety stool
He played that sad raggy tune like a musical fool.
    Sweet Blues!
Coming from a black man's soul.
    O Blues!
In a deep song voice with a melancholy tone
I heard that Negro sing, that old piano moan—
    "Ain't got nobody in all this world,
        Ain't got nobody but ma self
        I's gwine to quit ma frownin'
        And put ma troubles on the shelf."
Thump, thump, thump, went his foot on the floor.
He played a few chords then he sang some more—
    "I got the Weary Blues
        And I can't be satisfied.
        Got the Weary Blues
        And can't be satisfied—
        I ain't happy no mo'
        And I wish that I had died."
And far into the night he crooned that tune.
The stars went out and so did the moon.
The singer stopped playing and went to bed
While the Weary Blues echoed through his head.
He slept like a rock or a man that's dead.

18

The Era of Totalitarianism

Following World War I, fascist movements arose in Italy, Germany, and many other European countries. Although these movements differed—each a product of a history of separate national histories and the outlook of its leader—they shared a hatred of liberalism, democracy, and communism; a commitment to aggressive nationalism; and a glorification of the party leader. Fascist leaders cleverly utilized myths, rituals, and pageantry to mobilize and manipulate the masses.

Several conditions fostered the rise of fascism. One factor was the fear of communism among the middle and upper classes. Inspired by the success of the Bolsheviks in Russia, communists in other lands were calling for the establishment of Soviet-style republics. Increasingly afraid of a communist takeover, industrialists, landowners, government officials, army leaders, professionals, and shopkeepers were attracted to fascist movements that promised to protect their nations from this threat. A second factor contributing to the growth of fascism was the disillusionment of World War I veterans and the mood of violence bred by the war. The thousands of veterans facing unemployment and poverty made ideal recruits for fascist parties that glorified combat and organized private armies. A third contributing factor was the inability of democratic parliamentary governments to cope with the problems that burdened postwar Europe. Having lost confidence in the procedures and values of democracy, many people joined fascist movements that promised strong leadership, an end to party conflicts, and a unified national will.

Fascism's appeal to nationalist feelings also drew people into the movement. In many ways, fascism was the culmination of the aggressive racial nationalism that had emerged in the late nineteenth century. Fascists saw themselves as dedicated idealists engaged in a heroic struggle to rescue their nations from domestic and foreign enemies; they aspired to regain lands lost by their countries in World War I or to acquire lands denied them by the Paris Peace Conference.

Fascists glorified instinct, will, and blood as the true forces of life; they openly attacked the ideals of reason, liberty, and equality—the legacies of the Enlightenment and the French Revolution. At the center of German fascism (National Socialism or Nazism) was a bizarre racial mythology that preached the superiority of the German race and the inferiority of others, particularly Jews and Slavs.

Benito Mussolini, founder of the Italian Fascist party, came to power in 1922. Although he established a one-party state, he was less successful than Adolf Hitler, the leader of the German National Socialists, in controlling the state and the minds of the people. After gaining power as chancellor of the German government in 1933, Hitler moved to establish a totalitarian state.

In the 1930s, the term *totalitarianism* was used to describe the Fascist regime in Italy, the National Socialist regime in Germany, and the Communist regime in the Soviet Union. To a degree that far exceeds the ancient tyrannies and early modern autocratic states, these dictatorships aspired to and, with varying degrees of success, attained control over the individual's consciousness and behavior and all phases of political, social, and cultural life. To many people it seemed that a crises-riddled democracy was dying and that the future belonged to these dynamic totalitarian movements.

Totalitarianism was a twentieth-century phenomenon, for such all-embracing control over the individual and society could only have been achieved in an age of modern ideology, technology, and bureaucracy. The ideological aims and social and economic policies of Hitler and Stalin differed fundamentally. However, both Soviet Russia and Nazi Germany shared the totalitarian goal of monolithic unity and total domination, and both employed similar methods to achieve it. Mussolini's Italy is more accurately called authoritarian, for the party-state either did not intend to control all phases of life or lacked the means to do so. Moreover, Mussolini hesitated to use the ruthless methods that Hitler and Stalin employed so readily.

Striving for total unity, control, and obedience, the totalitarian dictatorship is the antithesis of liberal democracy. It abolishes all competing political parties, suppresses individual liberty, eliminates or regulates private institutions, and utilizes the modern state's bureaucracy and technology to impose its ideology and enforce its commands. The party-state determines what people should believe—what values they should hold. There is no room for individual thinking, private moral judgment, or individual conscience. The individual possesses no natural rights that the state must respect.

Unlike previous dictatorial regimes, the dictatorships of both the left and the right sought to legitimize their rule by gaining the masses' approval. They claimed that their governments were higher and truer expressions of the people's will. The Soviet and Nazi dictatorships established their rule in the name of the people—the German Volk or the Soviet proletariat.

A distinctive feature of totalitarianism is the overriding importance of the leader, who is seen as infallible and invincible. The masses' slavish adulation of the leader and their uncritical acceptance of the dogma that the leader or the party is always right promote loyalty, dedication, and obedience and distort rational thinking.

Totalitarian leaders want more than power for its own sake; in the last analysis, they seek to transform the world according to an all-embracing ideology, a set of convictions and beliefs, which, says Hannah Arendt, "pretend[s] to know the mysteries of the whole historical process—the secrets of the past, the intricacies of the present, the uncertainties of the future." The ideology constitutes a higher and exclusive truth, based on a law of history, and it contains a dazzling vision of the future—a secular New Jerusalem—that strengthens the will of the faithful and attracts converts.

Like a religion, the totalitarian ideology provides its adherents with beliefs that make society and history intelligible, that explain all of existence in an emotionally gratifying way. Again like a religion, it creates true believers, who feel that they are participating in a great cause—a heroic fight against evil—that gives meaning to their lives.

Not only did the totalitarian religion-ideology supply followers with a cause that claimed absolute goodness; it also provided a Devil. For the Soviets, the source of evil and the cause of all the people's hardships were the degenerate capitalists, the traitorous Trotskyites, or the saboteurs and foreign agents, who impeded the realization of the socialist society. For the Nazis, the Devil was the conspirator Jew. These "evil" ones must be eliminated in order to realize the totalitarian movement's vision of the future. Thus, totalitarian regimes liquidate large segments of the population designated as "enemies of the people." Historical necessity or a higher purpose demands and justifies their liquidation. The appeal to historical necessity has all the power of a great myth. Presented as a world-historical struggle between the forces of good and the forces of evil, the myth incites fanaticism and numbs the conscience. Seemingly decent people engage in terrible acts of brutality with no remorse, convinced that they are waging a righteous war.

Unlike earlier autocratic regimes, the totalitarian dictatorship is not satisfied with its subjects' outward obedience; it demands the masses' unconditional loyalty and enthusiastic support. It strives to control the inner person: to shape thoughts, feelings, and attitudes in accordance with the party ideology, which becomes an official creed. It seeks to create a "new man," one who dedicates himself body and soul to the party and its ideology. Such unquestioning, faithful subjects can be manipulated by the party.

The totalitarian dictatorship deliberately politicizes all areas of human activity. Ideology pervades works of literature, history, philosophy, art, and even science. It dominates the school curriculum and influences everyday speech and social relations. The state is concerned with everything its citizens do: there is no distinction between public and private life, and every institution comes under the party-state's authority. If voluntary support for the regime cannot be generated by indoctrination, then the state unhesitatingly resorts to terror and violence to compel obedience.

From the early days of his political career, Hitler dreamed of forging a vast German empire in central and eastern Europe. He believed that only by waging a war of conquest against Russia could the German nation gain the living space and security it required and, as a superior race, deserved. War was an essential component of National Socialist ideology; it also accorded with Hitler's temperament. For the former corporal from the trenches, the Great War had never ended. Hitler aspired to political power because he wanted to mobilize the material and human resources of the German nation for war and conquest. Whereas historians may debate the question of responsibility for World War I, few would disagree with French historian Pierre Renouvin that World War II was Hitler's war:

> It appears to be an almost incontrovertible fact that the Second World War was brought on by the actions of the Hitler government, that these actions were the expression of a policy laid down well in advance in *Mein Kampf,* and that this war could have been averted up until the last moment if the German government had so wished.

Western statesmen had sufficient warning that Hitler was a threat to peace and the essential values of Western civilization, but they failed to rally their people and take a stand until Germany had greatly increased its capacity to wage aggressive war.

World War II was the most destructive war in history. Estimates of the number of dead range as high as 50 million, including 25 million Russians, who sacrificed more than the other participants in both population and material resources. The consciousness of Europe, already profoundly damaged by World War I, was again grievously wounded. Nazi racial theories showed that even in an age of sophisticated science the mind remains attracted to irrational beliefs and mythical imagery. Nazi atrocities proved that people will torture and kill with religious zeal and machinelike indifference. The Nazi assault on reason and freedom demonstrated anew the precariousness of Western civilization. This assault would forever cast doubt on the Enlightenment conception of human goodness, secular rationality, and the progress of civilization through advances in science and technology.

1 The Rise of Nazism

Many extreme racist-nationalist and paramilitary organizations sprang up in postwar Germany. Adolf Hitler (1889–1945), a veteran of World War I, joined one of these organizations, which became known as the National Socialist German Worker's Party (commonly called the Nazi Party). Hitler's uncanny insight into the state of mind of postwar Germans and his extraordinary oratorical gifts enabled him to gain control of the party.

Adolf Hitler
Mein Kampf

In the "Beer Hall Putsch" of November 1923, Hitler attempted to overthrow the state government in Bavaria as the first step in bringing down the Weimar Republic. But the Nazis quickly scattered when the Bavarian police opened fire. Hitler was arrested and sentenced to five years' imprisonment—he served only nine months. While in prison, Hitler wrote *Mein Kampf* (My Struggle), in which he presented his views. The book came to be regarded as an authoritative expression of the Nazi world-view and served as a kind of sacred writing for the Nazi movement.

Hitler's thought—a patchwork of nineteenth-century anti-Semitic, Volkish, Social Darwinist, and anti-Marxist ideas—contrasted sharply with the core values of both the Judeo-Christian and the Enlightenment traditions. Central to Hitler's world-view was racial mythology: a heroic Germanic race that was descended from the ancient Aryans, who once swept across Europe, and was battling for survival against racial inferiors. In the following passages excerpted from *Mein Kampf,* Hitler presents his views of race, of propaganda, and of the National Socialist territorial goals.

THE PRIMACY OF RACE

Nature does not want a pairing of weaker individuals with stronger ones; it wants even less a mating of a higher race with a weaker one. Otherwise its routine labors of promoting a higher breed lasting perhaps over hundreds of thousands of years would be wiped out.

History offers much evidence for this process. It proves with terrifying clarity that any generic mixture of Aryan blood with people of a lower quality undermines the culturally superior people. The population of North America consists to a large extent of Germanic elements, which have mixed very little with inferior people of color. Central and South America shows a different humanity and culture; here Latin immigrants mixed with the aborigines, sometimes on a large scale. This example alone allows a clear recognition of the effects of racial mixtures. Remaining racially pure the Germans of North America rose to be masters of their continent; they will remain masters as long as they do not defile their blood.

The result of mixing races in short is: a) lowering the cultural level of the higher race; b) physical and spiritual retrogression and thus the beginning of a slow but progressive decline.

To promote such a development means no less than committing sin against the will of the eternal creator. . . .

Everything that we admire on earth—science, technology, invention—is the creative product of only a few people, and perhaps originally of only *one* race; our whole culture depends upon them. If they perish, the beauties of the earth will be buried. . . .

All great cultures of the past perished because the original creative race was destroyed by the poisoning of its blood.

Such collapse always happened because people forgot that all cultures depend on human beings. In order to preserve a given culture it is necessary to preserve the human beings who created it. Cultural preservation in this world is tied to the iron law of necessity and the fight to victory of the stronger and better. . . .

If we divide humanity into three categories: into founders of culture, bearers of culture, and destroyers of culture, the Aryan would undoubtedly rate first. He established the foundations and walls of all human progress. . . .

The mixing of blood and the resulting lowering of racial cohesion is the sole reason why cultures perish. People do not perish by defeat in war, but by losing the power of resistance inherent in pure blood.

All that is not pure race in this world is chaff. . . .

A state which in the age of racial poisoning dedicates itself to the cultivation of its best racial elements will one day become master of the world.

Modern anti-Semitism was a powerful legacy of the Middle Ages and the unsettling changes brought about by rapid industrialization; it was linked to racist doctrines that asserted the Jews were inherently wicked and bore dangerous racial qualities. Hitler grasped the political potential of anti-Semitism: by concentrating all evil in one enemy, he could provide non-Jews with an emotionally satisfying explanation for all their misfortunes and thus manipulate and unify the German people.

ANTI-SEMITISM

The Jew offers the most powerful contrast to the Aryan. . . . Despite all their seemingly intellectual qualities the Jewish people are without true culture, and especially without a culture of their own. What Jews seem to possess as culture is the property of others, for the most part corrupted in their hands.

In judging the Jewish position in regard to human culture, we have to keep in mind their essential characteristics. There never was—and still is no—Jewish art. The Jewish people made no original contribution to the two queen goddesses of all arts: architecture and music. What they have contributed is bowdlerization or spiritual theft. Which proves that Jews lack the very qualities distinguishing creative and culturally blessed races. . . .

The first and biggest lie of Jews is that Jewishness is not a matter of race but of religion, from which inevitably follow even more lies. One of them refers to the language of Jews. It is not a means of expressing their thoughts, but of hiding them. While speaking French a Jew thinks Jewish, and while he cobbles together some German verse, he merely expresses the mentality of his people.

As long as the Jew is not master of other peoples, he must for better or worse speak their languages. Yet as soon as the others have become his servants, then all should learn a universal language (Esperanto for instance), so that by these means the Jews can rule more easily. . . .

For hours the blackhaired Jewish boy lies in wait, with satanic joy on his face, for the unsuspecting girl whom he disgraces with his blood and thereby robs her from her people. He tries by all means possible to destroy the racial foundations of the people he wants to subjugate.

But a people of pure race conscious of its blood can never be enslaved by the Jew; he remains forever a ruler of bastards.

Thus he systematically attempts to lower racial purity by racially poisoning individuals.

In politics he begins to replace the idea of democracy with the idea of the dictatorship of the proletariat.

He found his weapon in the organized Marxist masses, which avoid democracy and instead help him to subjugate and govern people dictatorially with his brutal fists.

Systematically he works toward a double revolution, in economics and politics.

With the help of his international contacts he enmeshes people who effectively resist his attacks from within in a net of external enemies whom he incites to war, and, if necessary, goes on to unfurling the red flag of revolution over the battlefield.

He batters the national economies until the ruined state enterprises are privatized and subject to his financial control.

In politics he refuses to give the state the means for its self-preservation, destroys the bases of any national self-determination and defense, wipes out the faith in leadership, denigrates the historic past, and pulls everything truly great into the gutter.

In cultural affairs he pollutes art, literature, theatre, befuddles national sentiment, subverts all concepts of beauty and grandeur, of nobleness and goodness, and reduces people to their lowest nature.

Religion is made ridiculous, custom and morals are declared outdated, until the last props of national character in the battle for survival have collapsed. . . .

Thus the Jew is the big rabble-rouser for the complete destruction of Germany. Wherever in the world we read about attacks on Germany, Jews are the source, just as in peace and during the war the newspapers of both the Jewish stock market and the Marxists systematically incited hatred against Germany. Country after country gave up its neutrality and joined the world war coalition in disregard of the true interest of the people.

Jewish thinking in all this is clear. The Bolshevization of Germany, i.e., the destruction of the German national people-oriented intelligentsia and thereby the exploitation of German labor under the yoke of Jewish global finance are but the prelude for the expansion of the Jewish tendency to conquer the world. As so often in history, Germany is the turning point in this mighty struggle. If our people and our state become the victims of blood-thirsty and money-thirsty Jewish tyrants, the whole world will be enmeshed in the tentacles of this octopus. If, however, Germany liberates itself from this yoke, we can be sure that the greatest threat to all humanity has been broken. . . .

Hitler was a master propagandist and advanced his ideas on propaganda techniques in *Mein Kampf*. He mocked the learned and book-oriented German liberals and socialists who he felt were entirely unsuited for modern mass politics. The successful leader, he said, must win over the masses through the use of simple ideas and images, constantly repeated, to control the mind by evoking primitive feelings. Hitler contended that mass meetings were the most effective means of winning followers. What counted most at these demonstrations, he said, was will power, strength, and unflagging determination radiating from the speaker to every single individual in the crowd.

PROPAGANDA AND MASS RALLIES

The task of propaganda does not lie in the scientific training of individuals, but in directing the masses toward certain facts, events, necessities, etc., whose significance is to be brought to their attention.

The essential skill consists in doing this so well that you convince people about the reality of a fact, about the necessity of an event, about the correctness of something necessary, etc. . . . You always have to appeal to the emotions and far less to the so-called intellect. . . .

The art of propaganda lies in sensing the emotional temper of the broad masses, so that you, in psychologically effective form, can catch their attention and move their hearts. . . .

The attention span of the masses is very short, their understanding limited; they easily forget. For that reason all effective propaganda has to concentrate on very few points and drive them home through simple slogans, until even the simplest can grasp what you have in mind. As soon as you give up this principle and become too complex, you will lose your effectiveness, because the masses cannot digest and retain what you have offered. You thereby weaken your case and in the end lose it altogether.

The larger the scope of your case, the more psychologically correct must be the method of your presentation. . . .

The task of propaganda lies not in weighing right and wrong, but in driving home your own point of view. You cannot objectively explore the facts that favor others and present them in doctrinaire sincerity to the masses. You have to push relentlessly your own case. . . .

Even the most brilliant propaganda will not produce the desired results unless it follows this fundamental rule: You must stick to limiting yourself to essentials and repeat them endlessly. Persistence on this point, as in so many other cases in the world, is the first and most important precondition for success. . . .

Propaganda does not exist to furnish interesting diversions to blasé young dandies, but to convince above all the masses. In their clumsiness they always require a long lead before they are ready to take notice. Only by thousandfold repetition will the simplest concepts stick in their memories.

No variation of your presentation should change the content of your propaganda; you always have to come to the same conclusion. You may want to highlight your slogans from various sides, but at the end you always have to reaffirm it. Only consistent and uniform propaganda will succeed. . . .

Every advertisement, whether in business or politics, derives its success from its persistence and uniformity. . . .

The mass meeting is . . . necessary because an incipient supporter of a new political movement will feel lonely and anxiously isolated. He needs at the start a sense of a larger community which among most people produces vitality and courage. The same man as member of a military company or battalion and surrounded by his comrades will more lightheartedly join an attack than if he were all by himself. In a crowd he feels more sheltered, even if reality were a thousandfold against him.

The sense of community in a mass demonstration not only empowers the individual, but also promotes an esprit de corps. The person who in his business or workshop is the first to represent a new political creed is likely to be exposed to heavy discrimination. He needs the reassurance that comes from the conviction of being a member and a fighter in a large comprehensive organization. The sense of this organization comes first to him in a mass demonstration. When he for the first time goes from a petty workshop or from a large factory, where he feels insignificant, to a mass demonstration surrounded by thousands and thousands of like-minded fellows—when he as a seeker is gripped by the intoxicating surge of enthusiasm among three or four thousand others—when the visible success and the consensus of thousands of others prove the correctness of his new political creed and for the first time arouse doubts about his previous political convictions—then he submits to the miraculous influence of what we call "mass suggestion." The will, the yearning, and also the power of thousands of fellow citizens now fill every individual. The man who full of doubts and uncertain enters such a gathering, leaves it inwardly strengthened; he has become a member of a community. . . .

Hitler was an extreme nationalist who wanted a reawakened, racially united Germany to expand eastward at the expense of the Slavs, whom he viewed as racially inferior.

LEBENSRAUM

A people gains its freedom of existence only by occupying a sufficiently large space on earth. . . .

If the National Socialist movement really wants to achieve a hallowed mission in history for our people, it must, in painful awareness of its position in the world, boldly and methodically fight against the aimlessness and incapacity which have hitherto guided the foreign policy of the German people. It must then, without respect for "tradition" and prejudice, find the courage to rally the German people to a forceful advance on the road which leads from their present cramped living space to new territories. In this manner they will be liberated from the danger of perishing or being enslaved in service to others.

The National Socialist movement must try to end the disproportion between our numerous population and its limited living space, the source of our food as well as the base of our power—between our historic past and the hopelessness of our present impotence. . . .

The demand for restoring the boundaries of 1914 is apolitical nonsense with consequences so huge as to make it appear a crime—quite apart from the fact that our pre-war boundaries were anything but logical. They neither united all people of German nationality nor served strategic-political necessity. . . .

In the light of this fact we National Socialists must resolutely stick to our foreign policy goals, namely *to secure for the German people the territorial base to which they are entitled.* This is the only goal which before God and our German posterity justifies shedding our blood. . . .

Just as our forebears did not receive the soil on which we live as a gift from heaven—they had to risk their lives for it—so in future we will not secure the living space for our people by divine grace, but by the might of the victorious sword.

However much all of us recognize the necessity of a reckoning with France, it would remain ineffectual if we thereby limited the scope of our foreign policy. It makes sense only if we consider it as a rear-guard action for expanding our living space elsewhere in Europe. . . .

If we speak today about gaining territory in Europe, we think primarily of Russia and its border states. . . .

2 Totalitarianism and the Corruption of the Arts and Sciences

The totalitarian state seeks to fashion subjects who believe that the party's ideology is the supreme authority; its doctrines provide the final answers to the ultimate questions of history and life. Such unquestioning, faithful subjects can be manipulated by the party. The disinterested search for truth, justice, and goodness—the exploration of those fundamental moral, political, and religious questions that have characterized the Western intellectual tradition for centuries—is abandoned. Truth, justice, and goodness are what the party deems them to be, and ideological deviation is forbidden. "Propaganda does not have anything to do with truth!" Josef Goebbels (1897–1945), Nazi minister of propaganda, told his staff during World War II. "We serve truth by serving a German victory."

Intellectuals and creative artists are simply conveyors of official truths, "engineers of human souls," Stalin called them. "From now on it will not be your job to determine whether something is true but whether it is in the spirit of the National Socialist revolution," the Nazi minister of culture told university professors. Intellectual life is reduced to facilitating the smooth implementation of the ruling party's all-embracing blueprint. Intellectuals in totalitarian society, said Isaiah Berlin, are "technically trained believers who look on the human beings at their disposal as material which is infinitely malleable."

Yevgeny Yevtushenko
Literature as Propaganda

During the Stalin era, artists and writers were compelled to promote the ideals of the Stalin revolution. In the style of "socialist realism," their heroes were factory workers and farmers who labored tirelessly and enthusiastically to build a new society. Even romance served a political purpose. Novelists wrote love stories following limited, prosaic themes. For example, a young girl might lose her heart to a coworker who is a leader in the communist youth organization and who outproduces his comrades at his job; as the newly married couple is needed at the factory, they choose to forgo a honeymoon.

After Stalin's death in 1953, Soviet intellectuals breathed more freely, and they protested against the rigid Stalinist controls. In the following extract from his *Precocious Autobiography,* Russian poet Yevgeny Yevtushenko (b. 1933) looks back to the raw days of intellectual repression under Stalin.

Blankly smiling workers and collective farmers looked out from the covers of books. Almost every novel and short story had a happy ending. Painters more and more often took as their subject state banquets, weddings, solemn public meetings, and parades.

The apotheosis of this trend was a movie which in its grand finale showed thousands of collective farmers having a gargantuan feast against the background of a new power station.

Recently I had a talk with its producer, a gifted and intelligent man.

"How could you produce such a film?" I asked. "It is true that I also once wrote verses in that vein, but I was still wet behind the ears, whereas you were adult and mature."

The producer smiled a sad smile. "You know, the strangest thing to me is that I was absolutely sincere. I thought all this was a necessary part of building communism. And then I believed Stalin."

So when we talk about "the cult of personality," we should not be too hasty in accusing all those who, one way or another, were involved in it, debasing themselves with their flattery. There were of course sycophants [servile flatterers] who used the situation for their own ends. But that many people connected with the arts sang Stalin's praises was often not vice but tragedy.

How was it possible for even gifted and intelligent people to be deceived?

To begin with, Stalin was a strong and vivid personality. When he wanted to, Stalin knew how to charm people. He charmed Gorky and Barbusse. In 1937, the cruelest year of the purges, he managed to charm that tough and experienced observer, Lion Feuchtwanger.[1]

In the second place, in the minds of the Soviet people, Stalin's name was indissolubly linked with Lenin's. Stalin knew how popular Lenin was and saw to it that history was rewritten in such a way as to make his own relations with Lenin seem much more friendly than they had been in fact. The rewriting was so thorough that perhaps Stalin himself believed his own version in the end.

There can be no doubt of Stalin's love for Lenin. His speech on Lenin's death, beginning with the words, "In leaving us, Comrade Lenin has bequeathed . . ." reads like a poem in prose. He wanted to stand as Lenin's heir not only in other people's eyes, but in his own eyes too. He deceived himself as well as the others. Even [Boris] Pasternak[2] put the two names side by side:

Laughter in the village,
Voice behind the plow,

Lenin and Stalin,
And these verses now . . .

In reality, however, Stalin distorted Lenin's ideas, because to Lenin—and this was the whole meaning of his work—communism was to serve man, whereas under Stalin it appeared that man served communism.

Stalin's theory that people were the little cogwheels of communism was put into practice and with horrifying results. . . . Russian poets, who had produced some fine works during the war, turned dull again. If a good poem did appear now and then, it was likely to be about the war—this was simpler to write about.

Poets visited factories and construction sites but wrote more about machines than about the men who made them work. If machines could read, they might have found such poems interesting. Human beings did not.

The size of a printing was not determined by demand but by the poet's official standing. As a result bookstores were cluttered up with books of poetry which no one wanted. . . . A simple, touching poem by the young poet Vanshenkin, about a boy's first love, caused almost a sensation against this background of industrial-agricultural verse. Vinokurov's first poems, handsomely disheveled among the general sleekness, were avidly seized upon—they had human warmth. But the general situation was unchanged. Poetry remained unpopular. The older poets were silent, and when they did break their silence, it was even worse. The generation of poets that had been spawned by the war and that had raised so many hopes had petered out. Life in peacetime turned out to be more complicated than life at the front. Two of the greatest Russian poets, Zabolotsky and Smelyakov, were in concentration camps. The young poet Mandel (Korzhavin) had been deported. I don't know if Mandel's name will be remembered in the history of Russian poets but it will certainly be remembered in the history of Russian social thought.

He was the only poet who openly wrote and recited verses against Stalin while Stalin was alive. That he recited them seems to be what saved his life, for the authorities evidently thought him insane. In one poem he wrote of Stalin:

There in Moscow, in whirling darkness,
Wrapped in his military coat,
Not understanding Pasternak,
A hard and cruel man stared at the snow.

. . . Now that ten years have gone by, I realize that Stalin's greatest crime was not the arrests and the shootings he ordered. His greatest crime was the corruption of the human spirit.

---

[1]Gorky was a prominent Russian writer; Barbusse and Feuchtwanger were well-known western European writers.

[2]Pasternak was another prominent Russian writer.

Vladimir Polyakov
The Story of Fireman Prokhorchuk
AN ATTACK ON CENSORSHIP

The following reading by Soviet writer Vladimir Polyakov was published in Moscow the year Stalin died. This "story of a story" is a humorous attack on censorship.

(The action takes place in the editorial offices of a Soviet magazine. A woman writer—a beginner—shyly enters the editors' office.)

SHE Pardon me. . . . please excuse me. . . . You're the editor of the magazine, aren't you?

HE That's right.

SHE My name is Krapivina. I've written a little story for your magazine.

HE All right, leave it here.

SHE I was wondering whether I couldn't get your opinion of it right away. If you'll permit me, I'll read it to you. It won't take more than three or four minutes. May I?

HE All right, read it.

SHE It is entitled "A Noble Deed." (*She begins to read.*)
It was the dead of night—three o'clock. Everybody in the town was asleep. Not a single electric light was burning. It was dark and quiet. But suddenly a gory tongue of flame shot out of the fourth-floor window of a large gray house. "Help!" someone shouted. "We're on fire!" This was the voice of a careless tenant who, when he went to bed, had forgotten to switch off the electric hot plate, the cause of the fire. Both the fire and the tenant were darting around the room. The siren of a fire engine wailed. Firemen jumped down from the engine and dashed into the house. The room where the tenant was darting around was a sea of flames. Fireman Prokhorchuk, a middle-age Ukrainian with large black mustachios, stood in front of the door. The fireman stood and thought. Suddenly he rushed into the room, pulled the smoldering tenant out, and aimed his extinguisher at the flames. The fire was put out, thanks to the daring of Prokhorchuk. Fire Chief Gorbushin approached him. "Good boy, Prokhorchuk," he said, "you've acted according to the regulations!" Whereupon the fire chief smiled and added: "You haven't noticed it, but your right mustachio is aflame." Prokhorchuk smiled and aimed a jet at his mustachio. It was dawning.

HE The story isn't bad. The title's suitable too: "A Noble Deed." But there are some passages in it that must be revised. You see, it's a shame when a story is good and you come across things that are different from what you'd wish. Let's see, how does it start, your story?

SHE It was the dead of night—three o'clock. Everybody in the town was asleep. . . .

HE No good at all. It implies that the police are asleep, and those on watch are asleep, and. . . . No, won't do at all. It indicates a lack of vigilance. That passage must be changed. Better write it like this: It was dead of night—three o'clock. No one in the town was asleep.

SHE But that's impossible, it's nighttime and people do sleep.

HE Yes, I suppose you're right. Then let's have it this way: Everybody in the town was asleep but was at his post.

SHE Asleep at their posts?

HE No, that's complete nonsense. Better write: Some people slept while others kept a sharp lookout. What comes next?

SHE Not a single electric light was burning.

HE What's this? Sounds as if, in our country, we make bulbs that don't work?

SHE But it's night. They were turned off.

HE It could reflect on our bulbs. Delete it! If they aren't lit, what need is there to mention them?

SHE (*reading on*) But suddenly a gory tongue of flame shot out of the fourth-floor window of a large gray house. "Help!" someone shouted, "we're on fire!"

HE What's that, panic?

SHE Yes.

HE And it is your opinion that panic ought to be publicized in the columns of our periodicals?

SHE No, of course not. But this is fiction, . . . a creative work. I'm describing a fire.

HE And you portray a man who spreads panic instead of a civic-minded citizen? If I were you, I'd replace that cry of "help" by some more rallying cry.

SHE For instance?

HE For instance, say . . . ". . . We shall put it out!" someone shouted. "Nothing to worry about, there's no fire."

SHE What do you mean, "there's no fire," when there *is* a fire?

HE No, "there's no fire" in the sense of "we shall put it out, nothing to worry about."

SHE It's impossible.

HE It's possible. And then, you could do away with the cry.

SHE (*reads on*) This was the voice of the careless tenant who, when he went to bed, had forgotten to switch off the electric hot place.

HE The what tenant?

SHE Careless.

HE Do you think that carelessness should be popularized in the columns of our periodicals? I shouldn't think so. And then why did you write that he forgot to switch off the electric hot plate? Is that an appropriate example to set for the education of the readers?

SHE I didn't intend to use it educationally, but without the hot plate there'd have been no fire.

HE And would we be much worse off?

SHE No, better, of course.

HE Well then, that's how you should have written it. Away with the hot plate and then you won't have to mention the fire. Go on, read, how does it go after that? Come straight to the portrayal of the fireman.

SHE Fireman Prokhorchuk, a middle-aged Ukrainian . . .

HE That's nicely caught.

SHE . . . with large black mustachios, stopped in front of the door. The fireman stood there and thought.

HE Bad. A fireman mustn't think. He must put the fire out without thinking.

SHE But it is a fine point in the story.

HE In a story it may be a fine point but not in a fireman. Then also, since we have no fire, there's no need to drag the fireman into the house.

SHE But then, what about his dialogue with the fire chief?

HE Let them talk in the fire house. How does the dialogue go?

SHE (*reads*) Fire Chief Gorbushin approached him, "Good boy, Prokhorchuk," he said, "you've acted according to regulations!" Whereupon the fire chief smiled and added: "You haven't noticed it, but your right mustachio is aflame." Prokhorchuk smiled and aimed a jet at his mustachio. It was dawning.

HE Why must you have that?

SHE What?

HE The burning mustachio.

SHE I put it in for the humor of the thing. The man was so absorbed in his work that he didn't notice that his mustache was ablaze.

HE Believe me, you should delete it. Since there's no fire, the house isn't burning and there's no need to burn any mustachios.

SHE And what about the element of laughter?

HE There'll be laughter all right. When do people laugh? When things are good for them. And isn't it good that there's no fire? It's very good. And so everybody will laugh. Read what you have now.

SHE (*reading*) "A Noble Deed." It was the dead of night—three o'clock. Some people slept while others kept a sharp lookout. From the fourth-floor window of a large gray house somebody shouted: "We are not on fire!" "Good boy, Prokhorchuk!" said Fire Chief Gorbushin to Fireman Prokhorchuk, a middle-aged Ukrainian with large black mustachios, "you're following the regulations." Prokhorchuk smiled and aimed a jet of water at his mustachio. It was dawning.

HE There we have a good piece of writing! Now it can be published!

Johannes Stark
"JEWISH SCIENCE" VERSUS "GERMAN SCIENCE"

Several prominent German scientists endorsed the new regime and tried to make science conform to Nazi ideology. In 1934, Johannes Stark (1874–1957), who had won a Nobel Prize for his work in electromagnetism, requested fellow German Nobel Prize winners to sign a declaration supporting "Adolf Hitler . . . the savior and leader of the German people." In the following passage, Stark made the peculiar assertion that "German science" was based on an objective analysis of nature, whereas "Jewish science" (German Jews had distinguished themselves in science and medicine) sacrificed objectivity to self-interest and a subjective viewpoint.

But aside from this fundamental National Socialist demand, the slogan of the international character of science is based on an untruth, insofar as it asserts that the type and the success of scientific activity are independent of membership in a national group. Nobody can seriously assert that art is international. It is similar with science. Insofar as scientific work is not merely imitation but actual creation, like any other creative activity it is conditioned by the spiritual and characterological endowments of its practitioners. Since the individual members of a people have a common endowment, the creative activity of the scientists of a nation, as much as that of its artists and poets, thus assumes the stamp of a distinctive Volkish type. No, science is not international; it is just as national as art. This can be shown by the example of Germans and Jews in the natural sciences.

Science is the knowledge of the uniform interconnection of facts; the purpose of natural science in particular is the investigation of bodies and processes outside of the human mind, through observation and, insofar as possible, through the setting up of planned experiments. The spirit of the German enables him to observe things outside himself exactly as they are, without the interpolation of his own ideas and wishes, and his body does not shrink from the effort which the investigation of nature demands of him. The German's love of nature and his aptitude for natural science are based on this endowment. Thus it is understandable that natural science is overwhelmingly a creation of the Nordic-Germanic blood component of the Aryan peoples. Anyone who, in Lenard's classic work *Grosse Naturforscher* (Great Investigators of Nature), compares the faces of the outstanding natural scientists will find this common Nordic-Germanic feature in almost all of them. The ability to observe and respect facts, in complete disregard of the "I," is the most characteristic feature of the scientific activity of Germanic types. In addition,

there is the joy and satisfaction the German derives from the acquisition of scientific knowledge, since it is principally this with which he is concerned. It is only under pressure that he decides to make his findings public, and the propaganda for them and their commercial exploitation appear to him as degradations of his scientific work.

The Jewish spirit is wholly different in its orientation: above everything else it is focused upon its own ego, its own conception, and its self-interest—and behind its egocentric conception stands its strong will to win recognition for itself and its interests. In accordance with this natural orientation the Jewish spirit strives to heed facts only to the extent that they do not hamper its opinions and purposes, and to bring them in such a connection with each other as is expedient for effecting its opinions and purposes. The Jew, therefore, is the born advocate who, unencumbered by regard for truth, mixes facts and imputations topsy-turvy in the endeavor to secure the court decision he desires. On the other hand, because of these characteristics, the Jewish spirit has little aptitude for creative activity in the sciences because it takes the individual's thinking and will as the measure of things, whereas science demands observation and respect for the facts.

It is true, however, that the Jewish spirit, thanks to the flexibility of its intellect, is capable, through imitation of Germanic examples, of producing noteworthy accomplishments, but it is not able to rise to authentic creative work, to great discoveries in the natural sciences. In recent times the Jews have frequently invoked the name of Heinrich Hertz as a counter-argument to this thesis. True, Heinrich Hertz made the great discovery of electromagnetic waves, but he was not a full-blooded Jew. He had a German mother, from whose side his spiritual endowment may well have been conditioned. When the Jew in natural science abandons the Germanic example and engages in scientific work according to his own spiritual particularity, he turns to theory. His main object is not the observation of facts and their true-to-reality presentation, but the view which he forms about them and the formal exposition to which he subjects them. In the interest of his theory he will suppress facts that are not in keeping with it and likewise, still in the interest of his theory, he will engage in propaganda on its behalf.

Jakob Graf
Heredity and Racial Biology for Students

The following assignments from a textbook entitled *Hereditary and Racial Biology for Students* (1935) show how German youngsters were indoctrinated with racist teachings.

HOW WE CAN LEARN TO RECOGNIZE A PERSON'S RACE
Assignments

1. Summarize the spiritual characteristics of the individual races.

2. Collect from stories, essays, and poems examples of ethnological illustrations. Underline those terms which describe the type and mode of the expression of the soul.

3. What are the expressions, gestures, and movements which allow us to make conclusions as to the attitude of the racial soul?

4. Determine also the physical features which go hand in hand with the specific racial soul characteristics of the individual figures.

5. Try to discover the intrinsic nature of the racial soul through the characters in stories and poetical works in terms of their inner attitude. Apply this mode of observation to persons in your own environment.

6. Collect propaganda posters and caricatures for your race book and arrange them according to a racial scheme.

What image of beauty is emphasized by the artist (a) in posters publicizing sports and travel? (b) in publicity for cosmetics? How are hunters, mountain climbers, and shepherds drawn?

7. Collect from illustrated magazines, newspapers, etc., pictures of great scholars, statesmen, artists, and others who distinguish themselves by their special accomplishments (for example, in economic life, politics, sports). Determine the preponderant race and admixture, according to physical characteristics. Repeat this exercise with the pictures of great men of all nations and times.

8. When viewing monuments, busts, etc., be sure to pay attention to the race of the person portrayed with respect to figure, bearing, and physical characteristics. Try to harmonize these determinations with the features of the racial soul.

9. Observe people whose special racial features have drawn your attention, also with respect to their bearing when moving or when speaking. Observe their expressions and gestures.

10. Observe the Jew: his way of walking, his bearing, gestures, and movements when talking.

11. What strikes you about the way a Jew talks and sings

3 Intellectuals Confront Totalitarianism

A growing pessimism and disillusionment with traditional liberal-democratic values led many intellectuals to turn to fascism or communism as salvationist ideologies. "[I]t remains a paradoxical phenomenon," observes Karl Dietrich Bracher, "that writers and artists, philosophers and intellectuals, who more than anyone else are dependent on freedom and uncontrolled thought, seem to develop a strange weakness for revolutionary but intellectually closed systems of ideas." And George Lichtheim points out, "it is a myth that the Nazi movement represented only 'the mob.' It had conquered the universities before it triumphed over society. The SS leaders were for the most part academically trained." The appeal of fascism to intellectuals shattered the liberal assumption that educated people would reject irrational beliefs and support humanitarian causes.

Many intellectuals saw in fascism a way of awakening the soul and regenerating artistic creativity that had been deadened by a bourgeois civilization whose highest ideals were money and possessions. They hoped that these goals would be realized through the spiritual unity of the nation, the principal aim of fascism. Some intellectuals were attracted by fascism's activism (that not the word, but the deed gives life meaning), its elitism and cult of the hero (Nietzschean overman with the will to lead and to create), and its praise of war (the most genuine of life's experiences).

The economic misery of the depression and the rise of fascist barbarism led many intellectuals to find a new hope, even a secular faith, in communism. They praised the Soviet Union for supplanting capitalist greed with socialist cooperation, for recognizing the dignity of work and replacing a haphazard economic system marred by repeated depressions with one based on planned production, and for providing employment for everyone when joblessness was endemic in capitalist lands. Seduced by Soviet propaganda and desperate for an alternative to crisis-ridden democracy, these intellectuals saw the Soviet Union as a champion of peace and social justice.

American literary critic Edmund Wilson said that in the Soviet Union one felt at the "moral top of the world where the light never really goes out." British political theorists Sidney and Beatrice Webb declared that there was no other country "in which there is actually so much widespread public criticism and such incessant reevaluation of its shortcomings as in the USSR." To these intellectuals, it seemed that in the Soviet Union a vigorous and healthy civilization was emerging and that only communism could stem the tide of fascism. For many, however, the attraction was short-lived. Sickened by Stalin's purges and terror, the denial of individual freedom, and the suppression of truth, they came to view the Soviet Union as another totalitarian state and communism as another "god that failed."

Fascist irrationality and Stalin's terror frightened intellectuals committed to the Enlightenment tradition. These thinkers tried to reaffirm the ideals of rationality and freedom that had been trampled on by the totalitarian movements.

Ignazio Silone
Bread and Wine

Ignazio Silone (1900–1978), an Italian writer and a one-time communist, was expelled from his homeland by the Fascists. After viewing the performance of both Russian Communists and Italian Fascists once they had gained power, Silone grew disillusioned with ideologies: they promised earthly salvation but ended up oppressing people. Motivated by sincere compassion for the poor and oppressed, Silone believed that a combination of socialist idealism and Christian ethics offered the best approach to resolving society's problems. This synthesis figured in his political novels of the 1930s, especially *Bread and Wine* (1937), excerpts from which appear below. In the first passage, the protagonist Pietro tells his old schoolmaster Nunzio that the Fascist dictatorship must be resisted.

"One mustn't wait," Pietro said. "Those who emigrate spend their lives waiting too. That's the trouble. One must act. One must say: Enough, from this very day."

"But if there's no freedom?" Nunzio said.

"Freedom is not a thing you can receive as a gift," Pietro said. "One can be free even under a dictatorship on one simple condition, that is, if one struggles against it. A man who thinks with his own mind and remains uncorrupted is a free man. A man who struggles for what he believes to be right is a free man. You can live in the most democratic country in the world, and if you are lazy, callous, servile, you are not free, in spite of the absence of violence and coercion, you are a slave. Freedom is not a thing that must be begged from others. You must take it for yourself, whatever share you can."

Nunzio was thoughtful and troubled. "You are our revenge."

Wanted by the police for his antigovernment activities, Pietro disguises himself as the priest Don Paolo. To protest the Fascist state's suppression of liberty and its invasion of Ethiopia, Don Paolo scrawls antifascist slogans in several public places. As the police search for the dissident, Don Paolo explains the purpose of resistance to a young woman he has befriended.

"Why all the excitement?" Bianchina said. "Just because of a bit of charcoal on the wall? What a lot of fuss about nothing." In this case the girl's naïveté was genuine. "I really don't understand why people make such a fuss about a few words scrawled on a wall with charcoal," she said to Don Paolo.

Don Paolo, however, seemed pleased at the fuss, which showed no sign of abating, and he tried to explain the reason for it.

"The dictatorship is based on unanimity," he said. "It's sufficient for one person to say no and the spell is broken."

"Even if that person is a poor, lonely sick man?" the girl said.

"Certainly."

"Even if he's a peaceful man who thinks in his own way and apart from that does no-one any harm?"

"Certainly."

These thoughts saddened the girl, but they cheered Don Paolo.

"Under every dictatorship," he said, "one man, one perfectly ordinary little man who goes on thinking with his own brain is a threat to public order. Tons of printed paper spread the slogans of the regime; thousands of loudspeakers, hundreds of thousands of posters and freely distributed leaflets, whole armies of speakers in all the squares and at all the crossroads, thousands of priests in the pulpit repeat these slogans *ad nauseam,* to the point of collective stupefaction. But it's sufficient for one little man, just one ordinary, little man to say no and the whole of that formidable granite order is imperilled."

This frightened the girl, but the priest was cheerful again.

"And if they catch him and kill him?" the girl said.

"Killing a man who says no is a risky business," said the priest. "Even a corpse can go on whispering no, no, no, no with the tenacity and obstinacy that is peculiar to certain corpses. How can you silence a corpse? You may perhaps have heard of Giacomo Matteotti."[1]

"I don't think so," Bianchina said. "Who's he?"

"A corpse that no-one can silence," Don Paolo said.

Pietro also questions his allegiance to Communism. Has not a noble ideal been stifled by a political party that has evolved into "a decadent Church"?

He remembered his first joining a socialist group. He had left the Church, not because he doubted the correctness of its dogmas or the efficacy of the sacraments, but because it seemed to him to identify itself with a corrupt, petty, and cruel society that it should have combated. When he first became a socialist that had been his only motive. He was not yet a Marxist; that he became later after joining the socialist fold. He accepted Marxism "as the rule of the new community." In the meantime had that community not itself become a synagogue? "Alas for all enterprises the declared aim of which is the salvation of the world. They seem to be the surest traps leading to self-destruction." Don Paolo decided that his return to Italy had been basically an attempt to escape that professionalism, to return to the ranks, to go back and find the clue to the complicated issue.

These thoughts gave him no peace. At meals he was silent and more distracted than ever. Matalena tried talking to him, but in vain, he might have been deaf. To her great offence and sorrow he took not the slightest notice of what he was eating. As soon as he had finished his coffee he went out into the garden, sat on the bench under the rowan tree, and started writing again, with the notebook resting on his knees: "Is it possible to take part in political life, to put oneself in the service of a party and remain sincere? Has not truth for me become party truth and justice party justice? Have not the interests of the organization ended in my case too by getting the better of all moral values, which are despised as petty bourgeois prejudices, and have those interests not become the supreme value? Have I, then, escaped from the opportunism of a decadent Church only to end up in the Machiavellism of a political sect? If these are dangerous cracks in the revolutionary consciousness, if they are ideas that must be banished from it, how is one to confront in good faith the risks of the conspiratorial struggle?"

---

[1]Giacomo Matteotti (1885–1924) was a prominent Italian socialist leader and critic of Mussolini. His murder at the hands of fascist thugs caused opposition deputies to leave the Italian parliament in protest, facilitating Mussolini's consolidation of power.

Don Paolo reread what he had written and realised that all he had done was to write down a series of questions. Meanwhile a flock of sparrows and some wild pigeons had started hopping and fluttering about him as in an aviary. At one point some women who were watching the scene from a distance decided that he was talking to them; the poor priest, having no-one else to talk to, was in fact talking to himself. The women immediately hurried to the inn to spread the news of this marvel.

"Your priest," they said to Matalena, "is talking to the birds, just like St. Francis."

"Yes," she replied, "he's a saint, a real saint."

In the following dialogue between Pietro and Uliva, a disenchanted socialist, Silone shows his hostility to the power wielded by both fascist and communist bureaucracies. In both instances an oppressive state crushes the individual.

"Don't let yourself be taken in by appearances," said Pietro. "The strength of the dictatorship is in its muscles, not its heart."

"There you're right," said Uliva. "There's something corpse-like about it. For a long time it has no longer been a movement, . . . but merely a bureaucracy. But what does the opposition amount to? What are you? A bureaucracy in embryo. You too aspire to totalitarian power in the name of different ideas, which simply means in the name of different words and on behalf of different interests. If you win, which is a misfortune that will probably happen to you, we subjects will merely exchange one tyranny for another."

"You're living on figments of your imagination," said Pietro. "How can you condemn the future?"

"Our future is the past of other countries," Uliva replied. "All right, we shall have technical and economic changes, that I don't deny. Just as we now have state railways, state quinine, salt, matches and tobacco, so we shall have state bread, shoes, shirts and pants, and state potatoes and fresh peas. Will that be technical progress? Certainly, but it will merely serve as a basis for an obligatory official doctrine, a totalitarian orthodoxy that will use every possible means from the cinema to terrorism to crush heresy and terrorize over individual thought. The present black inquisition will be succeeded by a red inquisition, the present censorship by a red censorship. The present deportations will be succeeded by red deportations, the preferred victims of which will be dissident revolutionaries. Just as the present bureaucracy identifies itself with patriotism and eliminates all its opponents, denouncing them as being in foreign pay, so will your future bureaucracy identify itself with labour and socialism and persecute everyone who goes on thinking with his own brain as a hired agent of the industrialists and landlords."

"Uliva, you're raving," Pietro exclaimed. "You have been one of us, you know us, you know that that is not our ideal."

"It's not your ideal," said Uliva, "but it's your destiny. There's no evading it."

"Destiny is an invention of the weak and the resigned," said Pietro.

Uliva made a gesture as if to indicate that further discussion was not worthwhile. But he added, "You're intelligent, but cowardly. You don't understand because you don't want to understand. You're afraid of the truth."

Pietro rose to leave. From the door he said to Uliva, who remained impassively on the couch, "There's nothing in my life that entitles you to insult me."

"Go away and don't come back," Uliva said. "I have nothing to say to an employee of the party."

Pietro had already opened the door to leave, but closed it and went back and sat at the foot of the couch on which Uliva was lying. "I shan't go away until you have explained to me why you have become like this," he said. "What happened to you that changed you to this extent? Was it prison, unemployment, hunger?"

"In my privations I studied and tried to find at least a promise of liberation," Uliva said. "I did not find it. For a long time I was tormented by the question why all revolutions, all of them without exception, began as liberation movements and ended as tyrannies. Why has no revolution ever escaped that fate?"

"Even if that were true," Pietro said, "it would be necessary to draw a conclusion different from yours. All other revolutions have gone astray, one would have to say, but we shall make one that will remain faithful to itself."

"Illusions, illusions," said Uliva. "You haven't won yet, you are still a conspiratorial movement, and you're rotten already. The regenerative ardour that filled us when we were in the students' cell has already become an ideology, a tissue of fixed ideas, a spider's web. That shows that there's no escape for you either. And, mind you, you're still only at the beginning of the descending parabola. Perhaps it's not your fault," Uliva went on, "but that of the mechanism in which you're caught up. To propagate itself every new idea is crystallized into formulas, to maintain itself it entrusts itself to a carefully recruited body of interpreters, who may sometimes actually be appropriately paid but at all events are subject to a higher authority charged with resolving doubts and suppressing deviations. Thus every new idea invariably ends by becoming a fixed idea, immobile and out of date. When it becomes official state doctrine there's no more escape. Under an orthodox totalitarian régime a carpenter or a farm labourer may perhaps manage to settle down, eat, digest, produce a family in peace and mind his own business. But for an intellectual there's no way out. He must either stoop and enter the dominant clergy or resign himself to going hungry and being eliminated at the first opportunity."

Pietro had a fit of anger. He took Uliva by the lapels of his jacket and shouted in his face, "But why must that be our destiny? Why can there be no way out? Are we chickens shut up in a hen coop? Why condemn a régime that doesn't yet exist and that we want to create in the image of man?"

"Don't shout," Uliva calmly replied. "Don't play the propagandist here with me. You have understood very well what I have said, but you pretend not to understand because you're afraid of the consequences."

"Rubbish," said Pietro.

"Listen," said Uliva, "when we were in the students' cell I watched you a great deal. I then discovered you were a revolutionary out of fear. You forced yourself to believe in progress, you forced yourself to be an optimist, you forced yourself to believe in the freedom of the will only because the opposite terrified you. And you've remained the same."

Pietro made Uliva a small concession. "It's true," he said, "that if I did not believe in the liberty of man, or at any rate in the possibility of the liberty of man, I should be afraid of life."

"I've ceased to believe in progress and I'm not afraid of life," said Uliva.

Arthur Koestler
Darkness at Noon

Born in Budapest of Jewish ancestry and educated in Vienna, Arthur Koestler (1905–1982) worked as a correspondent for a leading Berlin newspaper chain. He joined the Communist party at the very end of 1931 because he "lived in a disintegrating society thirsting for faith," was sensitized by the Depression, and saw communism as the "only force capable of resisting the inrush of the primitive [Nazi] horde." In 1938, he broke with the party in response to Stalin's liquidations. *Darkness at Noon* (1941) was published three years later.

In the novel, Koestler explores the attitudes of the Old Bolsheviks, who were imprisoned, tortured, and executed by Stalin. These dedicated Communists had served the party faithfully—many were heroes of the Revolution—but Stalin, fearing opposition, hating intellectuals, and driven by megalomania, denounced them as enemies of the people. In *Darkness at Noon,* the leading character, the imprisoned Rubashov, is a composite of the Old Bolsheviks. Although innocent, and without being physically tortured, Rubashov publicly confesses to political crimes that he never committed. He is also aware of the suffering the Party has brought to the people. The following passage, a conversation between Rubashov and his prison interrogator Ivanov, is Koestler's powerful indictment of the Soviet Union.

"The greatest criminals in history," Ivanov went on, "are not of the type Nero and Fouché, but of the type Gandhi and Tolstoy. Gandhi's inner voice has done more to prevent the liberation of India than the British guns. To sell oneself for thirty pieces of silver is an honest transaction; but to sell oneself to one's own conscience is to abandon mankind. History is *a priori* amoral; it has no conscience. To want to conduct history according to the maxims of the Sunday school means to leave everything as it is. You know that as well as I do." . . .

"I don't approve of mixing ideologies," Ivanov continued. "There are only two conceptions of human ethics, and they are at opposite poles. One of them is Christian and humane, declares the individual to be sacrosanct, and asserts that the rules of arithmetic are not to be applied to human units. The other starts from the basic principle that a collective aim justifies all means, and not only allows, but demands, that the individual should in every way be subordinated and sacrificed to the community—which may dispose of it as an experimentation rabbit or a sacrificial lamb. The first conception could be called anti-vivisection morality, the second, vivisection morality. Humbugs and dilettantes have always tried to mix the two conceptions; in practice, it is impossible. Whoever is burdened with power and responsibility finds out on the first occasion that he has to choose; and he is fatally driven to the second alternative. Do you know, since the establishment of Christianity as a state religion, a single example of a state which really followed a Christian policy? You can't point out one. In times of need—and politics are chronically in a time of need—the rules were always able to evoke 'exceptional circumstances,' which demanded exceptional measures of defence. Since the existence of nations and classes, they live in a permanent state of mutual self-defence, which forces them to defer to another time the putting into practice of humanism." . . .

Rubashov looked through the window. The melted snow had again frozen and sparkled, an irregular surface of yellow-white crystals. The sentinel on the wall marched up and down with shouldered rifle. The sky was clear but moonless; above the machine-gun turret shimmered the Milky Way.

Rubashov shrugged his shoulders. "Admit," he said, "that humanism and politics, respect for the individual and social progress, are incompatible. Admit that Gandhi is a catastrophe for India; that chasteness in the choice of means leads to political impotence. In negatives we agree. But look where the other alternative has led us. . . ."

"Well," asked Ivanov. "Where?"

Rubashov rubbed his pince-nez on his sleeve, and looked at him shortsightedly. "What a mess," he said, "what a mess we have made of our golden age."

Ivanov smiled. "Maybe," he said happily. "Look at [the earlier revolutions]. . . . Up to now, all revolutions have been made by moralizing dilettantes. They were always in good faith and perished because of their dilettantism. We for the first time are consequent." . . .

"Yes," said Rubashov. "So consequent, that in the interests of a just distribution of land we deliberately let die of starvation about five million farmers and their families in one year. So consequent were we in the liberation of human beings from the shackles of industrial exploitation that we sent about ten million people to do forced labour in the Arctic regions and the jungles of the East, under conditions similar to those of antique galley slaves. So consequent that, to settle a difference of opinion, we know only one argument: death, whether it is a matter of submarines, manure, or the Party line to be followed in Indo-China. Our engineers work with the constant knowledge that an error in calculation may take them to prison or the scaffold; the higher officials in our administration ruin and destroy their subordinates, because they know that they will be held responsible for the slightest slip and be destroyed themselves; our poets settle discussions on questions of style by denunciations to the Secret Police, because the expressionists consider the naturalistic style counter-revolutionary, and *vice versa*. Acting consequently in the interests of the coming generations, we have laid such terrible privations on the present one that its average length of life is shortened by a quarter. In order to defend the existence of the country, we have to take exceptional measures and make transition-stage laws, which are in every point contrary to the aims of the Revolution. The people's standard of life is lower than it was before the Revolution; the labour conditions are harder, the discipline is more inhuman, the piece-work drudgery worse than in colonial countries with native coolies; we have lowered the age limit for capital punishment down to twelve years; our sexual laws are more narrow-minded than those of England, our leader-worship more Byzantine than that of the reactionary dictatorships. Our Press and our schools cultivate Chauvinism, militarism, dogmatism, conformism and ignorance. The arbitrary power of the Government is unlimited, and unexampled in history; freedom of the Press, of opinion and of movement are as thoroughly exterminated as though the proclamation of the Rights of Man had never been. We have built up the most gigantic police apparatus, with informers made a national institution, and with the most refined scientific system of physical and mental torture. We whip the groaning masses of the country towards a theoretical future happiness, which only we can see. For the energies of this generation are exhausted; they were spent in the Revolution; for this generation is bled white and there is nothing left of it but a moaning, numbed, apathetic lump of sacrificial flesh. . . . Those are the consequences of our consequentialness. You called it vivisection morality. To me it sometimes seems as though the experimenters had torn the skin off the victim and left it standing with bared tissues, muscles and nerves." . . .

"For a man with your past," Ivanov went on, "this sudden revulsion against experimenting is rather naïve. Every year several million people are killed quite pointlessly by epidemics and other natural catastrophes. And we should shrink from sacrificing a few hundred thousand for the most promising experiment in history? Not to mention the legions of those who die of undernourishment and tuberculosis in coal and quick-silver mines, rice-fields and cotton plantations. No one takes any notice of them; nobody asks why or what for; but if here we shoot a few thousand objectively harmful people, the humanitarians all over the world foam at the mouth. Yes, we liquidated the parasitic part of the peasantry and let it die of starvation. It was a surgical operation which had to be done once and for all; but in the good old days before the Revolution just as many died in any dry year—only senselessly and pointlessly. The victims of the Yellow River floods in China amount sometimes to hundreds of thousands. Nature is generous in her senseless experiments on mankind. Why should mankind not have the right to experiment on itself?"

He paused; Rubashov did not answer. He went on:

"Have you ever read brochures of an anti-vivisectionist society? They are shattering and heartbreaking; when one reads how some poor cur which has had its liver cut out, whines and licks his tormentor's hands, one is just as nauseated as you were to-night. But if these people had their say, we would have no serums against cholera, typhoid, or diphtheria." . . .

He emptied the rest of the bottle, yawned, stretched and stood up. He limped over to Rubashov at the window, and looked out.

George Orwell
1984

In *1984,* written while he was dying of tuberculosis, George Orwell (1903–1950), a British novelist and political journalist, warned that the great principles of reason, human dignity, and freedom were now permanently menaced by the concentration and abuse of political power. The society of 1984 is ruled by the Inner Party, which constitutes some 2 percent of the population. Heading the Party is Big Brother—most likely a mythical figure created by the ruling elite to satisfy people's yearning for a leader. Party members are conditioned to accept unquestionably the party's orthodoxy. The Ministry of Truth resorts to thought control to dominate and manipulate the masses and to keep Party members loyal and subservient. Independent thinking is destroyed. Truth is whatever the Party decrees at the moment. Anyone thinking prohibited thoughts is designated a Thought-criminal, a crime punishable by death. The Thought Police's agents are ubiquitous, using hidden microphones and telescreens to check on any signs of deviance from the Party's rules and ideology.

Orwell's antiutopian novel focuses on Winston Smith, who works for the Ministry of Truth and is arrested by the Thought Police for harboring antiparty sentiments. Smith rebels against the Party in order to reclaim his individuality, to think and feel in his own way rather than according to the Party's dictates. Tortured brutally, humiliated, and brainwashed, Smith confesses to crimes that both he and the Party know he did not commit. The Party does not kill Smith but "reshapes" him, "cures" him by breaking his will and transforming him into a true believer in Big Brother. Excerpts from Orwell's most famous work follow.

"Do you know where you are, Winston?" he said.

"I don't know. I can guess. In the Ministry of Love."

"Do you know how long you have been here?"

"I don't know. Days, weeks, months—I think it is months."

"And why do you imagine that we bring people to this place?"

"To make them confess."

"No, that is not the reason. Try again."

"To punish them."

"No!" exclaimed O'Brien. His voice had changed extraordinarily, and his face had suddenly become both stern and animated. "No! Not merely to extract your confession, nor to punish you. Shall I tell you why we have brought you here? To cure you! To make you sane! Will you understand, Winston, that no one whom we bring to this place ever leaves our hands uncured? We are not interested in those stupid crimes that you have committed. The Party is not interested in the overt act: the thought is all we care about. We do not merely destroy our enemies; we change them. Do you understand what I mean by that?"

He was bending over Winston. His face looked enormous because of its nearness, and hideously ugly because it was seen from below. Moreover it was filled with a sort of exaltation, a lunatic intensity. Again Winston's heart shrank. If it had been possible he would have cowered deeper into the bed. He felt certain that O'Brien was about to twist the dial out of sheer wantonness. At this moment, however, O'Brien turned away. He took a pace or two up and down. Then he continued less vehemently:

"The first thing for you to understand is that in this place there are no martyrdoms. You have read of the religious persecutions of the past. In the Middle Ages there was the Inquisition. It was a failure. It set out to eradicate heresy, and ended by perpetuating it. For every heretic it burned at the stake, thousands of others rose up. Why was that? Because the Inquisition killed its enemies in the open, and killed them while they were still unrepentant; in fact, it killed them because they were unrepentant. Men were dying because they would not abandon their true beliefs. Naturally all the glory belonged to the victim and all the shame to the Inquisitor who burned him. Later, in the twentieth century, there were the totalitarians, as they were called. There were the German Nazis and the Russian Communists. The Russians persecuted heresy more cruelly than the Inquisition had done. And they imagined that they had learned from the mistakes of the past; they knew, at any rate, that one must not make martyrs. Before they exposed their victims to public trial, they deliberately set themselves to destroy their dignity. They wore them down by torture and solitude until they were despicable, cringing wretches, confessing whatever was put into their mouths, covering themselves with abuse, accusing and sheltering behind one another, whimpering for mercy. And yet after only a few years the same thing had happened over again. The dead men had become martyrs and their degradation was forgotten. Once again, why was it? In the first place, because the confessions that they had made were obviously extorted and untrue. We do not make mistakes of that kind. All the confessions that are uttered here are true. We make them true. And, above all, we do not allow the dead to rise up against us. You must stop imagining that posterity will vindicate you, Winston. Posterity will never hear of you. You will be lifted clean out from the stream of history. We shall turn you into gas and pour you into the stratosphere. Nothing will remain of you: not a name in a register, not a memory in a living brain. You will be annihilated in the past as well as in the future. You will never have existed."

Then why bother to torture me? thought Winston, with a momentary bitterness. O'Brien checked his step as though Winston had uttered the thought aloud. His large ugly face came nearer, with the eyes a little narrowed.

"You are thinking," he said, "that since we intend to destroy you utterly, so that nothing that you say or do can make the smallest difference—in that case, why do we go to the trouble of interrogating you first? That is what you were thinking, was it not?"

"Yes," said Winston.

O'Brien smiled slightly. "You are a flaw in the pattern, Winston. You are a stain that must be wiped out. Did I not tell you just now that we are different from the persecutors of the past? We are not content with negative obedience, nor even with the most abject submission. When finally you surrender to us, it must be of your own free will. We do not destroy the heretic because he resists us; so long as he resists us we never destroy him. We convert him, we capture his inner mind, we reshape him. We burn all evil and all illusion out of him; we bring him over to our side, not in appearance, but genuinely, heart and soul. We make him one of ourselves before we kill him. It is intolerable to us that an erroneous thought should exist anywhere in the world, however secret and powerless it may be. Even in the instant of death we cannot permit any deviation. In the old days the heretic walked to the stake still a heretic, proclaiming his heresy, exulting in it. Even the victim of the Russian purges could carry rebellion locked up in his skull as he walked down the passage waiting for the bullet. But we make the brain perfect before we blow it out. The command of the old despotisms was 'Thou shalt not.' The command of the totalitarians was 'Thou shalt.' Our command is *'Thou art.'* No one whom we bring to this place ever stands out against us. Everyone is washed clean. Even those three miserable traitors in whose innocence you once believed—Jones, Aaronson, and Rutherford—in the end, we broke them down. I took part in their interrogation myself. I saw them gradually worn down,

whimpering, groveling, weeping—and in the end it was not with pain or fear, only with penitence. By the time we had finished with them they were only the shells of men. There was nothing left in them except sorrow for what they had done, and love of Big Brother. It was touching to see how they loved him. They begged to be shot quickly, so that they could die while their minds were still clean."

His voice had grown almost dreamy. The exaltation, the lunatic enthusiasm, was still in his face. He is not pretending, thought Winston, he is not a hypocrite; he believes every word he says. What most oppressed him was the consciousness of his own intellectual inferiority. He watched the heavy yet graceful form strolling to and fro, in and out of the range of his vision. O'Brien was a being in all ways larger than himself. There was no idea that he had ever had, or could have, that O'Brien had not long ago known, examined, and rejected. His mind *contained* Winston's mind. But in that case how could it be true that O'Brien was mad? It must be he, Winston, who was mad. O'Brien halted and looked down at him. His voice had grown stern again.

"Do not imagine that you will save yourself, Winston, however completely you surrender to us. No one who has once gone astray is ever spared. And even if we chose to let you live out the natural term of your life, still, you would never escape from us. What happens to you here is forever. Understand that in advance. We shall crush you down to the point from which there is no coming back. Things will happen to you from which you could not recover, if you lived a thousand years. Never again will you be capable of ordinary human feeling. Everything will be dead inside you. Never again will you be capable of love, or friendship, or joy of living, or laughter, or curiosity, or courage, or integrity. You will be hollow. We shall squeeze you empty, and then we shall fill you with ourselves." . . .

. . . "The real power, the power we have to fight for night and day, is not power over things, but over men." He paused, and for a moment assumed again his air of a schoolmaster questioning a promising pupil: "How does one man assert his power over another, Winston?"

Winston thought. "By making him suffer," he said.

"Exactly. By making him suffer. Obedience is not enough. Unless he is suffering, how can you be sure that he is obeying your will and not his own? Power is in inflicting pain and humiliation. Power is in tearing human minds to pieces and putting them together again in new shapes of your own choosing. Do you begin to see, then, what kind of world we are creating? It is the exact opposite of the stupid hedonistic Utopias that the old reformers imagined. A world of fear and treachery and torment, a world of trampling and being trampled upon, a world which will grow not less but *more* merciless as it refines itself. Progress in our world will be progress toward more pain. The old civilizations claimed that they were founded on love and justice. Ours is founded upon hatred. In our world there will be no emotions except fear, rage, triumph, and self-abasement. Everything else we shall destroy—everything. Already we are breaking down the habits of thought which have survived from before the Revolution. We have cut the links between child and parent, and between man and man, and between man and woman. No one dares trust a wife or a child or a friend any longer. But in the future there will be no wives and no friends. Children will be taken from their mothers at birth, as one takes eggs from a hen. The sex instinct will be eradicated. Procreation will be an annual formality like the renewal of a ration card. We shall abolish the orgasm. Our neurologists are at work upon it now. There will be no loyalty, except loyalty toward the Party. There will be no love, except the love of Big Brother. There will be no laughter, except the laugh of triumph over a defeated enemy. There will be no art, no literature, no science. When we are omnipotent we shall have no more need of science. There will be no distinction between beauty and ugliness. There will be no curiosity, no employment of the process of life. All competing pleasures will be destroyed. But always—do not forget this, Winston—always there will be the intoxication of power, constantly increasing and constantly growing subtler. Always, at every moment, there will be the thrill of victory, the sensation of trampling on an enemy who is helpless. If you want a picture of the future, imagine a boot stamping on a human face—forever."

Nicolas Berdyaev
MODERN IDEOLOGIES AT VARIANCE WITH CHRISTIANITY

To Nicolas Berdyaev, a Russian Christian philosopher who fled the Soviet Union, communism and Nazism were modern forms of idolatry in opposition to the core values of Christianity. Nationalism, he said, "dehumanizes ethics" and provokes hatred among peoples; Nazi racism, which demonizes Jews because of their genes, is "unworthy of a Christian." Only by a return to Christian piety, maintained Berdyaev, can we overcome the "collective demoniac possession" that is destroying European civilization. By Christian piety, he meant an active struggle for human dignity and social justice. Berdyaev expressed these views in *The Fate of Man in the Modern World* (1935), which is excerpted below.

Once the veil of civilization was torn aside by the war, the prime realities were revealed in all their nakedness. The faith in mankind which had existed for nineteen hundred years was finally shattered. Faith in God had been shaken earlier, and loss of one was followed by loss of the other. The humanist myth about man was exploded, and the abyss yawned at the feet of mankind. The wolf-like life of capitalist society was not able to encourage and support the faith in man. Man himself is left out of the picture. Economics, which should have aided man, instead of being for his service, is discovered to be that for which man exists: the non-human economic process. The war merely put into plain words what was already implicit in capitalism, that man is of no account, that he has not only ceased to be the supreme value, but value of any sort. And almost all the movements launched against capitalism since the war have accepted the same attitude toward man which characterized both capitalism and the war itself. This is the most characteristic process of our times. Man appears unable to withstand this process, to defend his own value, to find support within himself, and he grasps, as at a life-belt, at the collective, communist or national and racial, at the State as the Absolute here on earth, or at organized and technicalized forms of living. Man has lost his worth; it has been torn to tatters. Coming out of the war, there have appeared in the arena of history a series of human collectives, masses of men who have dropped out of the organized order and harmony of life, lost the religious sanctions for their lives and now demand obligatory organization as the sole means of avoiding final chaos and degeneration. . . .

. . . [W]e live in a very authoritarian epoch. The urge toward an authoritarian form of life is felt throughout the whole world: the liberal element seems completely discredited. . . .

The war was the catastrophic moment which disclosed that chaos moves beneath the false civilization of capitalism. The war was chaos, organized by forced labour. For chaos may wear an appearance of complete external organization. And since the war, man is not merely willing, but actively desires to live in the obligatorily-organized chaos which expresses itself in the authoritarian form of life. . . .

. . . The masses are easily subject to suggestion and often enter a state of collective demoniac possession. They may be possessed only by ideas which permit of a simple and elemental symbolism, a mode quite characteristic of our time. The search for leaders who can lead the masses, offer alleviation for woes, solve all problems, means simply that all the classic authorities have fallen, monarchy and democracy together, and that they must be replaced by new authorities, born of the collective "possession" of the mass. The leader must provide "bread and the theatre." . . .

. . . We are witnessing the process of dehumanization in all phases of culture and of social life. Above all, moral consciousness is being dehumanized. Man has ceased to be the supreme value: he has ceased to have any value at all. The youth of the whole world, communist, fascist, national-socialist or those simply carried away by technics . . . this youth is not only anti-humanistic in its attitudes, but often anti-human. . . .

. . . A bestial cruelty toward man is characteristic of our age, and this is more astonishing since it is displayed at the very peak of human refinement, where modern conceptions of sympathy, it would seem, have made impossible the old, barbaric forms of cruelty. Bestialism is something quite different from the old, natural, healthy barbarism; it is barbarism within a refined civilization. Here the atavistic, barbaric instincts are filtered through the prism of civilization, and hence they have a pathological character. . . . The bestialism of our time is a continuation of the war, it has poisoned mankind with the blood of war. The morals of wartime have become those of "peaceful" life, which is actually the continuation of war, a war of all against all. According to this morality, everything is permissible: man may be used in any way desired for the attainment of inhuman or anti-human aims. Bestialism is a denial of the value of the human person, of every human personality; it is a denial of all sympathy with the fate of any man. The new humanism is closing: this is inescapable.

We are entering an inhuman world, a world of inhumanness, inhuman not merely in fact, but in principle as well. Inhumanity has begun to be presented as something noble, surrounded with an aureole of heroism. Over against man there rises a class or a race, a deified collective or state. Modern nationalism bears marks of bestial inhumanity. No longer is every man held to be a man, a value, the image and likeness of God. For often even Christianity is interpreted inhumanly. The "Aryan paragraph" offered to German Christians is the project for a new form of inhumanity in Christianity. . . .

. . . The new world which is taking form is moved by other values than the value of man or of human personality, or the value of truth: it is moved by such values as power, technics, race-purity, nationality, the state, the class, the collective. The will to justice is overcome by the will to power. . . .

. . . National passion is tearing the world and threatening the destruction of European culture. This is one more proof of the strength of atavism in human society, of how much stronger than the conscious is the subconscious, of how superficial has been the humanizing process of past centuries. . . . [M]odern Nationalism means the dehumanization and bestialization of human societies. It is a reversion from the category of culture and history to that of zoology. . . .

. . . The results of the Christian-humanistic process of unifying humanity seem to be disappearing. We are witnessing the paganization of Christian society. Nationalism is polytheism: it is incompatible with monotheism.

This process of paganization takes shocking forms in Germany, which wishes no longer to be a Christian nation, has exchanged the swastika for the cross and demands of Christians that they should renounce the very fundamentals of the Christian revelation and the Christian faith, and cast aside the moral teaching of the Gospels. . . .

Nationalism turns nationality into a supreme and absolute value to which all life is subordinated. This is idolatry. The nation replaces God. Thus Nationalism cannot but come into conflict with Christian universalism, with the Christian revelation that there is neither Greek nor Jew, and that every man has absolute value. Nationalism uses everything as its own instrument, as an instrument of national power and prosperity. . . .

. . . Nationalism has no Christian roots and it is always in conflict with Christianity. . . .

. . . Nationalism involves not only love of one's own, but hatred of other nations, and hatred is usually a stronger motive than love. Nationalism preaches either seclusion, isolation, blindness to other nations and culture, self-satisfaction and particularism, or else expansion at the expense of others, conquest, subjection, imperialism. And in both cases it denies Christian conscience, contraverts the principle and the habits of the brotherhood of man. Nationalism is in complete contradiction to a personal ethic; it denies the supreme value of human personality. Modern Nationalism dehumanizes ethics, it demands of man that he renounce humanity. It is all one and the same process, in Communism as in Nationalism. Man's inner world is completely at the mercy of collectivism, national or social. . . .

[R]acialism . . . has no basis at all in Christianity. The mere consideration of the "Aryan paragraph" is unworthy of a Christian, although it is now demanded of Christians in Germany. Racialist anti-Semitism inevitably leads to anti-Christianity, as we see in Germany to-day. That Germano-Aryan Christianity now being promoted is a denial of the Gospels and of Christ Himself. The ancient religious conflict between Christianity and Judaism, a real conflict by the way, has taken such a turn in our difficult and uncertain times, that militant anti-Judaism turns out to be anti-Christianity. Truly Christian anti-Judaism is directed, not against the Bible or the Old Testament, but against the Talmudicrabbinic Judaism which developed after the Jews' refusal to accept Christ. But when religious anti-Judaism becomes racialist anti-Semitism, it inevitably turns into anti-Christianity, for the human origins of Christianity are Hebrew. . . . [I]t is impossible, it is forbidden, for a true Christian to be a racialist and to hate the Jews. . . .

. . . According to the race theory there is no hope of salvation, whatever: if you were born a Jew or a negro, no change of consciousness or belief or conviction can save you, you are doomed. A Jew may become a Christian: that does him no good. Even if he becomes a national-socialist, he cannot be saved.

4 The Great Depression: Literature as Social Protest

The Great Depression, which began in 1929 with the crash of the stock market in the United States, caused much misery throughout the world and was a major reason for the attraction of both fascism and communism.

More than any other novel of the period, John Steinbeck's *The Grapes of Wrath* (1939) captured the suffering of rural America during the Depression. In several southern and western states, prolonged drought and constant winds had deprived the land of top soil causing crops to fail and animals to die. Deprived of their livelihood, hundreds of thousands of families saw their property foreclosed or were forced to sell at a fraction of its value. Searching for a better life, they journeyed to California to work as migrant farmers under brutal conditions. Written during hard times, *The Grapes of Wrath* is both a cry of pain and an affirmation of life that urges people to be more humane, more compassionate, to recognize their moral obligation to care about others, particularly the downtrodden, with whom they share a common humanity.

Steinbeck's novel, which was the leading best-seller in 1939, came under attack, sometimes vicious, from conservatives and California farm groups. Rumors circulated that Steinbeck was a Jew and a communist—he was neither—out to undermine the American economy. In 1942, a Senate investigation confirmed the "shocking degree of human misery" endured by migrant farm workers.

John Steinbeck
The Grapes of Wrath

The Grapes of Wrath movingly described the ordeal of the Joad family, downtrodden Oklahoma farmers who headed to California to find work as farm laborers after being driven off their land. On the long journey west, the Joads suffer hardships: Grampa Joad, who did not want to leave his home, immediately suffers a fatal stroke; when Granma Joad dies, the family does not have the money for a proper burial.

When the Joads arrive in California, they stay at a squatters' camp where conditions are deplorable; California is not the "Promised Land" they had expected when they began their arduous journey. The migrants have to cope with filth, chaos, and abuse by brutal police and their deputies. The Joads move to another camp set up by the government. Because of effective management, including the active participation of the migrants themselves on committees, the camp is orderly and clean, a sign that common folk, organized and working together, can improve the conditions under which they live.

Knowing that the migrants are desperate for work, greedy orchard owners cut their pay and use the police to squash strikers, "them goddam reds," as they are referred to. Eight members of the Joad family—four men, two women, and two children—work all day picking peaches. At five cents a box, they earn only a dollar or so and are overcharged for food at the company store. Outside the orchards are pickets protesting that their pay had been slashed to two and one half cents a box. Tom Joad speaks with Jim Casy, who leads the pickets. Casy is an ex-preacher whose spiritual nature and humanitarian feelings draw him into fellowship with others. Casy tells Tom how the orchard owners have deceived and exploited the migrants.

"Lookie, Tom," he said at last. "We come to work there. They says it's gonna be fi' cents. They was a hell of a lot of us. We got there an' they says they're payin' two an' a half cents. A fella can't even eat on that, an' if he got kids— So we says we won't take it. So they druv us off. An' all the cops in the worl' come down on us. Now they're payin' you five. When they bust this here strike—ya think they'll pay five?"

"I dunno," Tom said. "Payin' five now."

"Lookie," said Casy. "We tried to camp together, an' they druv us like pigs. Scattered us. Beat the hell outa fellas. Druv us like pigs. They run you in like pigs, too. We can't las' much longer. Some people ain't et for two days. You goin' back tonight?"

"Aim to," said Tom.

"Well—tell the folks in there how it is, Tom. Tell 'em they're starvin' us an' stabbin' theirself in the back. 'Cause sure as cowflops she'll drop to two an' a half jus' as soon as they clear us out."

"I'll tell 'em," said Tom. "I don' know how. Never seen so many guys with guns. Don' know if they'll even let a fella talk. An' folks don' pass no time of day. They jus' hang down their heads an' won't even give a fella a howdy."

"Try an' tell 'em, Tom. They'll get two an' a half, jus' the minute we're gone. You know what two an' a half is—that's one ton of peaches picked an' carried for a dollar." He dropped his head. "No—you can't do it. You can't get your food for that. Can't eat for that."

"I'll try to get to tell the folks."

"How's your ma?"

"Purty good. She liked that gov'ment camp. Baths an' hot water."

"Yeah—I heard."

"It was pretty nice there. Couldn' find no work, though. Had a leave."

"I'd like to go to one," said Casy. "Like to see it. Fella says they ain't no cops."

"Folks is their own cops."

Casy looked up excitedly. "An' was they any trouble? Fightin', stealin', drinkin'?"

"No," said Tom.

"Well, if a fella went bad—what then? What'd they do?"

"Put 'im outa the camp."

"But they wasn' many?"

"Hell, no," said Tom. "We was there a month, an' on'y one."

Casy's eyes shone with excitement. He turned to the other men. "Ya see?" he cried. "I tol' you. Cops cause more trouble than they stop. Look, Tom. Try an' get the folks in there to come on out. They can do it in a couple days. Them peaches is ripe. Tell 'em."

"They won't," said Tom. "They're a-gettin' five, an' they don' give a damn about nothin' else."

"But jus' the minute they ain't strikebreakin' they won't get no five."

"I don' think they'll swalla that. Five they're a-gettin'. Tha's all they care about."

"Well, tell 'em anyways."

"Pa wouldn' do it," Tom said. "I know 'im. He'd say it wasn't none of his business."

"Yes," Casy said disconsolately. "I guess that's right. Have to take a beatin' 'fore he'll know."

"We was outa food," Tom said. "Tonight we had meat. Not much, but we had it. Think Pa's gonna give up his meat on account a other fellas? An' Rosaharn oughta get milk. Think Ma's gonna wanta starve that baby jus' 'cause a bunch a fellas is yellin' outside a gate?"

Casy said sadly, "I wisht they could see it. I wisht they could see the on'y way they can depen' on their meat— Oh, the hell! Get tar'd sometimes. God-awful tar'd. I knowed a fella. Brang 'im in while I was in the jail house. Been tryin' to start a union. Got one started. An' then them vigilantes bust it up. An' know what? Them very folks he been tryin' to help tossed him out. Wouldn' have nothin' to do with 'im. Scared they'd get saw in his comp'ny. Says, 'Git out. You're a danger on us.' Well, sir, it hurt his feelin's purty bad. But then he says, 'It ain't so bad if you know.' He says, 'French Revolution—all them fellas that figgered her out got their heads chopped off. Always that way,' he says. 'Jus' as natural as rain. You didn' do it for fun no way. Doin' it 'cause you have to. 'Cause it's you. Look a Washington,' he says. 'Fit the Revolution, an' after, them sons-a-bitches turned on him. An' Lincoln the same. Same folks yellin' to kill 'em. Natural as rain.'"

"Don't soun' like no fun," said Tom.

"No, it don't. This fella in jail, he says, 'Anyways, you do what you can. An',' he says, 'the on'y thing you got to look at is that ever' time they's a little step fo'ward, she may slip back a little, but she never slips clear back. You can prove that,' he says, 'an' that makes the whole thing right. An' that means they wasn't no waste even if it seemed like they was.'"

"Talkin'," said Tom. "Always talkin'. Take my brother Al. He's out lookin' for a girl. He don't care 'bout nothin' else. Couple days he'll get him a girl. Think about it all day an' do it all night. He don't give a damn 'bout steps up or down or sideways."

"Sure," said Casy. "Sure. He's jus' doin' what he's got to do. All of us like that."

The man seated outside pulled the tent flap wide. "God-damn it, I don' like it," he said.

Casy looked out at him. "What's the matter?"

"I don' know. I jus' itch all over. Nervous as a cat."

"Well, what's the matter?"

"I don' know. Seems like I hear somepin, an' then I listen an' they ain't nothin' to hear."

"You're jus' jumpy," the wizened man said. He got up and went outside. And in a second he looked into the tent. "They's a great big ol' black cloud a-sailin' over. Bet she's got thunder. That's what's itchin' him—'lectricity." He ducked out again. The other two men stood up from the ground and went outside.

Casy said softly, "All of 'em's itchy. Them cops been sayin' how they're gonna beat the hell outa us an' run us outa the county. They figger I'm a leader 'cause I talk so much."

The wizened face looked in again. "Casy, turn out that lantern an' come outside. They's somepin."

Casy turned the screw. The flame drew down into the slots and popped and went out. Casy groped outside and Tom followed him. "What is it?" Casy asked softly.

"I dunno. Listen!"

There was a wall of frog sounds that merged with silence. A high, shrill whistle of crickets. But through this background came other sounds—faint footsteps from the road, a crunch of clods up on the bank, a little swish of brush down the stream.

"Can't really tell if you hear it. Fools you. Get nervous," Casy reassured them. "We're all nervous. Can't really tell. You hear it, Tom?"

"I hear it," said Tom. "Yeah, I hear it. I think they's guys comin' from ever' which way. We better get outa here."

The wizened man whispered, "Under the bridge span—out that way. Hate to leave my tent."

"Le's go," said Casy.

They moved quietly along the edge of the stream. The black span was a cave before them. Casy bent over and moved through. Tom behind. Their feet slipped into the water. Thirty feet they moved, and their breathing echoed from the curved ceiling. Then they came out on the other side and straightened up.

A sharp call, "There they are!" Two flashlight beams fell on the men, caught them, blinded them. "Stand where you are." The voices came out of the darkness. "That's him. That shiny bastard. That's him."

Casy stared blindly at the light. He breathed heavily. "Listen," he said. "You fellas don' know what you're doin'. You're helpin' to starve kids."

"Shut up, you red son-of-a-bitch."

A short heavy man stepped into the light. He carried a new white pick handle.

Casy went on, "You don' know what you're a-doin'."

The heavy man swung with the pick handle. Casy dodged down into the swing. The heavy club crashed into the side of his head with a dull crunch of bone, and Casy fell sideways out of the light.

"Jesus, George. I think you killed him."

"Put the light on him," said George. "Serve the son-of-a-bitch right." The flashlight beam dropped, searched and found Casy's crushed head.

Tom looked down at the preacher. The light crossed the heavy man's legs and the white new pick handle. Tom leaped silently. He wrenched the club free. The first time he knew he had missed and struck a shoulder, but the second time his crushing blow found the head, and as the heavy man sank down, three more blows found his head. The lights danced about. There were shouts, the sound of running feet, crashing through brush. Tom stood over the prostrate man. And then a club reached his head, a glancing blow. He felt the stroke like an electric shock. And then he was running along the stream, bending low. He heard the splash of footsteps following him. Suddenly he turned and squirmed up into the brush, deep into a poison-oak thicket. And he lay still. The footsteps came near, the light beams glanced along the stream bottom. Tom wriggled up through the thicket to the top. He emerged in an orchard. And still he could hear the calls, the pursuit in the stream bottom. He bent low and ran over the cultivated earth; the clods slipped and rolled under his feet. Ahead he saw the bushes that bounded the field, bushes along the edges of an irrigation ditch. He slipped through the fence, edged in among vines and blackberry bushes. And then he lay still, panting hoarsely. He felt his numb face and nose. The nose was crushed, and a trickle of blood dripped from his chin. He lay still on his stomach until his mind came back. And then he crawled slowly over the edge of the ditch. He bathed his face in the cool water, tore off the tail of his blue shirt and dipped it and held it against his torn cheek and nose. The water stung and burned.

The black cloud had crossed the sky, a blob of dark against the stars. The night was quiet again.

Tom stepped into the water and felt the bottom drop from under his feet. He threshed the two strokes across the ditch and pulled himself heavily up the other bank. His clothes clung to him. He moved and made a slopping noise; his shoes squished. Then he sat down, took off his shoes and emptied them. He wrung the bottoms of his trousers, took off his coat and squeezed the water from it.

Along the highway he saw the dancing beams of the flashlights, searching the ditches. Tom put on his shoes and moved cautiously across the stubble field. The squishing noise no longer came from his shoes. He went by instinct toward the other side of the stubble field, and at last he came to the road. Very cautiously he approached the square of houses.

Once a guard, thinking he heard a noise, called, "Who's there?"

Tom dropped and froze to the ground, and the flashlight beam passed over him. He crept silently to the door of the Joad house. The door squalled on its hinges. And Ma's voice, calm and steady and wide awake:

"What's that?"

"Me. Tom."

"Well, you better get some sleep. Al ain't in yet."

"He must a foun' a girl."

"Go on to sleep," she said softly. "Over under the window."

He found his place and took off his clothes to the skin. He lay shivering under his blanket. And his torn face awakened from its numbness, and his whole head throbbed.

It was an hour more before Al came in. He moved cautiously near and stepped on Tom's wet clothes.

"Sh!" said Tom.

Al whispered, "You awake? How'd you get wet?"

"Sh," said Tom. "Tell you in the mornin'."

Pa turned on his back, and his snoring filled the room with gasps and snorts.

"You're col'," Al said.

"Sh. Go to sleep." The little square of the window showed gray against the black of the room.

Tom did not sleep. The nerves of his wounded face came back to life and throbbed, and his cheek bone ached, and his broken nose bulged and pulsed with pain that seemed to toss him about, to shake him. He watched the little square window, saw the stars slide down over it and drop from sight. At intervals he heard the footsteps of the watchmen.

At last the roosters crowed, far away, and gradually the window lightened. Tom touched his swollen face with his fingertips, and at his movement Al groaned and murmured in his sleep.

In the morning Ma sees Tom's battered face.

"Tom," she whispered, "what's the matter?"

"Sh!" he said. "Don't talk loud. I got in a fight."

"Tom!"

"I couldn' help it, Ma."

She knelt down beside him. "You in trouble?"

He was a long time answering. "Yeah," he said. "In trouble. I can't go out to work. I got to hide."

The children crawled near on their hands and knees, staring greedily. "What's the matter'th him, Ma?"

"Hush!" Ma said. "Go wash up."

"We got no soap."

"Well, use water."

"What's the matter'th Tom?"

"Now you hush. An' don't you tell nobody."

They backed away and squatted down against the far wall, knowing they would not be inspected.

Ma asked, "Is it bad?"

"Nose busted."

"I mean the trouble?"

"Yeah. Bad!"

Al opened his eyes and looked at Tom. "Well, for Chris' sake! What was you in?"

"What's a matter?" Uncle John asked. . . .

Pa clumped in. "[The store] was open all right." He put a tiny bag of flour and his package of lard on the floor beside the stove. "'S'a matter?" he asked.

Tom braced himself on one elbow for a moment, and then he lay back. "Jesus, I'm weak. I'm gonna tell ya once. So I'll tell all of ya. How 'bout the kids?"

Ma looked at them, huddled against the wall. "Go wash ya face."

"No," Tom said. "They got to hear. They got to know. They might blab if they don' know."

"What the hell is this?" Pa demanded.

"I'm a-gonna tell. Las' night I went out to see what all the yellin' was about. An' I come on Casy."

"The preacher?"

"Yeah, Pa. The preacher, on'y he was a-leadin' the strike. They come for him."

Pa demanded, "Who come for him?"

"I dunno. Same kinda guys that turned us back on the road that night. Had pick handles." He paused. "They killed 'im. Busted his head. I was standin' there. I went nuts. Grabbed the pick handle." He looked bleakly back at the night, the darkness, the flashlights, as he spoke. "I—I clubbed a guy."

Ma's breath caught in her throat. Pa stiffened. "Kill 'im?" he asked softly.

"I—don't know. I was nuts. Tried to."

Ma asked, "Was you saw?"

"I dunno. I dunno. I guess so. They had the lights on us."

For a moment Ma stared into his eyes. "Pa," she said, "break up some boxes. We got to get breakfas'. You got to go to work. Ruthie, Winfiel'. If anybody asts you—Tom is sick—you hear? If you tell—he'll—get sent to jail. You hear?"

"Yes, ma'am."

"Keep your eye on 'em, John. Don' let 'em talk to nobody." She built the fire as Pa broke the boxes that had held the goods. She made her dough, put a pot of coffee to boil. The light wood caught and roared its flame in the chimney.

Pa finished breaking the boxes. He came near to Tom. "Casy—he was a good man. What'd he wanta mess with that stuff for?"

Tom said dully, "They come to work for fi' cents a box."

"That's what we're a-gettin'."

"Yeah. What we was a-doin' was breakin' strike. They give them fellas two an' a half cents."

"You can't eat on that."

"I know," Tom said wearily. "That's why they struck. Well, I think they bust that strike las' night. We'll maybe be gettin' two an' a half cents today."

"Why, the sons-a-bitches——"

"Yeah! Pa. You see? Casy was still a—good man. Goddamn it, I can't get that pitcher outa my head. Him layin' there—head jus' crushed flat an' oozin'. Jesus!" He covered his eyes with his hand.

"Well, what we gonna do?" Uncle John asked.

Al was standing up now. "Well, by God, I know what I'm gonna do. I'm gonna get out of it."

"No, you ain't, Al," Tom said. "We need you now. I'm the one. I'm a danger now. Soon's I get on my feet I got to go."

Ma worked at the stove. Her head was half turned to hear. She put grease in the frying pan, and when it whispered with heat, she spooned the dough into it.

Tom went on, "You got to stay, Al. You got to take care a the truck."

"Well, I don' like it."

"Can't help it, Al. It's your folks. You can help 'em. I'm a danger to 'em."

Al grumbled angrily. "I don' know why I ain't let to get me a job in a garage."

"Later, maybe." Tom looked past him, and he saw Rose of Sharon {who is pregnant} lying on the mattress. Her eyes were huge—opened wide. "Don't worry," he called to her. "Don't you worry. Gonna get you some milk today." She blinked slowly, and didn't answer him.

Pa said, "We got to know, Tom. Think ya killed this fella?"

"I don' know. It was dark. An' somebody smacked me. I don' know. I hope so. I hope I killed the bastard."

"Tom!" Ma called. "Don' talk like that."

From the street came the sound of many cars moving slowly. Pa stepped to the window and looked out. "They's a whole slew a new people comin' in," he said.

"I guess they bust the strike, awright," said Tom. "I guess you'll start at two an' a half cents."

"But a fella could work at a run, an' still he couldn' eat."

"I know," said Tom. "Eat win'fall peaches. That'll keep ya up."

Ma turned the dough and stirred the coffee. "Listen to me," she said. "I'm gettin' cornmeal today. We're a-gonna eat cornmeal mush. An' soon's we get enough for gas, we're movin' away. This ain't a good place. An' I ain't gonna have Tom out alone. No, sir."

"Ya can't do that, Ma. I tell you I'm jus' a danger to ya."

Her chin was set. "That's what we'll do. Here, come eat this here, an' then get out to work. I'll come out soon's I get washed up. We got to make some money." . . .

Ma took a plate and a cup to Tom. "Better eat a little somepin."

"I can't, Ma. I'm so darn sore I couldn' chew."

"You better try."

"No, I can't, Ma,"

She sat down on the edge of his mattress. "You got to tell me," she said. "I got to figger how it was. I got to keep straight. What was Casy a-doin'? Why'd they kill 'im?"

"He was jus' standin' there with the lights on' 'im."

"What'd he say? Can ya 'member what he says?"

Tom said, "Sure. Casy said, 'You got no right to starve people.' An' then this heavy fella called him a red son-of-a-bitch. An' Casy says, 'You don' know what you're a-doin'.' An' then this guy smashed 'im."

Ma looked down. She twisted her hands together. "Tha's what he said—'You don' know what you're doin''?"

"Yeah!"

Ma said, "I wisht Granma could a heard."

"Ma—I didn' know what I was a-doin', no more'n when you take a breath. I didn' even know I was gonna do it."

"It's awright. I wisht you didn' do it. I wisht you wasn' there. But you done what you had to do. I can't read no fault on you." She went to the stove and dipped a cloth in the heating dishwater. "Here," she said. "Put that there on your face."

He laid the warm cloth over his nose and cheek, and winced at the heat. "Ma, I'm a-gonna go away tonight. I can't go puttin' this on you folks."

Ma said angrily, "Tom! They's a whole lot I don' un'erstan'. But goin' away ain't gonna ease us. It's gonna bear us down." And she went on, "They was the time when we was on the lan'. They was a boundary to us then. Ol' folks died off, an' little fellas come, an' we was always one thing—we was the fambly—kinda whole and clear. An' now we ain't clear no more. I can't get straight. They ain't nothin' keeps us clear. Al—he's a-hankerin' an' a-jibbitin' to go off on his own. An' Uncle John is jus' a-draggin' along. Pa's lost his place. He ain't the head no more. We're crackin' up, Tom. There ain't no fambly now. An' Rosasharn—" She looked around and found the girl's wide eyes. "She gonna have her baby an' they won't be no fambly. I don' know. I been a-tryin' to keep her goin'. Winfiel'—what's he gonna be, this-a-way? Gettin' wild, an' Ruthie too—like animals. Got nothin' to trus'. Don' go, Tom. Stay an' help."

"O.K.," he said tiredly. "O.K. I shouldn', though. I know it."

Ma went to her dishpan and washed the tin plates and dried them. "You didn' sleep."

"No."

"Well, you sleep. I seen your clothes was wet. I'll hang 'em by the stove to dry." She finished her work. "I'm goin' now. I'll pick. Rosasharn, if anybody comes, Tom sick, you hear? Don' let nobody in. You hear?" Rose of Sharon nodded. "We'll come back at noon. Get some sleep, Tom. Maybe we can get outa here tonight." She moved swiftly to him. "Tom, you ain't gonna slip out?"

"No, Ma."

"You sure? You won't go?"

"No, Ma. I'll be here."

"Awright. 'Member, Rosasharn." She went out and closed the door firmly behind her.

Tom lay still—and then a wave of sleep lifted him to the edge of unconsciousness and dropped him slowly back and lifted him again.

"You—Tom!"

"Huh? Yeah!" He started awake. He looked over at Rose of Sharon. Her eyes were blazing with resentment. "What you want?"

"You killed a fella!"

"Yeah. Not so loud! You wanta rouse somebody?"

"What da I care?" she cried. "That lady tol' me. She says what sin's gonna do. She tol' me. What chance I got to have a nice baby? . . . I ain't gettin' good food. I ain't gettin' milk." Her voice rose hysterically. "An' now you kill a fella. What chance that baby got to get bore right? I know— gonna be a freak—a freak! I never done no dancin'."

Tom got up. "Sh!" he said. "You're gonna get folks in here."

"I don' care. I'll have a freak! I didn' dance no hug-dance."

He went near to her. "Be quiet."

"You get away from me. It ain't the first fella you killed, neither." Her face was growing red with hysteria. Her words blurred. "I don' wanta look at you." She covered her head with her blanket.

Tom heard the choked, smothered cries. He bit his lower lip and studied the floor. And then he went to Pa's bed. Under the edge of the mattress the rifle lay, a lever-action Winchester .38, long and heavy. Tom picked it up and dropped the lever to see that a cartridge was in the chamber. He tested the hammer on half-cock. And then he went back to his mattress. He laid the rifle on the floor beside him, stock up and barrel pointing down. Rose of Sharon's voice thinned to a whimper. Tom lay down again and covered himself, covered his bruised cheek with the blanket and made a little tunnel to breathe through. He sighed, "Jesus, oh, Jesus!"

Outside, a group of cars went by, and voices sounded.

"How many men?"

"Jes' us—three. Whatcha payin'?"

"You go to house twenty-five. Number's right on the door."

"O.K., mister. Whatcha payin'?"

"Two and a half cents."

"Why, goddamn it, a man can't make his dinner!"

"That's what we're payin'. There's two hundred men coming from the South that'll be glad to get it."

"But, Jesus, mister!"

"Go on now. Either take it or go on along. I got no time to argue."

"But——"

"Look. I didn' set the price. I'm just checking you in. If you want it, take it. If you don't, turn right around and go along."

"Twenty-five, you say?"

"Yes, twenty-five."

At the book's end, the Joads and the other migrants, hungry, some to the point of starvation, penniless, and ill, have hit bottom. Yet the novel ends on a hopeful note. One of the Joads, Rose of Sharon, who has just given birth to a stillborn baby, offers her life-sustaining mother's milk to a starving stranger. Written during hard times, *The Grapes of Wrath* was both a cry of pain and an affirmation of life that urges people to be more humane, to be more compassionate, and to recognize their moral obligation to care about others, particularly the downtrodden, with whom they share a common humanity.

5 American Novelists and World War II

Among American novelists who produced memorable works about World War II are Norman Mailer, *The Naked and the Dead* (1948), Irwin Shaw, *The Young Lions* (1948), Herman Wouk, *The Caine Mutiny* (1951) and *The Winds of War* (1971), James Jones, *From Here to Eternity* (1951) and *The Thin Red Line* (1962), and Joseph Heller, *Catch-22* (1961). These novels explored many of the often conflicting emotions evidenced by men at war—fear, cowardice, brutality, fanaticism, patriotism, loyalty, courage, camaraderie, decency, altruism, longing; they showed men who loved war and the power it gave them, and delved into those elusive qualities of character demonstrated by effective leaders even under the most trying of circumstances. They contained powerful descriptions of the horror and tragedy of conflict that killed and maimed indiscriminately and in staggering numbers and touching scenes of compassion and loyalty. At times they analyzed the ideological and moral issues that were central to the war: the nature and appeal of fascism and its threat to freedom and civilized values. Several of the war novelists, reared on the social issues of the 1930s, were sensitive to bigotry that minorities, particularly Jews and blacks, fared in the service. Examining the prewar life of recruits who made up the heterogeneous American army, these novelists offered penetrating insights into American sexual behavior, social classes, and regional cultures.

Joseph Heller
Catch-22

Brooklyn-born Joseph Heller (1923–1999), author of *Catch-22,* enlisted in the United States Air Force in 1942, serving as a B-25 wing bombardier on his tour of duty in Europe. *Catch-22* is like no other war novel. It contains realistic accounts of men under attack on bombing missions, their panic and dying screams as their plane, hit by enemy fire, plummets to earth. But it also transcends the stark, documentary realism of traditional war novels. It is punctuated by outrageous satirical humor, which leads the reader into the bizarre world of the military bureaucracy, with its insane logic, and the Freudian world of mentally disjointed individuals. The comic satire that runs through the book mocks a romantic vision of war; for Heller, combat is not adventure, glory, or honor but madness. Also coming under satirical attack are bureaucratic authority, the profit motive, psychiatry, sexual encounters, religion, and patriotism.

The novel's principal character is Captain Yossarian, a paranoid American bombardier, who believes that people everywhere want to kill him. Knowing that the war is almost over, he no longer cares whether his bombs hit their target. He only wants to stay alive. He seeks to finish the number of missions needed to be sent home. But as soon the men of his squadron approach the figure, Colonel Cathcart raises it, and keeps raising it; and air force regulations require obedience to a commander's orders. This is Catch-22. Using this ploy, the colonel keeps Hungry Joe, who has now completed fifty missions—twice the number originally required—from going home. By now Hungry Joe is crazy; he experiences fearful nightmares and goes about Rome looking for women to photograph naked. Colonel Cathcart believes that setting a record for missions will make him a general and realize his dream of getting his picture in the *Saturday Evening Post.* From his desk, he bravely volunteers his squadron for the most dangerous missions.

Determined to stay alive, Yossarian does everything he can to avoid flying missions, including feigning sickness in order to gain the security of the hospital and ordering his plane to return to base before the mission is completed. On one mission, Snowden, the radio-gunner, is hit and spills his guts all over Yossarian. Traumatized by the ordeal, Yossarian walks around naked, refusing to wear the uniform that had been drenched with Snowden's blood. A frantic Yossarian begs Doc Daneeka to ground him because of insanity. But an army regulation, another Catch-22, states specifically that anyone asking to be grounded could not be insane because he is showing concern for his personal safety, which is a sign of mental health. A truly insane person is someone who cavalierly goes on missions showing no regard for his own life, a description that does not fit Yossarian. Yossarian's roommate, Orr, unknown to anyone, had been frequently crash-landing his plane as practice runs for an escape to neutral Sweden. When Yossarian learns that Orr had made it, he resolves to follow him to Sweden. In his determination to survive and to break free from an impersonal bureaucracy that is crushing his humanity—to take control over his own life in an increasingly irrational world—Yossarian affirms the enduring value of the individual.

The "death" of Doc Daneeka, who keeps complaining that the war has deprived him of his lucrative medical practice, exemplifies the military's macabre bureaucratic machinery. Fearful of flying, Doc Daneeka has the records falsified to show that he is collecting flight time. He is supposedly on a plane that crashes and learns that according to official records he is dead. "You didn't come down in a parachute, so you must have been killed in the crash," he is told. Following is Heller's treatment of this wacky situation.

THIRTY-ONE. Mrs. Daneeka

When Colonel Cathcart learned that Doc Daneeka too had been killed in McWatt's plane, he increased the number of missions to seventy.

The first person in the squadron to find out that Doc Daneeka was dead was Sergeant Towser, who had been informed earlier by the man in the control tower that Doc Daneeka's name was down as a passenger on the pilot's manifest McWatt had filed before taking off. Sergeant Towser brushed away a tear and struck Doc Daneeka's name from the roster of squadron personnel. With lips still quivering, he rose and trudged outside reluctantly to break the bad news to Gus and Wes, discreetly avoiding any conversation with Doc Daneeka himself as he moved by the flight surgeon's slight sepulchral figure roosting despondently on his stool in the late-afternoon sunlight between the orderly room and the medical tent. Sergeant Towser's heart was heavy; now he had *two* dead men on his hands—Mudd, the dead man in Yossarian's tent who wasn't even there, and Doc Daneeka, the new dead man in the squadron, who most certainly was there and gave every indication of proving a still thornier administrative problem for him.

Gus and Wes listened to Sergeant Towser with looks of stoic surprise and said not a word about their bereavement to anyone else until Doc Daneeka himself came in about an hour afterward to have his temperature taken for the third time that day and his blood pressure checked. The thermometer registered a half degree lower than his usual subnormal temperature of 96.8. Doc Daneeka was alarmed. The fixed, vacant, wooden stares of his two enlisted men were even more irritating than always.

"Goddammit," he expostulated politely in an uncommon excess of exasperation, "what's the matter with you two men anyway? It just isn't right for a person to have a low temperature all the time and walk around with a stuffed nose." Doc Daneeka emitted a glum, self-pitying sniff and strolled disconsolately across the tent to help himself to some aspirin and sulphur pills and paint his own throat with Argyrol. His downcast face was fragile and forlorn as a swallow's, and he rubbed the back of his arms rhythmically. "Just look how cold I am right now. You're sure you're not holding anything back?"

"You're dead, sir," one of his two enlisted men explained.

Doc Daneeka jerked his head up quickly with resentful distrust. "What's that?"

"You're dead, sir," repeated the other. "That's probably the reason you always feel so cold."

"That's right, sir. You've probably been dead all this time and we just didn't detect it."

"What the *hell* are you both talking about?" Doc Daneeka cried shrilly with a surging, petrifying sensation of some onrushing unavoidable disaster.

"It's true, sir," said one of the enlisted men. "The records show that you went up in McWatt's plane to collect some flight time. You didn't come down in a parachute, so you must have been killed in the crash."

"That's right, sir," said the other. "You ought to be glad you've got any temperature at all."

Doc Daneeka's mind was reeling in confusion. "Have you both gone crazy?" he demanded. "I'm going to report this whole insubordinate incident to Sergeant Towser."

"Sergeant Towser's the one who told us about it," said either Gus or Wes. "The War Department's even going to notify your wife."

Doc Daneeka yelped and ran out of the medical tent to remonstrate with Sergeant Towser, who edged away from him with repugnance and advised Doc Daneeka to remain out of sight as much as possible until some decision could be reached relating to the disposition of his remains.

"Gee, I guess he really is dead," grieved one of his enlisted men in a low, respectful voice. "I'm going to miss him. He was a pretty wonderful guy, wasn't he?"

"Yeah, he sure was," mourned the other. "But I'm glad the little fuck is gone. I was getting sick and tired of taking his blood pressure all the time."

Mrs. Daneeka, Doc Daneeka's wife, was not glad that Doc Daneeka was gone and split the peaceful Staten Island night with woeful shrieks of lamentation when she learned by War Department telegram that her husband had been killed in action. Women came to comfort her, and their husbands paid condolence calls and hoped inwardly that she would soon move to another neighborhood and spare them the obligation of continuous sympathy. The poor woman was totally distraught for almost a full week. Slowly, heroically, she found the strength to contemplate a future filled with dire problems for herself and her children. Just as she was growing resigned to her loss, the postman rang with a bolt from the blue—a letter from overseas that was signed with her husband's signature and urged her frantically to disregard any bad news concerning him. Mrs. Daneeka was dumfounded. The date on the letter was illegible. The handwriting throughout was shaky and hurried, but the style resembled her husband's and the melancholy, self-pitying tone was familiar, although more dreary than usual. Mrs. Daneeka was overjoyed and wept irrepressibly with relief and kissed the crinkled, grubby tissue of V-mail stationery a thousand times. She dashed a grateful note off to her husband pressing him for details and sent a wire informing the War Department of its error. The War Department replied touchily that there had been no error and that she was undoubtedly the victim of some sadistic and psychotic forger in her husband's squadron. The letter to her husband was returned unopened, stamped KILLED IN ACTION.

Mrs. Daneeka had been widowed cruelly again, but this time her grief was mitigated somewhat by a notification from Washington that she was sole beneficiary of her husband's $10,000 GI insurance policy, which amount was obtainable by her on demand. The realization that she and the children were not faced immediately with starvation brought a brave smile to her face and marked the turning point in her distress. The Veterans Administration informed her by mail the very next day that she would be entitled to pension benefits for the rest of her natural life because of her husband's demise, and to a burial allowance for him of $250. A government check for $250 was enclosed. Gradually, inexorably, her prospects brightened. A letter arrived that same week from the Social Security Administration stating that, under the provisions of the Old Age and Survivors Insurance Act of 1935, she would receive monthly support for herself and her dependent children until they reached the age of eighteen, and a burial allowance of $250. With these government letters as proof of death, she applied for payment on three life insurance policies Doc Daneeka had carried, with a value of $50,000 each; her claim was honored and processed swiftly. Each day brought new unexpected treasures. A key to a safe-deposit box led to a fourth life insurance policy with a face value of $50,000, and to $18,000 in cash on which income tax had never been paid and need never be paid. A fraternal lodge to which he had belonged gave her a cemetery plot. A second fraternal organization of which he had been a member sent her a burial allowance of $250. His county medical association gave her a burial allowance of $250.

The husbands of her closest friends began to flirt with her. Mrs. Daneeka was simply delighted with the way things were turning out and had her hair dyed. Her fantastic wealth just kept piling up, and she had to remind herself daily that all the hundreds of thousands of dollars she was acquiring were not worth a single penny without her husband to share this good fortune with her. It astonished her that so many separate organizations were willing to do so much to bury Doc Daneeka, who, back in Pianosa, was having a terrible time trying to keep his head above the ground and wondered with dismal apprehension why his wife did not answer the letter he had written.

He found himself ostracized in the squadron by men who cursed his memory foully for having supplied Colonel Cathcart with provocation to raise the number of combat missions. Records attesting to his death were pullulating [multiplying] like insect eggs and verifying each other beyond all contention. He drew no pay or PX rations and depended for life on the charity of Sergeant Towser and Milo, who both knew he was dead. Colonel Cathcart refused to see him, and Colonel Korn sent word through Major Danby that he would have Doc Daneeka cremated on the spot if he ever showed up at Group Headquarters. Major Danby confided that Group was incensed with all flight surgeons because of Dr. Stubbs, the bushy-haired, baggy-chinned, slovenly flight surgeon in Dunbar's squadron who was deliberately and defiantly brewing insidious dissension there by grounding all men with sixty missions on proper forms that were rejected by Group indignantly with orders restoring the confused pilots, navigators, bombardiers and gunners to combat duty. Morale there was ebbing rapidly, and Dunbar was under surveillance. Group was glad Doc Daneeka had been killed and did not intend to ask for a replacement.

Not even the chaplain could bring Doc Daneeka back to life under the circumstances. Alarm changed to resignation, and more and more Doc Daneeka acquired the look of an ailing rodent. The sacks under his eyes turned hollow and black, and he padded through the shadows fruitlessly like a ubiquitous spook. Even Captain Flume recoiled when Doc Daneeka sought him out in the woods for help. Heartlessly, Gus and Wes turned him away from the medical tent without even a thermometer for comfort, and then, only then, did he realize that, to all intents and purposes, he really was dead, and that he had better do something damned fast if he ever hoped to save himself.

There was nowhere else to turn but to his wife, and he scribbled an impassioned letter begging her to bring his plight to the attention of the War Department and urging her to communicate at once with his group commander, Colonel Cathcart, for assurances that—no matter what else she might have heard—it was indeed he, her husband, Doc Daneeka, who was pleading with her, and not a corpse or some imposter. Mrs. Daneeka was stunned by the depth of emotion in the almost illegible appeal. She was torn with compunction and tempted to comply, but the very next letter she opened that day was from that same Colonel Cathcart, her husband's group commander, and began:

> Dear Mrs., Mr., Miss, or Mr. and Mrs. Daneeka: Words cannot express the deep personal grief I experienced when your husband, son, father or brother was killed, wounded or reported missing in action.

Mrs. Daneeka moved with her children to Lansing, Michigan, and left no forwarding address.

6 The Holocaust

Against the Jews of Europe the Germans waged a war of extermination. Using the modern state's organizational capacities and the instruments of modern technology, the Nazis murdered 6 million Jews, including one and a half million children—two-thirds of the Jewish population of Europe. Gripped by a perverted mythical world-view, the SS, Hitler's elite units, carried out these murders with dedication and idealism; they believed that they were exterminating subhumans who threatened the German nation. Special squads of SS—the *Einsatzgruppen,* trained for mass murder—followed on the heels of the German army into Russia. Entering captured villages and cities, they herded Jews to execution grounds and slaughtered them by the thousands with rifle and machine-gun fire. Aided by Ukrainian, Lithuanian, and Latvian auxiliaries, the *Einsatzgruppen* massacred some 1.3 million Jews. To speed up the process, the Nazis constructed killing centers in Poland. Jews from all over Europe were jammed into sealed cattle cars; the victims traveled sometimes for days without food or water, choking from the stench of vomit and excrement, and shattered by the crying of children. When they were disgorged at a concentration camp, SS doctors quickly inspected the new arrivals, "the freight," as they referred to them. Those deemed unfit for arduous labor were immediately sent to the gas chambers. The Germans gassed some 2.5 to 3 million Jews in these death camps, the largest of which was Auschwitz-Birkenau.

Elie Wiesel
Night

The Holocaust has given rise to a vast and growing body of literature. During the war, Jews in the ghettos, concentration camps, or hiding, virtually all of whom eventually perished, wrote poems and kept diaries so that the world, which they felt had forsaken them, would know of their ordeal. These writings were also a means of spiritual sustenance and defiance during dark times. Anne Frank, a young girl who lived in a secret annex in Amsterdam, kept a diary of her experience that survived her capture and death in the notorious Bergen Belsen concentration camp. First published in 1947 and translated into many languages, *The Diary of a Young Girl,* has become a modern classic. Made into a play, in 1956 it was performed simultaneously in seven German cities before audiences that sat in stunned silence.

After liberation, survivors felt a compulsion to bear witness to the willful extermination of a people and a culture. One such survivor, Elie Wiesel (1928–), who received instant acclaim with the French publication of *Night* in 1958, has since become a distinguished man of letters. Among his many honors is the Nobel Peace Prize awarded in 1986. Born in a small village in Romania, which was ceded to Hungary in 1940, Wiesel was deported with his family to Auschwitz in May 1944. His mother and sister were gassed on arrival; his father, weakened by the death journey from Auschwitz to Buchenwald, much of it by foot in freezing weather and with little food, died in early 1945, shortly before the liberation. In this passage from *Night,* which has the quality of sacred poetry, Wiesel describes his entry into another planet—Auschwitz.

. . . We pressed against the windows. The convoy was moving slowly. A quarter of an hour later, it slowed down again. Through the windows we could see barbed wire; we realized that this must be the camp.

We had forgotten the existence of Madame Schächter. Suddenly, we heard terrible screams:

"Jews, look! Look through the window! Flames! Look!"

And as the train stopped, we saw this time that flames were gushing out of a tall chimney into the black sky.

Madame Schächter was silent herself. Once more she had become dumb, indifferent, absent, and had gone back to her corner.

We looked at the flames in the darkness. There was an abominable odor floating in the air. Suddenly, our doors opened. Some odd-looking characters, dressed in striped shirts and black trousers leapt into the wagon. They held electric torches and truncheons. They began to strike out to right and left, shouting:

"Everybody get out! Everyone out of the wagon! Quickly!"

We jumped out. I threw a last glance toward Madame Schächter. Her little boy was holding her hand.

In front of us flames. In the air that smell of burning flesh. It must have been about midnight. We had arrived—at Birkenau, reception center for Auschwitz. . . .

The cherished objects we had brought with us thus far were left behind in the train, and with them, at last, our illusions.

Every two yards or so an SS man held his tommy gun trained on us. Hand in hand we followed the crowd.

An SS noncommissioned officer came to meet us, a truncheon in his hand. He gave the order:

"Men to the left! Women to the right!"

Eight words spoken quietly, indifferently, without emotion. Eight short, simple words. Yet that was the moment when I parted from my mother. I had not had time to think, but already I felt the pressure of my father's hand: we were alone. For a part of a second I glimpsed my mother and my sisters moving away to the right. Tzipora held Mother's hand. I saw them disappear into the distance; my mother was stroking my sister's fair hair, as though to protect her, while I walked on with my father and the other men. And I did not know that in that place, at that moment, I was parting from my mother and Tzipora forever. I went on walking. My father held onto my hand.

Behind me, an old man fell to the ground. Near him was an SS man putting his revolver back in its holster.

My hand shifted on my father's arm. I had one thought—not to lose him. Not to be left alone.

The SS officers gave the order:

"Form fives!"

Commotion. At all costs we must keep together.

"Here, kid, how old are you?"

It was one of the prisoners who asked me this. I could not see his face, but his voice was tense and weary.

"I'm not quite fifteen yet."

"No. Eighteen."

"But I'm not," I said. "Fifteen."

"Fool. Listen to what *I* say."

Then he questioned my father, who replied:

"Fifty."

The other grew more furious than ever.

"No, not fifty. Forty. Do you understand? Eighteen and forty."

He disappeared into the night shadows. A second man came up, spitting oaths at us.

"What have you come here for, you sons of bitches? What are you doing here, eh?"

Someone dared to answer him.

"What do you think? Do you suppose we've come here for our own pleasure? Do you think we asked to come?"

A little more, and the man would have killed him.

"You shut your trap, you filthy swine, or I'll squash you right now! You'd have done better to have hanged yourselves where you were than to come here. Didn't you know what was in store for you at Auschwitz? Haven't you heard about it? In 1944?"

No, we had not heard. No one had told us. He could not believe his ears. His tone of voice became increasingly brutal.

"Do you see that chimney over there? See it? Do you see those flames? (Yes, we did see the flames.) Over there—that's where you're going to be taken. That's your grave, over there. Haven't you realized it yet? You dumb bastards, don't you understand anything? You're going to be burned. Frizzled away. Turned into ashes."

He was growing hysterical in his fury. We stayed motionless, petrified. Surely it was all a nightmare? An unimaginable nightmare?

I heard murmurs around me.

"We've got to do something. We can't let ourselves be killed. We can't go like beasts to the slaughter. We've got to revolt."

There were a few sturdy young fellows among us. They had knives on them, and they tried to incite the others to throw themselves on the armed guards.

One of the young men cried:

"Let the world learn of the existence of Auschwitz. Let everybody hear about it, while they can still escape. . . ."

But the, older ones begged their children not to do anything foolish:

"You must never lose faith, even when the sword hangs over your head. That's the teaching of our sages. . . ."

The wind of revolt died down. We continued our march toward the square. In the middle stood the notorious Dr. Mengele (a typical SS officer: a cruel face, but not devoid of intelligence, and wearing a monocle); a conductor's baton in his hand, he was standing among the other officers. The baton moved unremittingly, sometimes to the right, sometimes to the left.

I was already in front of him:

"How old are you?" he asked, in an attempt at a paternal tone of voice.

"Eighteen." My voice was shaking.

"Are you in good health?"

"Yes."

"What's your occupation?"

Should I say that I was a student?

"Farmer," I heard myself say.

This conversation cannot have lasted more than a few seconds. It had seemed like an eternity to me.

The baton moved to the left. I took half a step forward. I wanted to see first where they were sending my father. If he went to the right, I would go after him.

The baton once again pointed to the left for him too. A weight was lifted from my heart.

We did not yet know which was the better side, right or left; which road led to prison and which to the crematory. But for the moment I was happy; I was near my father. Our procession continued to move slowly forward.

Another prisoner came up to us:

"Satisfied?"

"Yes," someone replied.

"Poor devils, you're going to the crematory."

He seemed to be telling the truth. Not far from us, flames were leaping up from a ditch, gigantic flames. They were burning something. A lorry drew up at the pit and delivered its load—little children. Babies! Yes, I saw it—saw it with my own eyes . . . those children in the flames. (Is it surprising that I could not sleep after that? Sleep had fled from my eyes.)

So this was where we were going. A little farther on was another and larger ditch for adults.

I pinched my face. Was I still alive? Was I awake? I could not believe it. How could it be possible for them to burn people, children, and for the world to keep silent? No, none of this could be true. It was a nightmare. . . . Soon I should wake with a start, my heart pounding, and find myself back in the bedroom of my childhood, among my books. . . .

My father's voice drew me from my thoughts:

"It's a shame . . . a shame that you couldn't have gone with your mother. . . . I saw several boys of your age going with their mothers. . . ."

His voice was terribly sad. I realized that he did not want to see what they were going to do to me. He did not want to see the burning of his only son.

My forehead was bathed in cold sweat. But I told him that I did not believe that they could burn people in our age, that humanity would never tolerate it. . . .

"Humanity? Humanity is not concerned with us. Today anything is allowed. Anything is possible, even these crematories. . . ."

His voice was choking.

"Father," I said, "if that is so, I don't want to wait here. I'm going to run to the electric wire. That would be better than slow agony in the flames."

He did not answer. He was weeping. His body was shaken convulsively. Around us, everyone was weeping. Someone began to recite the Kaddish, the prayer for the dead. I do not know if it has ever happened before, in the long history of the Jews, that people have ever recited the prayer for the dead for themselves.

"*Yitgadal veyitkadach shmé raba*. . . . May His Name be blessed and magnified. . . ." whispered my father.

For the first time, I felt revolt rise up in me. Why should I bless His name? The Eternal, Lord of the Universe, the All-Powerful and Terrible, was silent. What had I to thank Him for?

We continued our march. We were gradually drawing closer to the ditch, from which an internal heat was rising. Still twenty steps to go. If I wanted to bring about my own death, this was the moment. Our line had now only fifteen paces to cover. I bit my lips so that my father would not hear my teeth chattering. Ten steps still. Eight. Seven. We marched slowly on, as though following a hearse at our own funeral. Four steps more. Three steps. There it was now, right in front of us, the pit and its flames. I gathered all that was left of my strength, so that I could break from the ranks and throw myself upon the barbed wire. In the depths of my heart, I bade farewell to my father, to the whole universe; and, in spite of myself, the words formed themselves and issued in a whisper from my lips: *Yitgadal veyitkadach shmé raba*. . . . May His name be blessed and magnified. . . . My heart was bursting. The moment had come. I was face to face with the Angel of Death. . . .

No. Two steps from the pit we were ordered to turn to the left and made to go into a barracks.

I pressed my father's hand. He said:

"Do you remember Madame Schächter, in the train?"

Never shall I forget that night, the first night in camp, which has turned my life into one long night, seven times cursed and seven times sealed. Never shall I forget that smoke. Never shall I forget the little faces of the children, whose bodies I saw turned into wreaths of smoke beneath a silent blue sky.

Never shall I forget those flames which consumed my faith forever.

Never shall I forget that nocturnal silence which deprived me, for all eternity, of the desire to live. Never shall I forget those moments which murdered my God and my soul and turned my dreams to dust. Never shall I forget these things, even if I am condemned to live as long as God Himself. Never.

Wiesel describes the execution by hanging of a young boy and the reaction among the inmates.

I witnessed other hangings. I never saw a single one of the victims weep. For a long time those dried-up bodies had forgotten the bitter taste of tears.

Except once. The Oberkapo of the fifty-second cable unit was a Dutchman, a giant, well over six feet. Seven hundred prisoners worked under his orders, and they all loved him like a brother. No one had ever received a blow at his hands, nor an insult from his lips.

He had a young boy under him, a *pipel,* as they were called—a child with a refined and beautiful face, unheard of in this camp.

(At Buna, the *pipel* were loathed; they were often crueller than adults. I once saw one of thirteen beating his father because the latter had not made his bed properly. The old man was crying softly while the boy shouted: "If you don't stop crying at once I shan't bring you any more bread. Do you understand?" But the Dutchman's little servant was loved by all. He had the face of a sad angel.)

One day, the electric power station at Buna was blown up. The Gestapo, summoned to the spot, suspected sabotage. They found a trail. It eventually led to the Dutch Oberkapo. And there, after a search, they found an important stock of arms.

The Oberkapo was arrested immediately. He was tortured for a period of weeks, but in vain. He would not give a single name. He was transferred to Auschwitz. We never heard of him again.

But his little servant had been left behind in the camp in prison. Also put to torture, he too would not speak. Then the SS sentenced him to death, with two other prisoners who had been discovered with arms.

One day when we came back from work we saw three gallows rearing up in the assembly place, three black crows. Roll call. SS all round us, machine guns trained: the traditional ceremony. Three victims in chains—and one of them, the little servant, the sad-eyed angel.

The SS seemed more preoccupied, more disturbed than usual. To hang a young boy in front of thousands of spectators was no light matter. The head of the camp read the verdict. All eyes were on the child. He was lividly pale, almost calm, biting his lips. The gallows threw its shadow over him.

This time the Lagerkapo refused to act as executioner. Three SS replaced him.

The three victims mounted together onto the chairs.

The three necks were placed at the same moment within the nooses.

"Long live liberty!" cried the two adults.

But the child was silent.

"Where is God? Where is He?" someone behind me asked.

At a sign from the head of the camp, the three chairs tipped over.

Total silence throughout the camp. On the horizon, the sun was setting.

"Bare your heads!" yelled the head of the camp. His voice was raucous. We were weeping.

"Cover your heads!"

Then the march past began. The two adults were no longer alive. Their tongues hung swollen, blue-tinged. But the third rope was still moving; being so light, the child was still alive. . . .

For more than half an hour he stayed there, struggling between life and death, dying in slow agony under our eyes. And we had to look him full in the face. He was still alive when I passed in front of him. His tongue was still red, his eyes not yet glazed.

Behind me, I heard the same man asking:

"Where is God now?"

And I heard a voice within me answer him:

"Where is He? Here He is—He is hanging here on this gallows. . . ."

That night the soup tasted of corpses.

At the end of the Jewish High Holy Days introducing the New Year, the Germans engage in a dreaded selection in which those deemed unfit for work are sent to the gas chambers.

Yom Kippur. The Day of Atonement.

Should we fast? The question was hotly debated. To fast would mean a surer, swifter death. We fasted here the whole year round. The whole year was Yom Kippur. But others said that we should fast simply because it was dangerous to do so. We should show God that even here, in this enclosed hell, we were capable of singing His praises.

I did not fast, mainly to please my father, who had forbidden me to do so. But further, there was no longer any reason why I should fast. I no longer accepted God's silence. As I swallowed my bowl of soup, I saw in the gesture an act of rebellion and protest against Him.

And I nibbled my crust of bread.

In the depths of my heart, I felt a great void.

The SS gave us a fine New Year's gift.

We had just come back from work. As soon as we had passed through the door of the camp, we sensed something different in the air. Roll call did not take so long as usual. The evening soup was given out with great speed and swallowed down at once in anguish.

I was no longer in the same block as my father. I had been transferred to another unit, the building one, where, twelve hours a day, I had to drag heavy blocks of stone about. The head of my new block was a German Jew, small of stature, with piercing eyes. He told us that evening that no one would be allowed to go out after the evening soup. And soon a terrible word was circulating—selection.

We knew what that meant. An SS man would examine us. Whenever he found a weak one, a *musulman* as we called them, he would write his number down: good for the crematory.

After soup, we gathered together between the beds. The veterans said:

"You're lucky to have been brought here so late. This camp is paradise today, compared with what it was like two years ago. Buna was a real hell then. There was no water, no blankets, less soup and bread. At night we slept almost naked, and it was below thirty degrees. The corpses were collected in hundreds every day. The work was hard. Today, this is a little paradise. The Kapos had orders to kill a certain number of prisoners every day. And every week—selection. A merciless selection. . . . Yes, you're lucky."

"Stop it! Be quiet!" I begged. "You can tell your stories tomorrow or on some other day."

They burst out laughing. They were not veterans for nothing.

"Are you scared? So were we scared. And there was plenty to be scared of in those days."

The old men stayed in their corner, dumb, motionless, hunted. Some were praying.

An hour's delay. In an hour, we should know the verdict—death or a reprieve.

And my father? Suddenly I remembered him. How would he pass the selection? He had aged so much. . . .

The head of our block had never been outside concentration camps since 1933. He had already been through all the slaughterhouses, all the factories of death. At about nine o'clock, he took up his position in our midst:

"Achtung!"

There was instant silence.

"Listen carefully to what I am going to say." (For the first time, I heard his voice quiver.) "In a few moments the selection will begin. You must get completely undressed. Then one by one you go before the SS doctors. I hope you will all succeed in getting through. But you must help your own chances. Before you go into the next room, move about in some way so that you give yourselves a little color. Don't walk slowly, run! Run as if the devil were after you! Don't look at the SS. Run, straight in front of you!"

He broke off for a moment, then added:

"And, the essential thing, don't be afraid!"

Here was a piece of advice we should have liked very much to be able to follow.

I got undressed, leaving my clothes on the bed. There was no danger of anyone stealing them this evening.

Tibi and Yossi, who had changed their unit at the same time as I had, came up to me and said:

"Let's keep together. We shall be stronger."

Yossi was murmuring something between his teeth. He must have been praying. I had never realized that Yossi was a believer. I had even always thought the reverse. Tibi was silent, very pale. All the prisoners in the block stood naked between the beds. This must be how one stands at the last judgment.

"They're coming!"

There were three SS officers standing round the notorious Dr. Mengele, who had received us at Birkenau. The head of the block, with an attempt at a smile, asked us:

"Ready?"

Yes, we were ready. So were the SS doctors. Dr. Mengele was holding a list in his hand: our numbers. He made a sign to the head of the block, "We can begin!" As if this were a game!

The first to go by were the "officials" of the block: *Stubenaelteste*, Kapos, foremen, all in perfect physical condition of course! Then came the ordinary prisoners' turn. Dr. Mengele took stock of them from head to foot. Every now and then, he wrote a number down. One single thought filled my mind: not to let my number be taken; not to show my left arm.

There were only Tibi and Yossi in front of me. They passed. I had time to notice that Mengele had not written their numbers down. Someone pushed me. It was my turn. I ran without looking back. My head was spinning: you're too thin, you're weak, you're too thin, you're good for the furnace. . . . The race seemed interminable. I thought I had been running for years. . . . You're too thin, you're too weak. . . . At last I had arrived exhausted. When I regained my breath, I questioned Yossi and Tibi:

"Was I written down?"

"No," said Yossi. He added, smiling: "In any case, he couldn't have written you down, you were running too fast. . . ."

I began to laugh. I was glad. I would have liked to kiss him. At that moment, what did the others matter! I hadn't been written down.

Those whose numbers had been noted stood apart, abandoned by the whole world. Some were weeping in silence. The SS officers went away. The head of the block appeared, his face reflecting the general weariness.

"Everything went off all right. Don't worry. Nothing is going to happen to anyone. To anyone."

Again he tried to smile. A poor, emaciated, dried-up Jew questioned him avidly in a trembling voice:

"But . . . but, *Blockaelteste*, they did write me down!"

The head of the block let his anger break out. What! Did someone refuse to believe him!

"What's the matter now? Am I telling lies then? I tell you once and for all, nothing's going to happen to you! To anyone! You're wallowing in your own despair, you fool!"

The bell rang, a signal that the selection had been completed throughout the camp. . . .

Several days had elapsed. We no longer thought about the selection. We went to work as usual, loading heavy stones into railway wagons. Rations had become more meager: this was the only change.

We had risen before dawn, as on every day. We had received the black coffee, the ration of bread. We were about to set out for the yard as usual. The head of the block arrived, running.

"Silence for a moment. I have a list of numbers here. I'm going to read them to you. Those whose numbers I call won't be going to work this morning; they'll stay behind in the camp."

And, in a soft voice, he read out about ten numbers. We had understood. These were numbers chosen at the selection. Dr. Mengele had not forgotten.

The head of the block went toward his room. Ten prisoners surrounded him, hanging onto his clothes:

"Save us! You promised . . . ! We want to go to the yard. We're strong enough to work. We're good workers. We can . . . we will. . . ."

He tried to calm them, to reassure them about their fate, to explain to them that the fact that they were staying behind in the camp did not mean much, had no tragic significance.

"After all, I stay here myself every day," he added.

It was a somewhat feeble argument. He realized it, and without another word went and shut himself up in his room.

André Schwartz-Bart
Last of the Just

In addition to the testimony of those who witnessed the Holocaust, creative writers, many not themselves survivors, have tried to express through their art happenings that exceed the bounds of historic experience and human imagination. Often for these authors, using the Holocaust to tell a story or to compose verse was a painful but necessary catharsis; they also regarded their words as a memorial to the millions who had suffered. Widely regarded as a memorable literary treatment of the Holocaust is the *Last of the Just* (1959) by André Schwartz-Bart, a French Jew who fought in the resistance and whose entire family perished in the Nazi death camps. In the book's last scene, excerpted below, the SS club Jewish men, women, children, and patriarchs into the gas chamber. Ernie Levy, whose family God has granted one Just Man for generations, tries to lessen the suffering of the little children he had been tending since the deportation from Drancy, a holding center for Jews in Paris.

A few freight trains, a few engineers, a few chemists vanquished that ancient scapegoat, the Jews of Poland. Taking strange roads (rivers to the sea where all was engulfed—river, lifeboat, man) the ancient procession of stake and fagot ended in the crematorium.

In the process of exterminating the Jewish people, the camp at Drancy was only one of many drains incited into Europe's passive flanks, one of the assembly points for the herd being led to the slaughter, quietly and without fuss, toward the discreet plains of Silesia, the new pastures of heaven. The Germans reached such perfection in *Vernichtungswissenchaft*—the science of massacre, the art of extermination—that for a majority of the condemned the ultimate revelation came only in the gas chambers. From profane measures to sacred, from registration to the Star of David, from assignment to transient camps, a prelude to the final mopping up, the mechanism functioned admirably, extorting obedience from the human animal, before whom a shred of hope was dangled to the very end.

So it was that at Drancy a belief was current in a distant kingdom called Pichipoi, where the Jews, guided by the staves of their blond shepherds, would be permitted to graze industriously on the grass of a fresh start.

And even those who had heard about the "final solution" did not trust their senses, their memory, their alerted minds. An interior voice reassured them, arguing plausibly that these things did not exist, that they could not exist, that they would never exist as long as the Nazis retained the faces of human beings. But when that voice was silent they foundered in the refuge of madness, or flung themselves from a seventh-story window onto a certain cement slab that became sadly famous in the camp. And yet they were silent to the end, leaping with lips sealed on their terrible secret. And if they had spoken it aloud, none would have believed them, for the soul is the slave of life. . . .

The locomotive whistled, shuddered, ground reluctantly to a halt. A ghostly tremor ran through the car. But when the first barking of dogs was heard, an electrifying fluid terror struck the outstretched bodies one by one, and a leaden Ernie stirred too, supporting Golda, who had been jolted out of her stupor. The surviving children screamed with all their poisonous breath, surrounding Ernie with a gaseous ring of decomposing entrails. Outside, pincers were already snipping through the seals affixed at the Drancy station, and the doors slid back, admitting the first S.S. death's-heads in a blinding flow of light. Carrying whips and bludgeons, restraining black mastiffs on taut leashes, they plunged with gleaming boots into the stormy tide of deportees, channeling it out onto the platforms with shouts and blows that roused even the dying, setting them suddenly into motion like a flock of sheep jostling and crushing. At dawn the platforms seemed unreal beneath the floodlights, and the jerry-built station opened out on a strange plaza bounded by a chain of S.S. men and dogs, and by a barracks dimly visible in the agonizing fog. Ernie never knew how, with Golda and a child clinging to his arms, he succeeded in running the length of the platform amid the mad panic of the survivors, many of whom were absurdly dragging bundles or suitcases. In front of them a woman tripped over her valise, which had burst open; her skirts flew up to her waist. Immediately a German stepped forward with one of those savage animals baying on his leash, and obviously addressing himself to the animal, he shouted before the terrified eyes of the motionless group, *"Man, destroy that dog!"* At the poor woman's outcry, Ernie started running again, aware of nothing but the crackle of his flaming brain and the pressure of Golda's and the child's hands. He wondered suddenly if that tiny, sharp shriek belonged to a girl or a boy. . . .

Beneath the blackish heights of the dawn, the plaza, trampled by hundreds of Jewish feet, also seemed unreal. But Ernie's wary eye soon noted alarming details. Here and there on the hastily swept pavement—just before the train's arrival, it was obvious—there still lay abandoned possessions, bundles of clothing, open suitcases, shaving brushes, enameled pots. . . . Where had they come from? And why, beyond the platform, did the tracks end suddenly? Why the yellowish grass and the ten-foot barbed wire? Why were the new guards snickering incomprehensibly at the new arrivals? These, catching their breath, were trying to settle into their new life, the men wiping their foreheads with kerchiefs, the girls smoothing their hair and holding their skirts when a breeze sprang up, the old men and women laboriously trying to sit down on their suitcases—silent, all of them, in a terrible silence that had fallen over the entire flock. Aside from the snickering and the knowing laughter, the guards seemed to have exhausted their anger, and while they calmly gave orders, blows and kicks, Ernie realized that they were no longer driven by hate but were going through the motions with the remote sympathy one feels for a dog, even when beating him. If the beaten animal is a dog, it may be supposed with a fair degree of probability that the beater is a man. But as he examined the barracks building, again a vague gleam shone through the fog, high in the gray sky, capped by a cloud of black smoke. At the same moment he became aware of the nauseating odor that hovered in the plaza, which differed from the stagnant effluvium of dysentery in that it had the pungency of organic matter in combustion. "You're weeping blood," Golda said suddenly in amazement. "Don't be silly," Ernie said, "nobody weeps blood." And wiping off the tears of blood that furrowed his cheeks, he turned away from the girl to hide from her the death of the Jewish people, which was written clearly, he knew, in the flesh of his face.

The crowd was thinning out in front of them. One by one the deportees passed before an S.S. officer bracketed by two machine gunners. With the end of his swagger stick, the officer directed the prisoners distractedly to left or right, gauging them with a quick, practiced glance. Those on the left, men between twenty and forty-five whose outward aspect was relatively sturdy, were lined up behind the chain of S.S. men along a row of roofless trucks that the lifting fog had just revealed to Ernie's haggard investigations. On one of those open trucks he even noticed a group of men apparently wearing pajamas, each of whom was holding a musical instrument. They composed a kind of peripatetic orchestra waiting farcically on the truck, wind instruments to their lips, drumsticks and cymbals raised, ready to blare forth. The prisoners on the right, all children, women, old men and invalids, huddled together raggedly near the barracks, shrinking before a wide grating set directly into the wall of that strange building. "They're going to separate us," Golda said coldly. And as if echoing her fears, the few children who had mysteriously found Ernie's trail through the crowd pressed closer around him, some of them simply offering the mute reproach of their heavy eyes, swollen like abscesses, and others clinging to his sleeve or the tail of his pitiful black jacket. Quite sure now of their imminent destiny, Ernie caressed their little heads, and contemplating Golda's anxious face and widening his eyes fogged by the blood congealing under the lids, he drank deeply one last time of the girl's beloved features, of her soul so well made for the simple marvels that earth dispenses to men, from which the curt movement of the S.S. doctor's swagger stick would shortly separate him forever. "No, no," he said, smiling at Golda while a fresh flow of blood streamed from his eyes, "we'll stay together, I swear it." And to the children, many of whom were now risking feeble groans, "Children, children," he reassured them, "now that we've come to the kingdom, do you think I'd stay out? We shall enter the kingdom together," he went on in the solemn, inspired voice, the one thing that could touch their souls so full of darkness and terror. "In a little while we shall enter it hand in hand, and there a banquet of tasty foods awaits us, a banquet of old wines, of tasty foods full of marrow, and of old wines, clear and good. . . . There, my little lambs . . ."

They listened without understanding, gentle smiles shadowing their tortured lips. . . ."

4

I am so weary that my pen can no longer write. "Man, strip off thy garments, cover thy head with ashes, run into the streets and dance in thy madness. . . ."

. . . Just one incident interrupted the ceremony of selection. Alerted by the smell, a woman suddenly cried, "They kill people here," which gave rise to a brief panic in the course of which the flock fell back slowly toward the platforms masked by the strange floodlit façade, like a stage set for a railway station. The guards went into action immediately, but when the flock was calm again, officers went through the ranks explaining politely—some of them even in unctuous, ministerial voices—that the able-bodied men had been called up to build houses and roads, and the remainder would rest up from the trip while they awaited assignment to domestic or other work. Ernie realized joyfully that Golda herself seemed to grasp at that fiction and that her features relaxed, suffused with hope. Suddenly the band on the truck struck up an old German melody. Stunned, Ernie recognized one of those heavily melancholy lieder that Ilse had been so fond of. The brasses glittered in the gray air, and a secret harmony came from the band in pajamas and their languidly glossy music. For an instant, a brief instant, Ernie was certain in his heart of hearts that no one could decently play music for the dead, not even that melody, which seemed to be of another world. Then the last brassy note died and, the flock duly soothed, the selection went on.

"But I'm sick, I can't walk," he murmured in German when at his turn the swagger stick had flicked toward the small group of healthy men who had been granted a reprieve.

Dr. Mengele, the physician in charge at the Auschwitz extermination camp, conceded a brief glance to the "Jewish dung" that had just pronounced those words. "All right," he said, "we'll fix you up."

The swagger stick described a half circle. The two young S.S. men smiled slyly. Staggering with relief, Ernie reached the sad human sea lapping at the edges of the barracks building. With Golda hugging him and the children's little hands tugging at him, he engulfed himself in it, and they waited. Finally they were all gathered together. Then an *Unterscharenführer* invited them, loudly and clearly, to leave their baggage where it was and to proceed to the baths, taking with them only their papers, their valuables and the minimum they needed for washing. Dozens of questions rose to their lips: Should they take underwear? Could they open their bundles? Would their baggage be returned? Would anything be stolen? But the condemned did not know what strange force obliged them to hold their tongues and proceed quickly—without a word, without even a look behind—toward the entrance, a breach in the wall of ten-foot barbed wire beside the barracks with its grating. At the far end of the plaza the orchestra suddenly struck up another tune and the first purring of the motors was heard, rising into a sky still heavy with morning fog, then disappearing in the distance. Squads of armed S.S. men divided the condemned into groups of a hundred. The corridor of barbed wire seemed endless. Every ten steps, a sign: "To the Baths and Inhalations." Then the flock passed along a tank-trap bristling with

chevaux-de-frise, then a sharp, narrow, rolled-steel wire, tangled like a briar, and finally down a long open-air corridor between yards and yards of barbed wire. Ernie was carrying a little boy who had passed out. Many managed to walk only by supporting one another. In the ever more crushing silence of the throng, in its ever more pestilential stench, smooth and graceful words sprang to his lips, beating time to the children's steps in reverie and to Golda's with love. It seemed to him that an eternal silence was closing down upon the Jewish breed marching to slaughter—that no heir, no memory would supervene to prolong the silent parade of victims, no faithful dog would shudder, no bell would toll. Only the stars would remain, gliding through a cold sky. "O God," the Just Man Ernie Levy said to himself as bloody tears of pity streamed from his eyes again, "O Lord, we went forth like this thousands of years ago. We walked across arid deserts and the blood-red Red Sea in a flood of salt, bitter tears. We are very old. We are still walking. Oh, let us arrive, finally!"

The building resembled a huge bathhouse. To left and right large concrete pots cupped the stems of faded flowers. At the foot of the small wooden stairway an S.S. man, mustached and benevolent, told the condemned, "Nothing painful will happen! You just have to breathe very deeply. It strengthens the lungs. It's a way to prevent contagious diseases. It disinfects." Most of them went in silently, pressed forward by those behind. Inside, numbered coathooks garnished the walls of a sort of gigantic cloakroom where the flock undressed one way or another, encouraged by their S.S. cicerones, who advised them to remember the numbers carefully. Cakes of stony soap were distributed. Golda begged Ernie not to look at her, and he went through the sliding door of the second room with his eyes closed, led by the young woman and by the children, whose soft hands clung to his naked thighs. There, under the showerheads embedded in the ceiling, in the blue light of screened bulbs glowing in recesses of the concrete walls, Jewish men and women, children and patriarchs were huddled together. His eyes still closed, he felt the press of the last parcels of flesh that the S.S. men were clubbing into the gas chamber now, and his eyes still closed, he knew that the lights had been extinguished on the living, on the hundreds of Jewish women suddenly shrieking in terror, on the old men whose prayers rose immediately and grew stronger, on the martyred children, who were rediscovering in their last agonies the fresh innocence of yesteryear's agonies in a chorus of identical exclamations: *"Mama! But I was a good boy! It's dark! It's dark!"* And when the first waves of Cyclon B gas billowed among the sweating bodies, drifting down toward the squirming carpet of children's heads, Ernie freed himself from the girl's mute embrace and leaned out into the darkness toward the children invisible even at his knees, and he shouted with all the gentleness and all the strength of his soul, "Breathe deeply, my lambs, and quickly!"

When the layers of gas had covered everything, there

was silence in the dark sky of the room for perhaps a minute, broken only by shrill, racking coughs and the gasps of those too far gone in their agonies to offer a devotion. And first a stream, then a cascade, an irrepressible, majestic torrent, the poem that through the smoke of fires and above the funeral pyres of history the Jews—who for two thousand years did not bear arms and who never had either missionary empires nor colored slaves—the old love poem that they traced in letters of blood on the earth's hard crust unfurled in the gas chamber, enveloped it, vanquished its somber, abysmal snickering: "SHEMA YISRAEL ADONOI ELOHENU ADONOI EH'OTH . . . Hear, O Israel, the Lord is our God, the Lord is One. O Lord, by your grace you nourish the living, and by your great pity you resurrect the dead, and you uphold the weak, cure the sick, break the chains of slaves. And faithfully you keep your promises to those who sleep in the dust. Who is like unto you, O merciful Father, and who could be like unto you . . . ?"

The voices died one by one in the course of the unfinished poem. The dying children had already dug their nails into Ernie's thighs, and Golda's embrace was already weaker, her kisses were blurred when, clinging fiercely to her beloved's neck, she exhaled a harsh sigh: "Then I'll never see you again? Never again?"

Ernie managed to spit up the needle of fire jabbing at his throat, and as the woman's body slumped against him, its eyes wide in the opaque night, he shouted against the unconscious Golda's ear, "In a little while, *I swear it!*" And then he knew that he could do nothing more for anyone in the world, and in the flash that preceded his own annihilation he remembered, happily, the legend of Rabbi Chanina ben Teradion, as Mordecai had joyfully recited it: "When the gentle rabbi, wrapped in the scrolls of the Torah, was flung upon the pyre by the Romans for having taught the Law, and when they lit the fagots, the branches still green to make his tor-

ture last, his pupils said, 'Master, what do you see?' And Rabbi Chanina answered, 'I see the parchment burning, but the letters are taking wing. . . . *"Ah, yes, surely, the letters are taking wing,"* Ernie repeated as the flame blazing in his chest rose suddenly to his head. With dying arms he embraced Golda's body in an already unconscious gesture of loving protection, and they were found that way half an hour later by the team of *Sonderkommondo* responsible for burning the Jews in the crematory ovens. And so it was for millions, who turned from *Luftmenschen* into *Luft* [that is, from human beings who breathe air into just air]. I shall not translate. So this story will not finish with some tomb to be visited in memoriam. For the smoke that rises from crematoriums obeys physical laws like any other: the particles come together and disperse according to the wind that propels them. The only pilgrimage, estimable reader, would be to look with sadness at a stormy sky now and then.

And praised. *Auschwitz.* Be. *Maidanek.* The Lord. *Treblinka.* And praised. *Buchenwald.* Be. *Mauthausen.* The Lord. *Belzec.* And praised. *Sobibor.* Be. *Chelmno.* The Lord. *Ponary.* And praised. *Theresienstadt.* Be. *Warsaw.* The Lord. *Vilna.* And praised. *Skarzysko.* Be. *Bergen-Belsen.* The Lord. *Janow.* And praised. *Dora.* Be. *Neuengamme.* The Lord. *Pustkow.*[1] And praised . . .

Yes, at times one's heart could break in sorrow. But often too, preferably in the evening, I can't help thinking that Ernie Levy, dead six million times, is still alive somewhere, I don't know where. . . . Yesterday, as I stood in the street trembling in despair, rooted to the spot, a drop of pity fell from above upon my face. But there was no breeze in the air, no cloud in the sky. . . . There was only a presence.

---

[1] All are places where the Germans persecuted and murdered Jews during the Holocaust.

19

The Contemporary Age

The decades since World War II have witnessed momentous changes in both Western and world history: the Cold War between the Soviet Union and the United States, both armed with weapons of mass destruction, ended with the collapse of the Soviet empire in Eastern Europe and the disintegration of the Soviet Union itself; the global map was rapidly altered as the European colonial powers surrendered their overseas empires.

In the twenty-first century, globalization continues relentlessly; the world is being knit together by the spread of Western ideas, popular culture, free market capitalism, and technology. High government officials and business and professional people all over the world are dressed in Western clothes. Women follow Western fashions in clothes, hairstyles, and makeup. Many people in non-Western lands follow Western lifestyles: they line up to eat at McDonald's or to see a movie made in Hollywood, to adopt the latest technology, to play baseball and basketball, and, in general, to seek to share in the benefits of Western modernity.

Advanced technology intensifies the means of communication, not only through television and radio, but also with faxes, e-mail, cellular phones, and the Internet—all means of instantaneous individual communication that have become commonplace in the past decade. These developments promote shared interests among individuals and businesses throughout the globe, reducing the importance of national frontiers.

The ideals of freedom and democracy, historical accomplishments of Western civilization, exert a powerful influence worldwide, but unlike technology, they cannot easily be put into practice outside the lands of their origin. However, they inspire human ambitions everywhere. They have even become part of the rhetoric of dictatorships.

At the same time, traditional ways of life persist, interacting, and often clashing, with the forces of modernity. All these factors combined are reshaping non-Western societies in a relentless process of cultural adjustment. A striking example of the clash of cultures is the hatred radical Muslim fundamentalists have for the West, which they view as a threat to traditional Islam. These Muslim militants, organized in an international network, al-Qaeda, with well-financed cells in dozens of countries, including the United States, were behind the bombing of the World Trade Center and the Pentagon on September 11, 2001, the worst terrorist attacks in history; in all, more than 3,000 people died.

Literature in the last half of the twentieth century reflected many of the concerns and problems faced by Europeans and Americans. With the United States emerging as a superpower and its popular culture spreading throughout the globe, the works of American writers assumed new importance.

The excerpts in this concluding chapter illustrate key themes discussed by both American and European novelists and thinkers since World War II.

1 Existentialism: Life with Meaning or Without

The philosophical movement that best exemplified the anxiety and uncertainty of Europe in an era of world wars and totalitarianism was existentialism. Like Nietzsche, existentialists maintained that the universe is devoid of any overarching meaning. Reality defies ultimate comprehension; there are no timeless truths, or essences, that exist independently of and prior to the individual human being. One becomes less than human in permitting one's life to be determined by a mental outlook—a set of rules and values—imposed by others. For the existentialist, the human being is alone and life is absurd. The universe is indifferent to our expectations and needs, and death is ever stalking us. There is no purpose to our presence in the universe. We simply find ourselves here; we do not know and will never find out why. When we face squarely the fact that existence is purposeless, we can give our life meaning. It is in the act of choosing freely from among different possibilities that the individual shapes an authentic existence. There is a dynamic quality to human existence; the individual has the potential to become more than he or she is.

Jean-Paul Sartre
EXISTENCE PRECEDES ESSENCE

Jean-Paul Sartre (1905–1980), the leading French existentialist, defined himself as an atheist and saw existentialism as a means of facing the consequences of a godless universe. For Sartre, existence precedes essence, that is, there arc no values that precede the individual metaphysically or chronologically to which he or she must conform. There exists no higher realm of Being and no immutable truths that serve as ultimate standards of virtue. It is unauthentic to submit passively to established values that one did not participate in making. It is the first principle of existentialism, said Sartre, that we must each choose our own ethics, define ourselves, and give our own meaning to our existence. In Sartre's view, a true philosophy does not engage in barren discourses on abstract themes. Rather it makes commitments and incurs risks. The realization that we have the freedom to decide for ourselves what meaning we give to our lives can be liberating and exhilarating. But it can also fill us with dread that immobilizes or that leads us to seek refuge in a role selected for us by others. When we abdicate this responsibility of choosing a meaning for our lives, said Sartre, we live in "bad faith." The selection below, drawn from a work published immediately after the war, summarizes the core principles of Sartre's existentialist philosophy.

Atheistic existentialism, which I represent . . . states that if God does not exist, there is at least one being in whom existence precedes essence, a being who exists before he can be defined by any concept, and that this being is man, or, as Heidegger says, human reality. What is meant here by saying that existence precedes essence? It means that, first of all, man exists, turns up, appears on the scene, and, only afterwards, defines himself. If man, as the existentialist conceives him, is indefinable, it is because at first he is nothing. Only

afterward will he be something, and he himself will have made what he will be. Thus, there is no human nature, since there is no God to conceive it. Not only is man what he conceives himself to be, but he is also only what he wills himself to be after this thrust toward existence.

Man is nothing else but what he makes of himself. Such is the first principle of existentialism. . . .

. . . [I]f existence really does precede essence, man is responsible for what he is. Thus, existentialism's first move is to make every man aware of what he is and to make the full responsibility of his existence rest on him. And when we say that a man is responsible for himself, we do not only mean that he is responsible for his own individuality, but that he is responsible for all men. . . .

. . . When we say that man chooses his own self, we mean that every one of us does likewise; but we also mean by that that in making this choice he also chooses all men. In fact, in creating the man that we want to be, there is not a single one of our acts which does not at the same time create an image of man as we think he ought to be. To choose to be this or that is to affirm at the same time the value of what we choose. . . .

If . . . existence precedes essence, and if we grant that we exist and fashion our image at one and the same time, the image is valid for everybody and for our whole age. Thus, our responsibility is much greater than we might have supposed, because it involves all mankind. . . . [I]f I want to marry, to have children; even if this marriage depends solely on my own circumstances or passion or wish, I am involving all humanity in monogamy and not merely myself. Therefore, I am responsible for myself and for everyone else. I am creating a certain image of man of my own choosing. In choosing myself, I choose man. . . .

. . . The existentialists say at once that man is anguish. What that means is this: the man who involves himself and who realizes that he is not only the person he chooses to be, but also a lawmaker who is, at the same time, choosing all mankind as well as himself, can not help escape the feeling of his total and deep responsibility. Of course, there are many people who are not anxious; but we claim that they are hiding their anxiety, that they are fleeing from it. Certainly, many people believe that when they do something, they themselves are the only ones involved, and when someone says to them, "What if everyone acted that way?" they shrug their shoulders and answer, "Everyone doesn't act that way." But really, one should always ask himself, "What would happen if everybody looked at things that way?" There is no escaping this disturbing thought except by a kind of double-dealing. A man who lies and makes excuses for himself by saying "not everybody does that," is someone with an uneasy conscience, because the act of lying implies that a universal value is conferred upon the lie. . . .

The existentialist . . . thinks it very distressing that God does not exist, because all possibility of finding values in a heaven of ideas disappears along with Him; there can no longer be an *a priori* Good, since there is no infinite and perfect consciousness to think it. Nowhere is it written that the Good exists, that we must be honest, that we must not lie; because the fact is we are on a plane where there are only men. Dostoievsky said, "If God didn't exist, everything would be possible." That is the very starting point of existentialism. Indeed, everything is permissible if God does not exist, and as a result man is forlorn, because neither within him nor without does he find anything to cling to. He can't start making excuses for himself.

If existence really does precede essence, there is no explaining things away by reference to a fixed and given human nature. In other words, there is no determinism, man is free, man is freedom. On the other hand, if God does not exist, we find no values or commands to turn to which legitimize our conduct. So, in the bright realm of values, we have no excuse behind us, nor justification before us. We are alone, with no excuses.

That is the idea I shall try to convey when I say that man is condemned to be free. Condemned, because he did not create himself, yet, in other respects is free; because, once thrown into the world, he is responsible for everything he does. The existentialist does not believe in the power of passion. He will never agree that a sweeping passion is a ravaging torrent which fatally leads a man to certain acts and is therefore an excuse. He thinks that man is responsible for his passion. . . .

. . . The doctrine I am presenting is the very opposite of quietism, since it declares, "There is no reality except in action." Moreover, it goes further, since it adds, "Man is nothing else than his plan; he exists only to the extent that he fulfills himself, he is therefore nothing else than the ensemble of his acts, nothing else than his life."

According to this, we can understand why our doctrine horrifies certain people. Because often the only way they can bear their wretchedness is to think, "Circumstances have been against me. What I've been and done doesn't show my true worth. To be sure, I've had no great love, no great friendship, but that's because I haven't met a man or woman who was worthy. The books I've written haven't been very good because I haven't had the proper leisure. I haven't had children to devote myself to because I didn't find a man with whom I could have spent my life. So there remains within me, unused and quite viable, a host of propensities, inclinations, possibilities, that one wouldn't guess from the mere series of things I've done."

Now, for the existentialist there is really no love other than one which manifests itself in a person's being in love. There is no genius other than one which is expressed in works of art; the genius of Proust is the sum of Proust's works; the genius of Racine is his series of tragedies. Outside of that, there is nothing. Why say that Racine could have written another tragedy, when he didn't write it? A man is involved in life, leaves his impress on it, and outside of that there is nothing. To be sure, this may seem a harsh thought to someone whose life hasn't been a success. But, on the other hand, it prompts people to understand that reality alone is what counts, that dreams, expectations, and hopes warrant no more than to define a man as a disappointed dream, as miscarried hopes, as vain expectations. In other words, to define him negatively and not positively. However, when we say, "You are nothing else than your life," that does not imply that the artist will be judged solely on the basis of his works of art; a thousand other things will contribute toward summing him up. What we mean is that a man is nothing else than a series of undertakings, that he is the sum, the organization, the ensemble of the relationships which make up these undertakings. . . .

Thus, I think we have answered a number of the charges concerning existentialism. You see that it can not be taken for a philosophy of quietism, since it defines man in terms of action; nor for a pessimistic description of man—there is no doctrine more optimistic, since man's destiny is within himself; nor for an attempt to discourage man from acting, since it tells him that the only hope is in his acting and that action is the only thing that enables a man to live. Consequently, we are dealing here with an ethics of action and involvement.

2 Anti-Utopianism: The Perilous Future

Thomas More's *Utopia* (1516), the first modern description of a perfect society, set the tone for Western utopian literature. A modern example of a utopian novel is B. F. Skinner's (1904–1990) *Walden Two* (1948), which describes an ideal community created on the basis of the principles of behaviorism—the idea that human behavior can be controlled by the conditioning of rewards and punishments. The authors of utopian literature hope that their vision of the future will come to pass.

The authors of anti-utopian novels also imagine the future—a bleak future where everything is controlled by a totalitarian government—but they hope that their visions will not come to pass. An early example of anti-utopian literature is Aldous Huxley's (1894–1963) *Brave New World* (1932), which describes a totalitarian government that dominates the World State by using science and technology. It is a society in which individuality and freedom have been sacrificed for social stability. Another famous anti-utopian novelist, George Orwell (1903–1950), also warns against the dangers of totalitarianism in his *1984* (1949)—under the ever-watchful eyes of Big Brother, the Party uses the Thought Police to control everyone in Oceana. Published in 1953, Ray Bradbury's *Fahrenheit 451* is a fourth notable anti-utopian novel.

Ray Bradbury
Fahrenheit 451

Fahrenheit 451 was written during a time when censorship was a reality in the United States. Writers, filmmakers, and artists came under the scrutiny of the House Un-American Activities Committee (HUAC), which was vigilant in its hunt for suspected Communists. Libraries were assailed for owning books about communism or books written by authors that HUAC considered to be subversive; in some cases, books were burned. *Fahrenheit 451* is about an American city in the future. In this society, reading books is against the law, and when a person is found to own books, the books and the house in which they are kept are torched by firemen. Therefore, the people have no interest in books. They live meaningless lives in large cities; they spend all of their leisure time driving fast cars and watching interactive television projected on all four walls of the parlor; and they listen to Seashells, radios in the ear that fill every minute with pop music and idle talk.

The protagonist is Guy Montag, a fireman who burns books and the homes that house them. One day, Montag meets Clarisse McClellan, an innocent seventeen-year-old girl who loves nature and has compassion for people. Moved by this remarkable young woman, Montag begins to think about the emptiness of his life. Other events make him even more reflective: his wife Mildred tries to commit suicide; an elderly woman chooses to burn with her forbidden books when the firemen are called; and Clarisse is killed by a car. As a result, Montag begins to accumulate books from the fires he has helped to start, and he wonders whether he ought to quit his job as a fireman. In the following excerpt, Montag talks to Mildred about the old woman and the books he burned.

"Mildred?" he called.

She returned, singing, snapping her fingers softly.

"Aren't you going to ask me about last night?" he said.

"What about it?"

"We burnt a thousand books. We burnt a woman."

"Well?"

The parlor was exploding with sound.

"We burnt copies of Dante and Swift and Marcus Aurelius."

"Wasn't he a European?"

"Something like that."

"Wasn't he a radical?"

"I never read him."

"He was a radical." Mildred fiddled with the telephone. "You don't expect me to call Captain Beatty, do you?"

"You must!"

"Don't shout!"

"I wasn't shouting." He was up in bed, suddenly, enraged and flushed, shaking. The parlor roared in the hot air. "I can't call him. I can't tell him I'm sick."

"Why?"

Because you're afraid, he thought. A child feigning illness, afraid to call because after a moment's discussion, the conversation would run so: "Yes, Captain, I feel better already. I'll be in at ten o'clock tonight."

"You're not sick," said Mildred.

Montag fell back in bed. He reached under his pillow. The hidden book was still there.

"Mildred, how would it be if, well, maybe, I quit my job awhile?"

"You want to give up everything? After all these years of working, because, one night, some woman and her books—"

"You should have seen her, Millie!"

"She's nothing to me; she shouldn't have had books. It was her responsibility, she should've thought of that. I hate her. She's got you going and next thing you know we'll be out, no house, no job, nothing."

"You weren't there, you didn't *see*," he said. "There must be something in books, things we can't imagine, to make a woman stay in a burning house; there must be something there. You don't stay for nothing."

"She was simple-minded."

"She was as rational as you and I, more so perhaps, and we burnt her."

"That's water under the bridge."

"No, not water; fire. You ever seen a burnt house? It smolders for days. Well, this fire'll last me the rest of my life. God! I've been trying to put it out, in my mind, all night. I'm crazy with trying."

"You should've thought of that before becoming a fireman."

"Thought!" he said. "Was I given a choice? My grandfather and father were firemen. In my sleep, I ran after them."

The parlor was playing a dance tune.

"This is the day you go on the early shift," said Mildred. "You should've gone two hours ago. I just noticed."

"It's not just the woman that died," said Montag. "Last night I thought about all the kerosene I've used in the past ten years. And I thought about books. And for the first time I realized that a man was behind each one of the books. A man had to think them up. A man had to take a long time to put them down on paper. And I'd never even thought that thought before." He got out of bed.

"It took some man a lifetime maybe to put some of his thoughts down, looking around at the world and life, and then I come along in two minutes and boom! it's all over."

"Let me alone," said Mildred. "I didn't do anything."

"Let you alone! That's all very well, but how can I leave myself alone? We need not to be let alone. We need to be really bothered once in a while. How long is it since you were *really* bothered? About something important, about something real?" . . .

At this point, Montag's boss, Captain Beatty, drops in to visit him.

Captain Beatty sat down in the most comfortable chair with a peaceful look on his ruddy face. He took time to prepare and light his brass pipe and puff out a great smoke cloud. "Just thought I'd come by and see how the sick man is."

"How'd you guess?"

Beatty smiled his smile which showed the candy pinkness of his gums and the tiny candy whiteness of his teeth. "I've seen it all. You were going to call for a night off."

Montag sat in bed.

"Well," said Beatty, "*take* the night off!" He examined his eternal matchbox, the lid of which said GUARANTEED: ONE MILLION LIGHTS IN THIS IGNITER, and began to strike the chemical match abstractedly, blow out, strike, blow out, strike, speak a few words, blow out. He looked at the flame. He blew, he looked at the smoke. "When will you be well?"

"Tomorrow. The next day maybe. First of the week."

Beatty puffed his pipe. "Every fireman, sooner or later, hits this. They only need understanding, to know how the wheels run. Need to know the history of our profession. They don't feed it to rookies like they used to. Damn shame." Puff. "Only fire chiefs remember it now." Puff. "I'll let you in on it."

Mildred fidgeted.

Beatty took a full minute to settle himself in and think back for what he wanted to say.

"When did it all start, you ask, this job of ours, how did it come about, where, when? Well, I'd say it really got started around about a thing called the Civil War. Even though our rule book claims it was founded earlier. The fact is we didn't get along well until photography came into its own. Then—motion pictures in the early twentieth century. Radio. Television. Things began to have *mass*."

Montag sat in bed, not moving.

"And because they had mass, they became simpler," said Beatty. "Once, books appealed to a few people, here, there, everywhere. They could afford to be different. The world was roomy. But then the world got full of eyes and elbows and mouths. Double, triple, quadruple population. Films and radios, magazines, books leveled down to a sort of paste-pudding norm, do you follow me?"

"I think so."

Beatty peered at the smoke pattern he had put out on the air. "Picture it. Nineteenth-century man with his horses, dogs, carts, slow motion. Then, in the twentieth century, speed up your camera. Books cut shorter. Condensations. Digests. Tabloids. Everything boils down to the gag, the snap ending."

"Snap ending," Mildred nodded.

"Classics cut to fit fifteen-minute radio shows, then cut again to fill a two-minute book column, winding up at last as a ten- or twelve-line dictionary resume. I exaggerate, of course. The dictionaries were for reference. But many were those whose sole knowledge of *Hamlet* (you know the title certainly, Montag; it is probably only a faint rumor of a title to you, Mrs. Montag) whose sole knowledge, as I say, of *Hamlet* was a one-page digest in a book that claimed: *now at last you can read all the classics; keep up with your neighbors.* Do you see? Out of the nursery into the college and back to the nursery; there's your intellectual pattern for the past five centuries or more."

Mildred rose and began to move around the room, picking things up and putting them down. Beatty ignored her and continued:

"Speed up the film, Montag, quick. *Click, Pic, Look, Eye, Now, Flick, Here, There, Swift, Pace, Up, Down, In, Out, Why, How, Who, What, Where, Eh? Uh! Bang! Smack! Wallop, Bing, Bang, Boom!* Digest-digests, digest-digest-digests. Politics? One column, two sentences, a headline! Then, in midair, all vanishes! Whirl man's mind around about so fast under the pumping hands of publishers, exploiters, broadcasters that the centrifuge flings off all unnecessary, time-wasting thought!" . . .

"School is shortened, discipline relaxed, philosophies, histories, languages dropped, English and spelling gradually neglected, finally almost completely ignored. Life is immediate, the job counts, pleasure lies all about after work. Why learn anything save pressing buttons, pulling switches, fitting nuts and bolts?" . . .

"Now let's take up the minorities in our civilization, shall we? Bigger the population, the more minorities. Don't step on the toes of the dog lovers, the cat lovers, doctors, lawyers, merchants, chiefs, Mormons, Baptists, Unitarians, second-generation Chinese, Swedes, Italians, Germans, Texans, Brooklynites, Irishmen, people from Oregon or Mexico. The people in this book, this play, this TV serial are not meant to represent any actual painters, cartographers, mechanics anywhere. The bigger your market, Montag, the less you handle controversy, remember that! All the minor minor minorities with their navels to be kept clean. Authors, full of evil thoughts, lock up your typewriters. They *did*. Magazines became a nice blend of vanilla tapioca. Books, so the damned snobbish critics said, were dishwater. No *wonder* books stopped selling, the critics said. But the public, knowing what it wanted, spinning happily, let the comic books survive. And the three-dimensional sex magazines, of course. There you have it, Montag. It didn't come from the Government down. There was no dictum, no declaration, no censorship, to start with, no! Technology, mass exploitation, and minority pressure carried the trick, thank God. Today, thanks to them, you can stay happy all the time, you are allowed to read comics, the good old confessions, or trade journals."

"Yes, but what about the firemen, then?" asked Montag.

"Ah," Beatty leaned forward in the faint mist of smoke from his pipe. "What more easily explained and natural? With school turning out more runners, jumpers, racers, tinkerers, grabbers, snatchers, fliers, and swimmers instead of examiners, critics, knowers, and imaginative creators, the word 'intellectual,' of course, became the swear word it deserved to be. You always dread the unfamiliar. Surely you remember the boy in your own school class who was exceptionally 'bright,' did most of the reciting and answering while the others sat like so many leaden idols, hating him. And wasn't it this bright boy you selected for beatings and tortures after hours? Of course it was. We must all be alike. Not everyone born free and equal, as the Constitution says, but everyone *made* equal. Each man the image of every other; then all are happy, for there are no mountains to make them cower, to judge themselves against. So! A book is a loaded gun in the house next door. Burn it. Take the shot from the weapon. Breach man's mind. Who knows who might be the target of the well-read man? Me? I won't stomach them for a minute. And so when houses were finally fireproofed completely, all over the world (you were correct in your assumption the other night) there was no longer need of firemen for the old purposes. They were given the new job, as custodians of our peace of mind, the focus of our understandable and rightful dread of being inferior: official censors, judges, and executors. That's you, Montag, and that's me." . . .

Beatty knocked his pipe into the palm of his pink hand, studied the ashes as if they were a symbol to be diagnosed, and searched for meaning.

"You must understand that our civilization is so vast that we can't have our minorities upset and stirred. Ask yourself, What do we want in this country, above all? People want to be happy, isn't that right? Haven't you heard it all your life? I want to be happy, people say. Well, aren't they? Don't we keep them moving, don't we give them fun? That's all we live for, isn't it? For pleasure, for titillation? And you must admit our culture provides plenty of these."

"Yes." . . .

"Colored people don't like *Little Black Sambo.* Burn it. White people don't feel good about *Uncle Tom's Cabin.* Burn it. Someone's written a book on tobacco and cancer of the lungs? The cigarette people are weeping? Burn the book. Serenity, Montag. Peace, Montag. Take your fight outside. Better yet, into the incinerator. Funerals are unhappy and pagan? Eliminate them, too. Five minutes after a person is dead he's on his way to the Big Flue, the Incinerators serviced by helicopters all over the country. Ten minutes after death a man's a speck of black dust. Let's not quibble over individuals with memoriums. Forget them. Burn all, burn everything. Fire is bright and fire is clean."

Montag meets a retired English professor, Faber, who helps him with his reading. The two of them concoct a plan to plant books in the houses of firemen and then turn them in. Later, Montag, angered by the silly talk of Mildred and two of her friends, reads to them from a book of poetry. After the women leave, Montag knowing that they will make a complaint against him, goes to the fire station and gives Beatty a book. While he is with Beatty, the alarm rings and the fire truck goes to Montag's own house. Beatty makes him burn the house to the ground and then arrests him. At this point, Montag kills Beatty with the flamethrower, knocks the other firemen unconscious, and flees. In the following excerpt, he joins a group of hobo intellectuals in the countryside. Rather than taking the chance of owning books, they have memorized the great books.

Granger touched Montag's arm. "Welcome back from the dead." Montag nodded. Granger went on. "You might as well know all of us, now. This is Fred Clement, former occupant of the Thomas Hardy chair at Cambridge in the years before it became an Atomic Engineering School. This other is Dr. Simmons from U.C.L.A., a specialist in Ortega y Gasset; Professor West here did quite a bit for ethics, an ancient

study now, for Columbia University quite some years ago. Reverend Padover here gave a few lectures thirty years ago and lost his flock between one Sunday and the next for his views. He's been bumming with us some time now. Myself: I wrote a book called *The Fingers in the Glove; the Proper Relationship between the Individual and Society,* and here I *am!* Welcome, Montag!"

"I don't belong with you," said Montag, at last, slowly. "I've been an idiot all the way."

"We're used to that. We all made the *right* kind of mistakes, or we wouldn't be here. When we were separate individuals, all we had was rage. I struck a fireman when he came to burn my library years ago. I've been running ever since. You want to join us, Montag?"

"Yes."

"What have you to offer?"

"Nothing. I thought I had part of the Book of Ecclesiastes and maybe a little of Revelation, but I haven't even that now."

"The Book of Ecclesiastes would be fine. Where was it?"

"Here." Montag touched his head.

"Ah." Granger smiled and nodded.

"What's wrong? Isn't that all right?" said Montag.

"Better than all right; perfect!" Granger turned to the Reverend. "Do we have a Book of Ecclesiastes?"

"One. A man named Harris in Youngstown."

"Montag." Granger took Montag's shoulder firmly. "Walk carefully. Guard your health. If anything should happen to Harris, *you* are the Book of Ecclesiastes. See how important you've become in the last minute!"

"But I've forgotten!"

"No, nothing's ever lost. We have ways to shake down your clinkers for you."

"But I tried to remember!"

"Don't try. It'll come when we need it. All of us have photographic memories, but spend a lifetime learning how to block off the things that are really *in* there. Simmons here has worked on it for twenty years and now we've got the method down to where we can recall anything that's been read once. Would you like, someday, Montag, to read Plato's *Republic?*"

"Of course!"

"I am Plato's *Republic.* Like to read Marcus Aurelius?[1] Mr. Simmons is Marcus."

"How do you do?" said Mr. Simmons.

"Hello," said Montag.

"I want you to meet Jonathan Swift,[2] the author of that evil political book, *Gulliver's Travels!* And this other fellow is Charles Darwin, and this one is Schopenhauer,[3] and this one is Einstein, and this one here at my elbow is Mr. Albert Schweitzer,[4] a very kind philosopher indeed. Here we all

---

[1]Roman emperor (r. 161–180) who wrote *Meditations.*
[2]English author (1667–1745).
[3]German philosopher (1788–1860).
[4]German philosopher, physician, and humanitarian (1875–1965).

are, Montag. Aristophanes[5] and Mahatma Gandhi[6] and Gautama Buddha[7] and Confucius[8] and Thomas Love Peacock[9] and Thomas Jefferson and Mr. Lincoln, if you please. We are also Matthew Mark, Luke, and John."

Everyone laughed quietly.

"It can't *be*," said Montag.

"It *is*," replied Granger, smiling. "*We're* book burners, too. We read the books and burnt them, afraid they'd be found. Microfilming didn't pay off; we were always traveling, we didn't want to bury the film and come back later. Always the chance of discovery. Better to keep it in the old heads, where no one can see it or suspect it. We are all bits and pieces of history and literature and international law. Byron,[10] Tom Paine,[11] Machiavelli,[12] or Christ, it's here. And the hour's late. And the war's begun. And we are out here, and the city is there, all wrapped up in its own coat of a thousand colors. What do you think, Montag?" . . .

"How many of you are there?"

"Thousands on the roads, the abandoned rail-tracks, tonight, bums on the outside, libraries inside. It wasn't planned, at first. Each man had a book he wanted to remember, and did. Then, over a period of twenty years or so, we met each other, traveling, and got the loose network together and set out a plan. The most important single thing we had to pound into ourselves is that we were not important, we mustn't be pedants; we were not to feel superior to anyone else in the world. We're nothing more than dust jackets for books, of no significance otherwise. Some of us live in small towns. Chapter One of Thoreau's *Walden*[13] in Green River, Chapter Two in Willow Farm Maine. Why, there's one town in Maryland, only twenty-seven people, no bomb'll ever touch that town, is the complete essays of a man named Bertrand Russell.[14] Pick up that town, almost, and flip the pages, so many pages to a person. And when the war's over, someday, some year, the books can be written again, the people will be called in, one by one, to recite what they know and we'll set it up in type until another Dark Age, when we might have to do the whole damn thing over again. But that's the wonderful thing about man; he never gets so discouraged or disgusted that he gives up doing it all over again, because he knows very well it is important and *worth* the doing."

---

[5]Greek playwright (c. 448–380 B.C.).

[6]Indian nationalist known for passive resistance and nonviolent protest against British rule (1869–1948).

[7]Religious teacher in India (c. 566–486 B.C.).

[8]Religious teacher in China (551–479 B.C.).

[9]English novelist and poet (1785–1866).

[10]Lord Byron, George Gordon, English poet (1788–1824).

[11]American philosopher and political writer (1737–1809).

[12]Italian Renaissance political theorist (1469–1527).

[13]An account of Thoreau's (1817–1862) life in the woods for two years in the 1840s.

[14]British philosopher and mathematician (1872–1970).

At this point, the war began and the city was totally destroyed by an atomic bomb. Afterward, the others think about the future in the following excerpt.

"Now, let's get on upstream," said Granger. "And hold onto one thought: You're not important. You're not anything. Someday the load we're carrying with us may help someone. But even when we had the books on hand, a long time ago, we didn't use what we got out of them. We went right on insulting the dead. We went right on spitting in the graves of all the poor ones who died before us. We're going to meet a lot of lonely people in the next week and the next month and the next year. And when they ask us what we're doing, you can say, We're remembering. That's where we'll win out in the long run. And someday we'll remember so much that we'll build the biggest goddamn steamshovel in history and dig the biggest grave of all time and shove war in and cover it up. Come on now, we're going to go build a mirror factory first and put out nothing but mirrors for the next year and take a long look in them." . . .

But now there was a long morning's walk until noon, and if the men were silent it was because there was everything to think about and much to remember. Perhaps later in the morning, when the sun was up and had warmed them, they would begin to talk, or just say the things they remembered, to be sure they were there, to be absolutely certain that things were safe in them. Montag felt the slow stir of words, the slow simmer. And when it came his turn, what could he say, what could he offer on a day like this, to make the trip a little easier? To everything there is a season. Yes. A time to break down, and a time to build up. Yes. A time to keep silence, and a time to speak.[15] Yes, all that. But what else. What else? Something, something . . .

And on either side of the river was there a tree of life, which bare twelve manner of fruits, and yielded her fruit every month; And the leaves of the tree were for the healing of the nations.[16]

Yes, thought Montag, that's the one I'll save for noon. For noon . . .

When we reach the city.

In the Coda to the present edition of the book, Bradbury relates that, unknown to him, a censored version of *Fahrenheit 451* was published in 1967.

There is more than one way to burn a book. And the world is full of people running about with lit matches. Every minority, be it Baptist/Unitarian, Irish/Italian/Octogenarian/Zen Buddhist, Zionist/Seventh-day Adventist, Women's Lib/Republican, Mattachine/FourSquareGospel feels it has the will, the right, the duty to douse the kerosene, light the fuse. Every dimwit editor who sees himself as the source of

---

[15]Ecclesiastes 3:1–7.

[16]Revelation 22:2.

all dreary blanc-mange plain porridge unleavened literature, licks his guillotine and eyes the neck of any author who dares to speak above a whisper or write above a nursery rhyme.

Fire-Captain Beatty, in my novel *Fahrenheit 451,* described how the books were burned first by minorities, each ripping a page or a paragraph from this book, then that, until the day came when the books were empty and the minds shut and the libraries closed forever.

"Shut the door, they're coming through the window, shut the window, they're coming through the door," are the words to an old song. They fit my lifestyle with newly arriving butcher/censors every month. Only six weeks ago, I discovered that, over the years, some cubby-hole editors at Ballantine Books, fearful of contaminating the young, had, bit by bit, censored some 75 separate sections from the novel. Students, reading the novel which, after all, deals with censorship and book-burning in the future, wrote to tell me of this exquisite irony. Judy-Lynn Del Rey, one of the new Ballantine editors, is having the entire book reset and republished this summer with all the damns and hells back in place.

3 The Dark Side of Human Nature

The dark, irrational side of human nature has intrigued ancient Greek dramatists, Christian moralists, and modern philosophers, psychologists, and novelists. It was central to the thought of such luminaries as Dostoevsky, Freud, and Conrad. The atrocities of World War II were a chilling reminder of the human being's capacity for evil and the precariousness of civilization. These themes found expression in the novels of William Golding (1911–1993), who served in the British navy during World War II.

William Golding
Lord of the Flies

Golding's most famous novel, *Lord of the Flies* (1954), takes place presumably during an atomic war. A plane carrying English schoolboys to safety is attacked and crashes on a deserted Pacific island. All the adults perished in the crash, and the stranded children, the oldest of whom is twelve and a few months and the youngest, the "little'uns," are about six or seven, are left to fend for themselves. The boys constitute a miniature society, and their interaction poses distressing questions about human nature and the future of civilization. Replete with symbols and inner meaning, the book is far more complex than a compelling adventure.

Chosen chief, Ralph attempts to maintain order, civility, and a proper focus: he keeps reminding the boys of the importance of constructing shelters and maintaining the fire that will signal rescue ships. His rival, Jack, organizes a pack of hunters who resist Ralph's attempt to sustain civilized ways and degenerate into a savage tribe, even painting their faces. Jack represents instinctual forces that inhabit our unconscious, forces that propel us into evil acts. Piggy, short, fat, near-sighted, and asthmatic, but wise, advises Ralph. Roger, an evil, sadistic member of Jack's tribe, delights in torturing pigs and the other boys and deliberately smashes Piggy with a heavy boulder that kills him. The two identical twins, Sam and Eric who do everything in concert, are referred to as one person, Samneric. Intimidated by Jack, they join his tribe and betray Ralph to Jack who is tracking Ralph in order to kill him and impale him like a pig.

Among the many metaphors and symbols employed by Golding, two stand out: the beast and the conch. The littl'uns spread a frightening tale that a beast dwelling on the island aims to harm them. In reality, there is no such creature; the real beast is something internal, a disfigured human nature that leads the boys to forsake civilization and descend to savagery. When Simon, sensitive, compassionate, and spiritual, discovers the truth about the beast, he himself is mistaken for the creature and is brutally murdered by the other boys. The conch shell symbolizes the order and civilized values so admired by English society. When a speaker holds the conch, the others are required to listen. Jack's increasing disregard of this rule and his eventual destruction of the conch symbolizes the boys' descent into anarchy.

Although the book contains several themes, Golding himself tells us the principal one—a demonic force inherent in human nature is a perpetual threat to civilized life:

> The theme is an attempt to trace the defects of society back to the defects of human nature. The moral is that the shape of a society must depend on the ethical nature of the individual and not on any political system however apparently logical or respectable. The whole book is symbolic in nature except the rescue in the end where adult life appears, dignified and capable, but in reality enmeshed in the same evil as the symbolic life of the children on the island. The officer, having interrupted a man-hunt, prepares to take the children off the island in a cruiser which will presently be hunting its enemy in the same implacable way. And who will rescue the adult and his cruiser?

In the following passage from the last chapter of *Lord of the Flies,* Ralph is fleeing Jack and his hunters who seek to kill him.

When the green glow had gone from the horizon and night was fully accomplished, Ralph came again to the thicket in front of the Castle Rock. Peeping through, he could see that the height was still occupied, and whoever it was up there had a spear at the ready.

He knelt among the shadows and felt his isolation bitterly. They were savages it was true; but they were human, and the ambushing fears of the deep night were coming on.

Ralph moaned faintly. Tired though he was, he could not relax and fall into a well of sleep for fear of the tribe. Might it not be possible to walk boldly into the fort, say—"I've got pax," laugh lightly and sleep among the others? Pretend they were still boys, schoolboys who had said, "Sir, yes, Sir"—and worn caps? Daylight might have answered yes; but darkness and the horrors of death said no. Lying there in the darkness, he knew he was an outcast.

"'Cos I had some sense."

He rubbed his cheek along his forearm, smelling the acrid scent of salt and sweat and the staleness of dirt. Over to the left, the waves of ocean were breathing, sucking down, then boiling back over the rock.

There were sounds coming from behind the Castle Rock. Listening carefully, detaching his mind from the swing of the sea, Ralph could make out a familiar rhythm.

"Kill the beast! Cut his throat! Spill his blood!"

The tribe was dancing. Somewhere on the other side of this rocky wall there would be a dark circle, a glowing fire, and meat. They would be savoring food and the comfort of safety.

A noise nearer at hand made him quiver. Savages were clambering up the Castle Rock, right up to the top, and he could hear voices. He sneaked forward a few yards and saw the shape at the top of the rock change and enlarge. There were only two boys on the island who moved or talked like that.

Ralph put his head down on his forearms and accepted this new fact like a wound. Samneric were part of the tribe now. They were guarding the Castle Rock against him. There was no chance of rescuing them and building up an outlaw tribe at the other end of the island. Samneric were savages like the rest; Piggy was dead, and the conch smashed to powder.

At length the guard climbed down. The two that remained seemed nothing more than a dark extension of the rock. A star appeared behind them and was momentarily eclipsed by some movement.

Ralph edged forward, feeling his way over the uneven surface as though he were blind. There were miles of vague water at his right and the restless ocean lay under his left hand, as awful as the shaft of a pit. Every minute the water breathed round the death rock and flowered into a field of whiteness. Ralph crawled until he found the ledge of the entry in his grasp. The lookouts were immediately above him and he could see the end of a spear projecting over the rock.

He called very gently.

"Samneric—"

There was no reply. To carry he must speak louder; and this would rouse those striped and inimical creatures from their feasting by the fire. He set his teeth and started to climb, finding the holds by touch. The stick that had supported a skull hampered him but he would not be parted from his only weapon. He was nearly level with the twins before he spoke again.

"Samneric—"

He heard a cry and a flurry from the rock. The twins had grabbed each other and were gibbering.

"It's me. Ralph."

Terrified that they would run and give the alarm, he hauled himself up until his head and shoulders stuck over the top. Far below his armpit he saw the luminous flowering round the rock.

"It's only me. Ralph."

At length they bent forward and peered in his face.

"We thought it was—"

"—we didn't know what it was—"

"—we thought—"

Memory of their new and shameful loyalty came to them. Eric was silent but Sam tried to do his duty.

"You got to go, Ralph. You go away now—"

He wagged his spear and essayed fierceness.

"You shove off. See?"

Eric nodded agreement and jabbed his spear in the air. Ralph leaned on his arms and did not go.

"I came to see you two."

His voice was thick. His throat was hurting him now though it had received no wound.

"I came to see you two—"

Words could not express the dull pain of these things. He fell silent, while the vivid stars were split and danced all ways.

Sam shifted uneasily.

"Honest, Ralph, you'd better go."

Ralph looked up again.

"You two aren't painted. How can you—? If it were light—"

If it were light shame would burn them at admitting these things. But the night was dark. Eric took up; and then the twins started their antiphonal speech.

"You got to go because it's not safe—"

"—they made us. They hurt us—"

"Who? Jack?"

"Oh no—"

They bent to him and lowered their voices.

"Push off, Ralph—"

"—it's a tribe—"

"—they made us—"

"—we couldn't help it—"

When Ralph spoke again his voice was low, and seemed breathless.

"What have I done? I liked him—and I wanted us to be rescued—"

Again the stars spilled about the sky. Eric shook his head, earnestly.

"Listen, Ralph. Never mind what's sense. That's gone—"

"Never mind about the chief—"

"—you got to go for your own good."

"The chief and Roger—"

"—yes, Roger—"

"They hate you, Ralph. They're going to do you."

"They're going to hunt you tomorrow."

"But why?"

"I dunno. And Ralph, Jack, the chief, says it'll be dangerous—"

"—and we've got to be careful and throw our spears like at a pig."

"We're going to spread out in a line across the island—"

"—we're going forward from this end—"

"—until we find you."

"We've got to give signals like this."

Eric raised his head and achieved a faint ululation by beating on his open mouth. Then he glanced behind him nervously.

"Like that—"

"—only louder, of course."

"But I've done nothing," whispered Ralph, urgently. "I only wanted to keep up a fire!"

He paused for a moment, thinking miserably of the morrow. A matter of overwhelming importance occurred to him.

"What are you—"

He could not bring himself to be specific at first; but then fear and loneliness goaded him.

"When they find me, what are they going to do?"

The twins were silent. Beneath him, the death rock flowered again.

"What are they—oh God! I'm hungry—"

The towering rock seemed to sway under him.

"Well—what—?"

The twins answered his question indirectly.

"You got to go now, Ralph."

"For your own good."

"Keep away. As far as you can."

"Won't you come with me? Three of us—we'd stand a chance."

After a moment's silence, Sam spoke in a strangled voice.

"You don't know Roger. He's a terror."

"And the chief—they're both—"

"—terrors—"

"—only Roger—"

Both boys froze. Someone was climbing toward them from the tribe.

"He's coming to see if we're keeping watch. Quick, Ralph!"

As he prepared to let himself down the cliff, Ralph snatched at the last possible advantage to be wrung out of this meeting.

"I'll lie up close; in that thicket down there," he whispered, "so keep them away from it. They'll never think to look so close—"

The footsteps were still some distance away.

"Sam—I'm going to be all right, aren't I?"

The twins were silent again.

"Here!" said Sam suddenly. "Take this—"

Ralph felt a chunk of meat pushed against him and grabbed it.

"But what are you going to do when you catch me?"

Silence above. He sounded silly to himself. He lowered himself down the rock.

"What are you going to do—?"

From the top of the towering rock came the incomprehensible reply.

"Roger sharpened a stick at both ends."

Roger sharpened a stick at both ends. Ralph tried to attach a meaning to this but could not. He used all the bad words he could think of in a fit of temper that passed into yawning. How long could you go without sleep? He yearned for a bed and sheets—but the only whiteness here was the slow spilt milk, luminous round the rock forty feet below, where Piggy had fallen. Piggy was everywhere, was on this neck, was become terrible in darkness and death. If Piggy were to come back now out of the water, with his empty head—Ralph whimpered and yawned like a littl'un. The stick in his hand became a crutch on which he reeled.

Then he tensed again. There were voices raised on the top of the Castle Rock. Samneric were arguing with someone. But the ferns and the grass were near. That was the place to be in, hidden, and next to the thicket that would serve for tomorrow's hideout. Here—and his hands touched grass—was a place to be in for the night, not far from the tribe, so that if the horrors of the supernatural emerged one could at least mix with humans for the time being, even if it meant . . .

What did it mean? A stick sharpened at both ends. What was there in that? They had thrown spears and missed; all but one. Perhaps they would miss next time, too.

He squatted down in the tall grass, remembered the meat that Sam had given him, and began to tear at it ravenously. While he was eating, he heard fresh noises—cries of pain from Samneric, cries of panic, angry voices. What did it mean? Someone besides himself was in trouble, for at least one of the twins was catching it. Then the voices passed away down the rock and he ceased to think of them. He felt with his hands and found cool, delicate fronds backed against the thicket. Here then was the night's lair. At first light he would creep into the thicket, squeeze between the twisted stems, ensconce himself so deep that only a crawler like himself could come through, and that crawler would be jabbed. There he would sit, and the search would pass him by, and the cordon waver on, ululating [howling] along the island, and he would be free.

He pulled himself between the ferns, tunneling in. He laid the stick beside him, and huddled himself down in the blackness. One must remember to wake at first light, in order to diddle [deceive] the savages—and he did not know how quickly sleep came and hurled him down a dark interior slope.

He was awake before his eyes were open, listening to a noise that was near. He opened an eye, found the mold an inch or so from his face and his fingers gripped into it, light filtering between the fronds of fern. He had just time to realize that the age-long nightmares of falling and death were past and that the morning was come, when he heard the sound again. It was an ululation over by the seashore—and now the next savage answered and the next. The cry swept by him across the narrow end of the island from sea to lagoon, like the cry of a flying bird. He took no time to consider but grabbed his sharp stick and wriggled back among the ferns. Within seconds he was worming his way into the thicket; but not before he had glimpsed the legs of a savage coming toward him. The ferns were thumped and beaten and he heard legs moving in the long grass. The savage, whoever he was, ululated twice; and the cry was repeated in both directions, then died away. Ralph crouched still, tangled in the ferns, and for a time he heard nothing.

At last he examined the thicket itself. Certainly no one could attack him here—and moreover he had a stroke of luck. The great rock that had killed Piggy had bounded into this thicket and bounced there, right in the center, making a smashed space a few feet in extent each way. When Ralph had wriggled into this he felt secure, and clever. He sat down carefully among the smashed stems and waited for the hunt to pass. Looking up between the leaves he caught a glimpse of something red. That must be the top of the Castle Rock, distant and unmenacing. He composed himself triumphantly, to hear the sounds of the hunt dying away.

Yet no one made a sound; and as the minutes passed, in the green shade, his feeling of triumph faded.

At last he heard a voice—Jack's voice, but hushed.

"Are you certain?"

The savage addressed said nothing. Perhaps he made a gesture.

Roger spoke.

"If you're fooling us—"

Immediately after this, there came a gasp, and a squeal of pain. Ralph crouched instinctively. One of the twins was there, outside the thicket, with Jack and Roger.

"You're sure he meant in there?"

The twin moaned faintly and then squealed again.

"He meant he'd hide in there?"

"Yes—yes—oh—!"

Silver laughter scattered among the trees.

So they knew.

Ralph picked up his stick and prepared for battle. But what could they do? It would take them a week to break a path through the thicket; and anyone who wormed his way in would be helpless. He felt the point of his spear with his thumb and grinned without amusement. Whoever tried that would be stuck, squealing like a pig.

They were going away, back to the tower rock. He could hear feet moving and then someone sniggered. There came again that high, bird-like cry that swept along the line. So some were still watching for him; but some—?

There was a long, breathless silence. Ralph found that he had bark in his mouth from the gnawed spear. He stood and peered upwards to the Castle Rock.

As he did so, he heard Jack's voice from the top.

"Heave! Heave! Heave!"

The red rock that he could see at the top of the cliff vanished like a curtain, and he could see figures and blue sky. A moment later the earth jolted, there was a rushing sound in the air, and the top of the thicket was cuffed as with a gigantic hand. The rock bounded on, thumping and smashing toward the beach, while a shower of broken twigs and leaves fell on him. Beyond the thicket, the tribe was cheering.

Silence again.

Ralph put his fingers in his mouth and bit them. There was only one other rock up there that they might conceivably move; but that was half as big as a cottage, big as a car, a tank. He visualized its probable progress with agonizing clearness—that one would start slowly, drop from ledge to ledge, trundle across the neck like an outsize steam roller.

"Heave! Heave! Heave!"

Ralph put down his spear, then picked it up again. He pushed his hair back irritably, took two hasty steps across the little space and then came back. He stood looking at the broken ends of branches.

Still silence.

He caught sight of the rise and fall of his diaphragm and was surprised to see how quickly he was breathing. Just left of center his heart-beats were visible. He put the spear down again.

"Heave! Heave! Heave!"

A shrill, prolonged cheer.

Something boomed up on the red rock, then the earth jumped and began to shake steadily, while the noise as steadily increased. Ralph was shot into the air, thrown down, dashed against branches. At his right hand, and only a few feet away, the whole thicket bent and the roots screamed as they came out of the earth together. He saw something red that turned over slowly as a mill wheel. Then the red thing was past and the elephantine progress diminished toward the sea.

Ralph knelt on the plowed-up soil, and waited for the earth to come back. Presently the white, broken stumps, the split sticks and the tangle of the thicket refocused. There was a kind of heavy feeling in his body where he had watched his own pulse.

Silence again.

Yet not entirely so. They were whispering out there; and suddenly the branches were shaken furiously at two places on his right. The pointed end of a stick appeared. In panic, Ralph thrust his own stick through the crack with all his might.

"Aaa-ah!"

His spear twisted a little in his hands and then he withdrew it again.

"Ooh-ooh—"

Someone was moaning outside and a babble of voices rose. A fierce argument was going on and the wounded savage kept groaning. Then when there was silence, a single voice spoke and Ralph decided that it was not Jack's.

"See? I told you—he's dangerous."

The wounded savage moaned again.

What else? What next?

Ralph fastened his hands round the chewed spear and his hair fell. Someone was muttering, only a few yards away toward the Castle Rock. He heard a savage say "No!" in a shocked voice; and then there was suppressed laughter. He squatted back on his heels and showed his teeth at the wall of branches. He raised his spear, snarled a little, and waited.

Once more the invisible group sniggered. He heard a curious trickling sound and then a louder crepitation as if someone were unwrapping great sheets of cellophane. A stick snapped and he stifled a cough. Smoke was seeping through the branches in white and yellow wisps, the patch of blue sky overheard turned to the color of a storm cloud, and then the smoke billowed round him.

Someone laughed excitedly, and a voice shouted.

"Smoke!"

He wormed his way through the thicket toward the forest, keeping as far as possible beneath the smoke. Presently he saw open space, and the green leaves of the edge of the thicket. A smallish savage was standing between him and the rest of the forest, a savage striped red and white, and carrying a spear. He was coughing and smearing the paint about his eyes with the back of his hand as he tried to see through the increasing smoke. Ralph launched himself like a cat; stabbed, snarling, with the spear, and the savage doubled up. There was a shout from beyond the thicket and then Ralph was running with the swiftness of fear through the undergrowth. He came to a pig-run, followed it for perhaps a hundred yards, and then swerved off. Behind him the ululation swept across the island once more and a single voice shouted three times. He guessed that was the signal to advance and sped away again, till his chest was like fire. Then he flung himself down under a bush and waited for a moment till his breathing steadied. He passed his tongue tentatively over his teeth and lips and heard far off the ululation of the pursuers.

There were many things he could do. He could climb a tree; but that was putting all his eggs in one basket. If he were detected, they had nothing more difficult to do than wait.

If only one had time to think!

Another double cry at the same distance gave him a clue to their plan. Any savage balked in the forest would utter the double shout and hold up the line till he was free again. That way they might hope to keep the cordon unbroken right across the island. Ralph thought of the boar that had broken through them with such ease. If necessary, when the chase came too close, he could charge the cordon while it was still thin, burst through, and run back. But run back where? The cordon would turn and sweep again. Sooner or later he would have to sleep or eat—and then he would awaken with hands clawing at him; and the hunt would become a running down.

What has to be done, then? The tree? Burst the line like a boar? Either way the choice was terrible.

A single cry quickened his heart-beat and, leaping up, he dashed away toward the ocean side and the thick jungle till he was hung up among creepers; he stayed there for a moment with his calves quivering. If only one could have quiet, a long pause, a time to think!

And there again, shrill and inevitable, was the ululation sweeping across the island. At that sound he shied like a horse among the creepers and ran once more till he was panting. He flung himself down by some ferns. The tree, or the charge? He mastered his breathing for a moment, wiped his mouth, and told himself to be calm. Samneric were somewhere in that line, and hating it. Or were they? And supposing, instead of them, he met the chief, or Roger who carried death in his hands?

Ralph pushed back his tangled hair and wiped the sweat out of his best eye. He spoke aloud.

"Think."

What was the sensible thing to do?

There was no Piggy to talk sense. There was no solemn assembly for debate nor dignity of the conch.

"Think."

Most, he was beginning to dread the curtain that might waver in his brain, blacking out the sense of danger, making a simpleton of him.

A third idea would be to hide so well that the advancing line would pass without discovering him.

He jerked his head off the ground and listened. There was another noise to attend to now, a deep grumbling noise, as though the forest itself were angry with him, a somber noise across which the ululations were scribbled excruciatingly as on slate. He knew he had heard it before somewhere, but had no time to remember.

Break the line.

A tree.

Hide, and let them pass.

A nearer cry stood him on his feet and immediately he was away again, running fast among thorns and brambles. Suddenly he blundered into the open, found himself again in that open space—and there was the fathom-wide grin of the skull, no longer ridiculing a deep blue patch of sky but jeering up into a blanket of smoke. Then Ralph was running beneath the trees, with the grumble of the forest explained. They had smoked him out and set the island on fire.

Hide was better than a tree because you had a chance of breaking the line if you were discovered.

Hide, then.

He wondered if a pig would agree, and grimaced at nothing. Find the deepest thicket, the darkest hole on the is-

land, and creep in. Now, as he ran, he peered about him. Bars and splashes of sunlight flitted over him and sweat made glistening streaks on his dirty body. The cries were far now, and faint.

At last he found what seemed to him the right place, though the decision was desperate. Here, bushes and a wild tangle of creeper made a mat that kept out all the light of the sun. Beneath it was a space, perhaps a foot high, though it was pierced everywhere by parallel and rising stems. If you wormed into the middle of that you would be five yards from the edge, and hidden, unless the savage chose to lie down and look for you, and even then, you would be in darkness—and if the worst happened and he saw you, then you had a chance to burst out at him, fling the whole line out of step and double back.

Cautiously, his stick trailing behind him, Ralph wormed between the rising stems. When he reached the middle of the mat he lay and listened.

The fire was a big one and the drum-roll that he had thought was left so far behind was nearer. Couldn't a fire outrun a galloping horse? He could see the sun-splashed ground over an area of perhaps fifty yards from where he lay, and as he watched, the sunlight in every patch blinked at him. This was so like the curtain that flapped in his brain that for a moment he thought the blinking was inside him. But then the patches blinked more rapidly, dulled and went out, so that he saw that a great heaviness of smoke lay between the island and the sun.

If anyone peered under the bushes and chanced to glimpse human flesh it might be Samneric who would pretend not to see and say nothing. He laid his cheek against the chocolate-colored earth, licked his dry lips and closed his eyes. Under the thicket, the earth was vibrating very slightly; or perhaps there was a sound beneath the obvious thunder of the fire and scribbled ululations that was too low to hear.

Someone cried out. Ralph jerked his cheek off the earth and looked into the dulled light. They must be near now, he thought, and his chest began to thump. Hide, break the line, climb a tree—which was the best after all? The trouble was you only had one chance.

Now the fire was nearer, those volleying shots were great limbs, trunks even, bursting. The fools! The fools! The fire must be almost at the fruit trees—what would they eat tomorrow?

Ralph stirred restlessly in his narrow bed. One chanced nothing! What could they do? Beat him? So what? Kill him? A stick sharpened at both ends.

The cries, suddenly nearer, jerked him up. He could see a striped savage moving hastily out of a green tangle, and coming toward the mat where he hid, a savage who carried a spear. Ralph gripped his fingers into the earth. Be ready now, in case.

Ralph fumbled to hold his spear so that it was point foremost; and now he saw that the stick was sharpened at both ends.

The savage stopped fifteen yards away and uttered his cry.

Perhaps he can hear my heart over the noises of the fire. Don't scream. Get ready.

The savage moved forward so that you could only see him from the waist down. That was the butt of his spear. Now you could see him from the knee down. Don't scream.

A herd of pigs came squealing out of the greenery behind the savage and rushed away into the forest. Birds were screaming, mice shrieking, and a little hopping thing came under the mat and cowered.

Five yards away the savage stopped, standing right by the thicket, and cried out. Ralph drew his feet up and crouched. The stake was in his hands, the stake sharpened at both ends, the stake that vibrated so wildly, that grew long, short, light, heavy, light again.

The ululation spread from shore to shore. The savage knelt down by the edge of the thicket, and there were lights flickering in the forest behind him. You could see a knee disturb the mold. Now the other. Two hands. A spear.

A face.

The savage peered into the obscurity beneath the thicket. You could tell that he saw light on this side and on that, but not in the middle—there. In the middle was a blob of dark and the savage wrinkled up his face, trying to decipher the darkness.

The seconds lengthened. Ralph was looking straight into the savage's eyes.

Don't scream.

You'll get back.

Now he's seen you. He's making sure. A stick sharpened.

Ralph screamed, a scream of fright and anger and desperation. His legs straightened, the screams became continuous and foaming. He shot forward, burst the thicket, was in the open, screaming, snarling, bloody. He swung the stake and the savage tumbled over; but there were others coming toward him, crying out. He swerved as a spear flew past and then was silent, running. All at once the lights flickering ahead of him merged together, the roar of the forest rose to thunder and a tall bush directly in his path burst into a great fan-shaped flame. He swung to the right, running desperately fast, with the heat beating on his left side and the fire racing forward like a tide. The ululation rose behind him and spread along, a series of short sharp cries, the sighting call. A brown figure showed up at his right and fell away. They were all running, all crying out madly. He could hear them crashing in the undergrowth and on the left was the hot, bright thunder of the fire. He forgot his wounds, his hunger and thirst, and became fear; hopeless fear on flying feet, rushing through the forest toward the open beach. Spots jumped before his eyes and turned into red circles that expanded quickly till they passed out of sight. Below him someone's legs were getting tired and the desperate ululation advanced like a jagged fringe of menace and was almost overhead.

He stumbled over a root and the cry that pursued him rose even higher. He saw a shelter burst into flames and the fire flapped at his right shoulder and there was the glitter of water. Then he was down, rolling over and over in the warm sand, crouching with arm to ward off, trying to cry for mercy.

He staggered to his feet, tensed for more terrors, and looked up at a huge peaked cap. It was a white-topped cap, and above the green shade of the peak was a crown, an anchor, gold foliage. He saw white drill, epaulettes, a revolver, a row of gilt buttons down the front of a uniform.

A naval officer stood on the sand, looking down at Ralph in wary astonishment. On the beach behind him was a cutter, her bows hauled up and held by two ratings. In the stern-sheets another rating held a sub-machine gun.

The ululation faltered and died away.

The officer looked at Ralph doubtfully for a moment, then took his hand away from the butt of the revolver.

"Hullo."

Squirming a little, conscious of his filthy appearance, Ralph answered shyly.

"Hullo."

The officer nodded, as if a question had been answered.

"Are there any adults—any grownups with you?"

Dumbly, Ralph shook his head, he turned a half-pace on the sand. A semicircle of little boys, then bodies streaked with colored clay, sharp sticks in their hands, were standing on the beach making no noise at all.

"Fun and games," said the officer.

The fire reached the coconut palms by the beach and swallowed them noisily. A flame, seemingly detached, swung like an acrobat and licked up the palm heads on the platform. The sky was black.

The officer grinned cheerfully at Ralph.

"We saw your smoke. What have you been doing? Having a war or something?"

Ralph nodded.

The officer inspected the little scarecrow in front of him. The kid needed a bath, a haircut, a nose-wipe and a good deal of ointment.

"Nobody killed, I hope? Any dead bodies?"

"Only two. And they've gone."

The officer leaned down and looked closely at Ralph.

"Two? Killed?"

Ralph nodded again. Behind him, the whole island was shuddering with flame. The officer knew, as a rule, when people were telling the truth. He whistled softly.

Other boys were appearing now, tiny tots some of them, brown, with the distended bellies of small savages. One of them came close to the officer and looked up.

"I'm, I'm—"

But there was no more to come. Percival Wemys Madison sought in his head for an incantation that had faded clean away.

The officer turned back to Ralph.

"We'll take you off. How many of you are there?"

Ralph shook his head. The officer looked past him to the group of painted boys.

"Who's boss here?"

"I am," said Ralph loudly.

A little boy who wore the remains of an extraordinary black cap on his red hair and who carried the remains of a pair of spectacles at his waist, started forward, then changed his mind and stood still.

"We saw your smoke. And you don't know how many of you there are?"

"No, sir."

"I should have thought," said the officer as he visualized the search before him, "I should have thought that a pack of British boys—you're all British, aren't you?—would have been able to put up a better show than that—I mean—"

"It was like that at first," said Ralph, "before things—" He stopped

"We were together then—"

The officer nodded helpfully.

"I know. Jolly good show. Like the Coral Island."

Ralph looked at him dumbly. For a moment he had a fleeting picture of the strange glamour that had once invested the beaches. But the island was scorched up like dead wood—Simon was dead—and Jack had. . . . The tears began to flow and sobs shook him. He gave himself up to them now for the first time on the island; great, shuddering spasms of grief that seemed to wrench his whole body. His voice rose under the black smoke before the burning wreckage of the island; and infected by that emotion, the other little boys began to shake and sob too. And in the middle of them, with filthy body, matted hair, and unwiped nose, Ralph wept for the end of innocence, the darkness of man's heart, and the fall through the air of the true, wise friend called Piggy.

The officer, surrounded by these noises, was moved and a little embarrassed. He turned away to give them time to pull themselves together; and waited, allowing his eyes to rest on the trim cruiser in the distance.

4 Feminism

In the advanced Western countries, the feminist movement, also called the women's liberation movement, has sought for two centuries to obtain legal and social rights for women, giving them equal status with men. Mary Wollstonecraft in *A Vindication of the Rights of Woman* (see page 99) proposed in 1792 that women receive the same education, work opportunities, and political rights as men. Since the 1960s, women's organizations have proliferated worldwide. Goals range from legal and cultural changes in developed countries, such as bans on gender-based discrimination and freedom of choice in matters related to childbearing, to elemental improvements in the Third World, such as the abolition of the bride price in some African countries. On some issues the movement does have opponents among women as well as men. Because of cultural differences, the extent to which women's rights are recognized varies from country to country, and there are still countries where women have few "rights," notably among the developing nations.

Simone de Beauvoir
The Second Sex

Simone de Beauvoir (1908–1986), the French philosopher and feminist, published *The Second Sex* in 1949. It described the role of women in a traditional society, in which the majority of women were married, depended on men for their role in society, and were tied to their home and their children; only a minority of women (including the author) led independent lives. De Beauvoir traced the role of women through history and through their contemporary life cycle as evidence for her thesis: because the forces of social tradition are controlled by men, women have been relegated to a secondary place in the world.

In the excerpts that follow, de Beauvoir argues that despite considerable change in their social status, women of her time are still prevented from becoming autonomous individuals and taking their places as men's equals. Marriage was still expected to be women's common destiny, with their identity defined in relation to their husbands. In discussing the status of newly independent women, de Beauvoir implied that because of their failure to escape the psychological trap of secondary status, they lacked confidence and creativity in their work.

. . . Woman has always been man's dependent, if not his slave; the two sexes have never shared the world in equality. And even today woman is heavily handicapped, though her situation is beginning to change. Almost nowhere is her legal status the same as man's, and frequently it is much to her disadvantage. Even when her rights are legally recognized in the abstract, long-standing custom prevents their full expression in the mores. In the economic sphere men and women can almost be said to make up two castes; other things being equal, the former hold the better jobs, get higher wages, and have more opportunity for success than their new competitors. In industry and politics men have a great many more positions and they monopolize the most important posts. In addition to all this, they enjoy a traditional prestige that the education of children tends in every way to support, for the present enshrines the past—and in the past all history has been made by men. At the present time, when women are beginning to take part in the affairs of the world, it is still a world that belongs to men—they have no doubt of it at all and women have scarcely any. To decline to be the Other, to refuse to be a party to the deal—this would be for women to renounce all the advantages conferred upon them by their alliance with the superior caste. Man-the-sovereign will provide woman-the-liege with material protection and will undertake the moral justification of her existence; thus she can evade at once both economic risk and the metaphysical risk of a liberty in which ends and aims must be contrived without assistance. Indeed, along with the ethical urge of each individual to affirm his subjective existence, there is also the temptation to forgo liberty and become a thing. This is an inauspicious road, for he who takes it—passive, lost, ruined—becomes henceforth the creature of another's will, frustrated in his transcendence and deprived of every value. But it is an easy road; on it one avoids the strain involved in undertaking an authentic existence. When man makes of woman the *Other*, he may, then, expect to manifest deep-seated tendencies towards complicity. Thus, woman may fail to lay claim to the status of subject because she lacks definite resources, because she feels the necessary bond that ties her to man regardless of reciprocity, and because she is often very well pleased with her role as the *Other*. . . .

Marriage is the destiny traditionally offered to women by society. It is still true that most women are married, or have been, or plan to be, or suffer from not being. The celibate woman is to be explained and defined with reference to marriage, whether she is frustrated, rebellious, or even indifferent in regard to that institution. We must therefore continue this study by analysing marriage.

Economic evolution in woman's situation is in process of upsetting the institution of marriage: it is becoming a union freely entered upon by the consent of two independent persons; the obligations of the two contracting parties are personal and reciprocal; adultery is for both a breach of contract; divorce is obtainable by the one or the other on the same conditions. Woman is no longer limited to the reproductive function, which has lost in large part its character as natural servitude and has come to be regarded as a function to be voluntarily assumed; and it is compatible with productive labour, since, in many cases, the time off required by a pregnancy is taken by the mother at the expense of the State or the employer. In the Soviet Union marriage was for some years a contract between individuals based upon the complete liberty of the husband and wife; but it would seem that it is now a duty that the State imposes upon them both. Which of these tendencies will prevail in the world of tomorrow will depend upon the general structure of society, but in any case male guardianship of woman is disappearing. Nevertheless, the epoch in which we are living is still, from the feminist point of view, a period of transition. Only a part of the female population is engaged in production, and even those who are belong to a society in which ancient forms and antique values survive. Modern marriage can be understood only in the light of a past that tends to perpetuate itself.

Marriage has always been a very different thing for man and for woman. The two sexes are necessary to each other, but this necessity has never brought about a condition of reciprocity between them; women, as we have seen, have never constituted a caste making exchanges and contracts with the male caste upon a footing of equality. A man is socially an independent and complete individual; he is regarded first of all as a producer whose existence is justified by the work he does for the group: we have seen why it is that the reproductive and domestic role to which woman is confined has not guaranteed her an equal dignity. Certainly the male needs her; in some primitive groups it may happen that the bachelor, unable to manage his existence by himself, becomes a kind of outcast; in agricultural societies a woman co-worker is essential to the peasant; and for most men it is of advantage to unload certain drudgery upon a mate; the individual wants a regular sexual life and posterity, and the State requires him to contribute to its perpetuation. But man does not make this appeal directly to woman herself; it is the men's group that allows each of its members to find self-fulfillment as husband and father; woman, as slave or vassal, is integrated within families dominated by fathers and brothers, and she has always been given in marriage by certain males to other males. In primitive societies the paternal clan, the gens, disposed of woman almost like a thing: she was included in deals agreed upon by two groups. The situation is not much modified when marriage assumes a contractual form in the course of its evolution; when dowered or having her share in inheritance, woman would seem to have civil standing as a person, but dowry and inheritance still enslave her to her family. During a long period the contracts were made between father-in-law and son-in-law, not between wife and husband; only widows then enjoyed economic independence. The young girl's freedom of choice has always been much restricted; and celibacy—apart from the rare cases in which it bears a sacred character—reduced her to the rank of parasite and pariah; marriage is her only means of support and the sole justification of her existence. It is enjoined upon her for two reasons.

The first reason is that she must provide the society with children; only rarely—as in Sparta and to some extent under the Nazi régime—does the Stare take woman under direct guardianship and ask only that she be a mother. But even the primitive societies that are not aware of the paternal generative role demand that woman have a husband, for the second reason why marriage is enjoined is that woman's function is also to satisfy a male's sexual needs and to take care of his household. These duties placed upon woman by society are regarded as a *service* rendered to her spouse: in return he is supposed to give her presents, or a marriage settlement, and to support her. Through him as intermediary, society discharges its debt to the woman it turns over to him. The rights obtained by the wife in fulfilling her duties are represented in obligations that the male must assume. He cannot break the conjugal bond at his pleasure; he can repudiate or divorce his wife only when the public authorities so decide, and even then the husband sometimes owes her compensation in money; the practice even becomes an abuse in Egypt under Bocchoris [Egyptian King] or, as the demand for alimony, in the United States today. Polygamy has always been more or less openly tolerated: man may bed with slaves, concubines, mistresses, prostitutes, but he is required to respect certain privileges of his legitimate wife. If she is maltreated or wronged, she has the right—more or less definitely guaranteed—of going back to her family and herself obtaining a separation or divorce.

Thus for both parties marriage is at the same time a burden and a benefit; but there is no symmetry in the situations of the two sexes; for girls marriage is the only means of integration in the community, and if they remain unwanted, they are, socially viewed, so much wastage. . . .

It must be said that the independent woman is justifiably disturbed by the idea that people do not have confidence in her. As a general rule, the superior caste is hostile to newcomers from the inferior caste: white people will not consult a Negro physician, nor males a woman doctor; but individuals of the inferior caste, imbued with a sense of their specific inferiority and often full of resentment towards one of their kind who has risen above their usual lot, will also prefer to turn to the masters. Most women, in particular, steeped in adoration for man, eagerly seek him out in the person of the doctor, the lawyer, the office manager, and so on. Neither men nor women like to be under a woman's orders. Her superiors, even if they esteem her highly, will always be somewhat condescending; to be a woman, if not a defect, is at least a peculiarity. Woman must constantly win the confidence that is not at first accorded her: at the start she is suspect, she has to prove herself. If she has worth she will pass the tests, so they say. But worth is not a given essence; it is the outcome of a successful development. To feel the weight of an unfavourable prejudice against one is only on very rare occasions a help in overcoming it. The initial inferiority complex ordinarily leads to a defence reaction in the form of an exaggerated affectation of authority.

Most women doctors, for example, have too much or too little of the air of authority. If they act naturally, they fail to take control, for their life as a whole disposes them rather to seduce than to command; the patient who likes to be dominated will be disappointed by plain advice simply given. Aware of this fact, the woman doctor assumes a grave accent, a peremptory tone; but then she lacks the bluff good nature that is the charm of the medical man who is sure of himself.

Man is accustomed to asserting himself; his clients believe in his competence; he can act naturally: he infallibly makes an impression. Woman does not inspire the same feeling of security; she affects a lofty air, she drops it, she makes too much of it. In business, in administrative work, she is precise, fussy, quick to show aggressiveness. As in her studies, she lacks ease, dash, audacity. In the effort to achieve she gets tense. Her activity is a succession of challenges and self-affirmations. This is the great defect that lack of assurance engenders: the subject cannot forget himself. He does not aim gallantly towards some goal: he seeks rather to make good in prescribed ways. In boldly setting out towards ends, one risks disappointments; but one also obtains unhoped-for results; caution condemns to mediocrity.

We rarely encounter in the independent woman a taste for adventure and for experience for its own sake, or a disinterested curiosity; she seeks "to have a career" as other women build a nest of happiness; she remains dominated, surrounded, by the male universe, she lacks the audacity to break through its ceiling, she does not passionately lose herself in her projects. She still regards her life as an immanent enterprise: her aim is not at an objective but, through the objective, at her subjective success. This is a very conspicuous attitude, for example, among American women; they like having a job and proving to themselves that they are capable of handling it properly; but they are not passionately concerned with the *content* of their tasks. Woman similarly has a tendency to attach too much importance to minor setbacks and modest successes; she is turn by turn discouraged or puffed up with vanity. When a success has been anticipated, one takes it calmly; but it becomes an intoxicating triumph when one has been doubtful of obtaining it. This is the excuse when women become addled with importance and plume themselves ostentatiously over their least accomplishments. They are for ever looking back to see how far they have come, and that interrupts their progress. By this procedure they can have honourable careers, but not accomplish great things. It must be added that many men are also unable to build any but mediocre careers. It is only in comparison with the best of them that woman—save for very rare exceptions—seems to us to be trailing behind. The reasons I have given are sufficient explanation, and in no way mortgage the future. What woman essentially lacks today for doing great things is forgetfulness of herself; but to forget oneself it is first of all necessary to be firmly assured that now and for the future one has found oneself. Newly come into the world of men, poorly seconded by them, woman is still too busily occupied to search for herself.

5 American Drama as Social Commentary

Modern American drama finds its roots in nineteenth century Europe. The Norwegian playwright Henrik Ibsen (see page 160) was the first to use drama to call attention to social problems. In his plays—such as *Pillars of Society* (1877) and *A Doll's House* (1879)—Ibsen dealt with contemporary social problems, including marital discord, capitalist greed and corruption, and the clash of generations. In plays such as *Mrs. Warren's Profession* (1893) and *Pygmalion* (1912), Irish dramatist George Bernard Shaw (see page 216) revealed a humanitarian concern for the poor and the exploited. German dramatist Bertolt Brecht also regarded the theater as an instrument of social change. He hoped that plays like *Life of Galileo* (1938–1939) and *Mother Courage and Her Children* (1939) would promote critical thinking among the audience and foster productive reforms.

Eugene O'Neill (see page 238), generally considered to be the first great American playwright, wrote drama that deals with social questions and religious and philosophical ideas. In his plays—such as *The Emperor Jones* (1920), *Beyond the Horizon* (1920), and *The Iceman Cometh* (1939)—O'Neill created the template for the new American tragedy, which developed during the twenty years following the end of World War II. This was a time when Americans experienced the onset of the Cold War, when more and more of them moved from the cities to the suburbs, and when African-Americans migrated to the North from the South. It was also a period of prosperity, when many people achieved the "American dream" of material success. Two Pulitzer Prize–winning playwrights, Arthur Miller and Tennessee Williams, launched this "golden age" of American drama, as they explored social and political themes in connection with contemporary American society.

Arthur Miller
Death of a Salesman

Arthur Miller (1915–) began to write plays while he was still a student at the University of Michigan. Soon after the conclusion of World War II, he found his first great success, with the production of *All My Sons*. Two years later, in 1949, Miller won the Pulitzer Prize for *Death of a Salesman: Certain Private Conversations in Two Acts and a Requiem.* Four years later, Miller's play, *The Crucible,* set in Salem, Massachusetts, during the witchcraft trials of 1692, was produced. The play was a means of exploring contemporary American politics during the so-called McCarthy Era, when Americans were accused of being Communists, just as those during the infamous Salem witchcraft trials were falsely accused and put to death.

Death of a Salesman reflects the growing domestic tensions in American society following World War II, tensions that Miller sees being exacerbated by the American dream that anyone can become wealthy and successful. Writing with compassion and in a simple style that befits his characters, Miller looks into the hearts of Willy Loman and his family and shows that the life of a common person can also be the subject of tragedy. The heroes of classical Greek and Shakespearean tragedies were monarchs and nobles, people of stature. Willy Loman, however, is just an ordinary American struggling to make it—to fulfill the American dream of success—but his life and suffering can also be treated as tragedy. Willy Loman is an insecure traveling salesman who believes in the American dream, but—still a traveling salesman in his sixties—he is never able to achieve it. He is self-delusional and boastful, and he cheats on his wife, Linda, when he is in Boston on sales trips. Linda, though she sees through Willy's delusions, is loyal and supportive. Their thirty-four-year-old son Biff, a football star in high school, has never been able to hold a job. His problems stem not only from his failure to graduate from high school because he failed math in his senior year, but also from his knowledge that his father is unfaithful to his mother. Neither Biff nor his younger brother, Happy, can live up to their father's aspirations for them.

In act 2, Willy approaches his boss, Howard, to ask him for a non-traveling job in New York. Howard had inherited the business from his late father, whom Willy regards as a prince. Willy even believes that he had given Howard his name when he was born. Howard, although much younger than Willy, treats him disrespectfully and blithely dismisses his years of service to the firm.

WILLY Pst! Pst!

HOWARD Hello, Willy, come in.

WILLY Like to have a little talk with you, Howard.

HOWARD Sorry to keep you waiting. I'll be with you in a minute.

WILLY What's that, Howard?

HOWARD Didn't you ever see one of these? Wire recorder.

WILLY Oh. Can we talk a minute?

HOWARD Records Things. Just got delivery yesterday. Been driving me crazy, the most terrific machine I ever saw in my life. I was up all night with it.

WILLY What do you do with it?

HOWARD I bought it for dictation, but you can do anything with it. Listen to this. I had it home last night. Listen to what I picked up. The first one is my daughter. Get this. (*He flicks the switch and "Roll out the Barrel" is heard being whistled.*) Listen to that kid whistle.

WILLY That is lifelike, isn't it?

HOWARD Seven years old. Get that tone.

WILLY Ts, ts. Like to ask a little favor if you . . .
      (*The whistling breaks off, and the voice of Howard's daughter is heard.*)

HIS DAUGHTER "Now you, Daddy."

HOWARD She's crazy for me! *Again the same song is whistled.* That's me! Ha! (*He winks.*)

WILLY You're very good!
      (*The whistling breaks off again. The machine runs silent for a moment.*)

HOWARD Sh! Get this now, this is my son.

HIS SON "The capital of Alabama is Montgomery; the capital of Arizona is Phoenix; the capital of Arkansas is Little Rock; the capital of California is Sacramento . . ." (*and on, and on.*)

HOWARD (*holding up five fingers*) Five years old, Willy!

WILLY He'll make an announcer some day!

HIS SON (*continuing*) "The capital . . ."

HOWARD Get that—alphabetical order! (*The machine breaks off suddenly.*) Wait a minute. The maid kicked the plug out.

WILLY It certainly is a—

HOWARD Sh, for God's sake!

HIS SON "It's nine o'clock, Bulova watch time. So I have to go to sleep."

WILLY That really is—

HOWARD Wait a minute! The next is my wife.
      (*They wait.*)

HOWARD'S VOICE "Go on, say something." (*Pause.*) "Well, you gonna talk?"

HIS WIFE "I can't think of anything."

HOWARD'S VOICE "Well, talk—it's turning."

HIS WIFE (*shyly, beaten*) "Hello." (*Silence.*) "Oh, Howard, I can't talk into this . . ."

HOWARD (*snapping the machine off*) That was my wife.

WILLY That is a wonderful machine. Can we—

HOWARD I tell you, Willy, I'm gonna take my camera, and my bandsaw, and all my hobbies, and out they go. This is the most fascinating relaxation I ever found.

WILLY I think I'll get one myself.

HOWARD Sure, they're only a hundred and a half. You can't do without it. Supposing you wanna hear Jack Benny, see? But you can't be at home at that hour. So you tell the maid to turn the radio on when Jack Benny comes on, and this automatically goes on with the radio . . .

WILLY And when you come home you . . .

HOWARD You can come home twelve o'clock, one o'clock, any time you like, and you get yourself a Coke and sit yourself down, throw the switch, and there's Jack Benny's program in the middle of the night!

WILLY I'm definitely going to get one. Because lots of time I'm on the road, and I think to myself, what I must be missing on the radio!

HOWARD Don't you have a radio in the car?

WILLY Well, yeah, but who ever thinks of turning it on?

HOWARD Say, aren't you supposed to be in Boston?

WILLY That's what I want to talk to you about, Howard. You got a minute? (*He draws a chair in from the wing.*)

HOWARD What happened? What're you doing here?

WILLY Well . . .

HOWARD You didn't crack up again, did you?

WILLY Oh, no. No . . .

HOWARD Geez, you had me worried there for a minute. What's the trouble?

WILLY Well, tell you the truth, Howard. I've come to the decision that I'd rather not travel any more.

HOWARD Not travel! Well, what'll you do?

WILLY Remember, Christmas time, when you had the party here? You said you'd try to think of some spot for me here in town.

HOWARD With us?

WILLY Well, sure.

HOWARD Oh, yeah, yeah. I remember. Well, I couldn't think of anything for you, Willy.

WILLY I tell ya, Howard. The kids are all grown up, y'know. I don't need much any more. If I could take home—well, sixty-five dollars a week, I could swing it.

HOWARD Yeah, but Willy, see I—

WILLY I tell ya why, Howard. Speaking frankly and between the two of us, y'know—I'm just a little tired.

HOWARD Oh, I could understand that, Willy. But you're a road man, Willy, and we do a road business. We've only got a half-dozen salesmen on the floor here.

WILLY God knows, Howard, I never asked a favor of any man. But I was with this firm when your father used to carry you in here in his arms.

HOWARD I know that, Willy, but—

WILLY Your father came to me the day you were born and asked me what I thought of the name of Howard, may he rest in peace.

HOWARD I appreciate that, Willy, but there just is no spot here for you. If I had a spot I'd slam you right in, but I just don't have a single solitary spot.
(*He looks for his lighter. Willy has picked it up and gives it to him. Pause.*)

WILLY (*with increasing anger*) Howard, all I need to set my table is fifty dollars a week.

HOWARD But where am I going to put you, kid?

WILLY Look, it isn't a question of whether I can sell merchandise, is it?

HOWARD No, but it's a business, kid, and everybody's gotta pull his own weight.

WILLY (*desperately*) Just let me tell you a story, Howard—

HOWARD 'Cause you gotta admit, business is business.

WILLY (*angrily*) Business is definitely business, but just listen for a minute. You don't understand this. When I was a boy—eighteen, nineteen—I was already on the road. And there was a question in my mind as to whether selling had a future for me. Because in those days I had a yearning to go to Alaska. See, there were three gold strikes in one month in Alaska, and I felt like going out. Just for the ride, you might say.

HOWARD (*barely interested*) Don't say.

WILLY Oh, yeah, my father lived many years in Alaska. He was an adventurous man. We've got quite a little streak of self-reliance in our family. I thought I'd go out with my older brother and try to locate him, and maybe settle in the North with the old man. And I was almost decided to go, when I met a salesman in the Parker House. His name was Dave Singleman. And he was eighty-four years old, and he'd drummed merchandise in thirty-one states. And old Dave, he'd go up to his room, y'understand, put on his green velvet slippers—I'll never forget—and pick up his phone and call the buyers, and without ever leaving his room, at the age of eighty-four, he made his living. And when I saw that, I realized that selling was the greatest career a man could want. 'Cause what could be more satisfying than to be able to go, at the age of eighty-four, into twenty or thirty different cities, and pick up a phone, and be remembered and loved and helped by so many different people? Do you know? when he died—and by the way he died the death of a salesman, in his green velvet slippers in the smoker of the New York, New Haven and Hartford, gong into Boston—when he died, hundreds of salesmen and buyers were at his funeral. Things were sad on a lotta trains for months after that. (*He stands up. Howard has not looked at him.*) In those days there was personality in it, Howard. There was respect, and comradeship, and gratitude in it. Today, it's all cut and dried, and there's no chance for bringing friendship to bear—or personality. You see what I mean? They don't know me any more.

HOWARD (*moving away, to the right*) That's just the thing, Willy.

WILLY If I had forty dollars a week—that's all I need. Forty dollars, Howard.

HOWARD Kid, I can't take blood from a stone, I—

WILLY (*desperation is on him now*) Howard, the year Al Smith was nominated, your father came to me and—

HOWARD (*starting to go off*) I've got to see some people, kid.

WILLY (*stopping him*) I'm talking about your father! There were promises made across this desk! You mustn't tell me you've got people to see—I put thirty-four years into this firm, Howard, and now I can't pay my insurance! You can't eat the orange and throw the peel away—a man is not a piece of fruit! (*After a pause*) Now pay attention. Your father—in 1928 I had a big year. I averaged a hundred and seventy dollars a week in commissions.

HOWARD (*impatiently*) Now, Willy, you never averaged—

WILLY (*banging his hand on the desk*) I averaged a hundred and seventy dollars a week in the year of 1928! And your father came to me—or rather, I was in the office here—it was right over this desk—and he put his hand on my shoulder—

HOWARD (*getting up*) You'll have to excuse me, Willy, I gotta see some people. Pull yourself together. *Going out:* I'll be back in a little while.

(*On Howard's exit, the light on his chair grows very bright and strange.*)

WILLY Pull myself together! What the hell did I say to him? My God, I was yelling at him! How could I! (*Willy breaks off, staring at the light, which occupies the chair, animating it. He approaches this chair, standing across the desk from it.*) Frank, Frank, don't you remember what you told me that time? How you put your hand on my shoulder, and Frank . . . (*He leans on the desk and as he speaks the dead man's name he accidentally switches on the recorder, and instantly*)

HOWARD'S SON "... of New York is Albany. The capital of Ohio is Cincinnati, the capital of Rhode Island is . . ." (*The recitation continues.*)

WILLY (*leaping away with fright, shouting*) Ha! Howard! Howard! Howard!

HOWARD (*rushing in*) What happened?

WILLY (*pointing at the machine, which continues nasally, childishly, with the capital cities*) Shut it off! Shut it off!

HOWARD (*pulling the plug out*) Look, Willy . . .

WILLY (*pressing his hands to his eyes*) I gotta get myself some coffee. I'll get some coffee . . .

(*Willy starts to walk out. Howard stops him.*)

HOWARD (*rolling up the cord*) Willy, look . . .

WILLY I'll go to Boston.

HOWARD Willy, you can't go to Boston for us.

WILLY Why can't I go?

HOWARD I don't want you to represent us. I've been meaning to tell you for a long time now.

WILLY Howard, are you firing me?

HOWARD I think you need a good long rest, Willy.

WILLY Howard—

HOWARD And when you feel better, come back, and we'll see if we can work something out.

WILLY But I gotta earn money, Howard. I'm in no position to—

HOWARD Where are your sons? Why don't your sons give you a hand?

WILLY They're working on a very big deal.

HOWARD This is no time for false pride, Willy. You go to your sons and you tell them that you're tired. You've got two great boys, haven't you?

WILLY Oh, no question, no question, but in the meantime . . .

HOWARD Then that's that. heh?

WILLY All right, I'll go to Boston tomorrow.

HOWARD No, no.

WILLY I can't throw myself on my sons. I'm not a cripple!

HOWARD Look, kid, I'm busy this morning.

WILLY (*grasping Howard's arm:*) Howard, you've got to let me go to Boston!

HOWARD (*hard, keeping himself under control:*) I've got a line of people to see this morning. Sit down, take five minutes, and pull yourself together, and then go home, will ya? I need the office, Willy. (*He starts to go, turns, remembering the recorder, starts to push off the table holding the recorder.*) Oh, yeah. Whenever you can this week, stop by and drop off the samples. You'll feel better, Willy, and then come back and we'll talk. Pull yourself together, kid, there's people outside.

(*Howard exits, pushing the table off left. Willy stares into space, exhausted.*)

Tennessee Williams
A Streetcar Named Desire

Tennessee Williams (1911–1983) first won recognition as a leading American playwright when *The Glass Menagerie* opened in New York in 1944. Three years later, Williams won the Pulitzer Prize for drama for his play *A Streetcar Named Desire.* The play, set in New Orleans, describes the moral and emotional demise of the former southern belle, Blanche DuBois. Although she still takes on airs as a femme fatale, Blanche's delusions are made painfully evident to the audience through the character of her brother-in-law, Stanley Kowalski, who is a new breed of southern male and in the prime of his life as a lover, a factory worker, and a brawler. For Williams, the brutal Stanley represents the new South, where gentility is dead.

Blanche had been an English teacher in Laurel, Mississippi, where she had married a tortured, young man who committed suicide when she discovered his homosexuality. Blanche then suffered an emotional collapse as she entered into a series of illicit sexual relationships for which she incurred the wrath of the Laurel community. Forced to leave her teaching position in Laurel, she arrives in New Orleans to stay with Stanley and her sister, Stella, who live in a lower level two-room apartment. Their friends, Eunice and Steve, live upstairs. In the following excerpt (with blues music in the background from the bar around the corner), Blanche tells Stella that their ancestral plantation, Belle Reve, has been lost.

BLANCHE (*in an uneasy rush*) I haven't asked you the things you probably thought I was going to ask. And so I'll expect you to be understanding about what *I* have to tell *you.*

STELLA What, Blanche? (*Her face turns anxious.*)

BLANCHE Well, Stella—you're going to reproach me, I know that you're bound to reproach me—but before you do—take into consideration—you left! I stayed and struggled! You came to New Orleans and looked out for yourself. *I* stayed at *Belle Reve* and tried to hold it together! I'm not meaning this in any reproachful way, but *all* the burden descended on *my* shoulders.

STELLA The best I could do was make my own living, Blanche.

(*Blanche begins to shake again with intensity*)

BLANCHE I know, I know. But you are the one that abandoned Belle Reve, not I! I stayed and fought for it, bled for it, almost died for it!

STELLA Stop this hysterical outburst and tell me what's happened? What do you mean fought and bled? What kind of—

BLANCHE I knew you would, Stella. I knew you would take this attitude about it!

STELLA About—what?—please!

BLANCHE (*slowly*) The loss—the loss . . .

STELLA Belle Reve? Lost, is it? No!

BLANCHE Yes. Stella.

(*They stare at each other across the yellow-checked linoleum of the table. Blanche slowly nods her head and Stella looks slowly down at her hands folded on the table. The music of the "blue piano" grows louder. Blanche touches her handkerchief to her forehead.)*

STELLA But how did it go? What happened?

BLANCHE *(springing up)* You're a fine one to ask me how it went!

STELLA Blanche!

BLANCHE You're a fine one to sit there *accusing me* of it!

STELLA *Blanche!*

BLANCHE I, I, *I* took the blows in my face and my body! All of those deaths! The long parade to the graveyard! Father, mother! Margaret, that dreadful way! So big with it, it couldn't be put in a coffin! But had to be burned like rubbish! You just came home in time for the funerals, Stella. And funerals are pretty compared to deaths. Funerals are quiet, but deaths—not always. Sometimes their breathing is hoarse, and sometimes it rattles, and sometimes they even cry out to you, "Don't let me go!" Even the old, sometimes, say, "Don't let me go." As if you were able to stop them! But funerals are quiet, with pretty flowers. And, oh, what gorgeous boxes they pack them away in! Unless you were there at the bed when they cried out, "Hold me!" you'd never suspect there was the struggle for breath and bleeding. You didn't dream, but I saw! *Saw! Saw!* And now you sit there telling me with your eyes that I let the place go! How in hell do you think all that sickness and dying was paid for? Death is expensive, Miss Stella. And old Cousin Jessie's right after Margaret's, hers! Why, the Grim Reaper had put up his tent on our doorstep! . . . Stella. Belle Reve was his headquarters! Honey—that's how it slipped through my fingers! Which of them left us a fortune? Which of them left a cent of insurance even? Only poor Jessie—one hundred to pay for her coffin. That was all, Stella! And I with my pitiful salary at the school. Yes, accuse me! Sit there and stare at me, thinking I let the place go! *I* let the place go? Where were *you!* In bed with your—Polack!

STELLA *(springing)* Blanche! You be still! That's enough! *(She starts out.)*

Blanche feigns dignity and position in front of Stanley, but he sees right through her pretensions and ridicules her. One night Stanley and his friends are drinking at a poker party at his place. One of them, Mitch, is attracted to Blanche, and they begin to talk. When Blanche tunes in some music on the radio Stanley becomes enraged, throws the radio out the window, and beats Stella, who is pregnant.

(Stanley stalks fiercely through the portieres into the bedroom. He crosses to the small white radio and snatches it off the table. With a shouted oath, he tosses the instrument out the window.)

STELLA *Drunk—drunk—animal thing, you!* *(She rushes through to the poker table)* All of you—please go home! If any of you have one spark of decency in you—

BLANCHE *(wildly)* Stella, watch out, he's—
    (Stanley charges after Stella.)

MEN *(feebly)* Take it easy, Stanley. Easy, fellow.—Let's all—

STELLA You lay your hands on me and I'll—
    (She backs out of sight. He advances and disappears. There is the sound of a blow. Stella cries out. Blanche screams and runs into the kitchen. The men rush forward and there is grappling and cursing. Something is overturned with a crash.)

BLANCHE *(shrilly)* My sister is going to have a baby!

MITCH This is terrible.

BLANCHE Lunacy, absolute lunacy!

MITCH Get him in here, men.
    (Stanley is forced, pinioned by the two men, into the bedroom. He nearly throws them off. Then all at once he subsides and is limp in their grasp.)
    (They speak quietly and lovingly to him and he leans his face on one of their shoulders.)

STELLA *(in a high, unnatural voice, out of sight)* I want to go away, I want to go away!

MITCH Poker shouldn't be played in a house with women.
    (Blanche rushes into the bedroom.)

BLANCHE I want my sister's clothes! We'll go to that woman's upstairs!

MITCH Where is the clothes?

BLANCHE *(opening the closet)* I've got them! *(She rushes through to Stella)* Stella, Stella, precious! Dear, dear little sister, don't be afraid!
    (With her arm around Stella, Blanche guides her to the outside door and upstairs.)

STANLEY *(dully)* What's the matter, what's happened?

MITCH You just blew your top, Stan.

PABLO He's okay, now.

STEVE Sure, my boy's okay!

MITCH Put him on the bed and get a wet towel.

PABLO I think coffee would do him a world of good, now.

STANLEY *(thickly)* I want water.

MITCH Put him under the shower!
    (The men talk quietly as they lead him to the bathroom.)

STANLEY Let the rut go of me, you sons of bitches!
    (Sounds of blows are heard. The water goes on full tilt.)

STEVE Let's get quick out of here!
> (*They rush to the poker table and sweep up their winnings on their way out.*)

MITCH (*sadly but firmly*) Poker should not be played in a house with women.

(*The door closes on them and the place is still. The Negro entertainers in the bar around the corner play "Paper Doll" slow and blue. After a moment Stanley comes out of the bathroom dripping water and still in his clinging wet polka dot drawers.*)

STANLEY Stella! (*There is a pause*) My baby doll's left me!
> (*He breaks into sobs. Then he goes to the phone and dials, still shuddering with sobs.*)

Eunice? I want my baby. (*He waits a moment; then he hangs up and dials again*) Eunice! I'll keep on ringin' until I talk with my baby!

(*An indistinguishable shrill voice is heard. He hurls phone to floor. Dissonant brass and piano sounds as the rooms dim out to darkness and the outer walls appear in the night light. The "blue piano" plays for a brief interval.*)

(*Finally, Stanley stumbles half dressed out to the porch and down the wooden steps to the pavement before the building. There he throws back his head like a baying hound and bellows his wife's name: "Stella! Stella, sweetheart! Stella!"*)

STANLEY Stell-*lahhhhh!*

EUNICE (*calling down from the door of her upper apartment*) Quit that howling out there an' go back to bed!

STANLEY I want my baby down here. Stella, Stella!

EUNICE She ain't comin' down so you quit! Or you'll git th' law on you!

STANLEY Stella!

EUNICE You can't beat on a woman an' then call 'er back! She won't come! And her goin' t' have a baby! . . . You stinker! You whelp of a Polack, you! I hope they do haul you in and turn the fire hose on you, same as the last time!

STANLEY (*humbly*) Eunice, I want my girl to come down with me!

EUNICE Hah! (*She slams her door.*)

STANLEY (*with heaven-splitting violence*) STELL-*LAHHHHH!*
> (*The low-tone clarinet moans. The door upstairs opens again. Stella slips down the rickety stairs in her robe. Her eyes are glistening with tears and her hair loose about her throat and shoulders. They stare at each other. Then they come together with low, animal moans. He falls to his knees on the steps and presses his face to her belly, curving a little with maternity. Her eyes go blind with tenderness as she catches his head and raises him level with her. He snatches the screen door open and lifts her off her feet and bears her into the dark flat.*)
> (*Blanche comes out on the upper landing in her robe and slips fearfully down the steps.*)

BLANCHE Where is my little sister? Stella? Stella?
> (*She stops before the dark entrance of her sister's flat. Then catches her breath as if struck. She rushes down to the walk before the house. She looks right and left as if for a sanctuary.*)
> (*The music fades away, Mitch appears from around the corner.*)

MITCH Miss DuBois?

BLANCHE Oh!

MITCH All quiet on the Potomac now?

BLANCHE She ran downstairs and went back in there with him.

MITCH Sure she did.

BLANCHE I'm terrified!

MITCH Ho-ho! There's nothing to be scared of. They're crazy about each other.

BLANCHE I'm not used to such—

MITCH Naw, it's a shame this had to happen when you just got here. But don't take it serious.

BLANCHE Violence! Is so—

MITCH Set down on the steps and have a cigarette with me.

BLANCHE I'm not properly dressed.

MITCH That don't make no difference in the Quarter.

BLANCHE Such a pretty silver case.

MITCH I showed you the inscription, didn't I?

BLANCHE Yes (*During the pause, she looks up at the sky*) There's so much—so much confusion in the world . . . (*He coughs diffidently*) Thank you for being so kind! I need kindness now.

The next day, Blanche tries to talk Stella into leaving Stanley, but Stella protests that she loves him. Blanche, not aware that he is secretly listening, mocks Stanley in the following excerpt.

BLANCHE Stella, I can't live with him! You can, he's your husband. But how could I stay here with him, after last night, with just those curtains between us?

STELLA Blanche, you saw him at his worst last night.

BLANCHE On the contrary, I saw him at his best! What such a man has to offer is animal force and he gave a wonderful exhibition of that! But the only way to live with such a man is to—go to bed with him! And that's your job—not mine!

STELLA After you've rested a little, you'll see it's going to work out. You don't have to worry about anything while you're here. I mean—expenses . . .

BLANCHE I have to plan for us both, to get us both—out!

STELLA You take it for granted that I am in something that I want to get out of.

BLANCHE I take it for granted that you still have sufficient memory of Belle Reve to find this place and these poker players impossible to live with.

STELLA Well, you're taking entirely too much for granted.

BLANCHE I can't believe you're in earnest.

STELLA No?

BLANCHE I understand how it happened—a little. You saw him in uniform, an officer, not here but—

STELLA I'm not sure it would have made any difference where I saw him.

BLANCHE Now don't say it was one of those mysterious electric things between people! If you do I'll laugh in your face.

STELLA I am not going to say anything more at all about it!

BLANCHE All right, then, don't!

STELLA But there are things that happen between a man and a woman in the dark—that sort of make everything else seem—unimportant. (*Pause.*)

BLANCHE What you are talking about is brutal desire—just—Desire!—the name of that rattle-trap street-car that bangs through the Quarter, up one old narrow street and down another . . .

STELLA Haven't you ever ridden on that street-car?

BLANCHE It brought me here.—Where I'm not wanted and where I'm ashamed to be . . .

STELLA Then don't you think your superior attitude is a bit out of place?

BLANCHE I am not being or feeling at all superior, Stella. Believe me I'm not! It's just this. This is how I look at it. A man like that is someone to go out with—once—twice—three times when the devil is in you. But live with? Have a child by?

STELLA I have told you I love him.

BLANCHE Then I *tremble* for you! I just—*tremble* for you. . . .

STELLA I can't help your trembling if you insist on trembling! (*There is a pause.*)

BLANCHE May I—speak—*plainly?*

STELLA Yes, do. Go ahead. As plainly as you want to.
(*Outside, a train approaches. They are silent till the noise subsides. They are both in the bedroom.*

(*Under cover of the train's noise Stanley enters from outside. He stands unseen by the women, holding some packages in his arms, and overhears their following conversation. He wears an undershirt and grease-stained seersucker pants.*)

BLANCHE Well—if you'll forgive me—he's *common!*

STELLA Why, yes, I suppose he is.

BLANCHE Suppose! You can't have forgotten that much of our bringing up, Stella, that you just *suppose* that any part of a gentleman's in his nature! *Not one particle, no!* Oh, if he was just—*ordinary!* Just *plain*—but good and wholesome, but—*no.* There's something downright—*bestial* about him! You're hating me saying this, aren't you?

STELLA (*coldly*) Go on and say it all, Blanche.

BLANCHE He acts like an animal, has an animal's habits! Eats like one, moves like one, talks like one! There's even something—sub-human—something not quite to the stage of humanity yet! Yes, something—ape-like about him, like one of those pictures I've seen in—anthropological studies! Thousands and thousands of years have passed him right by, and there he is—Stanley Kowalski—survivor of the stone age! Bearing the raw meat home from the kill in the jungle! And you—*you* here—*waiting* for him! Maybe he'll strike you or maybe grunt and kiss you! That is, if kisses have been discovered yet! Night falls and the other apes gather! There in the front of the cave, all grunting like him, and swilling and gnawing and hulking! His poker night!—you call it—this party of apes! Somebody growls—some creature snatches at something—the fight is on! *God!* Maybe we are a long way from being made in God's image, but Stella—my sister—there, has been *some* progress since then! Such things as art—as poetry and music—such kinds of new light have come into the world since then! In some kinds of people some tenderer feelings have had some little beginning! That we have got to make *grow!* And *cling* to, and hold as our flag! In this dark march toward whatever it is we're approaching. . . . *Don't—don't hang back with the brutes!*
(*Another train passes outside. Stanley hesitates, licking his lips. Then suddenly he turns stealthily about and withdraws through front door. The women are still unaware of his presence. When the train has passed he calls through the closed front door.*)

STANLEY Hey! Hey, Stella!

STELLA (*who has listened gravely to Blanche*) Stanley!

BLANCHE Stell, I—
(*But Stella has gone to the front door. Stanley enters casually with his packages.*)

STANLEY Hiyuh, Stella. Blanche back?

STELLA Yes, she's back.

STANLEY Hiyuh, Blanche. (*He grins at her.*)

STELLA You must've got under the car.

STANLEY Them darn mechanics at Fritz's don't know their ass fr'm—Hey!

> (*Stella has embraced him with both arms, fiercely, and full in the view of Blanche. He laughs and clasps her head to him. Over her head he grins through the curtains at Blanche.*)
> (*As the lights fade away, with a lingering brightness on their embrace, the music of the "blue piano" and trumpet and drums is heard.*)

A few weeks later, it is Blanche's birthday. Stella is preparing dinner for herself, Stanley, Blanche, and Mitch. In the following excerpt, Stanley has arrived to tell Stella that he has learned about Blanche's past in Laurel.

STANLEY Set down! I've got th' dope on your big sister, Stella.

STELLA Stanley, stop picking on Blanche.

STANLEY That girl calls *me* common!

STELLA Lately you been doing all you can think of to rub her the wrong way, Stanley, and Blanche is sensitive and you've got to realize that Blanche and I grew up under very different circumstances than you did.

STANLEY So I been told. And told and told and told! You know she's been feeding us a pack of lies here?

STELLA No, I don't, and—

STANLEY Well, she has, however. But now the cat's out of the bag! I found out some things!

STELLA What—things?

STANLEY Things I already suspected. But now I got proof from the most reliable sources—which I have checked on!
(*Blanche is singing in the bathroom a saccharine popular ballad which is used contrapuntally with Stanley's speech.*)

STELLA (*to Stanley*) Lower your voice!

STANLEY Some canary-bird, huh!

STELLA Now please tell me quietly what you think you've found out about my sister.

STANLEY Lie Number One: All this squeamishness she puts on! You should just know the line she's been feeding to Mitch. He thought she had never been more than kissed by a fellow! But sister Blanche is no lily! Ha-ha! Some lily she is!

STELLA What have you heard and who from?

STANLEY Our supply-man down at the plant has been going through Laurel for years and be knows all about her and everybody else in the town of Laurel knows all about her. She is as famous in Laurel as if she was the President of the United States, only she is not respected by any party! This supply-man stops at a hotel called the Flamingo.

BLANCHE (*singing blithely*) "Say it's only a paper moon, Sailing over a cardboard sea—But it wouldn't be make-believe If you believed in me!"

STELLA What about the—Flamingo?

STANLEY She stayed there, too.

STELLA My sister lived at Belle Reve.

STANLEY This is after the home-place had slipped through her lily-white fingers! She moved to the Flamingo! A second-class hotel which has the advantage of not interfering in the private social life of the personalities there! The Flamingo is used to all kinds of goings-on. But even the management of the Flamingo was impressed by Dame Blanche! In fact they were so impressed by Dame Blanche that they requested her to turn in her room-key—for permanently! This happened a couple of weeks before she showed here.

BLANCHE (*singing*) "It's a Barnum and Bailey world, Just as phony as it can be—
But it wouldn't be make-believe If you believed in me!"

STELLA What—contemptible—lies!

STANLEY Sure, I can see how you would be upset by this. She pulled the wool over your eyes as much as Mitch's!

STELLA It's pure invention! There's not a word of truth in it and if I were a man and this creature had dared to invent such things in my presence—

BLANCHE (*singing*) "Without your love,
It's a honky-tonk parade!
Without your love,
It's a melody played in a penny arcade . . ."

STANLEY Honey, I told you I thoroughly checked on these stories! Now wait till I finish. The trouble with Dame Blanche was that she couldn't put on her act any more in Laurel! They got wised up after two or three dates with her and then they quit, and she goes on to another, the same old line, same old act, same old hooey! But the town was too small for this to go on forever! And as time went by she became a town character. Regarded as not just different but downright loco—nuts.

(*Stella draws back.*)
And for the last year or two she has been washed up like poison. That's why she's here this summer, visiting royalty, putting on all this act—because she's practically told by

the mayor to get out of town! Yes, did you know there was an army camp near Laurel and your sister's was one of the places called "Out-of-Bounds"?

BLANCHE "It's only a paper moon, Just as phony as it can be—But it wouldn't be make-believe If you believed in me!"

STANLEY Well, so much for being such a refined and particular type of girl. Which brings us to Lie Number Two.

STELLA I don't want to hear any more!

STANLEY She's not going back to teach school! In fact I am willing to bet you that she never had no idea of returning to Laurel! She didn't resign temporarily from the high school because of her nerves! No, siree, Bob! She didn't. They kicked her out of that high school before the spring term ended—and I hate to tell you the reason that step was taken! A seventeen-year-old boy—she'd gotten mixed up with!

BLANCHE "Its a Barnum and Bailey world, Just as phony as it can be—"

(In the bathroom the water goes on loud; little breathless cries and peals of laughter are heard as if a child were frolicking in the tub.)

STELLA This is making me—sick!

STANLEY The boy's dad learned about it and got in touch with the high school superintendent. Boy, oh, boy. I'd like to have been in that office when Dame Blanche was called on the carpet! I'd like to have seen her trying to squirm out of that one! But they had her on the hook good and proper that time and she knew that the jig was all up! They told her she better move on to some fresh was territory. Yep, it was practickly a town ordinance passed against her!

Blanche does not know that Stanley has told Mitch everything that he has learned about her past, and when Mitch does not come to dinner, Blanche tries, unsuccessfully, to reach him on the telephone. In the following excerpt, Blanche, who has just taken a long hot bath, wonders why Mitch has not arrived.

BLANCHE *(she pauses reflectively for a moment)* I shouldn't have called him.

STELLA There's lots of things could have happened.

BLANCHE There's no excuse for it, Stella. I don't have to put up with insults. I won't be taken for granted.

STANLEY Goddam, it's hot in here with the steam from the bathroom.

BLANCHE I've said I was sorry three times. *(The piano fades out.)* I take hot baths for my nerves. Hydro-therapy, they

call it. You healthy Polack, without a nerve in your body, of course you don't know what anxiety feels like!

STANLEY I am not a Polack. People from Poland are Poles, not Polacks. But what I am is a one hundred percent American, born and raised in the greatest country on earth and proud as hell of it, so don't ever call me a Polack.
(The phone rings. Blanche rises expectantly.)

BLANCHE Oh, that's for me, I'm sure.

STANLEY *I'm* not sure. Keep your seat *(He crosses leisurely to phone.)* H'lo. Aw, yeh, hello, Mac.
(He leans against wall, staring insultingly in at Blanche. She sinks back in her chair with a frightened look. Stella leans over and touches her shoulder.)

BLANCHE Oh, keep your hands off me, Stella. What is the matter with you? Why do you look at me with that pitying look?

STANLEY *(bawling)* QUIET IN THERE!—We've got a noisy woman on the place.—Go on, Mac. At Riley's? No, I don't wanta bowl at Riley's. I had a little trouble with Riley last week. I'm the team-captain, ain't I? All right, then, we're not gonna bowl at Riley's, we're gonna bowl at the West Side or the Gala! All right, Mac. See you!
(He hangs up and returns to the table. Blanche fiercely controls herself, drinking quickly from her tumbler of water. He doesn't look at her but reaches in a pocket. Then he speaks slowly and with false amiability.)
Sister Blanche, I've got a little birthday remembrance for you.

BLANCHE Oh, have you, Stanley? I wasn't expecting any, I—I don't know why Stella wants to observe my birthday! I'd much rather forget it—when you—reach twenty-seven! Well—age is a subject that you'd prefer to—ignore!

STANLEY Twenty-seven?

BLANCHE *(quickly)* What is it? Is it for me?
(He is holding a little envelope toward her.)

STANLEY Yes, I hope you like it!

BLANCHE Why, why—Why, it's a—

STANLEY Ticket! Back to Laurel! On the Greyhound! Tuesday!
(The Varsouviana music steals in softly and continues playing. Stella rises abruptly and turns her back. Blanche tries to smile. Then she tries to laugh. Then she gives both up and springs from the table and runs into the next room. She clutches her throat and then runs into the bathroom. Coughing, gagging sounds are heard.)
Well!

STELLA You didn't need to do that.

STANLEY Don't forget all that I took off her.

STELLA You needn't have been so cruel to someone alone as she is.

STANLEY Delicate piece she is.

STELLA She is. She was. You didn't know Blanche as a girl. Nobody, nobody, was tender and trusting as she was. But people like you abused her, and forced her to change.
(He crosses into the bedroom, ripping off his shirt, and changes into a brilliant silk bowling shirt. She follows him.)
Do you think you're going bowling now?

STANLEY Sure.

STELLA You're not going bowling. *(She catches hold of his shirt)* Why did you do this to her?

STANLEY I done nothing to no one. Let go of my shirt. You've torn it.

STELLA I want to know why. Tell me why.

STANLEY When we first met, me and you, you thought I was common. How right you was, baby. I was common as dirt. You showed me the snapshot of the place with the columns. I pulled you down off them columns and how you loved it, having them colored lights going! And wasn't we happy together, wasn't it all okay till she showed here?
(Stella makes a slight movement. Her look goes suddenly inward as if some interior voice had called her name. She begins a slow, shuf-

fling progress from the bedroom to the kitchen, leaning and resting on the back of the chair and then on the edge of a table with a blind look and listening expression. Stanley, finishing with his shirt, is unaware of her reaction.)
And wasn't we happy together? Wasn't it all okay? Till she showed here. Hoity-toity, describing me as an ape. *(He suddenly notices the change in Stella)* Hey, what is it, Stella?
(He crosses to her.)

STELLA *(quietly)* Take me to the hospital.
(He is with her now, supporting her with his arm, murmuring indistinguishably as they go outside.)

When Stanley returns from the hospital later that night, he finds Blanche drunk. He informs her that the baby has not yet been born and won't come until morning. She tells him that she will be leaving to join a former boyfriend, Shep Huntleigh, who is now a millionaire. Stanley, knowing that this is a fabrication, mocks her, and refuses to get out of her way when she wants to walk by him. Blanche smashes a bottle and threatens to cut him with it. Stanley then rapes her.

Some time later, in the final scene, Blanche believes that she is about to leave with her millionaire. In reality, however, a doctor arrives and takes her away to an insane asylum as Stella, with the baby in her arms, sobs, while Stanley comforts her.

6 Jewish-American Writers: The Centricity of Moral Values

Even a partial listing demonstrates that since World War II Jewish-American writers have become a major force in American fiction: Arthur Miller, Saul Bellow, Bernard Malamud, Joseph Heller, Norman Mailer, Philip Roth, Cynthia Ozick, E. L. Doctorow, Herman Wouk. Some critics hold that Jewish writers do not constitute a separate category, that these writers are simply Americans of Jewish descent. Other critics hold that for many of these writers "Jewishness" was a formative experience that had a profound influence on their literary productions. Many Jewish-American writers reveal a compassion for the sufferer, a commitment to moral values, and a plea for social justice that reflect both prophetic morality and an awareness of the Jewish people's tragic history. Regardless of their commitment to Judaism, in raising and struggling to answer the question—What does it mean to be human?—they draw on thoughts and feelings that are deeply embedded in Jewish tradition.

Bernard Malamud
The Fixer

The popularity of Bernard Malamud (1914–1986) rests largely on *The Natural* (1952), a baseball fantasy that was made into a successful movie starring Robert Redford. However, in several of his other works, particularly *The Assistant* (1957) and *The Fixer* (1966), which won the National Book Award and the Pulitzer Prize, Jewish concerns are evident. Malamud used an actual event as the basis for *The Fixer.* In 1913, Mendel Beilis, a dispatcher at a factory in the Ukraine owned by a Jew, was accused of torturing and killing a young Christian boy in order to use his blood for a Jewish ritual. Malamud used the case to depict the virulence and irrationality of historic anti-Semitism and the grief and humiliation it inflicted on innocent Jews.

During the Middle Ages, Jews, who were seen as agents of Satan conspiring to destroy Christendom and as sorcerers employing black magic against Christians, were also accused of ritual murder: It was claimed that Jews, requiring Christian blood for baking matzoh used at Passover, sacrificed a Christian child and drained its blood. Despite the vehement denials of Jews and the protests of some enlightened Christian leaders, these vile and libelous accusations persisted, resulting in the torture, trial, murder, and expulsion of many Jews. Allegations of ritual murder and accompanying trials endured into the twentieth century (the libel is still widely circulated in the Muslim world) to the consternation and anger of enlightened people who regarded the charge as so much nonsense, a lingering medieval fabrication and superstition. (Into the early twentieth century, however, staunchly conservative Catholic clergy and publications insisted that the charge was true.)

In the Beilis case, evidence collected by the Russian police pointed to a gang of thieves as the likely murderers; apparently the boy had threatened to report their criminal activities to the authorities. Pressure by anti-Semitic officials within the tsar's government demanded a ritual murder trial, hoping to deflect attention away from the failures of the tsarist regime. These officials were supported by reactionary Russian nationalists and clerics who routinely circulated anti-Semitic literature and promoted pogroms, violent attacks against Jewish communities. Ultimately, the jury found Beilis not guilty.

Yakov Bok, the central character in *The Fixer,* was a simple repairman who seized an opportunity to manage a factory for a Russian gentile who was grateful to Yakov for helping him home after he had passed out in the snow in a drunken stupor. Yakov did not tell his anti-Semitic employer that he was Jewish and broke the law by living outside the Pale, the area in which Russian Jews were confined. When the young boy is found dead, several people, who now know Yakov is Jewish, fabricate a tale of ritual murder. The prosecuting attorney knows he is innocent, but driven by anti-Semitic hatred confines him to prison for more than two years while delaying an indictment. Placed in solitary confinement, Yakov endures numerous tortures and humiliations inflicted on him by the warden and guards.

At Beilis' actual trial, the prosecution provided a Catholic priest, Justin Pranaitis, as an expert witness. Two decades earlier, Pranaitis had published a pamphlet arguing that ritual murder was an integral part of Jewish tradition. At the trial, Pranaitis maintained that his awareness of Jewish wickedness derived from his deep familiarity with Jewish beliefs, including the Talmud, rabbinical commentary on Jewish law. The defense exposed the priest as a complete fraud who, in reality, was totally ignorant of the Talmud. It was as if someone claiming to be an expert in American history had never heard of the Civil War and thought that Pearl Harbor was a woman. In the following passage, from *The Fixer,* an Orthodox priest, whom the prosecution intends to call upon as an expert witness, tells Russian officials in the presence of Yakov that "ritual murder is meant to reenact the crucifixion of our dear Lord." Like Pranaitis, the priest is consumed by hatred and merely repeats ancient lies and calumnies.

"My dear children," said the priest to the Russians, wringing his dry hands, "if the bowels of the earth were to open to reveal the population of human dead since the beginning of the world, you would be astonished to see how many innocent Christian children among them have been tortured to death by Christ-hating Jews. Throughout the ages, as described in their holy books and various commentaries, the voice of Semitic blood directs them to desecrations, unspeakable horrors—for example, the Talmud, which likens blood to water and milk, and preaches hatred of gentiles, who are characterized as being not human, no more than animals. 'Thou shalt not kill' does not apply to us, for do not they also write in their books: 'Murder the good among gentiles'? This perfidy, too, is prescribed in their Kabbala, the book of Jewish magic and alchemy, wherein the name of Satan is invoked; hence there have been multitudes of slaughtered innocent children whose tears have not moved their murderers to mercy."

His eyes darted over the faces of the officials but no one moved.

"The ritual murder is meant to re-enact the crucifixion of our dear Lord. The murder of Christian children and the distribution of their blood among Jews are a token of their eternal enmity against Christendom, for in murdering the innocent Christian child, they repeat the martyrdom of Christ. Zhenia Golov, in the loss of his own warm blood, symbolizes to us our Lord's loss of his precious lifeblood, drop by cruel drop, as he hung in pain on the wooden cross to which the anti-Christ had nailed him. It is said that the murder of the gentile—any gentile—hastens the coming of their long-awaited Messiah. Elijah, for whom they eternally leave the door open but who has never, during all the ages since his first coming, bothered to accept the invitation to enter and sit in the empty chair. Since the destruction of their Temple in Jerusalem by the Legions of Titus there has been no sacrificial altar for animals in their synagogues, and it has come about, therefore, that the killing of gentiles, in particular innocent children, is accepted as a fitting substitute. Even their philosopher Maimonides, whose writings were suppressed in our country in 1844, orders Jews to murder Christian children. Did I not tell you they think of us as animals?

"In the recorded past," said Father Anastasy in his nasally musical voice, "the Jew has had many uses for Christian blood. He has used it for purposes of sorcery and witches' rituals, and for love potions and well poisoning, fabricating a deadly venom that spread the plague from one country to another, a mixture of Christian blood from a murdered victim, their own Jewish urine, the heads of poisonous snakes, and even the stolen mutilated host—the bleeding body of Christ himself. It is written that all Jews require some Christian blood for the prolongation of their lives else they die young. And in those days they considered our blood to be—this too is recorded—the most effective therapeutic for the cure of their diseases. They used it, according to their old medical books, to heal their women in childbirth, stop hemorrhages, cure the blindness of infants, and to alleviate the wounds of circumcision."

One of the Kiev police officials, Captain Korimzin, a man in a damp coat and muddy boots, secretly made the sign of the cross. Yakov felt faint. The priest, staring at him intently for a minute, went on, and although he spoke calmly his gestures were agitated. The Russians continued to listen with grave interest.

"There are those among us, my children, who will argue that these are superstitious tales of a past age, yet the truth of much I have revealed to you—I do not say it is all true— must be inferred from the very frequency of the accusations against the Jews. None can forever conceal the truth. If the bellman is dead the wind will toll the bell. Perhaps in this age of science we can no longer accept every statement of accusation made against this unfortunate people; however we must ask ourselves how much truth remains despite our reluctance to believe. I do not say that all Jews are guilty of these crimes and that pogroms should therefore be instituted against them, but that there are certain sects among them, in particular the Hasidim and their leaders, the tzadikim, who commit in secret crimes such as I have described to you, which the gentile world, despite its frequent experience with them, seems to forget until, lo! another poor child disappears and is found dead in this fashion: his hands tied behind his back, and his body punctured by a sharp weapon in several places, the number of wounds according to magic numbers: 3, 7, 9, 13, in the manner of such crimes of former times. We know that their Passover, though they ascribe to it other uses, is also a celebration of the crucifixion. We know that is the time they kidnap gentiles for their religious ceremonials. Here in our Holy City, during the Polovostian raids in the year 1100, the monk Eustratios was abducted from the Pechera Monastery and sold to the Jews of Kherson, who crucified him during Passover. Since they no longer dare such open crimes they celebrate the occasion by eating matzos and unleavened cakes at the Seder service. But even this act conceals a crime because the matzos and cakes contain the blood of our martyrs, though of course the tzadikim deny this. Thus through our blood in their Passover food they again consume the agonized body of the living Christ. I give you my word, my dear children, that this is the reason why Zhenia Golov, this innocent child who wished to enter the priesthood, was destroyed!"

The priest wiped one eye, then the other, with a white handkerchief. Two of the guards standing nearest the fixer edged away from him.

But then Yakov cried out, "It's all a fairy tale, every bit of it. Who could ever believe such a thing? Not me!" His voice quavered and his face was bloodless.

"Those who can understand will believe," said the priest. "Be respectful if you know what's good for you," Grubeshov said heatedly in an undertone. "Listen and learn!"

"How can it be so if the opposite is true," the fixer shouted, his throat thick. "It's all right to theorize with a fact or two but I don't recognize the truth in what's been said. If you please, your reverence, everybody knows the Bible forbids us to eat blood. That's all over the book, in the laws and everything. I've forgotten most of what I knew about the sacred books, but I've lived among the people and know their customs. Many an egg my own wife would throw out to the goat if it had the smallest spot of blood on the yolk 'Raisl,' I said, 'take it easy. We can't afford to live like kings,' but there was no getting the egg back on the table, either by hook or by crook, once she took it off, even admitting anyone wanted to, which I never did—you get used to the customs. What she did was final, your reverence. I never said, 'Bring back the bloody egg,' and she would have thrown it at me if I had. She also soaked for hours the little meat or chicken we ate, to wash out every fleck of blood, and then sprinkled it with salt so as to be sure she had drained out every last drop. The rinsings with water were endless. That's the truth of it, I swear. I swear I'm innocent of this crime you say I did, not you personally, your reverence, but some of the officials here. I'm not a Hasid and I'm not a tzadik. I'm a fixer by trade, it's a poorer trade than most, and formerly for a short time I was a soldier in the Imperial Army. In fact, to tell the whole truth, I'm not a religious man, I'm a free-thinker. At first my wife and I quarreled about this but I said a man's religion is his own business, and that's all there is to it, if you'll pardon me for saying so, your reverence. Anyway, I never touched that boy or any boy in my life. I was a boy myself once and it's a time I find hard to forget. I'm affectionate to children and I would have been a happy man if my wife had given birth to a child. It's not in my nature to do anything such as has been described, and if anyone thinks so it's mistaken identity for sure."

He had turned to the officials. They had listened courteously, even the two Black Hundreds representatives, though the shorter of them could not hide the distaste he felt for the fixer. The other now walked away. One man in a round cloth cap smiled sweetly at Yakov, then gazed impassively into the far distance where the golden cupolas of a cathedral rose above the trees.

"You'd be better off confessing," Grubeshov said, "instead of raising this useless stink." He asked the priest's pardon for his language.

"Confessing what, your honor, if as I told you I didn't do it? I can confess to you some things but I can't confess this crime. You'll have to excuse me there—I didn't do it. Why would I do such a thing anyway? You're mistaken, your honor. Somebody has made a serious mistake."

But no one would admit it and a heavy sadness settled on him.

"Confessing how it was done," Grubeshov replied. "How you enticed the boy into the stable with sweets, and then two or three of you pounced on him, gagged his mouth, tied him hand and foot, and dragged him up the stairs to your habitat. There you prayed over him with those black hats and robes on, undressed the frightened child, and began to stab him in certain places, twelve stabs first, then another making thirteen wounds—thirteen each in the region of the heart, on the neck, from which most of the blood is drawn, and on the face—according to your cabalistic books. You tormented and terrified him, enjoying the full shuddering terror of the child victim and his piteous pleas for mercy, in the meanwhile collecting his dripping lifeblood into bottles until you had bled him white. The five or six litres of warm blood you put into a black satchel, and this, if I understand the custom, was delivered by a hunchback Jew to the synagogue in time for making the matzos and afikomen. And when poor Zhenia Golov's heart was drained of blood and he lay on the floor lifeless, you and the tzadik Jew with the white stockings picked him up and carried him here in the dead of night and left his corpse in the cave. Then you both ate bread and salt so that his ghost would not haunt you and hurried away before the sun rose. Fearing the discovery of the bloodstains on your floor, you later sent one of your Jews to burn down Nikolai Maximovitch's stable. That is what you ought to confess."

The fixer, moaning, wrung his hands and beat them against his chest. He looked for Bibikov but the Investigating Magistrate and his assistant had disappeared.

"Take him up to the cave," Grubeshov ordered the guards.

Shutting his umbrella, he quickly preceded them, scampering up the steps, and entered the cave.

The leg chains were too short for Yakov to climb the steep steps, so he was seized under the arms by two of the gendarmes and dragged and pushed up, the other guards following directly behind. Then one guard went into the cave and the others shoved the fixer in through the narrow stone opening.

Inside the dank cave, smelling of death, in the dim light of a semicircle of dripping candles fastened on the wall, Grubeshov produced Yakov's tool sack.

"Aren't these your tools, Yakov Bok? They were found in your habitat in the stable by the driver Richter."

Yakov identified them in the candlelight.

"Yes, your honor, I've had them for years."

"Look at this rusty knife and these awls cleansed of blood with this rag, and now deny these instruments were used by you and your gang of Jews to perforate and bleed the body of a sweet and innocent Christian child!"

The fixer forced himself to look. He gazed at the gleaming point of the awl, and beyond it, into the depths of the cave which he now saw clearly, everyone present, among them Marfa Golov, her head wrapped in a black shawl, her wet eyes reflecting the candle lights, wailing on her knees at the bier of her Zhenia, disinterred from his grave for the occasion, lying naked in death, the wounds of his gray shrunken pitiful body visible in the light of two long thickly dripping white candles burning at his large head and small feet.

Yakov hastily counted the wounds on the child's bloated face, and cried out, "Fourteen!"

But the Prosecuting Attorney replied these were two magic groups of seven, and Father Anastasy, the stink of garlic rising from his head, fell on his knees and with a quiet moan began to pray.

Grubeshov, the prosecuting attorney who is a vicious anti-Semite, interviews Yakov in his cell.

"I have decided to send you to the preliminary confinement cell in the Kiev Prison to await your trial," Grubeshov said, blowing his nose and cleaning it slowly. "It is, of course, not easy to predict when it will begin, so I thought I would inquire whether you had become more cooperative? Since you have had time to reflect on your situation, perhaps you are now willing to tell the truth. What do you say? Further resistance will gain you only headaches. Cooperation will perhaps ease your situation."

"What else is there to say, your honor?" the fixer sighed sadly. "I've looked in my small bag of words and I have nothing more to say except that I'm innocent. There's no evidence against me, because I didn't do what you say I did."

"That's too bad. Your role in this murder was known to us before you were arrested. You were the only Jew living in the district, with the exceptions of Mandelbaum and Litvinov, Merchants of the First Guild, who weren't in Russia during the time of the commission of the crime, perhaps on purpose. We suspected a Jew at once because a Russian couldn't possibly commit that kind of crime. He might cut a man's throat in a fight, or suddenly kill a person with two or three heavy blows, but no Russian would maliciously torture an innocent child by inflicting forty-seven deadly wounds on his body."

"Neither would I," said the fixer. "It's not in my nature, whatever else is."

"The weight of the evidence is against you."

"Then maybe the evidence is wrong, your honor?"

"Evidence is evidence, it can't be wrong."

Grubeshov's voice became persuasive. "Tell me the honest truth, Yakov Bok, didn't the Jewish Nation put you up to this crime? You seem like a serious person—perhaps you were unwilling to do it but they urged it on you, made threats or promises of certain sorts, and you reluctantly carried out the murder for them? To put it in other words, wasn't it their idea rather than yours? If you'll admit that, I'll tell you frankly—I'll put it this way—your life would be easier. We will not prosecute to the full extent of our powers. Perhaps after a short while you will be paroled and your sentence suspended. In other words, there are 'possibilities.' All we ask is your signature—that's not so much."

Grubeshov's face glistened, as though he were making greater effort than was apparent.

"How could I do such a thing, your honor? I couldn't do such a thing. Why should I blame it on innocent people?"

"History has proved they are not so innocent. Besides I don't understand your false scruples. After all, you're an admitted freethinker, this admission occurred in my presence. The Jews mean very little to you. I size you up as a man who is out for himself, though I can't blame you. Come, here is an opportunity to free yourself from the confines of the net you have fallen into."

"If the Jews don't mean anything to me, then why am I here?"

"You are foolish to lend yourself to their evil aims. What have they done for you?"

"At the very least, your honor, they've let me alone. No, I couldn't sign such a thing."

"Then keep in mind that the consequences for you can be very grave. The sentence of the court will be the least of your worries."

"Please," said the fixer, breathing heavily, "do you really believe those stories about magicians stealing the blood out of a murdered Christian child to mix in with matzos? You are an educated man and would surely not believe such superstitions."

Grubeshov sat back, smiling slightly. "I believe you killed the boy Zhenia Golov for ritual purposes. When they know the true facts, all Russia will believe it. Do you believe it?" he asked the guards.

The guards swore they did.

"Of course we believe it," Grubeshov said. "A Jew is a Jew, and that's all there is to it. Their history and character are unchangeable. Their nature is constant. This has been proved in scientific studies by Gobineau, Chamberlain and others. We here in Russia are presently preparing one on Jewish facial characteristics. Our peasants have a saying that a man who steals wears a hat that burns. With a Jew it is the nose that burns and reveals the criminal he is."

He flipped open a notebook to a page of pen-and-ink sketches, turning the book so that Yakov could read the printing at the top of the page: "Jewish noses."

"Here, for instance, is yours." Grubeshov pointed to a thin high-bridged nose with slender nostrils.

"And this is yours," Yakov said hoarsely, pointing to a short, fleshy, broad-winged nose.

The Prosecuting Attorney, though his color had deepened, laughed thinly. "You are a witty man," he said, "but it won't do you any good. Your fate is foreseen. Ours is a humane society but there are ways of punishing hardened criminals. Perhaps I ought to remind you—to show you how well off you are—how your fellow Jews were executed in the not too distant past. They were hanged wearing caps full of hot pitch and with a dog hanging beside them to show the world how despised they were."

"A dog hangs a dog, your honor."

"If you can't bite don't show your teeth." Grubeshov, his neck inflamed, slashed the fixer across the jaw with a ruler. Yakov cried out as the wood snapped, one piece hitting the wall. The guards began to beat his head with their fists but the Prosecuting Attorney waved them away.

"You can cry to Bibikov[1] from now to doomsday," he shouted at the fixer, "but I'll keep you in prison till the flesh rots off your bones piece by piece. You will beg me to let you confess who compelled you to murder that innocent boy!"

Yakov's father-in-law, Shmuel, bribes the guard with forty rubles in order to speak with Yakov. The fixer, who has endured terrible suffering in prison while awaiting trial, reveals his innermost thoughts about God.

"Shmuel, I'm sorry for your forty rubles. It's a lot of money and what are you getting for it?"

"Money is nothing. I came to see you, but if it paves my way a foot into Paradise it's a fine investment."

"Run, Shmuel," the fixer said, agitated, "get out while you can or they'll shoot you in cold blood and call it a Jewish conspiracy. If that happens I'm doomed forever."

"I'm running," said Shmuel, cracking his knuckles against his bony chest, "but tell me first why they blame you for this terrible crime?"

"Why they blame me? Because I was a stupid ass. I worked for a Russian factory owner in a forbidden district. Also I lived there without telling him my papers were Jewish."

"You see, Yakov, what happens when you shave your beard and forget your God?"

"Don't talk to me about God," Yakov said bitterly. "I want no part of God. When you need him most he's farthest away. Enough is enough. My past I don't have to tell you, but if you knew what I've lived through since I saw you last." He began to say but his voice cracked.

"Yakov," said Shmuel, clasping and unclasping his excitable hands, "we're not Jews for nothing. Without God we can't live. Without the covenant we would have disappeared out of history. Let that be a lesson to you. He's all we have but who wants more?"

"Me. I'll take misery but not forever."

"For misery don't blame God. He gives the food but we cook it."

"I blame him for not existing. Or if he does it's on the moon or stars but not here. The thing is not to believe or the waiting becomes unbearable. I can't hear his voice and never have. I don't need him unless he appears."

"Who are you, Yakov, Moses himself? If you don't hear His voice so let Him hear yours. 'When prayers go up blessings descend.'"

"Scorpions descend, hail, fire, sharp rocks, excrement. For that I don't need God's help, the Russians are enough. All right, once I used to talk to him and answer myself, but what good does it do if I know so little in the first place? I used to mention once in a while the conditions of my life, my struggles, misfortunes, mistakes. On rare occasions I gave him a little good news, but whatever I said he never answered me. Silence I now give back."

"A proud man is deaf and blind. How can he hear God? How can he see Him?'"

"Who's proud if I ever was? What have I got to be proud of? That I was born without parents? I never made a decent living? My barren wife ran off with a goy? When a boy was murdered in Kiev, out of three million Jews in Russia they arrested me? So I'm not proud. If God exists I'll gladly listen to him. If he doesn't feel like talking let him open the door so I can walk out. I have nothing. From nothing you get nothing. If he wants from me he has to give first. If not a favor at least a sign."

"Don't ask for signs, ask for mercy."

"I've asked for everything and got nothing." The fixer, after a sigh, spoke close to the peephole. "'In the beginning was the word,' but it wasn't his. That's the way I look at it now. Nature invented itself and also man. Whatever was there was there to begin with. Spinoza said so. It sounds fantastic but it must be true. When it comes down to basic facts, either God is our invention and can't do anything about it, or he's a force in Nature but not in history. A force is not a father. He's cold wind and try and keep warm. To tell the truth, I've written him off as a dead loss."

"Yakov," said Shmuel, squeezing both hands, "don't talk so fast. Don't look for God in the wrong place, look in the Torah, the law. That's where to look, not in bad books that poison your thoughts."

"As for the law it was invented by man, is far from perfect, and what good is it to me if the Tsar has no use for it? If God can't give me simple respect I'll settle for justice. Uphold the Law! Destroy the Tsar with a thunderbolt! Free me from prison!"

"God's justice is for the end of time."

"I'm not so young any more, I can't wait that long. Neither can the Jews running from pogroms. We're dealing nowadays with the slaughter of large numbers and it's getting worse. God counts in astronomy but where men are con-

---

[1] A magistrate who knows that Yakov is being framed.

cerned all I know is one plus one. Shmuel, let's drop this useless subject. What's the sense of arguing through a little hole where you can barely see part of my face in the dark? Besides, it's a short visit and we're eating up time."

"Yakov," said Shmuel, "He invented light. He created the world. He made us both. The true miracle is belief. I believe in Him. Job said, 'Though he slay me, yet will I trust in Him.' He said more but that's enough."

"To win a lousy bet with the devil he killed off all the servants and innocent children of Job. For that alone I hate him, not to mention ten thousand pogroms. Ach, why do you make me talk fairy tales? Job is an invention and so is God. Let's let it go at that." He stared at the peddler with one eye. "I'm sorry I'm making you feel bad on your expensive time, Shmuel, but take my word for it, it's not easy to be a freethinker in this terrible cell. I say this without pride or joy. Still, whatever reason a man has, he's got to depend on."

"Yakov," said Shmuel, mopping his face with his blue handkerchief, "do me a favor, don't close your heart. No body is lost to God if his heart is open."

"What's left of my heart is pure rock."

"Also don't forget repentance," said Shmuel. "This comes first."

Zhitnyak appeared in a great hurry. "That's enough now, it's time to go. Ten minutes is up but you talked longer."

"It felt like two," Shmuel said. "I was just about to say what's on my heart."

"Run, Shmuel," Yakov urged, his mouth pressed to the peephole. "Do whatever you can to help me. Run to the newspapers and tell them the police have imprisoned an innocent man. Run to the rich Jews, to Rothschild if necessary. Ask for help, money, mercy, a good lawyer to defend me. Get me out of here before they lay me in my grave."

Shmuel pulled a cucumber out of his pants pocket. "Here's a little pickle I brought you." He attempted to thrust it through the spy hole but Zhitnyak grabbed it.

"None of that," the guard loudly whispered. "Don't try any Jew tricks on me. Also you shut up," he said to Yakov. "You've had your say and that's enough now."

He grabbed Shmuel by the arm. "Hurry up, it's getting towards morning."

"Goodbye, Yakov, remember, what I told you."

Saul Bellow
Mr. Sammler's Planet

The most honored American Jewish writer is Saul Bellow (1915–), who won the National Book Award three times (1953, 1965, and 1970) and both the Pulitzer Prize and the Nobel Prize for literature in 1976. In his many works, including *The Adventures of Augie March* (1953), *Herzog* (1964), *Mr. Sammler's Planet* (1970), and *Humboldt's Gift* (1975), Bellow deals with the moral dilemmas posed by contemporary society. His principal characters are usually urban Jews confronting misfortune and seeking to comprehend why. A concerned humanist, who values reason, kindness, decency, and family affection, Bellow is anguished by aspects of American life that undermine warm human relationships: selfishness, greed, unrestricted self-assertion, and the pursuit of instant gratification. He hopes that literature will promote social accord. In the tradition of the Hebrew prophets, he urges people to change their ways. Like many other Jews after the Holocaust, Bellow feels a responsibility to fight for humane and civilized values that the Nazis tried to destroy. From his Jewishness, he also acquired an attitude, strengthened by centuries of persecution, that one should reject despair and affirm the value of life.

In *Mr. Sammler's Planet,* Bellow angrily confronts the excesses of American society in the 1960s: rampant criminality, student radicalism, sexual promiscuity. Arthur Sammler, an elderly Polish-Jewish intellectual who barely survived the Holocaust, settles in New York after the war. He grows increasingly disenchanted with the unrestrained individualism—the self-indulgent and crazed quest for instinctual gratification—which he sees as a breakdown of Western civilization and a descent into barbarism. In an insightful essay on Saul Bellow, written twenty-five years after the publication of *Mr. Sammler's Planet,* literary critic Hilton Kramer noted:

> The first novel to give us a searing account of the moral collapse of the city (New York) and the class (the emancipated Jewish middle class) that were fundamental to our existence, it was also, among much else, a book about the failure of liberalism itself in the wake of the 60s rebellion, the sexual revolution, and the race war. It had taken the measure of the future of bourgeois urban life in America and pronounced it doomed.

In the following passage, Mr. Sammler reflects on a collapsing Western culture. He ridicules the generation of the 1960s, for its uncontrolled sexuality which is perceived as liberation of the self; he also condemns the generation's "petted intellectuals" who undermine cherished Western values in the name of the Marxist revolution, which they also perceive as human liberation. The philosophes' attack on irrational traditions and oppressive governments, says Sammler, has resulted in greater freedom for the individual. But this emancipation and democratization have also produced a "dark romanticism" that eschews restraint and self-discipline, revels in self-gratification, and searches for a higher truth "in being natural, primitive." The desire for liberation of the personality has not advanced the cause of human dignity, has not produced a desirable self. In our innermost heart, Bellow implies, we know those basic truths, those values, that civilized life requires we adhere to. We must not fall victim to unlimited desire that undermines reason and the moral discipline needed to abide by these values.

. . . The labor of Puritanism[1] now was ending. The dark satanic mills changing into light satanic mills.[2] The reprobates converted into children of joy, the sexual ways of the seraglio[3] and of the Congo bush adopted by the emancipated masses of New York, Amsterdam, London. Old Sammler with his screwy visions! He saw the increasing triumph of Enlightenment—Liberty, Fraternity, Equality, Adultery! Enlightenment, universal education, universal suffrage, the rights of the majority acknowledged by all governments, the rights of women, the rights of children, the rights of criminals, the unity of the different races affirmed, Social Security, public health, the dignity of the person, the right to justice—the struggles of three revolutionary centuries being won while the feudal bonds of Church and Family weakened and the privileges of aristocracy (without any duties) spread wide, democratized, especially the libidinous privileges, the right to be uninhibited, spontaneous, urinating, defecating, belching, coupling in all positions, tripling, quadrupling, polymorphous, noble in being natural, primitive, combining the leisure and luxurious inventiveness of Versailles with the hibiscus-covered erotic ease of Samoa.[4] Dark romanticism now took hold. As old at least as the strange Orientalism of the Knights Templar,[5] and since then filled up with Lady Stanhopes,[6] Baudelaires,[7] de Nervals,[8] Stevensons,[9] and Gauguins[10]—those South-loving barbarians. Oh yes, the Templars. They had adored the Muslims. One hair from the head of a Saracen was more precious than the whole body of a Christian. Such crazy fervor! And now all the racism, all the strange erotic persuasions, the tourism and local color, the exotics of it had broken up but the mental masses, inheriting everything in a

---

[1]The Puritans were morally rigorous, strict, disciplined Protestants in England and New England.

[2]"Dark satanic mills" is a phrase from "Jerusalem," a poem by William Blake. Although it may refer to the mills of the Industrial Revolution, it also is a reference to a situation where freedom and individuality are suppressed.

[3]A seraglio was the part of a Muslim palace that housed concubines; a harem.

[4]Samoa is an island nation in the South Pacific.

[5]The Knights Templars was a religious and military order established at Jerusalem during the Crusades (c. 1118) to protect pilgrims. They were called the Templars because they lived next to Solomon's Temple. It also is an order of Freemasonry that claims to descend from the medieval order.

[6]Lady Stanhope was an English aristocrat who traveled throughout the Middle East from 1810 to 1817.

[7]Charles Baudelaire was a nineteenth-century French poet who spent several weeks when he was young on the island of Mauritius in the Indian Ocean. He later used his impressions of tropical life in his highly symbolic poetry.

[8]Gerard de Nerval was a nineteenth-century French novelist who traveled in the orient and published his *Voyage to the Orient* in 1851.

[9]Robert Louis Stevenson, author of *Treasure Island,* sailed to Samoa in 1888. He died six years later and was buried on top of a mountain in Samoa.

[10]Paul Gauguin was a Postimpressionist painter who left Paris in 1891 to live and paint in Tahiti in the South Pacific.

debased state, had formed an idea of the corrupting disease of being white and of the healing power of black. The dreams of nineteenth-century poets polluted the psychic atmosphere of the great boroughs and suburbs of New York. Add to this the dangerous lunging, staggering crazy violence of fanatics, and the trouble was very deep. Like many people who had seen the world collapse once, Mr. Sammler entertained the possibility it might collapse twice. He did not agree with refugee friends that this doom was inevitable, but liberal beliefs did not seem capable of self-defense, and you could smell decay. You could see the suicidal impulses of civilization pushing strongly. You wondered whether this Western culture could survive universal dissemination—whether only its science and technology on administrative practices would travel, be adopted by other societies. Or whether the worst enemies of civilization might not prove to be its petted intellectuals who attacked it at its weakest moments—attacked it in the name of proletarian revolution, in the name of reason, and in the name of irrationality, in the name of visceral depth, in the name of sex, in the name of perfect instantaneous freedom. For what it amounted to was limitless demand—insatiability, refusal of the doomed creature (death being sure and final) to go away from this earth unsatisfied. A full bill of demand and complaint was therefore presented by each individual. Non-negotiable. Recognizing no scarcity of supply in any human department. Enlightenment? Marvelous! But out of hand, wasn't it?

7 Black American Writers: Critiques of Racism

In the 1950s and 1960s, American blacks and their white sympathizers, in what is known as the civil rights movement, actively fought to end legal segregation in the South. After the genocidal madness of Nazi racism, it became increasingly more difficult to defend southern racism. Because of its powerful indictment of racial injustice, Ralph Ellison's *Invisible Man* helped to stir public opinion in support of the struggle for civil rights

Ralph Ellison
Invisible Man

Ralph Waldo Ellison (1914–1994), whose grandparents were former slaves, was born in Oklahoma City and named for the transcendentalist essayist and poet, Ralph Waldo Emerson. As a young boy, Ellison loved literature, and as a teenager, he aspired to be a "Renaissance Man." He studied music, became an accomplished jazz trumpeter, played football, and dabbled in electronics. In 1933, Ellison left Oklahoma on a music scholarship to study at the Tuskegee Institute in Alabama, where he became fascinated with sociology and sculpture. There he met Langston Hughes and discovered the powerful language and symbols of T. S. Eliot's poem, *The Waste Land,* which later became a hallmark of Ellison's own writing. During the Depression, Ellison took up residence in Harlem, and he wrote literary reviews that focused on what he called the lack of a "conscious protagonist." Rather than having a black hero who is a victim of circumstance or of white America, Ellison wanted heroes whose blackness broke down stereotypical categories rather than encouraged them.

During World War II, Ellison joined the merchant marine and began his one and only novel: *Invisible Man* (1952). The story line of the five hundred-plus page novel is often convoluted, for it is replete with complex symbols, which have multiple layers of meaning, much like Eliot's *The Waste Land.* Ellison relates situations that cause men and women, both black and white, to be blind to people as unique individuals, preferring to see them as cogs in a piece of machinery or as some "thing" to help them further their own social or political agenda. This leads to a loss of personal identity. The unnamed narrator, the book's principal character, becomes increasingly aware that people seek to impose their values and expectations on him. By forcing him to become someone other than himself, by regarding him "simply {as} a material, a natural resource to be used," they deprive him of his identity, making him more invisible. This is why he has decided to live underground in a manhole, which is illumined by light bulbs electrified by his syphoning off power from New York City.

The series of puzzling, disenchanting, and debilitating events that led to the narrator's decision allow Ellison to explore his own feelings about race and to seek to understand the various ways black and white Americans relate to each other. In particular, he depicts the humiliations that black people of his generation had to endure. In the following passage, the narrator gets his first bitter taste of what it means to be invisible. He is to receive a scholarship, but before he gives his acceptance speech, his white benefactors decide to have a little "fun" with the young black man. He and his fellow blacks are led into a ballroom where a voluptuous blonde woman dances naked in front of them. They are then blindfolded and engage in a round robin boxing match.

We were led out of the elevator through a rococo hall into an anteroom and told to get into our fighting togs. Each of us was issued a pair of boxing gloves and ushered out into the big mirrored hall, which we entered looking cautiously about us and whispering, lest we might accidentally be heard above the noise of the room. It was foggy with cigar smoke. And already the whiskey was taking effect. I was shocked to see some of the most important men of the town quite tipsy. They were all there—bankers, lawyers, judges, doctors, fire chiefs, teachers, merchants. Even one of the more fashionable pastors. Something we could not see was going on up front. A clarinet was vibrating sensuously and the men were standing up and moving eagerly forward. We were a small tight group, clustered together, our bare upper bodies touching and shining with anticipatory sweat; while up front the big shots were becoming increasingly excited over something we still could not see. Suddenly I heard the school superintendent, who had told me to come, yell, "Bring up the shines, gentlemen! Bring up the little shines!"

We were rushed up to the front of the ballroom, where it smelled even more strongly of tobacco and whiskey. Then we were pushed into place. I almost wet my pants. A sea of faces, some hostile, some amused, ringed around us, and in the center, facing us, stood a magnificent blonde—stark naked. There was dead silence. I felt a blast of cold air chill me. I tried to back away, but they were behind me and around me. Some of the boys stood with lowered heads, trembling. I felt a wave of irrational guilt and fear. My teeth chattered, my skin turned to goose flesh, my knees knocked. Yet I was strongly attracted and looked in spite of myself. Had the price of looking been blindness, I would have looked. The hair was yellow like that of a circus kewpie doll, the face heavily powdered and rouged, as though to form an abstract mask, the eyes hollow and smeared a cool blue, the color of a baboon's butt. I felt a desire to spit upon her as my eyes brushed slowly over her body. Her breasts were firm and round as the domes of East Indian temples, and I stood so close as to see the fine skin texture and beads of pearly perspiration glistening like dew around the pink and erected buds of her nipples. I wanted at one and the same time to run from the room, to sink through the floor, or go to her and cover her from my eyes and the eyes of the others with my body; to feel the soft thighs, to caress her and destroy her, to love her and murder her, to hide from her, and yet to stroke where below the small American flag tattooed upon her belly her thighs formed a capital V. I had a notion that of all in the room she saw only me with her impersonal eyes.

And then she began to dance, a slow sensuous movement; the smoke of a hundred cigars clinging to her like the thinnest of veils. She seemed like a fair bird-girl girdled in veils calling to me from the angry surface of some gray and threatening sea. I was transported. Then I became aware of the clarinet playing and the big shots yelling at us. Some threatened us if we looked and others if we did not. On my right I saw one boy faint. And now a man grabbed a silver pitcher from a table and stepped close as he dashed ice water upon him and stood him up and forced two of us to support him as his head hung and moans issued from his thick bluish lips. Another boy began to plead to go home. He was the largest of the group, wearing dark red fighting trunks much too small to conceal the erection which projected from him as though in answer to the insinuating low-registered moaning of the clarinet. He tried to hide himself with his boxing gloves.

And all the while the blonde continued dancing, smiling faintly at the big shots who watched her with fascination, and faintly smiling at our fear. I noticed a certain merchant who followed her hungrily, his lips loose and drooling. He was a large man who wore diamond studs in a shirtfront which swelled with the ample paunch underneath, and each time the blonde swayed her undulating hips he ran his hand through the thin hair of his bald head and, with his arms upheld, his posture clumsy like that of an intoxicated panda, wound his belly in a slow and obscene grind. This creature was completely hypnotized. The music had quickened. As the dancer flung herself about with a detached expression on her face, the men began reaching out to touch her. I could see their beefy fingers sink into the soft flesh. Some of the others tried to stop them and she began to move around the floor in graceful circles, as they gave chase, slipping and sliding over the polished floor. It was mad. Chairs went crashing, drinks were spilt, as they ran laughing and howling after her. They caught her just as she reached a door, raised her from the floor, and tossed her as college boys are tossed at a hazing, and above her red, fixed-smiling lips I saw the terror and disgust in her eyes, almost like my own terror and that which I saw in some of the other boys. As I watched, they tossed her twice and her soft breasts seemed to flatten against the air and her legs flung wildly as she spun. Some of the more sober ones helped her to escape. And I started off the floor, heading for the anteroom with the rest of the boys.

Some were still crying and in hysteria. But as we tried to leave we were stopped and ordered to get into the ring. There was nothing to do but what we were told. All ten of us climbed under the ropes and allowed ourselves to be blindfolded with broad bands of white cloth. One of the men seemed to feel a bit sympathetic and tried to cheer us up as we stood with our backs against the ropes. Some of us tried to grin. "See that boy over there?" one of the men said. "I want you to run across at the bell and give it to him right in the belly. If you don't get him, I'm going to get you. I don't like his looks." Each of us was told the same. The blindfolds were put on. Yet even then I had been going over my speech. In my mind each word was as bright as flame. I felt the cloth pressed into place, and frowned so that it would be loosened when I relaxed.

But now I felt a sudden fit of blind terror. I was unused to darkness. It was as though I had suddenly found myself in a dark room filled with poisonous cotton-mouths. I could hear the bleary voices yelling insistently for the battle royal to begin.

"Get going in there!"

"Let me at that big nigger!"

I strained to pick up the school superintendent's voice, as though to squeeze some security out of that slightly more familiar sound.

"Let me at those black sonsabitches!" someone yelled.

"No, Jackson, no!" another voice yelled. "Here, somebody, help me hold Jack."

"I want to get at that ginger-colored nigger. Tear him limb from limb," the first voice yelled.

I stood against the ropes trembling. For in those days I was what they called ginger-colored, and he sounded as though he might crunch me between his teeth like a crisp ginger cookie.

Quite a struggle was going on. Chairs were being kicked about and I could hear voices grunting as with a terrific effort. I wanted to see, to see more desperately than ever before. But the blindfold was as tight as a thick skin-puckering scab

and when I raised my gloved hands to push the layers of white aside a voice yelled, "Oh, no you don't, black bastard! Leave that alone!"

"Ring the bell before Jackson kills him a coon!" someone boomed in the sudden silence. And I heard the bell clang and the sound of the feet scuffling forward.

A glove smacked against my head. I pivoted, striking out stiffly as someone went past, and felt the jar ripple along the length of my arm to my shoulder. Then it seemed as though all nine of the boys had turned upon me at once. Blows pounded me from all sides while I struck out as best I could. So many blows landed upon me that I wondered if I were not the only blindfolded fighter in the ring, or if the man called Jackson hadn't succeeded in getting me after all.

Blindfolded, I could no longer control my motions. I had no dignity. I stumbled about like a baby or a drunken man. The smoke had become thicker and with each new blow it seemed to sear and further restrict my lungs. My saliva became like hot bitter glue. A glove connected with my head, filling my mouth with warm blood. It was everywhere. I could not tell if the moisture I felt upon my body was sweat or blood. A blow landed hard against the nape of my neck. I felt myself going over, my head hitting the floor. Streaks of blue light filled the black world behind the blindfold. I lay prone, pretending that I was knocked out, but felt myself seized by hands and yanked to my feet. "Get going, black boy! Mix it up!" My arms were like lead, my head smarting from blows. I managed to feel my way to the ropes and held on, trying to catch my breath. A glove landed in my mid-section and I went over again, feeling as though the smoke had become a knife jabbed into my guts. Pushed this way and that by the legs milling around me, I finally pulled erect and discovered that I could see the black, sweat-washed forms weaving in the smoky-blue atmosphere like drunken dancers weaving to the rapid drum-like thuds of blows.

Everyone fought hysterically. It was complete anarchy. Everybody fought everybody else. No group fought together for long. Two, three, four, fought one, then turned to fight each other, were themselves attacked. Blows landed below the belt and in the kidney, with the gloves open as well as closed, and with my eye partly opened now there was not so much terror. I moved carefully, avoiding blows, although not too many to attract attention, fighting from group to group. The boys groped about like blind, cautious crabs crouching to protect their mid-sections their heads pulled in short against their shoulders, their arms stretched nervously before them, with their fists testing the smoke-filled air like the knobbed feelers of hypersensitive snails. In one corner I glimpsed a boy violently punching the air and heard him scream in pain as he smashed his hand against a ring post. For a second I saw him bent over holding his hand, then going down as a blow caught his unprotected head. I played one group against the other, slipping in and throwing a punch then stepping out of range while pushing the others into the melee to take the blows blindly aimed at me. The smoke was agonizing and there were no rounds, no bells at three minute intervals to relieve our exhaustion. The room spun round me, a swirl of lights, smoke, sweating bodies surrounded by tense white faces. I bled from both nose and mouth, the blood spattering upon my chest.

The men kept yelling, "Slug him, black boy! Knock his guts out!"

"Uppercut him! Kill him! Kill that big boy!"

Taking a fake fall, I saw a boy going down heavily beside me as though we were felled by a single blow, saw a sneaker-clad foot shoot into his groin as the two who had knocked him down stumbled upon him. I rolled out of range, feeling a twinge of nausea.

The harder we fought the more threatening the men became. And yet, I had begun to worry about my speech again. How would it go? Would they recognize my ability. What would they give me?

The boxing match is followed by this next horrific scene in which the young black men scurry for gold coins—their prize money—on an electrified carpet. None of the benefactors, however, sees anything wrong with what they have done.

Then the M.C. called to us, "Come on up here boys and get your money."

We ran forward to where the men laughed and talked in their chairs, waiting. Even seemed friendly now.

"There it is on the rug," the man said. I saw the rug covered with coins of all dimensions and a few crumpled bills. But what excited me, scattered here and there, were the gold pieces.

"Boys, it's all yours," the man said. "You get all you grab."

"That's right, Sambo," a blond man said, winking at me confidentially.

I trembled with excitement, forgetting my pain. I would get the gold and the bills, I thought. I would use both hands. I would throw my body against the boys nearest me to block them from the gold.

"Get down around the rug now," the man commanded, "and don't anyone touch it until I give the signal."

"This ought to be good," I heard.

As told, we got around the square rug on our knees. Slowly the man raised his freckled hand as we followed it upward with our eyes.

I heard, "These niggers look like they're about to pray!"

Then, "Ready," the man said. "Go!"

I lunged for a yellow coin lying on the blue design of carpet, touching it and sending a surprised shriek to join those rising around me. I tried frantically to remove my hand but could not let go. A hot, violent force tore through my body, shaking me like a wet rat. The rug was electrified. The hair bristled up on my head as I shook myself free. My muscles jumped, my nerves jingled, writhed. But I saw that this was not stopping the other boys. Laughing in fear and embarrassment, some were holding back and scooping up the coins knocked off by the painful contortions of the others. The men roared above us as we struggled.

"Pick it up, goddamnit, pick it up!" someone called like a bass-voiced parrot. "Go on, get it!"

I crawled rapidly around the floor, picking up the coins, trying to avoid the coppers and to get greenbacks and the gold. Ignoring the shock by laughing, as I brushed the coins off quickly, I discovered that I could contain the electricity—a contradiction, but it works. Then the men began to push us onto the rug. Laughing embarrassedly, we struggled out of their hands and kept after the coins. We were all wet and slippery and hard to hold. Suddenly I saw a boy lifted into the air, glistening with sweat like a circus seal, and dropped, his wet back landing flush upon the charged rug, heard him yell and saw him literally dance upon his back, his elbows beating a frenzied tattoo upon the floor, his muscles twitching like the flesh of a horse stung by many flies. When he finally rolled off, his face was gray and no one stopped him when he ran from the floor amid booming laughter.

"Get the money," the M.C. called. "That's good hard American cash!"

Toni Morrison
Song of Solomon

Chloe Anthony Wofford (1931–   ), best known as Toni Morrison, hoped to facilitate the creation of a canon of African-American writing, so that black writers would not feel indebted to white publishers and readers, and thus be free to focus their attention on the uniqueness of their own literary works. For her novels portraying the physical and spiritual desolation caused by slavery and how it shaped the identity of slaves, many of whom continued to feel alienated even after they were granted their freedom, Morrison received the Pulitzer Prize in 1988, and in 1993 she became the first black woman to be awarded the Nobel Prize for literature. Today, Morrison continues to write and is the Robert F. Goheen Professor in the Council of Humanities at Princeton University, making her the first African-American woman writer to occupy a named chair at an Ivy League college.

Morrison earned the National Book Critics Circle Award and garnered national attention for her novel *Song of Solomon* (1977). The loosely constructed plot traces Milkman Dead's search for his own identity, apart from his father's materialist hopes and dreams. When Milkman departs his home in Michigan, he sees the world materialistically, much like his father had, and he believes that material wealth will ensure him a unique identity. In the following passage, Milkman and his friend, Guitar, enter into a heated conversation about values in life. Guitar chastises Milkman for his "high-tone" waterfront friends on Honoré Island and his mad pursuit of women. On the other hand, Milkman is critical of Guitar's "super-serious" concern about race issues which is leading him down a dangerous path. To illustrate his point, Milkman recounts a dream he once had about his mother being suffocated by her flowers.

"Look, Milk, we've been tight a long time, right? But that don't mean we're not different people. We can't always think the same way about things. Can't we leave it like that? There are all kinds of people in this world. Some are curious, some ain't; some talk, some scream; some are kickers and other people are kicked. Take your daddy, now. He's a kicker. First time I laid eyes on him, he was kicking us out of our house. That was a difference right there between you and me, but we got to be friends anyway. . . ."

Milkman stopped and forced Guitar to stop too and turn around. "I know you're not going to give me a bullshit lecture."

"No lecture, man. I'm trying to tell you something."

"Well, tell me. Don't give me no fuckin' bullshit lecture."

"What do you call a lecture?" asked Guitar. "When *you* don't talk for two seconds? When you have to listen to somebody else instead of talk? Is that a lecture?"

"A lecture is when somebody talks to a thirty-one-year-old man like he's a ten-year-old kid."

"You want me to talk or not?"

"Go ahead. Talk. Just don't talk to me in that funny tone. Like you a teacher and I'm some snot-nosed kid."

"That's the problem, Milkman. You're more interested in my tone than in what I'm saying. I'm trying to say that we don't have to agree on everything; that you and me are different; that—"

"You mean you got some secret shit you don't want me to know about."

"I mean there are things that interest me that don't interest you."

"How you know they don't interest me?"

"I know you. Been knowing you. You got your high-tone friends and your picnics on Honoré Island and you can afford to spend fifty percent of your brain-power thinking about a piece of ass. You got that red-headed bitch and you got a Southside bitch and no telling what in between."

"I don't believe it. After all these years you putting me down because of where I live?"

Not where you live—where you hang out. You don't live nowhere. Not Not Doctor Street *or* southside."

"You begrudge me—"

"I don't begrudge you a thing."

"You're welcome everywhere I go. I've tried to get you to come to Honoré—"

"Fuck Honoré! You hear me? The only way I'll go to that nigger heaven is with a case of dynamite and a book of matches."

"You used to like it."

"I never liked it! I went with you, but I never liked it. Never."

"What's wrong with Negroes owning beach houses? What do you want, Guitar? You mad at every Negro who ain't scrubbing floors and picking cotton. This ain't Montgomery, Alabama."

Guitar looked at him, first in rage, and then he began to laugh. "You're right, Milkman. You have never in your life said a truer word. This definitely is not Montgomery, Alabama. Tell me. What would you do if it was? If this turned out to be another Montgomery?"

"Buy a plane ticket."

"Exactly. Now you know something about yourself you didn't know before: who you are and what you are."

"Yeah. A man that refuses to live in Montgomery, Alabama."

"No. A man that can't live there. If things ever got tough, you'd melt. You're not a serious person, Milkman."

"Serious is just another word for miserable. I know all about serious. My old man is serious. My sisters are serious. And nobody is more serious than my mother. She's so serious, she wasting away. I was looking at her in the backyard the other day. It was as cold as a witch's tit out there, but she had to get some bulbs in the ground before the fifteenth of December, she said. So there she was on her knees, digging holes in the ground."

"So? I miss the point."

"The point is that she wanted to put those bulbs in. She

didn't have to. She likes to plant flowers. She really likes it. But you should have seen her face. She looked like the unhappiest woman in the world. The most miserable. So where's the fun? I've never in my whole life heard my mother laugh. She smiles sometimes, even makes a little sound. But I don't believe she has ever laughed out loud."

Without the least transition and without knowing he was going to, he began to describe to Guitar a dream he had had about his mother. He called it a dream because he didn't want to tell him it had really happened, that he had really seen it.

He was standing at the kitchen sink pouring the rest of his coffee down the drain when he looked through the window and saw Ruth digging in the garden. She made little holes and tucked something that looked like a small onion in them. As he stood there, mindlessly watching her, tulips began to grow out of the holes she had dug. First a solitary thin tube of green, then two leaves opened up from the stem—one on each side. He rubbed his eyes and looked again. Now several stalks were coming out of the ground behind her. Either they were bulbs she had already planted or they had been in the sack so long they had germinated. The tubes were getting taller and taller and soon there were so many of them they were pressing up against each other and up against his mother's dress. And still she didn't notice them or turn around. She just kept digging. Some of the stems began to sprout heads, bloody red heads that bobbed over and touched her back. Finally she noticed them, growing and nodding and touching her. Milkman thought she would jump up in fear—at least surprise. But she didn't. She leaned back from them, even hit out at them, but playfully, mischievously. The flowers grew and grew, until he could see only her shoulders above them and her flailing arms high above those bobbing, snapping heads. They were smothering her, taking away her breath with their soft jagged lips. And she merely smiled and fought them off as though they were harmless butterflies.

He knew they were dangerous, that they would soon suck up all the air around her and leave her limp on the ground. But she didn't seem to guess this at all. Eventually they covered her and all he could see was a mound of tangled tulips bent low over her body, which was kicking to the last.

He described all of that to Guitar as though the dream emphasized his point about the danger of seriousness. He tried to be as light-hearted as possible in the telling, but at the end, Guitar looked him in the eyes and said, "Why didn't you go help her?"

"What?"

"Help her. Pull her out from underneath."

"But she liked it, She was having fun. She liked it."

"Are you sure?" Guitar was smiling.

"Sure I'm sure. It was my dream."

"It was *your* mother too."

"Aw, man, why you making something out of it that ain't there? You're making the whole thing into something super-serious, just to prove your point. First I'm wrong for

not living in Alabama. Then I'm wrong for not behaving right in my own dream. Now I'm wrong for dreaming it. You see what I mean? The least little thing is a matter of life and death to you. You're getting to be just like my old man. He thinks if a paper clip is in the wrong drawer, I should apologize. What's happening to everybody?"

Despite Milkman's cautionary words, Guitar joins a group called the "Seven Days"—seven black men who administer "justice" in the form of the biblical law of "an eye for an eye and a tooth for a tooth" toward the whites who are the perpetrators of injustice toward blacks. Milkman tries to demonstrate to Guitar that not all whites are bad by discussing the scientist, musician, and philosopher, Albert Schweitzer, and the philanthropist and wife of President Franklin D. Roosevelt, Eleanor Roosevelt. His words, however, only serve to agitate Guitar even more, for he believes he and his associates are engaged in an honorable struggle to bring about "balance" and "ratio" to "the earth, the land."

"[There's] something's going on with you. And I'd like to know what it is."

Guitar didn't answer.

"We've been friends a long time, Guitar. There's nothing you don't know about me. I can tell you anything—whatever our differences, I know I can trust you. But for some time now it's been a one-way street. You know what I mean? I talk to you, but you don't talk to me. You don't think I can be trusted?"

"I don't know if you can or not."

"Try me."

"I can't. Other people are involved."

"Then don't tell me about other people; tell me about you."

Guitar looked at him for a long time. Maybe, he thought. Maybe I can trust you. Maybe not, but I'll risk it anyway because one day . . .

"Okay," he said aloud, "but you have to know that what I tell you can't go any further. And if it does, you'll be dropping a rope around my neck. Now do you still want to know it?"

"Yeah."

"You sure?"

"I'm sure."

Guitar poured some more hot water over his tea. He looked into his cup for a minute while the leaves settled slowly to the bottom. "I suppose you know that white people kill black people from time to time, and most folks shake their heads and say, 'Eh, eh, eh, ain't that a shame?'"

Milkman raised his eyebrows. He thought Guitar was going to let him in on some deal he had going. But he was slipping into his race bag. He was speaking slowly, as though each word had to count, and as though he were listening carefully to his own words. "I can't suck my teeth or say 'Eh, eh, eh.' I had to do something. And the only thing left to do is balance it; keep things on an even keel. Any man, any woman, or any child is good for five to seven generations of heirs before they're bred out. So every death is the death of five to seven generations. You can't stop them from killing us, from trying to get rid of us. And each time they succeed, they get rid of five to seven generations. I help keep the numbers the same.

"There is a society. It's made up of a few men who are willing to take some risks. They don't initiate anything; they don't even choose. They are as indifferent as rain. But when a Negro child, Negro woman, or Negro man is killed by whites and nothing is done about it by *their* law and *their* courts, this society selects a similar victim at random, and they execute him or her in a similar manner if they can. If the Negro was hanged, they hang; if a Negro was burnt, they burn; raped and murdered, they rape and murder. If they can. If they can't do it precisely in the same manner, they do it any way they can, but they do it. They call themselves the Seven Days. They are made up of seven men. Always seven and only seven. If one of them dies or leaves or is no longer effective, another is chosen. Not right away, because that kind of choosing takes time. But they don't seem to be in a hurry. Their secret is time. To take the time, to last. Not to grow; that's dangerous because you might become known. They don't write their names in toilet stalls or brag to women. Time and silence. Those are their weapons, and they go on forever.

"It got started in 1920, when that private from Georgia was killed after his balls were cut off and after that veteran was blinded when he came home from France in World War I. And it's been operating ever since. I am one of them now."

Milkman had held himself very still all the time Guitar spoke. Now he felt tight, shriveled, and cold.

"You? You're going to kill people?"

"Not people. White people."

"But why?"

"I just told you. It's necessary; it's got to be done. To keep the ratio the same."

"And if it isn't done? If it just goes on the way it has?"

"Then the world is a zoo, and I can't live in it."

"Why don't you just hunt down the ones who did the killing? Why kill innocent people? Why not just those who did it?"

"It doesn't matter who did it. Each and every one of them could do it. So you just get any one of them. There are no innocent white people, because every one of them is a potential nigger-killer, if not an actual one. You think Hitler surprised them? You think just because they went to war they thought he was a freak? Hitler's the most natural white man in the world. He killed Jews and Gypsies because he didn't have us. Can you see those Klansmen shocked by him? No, you can't."

"But people who lynch and slice off people's balls—they're crazy, Guitar, crazy."

"Every time somebody does a thing like that to one of us, they say the people who did it were crazy or ignorant. That's like saying they were drunk. Or constipated. Why isn't cutting a man's eyes out, cutting his nuts off, the kind of thing you never get too drunk or ignorant to do? Too crazy to do? Too constipated to do? And more to the point, how come Negroes, the craziest, most ignorant people in America, don't get that crazy and that ignorant? No. White people are unnatural. As a race they are unnatural. And it takes a strong effort of the will to overcome an unnatural enemy."

"What about the nice ones? Some whites made sacrifices for Negroes. Real sacrifices."

"That just means there are one or two natural ones. But they haven't been able to stop the killing either. They are outraged, but that doesn't stop it. They might even speak out, but that doesn't stop it either. They might even inconvenience themselves, but the killing goes on and on. So will we." . . .

"You're missing the point. There're not just one or two. There're a lot."

"Are there? Milkman, if Kennedy got drunk and bored and was sitting around a potbellied stove in Mississippi, he might join a lynching party just for the hell of it. Under those circumstances his unnaturalness would surface. But I know I wouldn't join one no matter how drunk I was or how bored, and I know you wouldn't either, nor any black man I know or ever heard tell of. Ever. In any world, at any time, just get up and go find somebody white to slice up. But they *can* do it. And they don't even do it for profit, which is why they do most things. They do it for fun. Unnatural."

"What about . . ." Milkman searched his memory for some white person who had shown himself unequivocally supportive of Negroes. "Schweitzer. Albert Schweitzer. Would he do it?"

"In a minute. He didn't care anything about those Africans. They could have been rats. He was in a laboratory testing *himself*—proving he could work on human dogs."

"What about Eleanor Roosevelt?"

"I don't know about the women. I can't say what their women would do, but I do remember that picture of those white mothers holding up their babies so they could get a good look at some black men burning on a tree. So I have my suspicions about Eleanor Roosevelt. But *none* about Mr. Roosevelt. You could've taken him and his wheelchair and put him in a small dusty town in Alabama and given him some tobacco, a checkerboard, some whiskey, and a rope and he'd have done it too. What I'm saying is, under certain conditions they would *all* do it. And under the same circumstances we would not. So it doesn't matter that some of them *haven't* done it. I listen. I read. And now I know that they know it too. They know they are unnatural. Their writers and artists have been saying it for years. Telling them they are unnatural, telling them they are depraved. They call it tragedy. In the movies they call it adventure. It's just depravity that they try to make glorious, natural. But it ain't. The disease they have is in their blood, in the structure of their chromosomes."

"You can prove this, I guess. Scientifically?"

"No."

"Shouldn't you be able to prove it before you act on something like that?"

"Did they prove anything scientifically about us before they killed us? No. They killed us first and then tried to get some scientific proof about why we should die."

"Wait a minute, Guitar. If they are as bad, as unnatural, as you say, why do you want to be like them? Don't you want to be better than they are?"

"I am better."

"But now you're doing what the worst of them do."

"Yes, but I am reasonable."

"Reasonable? How?"

"I am not, one, having fun; two, trying to gain power or public attention or money or land; three, angry at anybody."

"You're not angry? You must be!"

"Not at all. I hate doing it. I'm afraid to do it. It's hard to do it when you aren't angry or drunk or doped up or don't have a personal grudge against the person."

"I can't see how it helps. I can't see how it helps anybody."

"I told you. Numbers. Balance. Ratio. And the earth, the land."

"I'm not understanding you."

"The earth is soggy with black people's blood. And before us Indian blood. Nothing can cure them, and if it keeps on there won't be any of us left and there won't be any land for those who are left. So the numbers have to remain static."

"But there are more of them than us."

"Only in the West. But still the ratio can't widen in their favor."

"But you should want everybody to know that the society exists. Then maybe that would help stop it. What's the secrecy for?"

"To keep from getting caught."

"Can't you even let other Negroes know about it? I mean to give us hope?"

"No."

"Why not?"

"Betrayal. The possibility of betrayal."

"Well, let *them* know. Let white people know. Like the Mafia or the Klan; frighten them into behaving."

"You're talking foolishness. How can you let one group know and not the other? Besides, we are not like them. The Mafia is unnatural. So is the Klan. One kills for money, the other kills for fun. And they have huge profits and protection at their disposal. We don't. But it's not about other people knowing. We don't even tell the victims. We just whisper to him, 'Your Day has come.' The beauty of what we do is its secrecy, its smallness. The fact that nobody needs the unnatural satisfaction of talking about it. Telling about it. We don't discuss it among ourselves, the details. We just get an assignment. If the Negro was killed on a Wednesday, the Wednesday man takes it; if he was killed on Monday, the Monday man takes that one. And we just notify one another when it's completed, not how or who." . . .

Milkman stared at his friend and then let the spasm he had been holding back run through him. "I can't buy it, Guitar."

"I know that."

"There's too much wrong with it."

"Tell me."

"Well, for one thing, you'll get caught eventually."

"Maybe. But if I'm caught I'll just die earlier than I'm supposed to—not better than I'm supposed to. And how I die or when doesn't interest me. What I die *for* does. It's the same as what I live for. Besides, if I'm caught they'll accuse me and kill me for one crime, maybe two, never for all. And there are still six other days in the week. We've been around for a long long time. And believe me, we'll be around for a long long time to come." . . .

8 A "Novel" Approach to the History of Philosophy

The late 1960s witnessed the rise of a movement that focused on what can loosely be called "alternative lifestyles" and a renewed interest in astrology, magic, the occult, and philosophies (both ancient and modern) emphasizing spirituality and mysticism. The movement was centered in the younger generation who demanded a greater voice in society, particularly politics. Finding traditional religious practices unsatisfactory in transporting them to a higher state of reality, many of them engaged in "transcendental meditation," yoga, or experimented with mind-expanding drugs, including LSD. This new age of spiritual/mystical transcendence was originally dubbed "The Age of Aquarius"—an age of peace, love, and understanding—as reputedly prophesied by astrologists. But during the 1970s the movement simply became known as the "New Age."

In 1991, a former Norwegian philosophy teacher, Jostein Gaarder (1952–) published his epistolary novel, *Sophie's World,* subtitled *A Novel about the History of Philosophy.* In his novel, Gaarder likens New Age philosophy to "a kind of pornography," and in an interview in 2000 with the Czech magazine *The New Presence,* he described it as an "instant philosophy" which gives readers "quick access to wonder and awe." Before Gaarder even knew it, his book was a runaway best-seller. For three consecutive years, it was the number one best-seller in Norway, and by 1995, it was the number one best-seller *in the world;* to date, it has been translated into more than forty-five languages.

Jostein Gaarder
Sophie's World

The occupations of Gaarder's parents instilled in him an interest in writing and teaching, for his father was the headmaster of a school in Oslo and his mother wrote children's books. At the University of Oslo, Gaarder studied theology and Scandinavian languages, and following his marriage in 1974, he contributed to books on theology and philosophy. In 1981, he moved his family to Bergen, where Gaarder became a high school philosophy teacher and began to write novels. His first novel was *The Diagnosis* (1986), which was followed by *The Children from Sukhavati* (1987), *The Frog Castle* (1988), and *The Solitaire Mystery* (1990), which won the Ministry of Cultural and Scientific Affairs Literary Prize, as well as the Norwegian Literary Critics' Award.

The heroine of *Sophie's World* is fourteen-year-old Sophie Amundsen, whose father, "the captain of a big oil tanker . . . was away for most of the year." In the days just before her fifteenth birthday, Sophie arrives home from school, checks the mailbox, and discovers an envelope with her name on it. Inside is a slip of paper with the solitary question "Who are you?" and nothing else. Later that day, she finds another envelope with another question: "Where does the world come from?" A three-page anonymous letter then arrives that answers these two questions. Thus begins Sophie's investigation into the history of philosophy from the time prior to Socrates until the existential philosophy of Jean-Paul Sartre and the concept of the "Big Bang." Eventually the reader learns that Sophie's guide is a man who calls himself Alberto Knox, a mysterious man who wears a beret.

But Sophie has another mystery to solve. One day she gets a mysterious postcard addressed to Hilde Møller Knag c/o Sophie Amundsen, wishing her a happy fifteenth birthday—a birth date, Sophie later learns, the two girls have in common. Through other mail that is addressed to Hilde, Sophie learns that Hilde also has an absentee father, Major Albert Knag, who serves with United Nations forces in Lebanon. (Halfway through the novel, the reader meets Hilde, who is a real girl, and discovers that Sophie is a fictional character in the novel *Sophie's World* written by Major Knag.) After Sophie has learned about philosophers such as Democritus, Socrates, Plato, Aristotle, Descartes, Locke, Kant, Hegel, Kierkegaard, Marx, Darwin, Freud, and Sartre, Alberto decides to introduce her to the fate of philosophy in an age of technology and globalization.

In the following selection, as Sophie and Alberto walk down a street lined with shops filled with technological equipment, Alberto indicates that such technological development is a type of second Renaissance that has united the world into a "planetary civilization." Suddenly, a television camera zooms in on UN soldiers, and Sophie sees someone holding a sign that reads: "Back soon, Hilde!" Sophie and Alberto then enter a bookstore filled with New Age "spiritism, astrology, and ufology" books. Alberto's critique of New Age philosophy mirrors

Gaarder's own critique, and the reader ultimately learns that true philosophers keep their eyes open to new possibilities, such as a "white crow," because they are often unaware of "underlying connections."

They walked out into the street where people were hurrying by like energetic moles in a molehill. Sophie wondered what Alberto wanted to show her.

They walked past a big store that sold everything in communication technology, from televisions, VCRs, and satellite dishes to mobile phones, computers, and fax machines.

Alberto pointed to the window display and said:

"There you have the twentieth century, Sophie. In the Renaissance the world began to explode, so to speak. Beginning with the great voyages of discovery, Europeans started to travel all over the world. Today it's the opposite. We could call it an explosion in reverse."

"In what sense?"

"In the sense that the world is becoming drawn together into one great communications network. Not so long ago philosophers had to travel for days by horse and carriage in order to investigate the world around them and meet other philosophers. Today we can sit anywhere at all on this planet and access the whole of human experience on a computer screen."

"It's a fantastic thought. And a little scary."

"The question is whether history is coming to an end—or whether on the contrary we are on the threshold of a completely new age. We are no longer simply citizens of a city—or of a particular country. We live in a planetary civilization."

"That's true."

"Technological developments, especially in the field of communications, have possibly been more dramatic in the last thirty to forty years than in the whole of history put together. And still we have probably only witnessed the beginning . . ."

"Was this what you wanted me to see?"

"No, it's on the other side of the church over there."

As they were turning to leave, a picture of some UN soldiers flashed onto a TV screen.

"Look!" said Sophie.

The camera zoomed in on one of the UN soldiers. He had a black beard almost identical to Alberto's. Suddenly he held up a piece of card on which was written: "Back soon, Hilde!" He waved and was gone.

"Charlatan!" exclaimed Alberto.

"Was that the major?"

"I'm not even going to answer that."

They walked across the park in front of the church and came out onto another main street. Alberto seemed slightly irritable. They stopped in front of LIBRIS, the biggest bookstore in town.

"Let's go in," said Alberto.

Inside the store he pointed to the longest wall. It had

three sections: NEW AGE, ALTERNATIVE LIFESTYLES, and MYSTICISM.

The books had intriguing titles such as *Life after Death?*, *The Secrets of Spiritism, Tarot, The UFO Phenomenon, Healing, The Return of the Gods, You Have Been Here Before,* and *What Is Astrology?* There were hundreds of books. Under the shelves even more books were stacked up.

"This is also the twentieth century, Sophie. This is the temple of our age."

"You don't believe in any of this stuff?"

"Much of it is humbug. But it sells as well as pornography. A lot of it is a kind of pornography. Young people can come here and purchase the ideas that fascinate them most. But the difference between real philosophy and these books is more or less the same as the difference between real love and pornography."

"Aren't you being rather cross?"

"Let's go and sit in the park."

They marched out of the store and found a vacant bench in front of the church. Pigeons were strutting around under the trees, the odd overeager sparrow hopping about amongst them.

"It's called ESP or parapsychology," said Alberto. "Or it's called telepathy, clairvoyance, and psychokinetics. It's called spiritism, astrology, and ufology."

"But quite honestly, do you really think it's all humbug?"

"Obviously it would not be very appropriate for a real philosopher to say they are all equally bad. But I don't mind saying that all these subjects together possibly chart a fairly detailed map of a landscape that does not exist. And there are many 'figments of the imagination' here that Hume[1] would have committed to the flames. Many of those books do not contain so much as one iota of genuine experience."

"Why are there such incredible numbers of books on such subjects?"

"Publishing such books is a big commercial enterprise. It's what most people want."

"Why, do you think?"

"They obviously desire something mystical, something different to break the dreary monotony of everyday life. But it is like carrying coals to Newcastle."

"How do you mean?"

"Here we are, wandering around in a wonderful adven-

---

[1]David Hume (1711–1776) was a Scottish philosopher who sought to develop a science of human faculties by describing the mind as consisting of "sense impressions" from which we form more complex ideas, such as causation, for which there is no rational proof.

ture. A work of creation is emerging in front of our very eyes. In broad daylight, Sophie! Isn't it marvelous!"

"I guess so."

"Why should we enter the fortune-teller's tent or the backyards of academe in search of something exciting or transcendental?"

"Are you saying that the people who write these books are just phonies and liars?"

"No, that's not what I'm saying. But here, too, we are talking about a Darwinian system."

"You'll have to explain that."

"Think of all the different things that can happen in a single day. You can even take a day in your own life. Think of all the things you see and experience."

"Yes?"

"Now and then you experience a strange coincidence. You might go into a store and buy something for 28 crowns. Later on that day Joanna comes along and gives you the 28 crowns she owes you. You both decide to go to the movies—and you get seat number 28."

"Yes, that would be a mysterious coincidence."

"It would be a coincidence, anyway. The point is, people collect coincidences like these. They collect strange—or inexplicable—experiences. When such experiences—taken from the lives of billions of people—are assembled into books, it begins to look like genuine data. And the amount of it increases all the time. But once again we are looking at a lottery in which only the winning numbers are visible."

"But there are clairvoyants and mediums, aren't there, who are constantly experiencing things like that?"

"Indeed there are, and if we exclude the phonies, we find another explanation for these so-called mysterious experiences."

"And that is?"

"You remember we talked about Freud's theory of the unconscious . . ."

"Of course."

"Freud showed that we can often serve as 'mediums' for our own unconscious. We might suddenly find ourselves thinking or doing something without really knowing why. The reason is that we have a whole lot of experiences, thoughts, and memories inside us that we are not aware of."

"So?"

"People sometimes talk or walk in their sleep. We could call this a sort of 'mental automatism.' Also under hypnosis, people can say and do things 'not of their own volition.' And remember the surrealists trying to produce so-called automatic writing. They were just trying to serve as mediums for their own unconscious."

"I remember."

"From time to time during this century there have been what are called 'spiritualist revivals,' the idea being that a medium could get into contact with a deceased person. Either by speaking in the voice of the deceased, or by using au-

tomatic writing, the medium would receive a message from someone who had lived five or fifty or many hundreds of years ago. This has been taken as evidence either that there is life after death or that we live many lives."

"Yes, I know."

"I'm not saying that all mediums have been fakes. Some have clearly been in good faith. They really have been mediums, but they have only been mediums for their own unconscious. There have been several cases of mediums being closely studied while in a trance, and revealing knowledge and abilities that neither they nor others understand how they can have acquired. In one case, a woman who had no knowledge of Hebrew passed on messages in that language. So she must have either lived before or been in contact with a deceased spirit."

"Which do you think?"

"It turned out that she had had a Jewish nanny when she was little."

"Ah."

"Does that disappoint you? It just shows what an incredible capacity some people have to store experience in their unconscious."

"I see what you mean."

"A lot of curious everyday happenings can be explained by Freud's theory of the unconscious. I might suddenly get a call from a friend I haven't heard from for many years just as I had begun to look for his telephone number."

"It gives me goose bumps."

"But the explanation could be that we both heard the same old song on the radio, a song we heard the last time we were together. The point is, we are not aware of the underlying connection."

"So it's either humbug, or the winning number effect, or else it's the unconscious. Right?"

"Well, in any case, it's healthier to approach such books with a decent portion of skepticism. Not least if one is a philosopher. There is an association in England for skeptics. Many years ago they offered a large reward to the first person who could provide even the slightest proof of something supernatural. It didn't need to be a great miracle, a tiny example of telepathy would do. So far, nobody has come forward."

"Hmm."

"On the other hand, there is a lot we humans don't understand. Maybe we don't understand the laws of nature either. During the last century there were a lot of people who thought that phenomena such as magnetism and electricity were a kind of magic. I'll bet my own great-grandmother would have been wide-eyed with amazement if I told her about TV or computers."

"So you don't believe in anything supernatural then."

"We've already talked about that. Even the term 'supernatural' is a curious one. No, I suppose I believe that there is only one nature. But that, on the other hand, is absolutely astonishing."

"But the sort of mysterious things in those books you just showed me?"

"All true philosophers should keep their eyes open. Even if we have never seen a white crow, we should never stop looking for it. And one day, even a skeptic like me could be obliged to accept a phenomenon I did not believe in before. If I did not keep this possibility open I would be dogmatic, and not a true philosopher."

Alberto and Sophie remained seated on the bench without saying anything. The pigeons craned their necks and cooed, now and then being startled by a bicycle or a sudden movement.

"I have to go home and prepare for the party," said Sophie at last.

"But before we part, I'll show you a white crow. It is nearer than we think, you see."

Alberto got up and led the way back into the bookstore. This time they walked past all the books on supernatural phenomena and stopped by a flimsy shelf at the very back of the store. Above the shelf hung a very small card. PHILOSO-PHY, it read.

Alberto pointed down at a particular book, and Sophie gasped as she read the title: *Sophie's World.*

"Would you like me to buy it for you?"

"I don't know if I dare."

Shortly afterward, however, she was on her way home with the book in one hand and a little bag of things for the garden party in the other.

9 The Controversy over the Canon

In 1984, William J. Bennett, who served as secretary of education under President Ronald Reagan, chaired a study group that published "To Reclaim a Legacy: A Report on the Humanities in Higher Education." The report was commissioned by the National Endowment for the Humanities (NEH). Bennett noted that when the NEH was founded in 1965, it "defined the humanities as specific disciplines: 'language, both modern and classical; linguistics; literature; history; jurisprudence; philosophy; archaeology; comparative religion; ethics; the history, criticism, and theory of the arts'; and 'those aspects of the social sciences which have humanistic content and employ humanistic methods.'" But the study group argued:

> [T]o define the humanities by itemizing the academic fields they embrace is to overlook the qualities that make them uniquely important and worth studying. Expanding on a phrase from Matthew Arnold [a nineteenth-century Victorian poet], I would describe the humanities as the best that has been said, thought, written, and other wise expressed about the human experience. The humanities tell us how men and women of our own and other civilizations have grappled with life's enduring, fundamental questions: What is justice? What should be loved? What deserves to be defended? What is courage? What is noble? What is base? Why do civilizations flourish? Why do they decline?

The report went on to criticize the effect the politically and socially charged culture of the 1960s had on higher education.

Bennett's report is now part of an ongoing controversy regarding what comprises the canon—the great works that should constitute the core of a Humanities curriculum. Traditionally, the great books included the works of Homer, Plato, Augustine, Dante, Shakespeare, Locke, Voltaire, and other luminaries who shaped the Western intellectual tradition. Although there was no unanimity among instructors as to what constituted "the best that has been said, thought, or written," there was agreement that prominent Western writers had something significant to say about the human condition and that their works were worthy of serious study.

In recent years, this traditional canon has come under attack. William Casement, professor of philosophy at St. Thomas University, succinctly defines the nature of the controversy. "On one side are defenders of the canon, who argue for the pedagogical superiority of the great books. On the other side are anticanonists, who believe that those books, and the tradition they represent, should give way to new books and an emphasis on new ways of thinking." Anticanonists, often a product of the intellectual turmoil that pervaded the 1960s, condemn the canon as elitist—it is concerned only with upper class people and their values; racist—it dismisses or denigrates non-European cultures; and sexist—it views women condescendingly. This ongoing debate has affected what books students should read in a Humanities curriculum. But it also has wider implications, for some radical anticanonists use the debate to attack and undermine the entire Western tradition, contending that it is fraught with gender, class, and racial bias.

Defenders of the Western heritage, on the other hand, argue that this heritage, despite all its flaws, still has a powerful message for us. They caution against devaluing and undermining the modern West's unique achievements: the tradition of *rationality,* which makes possible a scientific understanding of the physical universe and human nature, the utilization of nature for human betterment, and the identification and reformation of irrational and abusive institutions and beliefs; the tradition of *political freedom,* which is the foundation of democratic institutions; the tradition of *inner freedom,* which asserts the individual's capacity for ethical autonomy; the tradition of *humanism,* which regards individuals as active subjects, with both the right and the capacity to realize their full potential; the tradition of *equality,* which demands equal treatment under the law; and the tradition of *human dignity,* which affirms the inviolable integrity and worth of the human personality and is the driving force behind what is now a global quest for social justice and human rights. Defenders of the Western legacy insist that in this age of cultural and ethnic diversity, it is crucial that Westerners continually affirm and reaffirm the core values of their heritage and not permit this priceless legacy to be dismissed or negated.

James Atlas
"On Campus: The Battle of the Books"

The nature of the controversy over the canon is discussed in the following selection, "On Campus: The Battle of the Books," written by James Atlas for the *New York Times Magazine* in 1988. Atlas is not only the author of the celebrated biography of Saul Bellow, but he was nominated for the National Book Award for his book *Delmore Schwartz: The Life of an American Poet.* Moreover, he is the founding editor of Lipper/Viking Penguin Lives Series. In addition to writing for the *New York Times Magazine,* he has written for *Vanity Fair,* the *London Review of Books,* the *New York Review of Books,* the *New York Times Book Review,* and the *New Yorker.*

The philosopher George Santayana was once asked which books young people should read. It didn't matter, he replied, as long as they read the same ones. Generations of Eng. lit. majors in American colleges followed his advice. You started with the Bible, moved briskly through Beowulf and Chaucer, Shakespeare and Milton, the 18th-century novel, the Romantics, a few big American books like "The Scarlet Letter" and "Moby-Dick"—and so on, masterpiece by masterpiece, century by century, until you'd read (or browsed through) the corpus.

Occupational disputes broke out, reputations flourished and declined T. S. Eliot smuggled in the 17th-century meta-physical poets, Malcolm Cowley promoted Faulkner, there was a Henry James revival. For the most part, though, the canon was closed: You were either on the syllabus or off the syllabus.

It was in the academic journals that I first noticed the word *canon.* Originally, it referred to those works that the church considered part of the Bible; now, apparently, it had a new meaning. PMLA, the journal of the Modern Language Association, proposed a future issue on "the idea of the literary canon in relation to concepts of judgment, taste and value." This spring, the Princeton English department held a symposium on "Masterpieces: Canonizing the Literary."

Canon formation, canon revision, canonicity: the mysterious, often indecipherable language of critical theory had yielded up a whole new terminology. What was this canon? The books that constituted the intellectual heritage of educated Americans, that had officially been defined as great. The kind of books you read, say, in Columbia's famed lit. hum. course, virtually unchanged since 1937: Homer, Plato, Dante, Milton . . . The masterpieces of Western civilization. The Big Boys.

In the academic world, I kept hearing, the canon was "a hot issue." "Everything these days has to do with the canon," one of my campus sources reported. Then, early this year, a flurry of articles appeared in the press. "From Western Lit to Westerns as Lit," joked The Wall Street Journal in a piece about some English professors down at Duke University who have been teaching "The Godfather"—book and movie—"E.T." and the novels of Louis L'Amour. An article in The York Times, "U.S. Literature: Canon Under Siege," quoted a heretical brigade of academics who were fed up with hierarchies of literary value.

Why should Melville and Emerson dominate the syllabus? argued renegade professors from Johns Hopkins and Northwestern, Queens College and Berkeley. What about Zora Neale Hurston, a hero of the Harlem Renaissance? What about Harriet Beecher Stowe? "It's no different from choosing between a hoagy and a pizza," explained Houston Baker, a professor of literature at the University of Pennsylvania. (Did he mean that all literature, like all junk food, was essentially the same?) "To hell with Shakespeare and Milton, Emerson and Faulkner!" retorted Jonathan Yardley in The Washington Post, setting a high standard for the debate. "Let's boogie!"

By the end of March, when Stanford University announced plans to revise the series of Western culture courses it required of freshmen, eliminating the core list of classics and substituting works by "women, minorities and persons of color," what began as an academic squabble had burgeoned into a full-blown Great Books Debate. Comp. lit. and humanities professors, Afro-American specialists, historians, college administrators and government spokesmen entered the fray. All over the country, editorials appeared decrying the sorry developments at Stanford, where last year students on a march with Jesse Jackson had chanted, "Hey hey, ho ho, Western culture's got to go."

Days after the new course was unveiled, William J. Bennett, the Secretary of Education, showed up in Palo Alto, Calif., to deplore the university's decision. Speaking before an overflow crowd, Bennett expressed contempt for the faculty senate that had voted for the change.

"The West is the culture in which we live," Bennett asserted. "It has set the moral, political, economic and social standards for the rest of the world." By giving in to a vocal band of student radicals, "a great university was brought low by the very forces which modern universities came into being to oppose: ignorance, irrationality and intimidation."

Bennett's polemic ignored the fine print. Instead of dealing with 15 "classic texts," students would read the Old and New Testaments as well as the works of five authors: Plato, St. Augustine, Machiavelli, Rousseau and Marx. The other works assigned would concentrate on "at least one, non-European culture," with "substantial attention to issues of race, gender and class." No one was proposing to "junk Western culture," insisted Stanford's president, Donald Kennedy. The point was simply to reflect "the diversity of contemporary American culture and values."

Never mind. For Bennett, what happened at Stanford was another opportunity to rehearse one of his favorite themes: the decline of the West. In 1984, as chairman of the National Endowment for the Humanities, he published a report titled "To Reclaim a Legacy," which decried the influence of the 1960's on higher education in America, working in the obligatory reference to Matthew Arnold's famous definition of culture as the best that has been thought and said.

The trouble with this "Matthew Arnold view of literature and culture," as Gerald Graff, a professor at Northwestern University and one of the more reasoned commentators on the debate, observes, is that there never was any consensus about the best that has been thought and said—or, for that matter, why the West should have a corner on the high culture market. The idea of literature as a fixed and immutable canon—the Great Books, the Five-Foot Shelf—is a historical illusion. "Canon-busting is nothing new," Graff says. "There have always been politics. Teaching Shakespeare instead of the classics was a radical innovation."

So why is this debate over the canon different from all other debates? The fierce arguments about Socialist Realism that raged among American intellectuals in the 1930's and 40's were a lot more acrimonious. As for what's literature and what isn't, the critic Leslie Fiedler was anatomizing the cultural significance of Superman decades ago.

What's different is who's doing the debating. A new generation of scholars has emerged, a generation whose sensibilities were shaped by intellectual trends that originated in the 60's: Marxism, feminism, deconstruction, a skepticism about the primacy of the West. For these scholars, the effort to widen the canon is an effort to define themselves, to validate their own identities. In the 80's, literature is us.

On the shelves in Jane Tompkins's office at Duke are rows of 19th-century novels; she is one of the few who read them now. Her book "Sensational Designs: The Cultural Work of American Fiction 1790–1860" is a brilliant exhumation of what she considers lost masterpieces, the history of a different American literature from the one I read in college in the 1960's.

Writers like Charles Brockden Brown, Harriet Beecher Stowe and Susan Warner still deserve an audience, Tompkins argues with considerable persuasiveness. If they're no longer read, it's because our values have changed. The way to read these books is from the vantage of the past. Only by reconstructing the culture in which they were written and the audience to whom they were addressed can we learn to appreciate their intrinsic worth and see them for what they are: "man-made, historically produced objects" whose reputations were created in their day by a powerful literary establishment. In other words, the Great Books aren't the only books.

Tompkins is one of the jewels in the crown of Duke's English department, which in the last few years has assembled a faculty that can now claim to rival any in the country. Attracted by salaries that in some cases approach six figures and a university willing to let them teach pretty much whatever interests them, the new recruits compose a formidable team: Frank Lentricchia, the author of "After the New Criticism" and other works; Fredric Jameson, probably the foremost Marxist critic in the country; Barbara Herrnstein Smith, president of the Modern Language Association, and Tompkins's husband, Stanley Fish, chairman of the department. (Duke is known in academic circles as "the Fish tank.")

Canon revision is in full swing down at Duke, where students lounge on the manicured quad of the imitation-Cotswold campus and the magnolias blossom in the spring. In the Duke catalogue, the English department lists, besides the usual offerings in Chaucer and Shakespeare, courses in American popular culture; advertising and society; television, technology and culture.

Lentricchia teaches a course titled "Paranoia, Politics and Other Pleasures" that focuses on the works of Joan Didion, Don DeLillo and Michel Foucault. Tompkins, an avid reader of contemporary fiction—on a shelf in her office I spotted copies of "Princess Daisy" and "Valley of the Dolls"—is teaching all kinds of things, from a course on American literature and culture in the 1850's to one called "Home on the Range: The Western in American Culture."

Tompkins talks about her work with a rhetorical intensity that reminded me of the fervent Students for a Democratic Society types I used to know in college. Like so many of those in the vanguard of the new canonical insurrection, she is a child of the 60's and a dedicated feminist. In her book "Sensational Designs," she recounts how she gradually became aware of herself as a woman working in a "male-dominated scholarly tradition that controls both the canon of American literature and the perspective that interprets the canon for society." The writers offered up as classics didn't speak to Tompkins; they didn't address her own experience.

"If you look at the names on Butler Library up at Columbia, they're all white males," she notes one afternoon over lunch in the faculty dining hall. "We wanted to talk about civil rights in the classroom, to prove that literature wasn't a sacred lion above the heat and dust of conflict."

The English literature syllabus, Tompkins and her colleagues on other campuses discovered, was a potential instrument of change: "This is where it all came out in the wash." By the 1970's, Afro-American departments and women's studies majors had been installed on college campuses across the land. Books on gender, race, ethnicity poured from the university presses. Seminars were offered in Native American literature, Hispanic literature, Asian-American literature. "It wasn't only women, we'd neglected," says Marjorie Garber, director of English graduate studies at Harvard University. "It was the whole third world."

The ideology behind these challenges to the canon is as unambiguous as the vanity plates on Frank Lentricchia's old Dodge: GO LEFT. Pick up any recent academic journal and you'll find it packed with articles on "Maidens, Maps and Mines: the Reinvention of Patriarchy in Colonial South Africa" or "Dominance, Hegemony and the Modes of Minority Discourse." The critical vocabulary of the 1980's bristles with militant neologisms: *Eurocentrism, phallocentrism, logophallocentrism.* (Why not *Europhallologocentrism?*) "This is not an intellectual agenda, it is a political agenda," Secretary of Education Bennett declared on the "MacNeil/Lehrer News-Hour" the night after his Stanford speech.

Why should a revolutionary curricular struggle be happening at a time when radical politics in America is virtually extinct? Walk into any classroom and you'll find the answer. Enormous sociological changes have occurred in American universities over the last 20 years; the ethnic profile of both students and faculty has undergone a dramatic transformation.

There's a higher proportion of minorities in college than ever before. By the end of this century, Hispanic, black and Asian-American undergraduates at Stanford may well outnumber whites. Their professors, many of whom were on the barricades in the 60's, are now up for tenure.

"It's a demographic phenomenon," Jesse Tompkins says. "There are women, Jews, Italians teaching literature in universities. The people who are teaching now don't look the way professors used to look. Frank Lentricchia doesn't look like Cleanth Brooks."

I had never seen Cleanth Brooks, the eminent Yale professor emeritus, but I could imagine him striding across campus in a conservative gray suit and neat bow tie—not at all the way Frank Lentricchia looks. The photograph on the book jacket of "Criticism and Social Change" shows a guy in a sports shirt, posed against a graffiti-scarred wall—"the Dirty Harry of contemporary critical theory," a reviewer in The Village Voice called him.

In person, Lentricchia is a lot less intimidating. I found him mild-mannered, easygoing, and surprisingly conventional in his approach to literature. Standing before his modern poetry class in a faded blue workshirt open at the neck, he made his way through "The Waste Land" just the way professors used to, line by line, pointing out the buried allusions to Ovid and Dante, Marvell and Verlaine.

His work is densely theoretical, yet there's nothing doctrinaire about it. What comes through is a devotion to the classics that is more visceral than abstract. "I'm interested in social issues as they bear on literature, but what really interests me is the mainline stuff, like Faulkner," he says after class, popping open a beer—no sherry—on the porch of his comfortable home in the nearby town of Hillsborough. "I'm too American to be a Marxist."

One afternoon I talk with Stanley Fish, the chairman of Duke's English department, in his newly renovated office in the Allen Building. Fish has on slacks and a sports jacket, but he doesn't look any more like Cleanth Brooks—or my image of Cleanth Brooks—than Frank Lentricchia does. He's never been comfortable with the T. S. Eliot tradition, he says, though he's one of the leading Milton scholars in America.

Now 50, Fish is maybe a decade older than the generation of radical scholars who came of age in the 60's; but like many of them, he discovered his vocation largely on his own. "You come from a background where there were no books, the son and daughter of immigrants," he says. In such a world, Milton was a first name.

For American Jewish writers who grew up in the Depression, the art critic Clement Greenberg once noted, literature offered "a means of flight from the restriction and squalor of the Brooklyns and Bronxes in the wide open world which rewards the successful fugitive with space, importance and wealth." Making it in those days meant making it on others' terms: in this case, the terms established by tradition-minded English departments dominated by white, Anglo-Saxon Protestants, which even in the 1940's looked with skeptical distaste upon the Jewish assistant professors who were trying to storm the gates.

Diana Trilling has written movingly about the humiliation her celebrated husband, Lionel, suffered at the beginning of his career, when he was briefly banished from Columbia by the English department on the grounds that he was "a Freudian, a Marxist and a Jew." There was nothing subversive about Trilling's ambition; for him, as for Jewish critics like Philip Rahv and Harry Levin, literature was an escape from ethnic identity, not an affirmation of it.

Fish and his radical colleagues are no less ambitious. They, too, aspire to "space, importance and wealth," but on their own terms. Frank Lentricchia has a swimming pool in his backyard. In his work, though, he writes openly and with unashamed ardor, in the autobiographical fashion of the day, about his Italian-American origins, his grandfather in Utica, his working-class Dad.

"To become an intellectual from this kind of background means typically to try to forget where you've come from," he writes in "Criticism and Social Change." It means becoming "a cosmopolitan gentleman of the world of letters, philosophy and art."

That's not Lentricchia's style. For the scholars of his generation, it's no longer a matter of proving their claim on literature; that struggle has been won. What they're demanding now is a literature that reflects their experience, a literature of their own. "Assimilation is a betrayal," says Fish. "The whole idea of 'Americanness' has been thrown in question."

In a way, this was what the debate at Stanford was about.

"If you think we are talking about a handful of good books you are mistaken," Bill King, a senior and president of the university's Black Student Union, declared in an eloquent speech before the faculty senate. "We are discussing the foundations of education in America and the acceptance of Euro-America's place in the world as contribution, not creator." Why had he never been taught that Socrates, Herodotus, Pythagoras and Solon owed much of what they knew to African cultures in Egypt, or that "many of the words of Solomon" were borrowed from the black Pharaoh Amen-En-Eope? Where, in the great scheme of things, were *his* people to be found?

Yet "opening up the canon," as the effort to expand the curriculum is called, isn't as radical as it seems. It's a populist, grass-roots phenomenon, American to the core. What could be more democratic than the new "Columbia Literary History of the United States," which incorporates Chippewa poems and Whitman's "Song of Myself," Mark Twain and Jay McInerney? There are chapters on Afro-American literature, Mexican-American literature, Asian-American literature, on immigrant writers of the 19th century and slave narratives of the Civil War.

"There isn't just one story of American literature," says Emory Elliott, chairman of Princeton's English department and the volume's general editor. "Things are wide open."

No group has been more assiduous in the effort to institutionalize new canonical discoveries than the feminists. Gynocriticism, the study of women's literature, is a flourishing academic field. Catalogues list English department courses in "Feminism, Modernism and Post-Modernism," "Shakespeare and Feminism," "Feminist Theory and the Humanities." Margaret Williams Ferguson of Columbia University teaches a course on "Renaissance Women of Letters"—Christine de Pisan, Mary Sidney, Aphra Behn. "This is just the tip of the iceberg," says Harvard's Marjorie Garber. "These aren't just oddities or curiosities, but major writers."

But the feminist enterprise is more than a matter of introducing works by women into the curriculum, or "mainstreaming." Men and women, it is now believed, have different responses to literature. What is needed, says Princeton's Elaine Showalter, one of the most articulate feminist critics around, is a "defamiliarization of masculinity," "a poetics of the Other"—a critical methodology that addresses gender and sexual difference.

On campus bulletin boards I saw notices for lectures on "Coming Unstrung: Women, Men, Narrative and Principles of Pleasure"; "Men's Reading, Women's Writing: Canon-Formation and the Case of the 18th-Century French Novel"; "Abulia: Crises of Male Desire in Freud, Thomas Mann and Musil."

Lit. crit. in the 80's is like child-raising in the 80's: Both sexes share the burden. Lentricchia's work on Wallace Stevens attempts to sort out the poet's attitude toward his own masculinity—to "feminize" his image. At Harvard, Marjorie Garber is at work on a book about "cross-dressing" that discusses Sherlock Holmes, Laurie Anderson, old movies. "There's a lot of work to be done on cross-dressing," she says. Her most recent book is "Shakespeare's Ghost Writers: Literature as Uncanny Causality." "I'll sell you a copy," she offers. "I have a whole box of them." I put down my $14 and read it on the shuttle back to New York.

Garber has written a shrewd, idiosyncratic book, full of curious lore and lively speculation about hidden sexual motifs in Shakespeare's plays. But isn't the focus somewhat narrow? "They're looking for things to write," says Garber's colleague Walter Jackson Bate, the great biographer of Keats and Samuel Johnson. "You can't write the 40th book on the structure of 'Paradise Lost.'" Bate is convinced that the humanities are in "their worst state of crisis since the modern university was formed a century ago"—and that specialization is the cause. "The aim and tradition of literature is to give, if possible, the *whole* experience of life."

The idea that literature should reflect our unique identity is "the new academic shibboleth." Gertrude Himmelfarb, a historian and highly visible proponent of the traditional curriculum, objected last month on the Op-Ed page of The New York Times. "It used to be thought that ideas transcend race, gender and class, that there are such things as truth, reason, morality and artistic excellence, which can be understood and aspired to by everyone, of whatever race, gender or class." Now we have democracy in the syllabus, affirmative action in the classroom. "No one believes in greatness," Bate says mournfully. "That's gone."

All these "texts" that are being rediscovered, republished, "revalorized"—the sermons and spinsters' diaries, the popular fiction of 1850: Are any of them neglected masterpieces? Jane Tompkins makes a persuasive case for the merits of Susan Warner's "The Wide, Wide World" (reissued last year in paperback by the Feminist Press), and it *is* a powerful book. The story of a young woman orphaned and exiled to bullying relatives in Scotland, Warner's novel portrays an experience of physical and spiritual renunciation that was obviously familiar to its 19th-century audience. The writing is energetic and vivid, and the humiliations endured by the heroine recall the trials of Lily Bart in Edith Wharton's "The House of Mirth" or Dreiser's "Sister Carrie."

Only how do you know whether a book is "good" or not? Who decides and by what criteria? There are no universals, Tompkins insists: "It is the context—which eventually includes the work itself—that creates the value its readers 'discover' there." The critic is only part of the story.

What the Duke critics discovered was "the historicization of value," says Stanley Fish. It's not that texts have no literal meaning, as the deconstructors who dominated literary studies in the 1970's believed; they have "an infinite plurality of meanings." The only way that we can hope to interpret a literary work is by knowing the vantage from which we perform the act of interpretation—in contemporary parlance, where we're coming from.

Barbara Herrnstein Smith, a power at Duke and a specialist in matters canonical, has written the definitive text on value relativity. "Contingencies of Value," to be published this fall by Harvard University Press, is an exasperating book, especially in the first chapter, where Smith goes on about her life as a professor, and claims to be so close to Shakespeare's sonnets that "there have been times when I believed that I had written them myself."

Still, for all her confessional posturing, her self-professed "monstrous" immodesty, Smith is on to something. What is taste? What do we experience when we contemplate a work of art? Like Fish, Smith is less interested in the status of a given work than in how that status is established. Who decides what's in and what's out? Those who possess "cultural power." What is art? Whatever the literary establishment says it is.

Smith's recent work is, among other things, a shrewd polemic against "high-culture critics" intent upon "epistemic self-stabilization" (that is to say, maintaining the status quo). Just who are these critics? A tribe of "nonacculturated intellectuals," "post-modern cosmopolites," "exotic visitors and immigrants." In other words, professors.

The vanguard of this new professoriate has transformed the landscape of contemporary literature. Many of them are tenured; they publish books. So why do they cultivate an image of themselves as literary outlaws? Frank Lentricchia isn't the only heavy academic dude around. D. A. Miller, a professor of comparative literature at Berkeley, has adorned his latest book with a photograph that mimes Lentricchia's notorious pose on the back of "Critical and Social Change"—biceps rippling, arms folded across his chest like Mr. Clean.

Lentricchia's new book is titled "Ariel and the Police." Miller's is "The Novel and the Police." Both are ostensibly works of literary criticism—Lentricchia is writing largely about William James and Michel Foucault; Miller, about the Victorian novel—but their real subject is the repressive nature of society, power and the containment of power, how our culture "polices" us.

"Where are the police in 'Barchester Towers' (1857)?" Miller asks in a chapter on Trollope. Where, indeed? They're "literally nowhere to be found . . ." But not so fast. Their very absence is significant, Miller claims, proof that Victorian England was a repressed society. The novel, then, is a form of concealment as well as of disclosure. Its truths are latent, murky, undeclared. Miller's own aim as a critic is to "bring literature out of the classroom and into the closet."

What's going on here? Reading between the lines, one begins to get the message. The questioning of authority that's such a pervasive theme in criticism now is a theoretical version of the battles that were fought on campuses 20 years ago—with real police. "The new epistemology—structuralism, deconstruction—provided the interpretive framework for challenging the canon," says Tompkins. "It's out in the hinterlands now. It's everywhere."

How will the New Canonicity—to coin a term—affect

the way literature is taught in America? What will students in the next generation read? It would be presumptuous to guess. But at least the debate has focused public attention on books—not an easy thing to do.

"It's an issue that's made literary studies suddenly vital and exciting," says Geraid Graff. The struggle over who belongs in the canon and what it means is more than a literary matter, Tompkins asserts. "It is a struggle among contending factions for the right to be represented in the picture America draws of itself."

Credits

Chapter 10

Page 2: From J. H. Robinson and H. W. Rolfe, *Petrarch the First Modern Scholar and Man of Letters* (New York: G. P. Putnam's Son, 1909), pp. 208, 210, 213. *Page 3:* "Love for Greek Literature" from Henry Osborn Taylor, *Thought and Expression in the Sixteenth Century,* 2nd rev. ed. (New York: Frederick Ungar, 1930, repub. 1959), Vol. 1, pp. 36–37, 291. "On Learning and Literature" from *Vittorino da Feltre and Other Humanist Educators,* ed. W. H. Woodward (Cambridge: Cambridge University Press, 1897), pp. 124, 127–129, 132–133. *Page 5:* William Harrison Woodward, *Vittorino da Feltre and Other Humanist Educators,* 1897, pp. 102–109. *Page 7:* Pico della Mirandola "Oration on the Diginity of Man" from *The Renaissance Philosophy of Man* edited by Ernst Cassirer, Paul Oskar Kristeller, and John H. Randall, Jr., translated by Elizabeth L. Forbes (Chicago: University of Chicago Press, 1948). Copyright 1948 by The University of Chicago. All rights reserved. Used by permission of the publisher. *Page 9:* From Niccoló Machiavelli *The Prince,* translated by Luigi, revised by E. R. P. Vincent, (Oxford: Oxford University Press, 1935). Used by permission of Oxford University Press. *Page 12:* From *The Book of the Courtier* by Baldesar Castiglione, Illus. edited by Edgar Mayhew, translated by Charles Singleton, copyright © 1959 by Charles S. Singleton and Edgar de N. Mayhew. Used by permission of Doubleday, a division of Random House, Inc. *Page 15:* Francois Rabelais, *Celebration of the Worldly Life,* from *The Histories of Gargantua and Pantagruel,* translated by J. M. Cohen. Copyright J. M. Cohen, 1955. Reproduced by permission of Penguin Books Ltd. *Page 17:* From *Utopia: A Norton Critical Edition,* Second Edition by Sir Thomas More, translated by Robert A. Adams. Copyright © 1992, 1975 by W. W. Norton & Company, Inc. Used by permission of W. W. Norton & Company, Inc. *Page 20:* Excerpts from Frame, Donald M., translator, *The Complete Essays of Montaigne.* Copyright © 1958 by the Board of Trustees of the Leland Stanford Junior University. With permission of Stanford University Press, www.sup.org. *Page 23:* William Shakespeare from *The Tragedy of Hamlet, Prince of Denmark* in *The Riverside Shakespeare* 2/e (Boston: Houghton Mifflin Company, 1997). Used by permission of Houghton Mifflin Company. *Page 28:* Source line for Miguel Don Quixote.

Chapter 11

Page 33: Desiderius Erasmus from *In Praise of Follow,* translated by Clarence H. Miller, (New Haven, CT: Yale University Press, 1979). *Page 35:* Desiderius Erasmus, *Paraclesis,* from *Christian Humanism and the Reformation,* translated by John C. Olin. Copyright © 1965 by John C. Olin. Reprinted with permission of HarperCollins Publishers, Inc. *Page 37:* Martin Luther, "Address to the Christian Nobility of the German Nation Concerning the Efficacy of Indulgences," and "To the Christian Nobility of the German Nation Concerning the Reform of the Christian Estate, 1520," from *Luther's Works,* Volume 44, *The Christian in Society I,* James Atkinson, ed., Helmut T. Lehman, general ed. (Philadelphia: Fortress Press, 1966), Used by permission of Augsburg Fortress. *Page 37:* Martin Luther, "The Babylonian Captivity of the Church, 1520," from from *Luther's Works,* Volume 36, *Word and Sacrament II,* Abdel Ross Wentz, ed., Helmut T. Lehman, general ed. (Philadelphia: Fortress Press, 1959). Used by permission of Augsburg Fortress. *Page 37:* Martin Luther, "The Freedom of the Christian, 1520," from *Luther's Works,* Volume 31, *Career of the Reformer I,* Harold T. Grimm, ed., Helmut T. Lehman, general ed. (Philadelphia: Fortress Press, 1957). Used by permission of Augsburg Fortress. *Page 41–43:* Reproduced from CALVIN: Institutes of the Christian Religion (Library of Christian Classics) edited by John T. McNeill. Used by permission of Westminster John Knox Press. *Page 44:* From *The Spiritual Exercises of St. Ignatius* by Anthony Mottola, copyright © 1964 by Doubleday, a division of Random House, Inc. Used by permission of Doubleday, a division of Random House, Inc.

Chapter 12

Page 48: From Bishop Jacques-Benigne Bossuet, *Politics Drawn from the Very Words of Holy Scripture,* trans. & ed. by Patrick Riley, pp. 57, 58, 59, 60, 61, 81, 82, 83. Copyright © 1990. Press. *Page 49:* From *Select Statutes and Other*

Constitutional Documents Illustrative of the Reigns of Elizabeth and James I, 3rd Ed., ed. G. W. Prothero (Oxford: Clarendon Press, 1906), pp. 293–294, 400–401. *Page 51:* From *The English Works of Thomas Hobbes of Malmesbury, Leviathan, or the Matter Form and Power of a Commonwealth Ecclesiastical and Civil,* collected and ed. Sir William Molesworth (London: John Bohn, 1839), Vol. 3, pp. 110–113, 116, 117, 154, 157–158, 160–161. *Page 53:* John Milton, *Paradise Lost, The Harvard Classics: The Complete Poems of John Milton,* edited by Charles W. Eliot. From *The Harvard Classics,* 1980 edition. Copyright 1980 by Grolier Incorporated. Reprinted with permission. *Page 58:* John Bunyan's The Pilgrim's Progress (Old Tappan, New Jersey: Spire Books, 1982) pp.39–40; 141–142; 147; 249–251; 276. *Page 61:* From Pierre Corneille, "Le Cid" in *Three Masterpieces: The Liar, The Illusion, Le Cid,* translated by Ranjit Bolt. Oberon Books, 2000. Used by permission of Oberon Books. *Page 65:* From Moliere, "Tartuffe," from *The Misanthrope, Tartuffe, and Other Plays,* translated by Maya Slater. Oxford World Classics (Oxford: Oxford University Press, 2001). Reprinted by permission of Oxford University Press.

Chapter 13

Page 73: Galileo Galilei, *Letter to the Grand Duchess Christina and Dialogue Concerning the Two Chief World Systems,* translated by Stillman Drake, University of California Press, 1962. Used by permission of the University of California Press. *Page 75:* *Discourse on Method: Descartes* by Lafleur, © 1956. Reprinted by permission of Pearson Education, Inc., Upper Saddle River, NJ. pp. 3–7, 9–12, 20–21. *Page 78:* From *Candide and Other Writings* by Voltaire, edited by Haskell M. Block, copyright © 1956 and renewed 1984 by Random House, Inc. *Page 80:* From Denis Diderot, *The Encyclopedia Selections,* edited and translated by Stephen J. Gendzier, 1967. Used by permission of Stephen J. Gendzier. *Page 83:* From John Locke, *Two Treatises on Civil Government* (London: 1688, 7th reprinting by J. Whiston et al., 1772), pp. 292, 315–316, 354–355, 358–359, 361–362. *Page 85:* First printing of the Declaration of Independence, July 4, 1776, Papers of the Continental Congress No. 1, Rough Journal of Congress, III. *Page 86:* Reprinted with permission of Pocket Books, a Division of Simon & Schuster Adult Publishing Group, from *Candide and Zadig* by Voltaire, translated by Tobias George Smollett, edited by Lester G. Crocker. Copyright © 1962 by Washington Square Press. Copyright © renewed 1990 by Lester C. Crocker. *Page 91:* From Denis Diderot, *The Encyclopedia Selections,* ed. and trans. Stephen J. Gendzier, pp. 92–93, 104, 124–125, 134, 136, 153, 183–187, 199, 229–230. *Page 93:* From Montesquieu, *The Persian Letters* (Indianapolis, The Library of Liberal Arts, 1964), pp. 53–54, 88–89, 93–93, 165–166. *Page 98:* From Thomas Paine, *Rights of Man* (New York: Peter Eckler, 1892), pp. 94–96. *Page 99:* From Mary Wollstonecraft, *Vindication of the Rights of Woman.* *Page 102:* Copyright © 1996 Bedford/St. Martin's. From: *The French Revolution and Human Rights* edited and translated by Lynn Hunt. *Page 103:* Copyright © 1996 by St. Martin's Press, Inc. From *The French Revolution and Human Rights* by Lynn Hunt, ed.

Chapter 14

Page 106: From Edmund Burke, *Reflections on the Revolution in France* (London: Printed for J. Dodsley, 1791), pp. 51–55, 90–91, 116–117, 127–129. *Page 107:* From *The Odious Ideas of the Philosophes.* *Page 109:* From John Stuart Mill, *On Liberty* (Boston: Ticknor and Fields, 1863), pp. 22–23, 27–29, 35–36. *Page 110:* William Wordsworth, "Tables Turned," *The Poetical Works of William Wordsworth* (London: Edward Moxon, Son and Co., 1869), p. 361. *Page 111:* Wordsworth: Odes, "Tables Turned," *The Poetical Works of William Wordsworth* (London: Edward Moxon, Son and Co., 1869), p. 361. *Page 114:* From William Blake, *Milton: A Poem in Two Books* (London: Printed by William Blake, 1804), pp. 42–44. *Page 115:* From John Keats and Percy Bysshe Shelley: *Complete Poetical Works,* Bernnett A. Cerf and Donald S. Klopper, eds. (New York: The Modern Library, n.d.), pp. 277–279 and 185–186. *Page 116:* From John Keats and Percy Bysshe Shelley: *Complete Poetical Works,* Bernnett A. Cerf and Donald S. Klopper, eds. (New York: The Modern Library, n.d.), pp. 277–279 and 185–186. *Page 117:*